New Business Ventures and the Entrepreneur

New Business Ventures and the Entrepreneur

Third Edition

Howard H. Stevenson
Sarofim-Rock Professor of Business Administration
Harvard University Graduate School of Business Administration

Michael J. Roberts
Assistant Professor
Harvard University Graduate School of Business Administration

H. Irving Grousbeck
Lecturer in Business Administration
Stanford University Graduate School of Business

1989

IRWIN
Homewood, IL 60430
Boston, MA 02116

Sponsoring editor: William R. Bayer
Project editor: Paula M. Buschman
Production manager: Carma W. Fazio
Compositor: Carlisle Communications, Ltd.
Typeface: 10/12 Century Schoolbook
Printer: R. R. Donnelley & Sons Company

Library of Congress Cataloging-in-Publication Data
Stevenson, Howard H.
    New business ventures and the entrepreneur.

    Includes index.
    1. New business enterprises.   2. New business enter-
prises—United States.   I. Roberts, Michael J.
II. Grousbeck, H. Irving.   III. Title.
HD62.5.S75   1989   658.11   88–32060
ISBN 0-256-07576-X

Printed in the United States of America

    3 4 5 6 7 8 9 0 DO 6 5 4 3 2 1 0

To
Patrick Rooney Liles (1937–1983)
teacher
scholar of entrepreneurship
business leader
athlete
friend

Foreword

Entrepreneuring has come of age in the United States. In growing numbers, men and women of all ages are taking up careers in younger businesses, both startups and going concerns. On college campuses, it is now socially acceptable, even laudatory, to join an unknown company. Employment levels in larger companies have plateaued, even dipped. The tide is changing. This book is written to help those who want to participate directly in that change.

One element of the folklore of the times is that 9 out of 10 new businesses fail. While the statistic may have some historical validity, and may even be true today if every airport pretzel stand is included in the calculation, the folklore is misleading. The success rate for new businesses is much, much higher—over 50 percent—for companies that systematically take advantage of what is known today about making new ventures fly. This book pulls together and adds to the best of that knowledge. Building on the earlier work and format of the late Pat Liles, Howard Stevenson has developed a powerful teaching and learning device. The combination of truly interesting cases and concise, pertinent readings provides the necessary ingredients for a rich course on entrepreneuring at a time when the demand for such courses is increasing.

The team of Stevenson, Roberts, and Grousbeck is uniquely qualified to create this important work. They combine an exciting blend of successful, new venture operating experience and pedagogical prowess. They know whereof they write and teach. In addition, I sense in the fabric of the material a pervasive desire to be of real service to those who will guide our next generation of companies.

Steven C. Brandt
Stanford University
Graduate School of Business

Introduction

We have several objectives in writing this book. We believe that the topic of entrepreneurship is an exciting and important one. For those students of management who have decided to pursue a career as an entrepreneur, we think this book will provide some of the knowledge and skills required. For those who may be undecided, or perhaps committed to a more "traditional" career, many of the ideas in this book have value for those in more structured business settings. Executives are often called upon to deal with, and even to manage, entrepreneurs. Friends and acquaintances may contemplate starting new ventures and want the advice financial support of acquaintances in management positions.

Most importantly, we believe that all students of management have a great deal to learn from the study of entrepreneurship. The process of identifying and pursuing opportunity, the hallmark of the entrepreneur, has become increasingly important in restoring the competitive position of many U.S. industries in the international marketplace.

ORGANIZATION AND CONTENTS

This book is organized into four parts:

- *Part I:* Evaluating Opportunity and Developing the Business Concept. This first section of the book serves as an overview, and also looks at the first two steps in the process of starting a new venture. Its first two chapters provide both a working definition of entrepreneurship and a framework for understanding the entrepreneurial process. Remaining chapters look at methods of valuing business opportunities as well as the process of preparing a business plan. The cases require evaluating business opportunities and formulating strategies to exploit opportunities.

- *Part II:* Assessing and Acquiring Necessary Resources. This part looks at two of the entrepreneur's critical steps—assessing required resources and acquiring those resources. The chapters focus on understanding and techniques for acquiring both financial and nonfinancial resources. The cases cover a variety of issues, including deal structure, securities law, venture capital, and intellectual property.
- *Part III:* Acquiring an Existing Business. In this part, we look at another avenue to an entrepreneurial career: purchasing an existing business. Chapters describe the search process, as well as some of the tax and legal dimensions of acquisitions. The cases look at several examples of individuals who attempt to purchase a business.
- *Part IV:* Managing the Enterprise and Harvesting Value. Here we look at some of the unique challenges of managing an entrepreneurial firm. Included are some approaches to harvesting the economic value that the entrepreneur has created. Chapters look at managing growth, and cover the problem of bankruptcy, and the process involved in a public offering. Cases focus on the operating problems of new ventures and the issue or managing growth in a rapidly expanding business.

Together, these sections trace the entrepreneurial process from the initial idea through business operations to harvest.

Throughout the book, we have exhibited some of our own biases. One of which we are aware has to do with the material that has been included as exhibits. Whenever possible, we have included actual documents: business plans, prospectuses, leases, laws, and legal opinions. While some of this material is detailed and highly specific, it is well worth the effort. This is the stuff of which real business is made; better to discover some of the subtleties of the tax code or lease provisions now than when you're sitting down to form a real venture.

Although the detail is included, please do not consider the technical notes, the exhibits, and the appendices as substitutes for detailed current investigation of law, regulation, markets, and practices. This is a rapidly evolving field. Although every effort has been made to be clear, current, and complete, you must consult good attorneys, accountants, and investments advisers before proceeding.

ACKNOWLEDGMENTS

Patrick R. Liles taught the New Ventures course at Harvard from 1969 to 1977. In a very real sense, his early work in the field, his first edition of this book, and his vision of the entrepreneur provided a strong foundation on which to build. We dedicate this book to Pat, both in recognition of his accomplishments and our respect for them, and out of our own sense of loss.

In addition to Pat's involvement with the course, many others participated in its teaching and development over the past 40 years. We are indebted to Myles Mace, Frank L. Tucker, Malcom Salter, Thomas Raymond, Philip Thurston, Jim Morgan, Richard Reese, Richard Von Werssowetz, John Van Slyke and Matt Weisman for building the New Ventures course at Harvard and providing a solid foundation for our own work. Many other students and scholars of entrepreneurship not at Harvard have contributed helpful comments: Jeffry Timmons, Barry Unger, Steve Brandt, Zenas Block, Karl Vesper, and Neil Churchill.

Thanks are also due:

- Peter Tolnai and James H. Snider for their help with First Place (A).
- Peter Lombard and Ricardo Rodriquez for their help with Icedelights.
- Richard Von Werssowetz for his help with Commercial Fixtures, Inc., Duncan Field, Steven B. Belkin, Stratus Computer, and Michael Bregman.
- Paul Brountas, of the law firm of Hale & Dorr, Boston, for his work on Universal Robotics Corporation.
- Richard E. Floor, of the law firm of Goodwin, Procter & Hoar, Boston, for his help with Viscotech, Inc., and the chapters on Securities Law and Private Financing and Securities Law and Public Offerings.
- Martha Gershun for Eastwind Trading Company, Dragonfly Corporation and the chapter on bankruptcy.
- Jose-Carlos Jarillo Mossi for his help with R&R and Spinnaker Software Corporation.
- E. J. Walton for his help with CVD vs. A. S. Markham Corp., and the chapter on the Business Plan.
- E. J. Walton, Lynn Radlauer, Ned Lubell, David Hull, Byron Snider, Robert Stevenson, and Robert Winter for their help with Purchasing a Business: The Search Process.
- Susan Harmeling for her work on the Howard Head and Prince Manufacturing case, and for her help with Valerie Morgan.
- David Dodson, of Stanford Business School, for his work on Kirk Riedinger and Jamie Turner. We thank the Board of Trustees of the Leland Stanford Junior University for their permission to use this case.

The case writing and research was sponsored by the Division of Research; we are grateful to Jay Lorsch of the Division as well as to the Associates of the Harvard Business School, who provided much of the funding. Dean John McArthur has been a supporter of many of our efforts in the entrepreneurship area. Without the support of many alumni this activity would not have been possible. Arthur Rock and Fayez Sarofim gave the first chair at Harvard to reestablish a focus on entrepreneurship. Subsequently, the classes of 1954, 1955, 1960 and 1961 have each funded additional chairs. To further the work of the class of 1955, a chair was dedicated in memory of Dimitri d'Arbeloff, the entrepreneurial leader of Millipore. Joel Schiavone of the class of 1961 has also pledged to donate a chair. The depth of alumni interest and support has been most remarkable and rewarding as we have worked to build this area.

The task of compiling this text was an arduous one. We wish to express our appreciation to the word processing staff, under the direction of Rose Giacobbe, who expertly typed and revised the manuscript. Audrey Barrett was extremely helpful in securing the permissions needed to complete the book.

We are indebted to the entrepreneurs who gave so willingly of their time, energy, and ideas so that we could collect this case material. They provide one of the most critical elements of entrepreneurial success: role models. Robert Reiss, Steve Belkin, Heather Evans, Bob Donadio, Joe Connolly, Bill Foster, Michael Bregmann, Kirk Reidinger, Jamie Turner, Jim Southern, Vincent Lamb, Ralph Stayer, Bill Bowman, David Seuss and Howard Head are all real people who have shared their experiences with us; others have chosen to remain anonymous. To all we owe thanks for their cooperation. Ultimately, it is through the sharing of their experiences that we can learn.

Finally, each of us would like to make a more personal statement of thanks to our families:

- To Sarah and the boys: Willie, Charley, and Andy. Thanks for the patience in helping me to pursue this passion. And to my parents, Dorothy Stevenson and the late Ralph Stevenson, and aunt and uncle, Boyd and Zola Martin, thanks for helping me get a running start into this field.

H. H. S.

- To my parents, Herb and Joan Roberts, for all their love, support and encouragement.

M. J. R.

- To my wife Sukey for her love, laughter, adaptability, and constant encouragement, and to my mother Emily for loving lessons of the value of integrity and hard work.

H. I. G.

Contents

Part I

Evaluating Opportunity and Developing the Business Concept

In this first part of the book, we present, in Chapter 1, a framework for defining entrepreneurship. Following this, we look at the first two fundamental issues that the entrepreneur must address:

— Is this a good opportunity?

— What business strategy will most fully exploit the opportunity?

WHAT IS AN OPPORTUNITY?

One of the entrepreneur's most important tasks is to identify opportunities. The capacity to creatively seek out opportunity is the starting point of entrepreneurship for both the individual and the firm.

In order to qualify as a good opportunity, the situation must meet two conditions:

1. It must represent a future state that is desirable.
2. It must be achievable.

Obviously, this issue cannot be addressed in isolation. It is difficult to understand how attractive an opportunity is until one has developed an idea of what the business strategy will be, what resources will be required to pursue the opportunity, how much those resources will cost, and, finally, how much value will be left over for the entrepreneur. Nonetheless, the step of evaluating the opportunity is the starting point for this thought process.

In Chapter 2, "The Start-Up Process," we describe the key steps in starting a business, as well as some of the analytical thinking that drives the decisions that must be made at each juncture.

Chapter 3, "Valuation Techniques," looks at some of the quantitative techniques for assessing the financial value of a business opportunity. It is important to remember, though, that there may be significant nonfinancial value in an opportunity that these techniques cannot measure. Some opportunities, for example, may not be worth much but may open doors to other opportunities that have considerable value. For some entrepreneurs, the opportunity to work on an interesting idea, with good people, and to be one's own boss compensates for what may be only a mediocre opportunity in a financial sense.

Chapter 4, "The Business Plan," describes the uses of a business plan and how you can write one to meet your needs, as well as those of potential investors.

DEVELOPING THE BUSINESS CONCEPT

Once an opportunity is identified, the entrepreneur must develop a business concept and strategy to exploit the opportunity. Often, this strategy will proximately determine the success or failure of a business, even if the entrepreneur has identified a wonderful opportunity. Federal Express, for instance, decided to serve the same market that Emery Air Freight was serving. But Federal chose a much different strategy: a high fixed-cost hub system that was critically dependent on volume. Federal Express's strategy has allowed it to operate at lower costs and thus to surpass Emery in the express delivery market.

To maximize the odds of its success, a new venture should offer products or services that can profitably meet the needs of the markets it attempts to serve. But a new venture has an important advantage over an existing business. It can be created specifically to respond to market needs. Too often existing firms spend enormous resources searching for a market for the products or services produced by their operating assets.

THE CASES

First Place is a good introductory case, in that it describes a typically difficult time for an aspiring entrepreneur: Having developed an idea for a business, Jack Paston tries to raise the money he needs to pursue his opportunity. R&R and Eastwind Trading are really "bookends." R&R describes the brief—but successful—history of a business, while Eastwind looks at two women contemplating an entrepreneurial career.

Tru-Paint and Commercial Fixtures both deal with the issue of assessing and valuing an opportunity. These cases point out the difficulty of trying to evaluate an opportunity in a vacuum; clearly, these businesses are attractive at some price. But, what exactly is that price? On what does it depend? Finally, ICEDELIGHTS provides an overview of the start-up process that raises a host of issues, including opportunity evaluation, resource assessment and acquisition, and valuation and financing.

Chapter One

A Perspective on Entrepreneurship

The term *entrepreneurship* has entered the business vocabulary as the 1980s' equivalent of *professionalism,* the managerial buzzword of the 1970s. Many individuals aspire to be entrepreneurs, enjoying the freedom, independence, and wealth such a career seems to suggest. And larger corporations want to become more "entrepreneurial," their shorthand for the innovative and adaptive qualities they see in their smaller—and often more successful—competitors.

Our purpose in this chapter is to shed some light on the concept of entrepreneurship. We will define entrepreneurship as a management process and will discuss why we believe encouraging entrepreneurial behavior is critical to the long-term vitality of our economy. Finally, we will suggest that the practice of entrepreneurship is as important—if not more important—to established companies as it is to start-ups.

INCREASING INTEREST IN ENTREPRENEURSHIP

It would be difficult to overstate the degree to which there has been an increase in the level of interest in entrepreneurship. A strong indicator of such interest is provided by the unprecedented rise in the rate of new business formation. The number of annual new business incorporations has doubled in the last 10 years, from annual rates of about 300,000 to over 600,000.

This note was prepared by Howard H. Stevenson.

These trends are mirrored in the capital markets that fund these start-ups. The decade 1975–1984 saw explosive growth in the amount of capital committed to venture capital firms in the United States. There was a concurrent dramatic increase in the amount of money raised in the public capital markets by young companies.

In addition to interest on the part of individuals who wish to become entrepreneurs and investors who wish to back them, there has been a wave of interest in what some refer to as *intrapreneurship,* or entrepreneurship in the context of the larger corporation. Building on the wealth of books and articles on the subject, some large firms seem to have recognized their shortcomings on certain critical dimensions of performance and have structured themselves in an attempt to be more innovative.

Indeed, we believe that the strengthening of entrepreneurship is a critically important goal of American society. The first 30 years of the postwar period in the United States were characterized by an abundance of opportunity, brought about by expanding markets, high investment in the national infrastructure, and mushrooming debt. In this environment, it was relatively easy to achieve business success, but this is no longer true. Access to international resources is not as easy as it once was; government regulation has brought a recognition of the full costs of doing business, many of which had previously been hidden; competition from overseas has put an end to American dominance in numerous industries; technological change has reduced product life in other industries; and so forth. In short, a successful firm is one that is either capable of rapid response to changes that are beyond its control or is so innovative that it contributes to change in the environment. Entrepreneurship is an approach to management that offers these benefits.

DEFINING ENTREPRENEURSHIP

As we have discussed, there has been a striking increase in the level of attention paid to entrepreneurship. However, we've not yet defined what the term means.

As a starting point, it may be helpful to review some of the definitions scholars have historically applied to entrepreneurship. There are several schools of thought regarding entrepreneurship, which may roughly be divided into those that define the term as an economic function and those that identify entrepreneurship with individual traits.

The functional approach focuses on the role of entrepreneurship within the economy. In the 18th century, for instance, Richard Cantillon argued that entrepreneurship entailed bearing the risk of buying at certain prices and selling at uncertain prices. Jean Baptiste Say broadened the definition to include the concept of bringing together the factors of production. Schumpeter's work in 1911 added the concept of innovation to the definition of entrepreneurship. He allowed for many kinds of innovation including process innovation, market innovation, product innovation, factor innovation, and even organizational innovation. His seminal work emphasized the role of the entrepreneur in creating and responding to economic discontinuities.

While some analysts have focused on the economic function of entrepreneurship, still others have turned their attention to research on the personal characteristics of entrepreneurs. Considerable effort has gone into understanding the psychological and sociological sources of entrepreneurship—as Kent refers to it, "supply-side entrepreneurship." These studies have noted some common characteristics among entrepreneurs with respect to need for achievement, perceived locus of control, and risk-taking propensity. In addition, many have commented on the common—but not universal—thread of childhood deprivation and early adolescent experiences as typifying the entrepreneur. These studies—when taken as a whole—are inconclusive and often in conflict.

We believe, however, that neither of these approaches is sound. Consider, for example, the degree to which *entrepreneurship* is synonymous with *bearing risk, innovation,* or even *founding a company.* Each of these terms focuses on *some* aspect of *some* entrepreneurs. But, if one has to be the founder to be an entrepreneur, then neither Thomas Watson of IBM nor Ray Kroc of McDonald's will qualify; yet, few would seriously argue that both these individuals were not entrepreneurs. And, while risk bearing is an important element of entrepreneurial behavior, it is clear that many entrepreneurs bear risk grudgingly and only after they have made valiant attempts to get the capital sources and resource providers to bear the risk. As one extremely successful entrepreneur said, "My idea of risk and reward is for me to get the reward and others to take the risks." With respect to the "supply-side" school of entrepreneurship, many questions can be raised. At the heart of the matter is whether the psychological and social traits are either necessary or sufficient for the development of entrepreneurship.

Finally, the search for a single psychological profile of the entrepreneur is bound to fail. For each of the traditional definitions of the entrepreneurial type, there are numerous counter-examples that disprove the theory. We simply are not dealing with one kind of individual or behavior pattern, as even a cursory review of well-known entrepreneurs will demonstrate. Nor has the search for a psychological model proven useful in teaching or encouraging entrepreneurship.

ENTREPRENEURSHIP AS A BEHAVIORAL PHENOMENON

Thus, it does not seem useful to delimit the entrepreneur by defining those economic functions that are "entrepreneurial" and those that are not. Nor does it appear particularly helpful to describe the traits that seem to engender entrepreneurship in certain individuals. From our perspective, entrepreneurship is an approach to management that we define as follows: *the pursuit of opportunity without regard to resources currently controlled.*

This summary description of entrepreneurial behavior can be further refined by examining six critical dimensions of business practice. These six dimensions are the following: strategic orientation, the commitment to opportunity, the resource commitment process, the concept of control over resources, the concept of management, and compensation policy.

We shall define these dimensions by examining a range of behavior between two extremes. At one extreme is the "promoter" who feels confident of his or her ability to seize opportunity regardless of the resources under current control. At the opposite extreme is the "trustee" who emphasizes the efficient utilization of existing resources. While the promoter and trustee define the end points of this spectrum, there is a spectrum of managerial behavior that lies between these end points, and we define (overlapping) portions of this spectrum as entrepreneurial and administrative behavior. Thus, entrepreneurial management is not an extreme example, but rather a range of behavior that consistently falls at the end of the spectrum.

The remainder of this chapter defines these key business dimensions in more detail, discusses how entrepreneurial differs from administrative behavior, and describes the factors that pull individuals and firms toward particular types of behavior.

Strategic Orientation

Strategic orientation is the business dimension that describes the factors that drive the firm's formulation of strategy. A promoter is truly opportunity-driven. His or her orientation is to say, "As I define a strategy, I am going to be driven only by my perception of the opportunities that exist in my environment, and I will not be constrained by the resources at hand." A trustee, on the other hand, is resource-driven and tends to say, "How do I utilize the resources that I control?"

Within these two poles, the administrator's approach recognizes the need to examine the environment for opportunities, but is still constrained by a trustee-like focus on resources: "I will prune my opportunity tree based on the resources I control. I will not try to leap very far beyond my current situation." An entrepreneurial orientation places the emphasis on opportunity: "I will search for opportunity, and my fundamental task is to acquire the resources to pursue that opportunity." These perspectives are represented in Figure 1–1.

It is this dimension that has led to one of the traditional definitions of the entrepreneur as opportunistic or—more favorably—creative and innovative. But the entrepreneur is not necessarily concerned with breaking new ground; opportunity can also be found in a new mix of old ideas or in the creative application of traditional approaches. We do observe, however, that firms tend to look for opportunities where their resources are. Even those firms that start as entrepreneurial by recognizing opportunities often become resource-driven as more and more resources are acquired by the organization.

The pressures that pull a firm toward the entrepreneurial range of behavior include the following:

— Diminishing opportunity streams: Old opportunity streams have been largely played out. It is no longer possible to succeed merely by adding new options to old products.

— Rapid changes in:

• Technology: Creates new opportunities at the same time it obsoletes old ones.

FIGURE 1–1

Promoter	Strategic Orientation	Trustee
Driven by perception of opportunity	←————————→ Entrepreneurial Domain ←————————→ Administrative Domain	Driven by resources currently controlled
Pressures toward This Side		Pressures toward This Side
Diminishing opportunity streams Rapidly changing: Technology Consumer economics Social values Political rules		Social contracts Performance measurement criteria Planning systems and cycles

- Consumer economics: Changes both ability and willingness to pay for new products and services.
- Social values: Defines new styles and standards and standards of living.
- Political roles: Affects competition through deregulation, product safety, and new standards.

Pressures that pull a firm to become more administrative than entrepreneurial include the following:

— The "social contract":   The responsibility of managers to use and employ people, plant, technology, and financial resources once they have been acquired.

— Performance criteria: How many executives are fired for not pursuing an opportunity, compared with the number that are punished for not meeting return on investment targets? Capacity utilization and sales growth are the typical measures of business success.

— Planning systems and cycles: Opportunities do not arrive at the start of a planning cycle and last for the duration of a three- or five-year plan.

Commitment to Opportunity

As we move on to the second dimension, it becomes clear that the definition of the entrepreneur as creative or innovative is not sufficient. There are innovative thinkers who never get anything done; it is necessary to move beyond the identification of opportunity to its pursuit.

The promoter is willing to act in a very short time frame and to chase an opportunity quickly. Promoters may be more or less effective, but they are able to engage in commitment in a rather revolutionary fashion. The duration of their commitment, not the ability to act, is all that is in doubt. Commitment for the trustee is time-consuming and, once made, of long duration. Trustees move so slowly that it sometimes appears they are stationary; once there, they seem frozen. This spectrum of behavior is shown in Figure 1–2.

It is the willingness to get in and out quickly that has led to the entrepreneur's reputation as a gambler. However, the simple act of taking a risk does not lead to success. More critical to the success of the entrepreneurs is knowledge of the territory they operate in. Because of familiarity with their chosen field, they have the ability to recognize patterns as they develop and the confidence to assume that the missing elements of the pattern will take shape as they foresee. This early

FIGURE 1–2

Promoter	Commitment to Opportunity	Trustee
Revolutionary with short duration	⟵———————⟶ . Entrepreneurial Domain ⟵———————⟶ Administrative Domain	Evolutionary of long duration

Pressures toward This Side	Pressures toward This Side

Action orientation
Short decision windows
Risk management
Limited decision
    constituencies
	Acknowledgment of
	    multiple constituencies
	Negotiation of strategy
	Risk reduction
	Management of fit

recognition enables them to get a jump on others in commitment to action.

Pressures that pull a business toward this entrepreneurial end of the spectrum include:

— Action orientation: Enables a firm to make first claim to customers, employees, and financial resources.

— Short decision windows: Due to the high costs of late entry, including lack of competitive costs and technology.

— Risk management: Involves managing the firm's revenues in such a way that they can be rapidly committed to or withdrawn from new projects. As George Bernard Shaw put it, "Any fool can start a love affair, but it takes a genius to end one successfully."

— Limited decision constituencies: Requires a smaller number of responsibilities and permits greater flexibility.

In contrast, administrative behavior is a function of other pressures:

— Multiple decision constituencies: A great number of responsibilities, necessitating a more complex, lengthier decision process.

— Negotiation of strategy: Compromise in order to reach consensus and resultant evolutionary rather than revolutionary commitment.

— Risk reduction: Study and analysis to reduce risk slows the decision-making process.

— Management of fit: To assure the continuity and participation of existing players, only those projects that "fit" existing corporate resources are acceptable.

Commitment of Resources

Another characteristic we observe in good entrepreneurs is a multi-staged commitment of resources with a minimum commitment at each stage or decision point. The promoters, those wonderful people with blue shoes and diamond pinky rings on their left hands, say, "I don't need any resources to commence the pursuit of a given opportunity. I will boot-strap it." The trustee says, "Since my object is to use my resources, once I finally commit I will go in very heavily at the front end."

The issue for the entrepreneur is this: What resources are necessary to pursue a given opportunity? There is a constant tension between the amount of resources committed and the potential return. The entrepreneur attempts to maximize value creation by minimizing the resource set and must, of course, accept more risk in the process. On the other hand, the trustee side deals with this challenge by careful analysis and large-scale commitment of resources after the decision to act. Entrepreneurial management requires that you learn to do a little more with a little less. Figure 1–3 addresses this concept.

FIGURE 1–3

Promoter	***Commitment of Resources***	*Trustee*
Multistaged with minimal exposure at each stage	← Entrepreneurial Domain → Administrative Domain →	Single-staged with complete commitment upon decision

Pressures toward This Side	*Pressures toward This Side*
Lack of predictable resource needs Lack of long-term control Social needs for more opportunity per resource unit International pressure for more efficient resource use	Personal risk reduction Incentive compensation Managerial turnover Capital allocation systems Formal planning systems

On this dimension we have the traditional stereotype of the entrepreneur as tentative, uncommitted, or temporarily dedicated—an image of unreliability. In times of rapid change, however, this characteristic of stepped, multistaged commitment of resources is a definite advantage in responding to changes in competition, the market, and technology.

The process of committing resources is pushed toward the entrepreneurial domain by several factors:

— Lack of predictable resource needs: Forces the entrepreneurs to commit less up front so that more will be available later on, if required.

— Lack of long-term control: Requires that commitment match exposure. If control over resources can be removed by environmental, political, or technological forces, resource exposure should also be reduced.

— Social needs: Multistaged commitment of resources brings us closer to the "small is beautiful" formulation of E. F. Shumacher by allowing for the appropriate level of resource intensity for the task.

— International demands: Pressures that we use no more than our fair share of the world's resources (e.g., not the 35 percent of the world's energy that the United States was using in the early 1970s).

The pressures within the large corporation, however, are in the other direction—toward resource intensity. This is due to the following:

— Personal risk reduction: Any individual's risk is reduced by having excess resources available.

— Incentive compensation: Excess resources increase short-term returns and minimize the period of cash and profit drains—typically the objects of incentive compensation systems.

— Managerial turnover: Creates pressures for steady cash and profit gains, which encourages short-term, visible success.

— Capital allocation systems: Generally designed for one-time decision making, these techniques assume that a single decision point is appropriate.

— Formal planning systems: Once a project has begun, a request for additional resources returns the managers to the morass of analysis and bureaucratic delays; managers are inclined to avoid this by committing the maximum amount of resources up front.

Control of Resources

When it comes to the control of resources, the promoter mentality says, "All I need from a resource is the ability to use it." These are the people who describe the ideal business as the post office box to which people send money. For them, all additional overhead is a compromise of a basic value. On the other hand, we all know companies that believe they do not adequately control a resource unless they own it or have it on their permanent payroll.

Entrepreneurs learn to use other people's resources well; they learn to decide, over time, what resources they need to bring in-house. They view this as a time-phased sequence of decisions. Good managers also learn that there are certain resources you should never own or employ. For instance, very few good real estate firms employ an architect. They may need need the best, but they do not want to employ him or her, because the need for that resource, although critical to the success of the business, is temporary. The same is true of good lawyers. They are useful to have when you need them, but most firms cannot possibly afford to have the necessary depth of specialization of legal professionals constantly at their beck and call. Figure 1–4 illustrates this dimension.

FIGURE 1–4

Promoter	***Control of Resource***	*Trustee*
Episodic use or rent of required resources	← → Entrepreneurial Domain ← → Administrative Domain	Ownership or employment of required resources
Pressures toward This Side		*Pressures toward This Side*
Increased resource specialization Long resource life compared to need Risk of obsolescence Risk inherent in any new venture Inflexibility of permanent commitment to resources		Power, status, and financial rewards Coordination Efficiency measures Inertia and cost of change Industry structures

The stereotype of the entrepreneur as exploitative derives from this dimension: The entrepreneur is adept at using the skills, talents, and ideas of others. Viewed positively, this ability has become increasingly valuable in the changed business environment; it need not be parasitic in the context of a mutually satisfying relationship. Pressures toward this entrepreneurial side come from these:

— Increased resource specialization: An organization may have a need for a specialized resource like a VLSI design engineer, high-tech patent attorney, or state-of-the-art circuit test equipment, but only for a short time. By using, rather than owning, a firm reduces its risk and its fixed costs.

— Risk of obsolescence: Reduced by merely using, rather than owning, an expensive resource.

— Increased flexibility: The cost of exercising the option to quit is reduced by using, not owning, a resource.

Administrative practices are the product of pressures in the other direction, such as the following:

— Power, status, and financial rewards: Determined by the extent of resource ownership and control in many corporations.

— Coordination: The speed of execution is increased because the executive has the right to request certain action without negotiation.

— Efficiency: Enables the firm to capture, at least in the short run, all of the profits associated with an operation.

— Inertia and cost of change: It is commonly believed that it is good management to isolate the technical core of production from external shocks. This requires buffer inventories, control of raw materials, and control of distribution channels. Ownership also creates familiarity and an identifiable chain of command, which becomes stabilized with time.

— Industry structures: Encourage ownership to prevent being preempted by the competition.

Management Structure

The promoter wants knowledge of his or her progress via direct contact with all of the principal actors. The trustee views relationships more formally, with specific rights and responsibilities assigned through the delegation of authority. The decision to use and rent resources and not to own or employ them will require the development of an informal information network. Only in systems where the

FIGURE 1-5

Promoter	*Management Structure*	*Trustee*
Flat with multiple informal networks	←————————→ Entrepreneurial Domain ←————————→ Administrative Domain	Formalized hierarchy

Pressures toward This Side	*Pressures toward This Side*
Coordination of key noncontrolled resources Challenge to legitimacy of owner's control Employees' desire for independence	Need for clearly defined authority and responsibility Organizational culture Reward systems Management theory

relationship with resources is based on ownership or employment can resources be organized in a hierarchy. Informal networks arise when the critical success elements cannot be contained within the bounds of the formal organization. Figure 1–5 illustrates this range of behavior.

Many people have attempted to distinguish between the entrepreneur and the administrator by suggesting that being a good entrepreneur precludes being a good manager. The entrepreneur is stereotyped as egocentric and idiosyncratic and thus unable to manage. However, although the managerial task is substantially different for the entrepreneur, management skill is nonetheless essential. The variation lies in the choice of appropriate tools.

More entrepreneurial management is a function of several pressures:

— Need for coordination of key noncontrolled resources: Results in need to communicate with, motivate, control, and plan for resources *outside* the firm.

— Flexibility: Maximized with a flat and informal organization.

— Challenge to owner's control: Classic questions about the rights of ownership as well as governmental environmental, health, and safety restrictions undermine the legitimacy of control.

— Employees' desire for independence: Creates an environment where employees are unwilling to accept hierarchical authority in place of authority based on competence and persuasion.

On the other side of the spectrum, pressures that push the firm toward more administrative behavior include these:

— Need for clearly defined authority and responsibility: To perform the increasingly complex planning, organizing, coordinating, communicating, and controlling required in a business.

— Organizational culture: Often demands that events be routinized.

— Reward systems: Encourage and reward breadth and span of control.

Reward Philosophy

Finally, entrepreneurial firms differ from administratively managed organizations in their philosophy regarding reward and compensation. First entrepreneurial firms are more explicitly focused on the creation and harvesting of value. In start-up situations, the financial backers of the organization—as well as the founders themselves—have invested cash and want cash out. As a corollary of this value-driven philosophy, entrepreneurial firms tend to base compensation on performance (where performance is closely related to value creation). Entrepreneurial firms are also more comfortable rewarding teams.

As a recent spate of takeovers suggests, more administratively managed firms are less often focused on maximizing and distributing value. They are more often guided in their decision making by the desire to protect their own positions and security. Compensation is often based on individual responsibility (assets or resources under control) and on performance relative to short-term profit targets. Reward in such firms is often heavily oriented toward promotion to increasing responsibility levels. Figure 1–6 describes this dimension.

The pressures that pull firms toward the promoter end of the spectrum include the following:

— Individual expectations: Increasingly, individuals expect to be compensated in proportion to their contribution, rather than merely as a function of their performance relative to an arbitrary peer group. In addition, individuals seemingly have higher levels of aspiration for personal wealth.

— Investor demands: Financial backers invest cash and expect cash back, and the sooner the better. Increasingly, shareholders in publicly held firms are starting to press with a similar orientation.

— Competition: Increased competition for talented people creates pressure for firms to reward these individuals in proportion to their contributions.

On the other side, a variety of pressures pull firms toward more trustee-like behavior:

— Societal norms: We still value loyalty to the organization, and find it difficult to openly discuss compensation.

FIGURE 1–6

Promoter	Reward Philosophy	Trustee
Value-driven Performance-based Team-oriented	←————————→ Entrepreneurial Domain ←————————→ Administrative Domain	Security-driven Resource-based Promotion-oriented

Pressures toward This Side	Pressures toward This Side
Financial backers Individual expectations Competition	Societal norms Impacted information Demands of public shareholders

— Impacted information: It is often difficult to judge the value of an individual's contributions, particularly within the frame of the annual compensation cycle performance review that most firms use.

— Demands of public shareholders: Many public shareholders are simply uncomfortable with compensation that is absolutely high, even if it is in proportion to contribution.

SUMMARY

These characteristics have been gathered onto one summary chart (see Figure 1–7). In developing a behavioral theory of entrepreneurship, it becomes clear that entrepreneurship is defined by more than a set of individual traits and is different from an economic function. It is a cohesive pattern of managerial behavior.

This perspective on entrepreneurship highlights what we see as a false dichotomy: the distinction drawn between entrepreneurship and intrapreneurship. Entrepreneurship is an approach to management that can be applied in start-up situations as well as within more established businesses. As our definition suggests, the accumulation of resources that occurs as a firm grows is a powerful force that makes entrepreneurial behavior more difficult in a larger firm. But the fundamentals of the behavior required remain the same.

Still, our primary focus will be on the start-up. The situational factors that define a start-up situation do much to encourage entrepreneurship. As we look at the start-up process, however, it is worth keeping in mind that many of these lessons can be applied equally well in the large corporate setting.

FIGURE 1-7 Summary

Pressures toward This Side	Promoter	Key Business Dimension	Trustee	Pressures toward This Side
Diminishing opportunity streams Rapidly changing: Technology Consumer economics Social values	Driven by perception of opportunity	**Strategic Orientation** Entrepreneurial Domain ↕ Administrative Domain	Driven by resources currently controlled	Social contracts Performance measurement criteria Planning systems and cycle
Action orientation Short decisions windows Risk management Limited decision constituencies	Revolutionary with short duration	**Commitment to Opportunity** Entrepreneurial Domain ↕ Administrative Domain	Evolutionary of long duration	Acknowledgment of multiple constituencies Negotiation of strategy Risk reduction Management of fit
Lack of predictable resource needs Lack of long-term control Social need for more opportunity per resource unit Interpersonal pressure for more efficient resource use	Multistaged with minimal exposure at each stage	**Commitment of Resources** Entrepreneurial Domain ↕ Administrative domain	Single-staged with complete commitment upon decision	Personal risk reduction Incentive compensation Managerial turnover Capital allocation systems Formal planning systems

	Entrepreneurial Domain ⇕ Administrative Domain		
Increased resource specialization Long resource life compared to need Risk obsolescence Risk inherent in any new venture Inflexibility of permanent commitment to resources	Episodic use or rent of required resources	**Control of Resources**	Ownership or employment of required resources	Power, status, and financial rewards Coordination Efficiency measures Inertia and cost of change Industry structures
Coordination of key noncontrolled resources Challenge to legitimacy of owner's control Employees' desire for independence	Flat with multiple informal networks	**Management Structure**	Formalized hierarchy	Need for clearly defined authority and responsibility Organizational culture Reward systems Management theory
Individual expectations Competition Increased perception of personal wealth creation possibilities	Value-based Team-based Unlimited	**Compensation/Reward Policy**	Resource-based Driven by short-term data Promotion Limited amount	Societal norms IRS regulations Impacted information Search for simple solutions for complex problems Demands of public shareholders

Chapter Two

The Start-Up Process

"A Perspective on Entrepreneurship" describes a paradigm for understanding entrepreneurial behavior. The paradigm breaks general management down into a number of key dimensions: strategic orientation, commitment to opportunity, commitment of resources, control of resources, management structure, and reward structure. It describes a range of managerial behavior along each of these dimensions and discusses the type of behavior that can be characterized as entrepreneurial.

This note serves as a conceptual bridge between what entrepreneurial behavior *is* and an in-depth look at the *actual process of* entrepreneurship as it is practiced in the start-up of a business. Entrepreneurship involves the process of pulling together a unique package of resources to pursue an opportunity. Because the entrepreneur never controls *all* of the necessary resources, pursuing the opportunity requires "bridging the resource gap." Such a process requires a series of choices that must be made in a manner both internally consistent and externally appropriate to the environmental context.

This note will describe the elements of the entrepreneurial process as well as the analysis that can help with each step of the process. It is critical to think about these issues *before* actually starting a business. This activity is often called opportunity or "prestart" analysis. It is analogous to gauging the depth of the water before taking the plunge. There should be three dominant goals for this process:

This note was prepared by Michael J. Roberts under the direction of Howard H. Stevenson.

— To understand the dimensions of the opportunity and reach a conclusion regarding its attractiveness or unattractiveness.

— To understand the magnitude—and key elements—of the effort that will be required to exploit the opportunity.

— To identify a course of action—a strategy—for weaving one's way through the obstacles and the risks inherent in any venture.

A typical end product of this phase of analysis is a business plan, although it is entirely possible that the result will be a decision that the idea does *not* present an attractive opportunity.

The stages of prestart analysis flow in a natural order that corresponds to the process of starting a business: evaluating the opportunity, developing the business concept, assessing required resources, acquiring necessary resources, managing the venture, and harvesting and distributing value. Yet, to perform a thorough analysis, one must iterate through the full set of elements. For example, one dimension of the opportunity evaluation stage clearly involves an examination of potential financial returns. But, it is difficult to project these returns without first developing the business concept, assessing the resources required to execute it, and looking down the road to see what kinds of returns the providers of those resources will require at harvest. Thus, a thorough prestart analysis requires an examination of all these elements of the process before the first concrete step is taken. The remainder of this note will discuss each of the steps in this process in turn.

EVALUATING THE OPPORTUNITY

An attractive, well-defined opportunity is the cornerstone of all successful ventures. The way in which the opportunity is defined will shape the remainder of the venture. There are several key questions that need to be answered in order to adequately evaluate the opportunity.

What are the dimensions of the "window of opportunity"?

An opportunity has several critical dimensions: its raw size, the time span over which it is projected to exist, and the rate at which it is expected to grow over time.

The raw size of the market is naturally a critical dimension because it has a direct bearing on the potential sales volume of the new venture and, thus, financial returns. All things being equal, of course, bigger is better. But, things are not always equal. Large markets may attract large, powerful competitors and, thus, smaller niche markets may be more hospitable.

Growth rate is related to size, and, again, new ventures often thrive in rapid growth environments. By gaining—and holding on to—a piece of a small market and growing with that market, small ventures can become big business.

Every opportunity exists only for some finite amount of time, which varies greatly depending on the nature of the business. For example, in the popular music business, the opportunity for a new hit tune is usually only a few months. By contrast, in real estate, opportunities for even a single property may span several decades. It is important to understand (1) the time period and the economic life over which the opportunity will exist and (2) the appropriate time span for our own analysis of the opportunity. These are not always the same.

The risk and reward potential of an opportunity are also likely to vary over time. Certain parts of the economic life of the opportunity may have greater potential than others, and a careful analysis of the timing and magnitude of opportunities for harvesting can often indicate certain time limits to our analysis and plans. Looking again at real estate, for example, the syndication of tax shelters typically exploits only part of the total economic opportunity and over only a fraction of the total economic life of an income-producing property. Thus, it may be advantageous to pursue the underlying opportunity for only part of its total existence.

One key to exploiting the opportunity is to understand the forces that are creating it. Technological change, government regulation (or its relaxation), and shifts in consumer preferences and market demand can all create opportunity. By spotting patterns early, the entrepreneur can seize the initiative in creating a venture to exploit the opportunity.

The entrepreneur must identify the best period over which to pursue an opportunity, and match his or her concept of how value can be created with an analysis of his or her own goals, skills, and time frame.

Is the profit potential adequate to provide a satisfactory return on investment of capital, time, and opportunity costs?

An opportunity must earn a sufficient return to justify taking an entrepreneurial risk. *Adequate* is a relative term and depends on the amount of capital invested, the time frame required to earn the return, the risks assumed in the process, and existing alternatives for both capital and time.

Opportunities that demand substantial capital, require long periods of time to mature, and have large risks usually make little sense unless enormous value is being created. In all too many cases, such opportunities may create considerable value, but not for the original entrepreneurs. The numerous rounds of financing reduce the founders' percentage of ownership to such an extent that, ultimately, there is little recompense for the effort and risk.

Adequate also depends on our alternatives and opportunity costs, which vary with individuals, time, and circumstances. What may be attractive and viable for one person may be unrealistic for another, due to the availability of more attractive alternatives. Still, opportunities are likely to have the following financial characteristics:

— Steady and rapid growth in sales during the first five to seven years in some well-defined niche in the market.

— A high percentage of "recurring revenue." That is, once sold, a customer becomes a recurring source of revenue, not simply a one-time sale.

— High potential for operating leverage with increased experience and scale of operations.

— Internally generated funds to finance and sustain growth.

— Growing capacity for debt supported by:

  • Buildup of hard assets that can be used as collateral.

  • Increase in earnings and cash flow to service debt.

— Relatively short time frame during which significant value can be created and sustained—usually from three to five years.

— *Real* harvest options to turn equity into aftertax cash or equivalents.

— Rate of return on investment of 40 percent or more (after taxes).

Does the opportunity open up additional options for expansion, diversification, or integration?

Good opportunities create additional options in a variety of different ways. Since the future is often unknown, it is critical the entrepreneur *not* be locked into a single, unvarying course. Good opportunities allow for midcourse corrections.

Poorer opportunities foreclose or limit future options. Opportunities that consume resources, eliminate alliances, or narrow technological options are inferior to those that build in flexibility.

Will the profit stream be durable in the face of likely obstacles?

One thing is certain—circumstances will change over time, particularly if the venture is successful. This success will create all sorts of pressures on performance, including imitative competitors, product substitutions, changing technology, changing customer preferences, personnel turnover, and changing relationships with both suppliers and buyers. It is absolutely essential, therefore, to evaluate whether, having committed to the venture, it may become vulnerable to an erosion of its profit stream. This requires identifying and combatting potentially fatal vulnerabilities and recognizing that some are internal to the venture, such as personnel turnover, while others, such as competitive reactions, are external factors. Internal factors can be managed, and external ones must be carefully monitored.

Does the product or service meet a real need?

Successful products meet a real need in terms of functionality, price, distribution, durability, and/or perceived quality. The provision of real value is fundamental to any new venture. Except in pure trading or promotion activities, the creation of value ultimately depends on the ability to offer products and services that satisfy some real need among customers.

A new venture must convince potential customers of the need and the benefits of its products and services in a reasonable period of time and at an affordable marketing and selling cost.

Entrepreneurs often (a) fail to understand how or even if their products and services will meet a customer's real needs and (b) underestimate how much time and marketing expense will be required to achieve the required level of sales.

Summary

By undertaking an analysis of the opportunity, the entrepreneur should be able to identify critical risks that the venture will face. These can never be eliminated entirely, but it is certainly advantageous to know exactly what they are. Moreover, the judicious application of effort and resources should be of considerable help in managing these risks.

DEVELOPING THE BUSINESS CONCEPT

Having undertaken an analysis of the opportunity, it is appropriate to develop a business concept—or strategy—that fully exploits the opportunity. For instance, assume one felt that there existed an extraordinary opportunity in the retailing of fresh-baked breads. A strategy would still need to be developed to address the maze of choices the entrepreneur would face:

— Franchising versus company-owned stores.
— Mall versus free-standing sites.

— On-premise preparations and baking versus central preparation and frequent delivery.

— Specific geographic region to be targeted versus national rollout.

An investigation of the following issues will help the entrepreneur make some of these strategic choices.

Can barriers to entry be created?

Barriers to entry help sustain superior returns and can be created based on cost, distribution power, patents, trade secrets, product differentiation, and/or focus. Given a good idea, some real advantage, and success, a venture will, in fact, have only a finite lead time. Competition *will emerge*. Frequently, the first competitors will enter the market with a "copy and cut price" strategy for their products and pricing. Thus, we must anticipate competitive threats and devise measures to protect our lead time and our competitive advantage from encroachment over time. An often fatal error for the new firm is the failure to plan for expected competitive reaction and therefore to plan adequately for the renewal that must occur in order to assure that the advantages sought will be durable.

Are the customers identifiable, reachable, and open to change?

In order to successfully attract new customers, they must not only be identifiable and reachable, but must be willing to obsolete any investments they have made to other firms' people, procedures, and/or facilities and equipment.

Often a new venture's success depends on the ability to sell some sort of *change* to the customer: a new process, product, or service. In effect, the customer will be asked to do something different in order to do business with us. Typically, this requires some form of new investment or expenditures by the customer and involves changing the way he or she does business. Becoming integrated into the customer's procedures is often the most effective barrier to entry of competition; it is, however, often the major hurdle that a new product or process must overcome.

It is essential, therefore, that the change being sold be *affordable* to the customer and yield a clearly visible benefit. Assuming customers elect to buy our products and services, we must be able to satisfy and reward them with real benefits at prices and terms the customer can accept and is willing to pay.

It is particularly useful to identify *specific* groups of potential customers within markets and to compare the real benefits received with the products and services offered. Specificity as to the particular customer is an absolute prerequisite to the effective planning of distribution approaches. Those opportunities that postulate the existence of a generalized market are almost always less successful than those based on the knowledge of specific customers and the means by which to reach them.

Will the suppliers control critical resources and capture the innovative rents or profits?

As a result of "make or buy" analyses and the desire to be "lean and mean," new companies frequently elect for some period of time not to invest in certain facilities or technology on which their venture will depend. In such cases, the new venture may become dependent on its suppliers, who could be in a position to squeeze extra profits from the venture because they control critical resources.

Will the buyers be so strong as to demand uneconomic concessions?

This area is a potential mine field particularly in established markets. It is often the case when a new or small business attempts to break into a market or sell products or services to large corporations that the buyers enjoy such great advantages in purchasing (e.g., terms of delivery, price, credit, quality standards, etc.) that they wring concessions from the smaller business rendering the transactions uneconomic or excessively risky.

Summary

The process of developing the business concept is critical. The opportunity evaluation develops a perspective on a market need, but the entrepreneur must still develop a business strategy that meets that need in a way that generates a superior return. The forces that drive the development of the business strategy include both external market focus and the economics of various approaches to serving that market.

ASSESSING REQUIRED RESOURCES

An entrepreneur can be viewed as a person who finds ways to bridge the gap between what he or she has in the way of skills and resources and what is actually needed to pursue the opportunity. Those who already have the skills and resources under personal control are closer to "investors" rather than entrepreneurs.

Much entrepreneurial failure occurs because there is too great a mismatch between the resources controlled by the entrepreneur and those required to pursue the opportunity successfully. Every venture depends on having the ability to control a *minimum* set of critical skills, resources, and relationships, and to gain, as necessary, any required approvals. The key questions are: What is the minimum resource set required, and how can the entrepreneur get and maintain control over these resources?

In answering these questions, it is useful to ask several much more specific questions that test our ability to assemble this minimum package.

What skills, resources, and relationships does the entrepreneurial group already possess?

The creation of real and lasting value depends on the ability to bring something new to the table. The less one brings, the more fragile and vulnerable the venture will be. The more one brings that can be protected and sustained, the more unique and potentially durable will be the venture.

Rarely does an individual entrepreneur possess or even substantially control all of the skills, resources, and relationships that are required to pursue an opportunity over the longer term. It is important to assess and understand what skills, resources, and relationships are truly controlled by the venture and to understand the resulting advantages and vulnerabilities.

Who are the likely suppliers of the remainder of the resources?

The full set of resources required for the venture will include the following:

— Financial.
— Marketing and sales.
— Technological.
— Production.
— Product development.
— Personnel.
— Managerial.
— Systems.

Whatever we lack but need, we must come up with. The key to bridging the gap is to understand from where and how the needed resources can be obtained. Often one of the most difficult parts of the problem is simply *identifying* and understanding alternative sources of supply.

The "resourcefulness" of many entrepreneurs often shows most clearly in this area, particularly in their ability to "make do." The ability to find ingenious ways to get hold of and *use*—not necessarily *own* but *use*—needed resources is a survival skill. In-depth knowledge of an industry and a market is particularly useful in meeting this challenge. The entrepreneur can calibrate quality, honesty, cost, and risk through personal experience and knowledge.

Personal experience also improves credibility and increases the desire of potential suppliers of resources to participate. Suppliers prefer investing their own risk capital of time and product in a known quantity with whom they have personal experience or at least personal ability to calibrate knowledge and planning.

What skills and resources must be a part of the internal organization?

First, in order to achieve critical economies of scale, a certain critical mass must be obtained. The best companies include and control, as part of their internal organization, those elements and resources that yield distinctive competitive advantages as their experience level and scale of operations increase.

Next, if possible, competitors should be preempted from controlling critical resources. This is a particularly important strategic issue for small companies seeking to compete against larger established players, who may offer similar products or services. Human resources are often the major ones that can be preempted by start-up ventures. To accomplish this, however, careful attention must be paid early on to the venture's legal and economic structure.

Finally, for those resources that require continued coordination through direct authority relationships, internal control will be critical. Some resources can be managed through contractual relationships that are essentially self-enforcing (e.g., suppliers making product to specification). Creation of good alternative possibilities results in achievable price, quality, and delivery standards without direct authority over these items.

In other cases, direct contractual or other authoritative relationships must be established, an example being the creation of a new marketing organization. The feedback needs, the ambiguity of the task, and the requirements for noneconomic action such as missionary selling are often precursors to the need for direct authority-based control. In later stages as the marketing process becomes more routine and systematic, expansion can often be achieved without expanding employment.

For each resource or skill, what amount is required?

The entrepreneur must address the issue of how much of a given resource is optimal, versus the absolute minimum requirement. A bare-bones plan usually has lower costs but higher levels of operating risk. On the other hand, comfort usually means higher cost, but not necessarily lower operating risk.

Somewhere in the middle, there is usually a calculated level of risk that one is willing to assume. Often an entrepreneur believes his or her particular skills, knowledge, or experience allows risk to be managed differently than conventional wisdom might dictate. The entrepreneur therefore is prepared to assume a risk that others believe to be unwise, but in which, in fact, he or she believes there is minimal downside.

The keys are to understand what is needed for the venture, what causes increased risks and to devise an effective strategy to mitigate those risks assumed. The assumption that more resources provide less risk is clearly incorrect. The entrepreneur must know how and why that statement is incorrect.

What is really unique about the proposed business concept?

There are several bases on which to build a long-term competitive advantage, including:

— Cost structure.
√ — Technology.
— Product features or quality, including augmented product definitions.
√ — Marketing and sales channels.
— Financial resources.
— Focus.
— People.

It is absolutely essential to have a strategy in mind and a clear understanding of the venture's competitive basis, both in the short run and over time. Unless the entrepreneur controls the resources that generate the truly unique features in the approach, there is high vulnerability. Suppliers, customers, or innovative competitors can exploit this vulnerability to the long-term disadvantage of the venture.

What quality trade-offs can be made among the required skills and resources?

It is rarely necessary to have a uniform level of quality in every required resource. An important insight is understanding quality trade-offs. Many fine businesses have been built based on the utilization of used equipment. Management valued quality more highly in the output rather than in the appearance of the manufacturing floor.

What are the major requirements for regulatory compliance?

Compliance with governmental and other regulatory constraints is a critical but often overlooked step in the new venture analysis. Key aspects include:

— Licenses.
— Operating procedures.
— Product approvals and testing.
— Insurance and bonding.

It is a telling mark of inexperience and naïveté to pursue the opportunity without ensuring full compliance with the extensive sets of laws, regulations, and standards of business practice. We live in an extremely complex domestic and international environment; it is frequently necessary to obtain formal approval, licenses, or other sanctions in order to simply conduct our activities.

Some of the required sanctions and approvals can be obtained by complying with known laws and/or by compliance with regulations issued by federal, state, and local government agencies. Other sanctions and approvals, such as Underwriters Laboratory approval of the safety of certain kinds of consumer and industrial products, must be obtained from public and private organizations, which have lengthy and frequently expensive application, testing, and approval processes. Still, in other cases, such as in commercial building construction or many government and large private sector contracts, the standard business practice may require formal and legally enforceable bonding of supplier and/or contractor performance by insurance companies, and so forth.

What critical checkpoints will mark the lowering of risks?

Major long-term objectives are most relevant and useful when they can be broken down into achievable intermediate milestones. As a venture develops, it typically becomes more viable. Many entrepreneurs frequently think in terms of "plateaus" and "If only we could. . . . " Preplanning of these checkpoints and plateaus helps us understand how the risk of a venture can or will be reduced over time. These same plateaus act as useful benchmarks in the acquisition of additional resources. They mark times when new players can be induced to play, new types of financing become available, or new suppliers and subcontractors enter the picture based on risk stages having been passed. The entrepreneur who is conscious of passing these checkpoints and bases his or her strategy on passing plateaus can often maintain a higher percentage of ownership.

Are there adequate resources to surmount potential variations from the plan?

Things will go wrong and at the worst possible time. There is an old rule of thumb in business that new ventures can have variances of three and two: three times as much time and twice as much money, or vice versa. In times of financial distress the "golden rule" takes effect—the party with the gold (i.e., cash) rules. The refinancing of a venture in times of financial distress is most often done on a confiscatory basis. In the venture capital industry, this is called *down and dirty* financing.

The strain and bargaining disadvantage for an entrepreneur created by a major financial crisis provides a rare predatory opportunity for those with cash to exact excessive concessions from those with money already trapped in the deal. Rarely does new money coming into a deal ever agree to take (bail) old money out. The rule is last-in, first-out. To make matters worse, new money frequently demands not only that old money stay in the deal, but also that it retreat in terms of legal priority, control over the affairs of the venture, and any future opportunities to exit.

With this in mind, a plan without contingencies and reserves is no plan at all. The knowledgeable investor, supplier, customer, and employee will want to know what will be done and how it will affect their own expectations and rewards from the venture.

Obviously, however, it is not feasible to have enough resources available up front to surmount every potential contingency. On the other hand, the plan must deal with the *likely ones,* and the entrepreneur must have a back-up vision of the future that will allow survival in the face of potential misfortunes.

Summary

The process of critically assessing required resources is an important step in the venture creation process. One of the most important ways in which the entrepreneur can create value is by doing more with less. On the other hand, both the prudent management of risk and the maintenance of competitive advantage depends on sufficient amounts of the right resources.

ACQUIRING NECESSARY RESOURCES

It is always necessary to structure some kind of legal vehicle and organization for conducting the affairs of the venture and for controlling the skills and resources that must be assembled.

Having determined the resources that are critical to the venture, it is time to acquire them. Note that *acquire* does not translate into *own*. One of the most valuable techniques of leverage available to the entrepreneur is to obtain the desired measure of control—without ownership—through such approaches as rents, royalties, and other incentives to encourage the owners of resources to make them available for the entrepreneur's use.

For each critical skill or resource, what mechanisms for control are available?

In addition to the classic approach of ownership and direct control there are several alternatives for controlling resources, including:

— Contractual agreements.

— Long-term noncontractual supply arrangements.

— Ad hoc need fulfillment.

The analysis that determines which control mechanism should be used focuses on understanding the critical factors required for success in the business and evaluating how feasible it is to achieve the required level of performance from each resource under each of the alternative control mechanisms. In general, direct ownership and administrative control of a resource—hiring people, buying plant and equipment—is the most expensive approach and should only be followed for the most critical resources.

What are the critical agenda items for the potential providers of the required resources and skills?

The potential providers have complex and multi-item needs of their own that must be fulfilled in order to persuade them to allow you to use their resources. In addition to financial return, these needs may include:

— Financial reward.

— Professional advancement.

— Operating integration.

— Risk avoidance.

— Social status.

— Political response to outside constituency.

These factors frequently provide the foundation pieces for deals. One of the keys to unlocking someone else's resources on favorable terms is to know what the other person or organization values most. Frequently, there are complex factors at work that have little to do with money.

Can incentives be structured to meet the agenda items above?

It is difficult to establish and maintain meaningful control over any resource without providing incentives for the owner/possessor of the resource to cooperate with you.

"Thin" relationships and deals can be dangerous and unreliable over time. In cases where incentives are inadequate, it is often wise to enhance them to motivate others to work *actively* on your behalf. This keeps parties in the deal for positive reasons, but typically requires some kind of concession on the entrepreneur's part.

Will the opportunity provide enough return to meet the resource providers' needs and to provide the entrepreneurial reward?

New business ventures are always bounded in many ways and can support only so many players. However, there are many different types of "returns" in any venture, including noncash returns such as enhanced technical position, prestige, franchises on market segments, and so forth.

Skilled entrepreneurs know how to allocate all the important financial and other returns among the key players. The problem comes when the returns are just not sufficient to meet the expectations of the key players. These are known as *thin deals*.

Summary

The ability to obtain control over required resources in a creative manner is one of the hallmarks of the successful entrepreneur. By renting, leasing, or borrowing, and with the correct structuring of incentives and the clever use of subcontractors, entrepreneurs can substantially lower the resource requirements and fixed costs of the business. This both lowers risk and raises potential financial returns.

MANAGING THE VENTURE

Once the critical resources have been assembled, it's time to deploy them and actually start the business. The early days will be quite hectic, as the entrepreneur, assembled management team, and employees begin to learn the business and their jobs. Everything that happens will be happening for the first time, and someone will have to make a decision about how it should be handled. This raises a number of issues, including the following questions.

Does the management concept include both the critical internal and external elements of the organization?

Somehow, the entrepreneur must devise and apply a formal or informal system of management to the venture. This management system must include within its scope both what is going to be internal to the venture (e.g., people, production processes, etc.) and what will be kept outside of the venture's organization (e.g., key suppliers or distributors with whom the venture may have contracts and agreements).

Often the entrepreneurial venture is distinguished by the control that it exerts over resources that it does not legally own or employ. The control and influence can only be intelligently and purposefully exercised if there is a managerial relationship with those resources. The relationship is neither hierarchical nor a pure market transaction. It does provide for continuity, clear mechanisms for feedback and evaluation, and yet it must also be mutually beneficial over the long term if it is to endure.

How will employees be selected and attracted?

The task of selecting employees for the venture is complicated, given both the resource scarcity of the early days and natural uncertainty over the skills that will be required. Even if the entrepreneur could afford to hire proven managerial talent, it is not clear exactly what skills would be required.

Most entrepreneurs respond to this dilemma by hiring eager, young men and women who can be retained relatively inexpensively and who seem willing to perform a wide variety of tasks. Occasionally, these individuals can be groomed and become good managers. More often, however, it is necessary for the entrepreneur to bring in some seasoned professionals as the firm matures and is financially able to afford their services.

Thus, at the start, it is important for the entrepreneur to have a picture of the managerial resources that will be needed over the course of the venture and to work at developing them. When this approach fails, the entrepreneur must be willing to reach outside the firm for the required skills.

How will the evolution of the entrepreneur's role be managed?

The entrepreneur must be aware that his or her role will evolve considerably as the business grows and matures. As the scope of activity in the firm expands, the entrepreneur will have little choice but to delegate responsibility to a layer of middle managers. This, in turn, will create a new role for the entrepreneur as a "manager of managers," and new skills will be required to execute this role.

Summary

The management of the growing venture is an extremely challenging task, demanding skills that differ dramatically from those required to start the business. The ability to surmount these challenges depends on a recognition that they exist and that difficult changes in behavior and management style will be required.

HARVESTING AND DISTRIBUTING VALUE

If the business is successful, significant value will have been created. The issue then becomes harvesting and distributing that value. Outside investors will be one source of pressure, as they will want to turn their initial cash investment back into cash. The personal desires of the entrepreneur and key employees may also press for some form of harvest. This raises a number of issues, including the following questions.

Is there a specific mechanism for harvesting?

Not all ventures have the same alternatives for harvesting; some cannot be harvested at all and must simply be operated for cash. Often personal service businesses fall into this category. On the other hand, businesses that create assets are often harvestable even without the owner having to quit active business life.

Business ventures that have no realistic prospects for a harvest represent mainly investments that have been made in providing a job for oneself, one's partners, and employees. However, for those business ventures that can be harvested, it is important to understand the range of real options that the venture may have. These include:

— Acquisition by a larger company.

— Public offering of stock via:

  • IPO: typically new shares are issued by the company and sold to raise more financing and establish the market value of the stock.

  • Secondary offering: shares held by principles and early investors are sold to the public or new investors (may be part of IPO).

— Sale of the company:

  • To a third party.

  • To other management and employees.

— Liquidation and distribution of proceeds.

Of these mechanisms, acquisitions, mergers, and public offerings are most frequently used in venture capital situations. However, timing and market conditions are critical to the harvest. Public offerings are often the most elusive harvest form for entrepreneurs. On becoming paper millionaires, many founders find themselves the last to realize the aftertax cash gains from public offerings. Acquisitions and mergers have also often provided only illusionary harvesting mechanisms. The entrepreneur who substitutes his or her own undiversified holdings for undiversified holdings in another firm often loses both control and wealth.

It is critical to understand both the goals and the detailed mechanisms by which a harvesting strategy is to be executed.

Has the venture been structured financially and legally so as to maximize the aftertax yield from harvest?

Here is where the devil is in the details and where foresight is essential. The IRS has been as aggressive as taxpayers have been creative in pursuing aftertax dollars.

Substantial and frequently extensive legal and tax-related preplanning is always required. Some issues have significant lead times extending over several years. For example, achieving capital gains treatment of a partial liquidation and discontinuance of a line of business requires of a corporate vehicle that certain conditions be met for periods prior to and after the liquidation transaction.

What conditions will trigger a harvest?

Timing is everything. There may indeed be many factors that will determine when it is time to cash in. These could include the following items:

— Need for large amounts of capital to press on to a major stage of growth.
— Peaking of profit potential.
— Changes in tax laws.
— Changes in debt or public equity markets.
— Economic cycles.
— Age, health, and interests of principals and founders.

What conditions could preclude a harvest?

Depending on the nature of the venture, from time to time certain factors may work against harvesting or prevent it altogether. Among the more important external factors are these:

— Economic and market cycles.

— Tax law changes.

— Competitors.

— Changes in laws and regulations.

The more important internal factors include:

— Major management or operating problems.

— Loss of trade secrets.

How will responsibilities to other participants be fulfilled at harvest?

All of your creditors, investors, partners, and key employees have or develop expectations about what they will gain from the venture. If you ever intend to do business with them again after the harvest transaction, you will want to ensure that they come away from the experience reasonably happy.

Summary

The harvest is a bittersweet experience for many entrepreneurs. While it represents the culmination of a long effort to build financial value, it can also represent the end of an extremely rewarding managerial experience. Yet, the fear of "giving up the baby" should not be allowed to interfere with sound financial planning. Moreover, many entrepreneurs have a unique ability to build a business, but less of a competitive advantage in the actual management of the company over the long term. They should be willing to recognize where their strengths lie and focus on applying them in the appropriate situations.

CONCLUSION

Starting a new venture is obviously a complex activity. It entails foresight and planning regarding all of the issues required to manage and to eventually harvest the venture. In addition, it also requires a certain attitude—or point of view—on the general management task. This attitude stems from the unique role and responsibilities of the entrepreneur. Unlike other managers who may have responsibility for a certain aspect or a specific function, the entrepreneur is ultimately accountable for the entire venture. It is this extremely close identity with the business that makes success so very rewarding and failure so difficult. This unique role breeds a certain set of attitudes including:

— An action orientation: The entrepreneur cannot afford to merely elucidate the dimensions of the problem—he or she *must act*.

— An attention to detail: Because the entrepreneur is ultimately accountable for the venture, he or she cannot afford to delegate final responsibility for "details" to others, including trained professionals. The entrepreneur *must* be familiar with legal, financial, and tax details that can impact the business significantly.

Indeed, the whole process of entrepreneurship involves far more than the problem solving often associated with management. The entrepreneur is a finder and exploiter of opportunities. Consequently, successful students of entrepreneurship must develop a similar attitude toward case situations: going beyond analysis of the case problems to an elucidation of the range of alternatives and the selection of a particular plan of action designed to seize the opportunity.

You need not know the answer to everything before you start. You must, however, start with the expectation that it is your responsibility to know the answers and to respond adequately to those steel-hearted outsiders who will ask them of you. And they will ask.

It is an inescapable fact that whatever omissions you make and risks you fail to identify in the prestart phase will be automatically included in the venture. On the other hand, early identification and management of risk factors and the magnitude of the task can be opportunities for substantial profit.

One of the most common and often fatal mistakes for many first-time entrepreneurs is to believe that much of the responsibility for the prestart phase can be delegated (e.g., particularly to professionals and technical experts such as lawyers and accountants), while forgetting that the accountability for the venture's results always rests with the lead entrepreneur and his or her team.

Despite its potential difficulty and complexity, prestart analysis must have a very strong mandate in favor of decisiveness, timeliness, and go–no-go actions. You cannot get bogged down in "analysis paralysis."

If you can look across the scope of issues suggested in this note for your own prestart analysis and respond with well-considered answers, then you have passed through the first gate on the journey of your entrepreneurial venture.

Chapter Three

Valuation Techniques

One of the entrepreneur's critical tasks is determining value. This is important not only for the individual about to purchase a company, but also for the entrepreneur who is starting a firm and is attempting to estimate the value the business may have in the future. Finally, understanding value is a key step for the entrepreneur about to harvest a venture, either through sale or taking the business public.

Financial theorists have developed many techniques that can be used to evaluate a going concern. Of course, for a large public company, one could simply take the market value of the equity. For a going concern with a long history of audited financials, earnings and cash flow projections are possible. But the valuation of a small, privately held business is difficult and uncertain at best.

This note will briefly outline some of the more widely used valuation approaches, including:

— Asset valuations.
— Earnings valuations.
— Cash flow valuations.

ASSET VALUATIONS

One approach to valuation is to look at the underlying worth of the assets of the business. Asset valuation is one measure of the investor's exposure to risk. If within the company there are assets whose market value approximates the price of the company plus its liabilities, the immediate downside risk is low. In some instances an increase in the value of the assets of a company may represent a major portion of the investor's anticipated return. The various approaches to asset valuation are discussed below.

This note was prepared by Michael J. Roberts under the direction of Howard H. Stevenson.

Book Value

The most obvious asset value that a prospective purchaser can examine is the book value. In a situation with many variables and unknowns it provides a tangible starting point. However, it must be remembered that it is only a starting point. The accounting practices of the company as well as other things can have a significant effect on the firm's book value. For example, if the reserve for losses on accounts receivable is too low for the business, it will inflate book value and vice versa. Similarly, treatment of asset accounts such as research and development costs, patents, and organization expense can vary widely. Nevertheless, the book value of a firm provides a point of departure when considering asset valuation.

Adjusted Book Value

An obvious refinement of stated book value is to adjust for large discrepancies between the stated book and actual market value of tangible assets, such as buildings and equipment which have been depreciated far below their market value, or land which has substantially appreciated above its book value which stands at the original cost. An adjustment would probably also reduce the book value of intangible assets to zero unless they, like the tangible assets, also have a market value. The figure resulting from these adjustments should more accurately represent the value of the company's assets.

Liquidation Value

One step beyond adjusted book value is to consider the net cash amount that could be realized if the assets of the company were disposed of in a "quick sale" and all liabilities of the company were paid off or otherwise settled. This value would take into account that many assets, especially inventory and real estate, would not realize as much as they would were the company to continue as a going concern or were the sale made more deliberately. Also, calculation of a liquidation value would make allowances for the various costs of carrying out a liquidation sale.

The liquidation value, it should be noted, is only an indication of what might be realized if the firm were liquidated immediately. Should the company continue its operations and encounter difficulties, most likely a subsequent liquidation would yield significantly less than the liquidation value calculated for the company in its current condition.

The liquidation value of a company is not usually of importance to a buyer who is interested in the maintenance of a going concern. One would assume, however, that the liquidation value would represent some kind of a floor below which the seller would be unwilling to sell because he should be able to liquidate the company himself.

Replacement Value

The current cost of reproducing the tangible assets of a business can at times be significant in that starting a new company may be an alternative means of getting into the business. It sometimes happens that the market value for existing facilities is considerably less than the cost of building a plant and purchasing equivalent equipment from other sources. In most instances, however, this calculation is used more as a reference point than as a seriously considered possibility.

EARNINGS VALUATIONS

A second common approach to an investor's valuation of a company is to capitalize earnings. This involves multiplying an earnings figure by a capitalization factor or price-earnings ratio. Of course, this raises two questions: (1) Which earnings? and (2) What factor?

Earnings Figure

One can use three basic kinds of earnings:

— Historical Earnings: The logic behind looking at historical earnings is that they can be used to reflect the company's future performance; there is no logic in evaluating a company on the basis of what it has earned in the past. As will be discussed below, however, historical earnings should be given careful consideration in their use as a guide to the future. They should provide concrete realism to what otherwise would be just a best guess.

Historical earnings per se can rarely be used directly, and an extrapolation of these figures to obtain a picture of the future must be considered a rough, and frequently a poor, approximation. To gain the benefit from the information in a company's financial history of past operations, it is necessary to study each of the cost and income elements, their interrelationships, and their trends.

In pursuit of this study it is essential that random and nonrecurring items be factored out. Expenses should be reviewed to determine that they are normal and do not contain extraordinary expenses or omit some of the unusual expenses of operations. For example, inordinately low maintenance and repair charges over a period of years may mean that extraordinary expenses will be incurred in the future for deferred maintenance. Similarly, nonrecurring "windfall" sales will distort the normal picture.

In a small, closely held company, particular attention should be given to the salaries of owner-managers and members of their families. If these salaries have been unreasonably high or low in light of the nature and size of the business and the duties performed, adjustment of the earnings is required. An assessment should also be made of the depreciation rates to determine their validity and to estimate the need for any earnings adjustments for the future. The amount of federal and state income taxes paid in the past may influence future earnings because of carryover and carryback provisions in the tax laws.

— Future Earnings under Present Ownership: How much and in what ways income and costs are calculated for future operations depends to a large degree on the operating policies and strategies of management. The existing or future owners' approach will be influenced by a host of factors: management ability, economic and noneconomic objectives, and so on. In calculating future earnings for a company these kinds of things must be considered and weighed.

A calculation of value based on the future earnings of the company should provide an indication of the current economic value of the company to the current owner. To an investor, including the present owner as an investor, this figure should provide an economic basis for that individual's continued activity and investment in the company. (As we shall discuss later, there is usually more to a potential seller's position than just an economic analysis of his or her own future as an investor.) To an investor who anticipates a change in management with his investment, a calculation of value based on earnings from the current owner's continuing with the company is *not* a meaningful assessment of the value of the company to the investor.

— Future Earnings under New Ownership: These are the earnings figures that are relevant to the investor who is investing in the turnaround of a dying company or in the reinvigoration of a stagnant one. The basis for the figures—the assumptions, relationships between costs and income, and so on—will probably show significant variance from the company's past performance. Plans may be to change substantially the nature of the business. The evaluation and investment decision may also involve large capital investments in addition to the purchase price of the company.

It is the future earnings of the new operation of the business that are helpful in determining the value of the company to the entrepreneur as these are the earnings that will influence the economic return. Most likely these kinds of projections will have large elements of uncertainty, and one may find it helpful to consider the high, low, and most likely outcomes for financial performance.

In addition to deciding on an earnings period on which to focus, there is also the issue of "what earnings?" That is, profit before tax, profit after tax, operating income, or earnings before interest and taxes (EBIT). Most valuations look at earnings after tax (but before extraordinary items). Of course, the most important rule is to be consistent: don't base a multiple on earnings after tax, and then apply that multiple to EBIT. Beyond this, the most important factor to consider is precisely what you are trying to measure in your valuation. A strong argument can be made for using EBIT. This measures the earning power and value of the basic, underlying business, *without the effects of financing*. This is a particularly valuable approach if the entrepreneur is contemplating using a different financial structure for the business in the future.

Price-Earnings Multiple

Next, we have the issue of what multiple to use. Assuming that the investor's primary return is anticipated to result from sale of the stock at some future date, the investor should then ask the question: Given the anticipated pattern of earnings of this company, the nature of the industry, the likely state of the stock market, and so on, what will the public or some acquisitive conglomerate be willing to pay me for my holdings? In terms of some multiple of earnings, what prices are paid for stock with similar records and histories? To estimate with any degree of confidence the future multiple of a small company is indeed a difficult task. In many instances working with a range of values might be more helpful. This great uncertainty for a potential investor in estimating both a small company's future earnings *and* future market conditions for the stock of that company in part explains why his or her return on investment requirements for a new venture investment are so high.

Again, it is important to remember to be consistent: Always derive the multiple as a function of the same base you wish to apply it to—profit after tax, EBIT, or whatever.

Up until this point, we have been discussing methods of arriving at a value for the business as a whole. While the entrepreneur is naturally concerned with this issue, he or she is also concerned with the valuation of his or her piece of the business.

Residual pricing is a technique that addresses this issue. Essentially, residual pricing involves:

— Determining the future value of a company in Year n through one of the methods described above.

— Applying a target rate of return to the amount of money raised via the initial sale of equity.

— Using this information to develop a point of view on how much equity the entrepreneur must give up in order to get the equity financing required.

— The "residual," or remaining equity, can be retained by the entrepreneur as his return.

For example, if a company is projected to have earnings of $100,000 in Year 5, and if (after some analysis) it seems that the appropriate P/E for the company is 10, then we can assume that the company will be worth $1 million in Year 5. Now if we know that the entrepreneur needs to raise $50,000 from a venture capital firm (in equity) to start the business, and if the venture firm requires a 50 percent annual return on that money, then that $50,000 needs to be worth $50,000 \times (1 + 50 \text{ percent})^5 = \$380,000$. So in theory at least, the entrepreneur would have to give 38 percent of the equity to the venture firm in order to raise this money.

CASH FLOW VALUATIONS

Traditional approaches to evaluating a company have placed the principal emphasis on *earnings*. Assuming that the company will continue in operation, the earnings method posits that a company is worth what it can be expected to earn.

But this approach is only partially useful for the individual entrepreneur who is trying to decide whether or not to invest in a business. Again, the entrepreneur must distinguish between the value of the business as a whole and the portion of that value that can be appropriated for himself or herself. The entrepreneur must address the need to acquire resources from others and must understand that he or she will have to give up a portion of the value of the business in order to attract these resources. In addition to personal or subjective reasons for buying a business, the entrepreneur's chief criterion for appraisal will be return on investment. Because an entrepreneur's dollar investment is sometimes very small, it may be useful to think of return more as a return on his or her *time,* than a return on his or her dollar investment. To calculate the latter return, the entrepreneur must calculate his or her *individual* prospective cash flow from the business.

It is the entrepreneur's return *from* the business, rather than the return inherent in the business itself, which is important. As we shall see, there are several different types of cash flow that can accrue to the entrepreneur.

Operating Cash Flows

Cash or value that flows out of the business during its operations include:

— Perquisites: Perquisites are not literally cash at all, but can be considered cash equivalents in terms of their direct benefits. Business-related expenses charged to the company (e.g., company car and country club memberships) are received by the individual and are *not taxed* at either the corporate or personal level. Their disadvantage is that they are limited in absolute dollar terms.

— Return of Capital via Debt Repayment: This class of cash flow is a *tax-free* event at both the corporate and personal level. An additional advantage to this type of flow is that it can occur while enabling the entrepreneur still to maintain a continuous equity interest in the company. Its disadvantage is, of course, that it requires him or her to make the original investment.

— Interest and Salary: Both of these items constitute personal income and are taxed as such at the personal level. However, no tax is imposed at the corporate level.

— Dividends: As a means of getting cash from a venture, dividends are the least desirable as the resulting cash flow has undergone the greatest net shrinkage. Dividends incur taxes first at the corporate level (at the 15 percent or 34 percent rate as income accrues to the corporation) and then again at the personal level (at the personal income tax rate as the dividend payment accrues to the individual). At the maximum corporate income tax rate of 34 percent and the maximum personal income tax rate of 28 percent, we can see that this double taxation can reduce $1 of pretax corporate profit to $0.48 aftertax cash flow to the individual.

Terminal Value

Another source of cash is the money the entrepreneur pulls out of the business when the venture is harvested. Again, there are several elements to this aspect of return.

— Return of Capital via Sale: If the owner/manager sells all or part of the business, the amount he or she receives up to the amount of his or her cost basis is a *tax-free* event at both the corporate and personal level. Since a sale of his or her interest is involved, however, it is evident that unlike a return of capital via debt repayment, the owner/manager does not maintain his or her continuous equity interest in the concern. Also, like a cash flow based on debt retirement, an original investment is necessary.

— Capital Gain via Sale: When capital gains are realized in addition to the return of capital on the sale of stock, no tax is imposed at the corporate level; a sale of assets typically generates personal *and* corporate taxes.

Tax Benefits

While not precisely cash flow, tax benefits can enhance cash flow from other sources. For example, if a start-up has operating losses for several years, and if these losses can be passed through to the individual, then they create value by sheltering other income. Because entrepreneurs are often in a low-income phase when starting a business, these tax benefits may be of limited value to them. However, if properly structured, these tax benefits can provide substantial value to investors who can use them. In a situation where the structure and form of the organization (i.e., a corporation), does not permit the losses to flow through to the individual, these losses can be used to offset income of the corporation in prior or future years.

The entrepreneur must also take into account his negative cash flows. Three types of negative cash flows are particularly important:

— Cash portion of the purchase price.
— Deficient salary.
— Additional equity capital.

Frequently the most critical aspect of the cash portion of the purchase price is that it must be small enough for the entrepreneur to be able to pay in the first place. In this kind of situation the seller finances the purchase of his company by taking part of the purchase price in the form of a note. The seller then receives cash later on from future earnings of the company or from its assets. Of course, the less cash he or she is required to put up, the more cash the entrepreneur has available for other uses and the greater the opportunity he or she has to produce a high ROI. On the other hand, too much initial debt may hamstring a company from the start, thereby hurting the venture's subsequent financial performance and the entrepreneur's principal source of return—be it the cash withdrawn from the company or the funds received from eventual sale of the company.

The significance to the entrepreneur of a negative cash flow based on a deficient salary is clear—a lower income for personal use than could be obtained elsewhere. In addition, there is the effect that these early negative flows may have on the entrepreneur: Faced with an immediate equity requirement for working capital or fixed assets, the owner/manager may be forced to seek outside investors, thereby diluting his or her future value in the business and also introducing the possibility of divergent goals in the financial and other aspects of the company's operations.

At this point in our analysis it will appear obvious to some that the next step for the entrepreneur is to find the present value of the cash flow he or she predicts for the venture—in other words, discounting the value of future cash flows to arrive at a value of the venture in terms of cash today. We shall see, however, that in many respects this approach raises more questions than it answers, and therefore its usefulness to the analysis is questionable at best.

The essence of the problem is that present value is basically an investment concept utilizing ROI to determine the allocation of a limited supply of funds among alternatives, whereas the entrepreneur is faced basically with a personal situation where return on both investment and *time* are key. In addition, the entrepreneur may have made a considerable investment in generating the particular option, and it is difficult to weigh this tangible opportunity against unknown options. Because the entrepreneur does not have a portfolio of well-defined opportunities to choose from, he needs to define some standard of comparison. This is typically the salary that could be obtained by working.

In an investment analysis utilizing present value, the discount rate is selected to reflect uncertainty associated with cash flows; the higher the uncertainty, the higher the discount rate and, consequently, the lower the present value of the cash flows. In the corporate context there is usually a minimal ROI criterion for noncritical investments to keep the ROI greater than the firm's cost of capital.

For the individual entrepreneur, however, the decision to buy or to start a company is fundamentally a subjective one. Return on investment and time for this kind of decision is measured not only in terms of dollars, but also in terms of what he or she will be doing, who his or her associates will be, how much time and energy will have to be expended, and what lifestyle will result. Different kinds of ventures present *different kinds of return* on time. As cash to the entrepreneur is an important enabling factor for *some* of the things the entrepreneur is seeking, it is important that he or she calculate what these cash flows might be and when they can be expected. However, because decisions affecting cash flow also affect the other returns to the entrepreneur and because these other returns may be at least as important as the financial returns, a present value calculation often is not the most important measure.

In thinking about the attractiveness of a particular opportunity, an entrepreneur rarely has easily comparable alternatives. More than likely the decision is either to go ahead with a venture or to stay where he or she is until something else comes along. Perhaps the most useful way to think of this position is to imagine an individual looking down a corridor that will provide a range of opportunities—opportunities to achieve different levels of financial and other rewards with their accompanying risks and sacrifices. Financial theorists, for instance, have recently begun to study investments in terms of their ability to generate a future stream of growth opportunities.

SUMMARY

The previous discussion has outlined a variety of different approaches to the valuation of a firm. It is important to remember that no single approach will ever give the "right" answer. To a large extent, the appropriateness of any method of evaluation depends on the perspective of the evaluator. However, both in this course and in "real life" one must come to some point of view on the worth of a firm, no matter how scant the data. This is very important, even if the value is only a preliminary one, because it permits the individual to delve further into the issues at hand.

Nonetheless, the true purpose of the analysis is not to arrive at "the answer" but to:

— Identify critical assumptions.

— Evaluate the interrelationships among elements of the situation to determine which aspects are crucial.

— Develop *realistic* scenarios, not a best case/worst case analysis.

— Surface and understand potential outcomes and consequences, both good and bad.

— Examine the manner in which the value of the business is being carved up to satisfy the needs of prospective suppliers of resources.

No single valuation captures the true value of any firm. Rather, its value is a function of the individual's perception of opportunity, risk, the nature of financial resources available to the purchaser, the prospective strategy for operation, the time horizon for analysis, alternatives available given the time and money invested, and prospective methods of harvesting. Price and value are not equivalent. If the entrepreneur pays what the business is worth, he has not appropriated any value for himself. The difference is determined by information, market behavior, pressures forcing either purchase or sale, and negotiating skills.

Chapter Four

The Business Plan

A business plan is a document that articulates the critical aspects, basic assumptions, and financial projections regarding a business venture. It is also the basic document used to interest and attract support—financial and otherwise—for a new business concept. The process of writing a business plan is an invaluable experience, for it will force the entrepreneur to think through his or her business concept in a systematic way.

This note will raise and address issues that most entrepreneurs encounter as they prepare their business plans. One of the factors that makes crafting a good plan so difficult is the fact that it has a multitude of purposes. As described, the plan is a blueprint for the company itself, and, as such, is intended to help the firm's management. The plan is also typically used to attract potential investors. Finally, the plan may serve as the legal document with which funds are raised. These several uses highlight a constant conflict: To the extent that the plan is a "marketing document" for the company, it is likely to be more optimistic, one-sided presentation than a critical business analysis. For the purposes of legally raising funds, however, the document needs to contain a full disclosure of risks and legal "boilerplate" (see Securities Law and Public Offerings). Many a prospectus, for instance, contains the phrase—in big bold letters—"This investment is highly speculative and is suitable only for individuals who can afford a total loss of their investment." Thus, it

This note was prepared by Michael J. Roberts.

becomes extremely critical to understand exactly what purpose the "plan" is serving, and what audience such a purpose implies. Even if the document is clearly written to appeal to potential investors, it is important to know exactly what kind of investor. A busy venture capitalist or other professional investor will be more demanding than a private individual, who rarely invests in new enterprises. Similarly, a commercial banker reading the same document would have a different set of questions. Thus, the first rule is to keep in mind *who* the reader is and make sure the document addresses his or her particular concerns.

The bulk of this note will focus on preparing a business plan for the professional investor—venture capitalist or otherwise. A plan that meets the needs of this most demanding investor can be scaled down or used for other private individuals, who may well have professional financial advisors review the document anyway. This plan for investors may well include portions of an internal plan that includes far more detailed operating and contingency plans that would be suitable for investors.

To be clear, however, when we say a business plan, we do *not* mean a legal document for *actually* raising funds, although many entrepreneurs do think of these two documents as identical. First, a prospectus (or "offering memorandum," "investment memorandum," or "offering circular") needs to contain so much legal language and protective boilerplate as to be an ineffective marketing document. Second, we do not recommend proposing a "deal" (exact type and price of the security) in the business plan. Professional investors simply have far more expertise in crafting the security, and pricing is typically a matter of negotiation. Nonetheless, it is important to be clear on how much money you are seeking to raise and how it will be paid back. If money is being sought from less experienced private investors, the situation is more complicated. Not to propose a deal implies negotiating with many separate individuals who may have very different ideas about the type of security they are interested in and how it should be priced.

One approach that can be used to resolve these issues raised by the multiple objectives of the business plan is to follow the distribution of the plan with a more formal offering memorandum. In this way, only those investors who seem genuinely interested are actually solicited. And, this second offering memorandum can be used to meet the legal requirements of a fund-raising document.

THE PLAN

The following sections of this chapter will describe the various sections of a standard business plan. Overall, it is important that the plan be relatively short (40 or so pages in appropriate) and clearly written. Do not assume that the reader will be an expert in the technology or market you are interested in. Finally, think of the plan as an argument, for every point you make—the attractiveness of the market, the price you can charge for the product, its competitive advantages—offers evidence to support your claims.

To achieve this level of end product, it is often helpful to get others to read drafts of the plan. Certainly, members of the management team should prepare their section of the plan and read all of the others. Financial advisors or accountants can also play a valuable role. It is also a good idea to review other entrepreneurs' business plans to get a feel for how others have approached the task. If you can, talk to some of these individuals about their experiences writing the plan and raising funds. Finally, if you can speak with lawyers, accountants, and even some investors (whom you won't be targeting), you're bound to learn from them as well.

It is also a good idea to have a plan read by a legal advisor—presumably the same person who will help you incorporate and draft the other legal documents necessary for financing and starting the business. The securities laws are quite complicated, and you'll need expert advice to assure that you're not running afoul of them. (See Securities Law and Private Offerings.) Counsel will want to assure that you are not making any claims that could later pose problems (i.e., "Investors are guaranteed an attractive financial return"). In addition, there is some standard boilerplate that will help protect you from possible securities laws violations. Copies of the plans should all be individually numbered and a log kept detailing who received them.

The Executive Summary

These few pages are the *most* critical piece of any business plan. Investors will turn immediately to this section in order to get their first impression of the venture. To ensure that this section encompasses all that is should, it should be written last.

The executive summary must clearly but briefly explain:

— The company's status and its management.
— The company's products or services and the benefits they provide to users.
— The market and competition for the product.
— A summary of the company's financial prospects.
— The amount of money needed, and how it will be used.

The Company

This section should describe the company's origins, objectives, and management. The plan should describe how the company will be organized, who will fill these roles, and what their responsibilities will be. Some background on the founders should be given and their more extensive résumés referenced in an appendix. The "story" of how the company came into being should be briefly told so that potential investors get some sense of its history. The section should describe the current status of the company: number of employees, sales and profits (if any), products, facilities, and so forth. Finally, this section should paint a picture of where the company hopes to go and how it envisions getting there—its strategy.

The Product or Service

Having introduced the product in the previous section, the plan should describe it in more detail here. What needs does the product meet, especially compared to competitor's products. If the product exists and is in use, some detailed descriptions of that usage, the results, and some customer testimonials will prove valuable. If the product has yet to be manufactured, a description of how you intend to make it—and what the key milestones in the process are—is also important. If a patent or proprietary technology is employed, it should be explained here (although the proprietary aspects, of course, should not be divulged).

The Market

A common mistake is to deal with the marketing portion of the business plan in a cursory manner. Investors want evidence that the founders of a company have studied the market, understood it, and indeed are driven by their desire to satisfy its needs. To convey this, the plan should address:

— The size, rate of growth, and purchasing characteristics of the target market: Investors will be interested in—and will want to assure that the entrepreneurs are interested in and understand— market segments, the buying process, and how purchase decisions are made.

— The company's perspective on the market: Investors will be curious about the entrepreneur's perspective on the market. Why do you think the company is bringing something new to the market? What trends in the market does the company see, and what changes does the company anticipate in the future?

— The reaction the company expects from the market: What hurdles does the company expect in introducing its product? How will it overcome them? What features and benefits does the company expect will be particularly popular?

Competition

No business plan is complete without a section that describes the competitive firms and products. Again, investors want to be assured that the entrepreneurs understand whom they will be competing against. Information on competitors' products, prices, and marketing approaches should be included.

Sales and Marketing

This section of the plan should explain the manner in which the product will be sold. The plan should describe how target customers will be identified and how awareness will be built through advertising, promotion, or direct mail. The plan should also detail what distribution channel will be utilized, and how the product will be sold—by a direct sales force, reps, direct mail, and so forth. This section should also address how the company will introduce its product to the marketplace. This might include public relations, advertisement, special promotions, or targeted growth.

Operations

In this section, entrepreneurs should explain how the product will be manufactured: the facilities required, the use of subcontractors, and what equipment will be needed to actually produce the product. In general, investors would prefer to see a firm purchase or subcontract much of its manufacturing needs, at least initially. In addition, it is often desirable to lease facilities. The other aspects of operations, including distribution, should also be touched on.

Financials

In this section, investors expect to see realistic financial projections, typically for a five-year time horizon. The following information should be included: an income statement, balance sheet, cash flow forecast, and breakeven analysis. While the five-year forecasts should be relatively detailed, it is also important to highlight the key dimensions of the firm's financial performance—sales, earnings, and cash surplus (or deficit)—in some summary form.

It is critical that the financials be driven by *thoroughly documented assumptions*. For instance, don't just develop a sales forecast. Present detailed assumptions about unit volume and price. The same is true for expenses. This not only gives the investor the data he or she needs to evaluate your plan, it speaks volumes about your careful thinking. The financials should also clearly state the amount of money being sought and to what uses it will be put.

Investors will also be interested in how the venture plans on turning their cash investment back into cash. That is, what is the anticipated exit route for the investor: a public offering, a sale of the company, or a repurchase of shares by the firm? In the financial section, try to give potential investors some idea of how they can cash out.

While it's impossible to know what's going to happen in the future, investors will familiarize themselves with other firms in the industry in order to develop a sense of the appropriateness of the numbers forecasts. Once they are satisfied that the projections are realistic, investors will use these financials to help them value the firm and calculate a potential price for their investment.

Finally, some would-be entrepreneurs make use of public accounting firms to prepare their financials. They feel that the opportunity to present their projections on a prestigious account firm's stationery lends credibility to the numbers, and they may well be right. Some entrepreneurs are also anxious to use this approach to gain access to the network of wealthy private investors with which these accounting firms are well connected. While you may consider this approach on its merits, one point is clear. To use an accounting firm in such a manner is no substitute for having these critical financial skills as part of the venture's start-up team. Someone who is part of the team *must* have the ability to develop income statement and cash flow forecasts and budgets.

Appendix

The résumés of all key personnel and their responsibilities should be included in this section. In preparing the résumés, entrepreneurs should make sure that they portray themselves as a well-balanced team. In addition, any sample product literature, letters from customers or suppliers, and so forth can be included in the Appendix.

AFTER THE PLAN IS WRITTEN

When the plan is finished, it's time to distribute it to potential investors. It is wise to avoid simply sending the plan to all the venture capitalists you can find. Investors generally avoid plans that come in "over the transom" and far prefer to look at a plan that has been recommended by a financial advisor, lawyer, or company founder that they know and whose judgment they trust.

There are a number of different sources of capital available to entrepreneurs. They run the gamut from friends and family members, with limited or no experience providing capital, to professional investors, who manage a portfolio of investments in young firms. Each of these sources is attractive for different reasons, and it's up to the entrepreneur to understand the advantages and disadvantages of each (see Chapter 5, Alternative Sources of Financing). Within each category, *who* you raise money from is vitally important. The ability to attract successful, professional investors will lend credibility to your venture idea and will introduce you to a wide range of helpful contacts. Finally, many of these people are successful because they provide excellent guidance, and it will be to your benefit to avail yourself of it.

Because venture capital is such a visible portion of this spectrum of potential sources, it's worth knowing a bit about it. The venture capital industry is a highly fragmented network of individuals and small firms that accounts for $15 to $20 billion of capital. Other potential investors include Small Business Investment Corporations (SBICs) and the venture capital aims of larger corporations. Firms in the venture capital industry can be distinguished along four basic dimensions:

— The size of the investment pool: As with any industry, venture capital firms differ in the amount of money under management. Large firms might manage 10 to 20 times more capital than smaller firms.

— The stage(s) at which they prefer to invest: Venture capitalists tend to specialize in certain phases. Some prefer to invest in the seed and development stage so that they can own a larger part of the venture. Other VCs balk at the risks of this strategy and instead prefer to invest in later stage companies. Venture capitalists typically divide the investment process into four distinct rounds or stages.

  • Seed: This stage is the highest risk stage of investment because the company is usually newly organized and lacks an operational track record. In many situations the company is little more than an idea.

  • Development: This stage is also characterized by high risk. Companies in this stage are usually building a prototype product and exploratory marketing.

  • Revenue: Investments made in this stage are characterized by less risk than those made in the seed and development stages.

This is true because more information is available for venture capitalists to consider. Companies seeking funds in this stage usually have completed a prototype and have begun to market it to their customers.

- Profitable: Investments made in this stage are characterized by the least amount of risk. Venture capitalists prefer companies in this round because they are usually seeking capital to expand and grow.

— The minimum and maximum amount allocated in each investment: These amounts range anywhere from $150,000 to $5 million or more. Firms syndicate deals among many different companies to meet investment requests, which may be larger than the maximum amount considered.

— Preferred industries for investment: Venture firms may specialize by industry, believing that their ability to select attractive investments and add value is related to their degree of industry knowledge and expertise. Traditionally, high-technology industries such as microcomputers, telecommunications, and biotechnology have been popular with venture capitalists. More recently, low-tech and service sector businesses have become increasingly popular.

With these differences in mind, it's helpful to understand how venture capitalists tend to evaluate deals. They are quite busy and will rarely spend more than 5 to 10 minutes on an initial review of a plan. During this brief time, they will read the executive summary to get an understanding of the company's status and goals.

Plans that do not meet their criteria are rejected. Plans that seem to present an interesting investment opportunity are reviewed further. During this phase, venture capitalists try to understand and evaluate the key fundamentals of the business. These include:

— The management team: Professional investors are attracted by individuals with proven industry expertise and management ability, and some start-up experience is even better.

— The product/market: Venture capitalists like products that exist (in real life, not just in someone's mind), can be manufactured, and that have some evidence of acceptance into the market.

— The financials: Providers of capital like to see that their investment is likely to turn into value for them, typically within a three- to seven-year time horizon.

For all of these reasons, it is worth devoting some time and energy to a strategy to "get in the door." A 50-pound document and a form letter addressed to "To Whom It May Concern" is clearly a bad strategy. An introduction from a lawyer, another venture capitalist, or an entrepreneur whom the firm has backed are all superior options. Learn about the venture firm, its past investments, its strategy, and its people, and try to position your proposal in a way that fits with these elements.

Still, the process of evaluating a business plan is an imprecise art, not a science. Venture capitalists—who specialize in judging the potential of a business—make many investments that fail to live up to their expectations. Thus, many investors will use their "intuition" about a market, a business, and the entrepreneur to help make their decision.

SUMMARY

Essentially, the plan serves as a vehicle to get you in the door to talk to investors. They will probe you about the plan and also about your career and management experiences, and those of any other members of the team. A professional investor will present a good many potential problems. After all, the road to starting and managing a new venture is littered with unanticipated problems and difficult challenges. By gauging how you respond to the issues inherent in the fundraising process, the investor will be able to judge your diligence and business sense as well as the "fire in your belly"—sure to be as critical a factor in your success as a well-crafted plan.

First Place (A)

"My life plan when I left the Pacific Business School was to found a company and become a multimillionaire by the age of 30, take a Doctorate and pursue an academic career, and finally retire to the Bordeaux region of France to write. Given my experience, objectives, and time frame, I considered myself to be restricted to industries with a certain set of characteristics.

"I have long been fascinated with restaurants; however, my industry experience has been only a short period as a manager and several summers in hourly positions. I have never held a line marketing position with a restaurant organization, and my opinions and theories on restaurant marketing have developed through readings and personal observation. Having therefore not been indoctrinated with restaurant marketing techniques, I have had the opportunity to critique the traditional concepts as an industry spectator. I am convinced that the industry has misapplied traditional consumer marketing techniques.

"Despite my confidence in the First Place concept, I have spent considerable time considering the business risks caused by my relative lack of restaurant operations experience. In my opinion, the restaurant industry is one where the adage applies that 20 years of experience is only 1 year of experience repeated 20 times. I feel that I have had sufficient experience; I feel that I have surpassed the critical level of knowledge, following which my learning could only proceed in diminishing returns. I feel I am ready.

"I have spent the last four months researching the restaurant industry, especially the competitive structure and key operating pa-

This case was prepared by James Snider and Peter Tolnai under the direction of Howard H. Stevenson.

rameters of restaurants in the 'casual social and convenience middle market.' To find this information, I combed trade publications and traveled extensively to witness first-hand the most successful operations of my prospective competitors. Given my lack of industry experience, I have been guided by the belief that this comprehensive research is the best way for me to establish my credibility."

BACKGROUND

In June of 1978, Jack Paston graduated from the Pacific Business School and took a job as vice president of marketing for a computer software company. While working at this job, he developed a business plan to start his own restaurant. The following is an abridged version of this plan. (The full table of contents is shown on the following page, although some portions of the plan have been omitted.)

Business Plan for First Place
Table of Contents

Introduction

The restaurant industry has undergone dramatic changes over the past 20 years. What used to be a cottage industry composed of "mom and pop" operators is now a sophisticated, chain-dominated business. This transformation has been most evident in the fast-food segment of the industry where operators have introduced total standardization to all aspects of food service. During the 1960s and 1970s, the fast-food segment dominated the restaurant industry, and the operators who best served this market achieved spectacular growth.

The restaurant industry continues to evolve, however. There is considerable evidence that the fast-food segment of the industry has reached the maturity stage in its overall life cycle and that other segments of the industry will outperform the fast-food operators during the decades ahead. In particular, my research indicates that a "middle market" is developing as consumers' tastes and preferences shift away from the traditional fast-food eating experience. In this business plan I have outlined the marketing basis for this middle market opportunity and briefly presented the concept that I feel can be implemented to exploit this situation.

Evolution of the Middle Market

Growth Potential

The vast majority of concepts introduced during the 1960s and 1970s were in the fast-food segment of the industry. Restaurants opened featuring a wide array of food products, from soup to nuts and from muffins to baked potatoes. The fast-food segment was highly attractive to restaurant operators. This situation has now changed. The growth of the fast-food operators has leveled off. At the same time, consumer demand in the middle market has greatly increased. (See Exhibit 1 for 1978 growth rates of representative restaurants.) Since these shifts in consumer demand were not anticipated by the food service industry, the middle market is currently very underdeveloped. A clear opportunity exists for the introduction of new restaurant concepts that appeal to the middle market.

Concentration of the Industry

The increasing dominance of chain operators is a major trend within the industry. In 1975, chains accounted for 30.7 percent of industry sales; during 1980, their aggregate market share is forecasted to reach 50 percent. However, this statistic disguises the fact that chain market share varies greatly within each price segment of the industry. The table below demonstrates that as guest check averages increase, the aggregate market share maintained by chain operators decreases dramatically.

Segment Name	Price Range	Aggregate Chain Market Share within Each Segment
Fast food	$2.49 and under	86%
Upscale fast food	2.50 – $4.99	26
Middle	5.00 – 7.99	12
Gourmet	7.50 and up	8

Quite clearly, the fast-food segment is dominated by the sophisticated chains while the higher-priced market segments continue to be controlled by "mom and pop" operators.

Research indicates that the consumer acceptance of chain concepts will continue to increase. It is predictable that the upscale fast-food and middle-market segments will follow the example of the fast-food segment and become dominated by a few chain operators. Accordingly, this trend toward increased industry concentration will benefit those operators who have developed superior concepts and have the management ability to expand their operations without any loss of control. It therefore becomes important to quickly define, introduce, and expand a new concept in order to take advantage of this trend.

Consumer Behavior

Customers' Eating Out Frequency

Consumers' aggregate frequency of eating out has increased dramatically over the past two decades. This is clearly demonstrated by the fact that the ratio of grocery store sales to restaurant sales has decreased from 85:15 in 1963 to 75:25 in 1978.

This consumer behavior pattern is largely explained by two sociological phenomena. First, during the period 1950-1976, married female participation in the work force increased from 20 percent to 46 percent. Accordingly, the majority of wives now have considerably less time to plan and prepare meals at home and would prefer to eat out with their families instead. The extra income of these households with working female members also contributes to this increased eating out frequency. Second, eating out is no longer a "special event"; it is a generally accepted part of contemporary urban life. Consumers are willing to trade off the higher absolute cost of a restaurant meal for the factors of convenience, variety, and speed.

Since both of these phenomena are expected to continue, it appears that the overall rate of growth experienced by the restaurant industry will remain strong. The industry is forecasted to grow 3.4 percent per annum in real terms over the next five years.

Customers' Menu Preferences

Institutions Magazine annually conducts a "Menu Census" in which they survey restaurant operators to determine trends in consumer tastes and preferences for menu items. The scores for freshness and nutrition indicate that consumers are increasingly preferring fresh products which require less extensive cooking and preparation. The data also indicate that consumers are increasingly demanding portion size options in order to gain flexibility in their ordering patterns; this trend favors restaurants with a la carte menus with different portion sizes over those offering an entire "traditional dinner." Finally, the score for price/value indicates that although consumers maintain a definite price/value relationship, consumers' price sensitivity appears to be declining.

Six other editorial statements included in the 1979 Menu Census are as follows:

"Salads of all kinds continue to sell well."
"Soups sell. New entries and old favorites score well."
"Price increases have led some operators to cut back the number of entrees offered, but patrons are discovering new tastes."
"Fish and seafood prices have turned away some operators and patrons. The alternatives are innovative new offerings or the addition of 'healthy' foods."
"Hamburgers and cheeseburgers show signs of slipping."
"America's sweet tooth cannot be ignored, but patrons appear to be eating fewer desserts." (Note, however, ice cream obtained the highest score of all dessert products.)

A New Approach to Concept Development

The traditional approach to restaurant concept development has been quite simplistic. Operators would choose the most promising demo-

-3-

graphic segment as their target market, develop a menu traditionally favored by this group, and select a location where the concentration of these individuals was high. The operator might also implement a "gimmick" to distinguish his restaurant from others serving that market.

You will notice that this concept development process ignores the consumer behavior of the individuals making up the target demographic group. In my opinion, this concentration on overall demographic variables has led to an oversimplified approach to restaurant marketing. As an example, consider the weekly eating out habits of Mr. Smith, an average consumer.

On Monday, Mr. Smith has a business luncheon with a client at a fashionable downtown restaurant. On Tuesday, he and his family have a quick dinner at a restaurant close to their home before attending the movies. While shopping on Wednesday evening, Mr. Smith and his wife stop for hamburgers at a local fast-food restaurant. On Thursday, Mr. Smith's birthday, the couple dine at their favorite romantic restaurant. Friday, Mr. Smith has pizza and beer with old school friends while his wife shops. On Saturday, bringing the kids home from the baseball game, he stops at a fast-food outlet for take-home chicken.

An analysis of Mr. Smith's eating-out habits during that week indicates that, according to the traditional marketing approach, he entered virtually every market segment.

Monday: formal tablecloth
Tuesday: family
Wednesday: fast food (hamburgers)
Thursday: atmosphere
Friday: specialty (pizza)
Saturday: fast food (chicken)

However, during the week Mr. Smith obviously maintained a constant demographic profile—age, sex, marital status, family size, income level, etc. Therefore, although operators attempt to target their concepts toward specific demographic groups, the Mr. Smith example illustrates that any given demographic group may patronize any type of restaurant, depending on the individual customer's requirements at any given moment. Based on this observation, it is clear that demographics may be of limited use in selecting and attracting a target market.

I have developed an alternative approach for concept development which focuses upon the two real problems in restaurant marketing:

(A) Why do people eat out? (The Eating-Out Decision)
(B) How do they select specific restaurants? (The Restaurant Selection Process)

Instead of considering overall demographic variables, my approach considers the individual consumer's reason(s) for eating out and examines his or her expectations for the eating out experience.

(A) <u>The Eating-Out Decision.</u> It is my contention that people eat out for 10 basic reasons and that all restaurant visits can be assigned 1 of these 10 categories. THESE 10 CATEGORIES THEN REPRESENT THE SEGMENTS OF THE RESTAURANT INDUSTRY BASED ON THE CUSTOMER'S

ACTUAL MOTIVATION FOR EATING OUT. I have termed these 10 segments the Motivation Groups.

Of the 10 Motivation Groups, the two which are of particular interest are the Convenience and Casual Social segments, since they constitute the majority of the middle market.

Convenience. The convenience market segment describes restaurant occasions where consumers consider the extra cost of a restaurant meal to be less than the time and trouble of preparing food at home. The customer's "make-or-buy" decision is either impulse or a planned purchase.

Casual Social. The casual social market segment describes restaurant occasions where a group of people, who are quite familiar with each other on a social basis, meet for a meal.

It should be clear that the individuals who are motivated to eat out for convenience and casual social reasons may be drawn from virtually all demographic segments. Restaurant concepts should therefore be targeted to attract a specific Motivation Group, not a selected demographic segment. (See Exhibit 2 for descriptions of the other eight motivation groups.)

(B) The Restaurant Selection Process. How does a customer belonging to a specific Motivation Group select a restaurant? Consider the following argument.

The overall eating-out experience consists of four major components: food, service, atmosphere, and price. These four major components can be further broken down into their basic elements; these individual elements are called the PRODUCT ATTRIBUTES. It should be noted that all Product Attributes are relevant for all restaurant experiences, and that the Product Attributes are variable factors that are determined by the restaurant operator.

Furthermore, when a customer is a member of any given Motivation Group, the customer maintains a set of expectations that describes all aspects of his or her upcoming eating experience. Accordingly, CUSTOMERS WILL CHOOSE THE RESTAURANT THAT BEST FULFILLS THEIR NEEDS AND EXPECTATIONS AT THAT PARTICULAR TIME. Stated another way, customers will select the restaurant where the Product Attributes most closely correspond with the expectations of their Motivation Group.

A Summary of Expectations can be developed that describes the optimal condition for each of the Product Attributes for a given Motivation Group. If correctly developed, this Summary of Expectations then defines the Product Attributes that the restaurant operator must fulfill in order to attract a given Motivation Group.

I have prepared a Summary of Expectations for the Convenience and Casual Social Motivation Groups (see Exhibit 3). When these summaries are compared with each other, it becomes evident that they share very similar sets of Motivation Group expectations. Accordingly, it should be possible to attract both Motivation Group segments by "managing" the Product Attributes to appeal to one Motivation Group without offending the other. Furthermore, the customer-expected Product Attributes of these two Motivation Groups appear to coincide directly with the characteristics of the successful middle market restaurants. The specific characteristics of the First Place concept have therefore been developed to be consistent with the expectations of the Convenience and Casual Social Motivation Groups.

The First-Place Concept

The key characteristics of the first place concept are briefly summarized below. Further details on these aspects may be found in the Customer-Visible Operations section of the Business Plan.

Name. The name of the restaurant would be First Place. The accompanying promotional phrase to be included in the logo would be "Where Winners Can Be Choosers."

Theme. A sports theme would be developed with particular attention to individual sports such as skiing, swimming, cycling, track and field, in addition to the traditional team sports. Equal emphasis would be placed on men's and women's athletics. The theme would be implemented through authentic artifacts, photographs, menu descriptions, food server uniforms, etc.

Menu. Approximately 80 sandwiches would be available, of which 30 would be served hot. These would range from a simple "ham and swiss" to relatively exotic and complicated sandwiches with unusual ingredients. The menu would also offer 10 hamburgers, which would differ only in the toppings available. First Place would also offer approximately 25 salad products; of these, 5 would be pre-prepared specialty salads (e.g., Caesar), and 20 would be green garden salads assembled to order in the kitchen using different combinations of ingredients. About 15 hot and cold soup recipes would be developed and, of these, 6 would be available daily on a rotating basis. The principal dessert would be ice cream and related products, including banana splits, parfaits, and sundaes. The restaurant would be fully licensed for alcoholic beverages.

Site Selection. The concept is intended to be implemented in suburban and neighborhood areas with a high population density and a high mean household income level. An optimal location would be within a major suburban shopping mall. Approximately 5,000 square feet are required.

Service and Atmosphere. Full table service would be provided. The atmosphere would be casual and relaxed.

Pricing. The menu, portions and prices have been structured so that guest check averages will be between $6.50 and $6.75.

Turnover. The customer service and food production operations are designed to ensure that customers can complete a typical meal within 45 minutes without rushing.

Capacity. Approximately 180 seats.

Key Financial Characteristics

The projected annual sales volume is $2 million with a profit after tax of $312,000. The break-even sales volume would be slightly over $800,000. The total expected capital requirement is $296,000, which assumes that the building and primary kitchen equipment are fully leased. Exhibit 4 indicates the various pro forma operating results and capital requirements for various possible sales volumes.

Corporate Objectives

It is my intention to develop First Place into a major chain that can achieve a prominent position within the new generation of middle market restaurants. Accordingly, I would seek to verify the validity of the concept with the first unit, refine operations to a highly structured level, and sub-

sequently expand by the addition of new units both in Canada and the
United States.

All units would be company owned and operated, and growth
would proceed as financial resources and management capabilities permitted. There would be no franchising. It would be my intention to locate
four or five units within each selected market to achieve synergistic effects in marketing and management. I also feel that it is very important to
have an on-site regional manager responsible for no more than six units.

Direct Competition

During the past few years, various operators have recognized the
existence of the middle market opportunity and have developed new concepts. The success of these operators was noted in the 1978 Tableservice
Operations Report published by Laventhol & Horwath, an accounting firm
that is heavily engaged in consulting to the restaurant industry. The following statements were made by members of their consulting staff:

> A middle market segment is developing in Kansas City
> as a result of the escalating prices of the specialty restau-
> rants. This segment, characterized by heavy decor, full-
> service menus, youthful service personnel, and $3–$6 check
> averages is capitalizing on both young families and singles
> who demand specialty restaurant atmosphere and service but
> are value conscious.
>
> Especially noteworthy are those moderately priced res-
> taurants which have responded to clearly identified segments
> of demand by being innovative in service, menu, and decor.
>
> They (the customers) don't mind paying the price for
> food of good quality and quantity.

Moreover, it appears that success in the middle market is not restricted to any specific food type(s). Most important, a few restaurants
whose menus revolve around "exotic" sandwiches and salads have
opened quite successfully in various markets. In Exhibit 5, I have compared First Place with several of its most successful competitors along
certain key operating parameters.

This analysis demonstrates that the First Place concept is viable
and can be expected to achieve the financial projections indicated. It is
quite clear that the market will support a superior sandwich, soup, and
salad concept targeted towards the middle market.

First Place Unique Success Factors

For a new venture to be successful, it must possess definite conceptual, strategic, technological, or management advantages in order to effectively compete. The First Place concept possesses the following five
Unique Success Factors.

High Menu Variety: Limited Food Inventory

Although the menu offers a great variety within each product line,
(soups, salads, sandwiches, and desserts), it requires a very limited number of raw materials to execute. Through the various combinations and
permutations of ingredients, the 80 sandwiches, 25 salads, and large
number of desserts would require approximately 24 meats and cheeses,

19 produce products, 6 breads, 8 ice cream types, and sundry nonperishable seasonings and condiments to produce.

Product Assembly and Delivery Time

The entire menu has relatively high advance preparation requirements; the soups must be cooked beforehand, and all the ingredients for salads and sandwiches must be prepared prior to peak meal periods. When any given menu item is ordered by a customer, the product can be produced by the kitchen and available for customer delivery within five minutes of ordering.

Diversification of Ingredient Requirements

Many restaurant concepts suffer from very high exposure to volatile commodity prices of their primary raw materials. The raw material requirements for First Place are fully diversified across meats, dairy, produce, and baked goods. Furthermore, even within an ingredient line such as meat, the raw material requirements are diversified into beef, fowl, pork, etc. The First Place concept will therefore suffer very little cost pressure due to fluctuating *individual* commodity prices, and ingredient diversification assures that food costs will vary directly with the overall food price index.

Coincidence of High Volumes and Increased Gross Margin

Restaurant operations are typically very seasonal, with summer volumes being traditionally higher as demonstrated in Exhibit 6. This situation is aggravated in Canada by the severity of the winter season. Although the raw material ingredients are fully diversified overall, produce will clearly form a major component of the aggregate food cost. Since produce costs decline substantially during the summer months, overall food costs will be lowest when volumes are highest.

Less Variable Sales Patterns

Restaurants are typically busiest on Fridays and Saturdays, with significantly lower business volumes throughout the rest of the week. Exhibit 6 illustrates the typical distribution of meals by day of the week for the three principal types of restaurants described in the literature. Obviously, the key to success within the industry depends upon increasing sales Sunday through Thursday. If the Motivation Group approach to restaurant marketing is valid, it appears that the problem of highly variable daily sales volumes can be effectively managed within the First Place concept. It is evident that the weekend sales increases experienced by most operators are generated by the Sexual, Formal Social, Personal Event, and Entertainment Motivation Groups. First Place does not compete for these groups. Instead, First Place competes for the Convenience and Casual Social Motivation Groups whose restaurant occasions occur throughout the week as a result of the "fast-paced" contemporary North American lifestyle. First Place would therefore attract early week business at a significantly greater rate than the industry average, thereby establishing a much smoother weekly sales pattern.

Management of Risks

The restaurant industry has developed a reputation as a high-risk business. Many potential investors have felt that the apparent risks were unmanageable and that the food service industry should therefore be avoided as an investment possibility.

In my opinion, many of these risks can be minimized if the concept is fundamentally sound and the operations managed according to generally accepted management principles. This section lists five often mentioned risks and describes how they would be managed under the First Place concept.

1. "Labor costs are going up and up. Besides that, it's impossible to find the good people that you need to work in restaurants."

   Contrary to the popular view, it has been my experience that restaurant employees can be effectively managed if the proper policies are developed and implemented, and if sufficient management attention is paid to potential employee problem areas. In First Place, programs would be introduced for employee training and development, merit compensation, internal promotion, and tip pooling to provide employees with a well-structured working environment and incentives for superior performance.

2. "Restaurants don't do very well during recessions."

   During times of generally poor economic conditions, restaurants in the lower and middle price ranges do very well while expensive restaurants do quite poorly. Because of the trading down phenomenon and the increased disposable income spent on restaurant meals, middle and lower priced restaurants actually benefit from recessions.

3. "Employees will steal anything that's not chained down in a restaurant."

   Employee theft of both food and equipment is a major problem within the industry. But certain control and measurement systems have proven to be extremely effective in limiting employee theft in similar restaurants. Therefore, although the problem exists, it can be managed and minimized to an acceptable level.

4. "It will be very difficult to compete with the established fast-food chains if they decide to enter the middle market."

   The development of the middle market has not gone unnoticed by the major fast-food chains, and they are attempting to diversify their menus and upgrade their decors. However, the efforts of the fast-food chains to reposition themselves in the marketplace will be unsuccessful for several reasons. First, their existing consumer images are already very well established; the changes in consumer tastes and preferences for the overall eating-out experience far exceed their ability to upgrade their physical facilities from counter service and the production of a very limited menu, both of which are inconsistent with consumer preferences in the middle market. Finally, their sites were selected based upon consumer traffic patterns which favored fast-food purchases (e.g., highway interchanges). Many of their locations are therefore appropriate only as fast-food outlets, and it is doubtful that a chain would risk diluting its customer image by modifying some units to appeal to the middle market while not changing others.

5. "I don't think that a sandwich-oriented menu will attract customers for dinner on a consistent basis."

   Studies clearly demonstrate that the ratio of lunch to dinner business is remarkably constant between the fast food and middle market segments and that middle market restaurant occasions are relatively evenly split between lunch and dinner, regardless of food type.

Customer Visible Operations

Obviously, the most important factor that determines the lunch/ dinner mix is site selection. As mentioned previously, the First Place concept is designed to be implemented in major suburban shopping malls. Lunch business would consist of shoppers, the staff of the shopping center, and retailers and workers from nearby office buildings. Dinner business would be derived from shoppers, people returning home from the city, and area residents who wish to eat out for convenience and/or casual social reasons.

Site Selection

As explained previously, there are only two important considerations in restaurant site selection: traffic and personal disposable income. Due to the shopping and residency patterns which have evolved in most North American cities, exposure to these variables is maximized by locating in, or near, major suburban shopping malls.

The advantages of mall locations are well documented. First, the data indicate that the greatest absolute expenditure on food away from home is made by families residing in the neighborhood/suburban areas of the major metropolitan markets. Second, other research demonstrates that, over the past five years, restaurants located in these neighborhood/ suburban areas have had a sales growth rate which exceeds that of the industry by 29.5 percent. Finally, in 1975, the National Restaurant Association conducted a study in which they examined the eating-out habits of customers during shopping trips. Interestingly, 65 percent of the respondents indicated that they ate out either always, frequently, or fairly often during shopping trips. Their average evening expenditure on eating out was $4.22, or $6.07 in inflation-adjusted 1979 dollars.

Furthermore, as growth proceeds, it may prove worthwhile to develop free-standing units adjacent to major malls for three reasons. First, the comparative traffic and visibility characteristics for "in-mall" and "shopping center peripheral" locations are quite similar. However, free-standing sites have a significantly greater opportunity for attracting late evening business than do in-mall locations, which suffer when the rest of the mall closes at 9 or 10 P.M. Second, in-mall locations may attract too many weary shoppers who order minimal amounts; these shoppers are too lazy to make the effort to cross the parking lot. Finally, the previously mentioned National Restaurant Association study found that 41 percent of respondents preferred visiting restaurants within walking distance of their shopping location, instead of eating within the mall. This figure rose to 48 percent for families with incomes greater than $25,000.

Customer Invisible Operations

Kitchen Operations

1. Forecasting: Following the first month of operation, daily meal counts and the sales mix should become quite stable. Forecasting systems can then be implemented to ensure that raw material purchases and daily food preparation are adequate to meet daily requirements without overprocuring and sacrificing freshness.

2. <u>Purchasing</u>: All purchased food products would be specified by weight, size, quality, and brand name (if applicable). Only authorized products would be purchased. All purveyors would have to be approved by myself, and checks would only be issued to vendors on the approved listing.

3. <u>Receiving</u>: The quality of the incoming raw materials must obviously be maintained in order to serve a high quality product. Accordingly, all goods would be inspected for quality and freshness when received, and products that do not meet specifications would be returned. It has been my experience that purveyors will deliver only the best products to an account if they know that substandard products will be consistently returned.

4. <u>Food preparation and assembly</u>: All preparation procedures, specifications, recipes, and assembly instructions would be tightly specified. For example, based on the daily forecast, food preparation employees would know exactly how much of each ingredient to prepare (e.g., 15 pounds of ham to be sliced into 4-ounce portions at slicer setting 22). For the assembly of sandwiches, salads, and desserts, menu boards would be fixed on the wall in front of the respective work areas listing the contents of each product as well as assembly instructions. For example, Salad #16 (Large) might read as follows:

Endive/Iceberg lettuce mixture	2/3 bowl
15 carrot slices	sprinkled
15 mushroom slices	sprinkled
8 cherry tomatos	outside
8 cucumber slices	outside
3 tablespoons chopped scallions	sprinkled
4 cauliflower wedges	inside
1 broccoli stem	lay on top

5. <u>Other kitchen policies and procedures</u>
   a. Quality control testing.
   b. Clean-up procedures.
   c. Portion control checks.
   d. Movement of inventory from primary storage to secondary storage to current use.
   e. Production and rotation policies for soups.

EXHIBITS

1. Chain Restaurant Growth Analysis.
2. Remaining Eight Motivation Groups.
3. Product Attributes for the Convenience and Social Motivation Groups.
4. Pro Forma Income Statements.
5. Direct Competition Comparisons.
6. Patterns of Restaurant Sales.
7. Ingredients.
8. Calculation of Food Costs and Guest Check Average.
9. Kitchen Equipment Cost.
10. Leasehold Improvement, Furniture, and Fixture Costs.
11. Pre-Opening Expenses.
12. Occupancy and Equipment Leasing Costs.
13. Pro Forma Cash Flows.

Note: Unless otherwise stated, all exhibits and figures have been computed based on the following assumptions.

(1) The turnover cycle is 45 minutes.
(2) The Guest Check Average is $6.68.
(3) The restaurant contains 180 seats.
(4) The restaurant utilizes 5,000 square feet.   *$400*
(5) Total annual sales are $2 million.   *sq. foot*
(6) During the first two months of operations, sales volumes will reach forecasted levels due to the well documented "honeymoon" effect.
(7) During the first two months, food and labor costs will exceed normal levels by 20 percent due to start-up inefficiencies.

EXHIBIT 1   Chain Restaurant Growth Analysis (fiscal 1978)

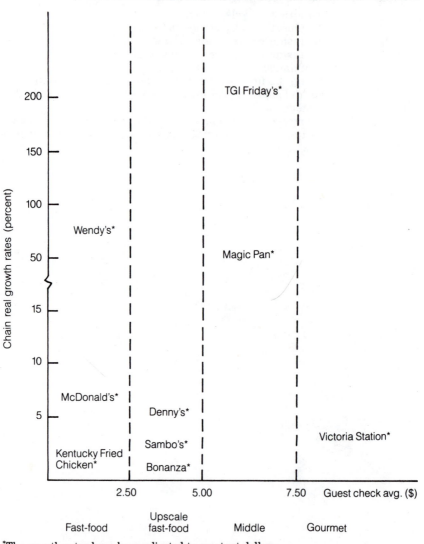

*The growth rates have been adjusted to constant dollars.

(4) Adequacy - No.

EXHIBIT 2   Remaining Eight Motivation Groups   *()Applicability   No*

1. Expediency
   The consumer's single reason for eating out is immediate hunger satisfaction.

2. Available at Restaurants Only
   In this market segment, the primary reason for eating out is to consume a food item that cannot be prepared at home.

3. Business
   The primary purpose for business meals is to provide the participants with a quiet and uninterrupted setting for private conversation.

4. Personal Events
   Dinners are typically used to celebrate memorable events such as birthdays, anniversaries, and promotions.

5. Institutional Events
   These are meals held by a group of coworkers (e.g., office parties), bowling leagues, civic organizations, etc.

6. Sexual
   Dinner dates provide a socially acceptable setting for couples to get further acquainted.

7. Formal Social
   The primary purpose for formal social restaurant visits is to entertain a person or group where circumstances dictate that proper decorum be observed.

8. Entertainment
   Within this segment, some form of entertainment forms a major component of the overall eating-out experience.

EXHIBIT 3   Product Attributes for the Convenience and Social Motivation Groups

Product Attributes	Expectations of Convenience Motivation Group	Expectations of Casual Social Motivation Group
Food	Food	Food
Food quality	Primary importance	Equal in importance to
Portion size	Quality	social aspects
Taste	Nutrition	Acceptable to all in
Nutrition level	Portion sizes	party
Menu variety	Limited menu may be	Portion size high
Freshness	inhibitor; standard	Quality must be
Liquor availability	menu should appear	moderate to high
Presentation	Interesting taste, not	Exotic menu,
Caloric content	too bland	substantial
		marketing
		Nutrition very
		important

EXHIBIT 3 *(concluded)*

Product Attributes	Expectations of Convenience Motivation Group	Expectations of Casual Social Motivation Group
Service	Service	Service
Turnover time	High service level	Friendly and easygoing
Reservations or not	Pacing of meal highly	Hostess to organize
Seating hostess or not	structured	seating
Friendliness of staff	Turnover cycle: 40–50	Reservations not
Customer/staff	minutes	required
interaction	Moderate seat comfort	Licensed lounge if
Payment method	required	customers have to
Entertainment	Knowledge of menu by	wait
Pacing of meal	foodserver high	Turnover cycle: 50–60
Flexibility in service	Most group sizes: 2's	minutes
style	and 4's	Payment: postmeal,
Attention to detail	Reservations not	foodserver, credit
	required	cards must be
	Hostess required to	accepted
	organize seating	Medium-size groups
	Licensed lounge not	(6–8 people)
	required	Flexibility in meal
		pacing
		Seating comfort is
		moderate
		Knowledge of menu by
		foodserver high
Atmosphere	Atmosphere	Atmosphere
Noise level	Moderate noise level	Informal and relaxed
Lighting	Music with moderate	Privacy varied but not
Intensity of theme	volume, relatively	too high
Degree of privacy	contemporary	Decor, noise level:
Decor	Some distractions, but	moderate
Seating comfort	able to be ignored	Ambient entertain-
Music (type, volume)	Privacy can be varied	ment but customer
	by choice	should be able to
	Casual and relaxed	ignore it
		Music: contemporary,
		medium volume
Price	Price	Price
Food	Guest check less than	Moderate prices
Beverage	$7.50	($5–$7.50 guest
Tipping patterns	Tipping pattern:	check averages)
	10–12%	Liquor prices not
		excessive
		Tipping pattern:
		approximately 12%

EXHIBIT 4 Pro Forma Income Statements   *Useful*

	Worst Case	Planned Volume	Best Case
Food	$ 883,000	$1,766,000	$2,649,000
Liquor/wine/beer	117,000	234,000	351,000
Total sales	1,000,000	2,000,000	3,000,000
Cost of goods	320,000	640,000	960,000
Gross margin	680,000	1,360,000	2,040,000
Direct labor	224,000	338,000	455,000
Management payroll	79,000	79,000	96,000
Payroll related expense	31,000	44,000	57,000
Employee bonus plan	0	20,000	30,000
Total labor	334,000	481,000	638,000
Maintenance and repairs	24,000	36,000	48,000
Laundry	9,000	18,000	27,000
Serviceware	15,000	22,000	29,000
Guest supplies	7,000	14,000	21,000
Utilities	25,000	35,000	45,000
Credit card commissions	15,000	30,000	45,000
Licenses	1,000	1,000	1,000
Miscellaneous (telephone, office, etc.)	4,000	5,000	6,000
Total other variables	100,000	161,000	222,000
Total operating costs	754,000	1,282,000	1,820,000
Equipment leasing	32,000	32,000	32,000
Occupancy costs	100,000	160,000	240,000
Taxes	8,000	8,000	8,000
Advertising and promotion	5,000	10,000	10,000
Insurance	10,000	10,000	10,000
Depreciation and amortization	18,000	18,000	18,000
Total overhead	173,000	238,000	318,000
Profit before tax	73,000	480,000	862,000
Income tax (assumes 35% effective tax rate)	25,000	168,000	302,000
Net earnings	$ 47,000	$ 312,000	$ 560,000

Note: During the first year of operation, pretax earnings would be decreased by $41,000, representing the write-off of pre-opening expenses.

EXHIBIT 5   Direct Competition Comparisons

Restaurant Name	Total Sales ($)	Annual Meals Served	Number of Seats	Guest Check Average ($)	Required Seat Turnover per Day
FIRST PLACE (at break-even sales volume)	$ 800,000	120,000	180	$6.67	1.85
FIRST PLACE (at expected sales volume)	2,000,000	300,000	180	6.67	4.63
MR. GREENJEANS (Toronto, Ontario)	2,000,000	312,000	160	6.41	5.41
D. B. KAPLAN'S (Chicago, Illinois)	3,000,000	650,000	300	4.61	6.05

(4) Adequacy - No
Sample size small.

EXHIBIT 6   Patterns of Restaurant Sales

Seasonality of Restaurant Sales

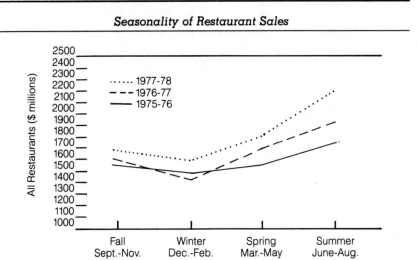

Meal Distribution by Week Day and Restaurant Type

	Noon Meal			Evening Meal		
Day of Week	Family	Fast-Food	Atmosphere	Family	Fast-Food	Atmosphere
Monday	13	10	11	7	9	8
Tuesday	12	14	15	12	17	10
Wednesday	16	15	20	11	15	14
Thursday	13	18	18	11	15	13
Friday	22	19	23	23	22	21
Saturday	13	17	8	20	13	22
Sunday	11	7	5	16	9	12
Totals	100	100	100	100	100	100

EXHIBIT 7 Ingredients

Meats	Salads	Miscellaneous	Miscellaneous	Ice Creams	Ice Cream Sauces/Toppings
Turkey	Iceberg lettuce	Tomato slices	Sauerkraut	Chocolate	Blueberry
Bacon	Romaine lettuce	Lettuce	Jelly	Vanilla	Chocolate-fudge
Hamburgers	Chickory (endive)	Onions (sauteed)	Tomato (broiled)	Strawberry	Pineapple
Ham	Asparagus	Beer mustard	Tartar sauce	Butterscotch	Strawberry
Crab meat salad	Beets	Cole slaw	Avocado slices	Banana	Cherry
Roast beef	Broccoli	Carbur's "Special" sauce	Sour cream	Black cherry	Marshmallow
Corned beef	Cabbage	Garlic mayonnaise	Honey	Pistachio nut	Peanuts
Shrimp salad	Carrots	Raw white onions	Marshmallow	Coffee	Jimmies
Steak (broiled)	Cauliflower	Avocado spread	Banana		Walnuts
Pastrami	Celery	Green peppers	Cottage cheese		Raisins
Knockwurst	Cucumbers	Russian dressing	Kidney beans		Marshmallows (mini)
(grilled)	Mushrooms	Taragon mayonnaise	Cucumbers		Smarties
Chicken livers	Onions (Bermuda)	Mushrooms (sauteed)	Hot crushed peppers		Chocolate chips
(grilled)	Onions (scallions)	Horseradish mayonnaise	Hot cherry peppers		Whipped cream
Tuna salad	Radishes	Mushrooms (raw)			Banana slices
Oysters (fried)	Spinach	Peanut butter			Strawberries
	Tomatoes	Blue cheese dressing			
Cheeses	Tomatoes (cherry)	Mayonnaise (plain)			
Swiss	Oranges	Bermuda onions (slices)			
Provolone		Chili mayonnaise			
American cheddar					
Sharp cheddar					
American colby					

EXHIBIT 8 Calculation of Food Costs and Guest Check Average

Product	(1) Average Product Price ($)	(2) Average Product Cost ($)	(3) Average Food Cost (%) (2) ÷ (1)	(4) Probability of Being Ordered by a Customer	Guest Check Average Excluding Liquor ($) (1) × (4)	Weighted Product Food Cost ($) (2) × (4)
Sandwiches	3.75	1.30	35	.75	2.8125	.984
Salad—Large	3.95	1.30	33	.20	.7900	2.610
—Small	2.55	.65	25	.50	1.2750	.319
Soup	1.55	.45	26	.25	.3875	.101
Beverage	.45	.20	44	.90	.4050	.178
Dessert	1.50	.55	33	.15	.2250	.074
Total					$5.895	$1.917

Sales mix weighted food cost: $\dfrac{\$1.917}{\$5.895} = 32.5\%$

Projected food revenue per person: $5.895
Projected liquor/wine/beer revenue per person: $.78
Projected total guest check average: $6.675

79

-20-

(1) Applicable   No

EXHIBIT 9   Kitchen Equipment Cost

Equipment	Cost
Dishwasher	$ 12,000
Walk-in cooler (18' by 6')	11,000
Garbage compactor (2,000 pounds per day)	10,000
Microwave ovens (2)	8,000
Slicers (2) (automatic, with portion control)	7,200
Shelving	5,500
Exhaust hood	5,000
Soup kettles (2) (1-50 gallons, 1-40 gallons)	5,000
Broiler	5,000
Ice machines (2) (1-200 pounds per day) (1-200 pounds per day)	4,000
Range (8 burners, with oven)	3,000
Undercounter freezer/work table (6-door, 120 cubic feet)	3,000
Shredder/dicer	3,000
Refrigerators (2) (72 cubic feet)	3,000
Beer cooler (4-door, self-contained compressor)	2,500
Fryolator	2,000
Ice cream freezer	2,000
Draft beer dispenser (including chiller)	2,000
Dishwashing sinks	1,500
Coffee machines (2) (5-pot)	1,500
Glass chiller	1,300
Plate chiller	1,300
Soda fountain system	1,000
Refrigerators (2) (14 cubic feet)	1,000
Spring-loaded ice bins (2)	1,000
Scales (3) (1-receiving) (2-portion control)	1,000
Kitchen smallware	15,000
Serviceware (adjusted to projected sales mix and sufficient for three complete turnovers)	11,000
Miscellaneous equipment	5,000
Total kitchen equipment cost	$133,800

EXHIBIT 10   Leasehold Improvements, Furniture, and Fixture Costs

Leasehold Improvements Cost

Item	Cost
Architect's professional fees	$ 20,000
Wall finishings	20,000
Partitions, other specialized interior finishings	15,000
Artifacts, photographs	15,000
Bar structure	10,000
Project manager	9,000
Carpets	7,000
Merchandising displays	6,000
Exterior signage	2,000
Miscellaneous	5,000
Total leasehold improvements cost	$109,000

Furniture and Fixture Costs

Item	Cost
Chairs	$ 9,000
Lighting (including emergency)	8,000
Tables	5,000
Music system	3,000
Safe, office furnishings and equipment	3,000
Washroom accessories	1,000
Burglary system	1,000
Miscellaneous	3,000
Total furniture and fixtures cost	$ 33,000

EXHIBIT 11   Pre-Opening Expenses

Item	Cost
Capitalized, leasehold improvements	
Architect's professional fees	$ 20,000
Construction—project manager	9,000
Subtotal	29,000
Capitalized, organization costs	
Professional fees, legal and accounting	15,000
Professional fees, restaurant design	15,000
Menu design	2,000
Subtotal	32,000
Expensed from earnings	
Salary (3 managers for 2 months)	10,000
Salary (1 secretary for 6 months)	7,000
Pre-opening hourly training	5,000
Manager recruiting (placement fees)	4,000
Menu printing	3,000
Menu development and testing	2,000
Hourly employee training materials	2,000
Licenses and applications	1,000
Miscellaneous pre-opening expenses (telephone, postage, office supplies, storage, printing, etc.)	7,000
Subtotal	41,000
Total pre-opening expenses	$102,000

EXHIBIT 12   Occupancy and Equipment Leasing Costs

It has been assumed that the occupancy cost for 5,000 square feet of space in a prime location would be the greater of either $20 per square foot ($100,000 per annum) or 8 percent of gross revenues. Under this assumption, the gross revenue leasing arrangement would come into effect at a sales volume of $1,250,000, which is well above breakeven. It has been further assumed that the landlord would be responsible for providing adequate heat, air conditioning, electrical, gas, and plumbing systems.

It has also been assumed that $108,000 of primary kitchen equipment would be obtained through some sort of leasing arrangement. The assumed terms were a closed five-year lease with an internal rate of return to the lessor of approximately 18 percent.

EXHIBIT 13 Pro Forma Cash Flows

Expense Item	Pre-Opening Cash Flow		Operating Cash Flows—First Fiscal Year			
	Q_1-1980	Q_2-1980	Q_3-1980	Q_4-1980	Q_1-1981	Q_2-1981
Professional fees						
Architects	$6,000	$ 6,000	$8,000	—	—	—
Tax and accounting	5,000	5,000	5,000	—	—	—
Restaurant design	5,000	5,000	5,000	—	—	—
Salaries						
Managers	—	10,000	—	—	—	—
Secretary	3,500	3,500	—	—	—	—
Construction—project manager	4,500	4,500	—	—	—	—
Management recruiting (placement fees)	—	4,000	—	—	—	—
Licenses and applications	500	500	—	—	—	—
Menu testing and development	2,000	—	—	—	—	—
Menu design and printing	1,000	4,000	—	—	—	—
Hourly training materials	—	2,000	—	—	—	—
Pre-opening hourly training	—	5,000	—	—	—	—
Miscellaneous pre-opening expenses	3,500	3,500	—	—	—	—

Serviceware	—	—	11,000	—	—	—
Smallware	—	—	15,000	—	—	—
Furniture and fixtures	—	—	33,000	—	—	—
Leasehold improvements	—	—	80,000	—	—	—
Working capital	—	—	122,000	—	—	—
Add: Funds provided by operations	—	—	51,000	$ 69,000	$ 62,000	84,000
Add: Depreciation and amortization	—	—	4,500	4,500	4,500	4,500
Total cash flow	($31,000)	($53,000)	($223,500)	$ 73,500	$ 66,500	$88,500
Total cumulative cash flow	($31,000)	($84,000)	($307,500)	($234,000)	($167,500)	($79,000)

85

R&R

During the summer of 1983, Bob Reiss observed with interest the success in the Canadian market of a new board game called *Trivial Pursuit.*® His years of experience selling games in the United States had taught him a rough rule of thumb: the sales of a game in the United States tended to be approximately 10 times those of sales in Canada. Since Trivial Pursuit had sold 100,000 copies north of the border, Reiss thought that trivia games might soon boom in the United States and that this might represent a profitable opportunity for him.

REISS' BACKGROUND

After his graduation from Harvard Business School in 1956, Reiss began working for a company that made stationery products. His main responsibility was to build a personalized pencil division, and he suggested that he be paid a low salary and a high sales commission. He was able to gain an excellent understanding of that market and by 1959 could start on his own as an independent manufacturer's representative in the same industry. His direct contact with stores that sold stationery products revealed that many of them were beginning to sell adult games. He decided to specialize in those products.

In 1973, Reiss sold his representative business to a small American Stock Exchange company in the needlecraft business in exchange for shares. He then set up a game manufacturing division and ran it for that company, building sales to $12 million in three years.

Reiss decided to go into business for himself again in 1979 and left the company. He incorporated under the name of R&R and worked with

This case was prepared by Jose-Carlos Jarillo Mossi under the direction of Howard H. Stevenson.

the help of a secretary from a rented office in New York; Reiss promised himself that he would keep overhead very low, even in good years, and never own or be responsible for a factory. In addition to being a traditional manufacturer's representative, he did some consulting for toy manufacturers, using his extensive knowledge of the market.

THE TOY AND GAME INDUSTRY

One of the main characteristics of the toy industry was that products generally had very short life cycles, frequently of no more than two years. Fads extended to whole categories of items: one class of toys would sell well for a couple of years and then fade away. Products that were part of categories tended to ride with the fate of that category, regardless to some extent of their intrinsic merit. Many new products were introduced every year, which made the fight for shelf space aggressive.

Promotional plans for a new product were a key factor in buy or no-buy decisions of the major retailers. At the same time, fewer and fewer retailers were dominating more of the market every year. The largest one, Toys "Я" Us, for example, had 14 percent of the entire market in 1984. The success of a product was often based on less than a dozen retailers.

A few large manufacturers were also becoming dominant in the industry, because they could afford the expensive TV promotional campaigns that retailers demanded of the products they purchased. Billing terms to retailers were extremely generous compared to other industries, thus increasing the need for financial strength. Financing terms ran from a low of 90 days to 9 to 12 months. In general, major retailers were reluctant to buy from new vendors with narrow product lines unless they felt that the volume potential was enormous. On the other hand, the large manufacturers tended to require a long lead time for introducing new products, typically on the order of 18 to 24 months.

The industry was also highly seasonal. Most final sales to the public were made in the four weeks prior to Christmas. Retailers decided what to carry for the Christmas season during the preceding January through March. There was a growing tendency among them, however, not to accept delivery until the goods were needed, in effect using the manufacturer as their warehouse.

THE TRIVIA GAME OPPORTUNITY

Trivial Pursuit was developed in Canada and introduced there in 1980. Its 1983 sales were exceptionally strong, especially for a product that had been promoted primarily via word of mouth. The game was introduced in the United States at the Toy Fair in February 1983 by Selchow & Righter, makers of Scrabble, under license from Horn & Abbot in Canada. Earlier, the game had been turned down by Parker Bros. and Bradley, the two largest game manufacturers in the United States.

Trivial Pursuit in the United States had a $19 wholesale price, with a retail price varying from $29.95 to $39.95, about 200 percent to 300 percent more expensive than comparable board games. Selchow was not known as a strong marketer and had no TV advertising or public relations budget for the game. The initial reaction at the Toy Fair in February had been poor. Yet, by August the game had started moving at retail.

Reiss thought that if the success of Trivial Pursuit in Canada spilled over to the United States, the large game companies would eventually produce and market their own similar products. This would generate popular interest in trivia games in general and constitute a window of opportunity for him. The only trivia game in the market as of September 1983 was Trivial Pursuit. Two small firms had announced their entries and were taking orders for the next season. Bob Reiss decided to design and market his own trivia game.

DEVELOPING THE CONCEPT

Reiss' first task was to find an interesting theme, one that would appeal to as broad an audience as possible. On one hand, he wanted to capitalize on the new "trivia" category that Trivial Pursuit would create; on the other, he wanted to be different, and therefore could not use a topic already covered by that game, such as movies or sports. Further, his game would have its own rules, yet be playable on the Trivial Pursuit board.

As was his custom, Reiss discussed these ideas with some of his closest friends in the manufacturer's representative business. Over the years, he had found them a source of good ideas. One of the reps suggested television as a topic. Reiss saw immediately that this had great potential: not only did it have a broad appeal (the average American family watches over seven hours of TV per day), it offered a great PR opportunity. A strong PR campaign would be needed since Reiss knew clearly that he was not going to be able to even approach the advertising budgets of the large manufacturers, which would probably surpass $1 million just for their own trivia games.

Because licensing was common in the toy industry and was a way to obtain both an easily recognizable name and a partner who could help promote the product, Reiss realized he could add strength and interest to his project if he could team up with the publishers of *TV*

Guide. This magazine had the highest diffusion in the United States, approaching 18 million copies sold each week. It reached more homes than any other publication and could be called a household name.

On October 17, 1983, Reiss sent a letter, printed below, to Mr. Eric Larson, publisher of *TV Guide.*

Mr. Eric Larson, Publisher   October 17, 1983
TV Guide
P.O. Box 500
Radnor, PA 19088

Dear Mr. Larson:

I am a consultant in the game industry and former owner of a game company.

Briefly, I would like to talk to you about creating a game and marketing plan for a TV GUIDE TRIVIA GAME.

In 1984, trivia games will be a major classification of the toy industry. I'm enclosing copy of a forthcoming ad that will introduce a game based on the 60 years of Time magazine. I am the marketer of this game and have received a tremendous response to the game, both in orders and future publicity.

This project can benefit both of us, and I would like to explore the opportunities.

Sincerely,

Robert S. Reiss

In a follow-up phone conversation, Mr. Bill Deitch, assistant to the publisher of the magazine, asked Reiss for some detailed explanation on the idea. Reiss sent the following proposal:

Mr. Bill Deitch   November 14, 1983
TV GUIDE
P.O. Box 500
Radnor, PA 19088

Dear Mr. Deitch:

In response to our phone conversation, I will attempt to briefly outline a proposal to do a TV Trivia Game by TV Guide.

WHY A TV GAME? It is a natural follow-up to the emerging craze of trivia games that is sweeping the country. This category should be one of the "hot" categories in the toy/game industry in 1984. This type of game got its start in Canada three years ago with the introduction of Trivial Pursuit. It continues to be the rage in Canada and was licensed in the United States this year. It is currently the top selling nonelectronic game. It retails from $29.95 to $39.95 and is projected to sell 1 million units. It is not TV promoted. The Time Game, with 8,000 questions covering six general subject areas, only began to ship two weeks ago and had an unprecedented initial trade buy, particularly with no finished sample available for prior inspection.

WILL TV GUIDE BE JUST ANOTHER TRIVIA GAME? No. The next step is to do specialty subjects. Trivial Pursuit has just done a Motion Picture Game with excellent success. Our research tells us that a TV-oriented game would have the broadest national appeal.

THE MARKETS. This type of game has wide appeal in that it is nonsexual and is of interest to adults and children. We feel we can place it in over 10,000 retail outlets ranging from upscale retailers like Bloomingdale's and Macy's to mass merchants like Toys "Я" Us, Sears, Penney, K mart, Target, etc. There is also a good mail-order market. The market is particularly receptive to good playing, social interactive games at this time. Video games are in a state of decline as their novelty has worn off. (To say nothing about profits.)

WHO WILL DEVELOP THE GAME? Alan Charles, a professional game developer who did the Time Game, is free at this moment to do work on the project. He has satisfied the strict standards Time, Inc. has set for putting its name on a product and mine for play value and product graphics in a highly competitive market. . . . No easy task.

WHO WILL PRODUCE AND MARKET THE GAME? There are two options for producing the game.

1. Give it to an established game company who would assume all financial risk as well as production and distribution responsibilities. Under this set-up, TV Guide would get a royalty on all goods sold.

2. TV Guide assumes all financial responsibilities for game. Production and shipping would be handled by a contract manufacturer. Bob Reiss would be responsible for hiring and supervising a national sales force to sell the game. This is not an unusual option, and I do have experience in this. All sales are on a commission basis. This way, TV Guide gets the major share of the profits.

   Attached exhibit explores some rough profit numbers for TV Guide, via both options.

POSITIONING OF GAME. We see the game as noncompetitive to Trivial Pursuit and Time Magazine Game. It can be developed to retail at $14.95, as opposed to $39.95 for Trivial Pursuit and $29.95 for Time. (Mass merchants generally discount from these list prices.) The TV Game should be able to be played by owners of both games as well as on its own. The name TV Guide is important to the credibility of the product. Sales of licensed products have been growing at geometric rates in the last decade. Consumers are more comfortable buying a product with a good name behind it.

PROMOTION OF GAME. Pricing of the product will have an ad allowance built into it. This will allow the retailers to advertise in their own catalog, tabloids and/or newspaper ads. An important part of promotion should be ads in TV Guide. Ads can be handled two ways: one, with mail order coupon and profits accruing to TV Guide; the other, with listing of retailers carrying the item. As you have so many regional splits, the listing could be rather extensive. Financially, you would probably opt for the first option on a royalty arrangement and the second if you owned the product.

This product lends itself perfectly to an extensive public relations program. This is an excellent product for radio stations to promote. This should be pursued vigorously.

BENEFITS TO TV GUIDE
- Profits from royalties or manufacturing.
- Extensive publicity through wide distribution on U.S. retail counter, including the prestigious retailers as well as the volume ones. This is the unique type of product that can bridge this gap.
- Good premium for your clients. Can be excellent premium for TV stations. Can be used as a circulation builder. In projecting profits, I have not included premiums. The numbers can be big, but they are difficult to count on.

TIMING. To effectively do business in 1984, all contracts must be done and a prototype developed for the American Toy Fair, which takes place in early February 1984. Shipments need not be made until late spring.

WHO IS BOB REISS? He is a graduate of Columbia College and Harvard Business School who started his own national rep firm in 1959, specializing in adult games when it became a distinct category in 1968. He sold his company in 1973 to an American Stock Exchange company. He remained there for five years and built Reiss Games to a dominant position in the adult-game field. For the last three years, he has been consulting in the game/toy industry and recently acted as broker in the sale of one of his clients, Pente Games, to Parker Bros.

I am enclosing some articles that have a bearing on the subject matter. I think what is needed, as soon as possible, is a face-to-face meeting, where we can discuss in greater detail all aspects of this proposal as well as responsibilities for all parties.

Sincerely,
Robert S. Reiss

RSR/ck
encl.

Rough Profit Potentials to TV Guide

Assumptions
1. Average wholesale cost of $7.15 after all allowances. (This would allow department stores and mail order to sell at $15. Discounters would sell at $9.95 to $11.95.)
2. Cost to manufacture, $3 each.
3. Royalty rate of 10 percent. (Range is 6 percent to 10 percent, depending on licensor support and name. Assuming 10 percent, based on fact you would run No Cost ads in TV Guide.)
4. Mail order retail in TV Guide is $14.95, and you would pay $4 for goods. Postage and handling would be a wash with small fee charged to customer.

Option I: Royalty Basis
Projected retail sales: 500,000 units.
*Royalty to TV Guide of $357,500.
Mail order sales: 34,000 units. (.002 pull on 17 million circulation.) Based on full-page ad with coupon. It is extremely difficult to project mail order sales without testing—too many variables. However, this is a product that is ideal for your audience.
*Profit to TV Guide of $372,300.

Option II: You Own Goods

Costs: (rough estimate)

Manufacture	$3.00
Royalties to inventor	.36
Fulfillment	.30
Sales costs	1.43
Amortization of start-up costs	.10
Total cost	$5.19
Profit per unit	$1.96

Profit on 500,000 units $980,000.00
(Does not include cost of money.)

Another phone conversation followed in which *TV Guide* showed a clear interest in pursuing the subject. Reiss answered with a new letter on December 12, 1983, that outlined clearly the steps that had to be followed by both parties should they want to go ahead with the venture. Reiss had to send still another letter with a long list of personal references that *TV Guide* could contact. *TV Guide* finally opted to be a licensor, not a manufacturer. They would give Bob Reiss a contract for him to manufacture the game or farm it out to an established manufacturer, provided he stayed involved with the project. *TV Guide* would receive a royalty that would escalate with volume. Royalties were normally paid quarterly, over shipments; Reiss, however, proposed to pay over money collected, which *TV Guide* accepted. As part of the final deal, *TV Guide* would insert, at no cost, five ads in the magazine worth $85,000 each. These would be "cooperative ads"; that is, the names of the stores selling the game in the area of each edition would also be displayed. Reiss thought that including the names of the stores at no cost to them would be a good sales argument and would help ensure a wide placement of the product.

DEVELOPING THE TV GUIDE TRIVIA GAME

The actual game was designed by a professional inventor, whom Reiss knew, in exchange for a royalty of 5 percent—decreasing to 3 percent with volume—per game sold. No up-front monies were paid or royalties guaranteed. Although the inventor delivered the package design in just a few weeks, the questions to be asked were not yet formulated, and Reiss realized he could not do this alone. *TV Guide*'s management insisted that their employees should develop them. Reiss would pay per question for each of the 6,000 questions he needed; employees could moonlight on nights and weekends. Reiss felt it was important to put questions and answers in books rather than cards like Trivial Pursuit. The cost would be considerably lower, and the most serious bottleneck in manufacturing—collating the cards—would be eliminated. Overall, the presentation of the game tried to capitalize on the well-known *TV Guide* name (Exhibit 1). The game also lent itself well to this approach, as the question books imitated the appearance of *TV Guide* magazine (Exhibit 2).

Initially, Reiss had not wanted to include a board with the game; he wanted people to use Trivial Pursuit's board and had made sure that the rules of the new game would take this into account. However, *TV Guide* wanted a complete game of its own, not just supplementary questions to be played on someone else's game. Another advantage of including a board, Reiss realized, was that a higher price could be charged.

Since *TV Guide* had opted for being merely a licensor, it was Reiss's responsibility to set up all the operations needed to take the game to market in time for the 1984 season, and there were only two months left until the February Toy Fair, where the game had to be introduced.

His first consideration was financial. He estimated that the fixed cost of developing the product would be between $30,000 and $50,000, but some $300,000 would be needed to finance the first production run. Those funds would be needed until the initial payments from sales arrived a few months later.

Reiss seriously considered raising the required money from the strongest among his manufacturer's representatives in the toy business, thinking they would push hard to sell the game to every account. Eventually, he decided against this approach: not only would it not contribute that much to the venture, reps could be motivated to sell in other ways. Perhaps more important, Reiss feared the prospects of perhaps 20 partners who "would be every day on the phone asking how things are going."

Another option that passed through his mind, which he dismissed promptly, was venture capital. He realized that he would have to give up too much and, even worse, that venture capitalists would not understand this kind of deal—one that had very attractive short-term profits but few long-term prospects.

TRIVIA INCORPORATED

With the agreement with *TV Guide* in hand, Reiss called Sam Kaplan—a long-time friend who lived in Chicago. Kaplan, 65 years old, had a sizable personal net worth, yet kept working at his small but successful advertising agency (25 employees) "for the fun of it," as he liked to say. Reiss thought that teaming up could be an important help, and Kaplan was indeed enthusiastic about the idea.

Reiss proposed to establish a company, Trivia Inc., that would develop the project. The equity would be split evenly among the two partners. Kaplan, besides lending his line of credit to purchase supplies for the initial run, would use his office to handle day-to-day details. (In fact, Trivia Inc. ended up having only one full-time employee.) Also, because of his vast knowledge of printing and his contacts, Kaplan could secure press time and paper supplies on short notice, and he would supervise the product's manufacturing. This was especially important, since the special paper stock on which the game was printed was then in short supply, and long lead times were generally needed to obtain it. Kaplan would also produce all the ads and the catalog sheets. Reiss would take responsibility for sales and marketing of the product and would pay all reps and coordinate the publicity and the relations with *TV Guide*. An important part of the agreement was that R&R (Reiss's company) would have the exclusive rights to market the game and would receive a commission of 20 percent of the wholesale price from which it would pay the commissions to the reps.

PRODUCTION, SHIPPING, AND BILLING

From the beginning, Reiss's intention was not to be a manufacturer. Through Kaplan's connections, they found not only good suppliers for the question books, the board, and the boxes, they even got lower costs than expected. But, they still had to tackle the problem of assembly and shipping. Kaplan was a long-time consultant to Swiss Colony, a manufacturer of cheese based in Madison, Wisconsin. This company specialized in mail sales and had developed a strong capability to process mail orders. As a result, Swiss Colony's management had decided several years earlier to offer that fulfillment capability to other companies. They took the orders, shipped the product, and billed to the retailer.

In the deal ultimately reached, Trivia Inc. would have the components sent by the different suppliers to Madison on a "just-in-time" basis, and Swiss Colony would put the boards, dice, and questions in the boxes, package, and ship them. Swiss Colony would charge $.25 per box, including billing for the games, and would send complete daily information on sales to Trivia Inc. Trivia Inc. would pay $2,500 for a customized computer program. With all these measures, Reiss and Kaplan were able to lower their estimated costs by 30 percent and attained the flexibility they wanted. The final cost of manufacturing, assembling, and shipping was about $3.10, not including the royalties paid to the inventor and to *TV Guide*.

A final point was financing the accounts receivable, once the sales started rolling in, and collecting the debts. Reiss was somewhat afraid that the bills of some of the smaller stores carrying the game would be very difficult to collect, since R&R did not have the resources to follow up closely on its collections; moreover, Trivia Inc. needed the leverage of a factor in order to collect from the larger retailers on time. He and Kaplan decided to use Heller Factoring to check credit, guarantee payment, collect the money, and pay Trivia Inc., all for a fee of 1 percent over sales. Trivia Inc. would not need any financing for operations: after 45 days of shipping, Trivia Inc. would always be in a positive cash flow. Thanks to Heller and Swiss Colony, Trivia Inc. had practically no administrative work left to itself.

SELLING THE GAME

Selling was the most important issue for Reiss. He knew that placing the goods in the stores and selling them to the public (selling through) were two distinct, many times unrelated, problems. In any case, however, he thought that the game needed to be priced below Trivial Pursuit to make up for both their lack of a complete national advertising campaign that major manufacturers would launch, and their lack of the kind of brand recognition that Trivial Pursuit was achieving. Accordingly, the wholesale price was set at $12.50, with a retail list price of $25.

Reiss distinguished carefully between two different channels: the mass merchandisers and the department/gift stores. An important part of the overall strategy was to sell quickly to upscale retailers who would establish a full retail mark-up (50 percent). These were mainly department stores, such as Bloomingdale's or Marshall Field's, and mail order gift catalogs and specialty gift stores. This, it was hoped, would help sell mass merchandisers and give them a price from which to discount. Such a two-tiered approach was not common in the industry. On long-life products, many times only the full-margin retailers got the product the first year. But Reiss felt that this could not be done with his product, because it could well be only a one-year product. Mass merchandisers, however, had to be reached, since they accounted for at least 70 percent of the market. (Exhibit 3 shows some of the stores Reiss thought had to be reached.)

Two different sets of reps were employed for the two different channels; on average, they received a 7 percent commission on sales. Reiss's personal knowledge of buyers for the major chains proved invaluable. He was able to obtain quick access to the important decision makers at the major chains. They also followed, when possible, the distribution pattern of *TV Guide* magazine. It was soon apparent that the statistics on demographics reached by *TV Guide*, which Reiss made sure all buyers saw (Exhibit 4), had a major impact. As Reiss said, "It appeared that every outlet's customers read *TV Guide*." The cooperative ads in the magazine, with the possibility of including the store's name, were also a powerful attraction for different buyers, as Reiss had expected: the name of their stores would be displayed in far more homes than it would with a conventional advertising campaign in national magazines. The stores would not be charged to have their name in the ads, but minimum purchase orders would be requested. Many large customers, such as K mart and Sears, placed large orders before the product was even finished. (Exhibit 5 shows a cover letter that was sent to supermarket buyers.)

PROMOTION

In order to promote the game to the public, Trivia Inc. had a four-part plan, beginning with the five ads in *TV Guide* (Exhibit 6). The first ad broke in mid-September 1984, and was strictly for upscale retailers, with $25 as the price of the game. *TV Guide* had eight regional issues, and different stores were listed in each area with a total of about 120, including Bloomingdale's, Marshall Field's, Jordan Marsh, and J. C. Penney. They all had to place minimum orders. The second ad, shown on October 6th, was just for Sears. The third, on November 10th, was devoted to mass merchandisers and did not include a retail price. The fourth, two weeks later, listed four of the most important toy chains: Toys "Я" Us, Child World, Lionel Leisure, and Kay Bee. The appeal to the public, then, was not just the ad: Reiss knew that showing well-known upscale stores carrying the game initially was the best way to obtain instant credibility for the product. Finally, K mart, the largest U.S. chain, gave Trivia Inc. an opening order to all their 2,100 stores, even before the game went into production, in exchange for the exclusivity in the fifth ad to be run in *TV Guide* on December 8, 1984. In that ad, K mart offered a three-day sale at $16.97.

The second part of the plan also tried to give credibility to the game. Trivia Inc. offered the department stores a 5 percent ad allowance (a 5 percent discount from wholesale price) if they put the product in newspaper ads, tabloids, or catalogs. For similar reasons, Reiss wanted to have the game placed in mail order gift catalogs. Their sales in the toy-game business were only moderate, but catalogs gave a lot of product exposure because of their large circulation figures.

The final part of the plan was to obtain free media publicity. The publisher of *TV Guide* magazine wrote a letter to be sent to the producers of such shows as "Good Morning, America," "CBS Morning News," "The Tonight Show," and to 25 top TV personalities, together with a sample of the game. Through *TV Guide*'s PR agency and the joint efforts of *TV Guide* and Trivia Inc., many newspapers, radio, and TV stations were reached. In all, more than 900 press kits were sent to media organizations. As a result, the game was mentioned on many talk shows (TV and radio), and news of it was published in many newspapers (Exhibit 7). The cost of this campaign was split between Trivia Inc. and *TV Guide*.

THE RESULTS

By October 1983, Selchow, manufacturer of Trivial Pursuit, started falling behind trying to meet the demand. By Christmas, when sales exploded, there was no hope of keeping up—and one of the most serious manufacturing problems was the bottleneck of collating the cards. By the February 1984 Toy Fair, most of the major manufacturers offered trivia games, which was projected to be the hottest category for the year.

R&R sold 580,000 units of the *TV Guide* Game in 1984 at the full wholesale price of $12.50. There were few reorders after mid-October, as the market became saturated with trivia games (over 80 varieties) and Trivial Pursuit flooded the market. By Christmas 1984, all trivia games became heavily discounted; many retailers ran sales on Trivial Pursuit at $14.95, having paid $19.00.

Bad debts for Trivia Inc. were about $30,000 on approximately $7 million billings, with hope of recovering $15,000. Losses from final inventory disposal (it was decided to close out the game) were less than $100,000.

TV Guide was extremely pleased with the royalty collected from the venture. Kaplan, through his 50 percent ownership in Trivia Inc., made over $1 million net. The total cost of designing and launching the product had been $50,000.

Commenting on the whole deal, Reiss said:

I think the critical aspects of success in being a contract manufacturer are to take care of your suppliers and to take care of your sales representatives. We want our suppliers to charge us full mark-up, so that we are a good customer to them, and we try hard to give them enough lead time to deliver. We pay on time always, no matter what happens. In exchange, we demand perfect work from them. They understand and like this relationship. We need their cooperation, because we are completely dependent on them.

The other aspect is how to deal with your customers, which for us are the manufacturer's representatives and the buyers of major chains. The manufacturer's reps are used to the fact that when sales really do pick up in any product and they can make a lot of money, many manufacturers try to "shave" their commissions, perhaps feeling that the reps are making too much money. I never do that: I am happy if they make millions, and they know it. I also pay on time always. With this, I have developed a loyal and experienced work force and have no fixed or up-front sales cost.

All of these factors allowed us to move quickly. My contacts enabled me to print and manufacture the game for the same cost as a big company. But, a Parker Bros. or Milton Bradley would have incurred fixed costs of roughly $250,000 just for design and development and would then have committed to an advertising and promotion budget of at least $1 million.

THE FUTURE

According to Reiss, the big question at the end of 1984 was, "Do we add on a new version of the *TV Guide* Game, do a new trivia game, or go onto something new in spite of the great market penetration and success of our game?"

He had been doing some planning for a new game to be called WHOOZIT? and, instead of questions, it would show photographs of famous people that the players would have to recognize. He had a preliminary royalty deal with Bettman Archives, who had the exclusive marketing rights to all the photographs of the news service UPI, in addition to their own extensive archives. But, he was unsure about what the best follow-up for the success of 1984 could be.

The market, however, did not seem to be in the best condition. The 1984 Christmas season had ended with large unsold inventories of Trivial Pursuit and other trivia games. Some major companies, like Parker Bros., Lakeside, and Ideal, had closed out their games at low prices, further flooding the market. Many buyers were saying that trivia games, as a category, were over, although they seemed to accept Selchow's estimate of 7 million units of Trivial Pursuit sold in 1985. That figure was well below the 20 million units sold in 1984 but was still an exceptionally high figure compared with other board games. Selchow had also announced a plan to spend $5 million to promote the game in 1985. Some upscale retailers, however, had announced their intention to abandon Trivial Pursuit and other trivia games, mostly because of the heavy discounting.

Reiss thought that one of the reasons why the public seemed to have lost interest in trivia games is that they were hard to play; too often, none of the players knew the answers. In retrospect, he thought that the *TV Guide* Game had had the same problem. But, that would be different with WHOOZIT?. He was thinking of making easier questions and giving several chances to each player, and he really expected the new game to be enjoyable.

In addition to improving the intrinsic playability of the game, Reiss wanted to have more flexibility selling it. He planned to offer three different price points, one of the versions having only the questions so it could be played on the Trivial Pursuit board. In spite of all these improvements, however, he was not sure whether he should try to replicate the success obtained with the *TV Guide* Game and wondered what his best strategy for a follow up could be.

EXHIBIT 1   Photo of the Game

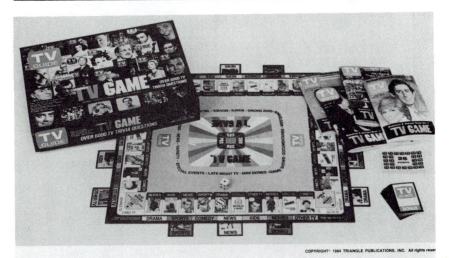

TV GUIDE'S TV GAME, the new board game for two to 20 players, contains more than 6,000 trivia questions and answers prepared and authenticated by the editors of TV GUIDE. It provides both a nostalgic trip through the days of Lucy and Uncle Miltie, and a journey through today's video environment...its people, its programs, and the world we all experience TV GUIDE'S TV GAME can be played as a family game (for ages 10 to adult), a party game with up to four teams with five or more players on a team, or without the board using just the questions and answers.

100

EXHIBIT 2 Book with Trivia Questions

TV GUIDE

Local Programs
July 25-31, 1981

The Royal Wedding: What It Means To Us
BY ANTHONY BURGESS
—Plus a Guide to Watching It

Question & Answer Book No. 2

TV GUIDE'S GAME

Name the three pitchers who each posted 20 victories for the 1956 Cleveland Indians. **Herb Score, Early Wynn & Bob Lemon**

Gene Stephens of the Red Sox shared the American League RBI title in 1949 and 1950—both times with teammates. Who were they? **Ted Williams (1949) and Walt Dropo (1950)**

On Oct. 19, 1957, this player scored a goal against Chicago's Glenn Hall—making him the first NHL star to score 500 goals in a career. **Maurice ("Rocket") Richard**

In 1921, Babe Ruth set an American league record with 171 runs batted in. Who held the old RBI mark? **Ty Cobb, who drove in 144 runs in 1911**

This Depression-era slugger was the first man to win back-to-back American League MVP honors. **Jimmy Fox (1932-33)**

Who was the last National Leaguer to win the Triple Crown? **Joe Medwick (St. Louis Cardinals, 1937)**

These two Hall of Famers are the only players to win baseball's Triple Crown twice. **Ted Williams (1942, 1947); Rogers Hornsby (1922, 1925)**

Joe DiMaggio's record 56-game hitting streak in 1941 broke a record that had stood since 1897 (44 games). Who held it? **Willie Keeler**

In 1962, he set a National League record by stealing 104 bases. **Maury Wills**

His 145 career knockouts is one boxing record that may never be broken. **Archie Moore**

He reigned over the heavyweight division for a record 11 years, nine months. **Joe Louis (1937-49)**

SPORTS

He sang "The Gold and Beyond" at the 1984 Winter Olympics. **John Denver**

Johnnie B. Baker Jr. is better known to baseball fans as _____. **Dusty Baker**

What two components make up skiing's Nordic combined event? **Cross-country skiing and jumping**

What is baseball manager Whitey Herzog's real first name? **Dorrel**

What is baseball player Biff Pocoroba's real first name? **Biff**

What is the maximum number of golf clubs a player may carry? **14**

The foil and saber are two of the three types of weapons used in fencing. What is the third? **Épée**

What is the maximum a professional middleweight boxer can weigh? **160 pounds**

What is the inside diameter of a regulation basketball hoop? **18 inches**

How high is the crossbar between a set of football goal posts? **10 feet**

Who was Joe Frazier's opponent in his final pro bout? **Jumbo Cummings**

As a freshman, he quarterbacked the University of Miami to a 31-30 upset of Nebraska and a national championship in early 1984. **Bernie Kosar**

In 1982, this team beat Stanford on a last-second five-lateral kickoff return that included a run through the Stanford marching band. **California**

13

EXHIBIT 3   Stores to Be Reached

Sears	879
Penney	450
Federated	451
Dayton Hudson	1,149
R. H. Macy	96
Allied Stores	596
Carter Hawley Hale	268
Associated Dry Goods	332
Mercantile	79
K mart	2,174
Woolworth	N/A
Wal-Mart	751
T.G.&Y.	754
Zayre	848
Bradlees	132
Murphy	386
Rose's	195
Kay Bee	500
Spencer Gifts	450
Hook's Drug	120
Toys "Я" Us	200

Bob Reiss thought that some 5,000 independent stores would be suitable targets, too.

EXHIBIT 4   Data on *TV Guide*'s Audience

February 3, 1984

Mr. Robert Reiss
President
R&R
230 Fifth Avenue
New York, New York 10001

Dear Bob:

I had our Research Department pull together some statistics about TV Guide that should be useful in discussing the audience dimensions of our magazine with major department stores and mass merchandisers.

First off, TV Guide's circulation averages over 17 million copies each week.

Included in TV Guide's average issue audience are:

1. 37,838,000 adult readers age 18 and over.
2. 8,829,000 teenage readers 12–17.
3. 46,667,000 total readers age 12 and over.
4. 19,273,000 readers 18–34.
5. 28,085,000 readers 18–49.
6. 10,312,000 adult readers in homes with one or more children 10–17 years of age.
7. 16,334,000 adult readers in homes with $25,000+ household income.
8. 11,815,000 adult readers with one or more years of college.
9. 4,344,000 adult readers who bought games or toys for children 12–17 in the past year.
10. 3,688,000 adult readers who bought games or toys for adults 18+ in the past year.

EXHIBIT 5   Letter to Supermarket Buyers

TRIVIA
INCORPORATED
Exclusive Marketing Agent
R&R
230 Fifth Avenue, New York, NY 10001
1-212-686-6003 Telex 238131-RR UR

June 29, 1984

Mr. Lamar Williams
General Mdse. Buyer
JITNEY JUNGLE STORES of AMERICA
P.O. Box 3409
453 N. Mill St.
Jackson, MI 39207

Dear Mr. Williams:

Once every decade a product comes along that is just right!

We think we have that product for you. It has two key elements:

1. It is licensed by TV Guide. I'm sure we don't have to tell you about the sales strength of TV Guide with its 17 million-plus weekly circulation, 46 million readers, etc. If your supermarket is typical, TV Guide is one of your best sellers and has earned its exalted position next to the cash registers.

2. The trivia game explosion has taken America by storm and duplicated its Canadian heritage, where trivia games have reigned for four years.

We have put these two elements together and, with TV Guide's help, developed a TV Guide Trivia Game with over 6,000 questions and answers. The enclosed catalog sheet gives full description and pricing. All our sales are final. We will advertise the game in five full page color ads in TV Guide this fall and will reach your customers.

We feel this game is ideally suited to be sold in your stores. We would be happy to send you a sample and/or answer any questions you may have.

We look forward to the opportunity of working with you.

Sincerely,

Bob Reiss

Robert S. Reiss

RSR/ck
encl.

EXHIBIT 6 Ads in *TV Guide* Magazine

EXHIBIT 7   Press Coverage of the Game

TV, too, gets into the trivia act

By BRUCE CHADWICK

Milburn Stone

Mary Tyler Moore

S O YOU KNOW who was the only vice president to resign. So what? Okay, you know who threw the ball that Babe Ruth hit into the seats for his 60th home run. Big deal. And you know the name of the drummer in Glen Miller's band. Who cares?

Think you're so smart at trivia? All right, in addition to Matt Dillon, who was the only other character seen during the entire run of "Gunsmoke"? What business did John Walton and his father run in "The Waltons"? In the early days of "All in the Family," what was the name of the company where Archie Bunker worked?

Gotcha, didn't we? Well, to find out all the answers, see below, and also see "TV Guide's TV Game," the latest in the avalanche of trivia games that are flooding stores.

What's different about this one, though, is that it is limited to television.

It's a board game with cards and dice. You land on squares that have questions in seven categories: drama, sports, comedy, news, kids, movies and other TV (questions are divided into three levels of difficulty and many are aimed at today's youngsters and yes, there is a Mr. T question). Whoever gets the most right answers wins. The game is designed for individual or team play.

"Trivia games are hot because people are tired of video games and computer games in which the player is isolated," said Bob Reese, head of Trivia Inc. and the game's founder. "People want to play games with other people and match wits with talking faces, not TV screens. That, plus the yen for nostalgia, is making all trivia games, not just ours, big sellers."

Reese wanted to get into trivia games when Trivial Pursuit became a best seller last fall. He needed something different and turned to television.

"Everyone watches television, so everyone will be interested in playing and, in fact, everyone will do reasonably well at this game," he said.

Reese turned to TV Guide because the magazine specializes in television coverage and has an extensive research department and library.

Researchers at TV Guide, led by Teresa Hagen, compiled a list of over 6,000 questions from over 20,000 submitted by writers there. Each question/answer had to have two written sources. Those that did not were dropped.

"It was harder than you'd think," said Hagen. "We needed a good balance of questions, easy to very difficult, and wanted a game that everyone, regardless of age, had a decent chance of winning."

The real research problems came in early television history.

"We had a very difficult time finding out firsts—the first comedy show, soap opera, president on TV, baseball game on TV—because early records were destroyed or sketchy."

They uncovered some unusual facts about television. As an example, the "Armed Forces Hour," an early '50's musical variety show, was only a half hour long. Dr. Ed Diethrich, owner of the USFL Arizona Wranglers, once performed open-heart surgery on live TV. Mary Tyler Moore's first major TV show was not "The Dick Van Dyke Show," but "Richard Diamond, Private Detective."

Hagen thinks the game is more than trivia. "We found that in playing it, we'd slide into conversations about what our own lives were like in relation to TV, like who our own heroes were, and our attitudes about things 20 years ago," she said. "We hope the game triggers conversations about life as well as TV."

The other continuing character on "Gunsmoke" was Doc Adams, played by Milburn Stone; the Waltons ran a lumber mill and Archie Bunker worked at Prendergast Tool and Die Co.

SOURCE: *Daily News,* New York: Burrelle's, June 12, 1984.

Eastwind Trading Company

Gail Pasternak and Martha Gershun sat down at their favorite table in the Prospect Restaurant in Kansas City, MO. Over the past several weeks, they had eaten more meals over meetings there than they cared to count. But today was the culmination of all those deliberations and all that number crunching. Today, they would decide whether or not they wanted to proceed with plans to form the Eastwind Trading Company and purchase the 6 million fresh water pearl buttons that would form the basis of the business.

HISTORY

Gail and Martha first started talking about their venture in the fall of 1984 when they worked together in the marketing department of a small computer software firm. Gail had come upon a unique collection of 6 million antique, handmade, fresh water pearl buttons in the basement of a local fabric shop (Exhibit 1). The fabric store owner and her husband, George and Susan Swanson, had been marketing the buttons to other fabric stores and had made money converting some of the buttons to jewelry. Gail and Martha decided to bid on the business with the intent of making jewelry out of the inventory that did not have predrilled holes. (Many antique buttons used metal shanks to give the seamstress a place to run the thread. These shanks could be cut off, leaving a lustrous, semiprecious stone that could be mounted as earrings, cufflinks, money clips, necklaces, or rings.)

This case was prepared by Martha Gershun under the direction of Howard H. Stevenson.

After two months of investigation into the jewelry business, the women decided they wanted to make the Swansons an offer for the business. They did not believe a bank would lend them money to buy such a fledgling firm with uncounted inventory and no real organization. They were reluctant to spend their savings to help buy the business because their own jobs at the software firm were so insecure. If they spent their money to buy the buttons and then lost their jobs, what would they do to live?

With the help of a local financial consultant, Gail and Martha offered the Swansons a deal requiring seller financing. They would work in the business full-time for no salary and over time earn 70 percent of the firm's stock. The women felt this was a good deal for the Swansons. They would own 30 percent of a firm of far greater size than their present operation. And the entrepreneurs would have built a company with no cash investment.

The Swansons did not see it that way. They viewed the deal as unfair to them and of questionable profitability. In January 1985, they sold their buttons to Michael Monroe, a contract construction executive from Branson, Missouri, for $200,000 in cash.

THE PRESENT

In November 1985, Gail received a call from Michael Monroe. He wanted to sell the buttons. He said that he had bought the company for his daughter to run. Now, she was getting married and moving to Africa as a missionary. He had put $40,000 into the business since he bought it. Did Gail and Martha want to buy it for $200,000?

The two women weren't sure. A lot had changed since they had offered to buy the company from the Swansons. The software firm where they had worked had sold out to a Canadian company. Martha had a new job that she loved, marketing cellular telephone service. Gail had built a freelance advertising business and was considering merging with a local advertising firm. Furthermore, they needed steady salaries more than ever. Martha had purchased a four-seater airplane that required steady cash to keep it in the air, and Gail was in the middle of a complex divorce settlement.

The women took a small-business consultant and flew Martha's plane down to Branson to take another look at the buttons. Michael Monroe had increased drastically the value of the business by organizing the inventory and developing a full-color catalog. The consultant advised Gail and Martha that he thought purchasing the buttons was "bankable." He offered to set them up with bankers in the Kansas City area who were willing to make loans to new ventures.

The women decided to buy the business. They would sell it to bankers as a pure button business, ignoring the more profitable, but riskier concept of selling the buttons as jewelry. They agreed that Gail would work in the business half-time, drawing a reasonable salary and keeping half of her freelance clients as supplemental income. Martha would continue her job, but would devote evenings and weekends to the business. They also decided to seek $300,000 in financing: $200,000 to buy the business and $100,000 in working capital.

Gail and Martha spent the next two weeks talking to bankers. (Exhibit 1 shows their business plan for the banks, and Exhibit 2 contains some pro forma projections.) In addition to their plan, they brought each banker a catalog from the business and several of the beautiful pearl buttons. Over and over they heard the same objections. If the business got into financial trouble, the banks were not prepared to try and sell off the buttons. Basically, the banks were not willing to bet on such an unconventional deal.

Finally, Stadium Bank offered to submit the loan to the Small Business Administration (SBA). If the SBA would guarantee the loan, then Stadium would lend the money. After another anxious two weeks, the SBA word came through—they would guarantee a loan of $225,000 to the Eastwind Trading Company at 1¾ percent over prime, adjusted quarterly, for 5½ years. The first six months would be interest-only payments. After that, payments would be $4,997/month. The time needed to pay off the loan would depend on fluctuations in the interest rate. There were only two major stipulations. Gail and Martha had to come up with $75,000 in equity before the loan would be granted. And they would each have to guarantee the loan personally.

Martha had stock, which her grandmother had given her over the years, now worth about $40,000. If she sold that, her tax liability could be as much as $5,000 at the end of the year. Additionally, each of the women had $5,000 in cash to invest in the business. They had other assets, too. Gail owned a grand piano and a BMW; Martha owned the airplane. While there were loans against these items, they certainly had value if the loans were paid off, possibly as much as $10,000 in total.

Gail and Martha decided that they needed outside financing. They recast the numbers they had shown the bank, pulling management salaries way down and adding payments to the outside board members; they also recast the financials using more optimistic projections (see Exhibit 3). They calculated that 1 percent of their business was worth $4,767 using a 35 percent discount rate and conservative numbers, and $9,142 using a 35 percent discount rate and more optimistic projections.

Over the next several weeks, Gail and Martha talked to many investors. Few wanted to invest funds; all wanted to give them advice.

Finally, they put together several options. Each investor had different reasons for being interested in the deal, and each one wanted different concessions before putting in money. Now, as Gail and Martha sat down at the Prospect yet again, they reviewed their list of potential investors to determine how to structure their business.

1. John Walsh, a wealthy local entrepreneur, was interested in investing $25,000 for 8 percent of the firm. He wanted reassurances that the business would be an ongoing concern, with Gail and Martha agreeing to exploit the distribution channels they would open up for the buttons with other follow-up products. He was concerned that the women had not been thorough enough in their evaluation of the implementation problems involved in shipping so many buttons, but he promised to keep his hands out of the firm and let Gail and Martha run their own show. He wanted cash kept in the firm, and thus preferred a straight corporate structure. Additionally, he wanted some mechanism to ensure that in the event of a liquidation, his paid-in capital would be returned before Gail and Martha made any profit.

2. Roger Johnson, one of Martha's close friends, offered to invest $15,000 for 4.8 percent of the firm's equity. He was willing to buy as much as 8 percent of the firm if Martha would loan him the additional $10,000 until he could get the cash—probably about 3 months. Roger had some interest in sitting on the firm's board of directors, but primarily agreed to let the women run the firm the way they wanted. He was interested in a contractual limit to their salaries and wanted cash dividends as soon as possible. Thus, he wanted the corporation to elect the tax advantages of an "S" corporation.

3. Dr. Dick Powell and Tom English, a local psychologist and a wealthy insurance executive, were interested in investing together. They offered Eastwind $65,000 for 25 percent of the firm as follows: $5,000 in equity financing, $45,000 loan to the business (subordinated to the SBA loan), and a $15,000 personal loan to Gail and Martha, repayable in the second year at 10 percent interest. Dick, in particular, showed a real fascination with the buttons and had lots of ideas about how they could be sold. He wanted to be actively involved in marketing the business and had lots of ideas for new product lines. The duo wanted the business to retain earnings for expansion and thus preferred a straight corporate structure.

4. Martha's sister Eleanor offered to pay $10,000 for 3.2 percent of the firm. She lived in New York and didn't really care about voting or how the business was run. Quite wealthy in her own right, she thought this investment would be a lark and might pan out well.

Martha turned to Gail and said:

Now that we have received approval on the SBA guarantee, we have really got to make our decisions about the start-up equity. It's fun so far, but business school just didn't prepare me for the amount of hassle we had to take from prospective investors. The worst ones are the ones who don't understand that what they are asking for isn't even good for them; the smart, but greedy ones, I can handle! We've got to figure out how to handle our minority investors. Because we are looking for relatively little cash, most of what I know about venture capital isn't so relevant.

Now, Gail and Martha had to make the tough decisions. Should they proceed with the business? How much outside money did they need? Who did they want as their minority shareholders? How much of their company should they give away? What price was their equity worth? How should the Eastwind Trading Company ownership and management be structured?

On a more personal level, Gail and Martha wondered: How much of their own money were they willing to risk? How poor were they willing to be? How did they feel about one of them putting in more money than the other?

EXHIBIT 1   Eastwind Trading Company Business Plan

Financing Request

We are seeking $300,000 in debt financing to purchase the Swanson Pearl Button Company, the world's only wholesale supplier of handmade fresh water pearl buttons. The loan will be secured by the finished goods inventory valued at between $1 million and $4 million. The loan will be paid out of business operations, over a seven-year period, with interest-only payments during the first year.

The total capitalization of $300,000 will be divided as follows:

— $200,000 to purchase the business, including all inventory, accounts receivable, customer lists, and related supplies.
— $100,000 working capital, used to reestablish marketing distribution through sales representatives.

The Swanson Pearls: What They Are, Where They Came From

The Swanson Pearl Buttons are the only remaining collection of handmade fresh water pearl buttons in the world. These 6 million buttons represent the final inventories of the factories that manufactured pearl buttons at the turn of the century in Muscatine, Iowa, the "Pearl Button Capital of the World." The factories closed when cheaply manufactured plastic buttons far underpriced pearl buttons in the 1920s. Today, with a resurgence of interest in high-quality materials, pearl buttons are in increasing demand for high-quality garments.

EXHIBIT 1   *(continued)*

Pearl buttons can no longer be manufactured in large quantities and wide varieties of colors. Not only has pollution seriously deteriorated oyster beds, but the labor intensive process by which they were manufactured is no longer cost-effective. The Japanese are currently manufacturing small quantities of "processed" pearl buttons of a very inferior quality with poor market acceptance.

Thus, the Swanson Pearls are unique and valuable. Their naturalness and quantity virtually identify them as a natural resource. Their history gives them value as antiques. Their finite quantity increases their value every year.

The pearls carry the Swanson name because they were discovered by George and Susan Swanson. Mrs. Swanson, a dressmaker for Kansas City socialites, had pursued a lengthy search for pearl buttons for her expensive custom clothing. When she exhausted all current manufacturer possibilities, she focused on finding pearl buttons that had possibly been left over from the early 1900s.

After an exhaustive and unproductive search, the Swansons accidentally happened upon this last collection of pearls, still in their original boxes, in an old fishery in Muscatine, Iowa, where they had been forgotten since their owner died in the 1950s.

The Swanson Pearl Button Company History

George and Susan Swanson, 1982–1985

The Swansons moved the buttons to Kansas City, placed them in a storeroom, separated 200 styles, and began to market them to fabric stores through a color flyer. Most of the buttons remained unseparated and in boxes. In the three years that they owned the buttons, the Swansons sold approximately 600,000 at an average of 65 cents apiece, or $390,000. The South provided most of the revenue through one effective sales representative. There was spotty distribution throughout the Mid- and Northwest.

The Swansons decided to sell the company when George Swanson developed health problems and could no longer manage the company.

Michael Monroe, 1985

In February 1985, the Swansons sold the buttons to Michael Monroe of Branson, Missouri, for $200,000 cash. Mr. Monroe bought the company for his daughter to run. This fall, she decided to move out of the country. During the time that he owned the buttons, Mr. Monroe invested $40,000 in mailing supplies and marketing. He developed internal control systems and sale processes and inventoried all of the buttons, increasing the available button styles to over 800. He developed a catalog, which he sent to 1,200 fabric stores.

Despite the fact that the company is now well organized, there is no selling effort beyond the initial catalog mailing. Even at this slow selling pace, the company has averaged $2,000 per month since February. The company is essentially sitting still, only filling orders for standing customers. In late November, Mr. Monroe announced that the buttons were up for sale again.

EXHIBIT 1   (*continued*)

No books or financial records were provided to Mr. Monroe when he purchased the buttons from George and Susan Swanson. At present, the only financial records are Mr. Monroe's lists of orders received and filled. The business currently has no outstanding debts or accounts payable. As the firm was purchased in February 1985, no income tax forms have yet been filed.

Our Plan

Current Status

Distribution is through catalog sales only and is confined to 100 accounts. Most accounts are in the Mid and Northwest. There are virtually no buttons sold east of the Mississippi and very few sold on the West Coast. They currently wholesale for an average of 65 cents apiece. Average order size is $25 per account per month.

Market Research

Our market research tells us that:

- There are over 14,000 fabric stores in the United States (Standard Rate and Data Service).
- Button pricing is very flexible, because of the unique nature of the buttons and the fact that they add little to the end cost of a garment. Current accounts felt that prices could be much higher.

Strategies for Increasing Revenue

Our plan is to:

- Raise the price of the buttons 30 percent to an average price of 85 cents each.
- Hire sales representatives at 20 percent commission to effectively cover the entire country.
- Provide retailers with selling incentives and merchandising assistance.
- Approach clothing manufacturers and designers for large sales of buttons for use on designer clothing.
- Implement a direct mail campaign to reach the remaining 12,000+ fabric stores.

Backgrounds of Key Personnel

Gail Pasternak

Gail Pasternak will bring to the business extensive experience in business management and all facets of marketing.

From 1977 to 1984, Ms. Pasternak was president and creative director of Pasternak, Kizer and Associates, a Kansas City advertising agency. During that time, she designed and implemented extensive marketing, public relations, and advertising programs for a wide variety of clients, including Data Phase, Continental Healthcare Systems, KLSI Radio, Cramer, Inc., Mid-America Health Network (HealthNet), and many others. She was responsible for many successful programs for her clients and received numerous creative awards for her work. During that time, she also managed the business, which employed from 4 to 10 people.

EXHIBIT 1   *(concluded)*

Ms. Pasternak also served as Director of Marketing Services for Data Phase Corporation. In that role, she was responsible for the development and implementation of marketing plans for the company's three computer products.

Since February, Ms. Pasternak has been working as a consultant and freelance writer for the advertising community. She is currently involved in such accounts as National Photo, Ralston Purina (protein division), Mid-America Health Network (HealthNet), Johnson County Bank, and International Soccer.

Ms. Pasternak holds a BA in Journalism, 1972, from Beaver College, Glenside, PA, and a BFA in Graphic Design, 1974, from the Kansas City Art Institute.

Martha Gershun

Martha Gershun will bring to the business extensive marketing, financial, and general management experience. She has worked for the data communications subsidiary of United Telecom, managing the corporate planning process and setting direction for new product introduction. She was responsible for the development of United Telecom's entry into the provision of data services for multitenant buildings.

Ms. Gershun also worked for Data Phase in Kansas City, as Product Manager for a new series of microcomputer software. In this capacity, she was responsible for the management of the product's development, documentation, marketing, and sales effort.

Ms. Gershun is presently employed with United TeleSpectrum, the subsidiary of United Telecom that provides cellular mobile and paging service to 27 markets nationwide. As Manager of Market Development, she is responsible for the company's cellular business, handling all advertising and public relations, sales material, billing implementation, market research, and new product development.

Additionally, Ms. Gershun has worked for the Boston Consulting Group, Boston, MA, doing strategic planning and acquisition studies, and for Amherst Associates, Chicago, IL, doing financial planning for the healthcare industry. She holds a BA *cum laude* from Harvard College, 1978, and an MBA from the Harvard Business School, 1983. She also holds a post-graduate diploma in economics from the University of Stirling, Scotland.

EXHIBIT 2 Financials

		Pro Forma Income Statement February 1986 to January 1987											
	February	March	April	May	June	July	August	September	October	November	December	January	FY 1986
Revenue													
Buttons:													
Shops/mail[a]	3,100	3,100	3,100	3,875	3,875	3,875	4,844	4,844	4,844	4,844	4,844	4,844	49,989
Shops/reps	—	—	—	5,000	6,500	8,000	9,500	11,000	11,000	11,000	11,000	11,000	84,000
Clothing mfg.	—	—	—	—	—	—	5,000	5,000	10,000	10,000	20,000	20,000	70,000
Total number	3,100	3,100	3,100	8,875	10,375	11,875	19,344	20,844	25,844	25,844	35,844	35,844	203,989
Sales	$ 2,015	$ 2,015	$2,635	$7,544	$ 8,819	$10,094	$16,442	$17,717	$21,967	$21,967	$30,467	$30,467	$172,149
Expenses													
Commissions	—	—	—	850	1,105	1,360	1,615	1,870	1,870	1,870	1,870	1,870	14,280
Rent[b]	500	500	500	500	500	500	500	500	500	500	500	500	6,000
Utilities	100	100	100	100	100	100	100	100	100	100	100	100	1,200
Moving expense	1,000	—	—	—	—	—	—	—	—	—	—	—	1,000
Stationery and miscellaneous	2,000	—	—	—	—	—	2,000	—	—	—	—	—	4,000
Supplies[c]	500	100	100	100	100	100	100	100	100	100	100	100	1,600

	P1	P2	P3	P4	P5	P6	P7	P8	P9	P10	P11	P12	Total
Computer	10,000	—	—	—	—	—	—	—	—	—	—	—	2,000
Advertising[d]	5,000	5,000	2,000	2,000	2,000	2,000	1,000	1,000	1,000	1,000	1,000	1,000	38,000
Travel[e]	2,000	2,000	2,000	1,000	1,000	1,000	1,000	1,000	1,000	1,000	640	640	14,000
Staff[f]	640	640	640	640	640	640	640	640	640	640	640	640	7,680
Insurance[g]	300	300	300	300	300	300	300	300	300	300	300	300	3,600
Management[h]	2,500	2,500	2,500	2,500	2,500	2,500	2,500	2,500	2,500	2,500	2,500	2,500	30,000
Professional[i] fees	1,700	200	200	200	4,450	200	200	200	200	200	200	3,200	11,150
Earnings before income tax	($17,225)	($11,325)	$8,705	($4,646)	$374	($2,856)	$5,487	$7,507	$13,757	$13,757	$22,257	$19,257	$37,639

[a]Current sales = 3,100 buttons with average price of .65/each. We will increase average price in April by 30 percent to .85.

[b]1,100 square feet commercial space.

[c]Business presently owns office furniture and mailing supplies.

[d]Direct mail to remaining 12,000 fabric stores.

[e]To recruit reps and manufacturing accounts and attend trade shows.

[f]Person to fill orders at $8/hr. × 20 hrs./wk.

[g]Buttons for $1 million and life insurance on both principals for $1 million.

[h]Gail full time at $30,000 until FY 1987, then at $60,000 (includes benefits); Martha full-time starting FY 1988.

[i]Legal, consulting, accounting, bookkeeping.

EXHIBIT 2 (continued)

Pro Forma Cash Flow Statement
February 1986 to January 1987

	February	March	April	May	June	July	August	September	October	November	December	January
Sources												
Sales	—	$ 2,015	$ 2,015	$ 2,635	$ 7,544	$ 8,819	$10,094	$16,442	$17,717	$21,967	$21,967	$ 30,467
Loan proceeds	$300,000	—	—	—	—	—	—	—	—	—	—	—
Cash from principals	10,000	—	—	—	—	—	—	—	—	—	—	—
Uses												
Purchase price	200,000	—	—	—	—	—	—	—	—	—	—	—
Commissions	—	—	—	—	850	1,105	1,360	1,615	1,870	1,870	1,870	1,870
Rent	1,000	500	500	500	500	500	500	500	500	500	500	500
Utilities	100	100	100	100	100	100	100	100	100	100	100	100
Moving expense	1,000	—	—	—	—	—	—	—	—	—	—	—
Stationery, miscellaneous	—	2,000	—	—	—	—	—	2,000	—	—	—	—
Supplies	—	500	100	100	100	100	100	100	100	100	100	100
Computer	—	—	2,000	—	—	—	—	—	—	—	—	—
Advertising	—	10,000	5,000	5,000	5,000	2,000	2,000	2,000	3,000	1,000	1,000	1,000
Travel	500	1,500	2,000	2,000	1,500	1,000	1,000	1,000	1,000	1,000	1,000	1,000
Staff	320	640	640	640	640	640	640	640	640	640	640	640
Insurance	3,600	—	—	—	—	—	—	—	—	—	—	—
Management	1,250	2,500	2,500	2,500	2,500	2,500	2,500	2,500	2,500	2,500	2,500	2,500
Professional fees	—	1,700	200	200	200	200	4,450	200	200	200	200	200
SBA charge	3,000	—	—	—	—	—	—	—	—	—	—	—
Cash position before debt service	$ 99,230	($17,425)	($11,025)	($ 8,405)	($ 3,846)	674	($ 2,556)	$ 5,787	$ 7,807	$14,057	$14,057	$ 22,557
Cumulative cash position before debt service	$ 99,230	$ 81,805	$ 70,780	$62,375	$58,529	$59,203	$56,647	$62,434	$70,241	$84,298	$98,355	$120,912

EXHIBIT 2   *(concluded)*

Pro Forma Income Statement
FY 1987–1990

	FY 1987	*FY 1988*	*FY 1989*	*FY 1990*
Revenue				
Buttons:				
Shops/mail	66,847	76,874	88,405	101,666
Shops/reps	144,000	172,800	207,360	248,832
Small manufacturing	300,000	400,000	500,000	600,000
Total number	510,847	649,674	796,400	950,498
Sales $	$434,212	$552,223	$676,400	$807,923
Expenses				
Commissions	$ 28,800	$ 34,560	$ 41,472	$ 49,766
Rent	6,000	6,000	6,000	6,000
Utilities	1,800	1,800	1,800	1,800
Moving expense	—	—	—	—
Stationery and miscellaneous	2,000	3,000	4,000	4,000
Supplies	6,000	9,000	12,000	17,000
Computer	10,000	—	—	—
Advertising	48,000	72,000	72,000	72,000
Travel	24,000	36,000	36,000	36,000
Staff	15,360	15,360	30,720	20,720
Insurance	3,600	3,600	3,600	3,600
Management	90,000	180,000	210,000	210,000
Professional fees	7,600	8,740	10,051	11,559
Earnings before income tax	$191,052	$182,163	$248,757	$365,478

Total buttons sold = 3,110,773

EXHIBIT 3 Financial Projections

| | | | | | Eastwind Scenario One | | | | |
	1986	1987	1988	1989	1990	1991	1992	1993	Total
Revenue									
Number of buttons:									
Shops/mail	49,989	66,847	76,874	88,405	101,666	101,666	101,666	101,666	688,779
Shops/reps	84,000	144,000	172,800	207,360	248,832	248,832	248,832	248,832	1,603,488
Clothing mfg.	70,000	300,000	400,000	500,000	600,000	600,000	600,000	600,000	3,760,000
Total number of buttons	203,989	510,847	649,674	796,400	950,498	950,498	950,498	950,498	5,762,267
Total sales[a]	$172,149	$434,212	$552,223	$676,400	$807,923	$807,923	$807,923	$807,923	$5,066,676
Expenses									
Commissions	$ 14,280	$ 28,800	$ 34,560	$ 41,472	$ 49,766	$ 49,766	$ 49,766	$ 49,766	$ 318,176
Rent	6,000	6,000	6,000	6,000	6,000	6,000	6,000	6,000	48,000
Utilities	1,200	1,800	1,800	1,800	1,800	1,800	1,800	1,800	13,800
Moving expenses	1,000	0	0	0	0	0	0	0	1,000
Stationery and miscellaneous	4,000	2,000	3,000	4,000	4,000	4,000	4,000	4,000	29,000

Supplies	1,600	6,000	9,000	12,000	17,000	17,000	17,000	17,000	96,600
Computer	2,000	10,000	0	0	0	0	0	0	12,000
Advertising	38,000	48,000	72,000	72,000	72,000	72,000	72,000	72,000	518,000
Travel	14,000	24,000	36,000	36,000	36,000	36,000	36,000	36,000	254,000
Staff	7,680	15,360	15,360	30,720	30,720	30,720	30,720	30,720	192,000
Insurance	3,600	3,600	3,600	3,600	3,600	3,600	3,600	3,600	28,800
Professional fees	11,150	7,600	8,740	10,051	11,559	11,559	11,559	11,559	83,777
Management	30,000	90,000	120,000	120,000	120,000	120,000	120,000	120,000	840,000
Board payments	4,000	4,000	4,000	4,000	4,000	4,000	4,000	4,000	32,000
Total expense	$138,510	$247,160	$314,060	$341,643	$356,445	$356,445	$356,445	$356,445	$2,467,153
Earnings before income tax	$ 33,639	$187,052	$238,163	$334,757	$451,478	$451,478	$451,478	$451,478	$2,599,523
Debt service	$ 42,000	$ 60,000	$ 60,000	$ 60,000	$ 0	$ 0	$ 0	$ 0	$ 282,000
Net income (before tax)	($ 8,361)	$127,052	$178,163	$274,757	$391,478	$451,478	$451,478	$451,478	$2,317,523
NPV at 25% $695,443									
NPV at 30% $572,310									
NPV at 35% $476,709									

1% of the business is worth $4,767 today. $50,000 = 10.5% of the business.
[a]Assumes no inflation

EXHIBIT 3 *(concluded)*

		Eastwind Scenario Two			
	1986	1987	1988	1989	1990	Total
Revenue						
Number of buttons:						
Shops/mail	49,989	66,847	153,748	176,810	203,332	650,726
Shops/rep	84,000	144,000	345,600	414,720	497,664	1,485,984
Clothing mfg.	70,000	300,000	800,000	1,000,000	1,200,000	3,370,000
Total number of buttons	203,989	510,847	1,299,348	1,592,800	1,900,996	5,506,710
Total sales[a]	$172,149	$434,212	$1,104,446	$1,352,800	$1,615,846	$4,679,453
Expenses						
Commissions	$ 14,280	$ 28,800	$ 34,560	$ 41,472	$ 49,766	$ 168,878
Rent	6,000	6,000	6,000	6,000	6,000	30,000
Utilities	1,200	1,800	1,800	1,800	1,800	8,400
Moving expenses	1,000	0	0	0	0	1,000
Stationery and miscellaneous	4,000	2,000	3,000	4,000	4,000	17,000

Supplies	1,600	6,000	9,000	12,000	17,000	45,600
Computer	2,000	10,000	0	0	0	12,000
Advertising	38,000	48,000	72,000	72,000	72,000	302,000
Travel	14,000	24,000	36,000	36,000	36,000	146,000
Staff	7,680	15,360	15,360	30,720	30,720	99,840
Insurance	3,600	3,600	3,600	3,600	3,600	18,000
Professional fees	11,150	7,600	8,740	10,051	11,559	49,100
Management	30,000	90,000	120,000	120,000	120,000	480,000
Board payments	4,000	4,000	4,000	4,000	4,000	20,000
Total expense	$138,510	$247,160	$314,060	$ 341,643	$ 356,445	$1,397,818
Earnings before income tax	$ 33,639	$187,052	$ 790,386	$1,011,157	$1,259,401	$3,281,635
Debt service	$ 42,000	$ 60,000	$ 60,000	$ 60,000	$ 60,000	$ 282,000
Net income (before tax)	($ 8,361)	$127,052	$ 730,386	$ 951,157	$1,199,401	$2,999,635
NPV at 25%	$1,231,196					
NPV at 30%	$1,057,254					
NPV at 35%	$ 914,225					

1% of the business is worth $9,142 today. $50,000 = 5.5% of the business.
[a]Assumes no inflation.

Tru-Paint, Inc.

On April 19, 1961, Warren G. Hamer received a telephone call from John M. Dublois, a finder, about a company that was for sale. After being reassured that he would receive a finder's fee of 5 percent of the purchase price, Dublois indicated that he would bring the information over to him in the morning. Dublois apologized for not thinking of Mr. Hamer earlier but only five days were left to submit a bid.

Mr. Dublois appeared early the next morning at Hamer's office with the three pages of information contained in Exhibit 1.

A quick check of the competitive situation with the Tru-Paint president disclosed that in the specific field of liquid paint dispensed in tubes for use in home decoration, Tru-Paint's sales were larger than any of its six competitors. Of the six competitors, only three distributed their products through the house-party plan. In the more general home hobbycraft and industrial markets, Tru-Paint had to meet intense competition with firms of significantly greater sales and resources.

There were certain aspects of the purchase that made Mr. Hamer apprehensive about the deal. First, the manner in which the company was being sold was very unusual, and the time period to evaluate the situation was very short. Second, no assurance could be given that the present management would stay on, and Mr. Hamer did not want to become actively involved in the management of a small company such as Tru-Paint. Finally, Mr. Hamer was worried about the restriction on contacting the company's distributors and the effects of the company's sale on their continued loyalty.

This case was prepared by Patrick R. Liles.

Copyright © 1971 by the President and Fellows of Harvard College
Harvard Business School case 9–371–202

Not wanting to commit a significant amount of his assets to the venture if he decided to undertake it, Mr. Hamer contacted a former associate, Mr. Blake. Edmund J. Blake, Jr., was a vice president of P. W. Brooks & Co., a medium-sized Wall Street investment banking firm that had specialized in unit financing programs, primarily in the utility and chemical industries, during the past 55 years.

On Friday, April 21, Messrs. Hamer and Blake met with Mr. Henry L. Aaron, president of the E-I Mutual Association and with Mr. Joseph Reimann, president of Tru-Paint, Inc. The company's office was in one corner of a large, basement room in an old commercial section of the city. The entire production facility consisted of vats and tanks for mixing and filling the ballpoint tubes and a shipping area for packaging the tubes after they were filled. The history of the company, presented by Aaron and Reimann, is summarized in Exhibit 2.

PARTY PLAN SELLING

There are three basic methods of house-to-house direct selling in which a salesman demonstrates and sells his products in a prospective customer's home: cold canvassing, coupon advertising, and party plan selling. The differentiating characteristic between these forms of direct selling is the method of generating prospects.

In cold canvassing a salesman, without first having made appointments, systematically knocks on every home or apartment door of a street until he encounters an interest in his product. If invited into the home, he demonstrates his product and attempts to make a sale.

Coupon advertising generates potential customers by means of reader service coupons attached to advertisements and promotional materials. When a reader of an advertisement or promotional handout sends in a reader service coupon requesting more information about a product, a salesman is sent to the reader's home to demonstrate and sell the product.

The party plan generates prospects by encouraging housewives to hostess a coffee and doughnut party for her friends; the stated purpose of the party to the guests is the opportunity for the company salesman to demonstrate and sell the company's products. The incentive for the housewife to hostess a party is the prospect of receiving a gift certificate from the company's hostess gift catalogue, which usually includes both company and noncompany home products. The value of the hostess's gift is a function of the dollar sales resulting from her party, the number of people who attend, and the number of additional hostesses recruited from the party.

For example, a Tru-Paint dealer (salesman/woman) might start developing a prospect-customer list by persuading a friend or relative to hostess a Tru-Paint embroidery party for a hostess gift. At this party the dealer would exhibit the range of materials to which Tru-Paint could be applied, available predesigned patterns, and all the necessary accessories needed to accomplish Tru-Paint embroidery. The dealer would receive from this party (1) a commission from the sales that were made and (2) leads on additional hostesses for future parties. Thus the party process frequently tends to snowball because of the "friends have different friends" phenomenon, which can generate a constant supply of new prospects for the distributor as well as produce a customer list for potential repeat sales.

The major advantage of home selling is that it focuses the attention of potential buyers only on the company product being sold. This elimination of competing products tends to make closing a sale easier than is possible in the more competitive environment of a retail outlet where similar and substitute products are displayed. Some advantages of the party plan over cold canvassing and coupon advertising as a means of home selling are (1) less sales resistance is met in the home because the hostess is sponsoring the product to her friends and the guests know in advance the selling purpose of the party; (2) customer and prospect lists grow faster and each sales call generates a larger sales volume since more than one family attends each party and hears each sales presentation; and (3) its respectability is generally greater in the eyes of the public because of its nonabrasive prospecting and straightforward selling approach.

Companies and products that employ the party plan selling method exclusively or in addition to cold canvassing and coupon advertising are:

Cosmetics	Apparel
Studio Girl Inc.	Beeline Fashions Inc.
Mary Kay Inc.	Queensway to Fashion Inc.
Fashion Two Twenty Inc.	Dutchmaid Inc.
Vanda-Beauty Counselor Inc.	Joya Fashions
a subsidiary of Dart Industries	a subsidiary of Jewel
Vivian Woodward Inc.	Fashions
a subsidiary of General Foods	
Lingerie	*Household Products*
Claire James Inc.	Tupperware Home Parties
Penny Rich Inc.	Stanley Home Products

EXHIBIT 1   Information and Terms and Conditions Relative to Proposed Sale by E-I Mutual Association of Its Wholly-Owned Subsidiary, Tru-Paint, Inc.

Tru-Paint, Inc., is located at 82 Main Street, West Orange, New Jersey. It manufactures and distributes, on a nationwide basis, liquid paint dispensed in ballpoint tubes. The product is sold under the registered trademarks "Tru-Paint" and "Liquid Embroidery" and is used primarily for hobby work of a decorative nature. It bears the Good Housekeeping Seal of Approval. In addition, Tru-Paint, Inc. manufactures or has manufactured a line of products accessory to its paints.

The product is distributed chiefly on the so-called party plan basis, with distributors located at various points throughout most of the United States.

The company has operated under its present ownership for the last five years, during which the volume and profit have steadily increased.

Terms and Conditions of Sale

1. Cash bids will be received up to and including April 24, 1961.
2. Bids shall be accompanied by a 5 percent deposit.
3. Bids shall be firm until 5 P.M., May 24, 1961. Acceptance may be made by a telegram filed before that date and hour or by letter postmarked prior to that date and hour.
4. Seller reserves the right to reject any or all bids.
5. Closing shall be at Seller's option between June 19 and June 23, 1961, inclusive.
6. Inspection of plant facilities is invited.
7. Bids shall be submitted subject to the understanding that Seller's distributors may not be contacted by, or on behalf of, Bidder and that any violation of this restriction shall result in automatic forfeiture of deposit.
8. Audited financial statements for 1957, 1958, 1959, and 1960 are annexed.
9. All bids shall be submitted to:

> Henry L. Aaron, President
> E-I Mutual Association
> 670 Q Street
> West Orange, New Jersey

Please mark the envelope *Confidential.* All inquiries shall also be directed to Mr. Aaron, who may be reached by telephone at REdwood 5-1234.

EXHIBIT 1 (*continued*) Balance Sheets

Assets	1960	1959	1958	1957
Current assets:				
Cash	$ 90,094	$ 89,790	$ 81,844	$ 70,639
Note receivable	23,902	—	—	—
Accounts receivable (less allowance for doubtful collections)	63,107	45,505	35,746	28,091
Inventories	91,079	75,704	59,050	59,261
Prepaid expenses	9,090	6,130	4,700	2,239
Total current assets	277,272	217,129	181,340	160,230
Furniture, fixtures, machinery and equipment, motor vehicles	22,669	17,604	15,328	15,148
Less accumulated depreciation	13,944	10,323	9,645	6,437
	8,725	7,281	5,683	8,711
Covenant not to compete, foreign license agreement, patents, etc.	82,180	122,180	192,180	193,180
Less accumulated amortization	24,566	52,264	51,915	35,963
	57,614	69,916	140,265	157,217
Goodwill	70,000	70,000	—	—
Total Assets	$413,611	$364,326	$327,288	$326,158

Liabilities	1960	1959	1958	1957
Current liabilities:				
Note payable	—	27,500	100,000	175,000
Accounts payable and accrued liabilities	22,397	19,683	11,781	9,993
Federal income tax payable	71,249	60,966	46,889	32,589
Total current liabilities	93,646	108,149	158,670	217,582
Capital stock and surplus:				
Authorized 1,000 shares of common, no par value—issued and outstanding	2,000	2,000	2,000	2,000
Earned surplus	317,965	254,177	166,618	106,576
Total capital stock and surplus	319,965	356,177	168,618	108,576
Total liabilities	$413,611	464,326	$327,288	$326,158

EXHIBIT 1 *(concluded)* Statement of Income and Surplus

	1960	1959	1958	1957
Net sales	$688,327	$597,603	$481,350	$466,580
Cost of goals sold	431,975	359,956	288,188	289,519
Gross profit	256,352	237,647	193,162	177,061
Selling, shipping, general, and administrative expenses	87,362	78,893	67,692	64,788
Operating profit	168,990	158,754	125,470	112,273
Other income	1,972	1,614	4,706	6,453
Net income	$170,962	$160,368	$130,176	$118,726
Other charges:				
Provision for amortization	12,301	12,801	16,952	17,452
Interest	624	4,121	6,293	9,185
	12,925	16,922	23,245	26,637
Profit before tax	158,037	143,446	106,931	92,089
Provision for federal income tax	71,249	60,966	46,889	32,589
Net profit for the year	$ 86,788	$ 82,480	$ 60,042	$ 59,500
Surplus January 1	$254,177	$166,618	$106,576	$ 47,076
Add: Partial disallowance by Treasury Department of amortization of foreign license agreement, patents, etc.		12,452		
		$179,070		
		7,375		
		$171,697		
Deduct: Additional federal income taxes		—	—	—
Dividends $23.00 per share	23,000			
	$317,965	$254,177	166,618	$106,576
Earned surplus December 31				

EXHIBIT 2   Background of the Company (summarized) as Described by
Messrs. Aaron and Reimann

Tru-Paint was organized in 1948 to exploit the possibilities of the ballpoint
paint dispenser. The company was the original manufacturer of ballpoint paint
dispensers and paint compounds suited to this use. The company originally
utilized both manufacturer's agents and direct contacts to sell their products
through large retail outlets. By 1954 Tru-Paint sales through the retail outlets
had grown to over $1 million.

By 1953, however, the large paint manufacturers were introducing competitive products with by-product pricing. The company foresaw that additional competition would create a substantial decline in the company's profit
margins. This factor coupled with disagreements within the management
group placed Tru-Paint on the sales block. Thus, in early 1954, the original
owners were approached by E-I Mutual with a purchase offer.

E-I Mutual Association was founded in 1949 by the son of Thomas A.
Edison, Mr. Theodore Edison, then president of Edison Electric, as an experiment in labor management relations. It was his thesis that if employees
became stockholders in other companies, they would be more sympathetic to
the needs of the stockholders and the management of their own company. He
set up the association with about $1 million worth of stock in Edison. The
original intent was that E-I Mutual should invest these funds in small
companies, but by 1954 it had sizable investments in American Telephone and
Telegraph, General Motors, General Electric, and other blue chip stocks. An
employee of Edison could purchase one share of E-I Mutual $3 dividend stock
at $10 a share for each year that he worked for the company up to a limit of 15
shares. If, for any reason, his employment was terminated, the employee had
to sell back to the association one share of his holdings each year following
separation at the same $10 per share price.

In 1954, Joseph Reimann, as president of E-I Mutual Association, learned
of the availability of Tru-Paint and recommended that E-I Mutual purchase
100 percent ownership for some $300,000. The membership voted and ap-
proved this recommendation. Subsequently, Mr. Reimann became president of
Tru-Paint.

Mr. Reimann realized that the Tru-Paint distribution system needed to be
revamped, and it was his idea to market the company's products under the
home party plan. By 1957, the company distributed its products to the
consumer market primarily through independent distributors under the home
party plan. In developing its distributor organization throughout the United
States, Tru-Paint entered into exclusive territorial franchise agreements with
its distributors.

Tru-Paint supplied kits consisting of its line of paint-filled ballpoint tubes,
various accessories such as embroidery hoops to hold the stamped materials
taut, and sample pieces of fabric printed with a design on which the novice
could practice. The distributor was free to make his own arrangements with
other suppliers to sell at the same parties, products such as stamped textiles,
glass, and leather to which the Tru-Paint line of color tubes could be applied.

EXHIBIT 2   (*concluded*)

The distributors were also free to create and manage their own organizations of demonstrators. The growth and selection of the independent distributors for Tru-Paint could be characterized as somewhat haphazard. Vast differences in population, size of territory, and normal trading areas were noticeable between distributors. By 1960, the company had 17 exclusive distributors.

Prior to the end of 1960, several of the company's distributors had indicated an interest in purchasing Tru-Paint if E-I Mutual decided to sell its interest.

In 1959, the company's products were awarded the Good Housekeeping Seal of Approval by *Good Housekeeping* magazine.

Commercial Fixtures, Inc.

It would take only a few quick strokes of his pen to fill out the bid form and but an instant to seal the envelope. Gordon Whitlock caught himself in momentary wonder that this simple form would have such a dramatic effect on the next few years of his life. Tomorrow, February 23, 1979, at 12 o'clock noon, the envelopes from Gordon and his partner, Albert Evans, would be opened to determine which of them would buy out the other and own Commercial Fixtures Inc., the company built by their fathers. After working together for over 25 years, the two partners had decided that this was the best way to resolve differences of opinion that had arisen over how to manage the company.

COMPANY DESCRIPTION

Commercial Fixtures Inc. (CFI) manufactured custom-engineered fluorescent lighting fixtures used for commercial and institutional applications. Sales in 1978 were $4 million with profits of $115,000.

Most sales were standard items within the nine major lines of products designed and offered by the company. Ten percent of sales were completely custom designed or custom built fixtures, and 15 percent of orders were for slightly modified versions of a standard product. In 1978, CFI shipped 66,000 fixtures. Although individual orders ranged from one unit to over 2,000 units, the average order size had been fairly consistently 15–20 fixtures. Modified and custom designed fixtures averaged about 25 per order. Gordon Whitlock, CFI president, described their market position:

> Our product marketing strategy is to try to solve lighting problems for architects and engineers. We design products that are architecturally

This case was prepared by Richard O. von Werssowetz and H. Irving Grousbeck under the direction of Philip H. Thurston.

Harvard Business School case 9–382–108

styled for specific types of building constructions. If an architect has an unusual lighting problem, we design a special fixture to fit his needs. Or if he designs a lighting fixture, we build it to his specifications. We try to find products that satisfy particular lighting needs that are not filled by the giant fixture manufacturers. We look for niches in the marketplace.

Having the right product to fit the architect's particular needs is the most important thing to our customer. Second is the relationship that the architect, the consulting engineer, or the lighting designer has with the people who are representing us. The construction business is such that the architect, engineer, contractor, distributor, and manufacturer all have to work as a team together on a specific project to ensure its successful completion. The architect makes a lot of mistakes in every building he designs, unless he just designs the same one over and over. Consequently, there's a lot of trading that goes on during the construction of a building, and everybody's got to give and take a little to get the job done. Then the owner usually gets a satisfactory job, and the contractors and manufacturers make a fair profit. It requires a cooperative effort.

Most of our bids for orders are probably compared with bids from half a dozen other firms across the country. Since a higher percentage of our orders are for premium-priced products, we are not as price sensitive as producers of more commonplace lighting fixtures. It is difficult for a small firm to compete in that market. As many as 30 companies might bid on one standard fixture job.

CFI owned its own modern manufacturing facility located outside Denver, Colorado. Production consisted of stamping, cutting, and forming sheet metal, painting, and assembly of the fixture with the electrical components that were purchased from outside suppliers. The company employed a total of 104 workers, with 34 in sales, engineering, and administration and another 70 in production and assembly.

The company sold nationwide through regional distributors to contractors and architects for new buildings and renovations. Prior to 1976, CFI sold primarily to a regional market. At that time, marketing activities were broadened geographically. This was the primary reason that sales had been increasing over the last few years even during a weak construction market. (See Exhibit 1 for historical sales, earnings, unit sales, and employment.)

BACKGROUND

Commercial Fixtures Inc. was formed in Golden, Colorado, in 1936 by Jonathan Whitlock and Julius Lacy. Each owned one half of the company. Whitlock was responsible for finance and engineering and Lacy for sales and design. They subcontracted all manufacturing for the lighting systems they sold.

After several years, differences in personal work habits led Whitlock to buy out Lacy's interest. Jonathan Whitlock then brought in Paul Evans as his new partner. Evans had been one of his sheet metal subcontractors. Paul Evans became president and Whitlock, treasurer. Ownership was split so that Whitlock retained a few shares more than half because of his experience with Lacy.

In 1940, CFI began manufacturing and moved its operations to a multifloor 50,000 sq. ft. plant also located in Golden. The company grew and was quite profitable during the war years and during the following boom in construction of the early 1950s. Whitlock and Evans were quite satisfied with the earnings they had amassed during this period and were content to let the company remain at a steady level of about $1 million in sales and about $15,000 in profit after taxes.

Jonathan Whitlock's son, Gordon, joined CFI as a salesman in 1956 after graduating from MIT and then Colorado Business School. Paul Evans' son Albert, who was a graduate of Trinity College, also became a CFI salesman in 1957 when he was discharged from the service. The two sons were acquaintances from occasional gatherings as they were growing up, but had not been close friends.

In 1959, Jonathan Whitlock had a heart attack and withdrew from the management of the business. Although he remained an interested observer and sometime advisor to his son, Jonathan was inactive in company affairs after this time. Paul Evans assumed complete management overview of the company.

Gordon Whitlock moved inside to learn about other parts of the company in 1960. His first work assignments were in manufacturing and sales service. Albert Evans joined his father in the manufacturing area a year later. Gordon became sales manager, Albert became manufacturing manager, and at Paul Evans' suggestion, another person was added as financial manager. These three formed a middle management triumvirate that worked well together, but major decisions were still reserved for Paul Evans, who spent less and less time in the office.

As the new group began revitalizing the company, a number of employees who had not been productive and were not responding to change were retired early or asked to leave. When the man who had been Paul Evans' chief aide could not work with the three younger managers, they ultimately decided he had to be discharged. Paul Evans became so angry that he rarely entered the plant again.

For several years the three managers guided the company as a team. However, there were some spirited discussions over the basic strategic view of the company. As sales manager, Gordon Whitlock pressed for responding to special customer needs. This, he felt, would be their strongest market niche. Albert Evans argued for smooth production flows and less disruption. He felt they could compete well in the "semistandard" market.

In 1962, the fathers moved to restructure the company's owner-ship to reflect the de facto changes in management. The fathers converted their ownership to nonvoting Class A stock. Each trans-ferred 44 percent of his nonvoting stock to his son. Jonathan Whitlock decided to relinquish his voting control at this time in an effort to help things work as the new generation took over. Accordingly, Gordon and Albert were each issued 50 percent of the Class B voting shares.

In 1961, Gordon Whitlock began to work with an individual in forming a company in the computer field that rented extra space from CFI. CFI provided management and administrative support, helping the new company with bidding and keeping track of contracts. Al-though Albert Evans was not active in this company, Gordon split his partial ownership in this new company with Albert because they were partners and because Gordon was spending time away from CFI with the computer company.

With the heavy demands of the start-up over the next three years, this new effort began to weaken the relationship between Gordon and Albert. At the same time, Albert and the financial manager began to have strong disagreements. These seemed to arise primarily from forays in cost analysis, which led the financial manager to question some of Albert's decisions. There were also differences of opinion over relations with the work force and consistency of policy. Albert pre-ferred to control the manufacturing operation in his own way. Gordon felt Albert could be more consistent, less arbitrary, and more support-ive of the work force. When the computer company was sold in 1968, the financial manager joined it as treasurer and resigned from CFI.

GROWING CONFLICT

The departure of the financial manager led to a worsening of the relationship between Gordon and Albert. Gordon had been made company president in 1963. Gordon recalled the decision:

> Paul Evans had resigned as president and the three of us were sitting around talking about who should be president. Albert Evans finally said, "I think you should be it." And I said, "OK."

Yet even with this change, the three managers had really operated together as a team for major decisions. Now, Gordon was upset that they had lost an excellent financial manager, someone critical to the operation (due, in his opinion, partially to the disagreements with Albert). There was also no longer a third opinion to help resolve conflicts. The financial manager was replaced with an old classmate of Albert's and the new manager became one of several middle level managers who had been hired as the company grew.

The pressures of growth created more strains between Gordon and Albert. Sales had reached $1 million and had begun to tax CFI's manufacturing capacity. Gordon felt that some of the problems could be alleviated if Albert would change methods that had been acceptable during slacker periods but hindered intense production efforts. Albert had different views. Both agreed to look for additional space.

The transition to a new factory outside Denver, Colorado, in 1970 eased the stresses between the partners. A major corporation had purchased an indirect competitor to obtain its product lines and sold CFI the 135,000 sq. ft. plant. CFI also entered into an agreement to manufacture some of the other company's light fixtures as a subcontractor. The plant was in poor condition and Albert Evans took over the project of renovating it and continuing production of the other company's lines. Gordon Whitlock remained in Golden running the CFI operation alone until it became possible to consolidate the entire operation in Denver. Gordon described this interlude:

The next year was a sort of cooling off period. Albert was immersed in his operation, and I was geared into the continuing operation. Albert had always enjoyed projects of this sort and was quite satisfied with this arrangement.

Then in 1972 we hired a plant manager to run the Denver plant, and Albert came back to work in Golden. By that time, of course, a lot of things had changed. All of Golden had been reporting to me. I had somewhat reshaped the operation, and the people had gotten used to my management style, which was different than Albert's.

Albert's reaction was to work with the design and engineering people, but he really wasn't involved very much with the daily manufacturing any more. He developed a lot of outside interests, business and recreation, that took up much of his time.

I was very happy with that arrangement because it lessened the conflict. But when he did come back, the disagreements were worse. I guess I resented his attempts to change things when he only spent a small amount of time in the company.

Then in 1973 we made the decision to sell the Golden plant and put the whole company in Denver. We were both involved in that. Most of our key people went with us. Albert and I were very active in pulling together the two groups, in integrating the operation.

That began a fairly good time. I was spending my time with the sales manager trying to change the company from a regional company to a national one and was helping to find new representatives all over the country. Evans spent his time in the engineering, design, and manufacturing areas. There was plenty of extra capacity in the new plant, so things went quite smoothly. In particular, Albert did an excellent job in upgrading the quality standards of the production force we acquired with the plant. This was critical for our line of products and our quality reputation.

This move really absorbed us for almost two years. It just took us a long time to get people working together, to produce at the quality level and rate we wanted. We had purchased the plant for an excellent price with a lot of new equipment and had started deleting marginal product lines as we expanded nationally. The company became much more profitable.

As the company expanded, a group of six people formed the operating team. Albert Evans concentrated on applications engineering for custom fixtures and new product design. In addition, there were a sales manager, financial manager, engineering manager, the plant manufacturing manager, and Gordon. Disagreements began again. Gordon recounted the problems:

> Our operating group would meet on a weekly or biweekly basis, whatever was necessary. Then we would have monthly executive committee meetings for broader planning issues. These became a disaster. Albert had reached the point where he didn't like much of anything that was going on in the company and was becoming very critical. I disagreed with him as did the other managers on most occasions. Tempers often flared and Albert became more and more isolated.
>
> He and I also began to disagree over which topics we should discuss with the group. I felt that some areas were best discussed between the two of us, particularly matters concerning personnel, and that other matters should be held for stockholders meetings. The committee meetings were becoming real battles.

In 1977, Paul Evans died. Although he had remained chairman of the board, he had been generally inactive since 1961. Jonathan and Gordon Whitlock and Albert Evans became the only directors.

SEARCH FOR A SOLUTION

Gordon Whitlock was discouraged by the continuing conflicts with his partner and had sought advice on how to remedy the situation from friends and associates as early as 1969. In 1977, Gordon was beginning to believe that he and Albert had just grown too far apart to continue together. However, Gordon had to find a mutually agreeable way to accomplish a separation. One partner could buy the other out, but they would have to agree on this and find an acceptable method. Albert seemed to have no interest in such an arrangement.

During 1977, the differences between the partners grew. The vacillations in leadership were disruptive to the operation and made other employees very uncomfortable.

By early 1978, the situation was growing unbearable. Gordon recalled the executive committee's annual planning meeting in January:

It was a total disaster. There were loud arguments and violent disagreements. It was so bad that no one wanted ever to participate in another meeting. We were all miserable.

What was so difficult was that each of us truly thought he was right. On various occasions other people in the company would support each of our positions. These were normally honest differences of opinion, but politics also started to enter in.

When Gordon returned from a summer vacation in August, he was greeted by a string of complaints from several of CFI's sales agents and also from some managers. Gordon decided that the problems had to be resolved. Gordon sought an intermediary:

I knew that Albert and I weren't communicating and that I had to find a mediator Albert trusted. I had discussed this before with Peter Dowling, our attorney. Peter was a boyhood friend who had grown up with Albert. I felt he had very high integrity and was very smart. Albert trusted him totally, and Peter was probably one of Albert's major advisers about things.

When I first talked to Dowling in March, he basically said, "Well, you have problems in a marriage, and you make it work. Go make it work, Gordon." He wasn't going to listen much.

Then in early September I went back to say that it wasn't going to work any more. I asked him for his help. Peter said that Albert had also seen him to complain about the problems, so Peter knew that the situation had become intolerable.

Dowling prepared a memorandum describing the various options of changing management and/or ownership that were available to partners who were having disagreements. Gordon decided to encourage one of Dowling's options that called for each partner to name a price for the business. Previously, some of Gordon's own advisers had suggested this same outlet.

Both directly and through Dowling, Gordon pressed Albert to agree to such an arrangement. Although Albert, too, was unhappy with their conflicts, he was hesitant to accede.

Gordon felt that there were several principal reasons for Albert's reluctance. One was the fact that Albert's only work experience was with CFI. This was limited primarily to managing manufacturing operations he had known for years. Second, Gordon thought Albert was very uncertain as to how to value the company since he had little formal training in financial analysis and had not been directly involved in the financial operations. Gordon felt that this made Albert's task of setting a bid price more difficult than his own. Finally, there was the emotional tie to the company and the avoidance of such a momentous decision.

As discussions began to result in the formulation of a buy-sell agreement, Albert's reluctance waxed and waned. Just before Christmas, Evans called Whitlock, who was sick at home, and said he had decided to fire the financial manager and become the treasurer of the company. He could look at the figures for a year or so and then make a better decision. Gordon felt the financial manager was essential and could not be discharged. He thought this was really more of an attempt to buy time.

After two more months of give and take in developing a formula and bid conditions, Whitlock and Evans finally signed a mutual buyout agreement on February 16, 1979. It called for sealed bids in a specific format with the partner offering the higher price buying out the other (Exhibit 2). The bids would be submitted in one week. Gordon credited Peter Dowling with convincing Albert to sign:

> I think Peter got him to sign it by sheer force of personality. By saying this situation is just not right, it's screwing up the company, you're not happy. You won't be happy until it's solved. This is a reasonable way to solve it, and you damn well ought to take the chance. Because later, if you pass this up, it's just going to get worse.

VALUING THE COMPANY

Before preparing his bid, Gordon reviewed the thinking he had done since first considering the idea of buying or selling the company. He began with the company's current position. With the serious discussions going on about the buyout agreement, preparation of the financial statements for 1978 had been accelerated, and they were already completed. (These are shown together with the results for 1977 and 1976 as Exhibit 3.)

Gordon had also begun developing the bank support he might need to fund a buyout. The company's banker indicated that he would loan Gordon funds secured by his other personal assets if Gordon was the buyer, but that since he had not worked with Albert, the bank would decline to finance an acquisition with Albert as the buyer. In addition, the bank would continue the company's existing line of credit, which was secured by CFI's cash and accounts receivable. The maximum that could be borrowed with this line was an amount equal to 100 percent of cash plus 75 percent of receivables. Both types of borrowing would be at 1 percent over the prime rate (then about 9 percent).

Gordon had worked with the banker to begin financial projections he could use in establishing his bid. These projections set out pro forma operating results *before* taking the bid conditions into consideration. By structuring the financial projections in this manner, the results of *operating* assumptions could be separated from *bid* structures. Various combinations of bid conditions could be easily tested based on this set of business operating results. Long-term debts that would be assumed with the business were included within the operating projections. Other bank financing requirements would be influenced by the bid terms and were left separate. The banker completed one sample projection using the minimum $500,000 bid and token $10,000 per year noncompete payments (Exhibit 4).

To be conservative, Gordon had made the sales projections about 10 percent lower each year than he really thought they would achieve. Because fixed costs would not rise appreciably with modest increases in sales, any improvements in sales volume would be particularly advantageous to profits. The asset and liability assumptions were based on company experience, but there could be fluctuations in items such as lengths of receivables and inventory turns. He felt he should consider how these various changes would impact his financing requirements and his price assessment.

Gordon also had sought out common evaluation techniques. By looking through business periodicals and talking to friends, he found these methods were not necessarily precise. Private manufacturing companies were then most often valued at between 5 and 10 times aftertax earnings. Book net asset value also helped establish business worth, but was often adjusted to reflect differences between the market values of assets and the depreciated values shown on balance sheets. For CFI, this was true because they had obtained their new plant at an excellent price. Gordon felt it alone was probably worth $200,000 more than stated book.

To Gordon, the variations in worth suggested by these different methods not only reflected the uncertainty of financial valuation techniques, but also showed that a business had different values to different people. His bid would have to incorporate other more personal and subjective elements.

One important consideration was what amount of personal resources he could and should put at risk. Both he and Albert were financially very conservative. Neither of them had ever had any personal long-term debt—even for a house. Gordon could gather a maximum of $650,000 of assets outside of CFI that could be pledged to secure borrowing. His bank had already confirmed that he could borrow against those assets. However, for him to put his entire worth at risk, he would want to be very comfortable that the price was a reasonable one. Gordon described his feelings:

> You get very protective about what you have outside the company. The problem you always have with a small company is that most of your worth is tied up in it, and you may have very little to fall back on if something goes sour. We both have never been big leverage buyers or anything like that.

Besides the element of increased financial risk, there were several other considerations that tempered Gordon's willingness to pay a very high price. Since they had moved to the plant in Denver, the one hour commute to work had been a bit burdensome. It would be nice not to have that drive. Gordon also felt he had good experience in the complete general management of a business, and his engineering undergraduate degree and MBA gave him a certain flexibility in the job market. This was important, because for both financial and personal reasons, he felt he would still have to work should he lose the bid.

On the other hand, some factors encouraged Gordon to be aggressive. His father cautioned him to be reasonable, but Gordon knew his father would be very disappointed if Gordon lost the company. And Gordon himself had strong emotional ties to CFI. Gordon also developed a point of view that in some ways he was buying the entire company rather than half:

> I'm sitting here with a company that I have no control over because of our disagreements. If I buy the other half share, I'm buying the whole company—I'm buying peace of mind, I could do what I want, I wouldn't have to argue. So I'd buy a "whole peace of mind" if I bought the other half of the company.

Gordon felt that differences in personal values had been the major reasons two friends had suggested two very different bids. Both had been business school friends and had been very successful entrepreneurs. However, one suggested a bid value for the other half of the company of $850,000 and the other suggested $1,100,000. Gordon commented:

> Philip, who suggested the lower bid, was much more similar to me in lifestyle. He was involved with his family and a number of other activities. Mark, who suggested the higher bid, was unmarried and intensely involved in his company. The company was his life. However, all of the many friends I consulted cautioned me that I would be better off financially if I bought the company and urged me not to "get cute" and undervalue it.

Finally, Gordon considered his competitive position versus Albert. Although Albert had not accumulated the personal resources that

Gordon had, he did have a relative with a private company that Gordon knew had an accumulated earnings problem and had the ability to match Gordon's resources. This relative would also be giving Albert financial advice in setting a value for the company. Albert also probably had fewer job prospects if he sold out. His undergraduate study was in liberal arts and his entire experience was within CFI. Gordon also thought Albert might have some doubts about his ability to manage the company on his own.

THE BID

The bid structure was a very simple one. The minimum bid was $500,000 in cash. Additional amounts could be added either to the cash portion and/or to a five-year noncompetition agreement. The bids would be evaluated on a present-value basis using an 8 percent discount rate. That rate was selected as equivalent to cash invested at the current return of AAA-rated bonds. Both Gordon Whitlock and Albert Evans were satisfied that was fair. The minimum cash payment had been established to protect the interests of the seller and to reduce possible future uncertainty and unpleasantness if the company's position should change substantially. The noncompetition payments would be obligations of CFI but also would be personally guaranteed by the buyer.

Now it was time to decide on a price and then try to get some sleep. Gordon put the form down and walked around the room. He sat down once again, uncapped his pen, and began to enter his bid.

EXHIBIT 1 Historical Performance

Year	Net Sales	Profit after Tax	Number of Fixtures Shipped	Total Employees	Hourly Employees
1978	$4,412,191	$115,209	66,000	104	70
1977	$3,573,579	$101,013	58,000	94	58
1976	$2,973,780	$106,528	52,000	82	52
1975	$2,935,721	$ 63,416	54,000	82	50

EXHIBIT 2   Buy/Sell Agreement

AGREEMENT made on this 17th day of February 1979, between Albert W. Evans of Denver, Colorado (hereinafter called *Evans*) and Gordon M. Whitlock of Denver, Colorado (hereinafter called *Whitlock*).

WHEREAS, Evans and Whitlock each own shares of the voting and nonvoting capital stock of Commercial Fixtures Inc. (CFI) and desire to arrange for the purchase by one (or the purchase by CFI) of all shares of capital stock of CFI owned by the other;

NOW, THEREFORE, in consideration of the foregoing and of the mutual agreements contained herein, Evans and Whitlock agree as follows:

1. Evans and Whitlock will each submit to David Austin, the named senior partner of CFI's accounting firm, by noon on February 23, 1979 (the "Bid Date"), a proposal to purchase (or to have CFI purchase some or all of) the other's shares of capital stock of CFI (such proposal to be on the Bid Form attached hereto as Attachment A):

   a. Such proposal shall include all of the stock owned by the other and shall specify the number of shares to be purchased by him, and by CFI and the purchase price, which price shall be not less than $500,000 in the aggregate and shall be paid in full at the Closing hereinafter specified, except as the parties shall otherwise agree.

   b. Such proposal shall specify the amount of the equal annual payments to be made by CFI over the five-year period from 1979 through 1983 in consideration of a noncompetition agreement for such period covering the United States to be executed by the seller in the form attached hereto as Attachment B [not included], such annual payments made in equal installments at the end of each calendar quarter commencing March 31, 1979.

2. If either Evans or Whitlock fails to submit such a proposal by the Bid Date (except for causes beyond his reasonable control in which event a new Bid Date will be established by Austin), the party so failing shall sell his capital stock to CFI upon the terms specified in the other's proposal. If neither party submits such a proposal by the Bid Date this agreement shall terminate.

3. With respect to each proposal, Austin shall add the amount of the purchase price submitted under Section 1(a) and the amount of the annual payment to be made under Section 1(b) above (discounted to present value as at January 1, 1979, as to all payments to be made on or after January 1, 1979, at the rate of 8 percent per annum), and thereby determine which of the submitted proposals is the highest price (the determination to be made as set forth in the Bid Form Computation attached hereto as Attachment C). The party submitting the highest proposal shall be the buyer (which term shall include CFI to the extent such proposal provides that it shall purchase shares). If both offers are determined by Austin to be equal, the buyer shall be determined by an auction as follows:

   a. The parties with such others as they choose to bring shall meet at Austin's offices at a time and a date specified by Austin.

   b. Commencing with Evans (unless he declines to raise his bid in which case commencing with Whitlock) the parties shall submit successive bids

EXHIBIT 2   (*continued*)

---

of not less than $5,000 in excess of the last bid submitted by the other party.

c. A party shall have 15 minutes after the bid of the other party in which to submit his own bid, and if he fails to submit a bid at least $5,000 higher than other party's last bid, then the last highest bid will be the buyer, except that if neither party raises his original bid then Austin shall determine the buyer by a flip of the coin.

d. If a party fails to attend such meeting, the other party shall be the buyer, unless such failure was for causes beyond the reasonable control of the party in which case Austin shall set a time and date for another meeting.

All determinations of Austin under this and the preceding Section, which shall include the question of whether causes beyond the reasonable control of a party prevented the party from acting, shall be final and binding on the parties. Compliance with this agreement shall be determined by Austin, and his determination thereof shall also be final and binding on the parties.

4. If Whitlock is the seller, Evans shall cause CFI at the Closing either (*a*) to redeem for $75,107.50 all shares of capital stock of CFI owned of record or beneficially by Jonathan Whitlock upon tender of certificates for the same endorsed to CFI or (*b*) to continue to pay a $10,000 annual pension to Jonathan Whitlock and to pay the premiums on the $75,000 life insurance policy held by CFI on Jonathan Whitlock's life and to place such insurance policy in a separate trust which trust shall be the beneficiary under such policy, all in such a manner as to place such policy and proceeds beyond the reach of CFI's creditors, and promptly upon receipt the proceeds of such policy shall be paid by the trust to Jonathan Whitlock's estate in consideration of the endorsement to CFI or the certificate for the shares of capital stock to CFI held by the estate. The bills of Peter Dowling to CFI, including those for arrangements leading to this agreement, shall be the responsibility of CFI regardless of which party is the buyer.

5. Austin shall notify the parties in writing promptly upon any determination that a party has failed to satisfy Section 2 hereof and promptly upon any determination made under Section 3 above. The closing date on which the buyer shall make his payment under Section 1(a) and the seller shall endorse his shares of capital stock to CFI to the buyer, shall be April 15, 1979, or such earlier date as the buyer shall designate. If the buyer shall fail to make the Section 1(a) payment at the Closing, the other party will become the seller upon the lower terms of the original seller's proposal, and Austin shall reschedule the Closing on a date within 90 days. If at the new Closing the new buyer fails to make the Section payment, this agreement shall terminate. Payment of amounts owed by CFI under Section 1(b) above (and under Section 4 if Whitlock is the seller) shall be personally guaranteed by Evans or Whitlock, as the case may be, and overdue payments of such amounts shall bear interest at the rate of 15 percent from the date due. There shall be credited against payment to be made under Section 1(b) with respect to 1979 commencing March 31, 1979, the amount of salary received by the seller for 1979. At the Closing the seller shall execute an agreement

EXHIBIT 2   (*concluded*)

not to compete with CFI for five years in the United States. The seller's employment, salary, Blue Cross/Blue Shield, group insurance, all other payments and benefits, except those provided herein, shall terminate at the Closing. The seller may retain the CFI automobile now used by him, and ownership thereof will be transferred to the seller by CFI.

WITNESS our hands and seals on the date first set forth above.

Albert W. Evans
_____

Gordon M. Whitlock
_____

Attachment A—Bid Form

PURCHASE PRICE (SECTION 1-a)	$_____
NONCOMPETITION AGREEMENT (SECTION 1-b)	$_____
AMOUNT PER YEAR	$_____
TOTAL AMOUNT (5 YEARS) (TO BE PAID IN EQUAL QUARTERLY PAYMENTS)	$_____

_____   _____
Date   Signature

Attachment C—Bid Computation Form

	Evans	Whitlock
Purchase price (1a):	$	$

Noncompetition agreement (1b):

	Evans	Whitlock		
Yearly amount for five years	$	$		
Discounted value (DV)			_____	_____
Adjusted purchase price			$_____	$_____

The discounted value shall be the present value of the yearly amount paid quarterly for 20 quarters discounted at an interest rate of 2 percent per quarter.

This shall be computed as follows:

$$DV = \frac{\text{Yearly amount}}{4} \times 16.3514 = \text{Yearly amount} \times 4.08786.$$

EXHIBIT 3   Financial Statements

COMMERCIAL FIXTURES INC.
Balance Sheets
Years Ended December 31

Assets	1978	1977	1976
Current assets:			
Cash	$ 51,248	$ 3,778	$ 70,520
Accounts receivable			
Customers	600,361	430,750	318,356
Refundable income			
taxes..................	23,001	—	—
Other	—	2,276	5,289
	623,362	433,026	323,645
Less allowance for			
doubtful receivables	3,500	3,500	3,500
	619,862	429,526	320,145
Inventories			
Raw materials..........	291,790	259,550	277,072
Work in process.........	534,438	483,357	316,113
	826,228	742,907	593,185
Prepaid insurance and			
other....................	14,028	20,134	26,070
Total current assets ..	1,511,366	1,196,345	1,009,920
Property, plant, and			
equipment:			
Buildings and			
improvements..........	341,426	325,686	295,130
Machinery and			
equipment	210,493	173,073	135,419
Motor vehicles	32,578	32,578	29,421
Office equipment.........	42,866	43,905	36,949
	627,363	575,242	496,919
Less accumulated			
depreciation	273,284	233,444	185,215
	354,079	341,798	311,704
Land	11,101	11,101	11,101
Total property, plant,			
and equipment	365,180	352,899	322,805
Other assets:			
Cash surrender value of			
life insurance policies			
(less loans of $19,748 in			
1978, $19,590 in 1977			
and $19,432 in 1976) ...	81,978	77,215	72,569
Total assets.................	$1,958,524	$1,626,459	$1,405,294

EXHIBIT 3 (*continued*)

Liabilities	1978	1977	1976
Current liabilities:			
Current maturities of			
long-term debt..........	$ 12,184	$ 10,558	$ 9,000
Note payable—bank*.....	325,000	200,000	—
Note payable—officer.....	—	30,000	39,000
Accounts payable:			
Trade	389,582	295,208	313,203
Employees'			
withholdings..........	4,875	3,197	3,070
Amount due for purchase			
of treasury stock........	—	—	75,000
Accrued liabilities:			
Salaries and wages	93,713	57,534	48,413
Commissions.............	41,474	26,010	12,878
Sundry..................	14,528	11,357	4,796
Income taxes...........	—	18,036	19,800
	149,715	112,937	85,887
Total current			
liabilities...........	881,356	651,900	525,160
Long-term debt..............	176,522	189,122	195,710
Stockholders' equity:			
Contributed capital			
6% Cumulative			
preferred stock—			
authorized 10,000			
shares of $10 par			
value; issued 2,000			
shares	20,000	20,000	20,000
Common stock			
Class A (nonvoting)			
Authorized 15,000			
shares of $10 par			
value; issued			
8,305 shares......	83,050	83,050	83,050
Class B (voting)			
Authorized 5,000			
shares of $10 par			
value; issued and			
outstanding 20			
shares............	200	200	200
	103,250	103,250	103,250
Retained earnings	892,396	777,187	676,174
	995,646	880,437	779,424

EXHIBIT 3 (*continued*)

Liabilities	1978	1977	1976
Less shares reacquired and held in treasury—at cost 2,000 shares 6% cumulative preferred stock.................	$ 20,000	$ 20,000	$ 20,000
2,308 shares Class A common stock	75,000	75,000	75,000
	95,000	95,000	95,000
Total stockholders' equity	900,646	785,437	684,424
Total liabilities..............	$1,958,524	$1,626,459	$1,405,294

*Converted to long-term debt in balance sheet projections in Exhibit 4.

EXHIBIT 3 *(continued)*

Statement of Earnings

	Year Ended December 31		
	1978	*1977*	*1976*
Net sales	$4,412,191	$3,573,579	$2,973,780
Cost of goods sold			
Inventories at beginning of year...	742,907	593,185	416,512
Purchases..........................	1,599,426	1,275,665	1,109,781
Freight in..........................	19,520	26,595	20,966
Direct labor.......................	430,154	360,568	328,487
Manufacturing expenses...........	977,299	802,172	673,643
	3,769,236	3,058,185	2,549,389
Inventories at end of year	826,228	742,907	593,185
	2,943,008	2,315,278	1,956,204
Gross profit	1,469,183	1,258,301	1,017,576
Product development expenses.......	131,746	128,809	102,299
Selling and administrative expenses.	1,112,542	915,140	740,801
	1,244,288	1,043,949	843,100
Operating income	224,895	214,352	174,476
Other deductions or (income)			
Interest expense	56,259	37,790	32,416
Payments to retired employee	10,000	10,000	20,000
Miscellaneous.....................	(923)	(1,551)	(6,193)
	65,336	46,239	46,223
Earnings before income taxes........	159,559	168,113	128,253
Provision for income taxes	44,350	67,100	49,000
Earnings before extraordinary			
income	115,209	101,013	79,253
Extraordinary income—life			
insurance proceeds in excess of			
cash surrender value..............	—	—	27,275
Net earnings	$ 115,209	$ 101,013	$ 106,528
Earnings per share of common stock	$19.15	$16.79	$13.10

EXHIBIT 3   (*continued*)

Statement of Changes in Financial Position

	Year Ended December 31		
	1978	1977	1976
Working capital provided from operations:			
Earnings before extraordinary income	$115,209	$101,013	$ 79,253
(Add item not requiring outlay of working capital)			
Depreciation	55,978	50,658	44,267
Working capital provided from operations	171,187	151,671	123,520
Extraordinary income from life insurance proceeds................	—	—	27,275
Capitalized equipment lease obligation	—	5,295	—
Proceeds from cash surrender value of life insurance policies	—	—	51,877
Total working capital provided ..	171,187	156,966	202,672
Working capital applied:			
Additions to property, plant, and equipment	68,259	80,752	47,107
Increase in cash surrender value of life insurance policies—net of loans...........................	4,763	4,646	5,954
Reduction of long-term debt	12,600	11,883	8,996
Purchase of 2,308 shares of nonvoting Class A stock.........	—	—	75,000
Total working capital applied .	85,622	97,281	137,057
Increase in working capital..........	$ 85,565	$ 59,685	$ 65,615
Net change in working capital consists of:			
Increase (decrease) in current assets:			
Cash	$ 47,470	$ (66,742)	$ 64,854
Accounts receivable—net........	190,336	109,381	(3,548)
Inventories......................	83,321	149,722	176,673
Prepaid expenses	(6,106)	(5,936)	(4,980)
	315,021	186,425	232,999

EXHIBIT 3   *(concluded)*

Statement of Changes in Financial Position

	Year Ended December 31		
	1978	1977	1976
Increase (decrease) in current liabilities:			
Current portion of long-term debt .	$ 1,626	$ 1,558	$ 500
Notes payable to bank...........	125,000	200,000	—
Note payable officer	(30,000)	(9,000)	—
Accounts payable................	96,052	(17,868)	107,153
Amount due for purchase of			
treasury stock..............	—	(75,000)	75,000
Contribution to profit-sharing			
trust........................	—	—	(20,000)
Accrued liabilities	54,814	28,814	(7,619)
Income taxes....................	(18,036)	(1,764)	12,350
	229,456	126,740	167,384
Increase in working capital..........	$ 85,565	$ 59,685	$ 65,615
Working capital at beginning of			
year...............................	544,445	484,760	419,145
Working capital at end of year.......	$630,010	$544,445	$484,760

EXHIBIT 4 Pro Forma Financial Statements

Income Statement for Projections

	Historical Percentages			Projected Percentages				Income Statement for Projections (thousands of dollars)		
	1976	1977	1978	1979	1980	1981		1979	1980	1981
Net sales	100.0	100.0	100.0	100.0	100.0	100.0		4,800	5,100	5,400
Cost of goods sold ...	65.78	64.79	66.70	67.0	67.0	67.0		3,216	3,417	3,618
Gross income	34.22	35.21	33.30	33.0	33.0	33.0		1,584	1,683	1,782
Operating general and admin.† ...	28.61*	29.28	28.25	28.0	28.0	28.0		1,344	1,428	1,512
Profit before taxes and purchase financing	5.61†	5.93	5.05	5.0	5.0	5.0		240	255	270
Noncompete payments								10	10	10
Interest for "other bank debt"‡ ...								74	70	63
Profit before taxes...								156	175	147
Taxes............	38.2§	39.9	27.8	39.0	39.0	39.0		61	68	77
Net earnings								95	107	120

*Historical and projected percentages include interest for long-term debt *only* as well as a $25,000 cost reduction for the reduced salary requirements of a replacement for Evans.

†Profit after adjustments to operating G&A.

‡Interest for "other bank debt" is assumed to be 10 percent times "other bank debt" outstanding at the end of the prior year.

§Effective tax rate.

Projected Beginning Equity Position

Total equity, December 31, 1978:	$900,646
Less cash payment of purchase price:	500,000
Beginning equity, January 1, 1979:	400,646

EXHIBIT 4 (continued)

Balance Sheet Accounts for Projections

(thousands of dollars)

	Historical			Projected			At Closing			
	1976	1977	1978	1979	1980	1981	1978	1979	1980	1981
Assets:										
Cash..........							50	50	50	50
Accounts receivable........ (Days)	39.3	43.9	51.3	52.0	52.0	52.0	620	684	727	769
Inventories........ (Turns)	3.3	3.1	3.6	3.8	4.0	4.1	826	846	854	882
Prepaids..........							14	15	15	15
Total current assets							1,510	1,595	1,646	1,716
Net fixed assets							365	370	370	370
(Assume policies cash in)							0	0	0	0
Total assets........							1,875	1,965	2,016	2,086
Liabilities and Equity:										
Operating accounts payable...... (Days)	59.0	47.0	48.9	50.0	50.0	50.0	394	441	468	496
Accrued expenses and taxes....							150*	150	150	150
Total existing long-term debt ..... ($000)	205	200	189				189	176	163	148
Liabilities from ongoing operations........							733	767	781	794
Other bank debt........							741	702	632	569
Total liabilities........							1,474	1,469	1,413	1,363
Equity at beginning of year†							401	401	446	603
Net earnings for year							NA	95	157	120
Total equity........							401	496	603	723
Total liabilities and equity......							1,875	1,965	2,016	2,086

*In a purchase by an *outside* buyer, this is often zero at closing. These liabilities are paid off rather than transferred, and new accruals are gradually rebuilt in the normal course of business.

†See calculations of beginning equity elsewhere in exhibit.

EXHIBIT 4   (*concluded*)

Sources and Uses of Funds
(thousands of dollars)

	1979	1980	1981
Sources:			
Net earnings............................	95	107	120
Plus depreciation	56	56	56
Funds provided by operations...........	151	163	176
Increase in accounts payable	47	27	28
Increase in accrual expenses and taxes..	0	0	0
Increase in other bank debt.............	—	—	—
Total sources	198	190	204
Uses:			
Increase in accounts receivables.........	64	43	42
Increase in inventories...................	20	8	28
Increase in prepaids	1	0	0
Increase in fixed assets*	61	56	56
Decrease in long-term debt	13	13	15
Decrease in other bank debt............	39	70	63
Total uses	198	190	204

Note: Total sources must equal total uses.
*Reinvestment in plant and equipment is assumed to equal depreciation after the first year.

ICEDELIGHTS

On March 10, 1983, Paul Rogers, Mark Daniels, and Eric Garfield walked out of their final negotiating session with ICEDELIGHTS. The three were negotiating for the Florida franchise rights to ICEDE-LIGHTS, a European-style cafe/ice cream shop selling a variety of beverages and frozen desserts.

The session had gone fairly well, and they felt as though they had gotten most of the concessions that they wanted. Yet, mixed with this air of excitement was a sense of trepidation. There was a great deal of work that remained to be done on the deal, not the least of which was the securing of additional financing. In addition, other issues remained: Did the Florida market offer good potential for an ice cream business? Did the deal make good business sense? Was it right for them personally at this point in their careers? Did they have the skills and resources to make the business work, assuming that the deal came off? Did the same factors that made them good friends make them good business partners?

BACKGROUND

Paul Rogers, Mark Daniels, and Eric Garfield were three second-year students at the New York School of Business (NYSB) who had all been classmates in their first year. (See resumes, Exhibit 1.) The idea of starting, or buying, their business arose during the week just prior to the start of second-year classes. The three had rented a house on Cape Cod for a week. Fresh from their summer jobs, they naturally

---

This case was prepared by Michael J. Roberts under the direction of Howard H. Stevenson.

Harvard Business School case 9–384–076

shared their views of what their summer experiences had been like, and what impact these experiences would have on their career choices.

— Paul, 26, had spent two-and-a-half years with State Street Bank in Boston. He had worked for the summer as an associate with the New York investment bank of Warburg Paribas Becker and had enjoyed the experience. Paul, however, was excited by the challenge and rewards of creating and managing an enterprise of his own at an early stage in his career.

— Mark, 25, had spent two years with McKinsey & Co. and had also turned to investment banking for the summer. While he had enjoyed this experience, Mark felt a genuine desire for the independence and satisfaction of owning and managing his own business. He was unsure how additional work in either consulting or investment banking would bring him closer to this goal.

— Eric, 30, had spent five years with Celanese in the international finance area. After pursuing positions with investment banks and consulting firms, Eric accepted a position with McKinsey's Atlanta office. Although he enjoyed the experience a great deal, Eric also felt drawn toward owning his own business. The independence, financial rewards, and opportunity to manage and truly create an organization seemed unequaled in any other career.

During that week on Cape Cod they spent a great deal of time on the beach and in the local bars discussing their experiences and speculating on what lay ahead. They talked about what they were looking for in a career: each of them wanted a job he would truly enjoy, independence, and great financial rewards. In addition, there was something incredibly appealing about building and managing an organization—really creating a business—being an entrepreneur. Moreover, it was clear that none of the "traditional" opportunities offered this. The idea of "having our own business" took hold.

Each of them had, at different times, thought that running his own business might be fun. During that week, they realized that this opportunity was the only option that would truly satisfy their objectives. Slowly, the focus of their thoughts turned to "How do we get there?"

Their discussions surfaced two fundamentally different approaches:

— The first approach, the "conservative" one, had two possibilities:

  • They could pick an industry, really try to learn a business, develop their management skills, and keep an eye out for opportunities; they were bound to learn a great deal, and they would be making their mistakes on someone else's money. In four or five years, they were bound to spot an opportunity and could then obtain the financing. Everyone says, "the money's there if you have a good idea."

- Or, they could get into the deal flow; go to work for a venture capital firm or the M&A area of an investment bank. They would learn how to evaluate deals and make contacts with people that could provide financing. Then they would buy something for themselves and run it!

— The second approach was, "Why wait?" They argued that they had the skills and abilities to run a business, not a high-tech or sophisticated manufacturing firm, but surely there were some businesses that they had the collective talent to manage—all they had to do was find one. Further, in four or five years, it would be much harder to do. One would be used to the financial security and lifestyle of corporate life; it wouldn't be easy to go back to $25,000 or $30,000 and 80-hour weeks. Finally, with a spouse, family, car payments, a mortgage, and a summer home or ski house on the way, the risks associated with failure would be far greater down the road.

As school began, they decided that it was certainly worth trying to find a business.

THE SEARCH

The three began talking with professors at the business school, lawyers, and business contacts. They asked for advice and mentioned that they were in the market to buy a company. It soon became clear that they needed some concrete specifications regarding the businesses they were interested in, both as a guide to potential sources of information and to show a minimum level of commitment to the project. A brief specifications sheet was pulled together (Exhibit 2), which described the businesses they would be interested in and included their resumes.

The process proceeded through October and November with little in the way of results. People were generally helpful and encouraging, but it was very tough to get specific leads.

In late November, Paul's father, Mr. Rogers, mentioned that some friends of the family had recently purchased the ICEDELIGHTS franchise for Oregon and California; he had heard that Florida might be available. The three were excited about the possibility even though retailing had not been one of the industries targeted in their specifications sheet. The skills required to run a food franchise seemed within their range of abilities. It sounded like a fun business, and the potential financial rewards seemed to be great.

ICEDELIGHTS

ICEDELIGHTS was a Boston-based chain of food outlets selling a variety of beverages, pastries, and frozen desserts. There were currently nine stores in the New England area (primarily Boston), with several more scheduled to be opened during 1983. ICEDELIGHTS had sold its first franchise rights (Oregon and California) in June 1982, and the first of these stores was scheduled to open in the summer of 1983.

The four of them met with ICEDELIGHTS on December 10. Bob Andrews, the chairman, revealed that they had received dozens of franchise requests for Florida. He mentioned seven individuals in particular, each with extensive experience in either the fast-food industry or Florida real estate and who clearly had the financial resources required. Yet he felt that, at this time, ICEDELIGHTS was stretched to its capacity. They had grown slowly and carefully and were committed to maintaining a quality operation. Managing their existing locations and their own expansion, as well as providing a high level of assistance to the California franchise, would consume their available resources for the near future.

ICEDELIGHTS' conservative approach was due in large part to problems the company had had in its early years. Bob Andrews purchased ICEDELIGHTS when it had two locations. Early expansion resulted in financial problems when the company did not have the necessary organization and control systems in place.

Following this meeting, they met with the president of ICEDELIGHTS—Herb Gross. As the chief operating officer, he provided the group with a more detailed description of the ICEDELIGHTS operation. He, too, stressed ICEDELIGHTS' commitment to slow, *quality* growth. He felt, however, that there was some possibility that a deal could be worked out. Paul, Mark, and Eric expressed their enthusiasm for the business and their desire to really get involved in the day-to-day, hands-on operations of ICEDELIGHTS. They left impressed with the quality of ICEDELIGHTS' management and its potential for growth.

During this conversation, Paul, Mark, and Eric gained a better understanding of how ICEDELIGHTS worked. The heart of the concept revolved around several factors: first, ICEDELIGHTS sold an Italian "gelati" type ice cream, which was extremely rich and "homemade" looking and tasting. Yet, through a great deal of effort, ICEDELIGHTS had been able to perfect the process of freezing this "homemade" ice cream. This enabled ICEDELIGHTS to manufacture each of the products centrally, freeze them, and then sell on the premises of each store location. Most shops with a high-quality ice cream made the product on the premises. Moreover, ICEDELIGHTS had built and developed a very impressive organization. Their ongoing standardization of production, training, accounting, and control systems, store management, and store design and construction convinced Paul, Mark, and Eric that they would receive a great deal of support as a franchise. Finally, by marketing the concept as a café, this chain was able to derive sales throughout the day from coffee, pastry, and light snacks as well as ice cream in the afternoon and evening.

At this point, Paul, Mark, and Eric felt that a real opportunity was finally within their grasp. They realized that a great deal of work lay ahead if they were to have any chance of pulling the deal off. The opportunity to do a field study in the New Ventures area seemed to be an excellent vehicle to both accomplish this effort and get some advice from a knowledgeable advisor. They put together a proposal (Exhibit 3), which was accepted.

The group met briefly with ICEDELIGHTS again in early January. Bob Andrews and Herb Gross indicated that they were interested in pursuing the Florida franchise further. They were very impressed with Paul's, Mark's, and Eric's abilities and willingness to get involved in the day-to-day operations of the franchise. The other groups had all been interested in purchasing the franchise as an investment. They viewed the desire to be involved in the operations as crucial to maintaining the quality of the operation. A dinner was scheduled for January 11 to discuss how to proceed.

THE DEAL

On January 11, Paul, Mark, Eric, and Mr. Rogers met Bob and Herb at a restaurant in Boston. ICEDELIGHTS indicated that they did want to go ahead with the Florida franchise, but because they were so stretched, they did not want to be legally bound to proceed. Nonetheless, they recognized that, because of their job search situation, Paul, Mark, and Eric did need some security that the deal would come off. So ICEDELIGHTS proposed the following terms:

The franchisee (Paul, Mark, Eric, and Mr. Rogers) would:

— Pay $200,000 up front.

- $100,000 development fee for the State of Florida.
- $100,000 in five prepaid franchise fees of $20,000 each. This was prepayment for the first five stores.

— Pay $20,000 per store opened (after the first five, which were prepaid as above).

— Pay a 5 percent royalty on sales.

In exchange, ICEDELIGHTS would allow them to use the ICEDE-LIGHTS name, sell them products for roughly 32 percent of suggested retail price, train them, train one manager per store opened, and provide them with assistance in finding real estate, selecting locations, and constructing stores. In effect, ICEDELIGHTS would provide them with the first few locations as "turnkey" operations.

Because ICEDELIGHTS did not wish to be legally obligated to proceed if they felt that their operation was still stretched to capacity, these terms would be subject to an option.

The parties would sign an option which specified the terms of the franchise agreement (as above):

— The franchisee (Paul, Mark, Eric, and Mr. Rogers) would make a deposit of $75,000. If ICEDELIGHTS did not agree to proceed within nine months, the group would get back its $75,000 plus interest.

— If ICEDELIGHTS did agree to proceed, the franchisee would pay the remainder of the up-front fee ($125,000) and proceed.

— If the franchisee did not agree to pay the remaining fee and proceed, they would forfeit the $75,000 deposit.

ICEDELIGHTS stressed that they were personally committed to going ahead with the Florida franchise as soon as California was running smoothly. They said that it was in everyone's best interest that they not be obligated to proceed if they did not feel that they could provide the franchisee with the level of support required. They further felt that by locking in the terms of the franchise, they were bringing something to the deal.

Another dinner was scheduled for January 25, two weeks hence, when Paul, Mark, Eric, and Mr. Rogers would deliver their decision to ICEDELIGHTS.

Paul, Mark, and Eric had two weeks to make a decision. The main issue now seemed to be financing. As the former president of a Boston-area bank, Mr. Rogers had a great many friends and associates who were potential sources of financing. Mr. Rogers began approaching them in hopes of finding one or two individuals to back the entire deal.

In the meantime, Paul, Mark, and Eric tried to pull together some financial data that would allow them to generate pro forma financials and estimate both the financing required and the attractiveness of the operation.

First, they compared the terms of the ICEDELIGHTS franchise with those of other leading franchises (Exhibit 4). On one hand, ICEDELIGHTS seemed expensive for a new and unproven franchise. Yet, it appeared to offer excellent profit potential, and they were obtaining the rights to the entire state of Florida.

They did try to get some idea of the market potential that Florida offered and pulled together the data shown in Exhibit 5.

Next, they looked at the store-level income statement (Exhibit 6). The operation appeared to be incredibly profitable, particularly in light of the investment required. At $160,000 investment per store, they estimated that they would require $750,000 in financing, as follows:

Up-front fee	$200,000
First three stores	480,000
Working capital	70,000
	$750,000

Next, they had to think about how to structure the deal and how much equity to keep: Could they keep enough to make it financially rewarding to them and attractive enough for investors? Would the operation require continued infusions of cash for growth?

They knew that the more debt they could put in the capital structure the better, due to the deductibility of interest payments, and the nondeductibility of dividends. They also knew that there were certain IRS regulations that limited the amount of debt they could have. They looked up the applicable section of the Tax Code, Sec. 385, and its explanation (see Exhibit 7). Further, debt and fixed interest payments would both restrict their growth and increase the riskiness of the venture.

After running some preliminary pro formas (Exhibit 8), they decided on a first cut at the deal capital structure. It seemed as though they could give 25 percent of their company away and still give investors an attractive return.

Mr. Rogers' contacts had said they were enthusiastic about the concept, but in the two-week period, they were unable to get any firm commitments. Mr. Rogers himself, however, had agreed to invest $75,000 in the venture.

On further reflection, Paul, Mark, and Eric decided that the deal was attractive to them even if they had to give up a good deal more than the 25 percent that they had projected. The enthusiasm that Mr. Rogers' contacts had expressed convinced them they would be able to raise the money. They decided to proceed.

On January 25, they met with ICEDELIGHTS and indicated that the terms were acceptable and that they wanted to go ahead with the deal. They agreed that their lawyers would be in touch to draw up the papers.

FINANCING

The following weekend, Paul, Mark, and Eric raced to produce a prospectus. They spent all day Saturday writing the document and hosted a previously planned dinner party Saturday evening for eight friends. At 1 A.M. Sunday morning, after a great dinner, a lot of wine, and a cut-throat game of charades, one guest suggested that they charge over to his office to type the document. A normally staid law firm was transformed as 11 typists pounded out the prospectus until 4:30 in the morning. The document, excerpted in Exhibit 9, presented the concept for the business and the proposed financing and capital structure.

During the next three weeks, they spoke to friends and associates of Mr. Rogers, presenting their business plan. At the end of three weeks, they had informal "commitments" for 15 units, or $405,000. With Mr. Rogers's $75,000, they had $480,000, and were only $270,000 shy.

During this time, it became clear that they would have to give up more than the original 25 percent they had planned. Not surprisingly perhaps, potential investors were somewhat put off by the 75/25 split in the deal. Paul, Mark, and Eric decided that as long as they were giving up more of the company they could raise a bit more money, and they revised the deal as shown in Exhibit 10.

In the process of determining the original deal, the three thought that investors would primarily be concerned with their overall return—ROI, IRR, NPV, or whatever. But, in fact, their requirements were more complex:

— Short-term repayment of original investment, with significant control during this phase.

— Long-term capital gain with reduction in investor control once original investment repaid.

There were also significant differences in the level of sophistication of potential investors. Some liked the concept, and that was sufficient. For others, a detailed analysis of investors' versus founders' risk and reward was required.

In addition, there were several other issues that remained to be settled, including:

— Form of organization. They had made a preliminary decision to use a straight corporation, but it was possible that a Sub-S or Limited Partnership made more sense.

— Legal counsel. They had decided to use Ernest Brooke, an acquaintance of Mr. Rogers who had indicated an interest in investing. Yet, a few weeks had gone by, and he now seemed more hesitant. Further, he did not have any particular expertise in securities or corporate law and had not been particularly helpful.

— The market. Was Florida really a good spot for this business? Throughout, they had attempted to obtain market information on Florida without spending the time and expense on a lengthy trip. The data they had obtained seemed inconclusive.

Throughout this period, the second-year recruiting season was in full swing. Because they were emotionally committed to the ICEDE-LIGHTS deal, and because it was consuming so much of their time, none of the three was actively pursuing other opportunities. Each of them had the opportunity to return to the firm where they had worked for the summer, as well as one or two other possibilities.

THE DECISION

It was now February 22, and they had gotten a preliminary set of documents to review. The time when they would actually have to sign papers and put down their $75,000 seemed to be drawing near. A meeting was set for March 10 to put the finishing touches on the agreement.

At this point, Mark began having some strong doubts about the advisability of proceeding. He expressed them this way:

I started getting these funny feelings in the pit of my stomach. I guess it was fear. It seemed to me that we had all gotten very caught up in the enthusiasm of the project and had not been as hard-nosed about the business decisions as we should have been.

First, we had not even been to Florida. Eric lived there and was home at Christmas, but we never thoroughly investigated the market. We didn't know if there was competition there, and if there *were* other ice cream shops/cafés, how were they doing? Who knew if the Florida market would be attracted to the rich and different style of ice cream we offered? Finally, this was a "mall-based" retail economy. Who knew how we would do in malls?

Second, I began to question the nature of our agreement and relationship with ICEDELIGHTS. It seemed to me that we were absolutely, critically dependent on them for real estate and product. We didn't have the credibility, contacts, or track record to get the prime real estate that we needed. We were dependent on Bob Andrews for that. Similarly, one of our real competitive advantages was the cost and quality of our product. They were under no legal obligation to supply us, and we had no right to build our own production facility. What happened if they decided to expand their own operation and couldn't supply us? This gelati is not like hamburger buns—you can't just pick it up anywhere. I thought that our agreements should recognize this dependency and that ICEDELIGHTS should take 25 percent of our company instead of the $200,000 up front. This would give them a real financial incentive to act in our best interests.

Finally, there was my relationship with Paul and Eric. There had been some tension lately. It was obvious that I was more conservative, more risk-averse than they. I was worried about how this might affect our working relationship. I was uncomfortable with the notion that I could be outvoted on a decision and committed to a course of action that I wasn't comfortable with.

At this same time, Mr. Rogers was in Florida and reported that there were a small number of ice cream shops/cafés serving gelati. Further, one of these shops was not doing too well. Obviously, there were a great many of the typical ice cream shops, including Häagen-Dazs, Baskin-Robbins, and several local chains. Still, he felt that there were ample locations to provide for a fast growing business. They also learned that there were two other operations with a similar focus on gelati—Gelateria Italia and Gelato Classico—which were centered in California, but had recently started to franchise.

In preparation for their March 10 meeting, they decided that they would:

1. Go to Florida over spring break to thoroughly investigate the market.
2. Press ICEDELIGHTS to provide further assurances that they would be able to deliver the real estate support and product that they needed.

The issue relative to their attorney was still dragging on. Mark had mentioned his concerns about Ernest Brooke to a friend, John Stors, who was an attorney with a prominent local law firm. John had offered to check with other lawyers in his firm to see if anyone had ever dealt with Brooke. Sure enough, a half-dozen or so lawyers in the office knew Brooke and had dealt with him on tax, real estate, divorce, and estate issues. One mentioned that he had won a case in court over Brooke, a case that Brooke should not have lost. And most damaging of all was the revelation that Brooke was known to be a very close, personal friend of Bob Andrews, ICEDELIGHTS chairman.

Based on this, they decided to use Evan Post and risk alienating Brooke, who seemed willing to invest $30,000 maximum. Post had a reputation as an excellent counsel for small start-ups, as well as good contacts with potential investors. They spoke with Brooke who was quite accommodating and who agreed that the lure of potential investors was attractive, and a legitimate reason for including Evan Post.

Finally, they had exhausted all of Mr. Rogers's contacts and were still about $400,000 short (some investors' "commitments" had evaporated over the past month). They had a meeting with a newly formed venture capital partnership just prior to their March 10 meeting. The venture capital firm indicated that they were extremely interested, but they would require more ownership in the company for their investment. This firm was a particularly attractive partner because its principals had extensive experience running a Kentucky Fried Chicken franchise.

At the March 10 meeting, ICEDELIGHTS responded to their concerns. First, they agreed that the franchisee would not have to pay the remaining $125,000 until ICEDELIGHTS had furnished them with one suitable location and the lease had been signed. Further, ICEDELIGHTS agreed that the franchisee would have the right to build a production facility if ICEDELIGHTS became unable to supply them with product.

The closing date for the deal was set for March 25; in two weeks they would have to put up their $75,000 and sign the franchise and option agreements.

During this time, they had to decide whether to proceed or not. Three major questions remained:

— Was there real potential for this business in the Florida market?

— Did the option and franchise agreement make good business sense?

— Did the returns justify the risks?

If they did decide to proceed, they had to resolve the remaining financial issues:

— How much of the company could they give up and still have the deal be attractive to them? They had revised the deal as shown in Exhibit 10, but knew that they might have to give up even more of the company.

— Should they go ahead and commit $75,000 under the option agreement before they had the full $825,000 of financing secured, hoping to obtain the remainder before the option was exercised?

— Should they go with less than $825,000 and plan a second offering after the first store was up and running?

Finally, they each had their own personal feelings about the deal.

Mark:

ICEDELIGHTS' concessions did reassure me to a certain extent, but I still have some very uncomfortable feelings.

First, the prospects for the business in Florida are still unclear to me; we haven't been to Florida yet, but I have the sense that we will find *some* attractive locations. But in order to meet our projections and investors' expectations, we have to grow extraordinarily quickly.

Second, even if the business does well, we are still critically dependent on ICEDELIGHTS. I think that real estate and product are our two key factors for success, and we really can't control them—they are in ICEDE-LIGHTS' hands. And if they don't perform, our only remedy is to sue. It really scares me to think that we will have the responsibility for $825,000 of other people's money, but can't control the two most important elements of the business.

Finally, I do question whether we have the skills to really make this work. I think that we have been pretty naive so far, and very much caught up in the excitement of actually doing a deal. Fortunately, it hasn't cost any money, and we've learned a lot.

Paul:

The concessions that we won from ICEDELIGHTS reassured me of their continuing commitment to the Florida franchise. We would have preferred giving ICEDELIGHTS a small equity stake in the company, but they were not interested in this proposition.

Like Mark, I am concerned about the market; I do want more than just a "gut feel" that the market is there. This issue is particularly pressing because the closing date of March 25 will come before we have a chance to get to Florida over spring break. We need some concrete research before that. Money is also still a problem. We have "informal commitments" for about $300,000 of the $825,000 needed; experience has taught us that these are often more "informal" than they are commitments. A venture capital firm has expressed very strong interest in a $400,000 to $500,000 investment, but we've grown skeptical of verbal commitments and are still looking for other investors.

Both Eric and I have picked up on Mark's concerns and feel that we are dealing with them. I've started to get the impression, though, that Mark is veiling a lot of his more personal concerns about the venture in terms of business risk.

As far as I'm concerned, we've been lucky so far—things have gone very smoothly. Now it is time to start running fast, tying up all the loose ends.

I'm exhilarated by the prospect of this, and the thought that we are really right on the verge of finally having our own company.

Eric:

I feel that we really have a great opportunity here. I'm really excited by the idea of creating and managing our own organization. It is a fairly simple business, and ICEDELIGHTS has done a great deal to build and standardize the organization. With their systems and support, I am very confident that we can be successful.

I spent Christmas break in Florida, and I believe that the market prospects are very good. The population base is an Eastern, upscale, sophisticated one. The economies of the business are such that we can be profitable even with a small volume. Finally, all of our investors believe that Florida is an attractive market.

I think that ICEDELIGHTS' concessions assured us of the product supply and real estate support that we needed. After we get a few stores up and running, we will have developed a name for ourselves and won't need their real estate assistance anyway.

I understand Mark's concerns, but there are always going to be risks. In this case, they are manageable, and the return justifies them. There is little to be gained by waiting to start our own business; in a few years the risks will seem even greater. Now we have very little to lose.

I really don't feel that any additional assurances will satisfy Mark's doubts. In fact, I think that Mark would be uncomfortable with *any* deal. His lack of commitment is a real problem at this point and needs to be cleared up before it becomes a personal and business problem for all of us.

EXHIBIT 1   Résumés

PAUL ROGERS

Education

1981–1983
NEW YORK SCHOOL OF BUSINESS
ADMINISTRATION   NEW YORK, NY
Candidate for the degree of Master in Business Administration in June 1983.

1974–1978
HARVARD COLLEGE   CAMBRIDGE, MA
Bachelor of Arts degree in June 1978. Majored in modern European history. Vice president of the Delphic Club; presently serves as graduate treasurer.

Work Experience

Summer 1982
WARBURG PARIBAS BECKER   NEW YORK, NY
Corporate Finance. Summer associate. Worked on the initial public offering of a manufacturer of computer memory devices. Assisted in the preparation of the prospectus, due diligence investigations, and marketing of this successful offering. In addition, performed preliminary debt rating analysis and lease-versus-buy analysis for prospective clients.

Summer 1981
NEWBURY, ROSEN & CO., INC.   BOSTON, MA
Corporate Finance. Wrote the prospectus for a $600,000 private placement for a start-up venture in the electronic test equipment rental industry. Performed industry, competitive, and market analyses.

STATE STREET BANK
AND TRUST COMPANY, INC.   BOSTON, MA
1981
Corporate Finance Department. Senior analyst. Worked with three-person team in structuring private placements and assembling prospectuses. Co-authored prospectus for $10 million private placement to regional retailing chain. Participated in presentations of services to a large high-technology firm.

1980–1981
Corporate Services Department. Senior analyst. Assisted vice president of department in establishing a Eurodollar loan syndication portfolio, in which State Street acted as lead manager and agent. Marketed this service to prospective clients. Made both individual and joint presentations to foreign banks interested in joining syndicates. Managed negotiations among the client, legal counsel, and the banking syndicate for a

EXHIBIT 1   *(continued)*

$10 million revolving loan syndication to a major toy manufacturer. Helped bring to a closing two additional term loan syndications totaling $14 million.

1978–1980
Commercial Credit Training Program. Trainee. Completed the training program in 18 instead of the stipulated 24 months.

1975–1978
HASTY PUDDING THEATRICALS   CAMBRIDGE, MA
Producer of this broadway-like musical comedy show. Selected script, hired professional director, set designer, music arranger, and costume designer, and coordinated an 80-person company. Budget for 1978: $110,000. Improved financial controls and initiated a fund drive.

Personal Background
Raised in Boston. Have lived and traveled extensively abroad. Flexible on relocation. Fluent in French.

References
Personal references available upon request.

November 1982

MARK DANIELS

Education
1981–1983
NEW YORK SCHOOL OF BUSINESS
ADMINISTRATION   NEW YORK, NEW YORK
Candidate for the degree of Master in Business Administration in June 1983. General management curriculum. Awarded First-Year Honors. Representative to Admissions and Financial Aid Advisory Committee.

1975–1979
HARVARD COLLEGE   CAMBRIDGE, MASSACHUSETTS
Awarded Bachelor of Arts, *cum laude,* in Economics, June 1979. Wrote Senior Honors Thesis on strategic implications of cost and market structure in the publishing industry. Served as Editor-in-Chief, Harvard Yearbook Publications; Treasurer, D.U. Club; Class Representative, 1979 Class Committee; Executive Committee member, Harvard Fund. Elected Trustee of Yearbook.

Business Experience
Summer 1982
MORGAN STANLEY & CO.   NEW YORK, NEW YORK
Worked as a summer associate in corporate finance and mergers and acquisitions areas. Assisted in the development and implementation of a

EXHIBIT 1 *(continued)*

strategy for divesting a client's shipping subsidiary. Assisted in the defense of an oil services client engaged in a hostile takeover.

1979–1981
McKINSEY & COMPANY   NEW YORK, NEW YORK
                                      TOKYO, JAPAN
Functioned as a consultant to top management of McKinsey's clients in the telecommunications, computer, and office products industries. Assessed the competitive cost position of a major international manufacturer of telecommunications products. Managed internal research project on Japanese competition in high technology industries. Transferred to McKinsey's Tokyo office to develop a strategy for a British client seeking to enter the Japanese office products market. Wrote and presented report to Board of Directors in London.

Current Activities
Currently teaching two courses at New York College, serving as business tutor at Kirk House (an undergraduate residence), and working as an admissions counselor at the New York Business School. Specific responsibilities include:

Tutor, New York College Economics Department, teaching Managerial Economics and Decision Theory.

Teaching Assistant, New York College General Education Department, teaching Business in American Life.

Nonresident Business Tutor, Kirk House, advising undergraduates on careers and graduate education.

Counselor, New York Business School Admissions Office, interviewing prospective students.

Personal Background
Enjoy sailing, racquet sports, travel, and photography.

References
Personal references available upon request.

September 1982

ERIC GARFIELD

Education
1981–1983
NEW YORK SCHOOL OF BUSINESS
ADMINISTRATION   NEW YORK, NEW YORK
Candidate for the degree of Master in Business Administration in June 1983. Pursuing a general management curriculum with emphasis on finance. Awarded COGME Fellowship.

EXHIBIT 1   *(concluded)*

1970–1974
UNIVERSITY OF FLORIDA   GAINESVILLE, FLORIDA
Earned a Bachelor of Science degree in Accounting with additional
concentration in Economics. Awarded membership in Beta Alpha Psi
and Phi Eta Sigma, two honorary scholastic fraternities.

Business Experience
Summer 1982
McKINSEY & COMPANY, INC.   ATLANTA, GEORGIA
Associate. Analyzed financial performance and product-line profitability,
as part of a strategy study, for a major pharmaceutical company.
Recommended a new pricing and production strategy. Prepared and
presented report to client.

CELANESE CORPORATION   NEW YORK, NEW YORK
1979–1981
International Finance Manager. Supervised the preparation and analysis
of strategic plans and operating budgets. Prepared financial analysis for
potential foreign acquisitions and divestitures. Collaborated in cost
reduction project resulting in annual savings of $5 million.

1978–1979
Financial Analyst. Prepared financial analysis for capital expenditure
projects and for actual monthly results versus budget.

1976–1978
International Auditor. Supervised audit team in performing operational
audits. Developed audit programs for foreign installations.

1975–1976
MINNESOTA MINING AND
MANUFACTURING (3M)   CARACAS, VENEZUELA
Senior Cost Analyst. Prepared product analysis required by the Venezu-
elan government for the introduction of new products. Analysis included
marketing, production, and financial data.

1974–1975
PRICE WATERHOUSE & CO.   MIAMI, FLORIDA
Staff Auditor. Performed financial audits of manufacturing and service
organizations.

Personal Background
Fluent in English and Spanish. Enjoy participative sports, reading
historical novels, and international travel.

References
Personal references available upon request.

September 1982

EXHIBIT 2 Specifications Sheet

Dear:

 We are currently second-year students at the New York School of Business and are interested in acquiring a company. We have the skills and abilities necessary to successfully manage a going concern and to create value for our backers and ourselves.

 As explained in the attached specification sheet, we seek to acquire a medium-size firm. We feel our skills are applicable to a broad range of industries—from general industrial to consumer goods.

 As the accompanying resumes indicate, the three of us have varied and complementary skills. We have backgrounds in planning, finance, control, operations, and general management. We believe that our abilities, combined with hard work and intense commitment, will enable us to succeed in such a venture.

 We would greatly appreciate the opportunity to discuss our ideas with you and would be grateful for any suggestions you might have.

Sincerely,

SPECIFICATIONS

GENERAL:	Established manufacturing firms engaged in the production of Industrial and/or Consumer Goods.
SALES VOLUME:	$5,000,000 – $10,000,000.
LOCATION:	Preferably, but not exclusively, Northeast.
PRODUCT:	Basic product with established market.
EXAMPLES:	Include, but are not limited to the following:

 Industrial equipment
 Food packaging and processing
 Control systems and equipment
 Electronic equipment
 Plastic molding
 Construction equipment
 Oil field machinery
 Sporting and athletic goods
 Precision instruments

EXHIBIT 3   Field Study Proposal

Outline of Proposed Field Study

STEP I.   Understand Existing Operations in New England, including: products, manufacturing, distribution, retail location strategy, advertising/merchandising strategy, cost structure, customer profile, management structure and systems, and personnel requirements.

STEP II.   Evaluate Implications for Franchise, including: potential profitability and growth, competition, cost impact, tailoring of concept, relations with franchisor, key risks, and financial requirements.

STEP III.   Evaluate and Structure Deal, including: management structure and responsibilities, form of organization, and legal/tax aspects.

STEP IV.   Prepare Business Plan, including: introduction, company description, risk factors, products, market, competition, marketing program, management, manufacturing, facilities, capital required and use of proceeds, and financial data and financial forecasts.

EXHIBIT 4   Food Franchises—Terms

	Franchise Fee per Location ($100)	*Royalty (percent of sales)*
ICEDELIGHTS	20	5
Gelateria Italia	15	0
Gelato Classico	30	0
Baskin-Robbins	0	0
Carvel	20	Varies
Swensen's	20	5.5
Häagen-Dazs	20	$0.60/gallon
Long John Silver Seafood	10	4
H. Salt Fish & Chips	10	Varies
Kentucky Fried Chicken	10	4
Church's Fried Chicken	15	4
McDonald's	12.5	11.5
Wendy's	15	4
Burger King	40	3.5
Burger Chef	10	4
Taco Bell	45	5
Domino's Pizza	10	5.5
Pizza Inn	15	4
Shakey's Pizza	15	4.5
Orange Julius	18	6

EXHIBIT 5 Population Growth and Income Levels in Florida

City	1980 Population (000)	1970–1980 Growth (percent)	1979 Median Family Income
Boston*	563	(12.0%)	$14,318
Jacksonville	540	7.1	17,646
Miami	456	3.6	13,384
Tampa	271	7.2	15,412
St. Petersburg	238	10.2	15,476
Ft. Lauderdale	153	10.1	19,275
Hialeah	145	42.2	17,070
Orlando	128	29.3	16,312
Hollywood	121	14.2	19,890
Clearwater	85	63.5	18,528
Gainsville	81	26.6	18,528
Largo	58	141.7	16,252
Pompano	52	36.6	20,447
Boca Raton	49	75.0	26,910
Sarasota	49	20.0	16,661

*For reference only.

EXHIBIT 6 Financials

Pro Forma Income Statement: Store Level

Sales		$550,000
Fixed costs:		
Rent (1,000 to 12,000 square feet)	$ 25,000	
Management salaries	30,000	
Variable costs:		
Cost of product	192,500	
Payroll	52,500	
Royalty to parent (5%)	27,500	
Shipping	16,500	
Advertising	5,500	
Other	11,000	
Rent override*	13,500	
Total costs		374,000
Pretax store contribution		$176,000

Capital Requirements per Store

Construction, leasehold improvements	$ 60,000
Equipment costs	85,000
Fees and miscellaneous expenses, capitalized	15,000
Total	$160,000

*A "percent-of-sales" bonus to the landlord after a base sales level is reached.

EXHIBIT 7   Section 385 of Tax Code and Accompanying Explanation

Law
Treatment of Certain Interests in Corporations as Stock or Indebtedness.

(a) *Authority to Prescribe Regulations.* The Secretary is authorized to prescribe such regulations as may be necessary or appropriate to determine whether an interest in a corporation is to be treated for purposes of this title as stock or indebtedness.

(b) *Factors.* The regulations prescribed under this section shall set forth factors which are to be taken into account in determining with respect to a particular factual situation whether a debtor-creditor relationship exists or a corporation-shareholder relationship exists. The factors set forth in the regulations may include among other factors:

(1) Whether there is a written unconditional promise to pay on demand or on a specified date a sum certain in money in return for an adequate consideration in money or money's worth and to pay a fixed rate of interest.

(2) Whether there is subordination to, or preference over, any indebtedness of the corporation.

(3) The ratio of debt to equity of the corporation.

(4) Whether there is convertibility into the stock of the corporation.

(5) The relationship between holdings of stock in the corporation and holdings of interest in question.

Explanation
The distinction between debt and equity is an important one, because of the different tax treatment accorded to each. Interest paid on debt is deductible, while dividends distributed on stock are not. Similarly, the repayment of principal is tax free.

In brief, in order to be classified as debt, a security must meet certain tests.

Essentially, the two key factors are:

— Proportionality: If debt is *not* held in proportion to equity, then the security will usually be treated as debt. If, however, the debt securities *are* held in proportion to equity, then the debt may be classified as equity if "debt is excessive."

— Excessive debt: Debt is typically *not* excessive if both of the following apply:
  • The outside debt/equity ratio is less than 10:1. The outside ratio includes *all* creditors.
  • The inside debt/equity ratio is less than 3:1. The inside ratio excludes debts to independent creditors.

However, even if debt is excessive by these tests, it still may not be excessive if the corporation pays a reasonable rate of interest on the debt, and the financial structure would be acceptable to a bank or similar lender.

EXHIBIT 8 Preliminary Pro Forma Cash Flow Statement (*in thousands of dollars*)

	Year 1	Year 2	Year 3	Year 4	Year 5	Year 6	Year 7	Year 8	Year 9	Year 10
Number stores, total	2	6	10	15	20	20	20	20	20	20
New stores	2	4	4	5	5	—	—	—	—	—
Existing stores	0	2	6	10	15	20	20	20	20	20
Sales	800	2,600	4,600	7,000	9,500	10,000	10,000	10,000	10,000	10,000
Operating income	130	470	390	1,375	1,900	2,100	2,100	2,100	2,100	2,100
Store opening expenses	100	200	200	250	250	—	—	—	—	—
Franchise fees	40	80	80	95	75	—	—	—	—	—
Corporation overhead	115	205	425	575	725	800	800	800	800	800
Income	(125)	(15)	185	455	850	1,300	1,300	1,300	1,300	1,300
Tax	(60)	(7)	35	200	380	580	580	580	580	580
AT income	(65)	(8)	150	255	470	720	720	720	720	720
– Store investment	250	500	500	625	625	—	—	—	—	—
– Corporation investment	10	20	50	50	50	—	—	—	—	—
+ Depreciation	40	120	200	300	400	400	400	400	400	400
+ Franchise fees (prepaid)	40	80	80	—	—	—	—	—	—	—
Case + or –	(180)	(320)	(270)	(375)	(175)	400	400	400	400	400
Total cash + or –	(305)	(335)	(120)	(120)	295	1,120	1,120	1,120	1,120	1,120
Cumulative cash + or –	(305)	(640)	(760)	(880)	(585)	535	1,655	2,775	3,895	5,015

EXHIBIT 9   Excerpts from Prospectus

THE OFFERING
Terms of the Offering

The Company is offering 25 Investment Units. Each Unit consists of 100 shares of its Class A Common Stock (zero par value), offered for $2,000 and $25,000 of the Company's Debentures.

	Per Unit	Total
Equity	$ 2,000	$ 50,000
Debentures	25,000	625,000
Total	$27,000	$675,000

All subscriptions shall be for at least one full unit. The Company currently plans to call for each subscription according to the following schedule:

Approximate Timing	Amount per Unit	Description
Immediately	$ 2,000	Equity
July 1–September 1, 1983	$15,000	Debentures
January 1–March 1, 1984	$10,000	Debentures

The Company reserves the right to accelerate or delay the timing of these contributions as its business requires, and will give investors thirty (30) days written notice of such requirements. Investors who are unable to meet subsequent contribution requirements will forfeit their contributions to date unless a suitable substitute can be found by the investor.
THE SECURITIES OFFERED HEREBY ARE NOT REGISTERED UNDER THE SECURITIES ACT OF 1933 AS AMENDED AND MAY NOT BE SOLD, TRANSFERRED, HYPOTHECATED OR OTHERWISE DISPOSED OF BY AN INVESTOR UNLESS SO REGISTERED OR, IN THE OPINION OF COUNSEL FOR THE COMPANY, REGISTRATION IS NOT REQUIRED UNDER SAID ACT.

Capitalization

The capitalization of the Company as of the conclusion of the Offering, assuming all units are sold, will be as follows:

Debt	$675,000
Equity	$ 75,000

EXHIBIT 9   (*continued*)

This capital consists of the $675,000 raised from the Offering *plus* $75,000 contributed by the Founders.

The Founders will purchase 7,500 shares of the Company's Class B Common Stock for $25,000 and will also contribute $50,000 in debt.

The resulting capitalization is detailed below:

Debt		
Investors	$625,000	
Founders	50,000	
		$675,000
Equity		
Investors	$ 50,000	
Founders	25,000	
		$ 75,000
Total capital		$750,000

Description of Shares and Debentures

The investment units each consist of 100 shares of the Company's Class A Common Stock (zero par value) representing 1 percent of the total outstanding Common Shares of the Company. In total, the Class A stockholders will have representation on the Board of Directors equal to 50 percent of the total number of directors. When the Debentures have been repaid in full, the Class A board representation will be reduced to a pro rata share.

The Founders' Class B stock will be restricted as to dividends until the Debentures have been repaid in full.

The Debentures will be issued with a face value of $5,000 each and will pay interest at 15 percent per annum, cumulative with the first payment deferred until the end of Year 2. Interest payments will be made annually. The Debentures will have a maturity of five (5) years and will be callable.

Use of Proceeds

The amount to be received by the Company from the sale of the Investment Units offered herein is $675,000. The Company intends to use these funds, in addition to the $75,000 contributed by the Founders, for the following purposes:

Development rights for the state of Florida	$100,000
Prepaid franchise rights for the first five stores	$100,000
Capital for three ICEDELIGHTS stores	$480,000
Working capital	$ 70,000
	$750,000

EXHIBIT 9 (*continued*)

Dividends

The Company plans to pay no dividends for a period of five (5) years, and until such time as the Debentures have been paid in full. Following this five-year period, the Company does have the intention of distributing dividends to its investors. No assurance can be made, however, that the Company will, in fact, be able to pay such dividends. Such payment is a matter to be determined from time to time by the Board of Directors and, of necessity, will be based upon the then existing earnings and cash position of the Company, as well as other related matters.

Reports to Stockholders

The Company will furnish its shareholders audited financial statements on an annual basis as well as unaudited quarterly reports of operations and financial condition.

Financial Projections

Following a period of identifying suitable real estate, negotiating loans, and equipping locations, the Company anticipates commencing retail operations no later than early 1984. Ten-year financial projections (attached) are based on the following assumptions.

Store Openings

The Company anticipates opening stores according to the following schedule:*

	Year									
	1	2	3	4	5	6	7	8	9	10
Number of stores opened	3	4	5	5	5	2	2	2	1	1
Cumulative number of stores in operation	3	7	12	17	22	24	26	28	29	30

Sales Level and Growth

Based on its knowledge of sales volumes in existing ICEDELIGHTS locations, and its knowledge of the Florida market, the Company estimates $550,000 in base-level sales. This base level for new stores inflates at the rate of 5 percent per year. Store-level sales grow as follows:

Year	Total Rate of Growth	Real Growth	Inflation
1	15%	10%	5%
2–10	13%	8%	5%

*The decline in the rate of openings after Year 5 reflects the Company's desire to show 10-year financial projections and does not serve to indicate the Company's estimate of the total potential of the Florida market.

EXHIBIT 9   (*continued*)

Capital Requirements

     Based on its knowledge of existing ICEDELIGHTS locations, the Company estimates a cost per store of $160,000. This breaks down as follows:

Construction costs	$60,000
Equipment costs	85,000
Fees and miscellaneous expenses	15,000
Total capital costs	$160,000

     The capital costs are depreciated or expensed as follows:

a. Construction costs over 10 years, the assumed life of a lease.
b. Equipment costs over five years.
c. Architectural fees and other expenses are expensed in the year incurred.

Store Expenses

     The Company estimates store level operating expenses as follows (as a percentage of sales):

Cost of product (including packaging)	35%
Payroll	15
Rent (1,000 to 1,200 square feet required)	7
Royalty	5
Shipping	3
Advertising	1
Other (telephone, cleaning, etc.)	2
Total expenses	68%

Amortization

     The $100,000 development rights are amortized over the 20-year life of the agreement.

THE ATTACHED PROJECTIONS REPRESENT OUR ASSESSMENT OF THE POTENTIAL FOR THE FLORIDA MARKET. THESE ESTIMATES ARE BASED ON DISCUSSIONS WITH MANAGEMENT AND OUR OWN INVESTIGATION OF THE EXISTING OPERATION. WE BELIEVE THAT THESE FIGURES ARE REPRESENTATIVE OF CURRENT OPERATIONS AND DO FAIRLY REFLECT THE LEVEL OF OPERATIONS ANTICIPATED IN FLORIDA. NONETHELESS, THEY ARE ONLY PROJECTIONS, AND MUST BE VIEWED AS SUCH.

EXHIBIT 9 (continued)

Projected Income Statement
(in thousands of dollars)

	Year									
	1	2	3	4	5	6	7	8	9	10
Net sales	$962	$3,340	$6,617	$10,815	$15,719	$20,392	$24,580	$29,386	$34,482	$39,839
Store level expenses:										
Variables	654	2,271	4,500	7,354	10,689	13,867	16,714	19,982	23,448	27,091
Fixed	53	174	330	521	730	900	1,025	1,160	1,784	1,398
Depreciation	69	165	295	430	575	585	574	545	480	415
Operating income	186	730	1,492	2,510	3,725	5,040	6,267	7,699	8,770	10,935
Start-up expenses	103	140	180	173	162	67	69	71	36	37
Corporate overhead	105	215	415	580	680	810	906	1,017	1,110	1,203
Amortization	5	5	5	5	5	5	5	5	5	5
Earnings before interest and taxes	(27)	370	892	1,752	2,878	4,158	5,287	6,606	7,619	9,690
Interest expense:										
Investor	0	216	101	101	75	0	0	0	0	0
Bank		15	15	15	0	0	0	0	0	0
Profit before taxes	(27)	139	776	1,636	2,803	4,158	5,287	6,606	7,619	9,690
Taxes	0	52	357	753	1,289	1,913	2,432	3,039	3,505	4,457
Net income	(27)	87	419	883	1,514	2,245	2,855	3,567	4,114	5,233

EXHIBIT 9 (continued)

Projected Balance Sheet
(in thousands of dollars)

					Year					
	1	2	3	4	5	6	7	8	9	10
Assets										
Cash	$320	$105	$ 24	$ 225	$ 936	$3,400	$6,445	$10,153	$14,537	$19,964
Prepaid fee	40	0	0	0	0	0	0	0	0	0
Development agreement	95	90	85	80	75	70	65	60	55	50
Net fixed assets	268	715	1,220	1,632	1,940	1,726	1,541	1,405	1,140	951
Total assets	$723	$910	$1,329	$1,937	$2,951	$5,196	$8,051	$11,618	$15,732	$20,965
Liabilities										
Bank debt	0	100	100	0	0	0	0	0	0	0
Investor debt	675	675	675	500	0	0	0	0	0	0
Total liabilities	675	775	775	500	0	0	0	0	0	0
Equity										
Paid-in capital	75	75	75	75	75	75	75	75	75	75
Retained earnings	(27)	60	479	1,362	2,876	5,121	7,976	11,543	15,657	20,890
Total equity	48	135	554	1,437	2,951	5,196	8,051	11,618	15,732	20,965
Total liabilities & equity	$723	$910	$1,329	$1,937	$2,951	$5,196	$8,051	$11,618	$15,732	$20,965

EXHIBIT 9 (continued)

Projected Cash Flow
(in thousands of dollars)

	Year									
	1	2	3	4	5	6	7	8	9	10
Net income	($ 27)	$ 87	$419	$ 883	$1,514	$2,245	$2,855	$3,567	$ 4,114	$ 5,233
Depreciation	69	165	295	430	575	585	575	545	480	415
Amortization	5	5	5	5	5	5	5	5	5	5
Prepaid expense	60	40	0	0	0	0	0	0	0	0
Cash from operations	107	297	719	1,318	2,094	2,835	3,434	4,117	4,599	5,653
Capital expenditures:										
Development agreement	100	—	—	—	—	—	—	—	—	—
Prepaid fees	100	—	—	—	—	—	—	—	—	—
Store construction and equipment	337	612	800	842	883	371	389	409	215	226
Cash generated: surplus/(deficit)	(430)	(315)	(81)	476	1,211	2,464	3,045	3,708	4,384	5,427
Financing:										
Equity	75	0	0	0	0	0	0	0	0	0
Debentures	675	0	0	(175)	(500)	0	0	0	0	0
Bank debt	0	100	0	(100)	0	0	0	0	0	0
Net cash flow	320	(215)	(81)	201	711	2,464	3,045	3,708	4,384	5,427
Beginning cash	0	320	105	24	225	936	3,400	6,445	10,153	14,537
Ending cash	$320	$105	$ 24	$ 225	$ 936	$3,400	$6,445	$10,153	$14,537	$19,964

EXHIBIT 9 (concluded)

Cash Flow and Internal Rate of Return to One Unit Shareholder
(in thousands of dollars)

	Year									
	0	1	2	3	4	5	6	7	8	9	10
Investment	$27	—	—	—	—	—	—	—	—	—	—
Interest	—	—	$8	$4	$4	$ 3	—	—	—	—	—
Return of principal	—	—	—	—	$4	$21	—	—	—	—	—
Share of cash flow (1%)	—	—	—	—	—	—	$25	$30	$37	$44	$ 54
Share of estimated market value at 10 times earnings*	—	—	—	—	—	—	—	—	—	—	$523
Net cash flow to investor	($27)	—	$8	$4	$8	$24	$25	$30	$37	$44	$577
Annualized internal rate of return = 49%											

*For illustrative purposes only.

EXHIBIT 10   Summary of Changes to the Offering

The Offering
    The Company is offering 25 investment units. Each unit consists of 150 shares of its Class A Common Stock (no par value), offered for $5,000 and $25,000 of the Company's 10% debentures.

	Per Unit	Total
Equity	$ 5,000	$125,000
Debentures	25,000	625,000
Total	$30,000	$750,000

    All subscriptions shall be for at least one full unit. The Company currently plans to call for each subscription according to the following schedule:

Approximate Timing	Amount per Unit	Description
Immediately	$ 2,500	Equity
July 1–September 1, 1983	17,500	Equity and 3 debentures
January 1–March 1, 1984	10,000	2 debentures

    The Company reserves the right to accelerate or delay the timing of these contributions as its business requires, and will give investors thirty (30) days written notice of such requirements. Investors who are unable to meet subsequent contribution requirements will forfeit their contributions to date, unless a suitable substitute can be found by the investor.
    The securities offered herein are not registered under the Securities Act of 1933 as amended and may not be sold, transferred, hypothecated or otherwise disposed of by an investor unless so registered or, in the opinion of counsel for the Company, registration is not required under said Act.

Capitalization
    The capitalization of the Company, as of the conclusion of the offering, assuming all units are sold, will be as follows:

Debt	$675,000
Equity	$150,000
Total	$825,000

The capital consists of $750,000 raised by the offering plus $75,000 contributed by the founders.
    The founders will purchase 6,250 shares of the Company's Class B Common Stock for $25,000 and will also contribute $50,000 in debt.

EXHIBIT 10 (*concluded*)

Revised Cash Flow and Internal Rate of Return to One Unit Shareholder
(*in thousands of dollars*)

					Year					
	0	1	2	3	4	5	6	7	8	9	10
Investment	$30	—	—	—	—	—	—	—	—	—	—
Interest	—	—	$5	$3	$3	$ 3	—	—	—	—	—
Return of principal	—	—	—	—	$5	$20	—	—	—	—	—
Share of cash flow (1½%)	—	—	—	—	—	—	$37	$46	$56	$66	$ 82
Share of estimated market Value at 10 times earnings*	—	—	—	—	—	—	—	—	—	—	$785
Net cash flow to investor	($30)	—	$5	$3	$8	$23	$37	$46	$56	$66	$867
Annualized internal rate of return = 52%											

*For illustrative purposes only.

185

Part II

Assessing and Acquiring Necessary Resources

This section addresses two of the most important issues faced by entrepreneurs as they start a new venture:

— What resources are needed?
— How are they to be acquired?

ASSESSING REQUIRED RESOURCES

In order to translate the business concept into a reality, the entrepreneur needs first to assess the resources that the venture will require. Entrepreneurs are often required to do more with less. By definition, they are attempting to achieve goals that will require considerably more resources than they currently control.

One of the key skills lies in distinguishing between those resources that are absolutely essential and those that would be nice to have but are not crucial.

Another technique is to distinguish between resources that must be "owned" and those that may be rented, contracted for, or even borrowed. Perhaps professional advice can be obtained based on friendship or the promise of future business. Doing more with less requires buying only what is needed and using the rest without actually owning it.

ACQUIRING NECESSARY RESOURCES

Having identified the required resources, it then becomes the entrepreneur's task to acquire them. This acquisition should be guided by a number of policies:

— First, the entrepreneur must commit quickly, and sometimes fully, in order to get to the next stage. This, perhaps, is why entrepreneurs are perceived as risk takers.

— Still, the entrepreneur must be flexible in these commitments, shifting resources once the desired end has been achieved.

— Finally, the individual must approach the acquisition process with the intention of giving up as little as possible in order to attract the needed resources. The rest of the value created thus accrues to the entrepreneur.

Financial Resources

Clearly, financial resources—dollars—are the most frequently needed. Chapter 5, "Alternative Sources of Financing," describes the spectrum of alternatives for obtaining financing. Chapter 6 looks at the technique of structuring a deal in order to obtain the required financial resources. Chapter 7 discusses the securities laws that impact the raising of funds and also describes the business plans and prospectuses that are typically used.

Nonfinancial Resources

The entrepreneur must also secure the nonfinancial resources that the venture needs—a building, plant or office space, technology, management, and other employees. Chapter 8, "Intellectual Property," describes the legal issues that surround ideas: patents, trademarks, trade secrets, confidentiality, and so forth. The entrepreneur must be aware of the serious repercussions that can result either from unfairly using someone else's idea or from failing to protect his or her own idea.

THE CASES

The Steven B. Belkin and Heather Evans cases both describe individuals attempting to raise funds to finance a start-up venture. In addition to the issues surrounding financing, there are other questions as well: Is the venture a good opportunity? Has the entrepreneur adequately detailed the business concept and the resources needed to exploit the opportunity? What kind of investors should be targeted?

The Duncan Field case looks at a situation where a would-be entrepreneur is attempting to purchase a cable TV business on the basis of little financial data. How should he value and finance the venture?

Clarion Optical Co. describes an interesting opportunity for some employees to purchase their current employer's business. The case exposes the student to some of the quantitative techniques that lie behind the structuring of a deal.

Viscotech concerns a young company that may have violated the securities laws in its search for funds. The student is asked to address this issue and to recommend a plan for proceeding in light of the potential violation.

Universal Robotics provides for a discussion of many of the technical and legal terms that accompany the structuring of venture financing.

CVD v. A. S. Markham describes a recent legal case in which employees of a large defense contractor left that firm to begin a competitive business. Did they take trade secrets with them or violate their employment agreements?

Finally, Stratus Computer offers the student an opportunity to evaluate one entrepreneur's efforts to raise several million dollars of equity capital for a new high-technology venture.

Chapter Five

Alternative Sources of Financing

One of the most common issues confronted by the entrepreneur revolves around securing financing for the venture. Questions of how and when to raise money and from whom are frequent topics of concern. This chapter will describe some common sources of capital and the conditions under which money is typically lent or invested. Chapter 6, "Deal Structure," discusses the specific terms and pricing of capital.

AN OVERVIEW

As in most transactions, the owners of capital expect to get something in return for providing financing for the venture. In evaluating potential opportunities, the providers of funds will typically use some form of a risk/return model. That is, they will demand a higher return when they perceive a higher risk.

The entrepreneur's objective, of course, is to secure financing at the lowest possible cost. The art of successful financing, therefore, lies in obtaining funds in a manner which those providers of funds view as relatively less risky.

The entrepreneur can do several things to structure the financing so it will be perceived as "less risky":

— Pledge personal or corporate assets against a loan.

— Promise to pay the money back in a short period of time when the investors can judge the health of the business, rather than over the long term when its financial strength is less certain.

This note was prepared by Michael J. Roberts under the direction of Howard H. Stevenson.

Copyright © 1984 by the President and Fellows of Harvard College
Harvard Business School note 9–384–187

— Give investors some measure of control over the business, through either loan covenants or participation in management (i.e., a seat on the board).

Note that these are only a few of the possible mechanisms.

The liabilities side of the balance sheet itself provides a good overview of the potential sources of financing. Because this side of the balance sheet is arranged in order of increasing risk, it follows that the lowest cost forms of financing will usually be available from the higher balance sheet items.

START-UP FINANCING

Start-up financing provides the entrepreneur with a host of unique challenges. The highest risk capital (and therefore potentially highest return capital) is at the bottom of the balance sheet as equity. When a business is in the start-up phase, it is at its riskiest point. Therefore, equity capital is usually an appropriate source of financing during this period. That is not to say that debt capital is unattractive. It may even be available when secured by assets of the business, such as a building or equipment. However, some equity is usually required to get a business "off the ground." There is virtually no getting around the fact that the first investment in the business will be equity capital. This is required to demonstrate commitment on the part of the entrepreneur. Investors perceive, and rightly so, that the individual entrepreneur will be more committed to the venture if she or he has a substantial portion of personal assets invested in the venture. It is this fact that has led some to claim that: "You're better off trying to start a business with $5,000 than with $100,000 in personal resources. If you are relatively poor, you can demonstrate your commitment for a smaller sum." This statement presumes that you will be seeking capital from some *outside* source. If you were going to fund the venture all by yourself, you would naturally prefer to have $100,000 instead of $5,000.

There is another, more practical reason why this start-up phase will usually be financed with the entrepreneur's own funds. In order to raise money, you typically need more than an idea. The entrepreneur will have to invest some money in the idea, perhaps to build a prototype or do a market study, in order to convince potential providers of capital that the idea has potential.

This is not to say that these funds must be equity capital in the purest sense. That is, the money need only be equity from the point of view of potential investors in the business. The entrepreneur can obtain these "equity funds" by mortgaging personal assets like a house or car, borrowing from friends or relatives, even from a personal bank loan or credit card advances. The important fact is that when the money goes into the business, it does so as equity, not as debt to be repaid to the entrepreneur.

Some specialized firms provide "seed capital." Most venture capital firms require that a business move beyond the idea stage before they will consider financing it. Yet, some businesses require a good deal of work (and money) to get from the concept phase to the point where they can obtain venture capital financing. Seed funds can provide this kind of capital.

OUTSIDE EQUITY CAPITAL

Typically, the entrepreneur will exhaust his or her own funds before the business is a viable operation. At this point, it is usually still too early to obtain all of the required financing in the form of debt. The entrepreneur must approach outside sources for equity capital.

Private Investors

One popular source of equity capital is private investors, also known as *wealthy individuals*. These investors may range from family and friends with a few extra dollars to extremely wealthy individuals who manage their own money. Doctors frequently come to mind, and do, in fact, represent a significant source of private equity capital. Wealthy individuals may be advised by their accountants, lawyers, or other professionals, and the entrepreneur must deal with these people as well.

In order to approach wealthy individuals, you will usually need at least a business plan. A formal offering memorandum has the advantage of providing more legal protection for the entrepreneur in the form of disclaimers and legal language. However, it suffers from appearing overly negative, being more costly to prepare (it usually requires legal counsel), and also being limited by the SEC laws in terms of its distribution. That is, some of the SEC rules permit only 35 "offerees." Some legal advisers believe that you can show the business plan to more individuals and then formally "offer" to only those individuals who have a real interest in investing.

One of the best ways to find wealthy investors is through a network of friends, acquaintances, and advisers. For instance, if you have used a local lawyer and accountant to help you prepare a business plan or offering document, these advisers may know of wealthy individuals who invest in ventures like yours.

At this point, it is worth reiterating the importance of following the securities laws and obtaining the advice of counsel. Because many of these wealthy individuals are "unsophisticated," they can (and often do, if the venture is unsuccessful) claim that they were misled by you, the conniving entrepreneur. A carefully drawn offering document is the key to legal protection in this instance.

Wealthy investors may be well-suited to participation in equity financings that are too small for a venture capital firm to consider (e.g., under $500,000). Wealthy investors are also typically thought of as being a less expensive source of equity than venture capital firms. This may be true. It is also true that:

— Wealthy individuals do not often possess the expertise or time to advise the entrepreneur on the operations of the business.

— Wealthy investors are far less likely to come up with additional funds if required.

— These investors are more likely to be a source of "problems" or frustration, particularly if there is a large number of them. Phoning frequently, or complaining when things are not going according to plan, they can create headaches for even the most well-intentioned of entrepreneurs.

Venture Capital

Venture capital refers to a pool of equity capital that is professionally managed. Wealthy individuals invest in this fund as limited partners, and the general partners manage the pool in exchange for a fee and a percentage of the gain on investments.

In order to compensate for the riskiness of their investments, give their own investors a handsome return, and make a profit for themselves, venture firms seek a high rate of return on their investments. Target returns of 50 percent or 60 percent are not uncommon hurdles for firms to apply to prospective venture capital investments.

In exchange for this high return, venture firms will often provide advice to their portfolio companies. These people have been through many times what the entrepreneur is usually experiencing for the first time. They can often provide useful counsel on the problems a company may experience in the start-up phase.

Venture firms can differ along several dimensions. Some prefer investing in certain kinds of companies. "High-tech" is popular with most, although perceptions of what precisely this is will vary widely. Some firms have a reputation for being very involved with the day-to-day operations of the business; others exhibit a more hands-off policy.

In approaching venture capitalists, the entrepreneur needs a business plan to capture the firm's interest. Here the document serves a far different purpose than it would in the case of wealthy individuals.

A venture capital firm will expend a good deal of effort investigating potential investments. Not only is this sound business practice on their part, but they have legal obligations to their own investors.

Therefore, a business plan targeted to venture firms should be short, concise, and attempt to stimulate further interest, rather than present the business in exhaustive detail.

Most venture capitalists also report that it is only the naive entrepreneur who will propose the actual terms of the investment in the initial document. While the plan should certainly spell out how much financing the entrepreneur is seeking, to detail the terms (e.g., "for 28 percent of the stock. . .") is viewed as premature for an initial presentation.

One topic, which is frequently of concern to entrepreneurs, is confidentiality. On the one hand, it seems wise to tell potential investors about your good ideas to get them interested in the company; on the other, what if someone else takes them? In general, venture capitalists are a professional group and will not disclose confidential information. It is more difficult, however, to make this statement about private sources of capital, like wealthy individuals.

Whatever the target investor audience, it is generally *not* a good idea to put truly proprietary material in a business plan. These plans are frequently copied and could certainly be left accidentally on a plane or in an office. A business plan might, for example, describe the functions a new product would perform, but should probably not include circuit designs, engineering, drawings, etc.

Venture firms may not invest via a pure equity security. Some may invest a package of debt and equity, convertible debt, or convertible preferred. Each of these has its advantages:

— A debt/equity package provides for the venture firm to get some of its funds back via interest, which is deductible to the company, and results in a tax savings. The investor can also recover tax free cash based on repayment of loan principal.

— Convertible debt or preferred gives the venture firm a liquidation preference. If the venture should fail, the venture capitalist will have a priority claim on the assets of the business. Often too, the terms can force eventual repayment even if the firm never achieves "public" status.

Venture firms will usually "syndicate" a large investment. That is, they will attempt to interest other firms in taking a piece of the investment. This permits the firm to invest in a larger number of companies and thus spread its risk. This is particularly important on subsequent "rounds" or stages of financing. Other venture firms will want to see that the original firm(s) will continue their investment in the company. If the existing, more knowledgeable investors aren't interested in the company, why should a new venture firm be interested?

Public Equity Markets

Of course, the largest source of equity capital remains the public equity markets: The New York, American, and over-the-counter stock exchanges. Typically, however, a firm must have a history of successful operation before it can raise money in this way. In "hot" markets, some smaller, start-up companies have been able to raise public equity. The process is lengthy, detailed, and expensive. See "Securities Law and Going Public" for a discussion of the public equity markets.

Whether the investment is made by wealthy individuals or a venture capital firm, terms will have to be negotiated. In exchange for their investment, the investor will receive a "security," which represents the terms of his or her investment in the company. In the case of a public offering, the investment bank negotiates the terms on behalf of its clients. Venture capital firms and investment banks, of course, tend to be more sophisticated than the average wealthy investor.

DEBT CAPITAL

The other large category of capital is debt. Debt is presumed to be lower risk capital because it is repaid according to a set schedule of principal and interest.

In order to have a reasonable expectation of being paid according to this schedule, creditors lend against:

— Assets: Firms can obtain asset-based financing for most hard assets that have a market value. A building, equipment, or soluble inventory are all assets that a company could borrow against.

— Cash flow: Lenders will allow firms to borrow against their expected ability to generate the cash to repay the loan. Creditors attempt to check this ability through such measures as interest coverage (EBIT ÷ interest payments) or debt/equity ratio. Obviously, a healthy business with little debt and high cash flow will have an easier time borrowing money than a new venture.

Cash Flow Financing

Cash flow or unsecured financing is of several types and can come from different sources.

— Short-term debt: Short-term unsecured financing is frequently available to cover seasonal working capital needs for periods of less than one year, usually 30 to 40 days.

— Line-of-credit financing: A company can arrange for a line of credit, to be drawn upon as needed. Interest is paid on the outstanding principal, and a "commitment fee" is paid up front. Generally, a line of credit must be "paid-down" to an agreed-upon level at some point during the year.

— Long-term debt: Generally available to solid "creditworthy" companies, long-term debt may be available for up to 10 years. Long-term debt is usually repaid according to a fixed schedule of interest and principal.

Cash flow financing is most commonly available from commercial banks, but can also be obtained from savings and loan institutions, finance companies, and other institutional lenders (e.g., insurance companies, pension funds). Because cash-flow financing is generally riskier than asset-based financing, banks will frequently attempt to reduce their risk through the use of covenants. These covenants place certain restrictions on a business if it wishes to maintain its credit with the bank. Typical loan covenants concern:

— Limits on the company's debt/equity ratio.

— Minimum standards on interest coverage.

— Lower limits on working capital.

— Minimum cash balance.

— Restrictions on the company's ability to issue senior debt.

These, and other covenants, attempt to protect the lender from actions that would increase the likelihood of the lender not getting its money back.

Asset-Based Financing

Most assets in a business can be financed. Because cash-flow financing usually requires an earnings history, far more new ventures are able to obtain asset-based financing. In an asset-based financing, the company pledges or gives the financier a first lien on the asset. In the event of a default on the financing payments, the lender can repossess the asset. The following types of financing are generally available:

— Accounts receivable: Up to 90 percent of the accounts receivable from creditworthy customers can usually be financed. The bank will conduct a thorough investigation to determine which accounts are eligible for this kind of financing. In some industries, such as the government business, accounts receivable are often "factored." A factor buys approved receivables for a discount from their face value, but collects from the accounts.

— Inventory: Inventory is often financed if it consists of merchandise that could be easily sold. Typically, 50 percent or so of finished goods inventory can be financed.

— Equipment: Equipment can usually be financed for a period of 3 to 10 years. One-half to 80 percent of the value of the equipment can be financed, depending on the salability or "liquidity" of the assets. Leasing is also a form of equipment financing where the company never takes ownership of the equipment, but rents it.

— Real estate: Mortgage financing is usually readily available to finance a company's plant or buildings; 75 to 85 percent of the value of the building is a typical figure.

— Personally secured loans: A business can obtain virtually any amount of financing if one of its principals (or someone else) is willing to pledge a sufficient amount of assets to guarantee the loan.

— Letter-of-credit financing: A letter of credit is a bank guarantee that a company can obtain to enable it to purchase goods. A letter of credit functions almost like a credit card, allowing businesses to make commitments and purchases in other parts of the world where the company does not have relationships with local banks.

— Government-secured loans: Certain government agencies will guarantee loans to allow businesses to obtain financing when they could not obtain it on their own. The Small Business Administration, the Farmers Home Administration, and other government agencies will guarantee bank loans.

Asset-based financing is available from commercial banks and other financial institutions. Insurance companies, pension funds, and commercial finance companies provide mortgages and other forms of asset-backed financing. Entrepreneurs themselves can also provide debt capital to a business once it has passed out of the risky start-up period.

INTERNALLY GENERATED FINANCING

A final category of financing is internally generated. This term describes:

— Credit from suppliers: Paying bills in a less timely fashion is one way to increase working capital. Sometimes, suppliers will charge you interest for this practice. In other instances, the costs may be more severe if a key supplier resource decides to stop serving you.

— Accounts receivable: Collecting bills more quickly will also generate financing.

— Reducing working capital: A business can generate internal financing by reducing other working capital items: inventory, cash, and so forth.

— Sale of assets: Perhaps a more drastic move, selling assets will also generate capital.

Each of these techniques represents an approach to generating funds internally, without the help of a financial partner. Although the purely financial costs are low, the entrepreneur must be wary of attempting to run the business "too lean."

SUMMARY

We've attempted to describe the spectrum of financial sources that an entrepreneur can tap both during the start-up phase and as a going concern. Figure 5–1 is an attempt to summarize these sources. Along the horizontal axis, we've tried to note whether the provider of capital tries to manage the risk/reward ratio by (1) increasing reward by raising the cost of funds or (2) decreasing risk by asserting some measure of control over the business. This is not an exhaustive list, but an overview of the most popular sources. In every case, there is a high premium on understanding both your own needs and the specific needs of the financier.

FIGURE 5-1 Alternative Sources of Financing

Source	Cost								Control	
	Zero	Fixed Rate Short-term	Fixed Rate Long-term	Floating Rate Short-term	Floating Rate Long-term	Percent of Profits	Equity	Covenants	Voting Rights	Guarantee of Debt
Self	X		X				X		X	X
Family and friends		X	X	X	X		X		X	X
Suppliers and trade credit		X				X				X
Commercial banks		X		X				X		X
Other commercial lenders		X	X		X			X		X
Asset-based lenders/lessors			X			X	X	X		
Specialized finance companies		X	X			X	X	X		
Institutions and insurance companies			X		X	X		X		
Pension funds			X			X	X	X		
Venture capital		X	X				X	X	X	X
Private equity placements							X	X	X	
Public equity offerings						X	X		X	
Government agencies (SBIC)			X		X	X				X
Other government programs			X					X		X

Chapter Six

Deal Structure

A critical aspect of the entrepreneur's attempt to obtain resources is the development of an actual "deal" with the owner of the resources. Typically, the entrepreneur needs a variety of resources, including dollars, people, and outside expertise. As in any situation, the individual who desires to own, or use, these resources must give up something. Because the entrepreneur typically has so little to start with, she or he will usually give up a claim on some future value in exchange for the ability to use these resources now.

Entrepreneurs can obtain funds in the form of trade credit, short- and long-term debt, and equity or risk capital. This chapter will focus on the structure and terms of the deal that may be used to obtain the required financial resources from investors. The note will center on financial resources because raising capital is a common problem that virtually all entrepreneurs face.

WHAT IS A *DEAL?*

In general, a *deal* represents the terms of a transaction between two (or more) groups or individuals. Entrepreneurs want money to use in a (hopefully) productive venture, and individuals and institutions wish to earn a return on the cash that they have at risk.

The entrepreneur's key task is to make the whole equal to more than the sum of the parts. That is, to carve up the economic benefits of the venture into pieces that meet the needs of particular financial backers. The entrepreneur can maximize his or her own return by selling these pieces at the highest possible price, that is, to individuals

This note was prepared by Michael J. Roberts under the direction of Howard H. Stevenson.

who demand the lowest return. And the individuals who demand the lowest return will typically be those that perceive the lowest risk.

THE DEAL

In order to craft a deal that maximizes his or her own economic return, the entrepreneur must:

— Understand the fundamental economic nature of the business.

— Understand financiers' needs and perceptions of risk and reward.

— Understand his or her own needs and requirements.

Understanding the Business

The first thing the entrepreneur must do is assess the fundamental economic nature of the business itself. Most business plans project a set of economics that determine:

— The amount of the funds required.

  • The absolute amount.

  • The timing of these requirements.

— The riskiness of the venture.

  • The absolute level of risk.

  • The factors that determine risk.

— The timing and potential magnitude of returns.

It is important to remember that the venture itself does not necessarily have an inherent set of economics. The entrepreneur determines the fundamental economics when she or he makes critical decisions about the business. Still, there may be certain economic characteristics that are a function of the industry and environment and that the entrepreneur will generally be guided by.

For instance, a venture such as a genetics engineering firm has characteristics that differ greatly from those of a real estate deal. The genetics firm may require large investments over the first several years, followed by years with zero cash flow, followed by a huge potential return many years out. The real estate project, on the other hand, may require a one-time investment, generate immediate cash flow, and provide a means of exit only several years down the road.

One technique for understanding a venture's economic nature is to analyze the potential source of return. Let's take this example—a paint business with the following projected cash flows:

	Year					
	0	1	2	3	4	5
Cash flow [$000 omitted]	(1,000)	400	400	400	400	5,600

Now, we can break this cash flow down into its components:

— Investment: money required to fund the venture.

— Tax consequences: not precisely a cash flow, but nonetheless a cash benefit that may accrue if an investment has operating losses in the early years.

— Free cash flow: cash that the business throws off as a result of its operations before financing and distributions to providers of capital.

— Terminal value: the after-tax cash that the business returns as a result of its sale. Here, this is assumed to occur at the end of Year 5.

Let's assume that these flows are as follows:

	Year					
Cash Flows ($000)	0	1	2	3	4	5
Original investment	(1,000)					
Tax consequences	—	300	300	0	(100)	(200)
Free cash flows	—	100	100	400	(500)	(800)
Terminal value (after tax)						5,000
Total	(1,000)	400	400	400	400	5,600

Now, we can calculate the IRR of the total investment: 64.5 percent.
Next, we calculate the present value of each of the individual elements of the return *at that IRR,* and then the percent that each element contributes to the total return. Of course, the present value of the total return will be equal to the original investment.

Element	Present Value @ 64.5% ($000)	Element's Percent of Total
Tax consequences	263	26.3
Free cash flows	322	32.2
+ Terminal value	415	41.5
Total	$1,000	100.0%

This analysis illuminates the potential sources of return inherent in the business, as projected.

The task of the entrepreneur is now to carve up the cash flows and returns and sell them to the individuals/institutions that are willing to accept the lowest return. This will leave the biggest piece of the economic pie for the entrepreneur. To do so requires an understanding of the financiers' needs and perceptions.

Understanding Financers

Providers of capital clearly desire a "good" return on their money, but their needs and priorities are far more complex. Figure 5–1 in Chapter 5 depicts some of the differences that exist among different financial sources. They vary along a number of dimensions, including:

— Magnitude of return desired.

— Magnitude and nature of risk that is acceptable.

— Perception of risk and reward.

— Magnitude of investment.

— Timing of return.

— Form of return.

— Degree of control.

— Mechanisms for control.

The priorities attached to the various elements may differ widely. For instance, institutions such as insurance companies and pension funds have legal standards, which determine the type of investment that they can undertake. For others, the time horizon for their return may be influenced by organizational or legal constraints.

Certain investors may want a high rate of return and be willing to wait a long period and bear a large amount of risk to get it. Still other investors may consider any type of investment, as long as there exists some mechanism for them to exert their own control over the venture. To the extent that the entrepreneur is able to break down the basic value of the business into components, which vary along each of these dimensions, and then find investors who want this specific package, the entrepreneurs will be able to structure a better transaction; a deal that creates more value for himself or herself.

If we return to our example of the paint business, which requires a $1 million investment, we can see how the entrepreneur can take advantage of these differences in investor characteristics.

— The tax benefits, for example, are well suited for sale to a risk-averse wealthy individual in a high marginal tax bracket. Because the benefits accrue as a result of operating losses, if the business does poorly, the tax benefits may be even greater. But let's assume that the wealthy individual believes that these forecasts are realistic and requires a 25 percent return. If we discount the tax benefits at this 25 percent required return, we arrive at a present value of $325,500. Therefore, this individual should be willing to invest $325,500 in order to purchase this portion of the cash flows. There must be economic substance to the transaction other than tax benefits. Care must be taken so that the investor can show prospect for economic gain. For this analysis, this tax-based requirement is ignored.

— The operating cash flows would, in total, be perceived as fairly risky. However, some portion of them should be viewed as a "safe bet" by a bank. Let's assume that the entrepreneur could convince a banker that no less than $60,000 would be available in any given year for interest expenses. Further, if the banker were willing to accept 12 percent interest and take all of the principal repayment at the end of Year 5 (when the business is sold), then she or he should be willing to provide $60,000 ÷ .12 = $500,000 in the form of a loan.

Now the entrepreneur has raised $825,500 and needs only $174,500 to get into business.

— The terminal value, and the riskier portion of the operating cash flows, remain to be sold. Let's assume that a venture investor would be willing to provide funds at a 50 percent rate of return.

First, we need to see precisely what cash flows remain:

	Year				
	1	2	3	4	5
Total	400	400	400	400	5,600
− Wealthy investor	300	300	0	(100)	(200)
− Bank	60	60	60	60	560
= Remaining	40	40	340	440	5,240

The remaining cash flows in Years 1 through 5 have a present value, at the venture firm's 50 percent discount rate, of $922,140. If we need $174,500, we need to give up $174,500 ÷ $922,140 = 18.9 percent of these flows in order to entice the venture investor to provide risk capital. These flows might well be sold to the tax-oriented investor in order to meet the requirements for economic substance. This leaves the entrepreneur with a significant portion of the above "remaining" flows.

One can see how these differences in needs and perceived risk allow the entrepreneur to create value for himself or herself.

Understanding the Entrepreneur's Own Needs

The example we have just worked through was based on the assumption that the entrepreneur wants to obtain funds at the lowest possible cost. While this is generally true, there are often other factors that should affect the analysis.

The entrepreneur's needs and priorities do vary across a number of aspects including the time horizon for involvement in the venture, the nature of that involvement, degree of business risk, and so on. All of these variables will affect the entrepreneur's choice of a venture to pursue. However, once the entrepreneur has decided to embark on a particular business, his or her needs and priorities with respect the *financing* of the venture will vary with respect to:

— Degree of control desired.
— Mechanisms of control desired.
— Amount of financing required.
— Magnitude of financial return desired.
— Degree of risk that is acceptable.

For instance, in the above example, the entrepreneur could have decided to obtain an additional $100,000 or $200,000 as a cushion to make the venture less risky. This would certainly have lowered the economic return, but might have made the entrepreneur more comfortable with the venture.

Similarly, the bank, which offered funds at 12 percent, or the venture investor might have imposed a series of very restrictive covenants. Rather than accept this loss of control, the entrepreneur might rather have given up more of the economic potential.

In addition, the entrepreneur may need more than just money. There are times when some investors' money is better than others. This occurs in situations where once an individual is tied into a venture financially, she or he has an incentive to help the entrepreneur in nonfinancial ways. For instance, an entrepreneur starting a business that depends on securing good retail locations would prefer to obtain financing from an individual with good real estate contacts than from someone without those contacts. Venture capital firms are frequently cited for providing advice and support in addition to financing.

SUMMARY

Once the fundamental economics of a deal have been worked out, the entrepreneur must still structure the deal. This requires the use of a certain legal form of organization and a certain set of securities.

The vehicles through which the entrepreneur can raise capital include the general partnership, the limited partnership, the S corporation, and the corporation. While these forms of organization differ with respect to their tax consequences, they also differ substantially regarding the precision with which cash flows may be carved up and returned to various investors. In a limited partnership, for instance, virtually *any* distribution of profits and cash flow is feasible so long as it is spelled out clearly and in advance in the limited partnership agreement. (Losses, however, are usually distributed in proportion to capital provided.) In an S corporation, on the other hand, where only one class of stock is permitted, investors can get a return in the form of tax losses that can be passed through, but founder's stock is equivalent to investors' stock, and it is difficult to draw any distinctions in the returns that accrue to the two groups.

Securities can involve debt, warrants, straight or preferred equity, and a host of other legal arrangements. The structuring of securities requires the assistance of good legal counsel with expertise in securities and corporate law, as well as intimate knowledge of the tax code.

In the previous chapter, we looked at alternative sources of financing. Here, we've attempted to describe how the entrepreneur can structure a deal with these potential sources of capital. A well-structured deal will provide the financier with his or her desired return and still create substantial value for the entrepreneur.

Chapter Seven

Securities Law and Private Financing

Many business financing transactions are regulated by state and federal securities laws. The Securities and Exchange Commission (SEC) administers federal securities laws, and state securities laws (Blue Sky laws) are enforced by the respective states.

Securities laws apply to private business transactions as well as to public offerings in the stock markets. This piece will focus on private financing; see Securities Law and Public Offerings for information on the public financing markets. Like tax laws, securities laws are complex and not always grounded in logic. The consequences of violation (even technical violation) can be vastly disproportionate to the harm inflicted and can include severe personal liabilities for management (including innocent management). In addition, a violation can preclude present and future business financings. Treatment and cure of violations, when possible, can be time-consuming and expensive. To complicate matters, securities regulation has changed dramatically over the past dozen years first in response to the speculative abuses of the late 60s and, more recently, in an attempt to modify regulations that would facilitate capital formation.

Statements contained in this piece are of necessity general in nature and become outdated with the passage of time, and therefore they should not be relied on in formulating definitive business plans, but used rather as an indication of the nature and extent of securities regulation that may be applicable in various circumstances. In this regard, it should be borne in mind that in addition to the federal securities laws, there are securities laws in each of the 50 states— many of which vary substantially from state to state.

This note was prepared by Michael J. Roberts and Richard E. Floor under the direction of Howard H. Stevenson.

WHAT IS A SECURITY?

The securities laws are applicable only if a *security* is involved in the transaction. The statutory definition of security includes common and preferred stock, notes, bonds, debentures, voting-trust certificates, certificates of deposit, warrants, options subscription rights, and undivided oil or gas interests. In fact, the definition is broad enough to encompass just about any financing transaction, whether or not a certificate evidencing the investor's participation is issued, so long as the investor's participation in the business is passive or nearly so. Generally, a security is involved whenever one person supplies money or some item of value with the expectation that it will be used to generate profits or other monetary return for the investor primarily from the efforts of others. Thus, a limited partnership interest is a security. So is a cow, if purchased together with a maintenance contract whereby someone else will raise, feed, and sell the cow without the participation of the investor. Similarly, an orange grove is a security if coupled with an agreement to maintain, harvest, and sell the orange crop; a condominium unit is a security if coupled with an agreement to rent the unit to others when not occupied by the owner; and parcels of oil property may be securities if sold with the understanding that the promoter will drill a test well on adjoining land. A franchise may or may not be a security, depending on the extent of the participation of the investor. Generally, a transaction involves a security if there is an expectation of a "profit" or monetary return.

Despite the broadness of the above generalizations, there are some financing transactions that are deemed not to involve securities merely because they traditionally have not been considered to involve them. Thus, a note given in connection with a long-term bank loan is generally not considered a security although it falls squarely within the statutory definition. On the other hand, bank transactions only modestly removed from normal commercial practice may be deemed to involve securities. Active participation in the solicitation of a pledge of a third party's securities in connection with an outstanding loan to another party, for instance, would fit within the definition and thus be subject to the securities laws.

BUSINESS FINANCING DISCLOSURES

The financing of a business frequently involves the investment of money or some other item of value by a person who is not a part of management or otherwise familiar with all of the material aspects of the business. In order for an outside investor to make an informed investment decision, she or he must be made aware of the material factors that bear upon the present condition and future prospects of the business and of the pertinent details regarding participation in the business and its profits. The securities laws thus impose an obligation upon a business and its management to disclose such information to a potential investor together with the factors that adversely affect the business or which may reasonably be foreseen to do so in the future. In addition to financings by a company, these laws impose similar disclosure requirements whenever a member of management or a principal equity owner sells his personal security holdings to an outsider.

In financings involving outsiders, it is common practice (whether required or not) for management to prepare a prospectus, offering circular, or memorandum describing the nature, condition, and prospects of the business and the nature and extent of the investor's participation in it (see Chapter 4). In this manner the pertinent disclosures are set forth in a permanent written record so that there can be no argument as to whether or not the disclosures have been made or what they were. Such a document traditionally discloses the terms of the offering, the use of the proceeds, the capitalization of the business (before and after the financing), contingent liabilities (if any), the operations of the business, its sources of supply, marketing techniques, competitors and market position, its personnel, government regulation and litigation, its management and management's remuneration, transactions between the company and management, the principal equity owners of the business, and balance sheets and earnings statements of the business.

Historically, the SEC has discouraged the disclosure of forward-looking information such as projected earnings or dividends per share, and in fact has implied that disclosure of such information might be inherently misleading. In recent years, however, the commission has changed its view and has issued a series of rulings authorizing the disclosure of projections concerning revenues, income, earnings, dividends, and company objectives, under certain circumstances. In disclosing such information to prospective investors, management must act reasonably and in good faith, disclose any underlying assumptions, and correct information that becomes false or misleading over time.

Despite the fact that disclosure documents are often prepared and reviewed by attorneys and accountants, the law imposes the primary obligation for complete and accurate disclosure upon the company, its management, and principal equity owners.

It thus is essential that each member of management (including outside directors) and each principal equity owner be satisfied that the information in the disclosure document is accurate and complete based on his own personal knowledge of the company and its records. The financial statements, for instance, are generally deemed to be the company's disclosures rather than the accountant's, and the company itself remains principally responsible for their accuracy, even when an audit has been performed. In fact, the company has no "due diligence" defense at all in a federally registered offering and is absolutely liable if any material misstatements or omissions occur anywhere in the prospectus.

A disclosure document that satisfies these disclosure standards often appears negative in its presentation. Such a document need not be unduly so in order to provide the necessary protection, and, in any event, what appears "negative" to management may not necessarily appear negative to the financial community, which is accustomed to reading disclosure documents of this type.

In order to alleviate this negative effect, some entrepreneurs will first prepare a "business plan," which is *not* an offering/disclosure document. The purpose of this document will be to stimulate investor interest. Having screened investors, the entrepreneur will then circulate a more formal offering/disclosure document. This technique is often effective, but still imposes a duty on the entrepreneur not to make any misleading claims in the business plan. In a public offering, such an approach (called *gun-jumping*) would clearly be illegal. See Figure 7–1 for an outline of a business plan and prospectus.

PRIVATE OFFERINGS

Private offerings are distinct from public offerings in a number of ways. Public offerings typically involve larger sums of money and may be sold through brokers. Public offerings require that the company go through an expensive and lengthy "registration" process to register the securities with the SEC. This process is discussed more fully in the chapter Securities Law and Public Offerings.

Federal securities laws and many state securities laws have long reflected the view that some potential investors are sufficiently sophisticated in business investment matters to be as able to investigate a business and assemble relevant data as are management and regulatory authorities. More recently, Congress has recognized that small businesses wishing to attract capital may be unduly hampered by burdensome filing requirements. In either circumstance, preparation of an orderly and systematic discussion of the business in a formal prospectus and the review of this presentation by government agents is deemed unnecessary because the offerees are competent to assess the venture independently, or because the issuer seeks to raise very limited amounts of capital. Thus, registration is unnecessary, and the company and its management and principal equity owners may rely upon one of the so-called private offering exemptions. (Local state securities laws in every state where a *purchaser* is residing should always be reviewed.)

Historically, the principal criteria of the availability of the private offering exemption have been business acumen or "sophistication" of the offerees, access to material information concerning the company, and the number of offerees (*not purchasers*). All of these items were highly subjective, and the absence of guidelines often resulted in liability for issuers who mistakenly believed they came within the exemption. Beginning in the 1970s, however, the SEC attempted to bring more order to this area by releasing a series of rules that provide "safe harbors" within the general ocean of uncertainty embodied in these three traditional criteria. Regulation D represents the commission's most recent attempt to foster coherence and certainty.

Regulation D: The Various Rules

Six administrative rules, three of which set forth general definitions and three of which provide safe harbors for certain private offerings, comprise Regulation D. The operative rules—504, 505, and 506—broaden the scope of private offering exemption. Collectively, they are designed to simplify the existing rules and regulations, to eliminate unnecessary restrictions on small issuers' ability to raise capital, and to create regulatory uniformity at the federal and state levels. Each of the rules requires that a notice be filed with the SEC on Form D.

Rule 504.   The first exemption, Rule 504, is especially useful to issuers seeking to raise relatively small amounts of capital from numerous investors. It permits an issuer to sell up to $1 million of its securities during any 12-month period as long as more than $500,000 of the aggregate offering price is attributable to offers and sales that are not registered under a state's securities laws. (Thus, up to $500,000 may be sold during any 12-month period without registration under *either* federal or state law.) Rule 504 does not limit the number or sophistication of the investors or prescribe the specific form of disclosure. The issuer may not, however, engage in general solicitation or advertising, and purchasers may not resell their shares without registration unless the offering is registered in states that require delivery of a disclosure document. The effect of the rule, then, is to delegate substantial responsibility regulating small issuers to the state agencies. Because Rule 504 is designed to assist small businesses, moreover, it is unavailable to investment companies or companies required to file periodic reports under the Securities Exchange Act.

Rule 506.   In contrast to Rule 504, Rule 506 permits an issuer to sell an unlimited amount of its securities but only to certain investors. In this regard, the rule represents a continuation of the SEC's effort to codify some of the practices developed by lawyers and courts in applying the general private placement standards of sophistication, information, and numbers and permits issuers to raise potentially substantial amounts of capital without registration. Rule 506 is available for transactions that do not involve more than 35 purchasers. Sales to accredited investors (defined below), relatives of investors, or entities controlled by investors are excluded from this total. The issuer must determine that each nonexempt investor meets the sophistication test, either individually or through a knowledgeable "purchaser representative," but no longer need inquire as to the investor's ability to bear the financial risk of his or her investment. In determining sophistication, the issuer can insist that each purchaser or group of purchasers be represented by a person who would clearly meet any test of sophistication. Subject to certain exceptions, the representative cannot be an affiliate, director, officer, employee or 10 percent beneficial owner of the company (although he can be paid by the company as long as this is disclosed) and must be accepted by the purchaser in writing as his representative.

Perhaps the most significant aspect of Rule 506 is the "accredited investor" concept. Such investors are presumed to be sophisticated and thus do not count against the 35 investor limitation. They include institutional investors such as banks, savings and loan associations, broker-dealers, insurance companies, investment companies, certain ERISA employee benefit plans, private business development companies, corporations, certain trusts, partnerships and tax-exempt organizations, the issuer's directors, executive officers, and general partners. In addition, individuals whose net worth exceeds $1 million at the time of the purchase, or individuals with incomes in excess of $300,000 (or joint income with spouse in excess of $300,000) in each of the last two years, are considered accredited investors.

When an issuer sells securities under Rule 506 to accredited investors only, it is not compelled to make disclosures of any sort. If the sale involves both accredited and nonaccredited investors, by contrast, the disclosure requirements are more complex. Nonreporting companies must disclose (i) the information contained in Part II of Form 1-A for offerings of up to $2 million of their securities (including an audited balance sheet), (ii) the information contained in Part I of Form S-18 or available registration when offering up to $7.5 million of their securities (including two-year financials audited for the most recent year), and (iii) the information contained in Part I of an available form of registration when offering more than $7.5 million of their securities. If obtaining audited financial statements requires "undue effort and expense" for an issuer other than a limited partnership (to which separate provisions apply), then only a balance sheet as of 120 days prior to the offering need be audited. Reporting companies, on the other hand, must furnish (a) their most recent Rule 14a-3 annual report, definitive proxy statement, and Form 10-K if requested, *or* the information contained in their most recent Form S-1, Form 10, Form S-11, Form S-18, or Form 10-K, and (b) any other reports or documents required to be filed under the Securities Exchange Act subsequent to distribution or filing of special reports or registration statements together with information concerning the offering and material changes, regardless of the size of the offering. All companies selling securities to accredited and nonaccredited investors must also furnish nonaccredited investors a written description of any written information accredited purchasers receive, and must give all purchasers an opportunity to ask questions and receive answers and to obtain any additional information which the issuer possesses or can acquire without unreasonable effort or expense prior to the sale. Finally, no issuer utilizing Rule 506 may engage in general solicitation or advertising.

Rule 505.   Rule 505 adds some flexibility to Rule 506 for certain issuers. It permits the sale of up to $5 million of unregistered securities over any 12-month period to any 35 investors in addition to an unlimited number of accredited investors. The primary advantage of Rule 505, therefore, is the elimination of the sophistication test for unaccredited investors entirely and with it the elimination of the need for a purchaser representative.

Investment companies and issuers disqualified under Regulation A are ineligible to use Rule 505. Like Rule 506, Rule 505 prohibits general advertising or solicitation through public media of any kind and imposes disclosure requirements identical to the Rule 506 requirements discussed above.

Section 4(6).   Section 4(6) of the Securities Act, enacted as part of the Small Business Investment Incentive Act of 1980 and not technically a part of Regulation D, permits companies to issue up to $5 million of their securities in any single offering without registration and restricts the class of purchasers in any such transaction to accredited investors. Issuers are not required to disclose any specific information and may not engage in any form of solicitation in connection with offers or sales. Given these requirements, any issuer who can meet the requirements of Section 4(6) can also qualify under Rules 505 or 506.

Regulation D: Other Information

In addition to these specific exemptions, Regulation D includes a number of broadly applicable provisions designed to streamline and simplify private offerings. For example, when calculating dollar limitations, issuers must integrate the proceeds from all offers and sales made more than six months before or after a Regulation D offering. The regulation also provides that any securities issued pursuant to one of its exempting provisions (other than securities registered at the state level and issued under Rule 504) may not be resold without registration. In this regard the company must exercise reasonable care to prevent further distribution and should accordingly place restrictive legends on its certificates, enter "stop-transfer" orders, advise purchasers of the restrictions on resale, and secure representations that the securities are purchased for the individual's own account and not with any intention to redistribute. The issuer in a Regulation D or Section 4(6) private offering must file five copies of Form D with the commission not later than 15 days after the first sale.

The burden of proving the availability of an exemption is on the person asserting it. In order for the risk of nonavailability of the exemption to be reduced to an acceptable level, the issuer must complete positive and compelling documentary proof that each of the requirements for exemption has been met. This is particularly important if none of the safe-harbor rules applies. The sophistication of offerees should be thoroughly investigated *before* they are approached, and a memorandum setting forth their background and the reasons for their sophistication placed in the log. In making the initial presentation, use of a private placement memorandum should be made, each such memorandum being numbered and containing a legend that is not to be reproduced or disclosed to outsiders. The number of the memorandum and the date on which it is submitted to the offeree should be set forth in the log. If the offeree becomes an investor, the date on which he or his representative reviews the books and the records of the company, the books and records so reviewed, and the date on which he or his representative engaged in face-to-face negotiation should be recorded in the log. At the end of the offering, a memo should be placed in the log stating that no persons other than those set forth in the log were contacted or offered any of the securities, such memo reciting that *offer* is understood to mean nothing more than creating a situation that can be construed as seeking a commitment (even informal) to acquire a security to be issued by a described company at a given price. The log should be placed in the company's permanent files as evidence of the availability of the private offering exemption as to the financing.

Finally, and perhaps most important, an issuer must remember that all offerings, even if exempt from federal registration, remain subject to the antifraud and civil liability provisions of the federal securities laws and to the general requirements of state Blue Sky laws. Particular note should be taken of the fact that the safe-harbor exemptions provided under Regulation D are generally not available under state Blue Sky laws and that registration may be necessary in a given state for an offering that fully complies with Rules 504, 505, or 506.

RESALE OF RESTRICTED SECURITIES

Securities issued under one of the private offering exemptions or held by a member of management or a principal equity owner of the company (no matter how acquired, and whether registered or not) are subject to restrictions on resale that severely limit their liquidity unless the securities are subsequently registered under the Securities Act of 1933. For this reason, it is common practice for venture capital firms, private placement investors, management, and such owners to obtain an agreement from the company to register the securities upon demand or to include them "piggyback" in any other SEC registration that the company might undertake.

If the securities are not registered or covered by Regulation A when they are resold, as a practical matter the resales must be made under SEC Rule 144, or one of the private offering exemptions (not including the Regulation D exemptions for this purpose). Absent such an exemption, the resales will constitute unregistered offerings and subject the issuer and seller to potential liability. In addition, if the securities are transferred without consideration—by gift or upon death, for example—the restrictions generally bind the recipient.

Restrictions upon subsequent resale must be disclosed to potential investors in a private placement or the financing will be deemed by the SEC to violate the antifraud provisions of federal securities laws. This disclosure is often recited as part of the "investment letter" signed by the investor.

CONSEQUENCES OF VIOLATION

As a practical matter, in the past a vast majority of securities laws violations have not been investigated or litigated. However, the possibility of nonenforcement provides little comfort to potential defendants when commercial transactions of any size are involved. Moreover, transactions of today are potential lawsuits five years from now, when investors may be more aware of their rights under the securities laws and more inclined to enforce them.

The consequences of violation of the securities laws in connection with a company's prior financings are rarely serious so long as its operations continue to be successful and this success is reflected in the price of its securities. If public estimates of a company's success have been too conservative, however, an investor who has sold his securities too cheaply may complain. Investors and regulators tend to scrutinize company disclosures in minute detail when a business turns sour, with the hopes of discovering some technical or other securities law violation to use in unwinding a financing, or holding management responsible.

The most serious consequence of violation of the securities laws is potential civil liability that may be incurred by those persons deemed to have violated such laws or to have aided and abetted violations. When a corporation or other business entity is involved, management (i.e., officers and directors, general partners, etc.) and the company's principal equity owners may be held liable as controlling persons. In this regard, the corporate entity, which serves as an effective shield from liability in other situations, affords no protection from securities laws violations. The magnitude of the liabilities that may thus be incurred can be enormous. If a violation involves improper disclosure, the applicable statute of limitations does not begin until the person harmed discovers or reasonably should discover the improper disclosure. Furthermore, agreements to indemnify management and owners from liability for securities laws violations are of little use. Insurance from these liabilities is expensive and often difficult to obtain.

Suit under the securities laws by damaged investors or others is relatively easy to bring. Such suit may be brought in federal court in any jurisdiction in which any defendant is found or lives or transacts business, and service of process may be made anywhere in the world. A single plaintiff may bring a class action on behalf of all persons similarly situated, and courts award attorneys' fees liberally to successful or settling plaintiffs' attorneys as an inducement to bring such suits as private guardians of the public.

A company that makes an offer to an ineligible offeree in a nonregistered offering in which the private or intrastate offering exemption is relied on is thus subject to a contingent liability to all investors in the offering for the aggregate amount of their investment. Under past practice, this contingent liability was deemed by the SEC staff to be cured by a subsequent registered or Regulation A offer to the investors to repurchase the shares sold in violation of the registration provisions. Subsequent financings without either the offer to repurchase or a disclosure of the contingent liability violate the antifraud provisions of the securities laws. Under recent SEC staff interpretations, even a registered offer to repurchase may not remove the contingent liability, and the contingent liability must be disclosed in subsequent financings until the three-year statute of limitations has run, or else an antifraud violation will occur.

Uncorrected securities laws violations can preclude subsequent Regulation A or registered financings. The SEC may take administrative, civil, or criminal action, which can result in fine, imprisonment, court order requiring restoration of illegal gains, order suspending or barring activities with or as a broker-dealer, or other sanctions reflecting the nature and seriousness of the violation.

SUMMARY

Like many areas of the law, securities regulation is complex territory, fraught with countless opportunities for the entrepreneur to stumble. In the case of securities laws, an error can be particularly costly, making it difficult for the individual or the company to raise funds. For this reason, competent legal counsel is vitally important.

FIGURE 7–1   Business Plan and Prospectus Outline

Business Plan

1. Introduction (or Executive Summary)
   Short description of:
   — Business Objectives
   — Product
   — Technology and Development Program
   — Market and Customers
   — Management Team
   — Financing Requirements
2. Company Description
   — History and States
   — Background and Industry
   — Company's Objectives
   — Company's Strategies
3. Risk Factors
4. Products
   — Product Description and Comparisons
   — Innovative Features (Patent Coverage)
   — Applications
   — Technology
   — Product Development
   — Product Introduction Schedule and Major Milestones
5. Market
   — Market Summary and Industry Overview
   — Market Analysis and Forecasts
   — Industry Trends
   — Initial Product(s)
6. Competition
7. Marketing Program
   — Objectives
   — Marketing Strategy
   — Sales and Distribution Channels
   — Customers
   — Staffing
8. Management
   — Founders
   — Stock Ownership
   — Organization and Personnel
   — Future Key Employees and Staffing
   — Incentives (Employee Stock Purchase Plan)
9. Manufacturing
10. Service and Field Engineering
11. Future Products (Product Evolution)
    — Engineering Development Program
    — Future R&D

FIGURE 7–1   (*concluded*)

12. Facilities
13. Capital Requirements
14. Financial Data and Financial Forecasts
    — Assumptions Used
    — 3-Year Plan
    — 5-Year Plan
15. Appendixes
    — Detailed Management Profiles
    — References
    — Product Descriptions, Sketches, Photos
    — Recent Literature on Product, Market, etc.
    Prospectus
    When used as a legal prospectus, or offering memorandum, the
    following additions or changes should be made:
    — Affix federal and state securities legends.
    — Affix disclosures.
    — Add a detailed use of Proceeds section.
    — Add a section that describes the securities offered, in detail.
    — Expand on the Risk Factors section to include dilution,
      nontransferability, and other risk factors that relate specifically to
      the securities being offered.

Remember—Obtain the counsel of a competent securities attorney.

Note: Use and dissemination should be restricted; document should be treated as confidential.

Chapter Eight

Intellectual Property

In recent years, the world's major industrial economies have become considerably more knowledge-based. That is, high value-added, knowledge-intensive industries (such as electronics and service businesses) have grown at the expense of resource-based and commodity businesses. The rationale for this trend is clear: The major economic powers have focused their efforts on developing knowledge-intensive industries as a way to increase the income and standard of living of their populace, while decreasing their economy's dependence on diminishing natural resources.

As the U.S. economy has become more knowledge-intensive, legal minds have grappled with the issue of intellectual property. Who owns an idea? How can valuable knowledge and information be protected?

This note will address the various categories of protection afforded by the law, describe the nature of what can be protected, and discuss how that protection is achieved.

INTELLECTUAL PROPERTY

The area of intellectual property has challenged the legal system for hundreds of years and continues to do so. Common law has historically protected the property rights of individuals and corporations. But the area of intellectual property has presented new challenges to the legal system. If someone stole your wedding band, it would be fairly easy to prove—that individual would have the ring, and you would be without it.

Yet, how can you tell when someone has taken an idea or a concept? Intellectual property issues are particularly relevant in situations where an individual is working on some state-of-the-art

This note was prepared by Michael J. Roberts under the direction of Howard H. Stevenson.

process for his or her employer. During the course of developing the design, the employee has some "inspiration" that is outside the scope of the project's original bounds. Does this idea belong to the employer or the employee? Does it matter whether the inspiration occurred on the company's premises or while the employee was at home in the shower? Could the employee continue to work for the employer, but set up an independent business to exploit the idea?

A special patent law and patent court system was developed to deal specifically with these questions. Recently, however, intellectual property issues have arisen outside the bounds of traditional patent and trade secret law. The legal system is currently in the midst of grappling with these perplexing issues.

INTELLECTUAL PROPERTY AND THE LAW

Historically, it has been a specific goal of U.S. public policy to create the incentives required for the progress of technology. One of the means to this end has been through the system of patents and copyrights. These classes of intellectual property have arisen out of the statutes of the United States government, which are, quite literally, the laws of the United States as passed by Congress.

They include subjects such as:

— Title 11: Bankruptcy
— Title 23: Highways
— Title 39: Postal Service
— Title 50: War and National Defense

Each of the titles lays down the law relating to the subject at hand, as well as the administrative systems the U.S. government will put in place to support each of the areas.

Specifically relating to intellectual property are two titles:

— Title 17: Copyrights
— Title 35: Patents

Patents and copyrights receive protection directly under this statutory framework, but the law in these areas is not governed exclusively by the language of the U.S. Code itself. Through their application and interpretation of the statutes in individual cases, judges define (and, indeed create) relevant legal standards. Such "common law," or judge-made law, adapts the patent and copyright laws to modern circumstances (short of congressional amendments of the statutes themselves).

Out of common law principles have grown other areas of law that address intellectual property issues. These areas include trademarks, trade secrets, and confidential business information. Each of these topics will be explored in detail.

Patents

Patents are issued by the U.S. Patent and Trademark Office. There are three specific types of patents:

— Utility Patents: for new articles, processes, machines, etc.
— Design Patents: for new and original ornamental designs for articles of manufacture.
— Plant Patents: for new varieties of plant life.

It is important to understand the concept of a patent. A patent *does not* grant an individual exclusive rights to an invention. The inventor *already* has that exclusive right by dint of having invented the device in the first place; he or she can merely keep the invention a secret and enjoy its exclusive use.

Rather, the government grants the inventor the "negative right" to exclude others from making or using the invention. This right is granted in exchange for placing the information in the public domain.[1]

For instance, let's assume that the electronic calculator was a patentable invention, and that Mr. B was issued a patent on the device. Now, let us further assume that the idea of a checkbook holder with an electronic calculator was also patented, and that Mr. C was issued a patent on this invention. Mr. C would have the right to prevent others, including Mr. B, from manufacturing this device. However, Mr. C *could not* produce his article without the consent of Mr. B. In the event that patent infringement does occur, the patent holder can sue in civil court for damages. Should the patent holder become aware of potential infringement before the actual infringement occurs, he or she can sue for an injunction to prevent the infringement from actually occurring.

As mentioned, these kinds of legal battles occur in the civil courts. The purpose of the patent court system is to mediate patent claims. For example, when a patent claim is published in the *Patent Gazette,* others could come forward and challenge the patentability of the invention in the patent court system. One basis of challenge is for another inventor to claim that he or she was actually the first inventor. For this reason, it is recommended that inventors keep a daily record of their progress

---

[1]David A. Burge, *Patent and Trademark Tactics and Practice* (New York: John Wiley & Sons, 1980), p. 25.

in a notebook. These notes should record the inventor's progress and be signed and witnessed on a daily basis. In the event of a challenge, such a record will prove invaluable.

The three types of patents each cover different kinds of intellectual property and are governed by different regulations.

Utility Patents. A utility patent is issued to protect new, useful processes, devices, or inventions. First, what constitutes a patentable invention? The invention must meet several requirements:

— It must fall within one of the statutory categories of subject matter. There are four broad classes of subject matter: machines, manufacture, composition of matter, and processes.

— Only the actual, original inventor may apply for patent protection. In the case of corporations, for instance, the patent, when issued, is always granted to the individual and then *assigned* to the corporation.

— The invention must be new. That is, it will be considered novel if it is:

  • Not known or used by others in the United States.

  • Not patented or described by others in a printed publication in this or a foreign country.

  • Not patented in this country.

  • Not made in this country by another who had not abandoned, suppressed, or concealed it.

— The invention must be useful, even if only in some minimal way.

— The invention must be nonobvious. If the invention has been obvious to anyone skilled in the art, then it is not patentable.[2]

Finally, even if an invention meets all of these requirements, a patent can be denied if the application was not filed in a timely fashion. Specifically, if you used, sold, described in print, or attempted to secure a foreign patent application *more than one year prior* to your U.S. application, the patent will be denied.

Utility patents are issued for a term of 17 years.

The process of obtaining a patent is quite laborious. Patent attorneys, who specialize in the area, will draft the patent application which includes specific claims for the patentability of the invention.

---

[2]llinois Institute for Continuing Legal Education, *Intellectual Property Law for the General Business Counselor* (Chicago: Illinois Bar Center, 1973), pp. 1–16 through 1–24.

After several iterations of discussions with the patent office, some or all of the claims may be approved. This process frequently takes two years or longer.

Following acceptance of the patent by the Patent Office, a general description of the invention is published in the *Patent Gazette*. Interested parties may request a copy of the full patent from the Patent Office for a very nominal fee.

During the time between application for a patent and its issue, the invention has "patent pending" status. In some ways, this offers more protection than the actual patent. The invention will not be revealed by the government during this time, and others may be afraid to copy the invention for fear of infringing on the forthcoming patent.

Design Patents.   A design patent protects the nonfunctional features of useful objects. In order to obtain a design patent, the following requirements must be met:

— Ornamentality: The design must be aesthetically appealing and must not be dictated solely by functional or utilitarian considerations.

— Novelty: The design must be new. The same criteria used for a utility patent will be applied here.

— Nonobvious: The design must not be obvious to anyone skilled in the art. This is a difficult standard to apply to a design and is quite subjective.

— Embodied in an article of manufacture: The design must be an inseparable part of a manufactured article.[3]

Design patents are issued for 3½, 7, or 14 years, depending on the election of the applicant at the time of the application.

Plant Patents.   A plant patent is obtainable on any new variety of plant that that individual is able to reproduce asexually. The new plant must be nonobvious. A plant patent is issued for a term of 17 years.

Copyrights

Copyright protection is afforded to artists and authors, giving them the sole right to print, copy, sell, and distribute the work. Books,

---

[3]Burge, *Patent and Trademark*, pp. 137–38.

musical and dramatic compositions, maps, paintings, sculptures, motion pictures, and sound recordings can all be copyrighted.

To obtain copyright protection, the work must simply bear a copyright notice, which includes the symbol © or the word *copyright*, the date of first publication, and the name of the owner of the copyright.

Copyrighted works are protected for a term of 50 years beyond the death of the author.

Trademarks

A trademark is any name, symbol, or configuration that an individual or organization uses to distinguish its products from others.

Trademark law is *not* derived from statutes of the Constitution, but is an outgrowth of the common law dealing with unfair competition.

Unfair competition is deemed to exist when the activities of a competitor result in confusion in the mind of the buying public.

Trademarks are typically brand names that apply to products, and servicemarks are names that apply to services.

There are several regulations that govern the proper use and protection of trademarks.[4] The scope of protection under the law is a function of the nature of the mark itself. Principal categories are:

— Coined marks: A newly coined, previously unknown mark is afforded the broadest protection (e.g., Xerox as a brand of copier, Charmin as a brand of toilet tissue).

— Arbitrary marks: A name already in use and applied to a certain product by a firm, but without suggesting any of the product's attributes (e.g., Apple Computer, Milky Way candy bars).

— Suggestive marks: A name in use, but suggesting some desirable attribute of the product (e.g., Sweet-n-Low as a low-calorie sweetener, White-Out correction fluid).

— Descriptive marks: A name that describes the purpose or function of the product. Descriptive marks cannot be registered until, over time, they have proven to be distinctive terms (e.g., *sticky* would probably not be approved as a trademarked brand name for glue).

— Unprotectable terms: Generic names, which refer to the general class of product. Escalator, for instance, once a trade name, is now a generic term for moving staircases. One could not introduce a new brand of orange juice and call it *O.J.*

---

[4]Burge, *Patent and Trademark,* p. 114.

In order to maintain a trademark, an owner must continue to use it and protect it. In this vein, some consumer product companies routinely produce and sell a few hundred items of several brand names which they have trademarked and wish to protect, but are not in normal production. Similarly, Coca-Cola has a crew of agents who routinely order "a coke" in establishments that do not serve Coca-Cola. If they are served a soda, they prosecute. In this way, they can maintain that they have attempted to keep their brand name from becoming a generic term. Aspirin, Cellophane, Zipper, and Escalator are all names which have lost their trademark status.

Until a trademark is registered with the Patents and Trademark Office, it is desirable to use the ^{TM} symbol after the name of a product, ^{SM} for services. After registration, the legend ® should be used.

Trade Secrets

A trade secret is typically defined as any formula, device, process, or information that gives a business an advantage over its competitors. To be classified as a trade secret, the information must not be generally known in the trade.

One cannot, by definition, patent a trade secret because the patent laws require that the invention be fully disclosed.

One advantage of a trade secret is that the protection will not expire after the 17-year term of the patent. Coke, for instance, maintains its recipe as a trade secret rather than patent it. Yet, should the information become public knowledge, their advantage could disappear quickly, and the inventor would have no claim on the process because it had not been patented.

Finally, should a firm decide to maintain a patentable advantage as a trade secret, and should another firm independently discover and patent that invention, this "second" inventor will have the right to collect royalties or force the "first" inventor to cease patent infringement. For this reason, many corporations routinely "defensively patent" and publish inventions so that others cannot.

In order for a company to maintain trade secret status for advantageous information, the company must keep the information secret and take precautions to keep it secret. These precautions include:

— Having certain policies relating to secret information.

— Making employees sign confidentiality and noncompete agreements.

— Marking documents *confidential* or *secret*.

Confidential Business Information

The courts have also seen fit to protect a class of information less "secret" than a trade secret, but which is nonetheless confidential. The key here is that the information is disclosed in confidence, with the clear understanding that the information is confidential. Even if the information is in the public domain, if the recipient derives some value from the confidential disclosure he or she can be held liable for claims of unjust enrichment. There are several cases, for instance, where an inventor disclosed an idea to a second party; the second party searched out the idea in *existing* U.S. patents, found the idea was already the subject of a patent, and bought that patent from the holder. The courts held that the second party had to give the patent to the inventor because of the confidential nature of their relationship.[5]

EMPLOYEE'S RIGHTS

Much of the law has evolved in an attempt to protect the rights of the enterprise. This has always been balanced, however, by the employee's right to earn a livelihood in the *best* potential source of livelihood. For instance, as an atomic engineer, the courts would protect my right to make a living as an atomic engineer, not merely earn a wage as a waiter or a bartender.

When a relationship between an employee and employer is severed, it is often the content of the written documents that will govern who has rights to what. Employment contracts, confidentiality, non-disclosure, and noncompete agreements all come into play. For this reason, prospective employees are well advised to read these documents carefully and negotiate, rather than merely sign all of the papers that are typically associated with the first day on the job.

An employee can bargain away some of his or her rights in this area by signing inventions agreements, noncompete contracts, or employment agreements. However, the courts will not let an employee bargain away his or her fundamental right to earn a living from the best potential source.

If an employee signed an agreement, which the courts found to be overly restrictive, the entire agreement would be thrown out. It is this fact that gives rise to the lawyer's advice that "It is better to sign an unreasonable employment agreement than a reasonable one."

---

[5]Illinois Institute for Continuing Legal Education, *Intellectual Property Law*, pp. 6–9, 10.

There are three dimensions to the reasonableness test that the courts apply to employment agreements:

— Time horizon.
— Geographic scope.
— Nature of employment.

For instance, an employment contract that required an employee not to compete for six months, in the state of New York, as a designer of petroleum process facilities might be viewed as reasonable, while an agreement that specified a time horizon of one year and a geographic area of the United States would probably be viewed as unreasonable.

SUMMARY

It is clear that the body of legal knowledge in the intellectual property area is evolving rapidly. Yet, the processes that the law prescribes remain vitally important; in this area in particular, dotting the "i's" and crossing the "t's" is key. Whether it be keeping notebooks and records, filing patent claims, or reading the fine print on an employment contract, it is hard to overemphasize the importance of understanding the details.

In order to gain sufficient command of the relevant body of law, specialized legal counsel is called for. In an area that is changing so rapidly, one cannot rely on prior practices and "industry standard policies" for protection.

REFERENCES

American Bar Association. *Sorting out the Ownership Rights in Intellectual Property: A Guide to Practical Counseling and Legal Representation.* Chicago: American Bar Association, 1980.

Burge, David A. *Patent and Trademark Tactics and Practice.* New York: John Wiley & Sons, 1980.

Gallafent, R. J.; N. A. Eastway; and V. A. F. Dauppe. *Intellectual Property Law and Taxation.* Kensington, Calif.: Oyez, 1981.

Illinois Institute for Continuing Legal Education. *Intellectual Property Law for the General Business Counselor.* Illinois Bar Center, 1983.

Johnston, Donald F. *Copyright Handbook.* New York: R. R. Bowker Company, 1978.

Lietman, Alan. *Howell's Copyright Law.* BNA Incorporated, 1962.

White, Herbert S. *The Copyright Dilemma.* Chicago: American Library Association, 1977.

Steven B. Belkin

Wake up, Steven! It must be some mistake, but American Express is calling and says it's important. It's something about your credit rating.

His wife's voice roused Steven Belkin from a fitful sleep. A cascade of problems swept through his mind as Joan handed him the telephone:

This must be about my $15,000 overdue credit card bill. Joan hasn't realized I'm in quite so deep . . . she's going to be a bit shaken by this. I can see I'd better reassure her when I get off the phone . . . but to tell the truth, if I don't find investors soon, I'm really in trouble.

It was 11:30 the night of December 5, 1973. Steven Belkin had charged many of his expenses while trying to set up a new group travel business. Finding investors was proving much more difficult than he had anticipated, and he had had to let his bill slip for a couple of months. Steven was going to have to find a new financing strategy fast to keep The Travel Group from being a one-way ticket to disaster.

BACKGROUND

Steven Belkin, age 26, had lived in Grand Rapids, Michigan, as a youth. There he had his earliest business experiences. When he was 12, his grandfather had given him some salvaged automatic letter openers. Steven decided to set up a raffle with $1 tickets and the letter openers as the prize. He enjoyed selling the tickets and felt wonderful telling the purchasers who had won. Another time he sold light bulbs door-to-door. Taking the idea from a school fund-raising project, he

---

This case was prepared by Richard O. von Werssowetz under the direction of Howard H. Stevenson.

made it a summer job for his own profit. Steven's parents were of modest means, and financial pressures were a source of family discord. Steven resolved that his own excellence and success would provide family happiness.

Several people advised Steven that the way to success was to couple engineering with business school. After graduating from high school where he had been captain of his basketball and tennis teams, Steven received an industrial engineering degree from Cornell. He concentrated on obtaining good grades at Cornell and also was active in student government and other school activities to improve his chances for admittance to graduate school. After graduation in 1969, Steven entered the MBA program at Harvard. Steven recalled an interview he had set up:

> I tried to figure out how best to improve my odds to get in. I came down and had an interview and talked to different people. I don't know if it helped—they say it doesn't, but I don't know. I always took the attitude to absolutely give everything you have. Then if you don't make it, at least you have given all you've got.

Steven saw life as a series of plateaus. At Cornell, grades had been important to reach the next level. Having reached business school, Steven now wanted to concentrate on learning about different kinds of business and on getting to know his classmates. Steven recalled:

> I felt I needed to get there faster than the usual course. It wasn't okay for me to get there in the regular process, riding someone else's wave. I needed to get ready to jump on my own wave. In order to do that, to speed up the process, I needed to have more experience and contacts than my years. You get that extra knowledge from the experiences of others. And the families and friends of your classmates are a wealth of contacts.

Steven and another student obtained the resume concession at Harvard Business School, which not only helped with expenses but also gave him a chance to meet all members of his class.

Innovative Management

During the summer between the first and second years of the MBA program, Steven decided he wanted to do consulting for small businesses. He asked friends and professors for leads, with little success. However, he did find that four graduating students were starting a new consulting company in that area which they would name Innovative Management (IM). Actually, one student had some possible business sources and had found a financial backer who would provide $50,000 for working capital. That student had asked the others to join for a salary and 5 percent portions of equity. Steven joined in the same fashion and the group quickly got underway. Steven described their start-up:

> We would go to bankers and individual venture capitalists who had made loans or investments in companies that weren't doing as well as they had hoped. We offered to go in and analyze the situation and either suggest that they write off the situation or propose a plan to improve the company. Then we would actually go in and implement our suggestions.
>
> The bankers and private investors we approached often didn't have the time or the ability to do this type of analysis. So they would go to the head of a company in trouble and point out that things weren't going very well, then suggest that the company employ us for the study as a condition of providing more funds. The companies would pay our fees which usually were $4,000 to $5,000.
>
> Initially, we would approach a new source of projects and offer to do the first job at no cost. After we showed what we could do, they would usually give us additional assignments.
>
> Our customers were companies with annual sales from $2 million to $10 million. Most were fairly new entities. Usually we could provide a needed control system, a marketing strategy—an entire business plan. Although the owners usually were under considerable pressure to let us in, they often were very stimulated by what we did. They knew they had problems and they didn't have the luxury of our education. After we gave our report to the financial backer, we also gave it to the company. Often we could provide our recommendation in only three or four days.
>
> By the end of the summer, we were so successful that we began hiring additional business school graduates. I continued to manage several others during my second year of school.

In addition to running the resume service and continuing his consulting business, Steven did a survey of interest in small business among students in the top 10 business schools as his second year project.

> My purpose was to show that there was a strong interest among these students in new ventures and starting your own company even though most schools were not teaching that. The survey confirmed this, and I used the data to write some articles that we used to publicize our consulting firm. For example, we had stories in the *Boston Globe* and the SBANE [Small Business Association of New England] paper.
>
> People are always fascinated about people who do surveys and who have statistics. It makes you an instant expert to have a survey! It bought us new contacts and more credibility.

Looking back, Steven commented that he had done too much during the second year:

> I was incredibly busy. I cut a lot of classes. But the income was tempting, and I was just ready to get the second year over with. But you are always going to have work, yet you only have the second year of business school

once. I missed an awful lot. I didn't realize then that the cases contained so much practical experience—I felt they were "text booky." I just didn't absorb that they really reflected day-to-day problems.

During the last half of the second year, Steven explored the job market, interviewing primarily with consulting firms. Although none of the firms caught his fancy, Steven thought the process was worthwhile:

It was a terrific educational experience to be able to talk to these high caliber people in the different companies where they were trying to sell you and tell you all about their companies. But I guess I was a bit spoiled after already having my teeth in it, giving suggestions to people and seeing them implement them the next week. The big companies seemed a little academic—nothing, really, compared to what I was doing.

Steven remained with Innovative Management when he graduated in June 1971. A year later, however, the company was sold and Steven decided to leave. Steven explained:

We grew from 5 people to 22 in that first two years. Then one of the individual venture capitalists who had given us some work wanted to buy the company. The other four founders wanted to sell, but I thought that we would lose our objectivity as an affiliated consultant. I wasn't very happy about it, so I left the firm.

Group Touring Associates

Having decided to leave Innovative Management, Steven Belkin reviewed his situation. Financially, he had limited resources. Steven had been earning almost twice the $12,000 typical starting salary of his class. Joan, whom he had married just after graduation, worked as a teacher for a smaller salary. Steven had received $15,000 for his interest in the consulting company but also still owed several school loans that were not yet due for payment. Their net worth was about $10,000. Steven had no special ideas for starting a different business and was not attracted to seeking a job with a larger company. It appeared to him that he should continue small business consulting on his own.

The sale of IM took place at the end of the summer of 1972. Before Steven embarked on an independent course, however, he was approached by Frank Rodgers, the original investor in Innovative Management. Rodgers had been squeezed out of that investment when the company was sold. Rodgers said he would like Steven to work for him helping other companies in which Rodgers had investments and Steven agreed.

Steven found he had a special attraction for a group travel company that was one of Rodgers' first assignments. This company, Group Touring Associates (GTA), developed tours that were sold to various groups by mail using their membership lists. GTA had been started by Robert Goode in 1966 with the backing of Rodgers and a few other private investors. Rodgers had invested $200,000 to date; the others, another $200,000.

Sales had grown to $1.8 million over the past year, but GTA had yet to make a profit. Losses had been increasing from $50,000 four years ago to over $250,000 last year. Robert Goode had convinced his investors to continue their backing by pointing to the rising sales. He contended that the front-end marketing costs of mailings and of setting up the trips would cause him to show losses as he grew. On the other hand, the unearned customer deposits made prior to the trips provided much of the cash needed for the growing operation. Rodgers agreed that some losses might have been necessary as the company got its start, but now was alarmed by the continuing deficits. Rodgers felt that the deposit cash flow was disguising more fundamental problems and wanted Steven to help the situation.

After a brief analysis of the business, Steven felt GTA had excellent potential and that it could be built profitably with better management. He accepted an offer to join the company and became GTA's executive vice president:

> Looking back at my other consulting clients, there wasn't one business that I wanted to do. I had done one project for another tour operator, but they marketed through travel agents and student groups. The combination of group travel with direct mail made this very fascinating to me—this was the business for me. Okay, I needed solid experience in this one. This was a good opportunity, and I could earn a piece of the action.

A year later, Steven could point with pride to sales that had grown 50 percent and to a profit of over $150,000. Steven credited the turnaround to basic planning and well-managed execution:

> There was little organization when I came: no business plan, budgets, or anything like that. What I did was to clearly define our product and focus our operational and selling efforts. All within a budget and a plan. Before, the salespeople would try to find what trips various groups might be thinking about and come back and try to put one together. I introduced the strategy of defining the trips with the greatest general demand, then putting the trips together, and having the salespeople fill them up.
>
> This strategy let us buy better, put together better promotional material, and better control our costs. I was very sensitive to the fact that we were in the direct mail business rather than just the group travel business. We had to provide better value for the travel dollar and promote it well by mail.

At the end of his first year as executive vice president, Steven reopened discussion about his future role in GTA with Robert Goode. He had initially accepted a salary of $22,000 with the understanding that they would renegotiate his position after Steven had proven himself. Now Steven felt he should receive a $30,000 salary and also be given 10 percent of the company. Robert would not agree. Steven recalled:

> Robert and I went back and forth quite a bit. GTA was finally making money, and I felt I deserved part ownership. Robert wouldn't go over $25,000 in salary and wanted to wait another year for the equity.
>
> As we reached an impasse, Frank Rodgers arranged several more meetings between us. However, now that the company was profitable, Goode no longer needed more equity, and Rodgers didn't have enough power to force Goode to agree to my demands. I think Robert also felt that he had run the company for six years and, now that I had gotten GTA over the hurdle, he wanted to be the boss again.
>
> I tried very hard to reach an agreement; I wanted to stay. I felt that if I could be earning the $30,000 and have 10 percent of a profitable, growing company, I would be on my way to being successful. I was really running the show; I felt I was going to make money; I was fulfilling my entrepreneurial goals.

CONSIDERING AN INDEPENDENT COURSE

As Robert Goode's position hardened, Steven began to consider leaving GTA to start his own group travel packager. Looking at the industry structure made him feel this segment was a good opportunity. Potential air travelers could arrange pleasure trips directly on their own, choose ground packages offered by "tour wholesalers" such as American Express, or select complete air/ground packages such as those organized by GTA using chartered airlines. Traits of these choices are shown in Table 1.

Although the group air charter industry had only developed over the last 10 years after the introduction of jet air service, this mode of touring had already become a popular travel alternative. Steven felt the key attractions were lower cost, professional tour management, and the comfort and peace of mind of the sponsoring organizations' endorsements.

The lower costs were the direct result of the use of chartered aircraft—the group tour organizer guaranteed to pay for all seats and took the risk of filling the flight. Many travelers were willing to accept the fixed schedules of charters to take advantage of the lower prices. The offer of complete tour packages with professional tour guides was convenient, especially for travelers unfamiliar with the desired desti-

TABLE 1   Comparison of Pleasure Travel Options

	Direct Selection by Traveler	Use of "Tour Wholesaler"	Charter Tours
Air travel	Via scheduled airline	Via scheduled airline	Chartered airplane
Land arrangements	Individual plans and arranges directly with provider or through retail travel agents	Provided by tour wholesaler	Provided by group travel wholesaler
Flexibility	Complete	Travel timing flexible Only selected destinations and accommodations	Fixed departure and return schedules Only selected destinations and accommodations
Usual cost	Highest price	Sold as service; cost often same as direct	30 percent to 40 percent lower
Sold by	Individual carriers, hotels, etc.; retail travel agents	Retail travel agents	Group-sponsored direct mail, some retail travel agents
Other limitations			Must be member of "affinity group"

nation. Also, each traveler was a member of a group that sponsored the tour and could feel that his or her own representative would make sure the tour was a good trip and that the group would receive everything for which they had paid. This was particularly important in 1973 because there had been some recent publicity about tours that had been stranded or given inferior accommodations or service.

Steven saw these advantages as clear distinctions between group charter companies and tour wholesalers that used scheduled air carriers. The tour wholesalers also marketed primarily through retail travel agents whereas charter tours were normally sold using direct mail.

Looking at competition, Steven knew there were 10 major group tour operators in the United States. GTA ranked about seventh in that list. Where GTA provided tours for about 8,000 people per year, the largest U.S. operators moved about 50,000 customers yearly. As he viewed the market, he felt there was certainly room for one more:

> In the United States, there were regulations that you had to belong to an organization to go on a group trip. These had been eliminated about six years ago in Europe. With that, some of the group tour operators did more business than some of the scheduled carriers. The largest European companies running group charters were moving over a million people per year each. These regulations were relaxing in the United States, so I felt there would be great opportunities.

Steven received encouragement from Alan Lewis, GTA's most productive salesman. During Steven's negotiations with Robert Goode, Steven had described his growing frustration to Lewis. When Steven mentioned that he would be happy for Alan to join him if he left, Alan suggested that Steven should go out on his own whether or not Goode agreed to his demands. Alan would like to join him and was anxious to get an ownership position himself.

Steven's discussions with Goode made no further progress, so Steven resigned and left in early September 1973. Alan Lewis also resigned, and the two of them began to develop The Travel Group, their own group travel business.

THE TRAVEL GROUP

Steven's idea for The Travel Group (TTG) was to duplicate the strategy that had been successful for Group Touring Associates. They would start with limited tour offerings to the most popular destinations, then expand as their reputation grew. They would use five sales representatives to call on groups across the United States to develop sponsors for direct mail promotions. They would carefully control their customer service and tour operations to minimize costs and gain customer satisfaction.

The tours they would offer were complex logistical tasks with large financial commitments. Running a tour meant chartering an entire plane, which would accommodate up to 200 passengers. The company would also have to commit to blocks of hotel rooms and meals and provide ground transportation and other assorted support services. Once the package was planned, promotional material had to be written, printed, and distributed. Then inquiries had to be answered and reservations made.

To run the company, Steven would be president and major shareholder. He would be responsible for raising the capital they would need, for negotiating the trip arrangements, and for setting up the internal operations. Alan Lewis would be executive vice president. He would hire and manage the sales force, cover key clients personally, and work with sponsoring groups to fill the tours. Steven described their deal:

> I had planned to give five key salespeople 5 percent of the company each. Alan convinced me to give him the entire 25 percent, and he would give away whatever was necessary to hire the others. Thus we became partners, but I would have a minimum of 51 percent ownership, Alan up to 25 percent, and the remainder would be for me or the investors. He ended up keeping all 25 percent after hiring four other excellent salespeople. Equity for our financial backers would come out of my share.

Steven and Alan immediately swung into action. Steven concentrated first on creating a business plan, while Alan began his search for salespeople and selling efforts for an initial tour he and Steven had outlined. By October 1, 1973, the business plan was finished, and Steven prepared to raise $250,000:

> Developing the plan was fairly straightforward. We knew the basic charter travel destinations and seasons. We planned to run one airplane a week in season during the first year, two planes a week the second, and build each year. It was important to run "back to back" tours as much as possible so that the chartered plane could take one tour and return with the prior week's group. I added cost projections and made cash flow assumptions to give an overall financial plan.
>
> The plan showed an accumulated deficit of $155,000 for the five months before our first tour. Then I expected profits and tour deposits to provide cash for growth. I felt I should raise $250,000 for a safe cushion to fund that deficit with room for unexpected costs, delays, or errors.

The business plan for The Travel Group is shown in Exhibit 1. Steven intended this document to be a simple, easy to follow business plan rather than a formal investment memorandum. He explained his reasoning:

> Most people make business plans so complicated that people understand nothing and get scared by them. If you repeat things two or three times, then they say, "Oh, yes. I understand that." They think they understand what they are investing in. If you keep giving them more and more inputs and ideas, they just can't absorb it.
>
> When people finish reading my verbal description, they understand what I have said. That does not mean they understand the business. But they have understood what I said, so therefore they think they understand the business.

Financing Strategy

Steven and Alan had direct experience in the operational tasks confronting them. Finding the needed financing was less familiar.

However, several of Steven's earlier IM consulting assignments had involved raising money for smaller companies. Steven described IM's role:

> Some situations we investigated needed more equity along with the strategic and management changes we might suggest. If asked to implement our plan, we would agree to raise the money along with providing an executive vice president to bolster management and increase the company's credibility to investors. In return, we would receive part of the equity.
>
> We tried to keep this from being threatening to the president. Rather, we worked to convince the president that we'd be adding some new skills and helping to make the company valuable. Not like we were after the president's job.
>
> We'd approach individual venture capitalists for investments of $25,000 to $50,000 each. Our total needs were usually $100,000 to $200,000. The Rodgers family was very well connected, and we had developed other contacts in the course of our projects.
>
> Pricing was rather arbitrary. The company probably didn't have earnings, and we were selling the future. There was no scientific approach. We tried to show that the investors would double their money in a three-year period, then double it again to a value four times their original investment by the end of year five.
>
> Structurally, these investments sometimes ended up as a combination of debt and equity. This might be a loan with stock warrants. If all went well, they'd get most of their money back in a year or so and keep an equity ride with the warrants. The investors were very interested in not losing—not making mistakes, and less worried about how to get their equity out. That was less well structured—something down the road.

With this limited fund-raising experience, Steven developed a financing strategy. First, he assessed the situation from an investor's point of view. TTG had a large upside. Few start-ups could show the rapid sales growth Steven had projected. There were good margins that gave an excellent profit potential and unusually attractive cash flows. The management team had strong credentials. Steven's education was a plus, and both he and Alan had been successful running a similar company. They would also be using an experienced sales force. The group travel market in the United States had much less penetration than in Europe and should grow rapidly. Finally, there was little sophisticated competition in this industry, so their management skills would give them an extra advantage.

To demonstrate long-term potential, Steven could also show evidence that a group tour operator could be attractive as a public stock offering. One large U.S. tour operator had gone public in 1967 at a price of $10 per share. Within two years, the price had risen as high as $93 per share. The shares were currently trading for about $8, but this was primarily the result of that company's poor results in diversifying into restaurants, cruise ships, and hotels.

Steven decided that this set of characteristics made TTG a good deal for institutional venture capital groups. He would attempt to raise the $250,000 in five units of $50,000. He hoped that two or three investors would subscribe to the entire total. Steven felt this was a better alternative than going to wealthy individual investors for smaller units:

> I thought the larger shots would be easier. I had the right background and credentials and a good business plan. I was sophisticated enough to present it to institutional investors. I felt this was a good package to offer, that they would buy me and would buy the business plan.

As insurance, Steven would also present the plan to a few individual investors, but his main thrust would be the institutional groups.

For leads, Steven turned to the "hit" list he had been developing since he had been in business school:

> I kept a notebook of people I met who might be good contacts. I'd put in notes on meetings and phone calls, addresses, correspondence. Some were filed in various institutional categories—others were just alphabetical.
>
> I put the people I would approach in priority by relationships. I wasn't going to ask people directly to invest. Rather, I would ask for their help: "What should I do to raise money?" I didn't want to put them on the defensive—once you ask them if they'd invest they have to protect themselves. This way, they could talk to me totally straight and really give me advice. If they *were* interested, then they would say they'd like to look at my plan further. Either way, they'd often recommend someone else to see.

Prospects, 5: Investors, 0

Steven had contacts with five well-known institutional venture capital companies. He approached each, describing his idea and asking advice. Out of these five, two were interested enough to ask to consider his plan. After being initially encouraged by this interest, Steven soon began to feel that none of these firms was likely to invest. He described the problem areas he encountered:

> First, I was confronted with the developing fuel crisis. There were headlines in the newspapers saying airlines were cancelling charter flights. Only needed scheduled flights would be flying. There I was telling people I was starting a new charter company just as TWA was grounding all of its charters!

I had to explain that I could buy space on regular flights if necessary, but that the *charter airlines* would continue to run. The charter airlines were separate airlines encouraged by the government so that additional aircraft would be available in a national emergency. They only flew charters and were not canceling their flights. I also argued that if flights were rationed, my old relationships with the airlines and the professionalism we would be bringing in would give us preference in charter assignments.

I felt I was making some of the venture capital companies comfortable about the fuel problem, but I also found them reluctant to invest because there were no hard assets to "lend" against. They'd say, "There's nothing there! You aren't buying any machinery; all the money's going for working capital. There's no product line, no proprietary technology."

I believe they were thinking that if it didn't work, with hard assets they could still minimize their losses somehow and get something out of it. I got the feeling they were just more liberal bankers, which was different from my earlier concept of venture capitalists.

Approaching Wealthy Individuals

Scheduling appointments and follow-up visits with the venture capital companies took most of October with some discussions continuing into November. At the same time, Steven also was calling on wealthy acquaintances in a more casual way:

I'd say, "You know I'm raising money on Wall Street, but this might be something you'd be interested in. I'd like to get your input. Do you have any suggestions?" I'd mostly ask for advice and references to other venture capitalists or investment bankers.

As it became evident that the venture capital companies were not showing great enthusiasm, Steven more seriously pursued wealthy individuals:

I primarily approached other successful business executives who either still ran their own businesses or had sold their businesses in the last few years. I thought that a $50,000 investment would be easy for them. It was a lot tougher than I thought.

By November, I was letting everyone know I was trying to start this company. I was using every contact I could to get referrals to wealthy investors.

Out of all of his contacts, Steven developed two serious leads. One investor who was also a friend indicated he might provide $20,000. The other wanted Steven to come back when he had raised most of the remainder of the offering. Steven had expected wealthy individuals to be excited by the opportunity he saw in TTG. Now he found that wealthy individuals were going to be more difficult to attract as investors than he had anticipated.

Offer of a Bank Loan

Steven's discussions with the wealthy individual who knew him did lead to an unexpected offer of debt financing. Steven explained:

I didn't think any part of my deal was bankable at all. I clearly felt that all equity money would be required. Yet the one wealthy individual who was my friend said he did think the idea had merit and that he would introduce me to his bank. He gave me a very strong personal endorsement and to my surprise, his banker said he would match every dollar of equity I raised with one dollar of debt!

Once this bank opened my eyes, I approached several downtown banks to see what they would do. They wouldn't have any part of a loan—there were no assets to lend against.

The bank willing to give me a credit line was located outside of the main metropolitan area. They were more aggressive to compete, but they also saw TTG as a good cash flow generator and needed the deposits.

The loan offer opened welcome new possibilities to Steven. Now if he could raise as little as $125,000 in equity, the total of $250,000 would be available to him. However, the use of the debt line would greatly increase his own exposure because the bank would be lending against his personal guarantee. He was not anxious to do this himself, and the idea was frightening to Joan:

I was signing a $125,000 note, but my net worth was less than $10,000. Sure. I decided it didn't make any difference—if things went bad, I couldn't pay it anyway, so why worry about it? I would be more concerned about signing a $25,000 note because I conceivably could pay that.

But they also required Joan to sign it, and this was very, very stressful for her. It was overwhelming and very upsetting. We talked about it, and I said it was the same way for me too. But if it's $125,000 or it's a million, it doesn't make any difference right now.

The note Steven and Joan Belkin signed was a contingent line of credit at 2 percent over the prime lending rate. The credit line would equal the amount of TTG's equity up to a maximum of $125,000. Steven could draw on the line at his discretion. However, both he and Joan were very anxious not to use this credit so that they would not actually incur the personal liability of their guarantee.

Growing Pressures

Signing the credit line agreement and the slow progress in raising the needed equity were not the only sources of the pressures Steven felt building. There was also the hectic pace of beginning TTG operations.

If TTG was to run its first tour during the late winter season, the package must be put together and ready for sale by the beginning of

January. To do this, Steven and Alan had been continually working to develop their first trip and get their sales effort underway since October. By October 15, they had hired a secretary who had worked with them at GTA and set up operations in Steven's apartment. By the end of October, they had added another secretary and the first additional salesman. Steven described what it was like:

> We just assumed we would get the money and that we had to make it work. So we had to get the sales.
>
> Joan was teaching, so she went off to work at seven o'clock and came home about 3:30. She had been very, very helpful in putting together the business plan, but she's a very organized person and had her own work to do. When all the people were in the apartment, that started getting to her. Not only would there be no privacy and no quiet to plan her classes and grade papers, but sometimes we'd raid the refrigerator for lunch, and she'd find that what she had planned for supper had disappeared. We would often work past seven o'clock talking to the West Coast. She could go into a bedroom by herself, but in that small two bedroom apartment, it was more of a prison than a refuge.
>
> On November 15, we rented a 10' by 20' office that had been the rental office in my apartment building so things were a bit better, but we still used my apartment. We were sharing desks and had no place to have meetings with potential backers or sales contacts. I always met people at the airport, said I was just leaving on a flight, then waited until they had gone before going back to our office.

Steve Belkin and Alan Lewis were funding the office expenses and salaries for the other employees from their own pockets. So far they had invested almost $10,000 in cash. In addition, each of them was charging every possible expense on their personal American Express credit cards. Since both of them were traveling around the United States and Europe to talk to group sales prospects, interview sales representative candidates, and set up the first tour, they had accumulated outstanding charges of about $15,000 each. They had both been heavy users of their credit cards before, which gave them high credit limits. They had made no payments since September and were starting to get overdue reminder letters, which emphasized they were about to lose their hard-earned credit.

As business paused for the Thanksgiving holiday, Steven wasn't quite sure how much he should be thankful. There was little progress finding equity investors, and Steven's bills and responsibilities grew.

He felt he had to provide others emotional support just when he was the least sure of what he might have done to his own position:

> I was having to play Mr. Completely-in-Control: "Everything is great. We're going to get our money." The only one who was really starting to worry was Alan. He was the only one I really talked to. He hadn't had

much exposure to raising money. I was starting to let him know I was getting nervous, and he didn't know how to read that. "What does it mean when Steve's nervous?"

I'd also gone far enough that everyone knew I was doing this. It's not like I could have a quiet failure. I'd gone to close friends and family for contacts—the ones I'd worked so hard to impress. I'd always been Mr. Successful: "Here's Steve. He went to Harvard, was captain of his tennis team and basketball team, and always got good grades. He had his own consulting firm." Now Mr. Successful was starting his own company, and Mr. Successful was in trouble.

WHAT NOW?

By the first week of December, Steven knew he had only a few weeks left before TTG would start to unravel. Finding money was the key:

I felt I really had to switch gears here. I had to scrape it together. Initially I wanted to do it the business school way. Now, I had to become a street fighter. I might have to go out and beg, and it would be very difficult for me to go to people and say, "I need your help."

I only had a little time. Should I put more emphasis on the venture capital route and really try to close one of those? Should I continue with the wealthy investors? Or should I go to friends and relatives and try to piece it together in fives and tens? Because I had so little time left, I really felt the main options I should consider were to find one venture capitalist for $250,000 or to go to friends for small amounts.

In deciding on his last ditch strategy, Steven also contemplated whether he should change his offering to be more attractive. Pricing had never been explicitly discussed with the institutional venture firms. When talking to wealthy individuals, Steven was offering to sell 250,000 shares at $1 per share. He and Alan would be issued 750,000. What ways of repricing or restructuring the deal would help him to raise his equity fast?

"This is not exactly how I thought it would be," Steven thought to himself as he struggled to find a creative solution that December evening. "This is a good opportunity. Why haven't I been successful raising the money yet? I wonder if it was a mistake to resign so quickly? Well, here I am. Maybe I'll think of something tomorrow." It seemed that he had just drifted away, when the phone rang.

EXHIBIT 1   TTG Business Plan—October 1, 1973

[The entire narrative of the business plan is reproduced below. Title pages have been removed and the layout has been condensed. Only selected financial exhibits are included.]

I. THE INTRODUCTION

The Travel Group is being formed to meet the tremendous need for low cost group travel. People now have more leisure time than ever before, and they are becoming aware that group vacations are available at prices almost everyone can afford. A week in Europe or the Caribbean for $199 per person is an affordable price for most people.

The group travel industry is less than 10 years old. The market penetration for this new industry has barely begun. There are unlimited groups available. Alumni organizations, professional associations, religious groups, fraternal organizations, employee associations, unions, corporations, women's clubs, etc. The Travel Group will be concentrating on "prime groups." These are organizations that are known to be extremely responsive to group travel (e.g., Shriners, medical associations, bar associations, teacher associations).

The Travel Group will provide "deluxe" group tours. The attitude of management is to send "prime groups" during "prime season." Hotel accommodations will be at deluxe hotels (e.g., Hilton, Sheraton, Hyatt), and air transportation will be via scheduled carriers (e.g., United, Braniff, American) when possible.

The Travel Group will be classified as a "back-to-back wholesaler" in the travel industry. The corporation will market its group tours to travel agents throughout the United States. This should comprise less than 10 percent of the sales during the first two years, but eventually should produce 25 percent of the sales volume.

The primary source of sales for The Travel Group will be through direct sales. The corporation will have their own sales force, and each salesman will be assigned a different territory.

During the first year of operations, The Travel Group projects the movement of only 6,861 passengers. The four salesmen that management will offer positions currently move more than 18,000 passengers per year. Thus, the first year projection of less than 7,000 passengers is quite conservative. Management has also allowed six months before the departure of the first flight. This will provide the sales force with more than sufficient time to sell the first back-to-back charters to Hawaii.

Sales of $2,766,397 are projected during this first year and a profit of $169,223.

The second year of operations, 1975, should produce sales of $8,059,589 with a profit before tax of $832,636. In five years, 1978, The Travel Group should achieve a sales volume of $18,241,542 and a before tax profit of $2,150,121.

There is a tremendous positive cash flow in the group charter business. This allows for rapid expansion without additional financing. The potential of The Travel Group is open-ended, but management will expand cautiously.

EXHIBIT 1 (*continued*)

II. THE INDUSTRY

The back-to-back group charter business is in the early stages of growth. The industry is less than 10 years old. The management in the industry is quite unsophisticated. Financial and management controls are lacking. The market penetration of group charters has barely begun. Few companies have creative and organized marketing programs.

The main regulatory organization in the industry is the Civil Aeronautics Board (CAB). The trend in the past two years has been for more and more "low cost group travel." The CAB is oriented toward making travel available at a cost affordable for the mass public. This is very favorable for firms like The Travel Group, and, thus, governmental regulation should be beneficial to the company.

The United States is several years behind Europe in low cost vacations. In 1972 group vacation charters provided more revenue to the European airlines than the regularly scheduled flights.

In the United States, the same growth pattern is developing. In the past four years, charters on the North Atlantic have grown at the rate of 58 percent per year. In 1972 charter flights accounted for 30 percent of all passengers flown on the North Atlantic.

It is easy to understand this tremendous growth in the group charter business by simply looking at the money saved by a typical vacationer.

Assume an individual would like to travel to Hawaii for one week. He departs on a weekend, flies coach class, and all accommodations are deluxe:

	Regular Rate	Group Charter Rate	Savings
Air fare	$510	$225	$285
Hotel	140	84	56
Dinners	56	40	16
Transfers	20	10	10
Tour operator's fee	0	113	− 113
Total cost	$726	$472	+ $254
	****	****	*****

Thus, an individual can save 35 percent, or $254, during a one week visit to Hawaii.

III. THE COMPANY

The Travel Group will be selling deluxe back-to-back group charters. *Back-to-back* means that, for a set period of time, groups will be sent <u>every</u> week to a particular destination. The aircraft, which takes one

EXHIBIT 1   (*continued*)

group to the destination, will pick up the group that is ending their vacation. This allows substantial savings on air fare. There is also tremendous buying power at the hotels because rooms are utilized every week.

These cost advantages will allow The Travel Group to sell vacations to destinations all over the world at savings of 35 percent or more (see Industry section).

The Travel Group will have salesmen assigned to different territories in certain sections of the country. These salesmen will call on prime traveling groups. They will be selling deluxe packages, principally during prime season. The "sell" is usually easy because the organization has nothing to lose and much to gain. The Travel Group will pay for the mailing of a brochure describing the vacation to all the members of the organization. For each reservation the group produces, the organization will be given about $15. Thus, if a group fills a 150-seat airplane, the organization will receive $2,250 (150 × $15) and will have provided vacations for its members at substantial savings.

Groups that will be approached by the sales force include Shriners, Masons, medical associations, bar associations, Elks, Moose, alumni associations, teacher associations, unions, employee groups, and Knights of Columbus. There is an unlimited number of groups. Management will develop a mailing list of all the prime groups in the country to provide additional direction for the sales force.

The cash flow in the business is very favorable. Deposits from passengers are often received more than 90 days in advance. Final payments from passengers are due 45 days before departure. Payments to the airlines occur 30 days before departure, and hotel bills are not paid until 30 days after departure. Thus, the majority of receipts are in-house 45 days in advance of departure while disbursements occur 15 to 90 days after the initial receipts are in.

IV. THE COMPETITION

The group travel industry is in its early stages of growth. The industry is less than 10 years old, and there is only a limited number of group tour operators. Sophisticated and experienced management is scarce in the industry. The few back-to-back group travel companies, which do exist, have had substantial sales growth in the past three years. In the last eighteen months, there have been several new companies started that have been running back-to-back charters. One of these companies had sales of close to $8 million during its first year and before tax profits of over $500,000.

Competition in the industry has not developed to the point of pricing of the same packages. Sales growth is achieved by contacting the proper groups and then appropriately following up these leads.

Back-to-back operators always concentrate on a few destinations. With the vast number of destinations, there is limited competition among tour operators in providing packages to the same place. For instance, one of the new tour operators is just specializing in running trips to Greece, while another has programs just to the Orient.

EXHIBIT 1   (*continued*)

Currently the East Coast is the only section of the country that has become familiar, to some extent, with group charters. Amazingly, 60 percent of all charter flights are out of New York. The South, Midwest, and Central States have barely been touched.

Less than five back-to-back tour operators have a national sales force. The Travel Group's national sales force will be comprised of experienced travel salesmen who are currently working in different territories throughout the United States for other tour operators.

V. THE MANAGEMENT

There are two key departments in the group charter business. One is sales, and the other is operations. By providing a well-organized business plan and by making equity available, The Travel Group has attracted some of the most qualified people in the industry.

Mr. Steven B. Belkin will be president. He will be responsible for directing the operations of the company. Mr. Belkin is thoroughly familiar with the day-to-day operations as well as the overall business planning of a back-to-back tour operator.

He is a graduate of Cornell University and Harvard Business School. He was one of five founders of Innovative Management, a small business consulting firm in the Boston area. Some of his consulting projects included the development and implementation of a marketing program for a ski charter travel firm, running a chain of sporting goods stores with sales of over $6 million, and serving as president of a film school and production company. When Mr. Belkin left and sold his interest in this consulting firm, it had grown to 22 full-time consultants.

For more than a year, Mr. Belkin has been devoting full time to a travel group charter firm, which was in severe financial difficulties. With the development and implementation of a new business plan, creation of a national sales force, and tighter management and financial controls, this firm has now been turned around. The year before Mr. Belkin's involvement, the firm had sales of approximately $1 million with a loss of over $250,000. This year the company has already reported a respectable profit for the first six months and has more than doubled the previous year's sales.

The sales force that is available is comprised of some of the best salesmen in the industry. Each man has thorough familiarity and personal contacts with the prime groups in the different sections of the country.

The sales team will have a minimum of six months before the first back to back charter will start. This should provide more than sufficient time to sell the program. During the first year of operations, the sales force needs to move only 6,861 passengers. This year the four salesmen being considered moved more than 18,000 passengers. Thus, the first year programs should be sold fairly easily, and this will allow the sales team to start concentrating on the second year programs well in advance.

EXHIBIT 1   (*continued*)

VI. THE FINANCIALS
                           [Some exhibits omitted.]
  A. TRIP COST ANALYSIS
        Exhibit   I   Hawaii
        Exhibit   II   San Juan
        Exhibit   III   Ad hoc
        Exhibit   IV   Acapulco
        Exhibit   V   Spain

  B. PROFIT AND LOSS STATEMENTS 1974 and 1975
        Exhibit   VI   Pro Forma Profit and Loss Statement (1974 and
                         1975)
        Exhibit   VII   Plane and Passenger Projections (First Year 1974)
        Exhibit VIII   Monthly Pro Forma Profit and Loss Statement
                         (First Year 1974)
        Exhibit   IX   General and Administrative Expenses
        Exhibit   X   Plane and Passenger Projections (Second Year
                         1975)
        Exhibit   XI   Monthly Pro Forma Profit and Loss Statement
                         (Second Year 1975)

  C. CASH FLOW ANALYSIS
        Exhibit   XII   Cash Flow Assumptions
        Exhibit XIII   Monthly Cash Flow Projections (First Year 1974)
        Exhibit   XIV   Monthly Cash Flow Projections (Second Year 1975)

  D. FIVE YEAR PROJECTIONS
        Exhibit   XV   Pro Forma Profit and Loss Statements (1974–1978)

A great deal of time and effort has been devoted to the preparation of the following financial exhibits. Management will use them for budgeting as well as for projections.

The Trip Cost Analysis section clearly outlines the revenues and expenses associated with each trip on both a per passenger and per airplane basis. The air fare, hotel, meals, transfers, mailing, giveaways, and load factor are all expenses that have been determined by historical statistics and actual experience.

The Profit and Loss Statements for the first two years have been prepared on a month-to-month basis. Management has determined the number of planes and passengers that can be accommodated each month to a particular destination. During the first year of operation, no passengers are projected to be moved until June. There is a good possibility that ad hoc programs will be sold before this time, so sales and profit could be greater than projected.

The Cash Flows have been prepared for the first two years on a month-to-month basis. The cash flow assumptions are very important, and management feels the assumptions made are conservative.

The five-year, pro-forma profit and loss statement illustrates the potential of this new and growing business. The Travel Group hopes to have sales of over $18 million within five years and profits before tax of over $2 million.

EXHIBIT 1   (*continued*)

EXHIBIT I
COST ANALYSIS PER PASSENGER
HAWAII

Selling Price		$429 + 10% =	$471.90
Direct Costs: Air	$225		
Hotel	84		
Meals	40		
Transfers	10		−359.00
Gross profit before acquisition costs			$112.90

Acquisition costs:
Mailing costs 10¢ brochure
+ Nonprofit mailer

(.50% return rate)	$ 20.00	
Giveaways ($20/reservation)	20.00	
Load factor (90%) → *Too high*	20.00	−60.00
Gross profit		$ 52.90
		*********

****

Hawaii Trip Analysis per Plane

Total sales	=$471.90 × 135 passengers	=$63,706
Cost of sales	=$419.00 × 135 passengers	=$56,565
Total profit	=$ 52.90 × 135 passengers	=$ 7,141

Options: $10 net/passenger = $1,350/plane
(Options include additional profit on such items as bus tours, which
are arranged through the charter operator.)

EXHIBIT VI
THE TRAVEL GROUP, INC.
PRO FORMA PROFIT AND LOSS STATEMENT (1974 AND 1975)

	1974	1975
SALES	$2,766,397	$8,059,589
Cost of sales	2,345,594	6,870,953
Gross profit	$ 420,803	$1,188,636
General and administrative	251,580	356,000
Profit (before tax)	$ 169,223	$ 832,636
	***********	***********
Earnings per share	$ .17	$ .83
Value/share (10 multiple)	$1.70	$8.33
Number of planes	44	128
Number of passengers	6,861	22,183

3 times

fuel costs very high

EXHIBIT 1 (*continued*)

EXHIBIT VII
THE TRAVEL GROUP, INC.
PLANE AND PASSENGER PROJECTIONS
FIRST YEAR OF OPERATION (1974)

	January	February	March	April	May	June	July	August	September	October	November	December	Total
HAWAII													
Passengers						750	600	750	600	600	750	600	4,650
Planes						5	4	5	4	4	5	4	31
SAN JUAN													
Passengers											895	716	1,611
Planes											5	4	9
AD HOC													
Passengers						150	150	150	150				600
Planes						1	1	1	1				4
TOTAL PASSENGERS	0	0	0	0	0	900	750	900	750	600	1,645	1,316	6,861
TOTAL PLANES	0	0	0	0	0	6	5	6	5	4	10	8	44

EXHIBIT VIII

THE TRAVEL GROUP, INC.
PRO FORMA PROFIT AND LOSS STATEMENT
FIRST YEAR OF OPERATION (1974)

	January	February	March	April	May	June	July	August	September	October	November	December	Total
SALES													
Hawaii (150-seat plane) (31 planes) (4,650 passengers)						318,530	254,824	318,530	254,824	254,824	318,530	254,824	
Hawaii options (net)						7,500	6,000	7,500	6,000	6,000	7,500	6,000	
San Juan (179 seat plane) (9 planes) (1,611 passengers)											263,120	210,496	
San Juan options (net)											4,475	3,580	
Ad hoc programs (4 planes) (600 passengers)						65,835	65,835	65,835	65,835				
TOTAL SALES 44 planes 6,881 passengers						391,865	326,659	391,865	326,659	260,824	593,625	474,900	2,766,397
COST OF SALES													
Hawaii						276,070	220,856	276,070	220,856	220,856	276,070	220,856	
San Juan											219,200	175,360	
Ad hoc programs						59,850	59,850	59,850	59,850				
TOTAL COST OF SALES						335,920	280,706	335,920	280,706	220,856	495,270	396,216	2,345,594
General and administrative costs	15,000	15,000	18,000	18,000	22,716	22,716	22,716	22,716	22,716	24,000	24,000	24,000	251,580
Net profit (before tax)													$ 169,223

251

–8–

EXHIBIT 1 (*continued*)

EXHIBIT XII
CASH FLOW ASSUMPTIONS

A. Receipts
 1. Deposits and final payments are only received 15 days before the date of the trip (very conservative since final payments are due 45 days before departure, and deposits are often received 90 days in advance).
 2. Net Operational Tour Receipts are received the week of the trip.

B. Disbursements
 1. Airlines are paid 30 days in advance.
 2. Hotels are paid 30 days after the trip (requires letter of credit and cash deposits).
 3. Meals and transfers are paid 30 days after the trip.
 4. Acquisition costs are paid 30 days in advance.
 5. Ad hoc program payments require $10,000 deposit 30 days before departure and the balance paid the week before departure.
 6. General and administrative expenses are assumed to be paid/disbursements during the month they are expensed. (Conservative since telephone and travel and entertainment expenses are usually not disbursed until a minimum of 30 days after being expensed. These two expense categories are approximately 20% of G + A expenses.)

EXHIBIT XIII
THE TRAVEL GROUP, INC.
CASH FLOW PROJECTIONS
FIRST YEAR OF OPERATION (1974)

	January	February	March	April	May	June	July	August	September	October	November	December
RECEIPTS												
Hawaii					159,265	286,677	286,677	286,677	254,824	286,677	286,677	254,824
Hawaii options (net)						7,500	6,000	7,500	6,000	6,000	7,500	6,000
San Juan										131,560	236,808	210,496
San Juan options (net)											4,475	3,580
Ad hoc programs					32,918	65,835	65,835	65,835	32,918			118,504
TOTAL RECEIPTS	—	—	—	—	192,183	360,012	358,512	360,012	293,742	424,237	535,460	593,404
DISBURSEMENTS												
Hawaii					192,375	153,900	282,825	226,260	244,350	264,735	226,260	244,350
San Juan						59,850	59,850	59,850	49,850	100,000	80,000	199,200
Ad hoc					10,000							92,880
General + administrative	70,608	15,000	18,000	18,000	22,716	22,716	22,716	22,716	22,716	24,000	24,000	24,000
TOTAL DISBURSEMENTS	70,608	15,000	18,000	18,000	225,091	236,466	365,391	308,825	316,916	388,735	330,260	560,430
MONTHLY CASH SURPLUS (DEFICIT)	(70,608)	(15,000)	(18,000)	(18,000)	(32,908)	123,546	(6,879)	51,186	(23,174)	35,502	205,200	32,974
BEGINNING CASH BALANCE	—	(70,608)	(85,608)	(103,608)	(121,608)	(154,516)	(30,970)	(37,849)	13,337	(9,837)	25,665	230,865
ENDING CASH BALANCE	(70,608)	(85,608)	(103,608)	(121,608)	(154,516)	(30,970)	(37,849)	13,337	(9,837)	25,665	230,865	263,839

EXHIBIT 1 *(concluded)*

EXHIBIT XIV
THE TRAVEL GROUP, INC.
CASH FLOW PROJECTIONS
SECOND YEAR OF OPERATION (1975)

	January	February	March	April	May	June	July	August	September	October	November	December
RECEIPTS												
Hawaii	254,824	286,677	286,677	254,824	254,824	286,677	286,677	286,677	286,677	286,677	286,677	382,236
Hawaii options (net)	6,000	6,000	7,500	6,000	6,000	6,000	7,500	6,000	7,500	6,000	7,500	6,000
San Juan	210,496	236,808	236,808	157,872	52,624					105,248	210,496	315,744
San Juan options (net)	3,580	3,580	4,475	3,580	1,790						3,580	3,580
Acapulco	237,008	266,634	266,634	177,756	59,252				118,504	118,504	237,008	355,512
Acapulco options (net)	5,400	5,400	6,750	5,400	2,700						5,400	5,400
Spain					148,006	333,014	333,014	333,014	333,014	148,006		
Spain options (net)						4,500	5,625	4,500	5,625	4,500		
TOTAL RECEIPTS	717,308	805,099	808,844	605,432	525,196	630,191	632,816	630,191	632,816	668,935	750,661	1,068,472
DISBURSEMENTS												
Hawaii	226,260	264,735	226,260	244,350	226,260	264,735	226,260	282,825	226,260	282,825	226,260	398,250
San Juan	175,360	195,360	175,360	159,200	95,360	47,680				80,000	80,000	255,360
Acapulco	92,880	234,900	211,680	194,940	118,800	59,400	252,900	316,125	252,900	92,880	92,880	304,560
Spain					174,600	218,250				97,875	78,300	
General and administrative	28,000	28,000	28,000	28,000	28,000	30,000	30,000	30,000	30,000	32,000	32,000	32,000
TOTAL DISBURSEMENTS	522,500	722,995	641,300	626,490	643,020	620,065	509,160	628,950	509,160	585,580	509,440	990,170

254

MONTHLY											
CASH SURPLUS/ (DEFICIT)	194,808	82,104	167,544	(21,058)	(117,824)	10,126	123,656	1,241	123,656	83,355	241,221	78,302
BEGINNING CASH BALANCE	263,839	458,647	540,751	708,295	687,237	569,413	579,539	703,195	704,436	828,092	911,447	1,152,668
ENDING CASH BALANCE	458,647	540,751	708,295	687,237	569,413	579,539	703,195	704,436	828,092	911,447	1,152,668	1,230,970

EXHIBIT XV
THE TRAVEL GROUP, INC.
PRO FORMA PROFIT AND LOSS (1974–1978)

	1974	1975	1976	1977	1978
SALES	$2,766,397	$8,059,589	$12,029,894	$15,124,878	$18,241,542
Cost of sales	$2,345,594	$6,870,953	$10,305,490	$12,910,496	$15,481,421
Gross profit	420,803	1,188,636	1,724,404	2,214,382	2,760,121
General and administrative	251,580	356,000	480,000	540,000	610,000
Profit (before tax)	$ 169,223	$ 832,636	$ 1,244,404	$ 1,674,382	$ 2,150,121
Earnings per share	$.17	$.83	$1.24	$1.67	$2.15
Value/share (10 price/ earnings)	$1.70	$8.33	$12.44	$16.74	$21.50
Number of planes	44	128	192	240	288
Number of passengers	6,861	22,183	33,275	41,595	49,915

Heather Evans

It was May 10, 1983, and Heather Evans's graduation from Harvard Business School was less than a month away. Although she had just taken the last of her final exams that morning, Heather's thoughts could not have been further from school as she boarded the Eastern Shuttle and headed back to New York. The trip was a familiar one, for Heather had been commuting between school and Manhattan in an attempt to get her dress company off the ground.

Many of the elements of the business were falling into place, but the securing of $250,000 in financing remained elusive. Her business plan had been in the hands of potential investors for over a month now, and her financing group was simply not coming together. Her contact at Arden & Co., a New York investment firm and hoped-for lead investor, was not even returning her phone calls. A number of small, private investors had been stringing along for some weeks, but whenever Heather tried to go that next step and negotiate specific financing terms with any one of them, the rest of the group seemed to move further away. Heather expressed her frustration:

> I was really counting on Arden & Co. to be my lead investor; this would lend both credibility to the deal and give me *one* party to negotiate terms with. Then I could go to these private investors, point to the deal I'd struck with Arden and say, "These are the terms—make a decision."
>
> Now, if I give each of these investors what they want, I'll end up giving the company away. But I do need the money, and fast. In order to get out a holiday (winter) line, I need to start placing orders for fabric in the next month. All this, in addition to the rent and salaries I'm committed to.
>
> I don't know whether I should stick with the private investors I have and somehow try to hammer out a deal; or really work on getting a

This case was prepared by Michael J. Roberts under the direction of Howard H. Stevenson.

venture firm as a lead investor—maybe there is still a chance of bringing Arden & Co. around. Maybe I should try to get less money, or move back my timetable and wait for spring to introduce a line.

HEATHER EVANS

Heather Evans graduated from Harvard College in 1979, having earned her bachelor's degree in philosophy in three years. A Phi Beta Kappa graduate, Heather had been a working model throughout her college career, appearing in such publications as *Mademoiselle, Seventeen, and GQ*. (See Exhibit 1.)

Heather applied to the Harvard Business School during her senior year, and was accepted with a two-year deferred admit to the class entering in 1981. She accepted a position with Morgan Stanley as a financial analyst. Heather explained the origin of her interest in a business career:

> My father is an attorney with a Wall Street firm, and many of my parents' friends were "deal-makers" who had gone to the Business School. I thought that I would like that kind of work and the lifestyle that went along with it. In addition, my career as a model gave me a taste of running my own business—the independence, the travel, the people—and I loved it. I knew, though, that I would need a good solid background to gain the skills and credibility necessary for success.
>
> I thought that working for an investment bank like Morgan Stanley would give me the technical and financial training that I would need during my career.

Heather left Morgan Stanley and began her two years at HBS with her basic orientation unchanged:

> I was still focused primarily on a deal-making, venture-capital type of career. I had always been interested in the fashion business and thought that I might, at some point, financially back a designer. I decided to work on Seventh Avenue for the summer and got a job as the assistant to Jackie Hayman, president of a woman's clothing company.

Heather saw the business and financial side of the business as well as the design and marketing aspects:

> I was convinced and confident that I could run a business like this. That summer was actually the first time I believed that business school education had much value at all. I was able to understand the business very well, and my education and experience allowed me to grasp the fundamental issues quickly.

Heather returned to HBS in September, committed to starting her own venture in the garment industry.

THE EVOLUTION OF HEATHER EVANS INCORPORATED

Heather began by defining the concept of the company and its product line. Based on her experience in investment banking and at business school, Heather was convinced that the current mode of business dress for women—primarily suits—was, in fact, ill-suited to the demands and desires of businesswomen. Heather conceived a line of dresses in natural and wear-worthy fabrics that would better meet these women's needs (see business plan for full description).

In September, she began working with Robert Vin, an assistant designer in New York, in an attempt to transfer her concepts to finished design sketches and patterns. By November, it was clear to Heather that this arrangement was not going to work out; she decided that she would be both the chief designer and operating manager of her firm. Although it was an extremely untraditional approach to a start-up in the garment business, Heather reasoned that it would make more sense for her:

> First, I didn't get along that well with Robert on a personal level. More important, though, I found myself doubting both his design sense and my own ability to judge someone else's design sense. Fundamentally, I had more trust in myself and my abilities as a designer.

Thus was Heather Evans Incorporated born.

Heather spent November and December flying between Boston and New York and developing, in further detail, her concept of the business. By December, Heather had put together a plan of action, which she submitted for approval as a field study (see Exhibit 2). After her first-semester exams ended, Heather moved to New York. She scheduled all of her classes on Monday and Tuesday and planned to spend the rest of her time in New York getting the key elements of her business in place.

Staff

Heather decided that the first person she needed was an assistant designer. "I wanted someone who had the technical training and experience in design that I lacked. I needed someone who knew more about design than I did, but who didn't mind working for me as an assistant."

Heather interviewed several individuals and in early February offered the position to Belinda Hughes, who had served as an assistant designer with two major firms. Heather began paying Belinda (out of her own pocket) to do free lance work based on detailed discussions with Heather about the content of the line, with the promise that full-time employment would begin in April or May.

Heather also began looking for a pattern-maker: someone who could transform a sample dress into specifications and a design for production.

Heather asked several industry acquaintances, and a vice president at Marjori (a major fashion manufacturer) recommended Barbara Tarpe. Heather called Barbara and the two hit it off. During their meeting, Barbara indicated that she would like an equity position in the company. Heather thought that Barbara could make a significant contribution and that her request was reasonable. Heather genuinely liked Barbara and thought that she would make a good partner.

One week later, before proceeding further, Heather decided to call another friend in the industry who might know Barbara.

> Martin is an old friend, and I trust his judgment; he told me that Barbara was a terrible liar and had no real talent. I looked back at my original notes after our meeting: "Very good rapport with Barbara. She seems *HONEST*. Feel she can run entire inside of business." I didn't hire Barbara and was shocked at how wrong I could be about someone. I had always felt comfortable trusting my own judgment.

Office and Showroom Space

Heather spent countless afternoons scouring New York's garment district (around Seventh Avenue from 42nd to 34th Streets) for potential showroom, office, and working space. Showroom space is very important, because store buyers visit here during the buying season to make their decisions.

> I decided that I needed about 1,500 square feet of space for an office, sample and pattern-making space, and a showroom. For $7 or $8 per square foot, I could get space in buildings which were somewhat off the main center of the district and which housed other relatively "unknown" designers. For $20–$25 per foot, I could be in a building that was more centrally located and that housed better-known firms.

By late February, Heather had decided to lease 1,500 square feet of space in a building at $10 per foot, for $1,500 per month.

Although the building was in a less desirable location, and would get less traffic from buyers than more expensive buildings, Heather reasoned that she should attempt to conserve as much cash as possible. Heather sent a deposit on this space and would begin paying rent May 1.

A month later, an acquaintance in the garment business called and offered Heather space in 550 Seventh Avenue—the most prestigious building in the garment center, housing such designers as Ralph Lauren, Oscar de la Renta, and many other famous names. Heather would have her own office space and would share the showroom space with another designer (who sold a line of clothing that would not compete directly with Heather's). Heather accepted his offer on the spot, even though she would have to start paying rent as of March 15, and the rent was $2,000, substantially more than the other building, and there was less space.

Financing

In the fall, Heather had begun talking informally with potential investors—friends at school and former colleagues in the investment banking and garment industry. She was hesitant, however, to do more than this until she had a business plan and a proposed deal.

Then in February, a friend and recent Business School graduate called to suggest that the two get together for a drink.

> Anne Snelling and I had both worked for Morgan Stanley and then gone on to the Business School. She had graduated one year earlier than I and gone to work for Arden & Co. (a private investment bank). I assumed that our meeting would be social, but Anne was soon putting on the hard-sell for Arden, convincing me that they should do the whole deal. I was quite surprised and pleased. Arden had an excellent reputation, and their financing would be a "stamp of approval" on the deal.

Heather and Anne met once or twice during January and February, and Anne asked Heather to accompany her to Vail for a week of skiing over spring break the first week in March. Heather reasoned that it would be a wise move to go.

> I didn't really feel comfortable taking off for a week—I had an incredible amount to do. Yet, I was anxious for Arden's participation, so off to Vail I went. I was unsure whether Anne intended our week to be business or pleasure, but I brought along all of my papers and was prepared to negotiate a deal.
>
> Once we got there, Anne said she wanted to talk about the deal, but was constantly on the phone pursuing other business. I came back to New York feeling pretty discouraged; we had never had a chance to really discuss my business.

Heather called Anne that next week and voiced her concern: time was running out, and Heather still had no clear idea where Arden or Anne stood on the issue.

> Anne suggested that we get together for dinner that evening and tie things up—I was relieved. But when I walked into the restaurant, Anne

was sitting there with her sister, Susan, and Susan's fiance. She apologized—they had just flown into the city, and Anne had asked them to join us. I was livid.

At this point, Heather realized that the financing was not going to come as easily as she had hoped, and she began pushing some of her other potential investors to get a sense of their interest. She raced to finish the business plan (see Exhibit 3) and sent this out to Arden & Co. and 15 individual investors during the first week in April.

DOWN TO THE WIRE

During the month of April, the pace of Heather's efforts accelerated and the business began eating up more cash. Belinda's part-time salary was now running about $1,000 per month; rent was running $2,000 per month. Finally, Heather had begun shopping the fabric market and would soon have to order and pay for $3,000 worth of sample fabric.

Heather had already invested about $10,000 of her own funds in the business, and her remaining resources were dwindling quickly. Because of the timing of the cycles in the garment industry (see Exhibit 4) Heather would have a great many more expenses before any cash came back into the business; most significantly, she would have to pay for the fabric for the entire holiday line—about $40,000 worth.

Yet Heather was having a difficult time bringing the investor group together. Anne Snelling was not returning her phone calls, and the private investors were interested, but had made no firm commitments. Heather's major problem was trying to negotiate with all of these potential investors individually; without a lead investor, there was no one party to negotiate the terms of a deal with.

The process of raising funds was hampered by Heather's extremely busy schedule. Besides talking to retailers, working on designs, and getting settled in her new office space, Heather was still going to school during this time, and exams were coming up. Heather commented on the strain:

> The spring semester was a rough one; trying to get my company started really took its toll. I had always considered myself a responsible student. I prepared about a half-dozen cases the entire semester and only made it to half my classes. I felt bad about it, but I knew I had to do it to get my business going.

FINANCING OPTIONS

Heather had several options available, but knew that she did not have sufficient time to pursue them all.

Arden & Co.

Heather held out some hope that Arden was still interested in the deal. Perhaps if she really pushed for a commitment, Arden would come through.

Venture Capital Firms

Heather had spoken with one or two firms that had indicated some interest. She knew that starting fresh with people who were unfamiliar with the company, as well as dealing with the bureaucratic decision-making process, would take a great deal of time. In addition, Heather suspected that they might drive a harder bargain than private investors, but at this point she welcomed the opportunity to negotiate with anyone just to get an idea of what valuation to put on the company.

Helen Neil Fashions, Inc.

Heather had approached another small venture capital firm which had Helen Neil Fashions, Inc. in its portfolio of companies. Helen Neil herself was a proven designer, and the company had established a base of relationships with manufacturers and retailers. The company, however, lacked any real operating management. This venture firm had indicated an interest in financing Heather if she would ally herself with Helen Neil and essentially embark on a joint venture. This idea had not yet been broached with Helen Neil, however, and Heather knew that any deal was dependent on the approval of Helen and her company's management.

Private Investors

Heather had a pool of 20 or so private individuals who seemed interested in investing in the company. The problem here was the amount of time it took to negotiate with each of these people individually, and their diverse desires for the terms of the investment. Heather was unsure how to structure the deal to satisfy the divergent interests of these individuals whom she was fairly sure would invest under any reasonable set of terms. She had spoken to a small sample of these investors (see Exhibit 5) to get their point of view, but was hesitant to speak to any more investors before she could present them with a deal.

HEATHER'S REQUIREMENTS

Heather had given some thought to the different aspects of the deal and had decided that the following terms were important to her:

— Control of the company: Heather felt that she should be able to control over 50 percent of the equity, as well as have a majority of the voting control of the company.

— License of the name *Heather Evans:*   Heather felt that she had already expended considerable effort in building up her own name, and that if she left the company, she should have the right to use it.

— Ability to remain private: Heather did not want to be in a position where her investors could force her to become a public company. Liz Claiborne, a successful women's clothing company, had recently gone public, and potential investors were naturally excited by the returns inherent in a public offering. (See Exhibit 6 for excerpts from the Liz Claiborne prospectus.) Heather knew that she had to offer her investors some means of exit and getting a return on their investment.

With exams finally over, Heather could concentrate her full energies on pulling together her financial backing and getting the business off the ground.

EXHIBIT 1   Heather Evans Modeling One of Her Designs

EXHIBIT 2   Field Study Plan

The purpose of this project is to develop a business plan and a strategy for approaching investors for a women's designer clothing manufacturing company, which I will form upon graduation from HBS. This company will offer high price, high quality dress and jacket combinations to executive women, ages 27 to 45.

The business plan will include:

 I. A marketing plan, including an analysis of the relevant market, how I will position my product (in terms of price and image), and a retailing and promotion strategy.
 II. A description of the organization, including people and physical plant.
 III. Pro forma financial statements, based on sales projections from I, and operating costs from II.
 IV. A financing proposal.

The attached time schedule outlines the process of putting together this plan. You will note that I have allotted substantial time to drafting and redrafting the plan, relative to research. This is because I have already spent a lot of time gathering information and find that I now need to organize that information in order to see what is missing. I will, however, spend the first half of January meeting with department store buyers to refine my retailing strategy, which I recognize is weak.

The final product for my Independent Research Report (IRR) will be the business plan actually presented to investors and a broader strategic document describing how the plan fits into my investor strategy.

Field Study Project Schedule Week of:

December 13, 1982	—Settle issue of adviser for IRR.
	—Gather examples of business plans.
December 20	—Complete survey of existing market research and financial information on comparable companies. (Sources: Fairchild Publications' library; 10-Ks ordered from companies.)
December 27	—Vacation.
January 3, 1983	—Prepare preliminary outline of plan.
	—Review outline with adviser.
	—Set up meetings with buyers from Filene's, Nieman's, Macy's, Bergdorf, Saks, Bloomingdales, Nordstrom, and others.
January 10 and 17	—Prepare first draft of plan Parts I and II.
	—Meet with buyers.
January 24 and 31	—Talk with various industry contacts to fill information "holes," especially regarding Part II of plan (e.g., salary levels for various employees, equipment needs and costs, and optimal showroom and design studio locations).

EXHIBIT 2 *(concluded)*

February 7	—Prepare second draft of plan, including detailed pro formas (Part III).
	—Begin interviewing candidates for design assistant, sales/PR director, and business manager positions. (These individuals should be named in the plan.)
February 14	—Review second draft with adviser.
	—Present plan to CPA for review.
	—Prepare list of potential investors and consider order of approach.
	—Select law firm.
February 21 and 28	—Select and recruit key employees.
	—Revise plan, Parts I–III.
	—Present revised plan to lawyer.
	—Explore financial structure alternatives with lawyer, adviser, and others.
March 7	—Draft Part IV of plan.
	—Determine preferred investor group profile and strategy for approaching investors.
	—Select factor and discuss terms, to the extent appropriate at that point.
March 14, 21, 28	—Vacation.
April 4 and 11	—Meet informally with key investors.
	—Finalize plan.
April 18	—Distribute plan to potential investors.

EXHIBIT 3 Heather Evans Incorporated Business Plan, April 7, 1983 *(Confidential)*

TABLE OF CONTENTS

HEATHER EVANS INCORPORATED BUSINESS PLAN
I. SUMMARY

COMPANY   HEATHER EVANS INCORPORATED, incorporated in New York on March 9, 1983, and located in New York City.

EXHIBIT 3 *(continued)*

BUSINESS	The Company will design, contract for the manufacture of, and market a line of clothing for professional women.
MANAGEMENT	*Heather H. Evans, President and Designer* Ms. Evans will graduate from Harvard Business School in June 1983. She has worked as assistant to the president of Catherine Hipp, a designer clothing firm; as a financial analyst at Morgan Stanley, an investment bank; and as a photographic model, with Ford Models.
	Belinda Hughes, Assistant Designer Most recently, Ms. Hughes was head designer at Creations by Aria. For two years before that, after her graduation from Parsons School of Design, she worked as Mr. Kasper's assistant at Kasper for J.L. Sports.
CONCEPT	The Company will offer a "designer" line to fit the lifestyle of professional women. Based on her experience in investment banking and at business school, Ms. Evans has conceived a style of clothing, based primarily on dresses, which better fits the lifestyle and demands of businesswomen than the suits and other looks currently offered to them by existing clothing manufacturers.
STATUS	The Company has already begun designing its holiday line, obtained showroom and studio space in a prestigious designer building, reserved production capacity in a high-quality factory, and arranged for credit with an apparel industry factor.
	In order to present its first line for the Holiday 1983 season, the Company must be assured financing prior to May 1983. The Company is seeking $250,000, to cover start-up expenses, to fund development of its first line, and to provide initial working capital. Thereafter, the Company anticipates that it will generate sufficient cash from operations, which, together with normal industry factoring, will fund growth internally.
Legal Counsel:	Kaye, Scholer, Fierman, Hays & Handler
Accountants:	Rashba & Pokart
Bank:	Citibank

II. CONCEPT

HEATHER EVANS INCORPORATED aims to become a substantial apparel company. Its success formula is a combination of powerful elements:

— a new look,
— for an unmet and quickly growing market,
— promoted and sold by a unique individual, Heather H. Evans,
— within a professionally managed and controlled organization.

EXHIBIT 3   (*continued*)

Ms. Evans recognized the need for a *new look* for professional women when she shopped for clothes to wear to her job at an investment bank. She found few clothes that fit the functional demands of her work, while having some "style." Since then, she has spoken with hundreds of professional women who voice the same complaint. They work in an environment that strictly defines what is considered appropriate; "Seventh Avenue" does not understand these women.

The HEATHER EVANS "look" will be based on dresses, worn with untailored or softly tailored jackets, with:

— A clean and elegant silhouette.
— Distinctiveness through cut and line, without frills, excessive detail, or sexual suggestiveness.
— Undistracting colors, in solids or subtle patterns (e.g., Glen plaid or pinstripe).
— Comfortable fit.
— Travel-worthy fabrics in all-natural fibers, such as silk-wool blends.
— Quality construction.

Dresses and jackets will be priced and sold separately, along with coordinated skirts and tops, as a *complete* line:

— To permit the customer to coordinate an entire workplace wardrobe from the line.
— To position the line in "sportswear" departments of department stores, which are more updated and better displayed than "dress" departments.
— To avoid resistance to the high price tag of a combined outfit, from a customer who usually buys sportswear pieces.

Each collection will include 30 to 70 pieces, depending on the season, which is comparable to other complete designer sportswear lines. The Company will sell five collections: for the holiday, early spring, spring, transition, and fall seasons. These are the regular "sportswear" market periods.

Unlike most designer collections, which include many kinds of clothes for different activities and different times of day, the HEATHER EVANS collection will include only clothes appropriate for the conservative workplace. This focus is critical in establishing the confidence of upper-strata professional women in the "look" for officewear. Later, the Company can introduce other lines (e.g., leisurewear) under the HEATHER EVANS name, in order to benefit from its reputation and customer franchise.

HEATHER EVANS clothes will be sold through better department and specialty stores. The line will be marketed as "designer" clothing, but will be priced at the upper end of the "bridge" category, which is the next lower price category. The bridge category was born and grew dramatically with such lines as Liz Claiborne and Evan Picone, which targeted the flood of women into the workplace over the past decade; HEATHER EVANS will capitalize on the second stage of this demographic trend, as women become accepted in large numbers in better-paid, professional and managerial roles. Positioning the line at the top of the bridge category:

EXHIBIT 3 (*continued*)

— Will place the line in stores next to other lines currently bought by the target customer (e.g., Tahari, Harve Bernard, Nipon Collectibles).
— Responds to growing price resistance among customers, *but*
— Permits the Company to create a quality garment.
— Develops the HEATHER EVANS label for future licensing potential.

Heather H. Evans:

Ms. Evans is uniquely qualified to develop and sell a new style of clothing for conservative businesswomen. As a former investment banker and a graduate of Harvard Business School,

— She has lived the lifestyle of these women, and knows their needs.
— She understands the limits of appropriateness within a formal office environment, which Seventh Avenue designers, who have tried to capture this customer, clearly do not.
— She can gain the confidence of the target customer through identification of her own background with their own lives.

Moreover, as a former model, Ms. Evans has experience at projecting herself through the media and can attract publicity as a designer/personality. She will actively seek to publicize the Company in business media, as well as fashion media, to reach the target customer. She is currently working on stories about the Company with writers from *Vogue* and *Savvy*. (Ms. Evans's resume is included as Appendix A.)

III. MARKET

HEATHER EVANS will initially position its products as designer clothing for the "formal" professional woman to wear to the office. Later, the Company can serve a virtually unlimited number of markets based on its reputation for quality and taste, as established through its original line of clothing.

PROFESSIONAL WOMEN'S CLOTHING

Target Market:

HEATHER EVANS will target the upper end of a subsegment of the working women's clothing market, identified as "formal professional" women in a 1980 market study by Celanese.

These women are an extremely attractive market because they are:

— a large, fast-growing group,
— with high disposable incomes,
— who are concentrated in metropolitan areas,
— where they buy at a select group of better department and specialty stores,
— with relative insensitivity to price,
— attention to quality,
— apparel brand loyalty,
— and *still-developing tastes and preferences in professional clothing.*

Celanese found the formal professional segment to be a well-defined purchasing group: it "includes accountants, lawyers, sales managers, executives, and administrators who work in highly structured and formal environments. They can be characterized by a strict dress code

EXHIBIT 3   (*continued*)

and overriding concern with presenting a professional image. Members of this group wish to convey occupational status at work and in nonwork activities and can be considered investment dressers."
— 4.3 million women fall within this group.
— They spend $5 billion per year on clothes.
— They represent the fastest growing segment of the working women's clothing market, with real growth forecast at 8–10 percent per year.

HEATHER EVANS will target the upper end of this group, whose concerns about quality and appropriateness are highest, commensurate with their level of income and responsibility.

The following statistics suggest that the upper end of the market is growing even faster than the formal professional market as a whole:
— In 1980, 793,000 women made over $25,000 per year.
— 147,000 women made over $50,000 per year, up 22 percent from the previous year.

Thus, HEATHER EVANS will target the new ranks of established executive and professional women. Whereas Liz Claiborne and others capitalized on the initial entry of women into the work force in the 70s, HEATHER EVANS will capitalize on their acceptance in positions of responsibility in the 80s.

Style Trends:

Formal professional women are a ripe market for a well-conceived new clothing label because their tastes and habits in officewear are evolving, but they have few options among existing clothes.

Women in the upper end of the market, HEATHER EVANS's target, are still wearing mostly classic or modified tailored suits, with a blouse and neck ornament. The lower end shows movement toward softer looks and, particularly, dresses. Ms. Evans believes that this trend toward more varied looks will also be seen in the upper end of the market. However, the existing untailored bridge lines, dress lines, and designer sportswear lines are inappropriately styled for that segment.

Manufacturers have recently seen the demand for suits flatten, as interest in dresses has renewed. Responding to this trend, Liz Claiborne and Albert Nipon both opened dress divisions aimed at executive women, priced in the "better" range. The president of Liz Claiborne Dresses voiced the expectations of many in the industry when she told *Women's Wear Daily* that, unlike the 70s when working women wore mostly tailored sportswear for fear of standing out, "in the 80s I think they're going to be a lot more adventuresome in what they wear." As evidence, the dress division of Liz Claiborne hit around $10 million in wholesale sales in less than a year, approximately 10 percent of the entire company's sales.

These examples illustrate the receptivity of the working women's market to new styles and designers. However, the offerings of these companies and others are inappropriate for the more conservative elements. HEATHER EVANS intends to fill this gap.

EXHIBIT 3   (*continued*)

Competition:
The "designer" fashion market is a relatively easy one to enter, because—

— *Competition is fragmented.* For example, although there are no comprehensive trade statistics available, it is worth noting that Liz Claiborne, which is one of the two largest companies in the market, can claim less than 3 percent of the market, with $155 million in latest 12 months sales.
— *Channels welcome new products.* Department store buyers are responsible for identifying and promoting new, promising lines, so that customers perceive the buyer's store as a fashion leader. In particular, major department store chains are seeking new lines in the bridge price range, in which HEATHER EVANS will position its products. They foresee this price category becoming increasingly important.

Retailers are encountering consumer price resistance, which suggests that the designer-priced sportswear market has matured: the continual "trading-up" by customers in the 70s has ended. In response, manufacturers are generally lowering prices, both within existing lines and by introducing new lines in lower price categories. Many designer companies will target the bridge market, where customers are value-conscious, but have disposable income. The Company anticipates that the opportunities created by renewed interest in this area will favor the Company's strategy and outweigh the threat of other new entrants and competition.

DESIGNER PRODUCTS MARKET
Once it has established a franchise in the expensive businesswear market, HEATHER EVANS can expand into any of several immediately related markets:

— Accessories (e.g., belts, shoes, scarves) in a similar price category to coordinate with the original clothing line.
— Leisure clothing in the same price range for the same customer as the original line.
— Lower-priced office-wear for a different, wider customer group (i.e., the rest of the 4.3 million formal professional women).

Finally, numerous tertiary markets exist for a well-managed designer name. For example, Bill Blass has licensed his name for chocolates, while Ralph Lauren has licensed his for a full line of home furnishings.

In the past, these designers have developed their names in the couture or designer sportswear levels; however, the extraordinary success of Norma Kamali, whose clothes retail for $30 to $100, demonstrates that a "designer" name can be made in any price range.

Thus, the Company can serve a virtually unlimited number of markets based on its reputation for taste and quality, as established through its original line of clothing. In Calvin Klein's case, his name is used on products with combined retail sales of $1 billion.

EXHIBIT 3   (*continued*)

Licensing:
     Designers profit enormously from licensing agreements, through which they attach their names to products in return for a 5-10 percent royalty. These products are manufactured and marketed—and often designed—by the licensee. For example,
— Pierre Cardin reaps over $50 million a year in royalties on $1 billion of wholesale sales on 540 licenses, with minimal related expenses.
— The top 10 designers collect over $200 million in royalties between them each year.

Long-Run View:
     The designer label has replaced the better department store label as the arbiter of taste and quality for the American consumer. After some designers (most notably Cardin) licensed their names indiscriminately in the name-craze of the mid-70s, consumers became more evaluative about the value of a given designer's name, but they continue to purchase according to that name.
     This shift has been disastrous for department stores, which have lost their business to discounters, which carry the same designer names for less with comparable service, and to specialty stores, which offer superior service at comparable prices. Although this shake-up in the retail industry will have repercussions for designers, it is unlikely to reverse a now well-entrenched phenomenon.

IV. MANAGEMENT AND OPERATIONS

ORGANIZATION AND PEOPLE

Design:
     The design group is the core of the Company: it creates five new product lines each year, on which the eventual success of the Company will depend. It is important to recognize that sales of the line will depend as much on existing specifications of fit, construction, fabrics, and coordination of pieces within the line as on the design sketches themselves; these are all parts of the design function.
     The design process for each line takes approximately nine months, so that several lines are being worked on in various stages at any time. For each line, the design function is to—
— Plan the line; determine the number of styles, colors, and fabric groups, on the basis of overall line balance, ranges of buyer climates and tastes, and other marketing factors.
— Define the theme and tone of the line.
— Choose and order specific fabrics and other supplies, after surveying the market for these products.
— Create and select sketches.
— Cut, drape, and sew samples. Perfect fit of samples.
— Select final samples for the collection.
— Prepare patterns for production and communicate with normal industry contract manufacturers.

EXHIBIT 3   (*continued*)

Ms. Evans will spend 40 percent of her time on design and production functions. She will oversee the entire process, with emphasis on *planning* and defining the theme of each line, and *selecting* fabrics, sketches, and final samples.

Ms. Hughes and Ms. Evans will work as a team on all design-related tasks. Ms. Hughes has significant expertise in the creative and technical aspects of fashion design. She is experienced in creating specific styles from a general concept for a line. Her vocabulary of stylistic detail, production feasibility, and textile characteristics complement Ms. Evans's market-driven design direction. (Ms. Hughes's backgound is described in Appendix B.)

Ms. Hughes has already been retained by Ms. Evans on a freelance basis and is designing a Holiday line. It is expected that Ms. Hughes will join the company on a full-time basis shortly after funding is received.

The Company plans to hire a design assistant in June. The design assistant will make sample patterns, cut the samples, and oversee the sample makers. She will work with an outside pattern maker on production patterns and with the factory to assure that the final product meets the specifications of the sample garments.

The Company plans to hire one sample maker in June and another in September 1983.

Production:

The production function manages the process from the sample through the shipment of the final garment to the stores. The concerns of the production staff are quality, timely delivery, and cost. During the first two years, Ms. Evans and the design assistant will oversee production as part of their design responsibilities.

Following normal industry practice, the Company will subcontract all manufacturing, including the grading and marketing of its patterns, cutting of its piece goods, and sewing of its garments, to independent suppliers. Initially, all its suppliers will be located in New York City and other locations in the northeastern United States. There is capacity available in suitable shops in this area, where management can carefully monitor the quality and timing of production. As production volume increases, the Company may consider manufacturing in Hong Kong, Taiwan or elsewhere, where manufacturing costs for quality workmanship may be lower.

Malcolm Wong, a contractor located at 226 West 37th Street, has agreed to reserve time to produce production patterns and sew the Company's entire first collection. Mr. Wong's factory is a high-quality, non-union shop, with 20 operators. Ms. Evans may use other contractors for all or part of the line, if these contractors offer a more favorable price.

The Company has arranged for its shipping to be done through Fernando Sanchez, as part of its rental arrangement with that firm (see Facilities and Equipment). Fernando Sanchez will provide space, shipping personnel, and shipping supplies. After July 1984, the Company expects to add one shipping employee of its own.

EXHIBIT 3   *(continued)*

Sales and Promotion:

Sales are made during "market weeks," which last approximately three weeks for each of the five seasons, spread through the year. Store buyers write orders based on the sample line, which they view in the Company's showroom or in one of several regional marketplaces. The Company plans to join the New York Fashion Council, Inc. and has tentatively arranged through this group to reserve space in the key regional market shows.

Ms. Evans will spend 40 percent of her time in sales and promotion.

Initially, Ms. Evans will handle all department store sales and some specialty store sales, in the showroom and in "trunk shows" to the Dallas and L.A. markets. Ms. Evans's personal attention is important in this stage to communicate the philosophy of the line, to use her Harvard Business School contacts in department store managements, and to save money.

The Company plans to retain an established, independent representative to sell the line to specialty stores in the Northeast (except New York City). Ms. Evans is currently negotiating with a well-known representative for several designer lines, with whom she has worked previously. The representative will show the line to his customers in the Company's showroom.

Once critical customer relationships have become established and sales volume warrants, Ms. Evans will hire full-time, experienced showroom personnel and, possibly, retain additional independent sales representatives. Ms. Evans will then direct her efforts to more promotional activities and to managing the sales personnel.

Ms. Evans will also carry out an active campaign of nonsales promotion. She will communicate with customer fashion directors, concerning use of samples in cooperative advertising and scheduling personal in-store appearances, and with newspaper and magazine editors to encourage editorial coverage. She will also oversee production of promotional materials to announce the opening of each collection.

Control:

Financial and production control will occupy 20 percent of Ms. Evans' time. These functions are critical to, but often neglected in, apparel manufacturing companies. In particular, fabric purchasing and production decisions must be made so as to maximize sales, yet minimize inventory at the end of the season when it becomes obsolete. Ms. Evans' experience in financial analysis and her business school training are valuable assets in the control function.

The Company plans to hire a part-time bookkeeper during its first months of operation. In July 1984 or thereafter, the Company will retain a full-time office manager.

FACILITIES AND EQUIPMENT

The Company has arranged for showroom and design studio space in the 550 Seventh Avenue building. This is one of the most prestigious buildings in the garment district, with such other tenants as Bill Blass, Halston, Ralph Lauren, and Oscar de la Renta.

EXHIBIT 3 (*continued*)

HEATHER EVANS' showroom will be within the showroom of
Fernando Sanchez, a new and successful high-priced, designer line. Ms.
Evans feels that the exposure of the HEATHER EVANS line alongside the
Sanchez line and within the 550 Seventh Avenue building will be very
beneficial for the Company. The Company's line does not compete with
the Sanchez line and will often be bought by different buyers from a
given store.

The Company's design studio and office space will be adjacent to
the Fernando Sanchez showroom, with its own entrance. The Company
will be provided with shipping space at another location, 226 West 37
Street, as part of its arrangement with Fernando Sanchez. These facilities
should be adequate for the first two years of operation.

V. FINANCIALS

The Company anticipates raising $250,000 in equity capital. This
level of capitalization is adequate, together with normal industry factoring, to develop and to grow a substantial apparel company, without additional equity financing. This is a business plan and is not intended, of
itself, to be an offering of stock or debt.

Industry Financial Characteristics:
High fashion apparel manufacturing offers high returns on capital
within a short time frame to those companies whose clothing becomes
"fashion."

— Margins run 40 to 60 percent.
— Operating costs after cost of goods sold and sales commissions (approximately 10 percent of sales) are relatively fixed. Basically, the cost
  of designing a line is the same at $1 million in sales as at $20 million.
— Investment in working capital is low: with 60-day terms from fabric
  suppliers and receivables factoring, cash received from shipment of
  finished goods can be applied to the cost of those same goods.
— Investment in fixed assets is limited to equipping and remodeling
  showroom, studio, and shipping space. All manufacturing is subcontracted.
— After an initial introductory period of one to two years, acceptance of a
  line may proceed extremely rapidly, with annual sales growth rates of
  100 to 500 percent not unusual.

Whether a line does become "fashion" and to what extent depends
on a number of variables that cannot be tested or foreseen until the clothing is presented to the fashion press and the consumers. These variables
include the appeal of the specific styles and fit of the line, general fashion trends and specific competitive styles offered at the time the line is
presented, and media interest in the line. Thus, investors are rewarded
for putting at risk the cost of developing, producing, and marketing a line
of clothing during an initial introductory period.

EXHIBIT 3   *(continued)*

Sales Projections:
   The Company has prepared sales projections for the first two years of operation, as presented in Exhibit I. These projections are based on typical order sizes for new lines in the Company's price range and reasonable rates of trial by stores, taking into account supplier credit limits.
   For reasons mentioned above, having to do with the nature of fashion, the Company cannot meaningfully forecast sales growth beyond the introductory period.

Financial Statements:
   Projected financial statements for the company's first and second years of operation are included as Exhibits II and III, respectively. These forecast net income of $167,173 on sales of $1,712,500 in the second year.
   A detailed list of assumptions for the forecasted financial statements is included as Exhibit IV. These estimates were developed by Ms. Evans, based on the experience of comparable companies, and discussed in detail with Rashba & Pokart, certified public accountants, who have extensive experience with apparel industry clients.

EXHIBIT 3 (continued)

EXHIBIT I

HEATHER EVANS INCORPORATED

Sales Projections

			Specialty Store			Department Store			Total ($000)
Season	Market Period	Shipping Period	Number of Orders	Avg. Order Size ($000)	Sales Volume ($000)	Number of Orders	Avg. Order Size ($000)	Sales Volume ($000)	
Year 1									
Holiday	August	October-November	38	$ 2	$ 75	9	$ 8	$ 75	$ 150
Early spring	September	December-January	50	1	50	12	4	50	100
Spring	October	February-April	50	3	150	12	12	150	300
Transition	February	May-June	58	1	57.5	14	4	57.5	165
Total									$ 715
Year 2									
Fall	March	July-September	62	3.5	217.5	15	14	217.5	435
Holiday	August	October-November	60	2	120	15	8	120	240
Early spring	September	December-January	75	1	75	19	4	75	150
Spring	October	February-April	94	4	375	23	16	375	750
Transition	February	May-June	80	1	80	20	4	80	160
Total									$1,735

EXHIBIT 3 *(continued)*

EXHIBIT II

HEATHER EVANS INCORPORATED

Projected Statement of Income

Year Ended May 31, 1984

	TOTAL	JUNE	JULY	AUG.	SEPT.	OCT.	NOV.	DEC.	JAN.	FEB.	MAR.	APRIL	MAY
TOTAL SALES	607500	0	0	0	0	75000	75000	50000	50000	100000	100000	100000	57500
LESS: DISCOUNTS	48600	0	0	0	0	6000	6000	4000	4000	8000	8000	8000	4600
NET SALES	558900	0	0	0	0	69000	69000	46000	46000	92000	92000	92000	52900
COST OF GOODS SOLD													
INVENTORY—BEGINNING	0	0	0	0	24375	61875	53750	41250	57500	82500	82500	68688	48750
PIECE GOODS & TRIMMINGS	257438	0	0	24375	24375	16250	16250	32500	32500	32500	18688	20000	40000
CONTRACTING COSTS	116313	0	0	0	13125	13125	8750	8750	17500	17500	17500	10063	10000
TOTAL	373750	0	0	24375	61875	91250	78750	82500	107500	132500	118688	98750	98750
LESS: INVENTORY—ENDING	70000	0	0	24375	61875	53750	41250	57500	82500	82500	68688	48750	70000
COST OF GOODS SOLD	303750	0	0	0	0	37500	37500	25000	25000	50000	50000	50000	28750
GROSS PROFIT	255150	0	0	0	0	31500	31500	21000	21000	42000	42000	42000	24150

OPERATING EXPENSES:												
PRODUCTION	149100	11300	11300	11300	12800	12800	12800	12800	12800	12800	12800	12800
SELLING AND SHIPPING	53513	1000	1000	1700	1000	8825	5125	3750	3750	6500	10200	6500
GENERAL AND ADMINISTRATIVE	120369	9727	9727	9727	10132	10132	10132	10132	10132	10132	10132	10132
FACTOR'S CHARGES	24300	0	0	0	0	3000	3000	2000	2000	4000	4000	4000
TOTAL OPERATING EXPENSES	347282	22027	22027	22727	23932	34757	31057	28682	28682	33432	37132	33432
NET INCOME (-LOSS)	-92132	-22027	-22027	-22727	-23932	-3257	443	-7682	-7682	8568	4868	8568

(continued)

12800
4163
10132
2300
29395
-5245

SEE ACCOMPANYING SUMMARY OF SIGNIFICANT PROJECTION ASSUMPTIONS AND SUMMARY OF SIGNIFICANT ACCOUNTING POLICIES.

PRELIMINARY DRAFT
   For discussion purposes only; all exhibits are tentative and subject to change.

-14-

EXHIBIT 3 (*continued*)

EXHIBIT II

HEATHER EVANS INCORPORATED

Projected Schedule of Operating Expenses
Year Ended May 31, 1984

	TOTAL	JUNE	JULY	AUG.	SEPT.	OCT.	NOV.	DEC.	JAN.	FEB.	MAR.	APRIL	MAY
PRODUCTION EXPENSES:													
DESIGNER'S SALARY	30000	2500	2500	2500	2500	2500	2500	2500	2500	2500	2500	2500	2500
ASSISTANT DESIGNER AND SAMPLEHAND'S SALARIES	55500	3500	3500	3500	5000	5000	5000	5000	5000	5000	5000	5000	5000
PATTERN MAKER SALARY	39600	3300	3300	3300	3300	3300	3300	3300	3300	3300	3300	3300	3300
DESIGN ROOM SUPPLIES	24000	2000	2000	2000	2000	2000	2000	2000	2000	2000	2000	2000	2000
TOTAL	149100	11300	11300	11300	12800	12800	12800	12800	12800	12800	12800	12800	12800
SELLING AND SHIPPING:													
SALESMEN'S COMMISSIONS	30375	0	0	0	0	3750	3750	2500	2500	5000	5000	5000	2875
TRAVEL AND ENTERTAINMENT	20100	1000	1000	1700	1000	4700	1000	1000	1000	1000	4700	1000	1000
FREIGHT OUT	3038	0	0	0	0	375	375	250	250	500	500	500	288
TOTAL	53513	1000	1000	1700	1000	8825	5125	3750	3750	6500	10200	6500	4163

GENERAL AND
ADMINISTRATIVE:

	Total	1	2	3	4	5	6	7	8	9	10	11	12
RENT	24000	2000	2000	2000	2000	2000	2000	2000	2000	2000	2000	2000	2000
OFFICE SALARY	9600	800	800	800	800	800	800	800	800	800	800	800	800
TELEPHONE	8400	700	700	700	700	700	700	700	700	700	700	700	700
STATIONERY AND OFFICE	12000	1000	1000	1000	1000	1000	1000	1000	1000	1000	1000	1000	1000
LEGAL AND AUDIT	12000	1000	1000	1000	1000	1000	1000	1000	1000	1000	1000	1000	1000
DUES AND SUBSCRIPTIONS	3600	300	300	300	300	300	300	300	300	300	300	300	300
DEPRECIATION AND AMORTIZATION	2700	225	225	225	225	225	225	225	225	225	225	225	225
INSURANCE	7200	600	600	600	600	600	600	600	600	600	600	600	600
BUSINESS AND PAYROLL TAXES	13470	1010	1010	1010	1160	1160	1160	1160	1160	1160	1160	1160	1160
UTILITIES	4500	375	375	375	375	375	375	375	375	375	375	375	375
EMPLOYEE BENEFITS	22899	1717	1717	1717	1972	1972	1972	1972	1972	1972	1972	1972	1972
TOTAL	120369	9727	9727	9727	10132	10132	10132	10132	10132	10132	10132	10132	10132

SEE ACCOMPANYING SUMMARY OF SIGNIFICANT PROJECTION ASSUMPTIONS AND SUMMARY OF SIGNIFICANT ACCOUNTING POLICIES.

PRELIMINARY DRAFT
For discussion purposes only; all exhibits are tentative and subject to change.

EXHIBIT 3 *(continued)*

EXHIBIT II

HEATHER EVANS INCORPORATED

Forecasted Balance Sheets
June 1983 through May 1984

ASSETS	JUNE	JULY	AUG.	SEPT.	OCT.	NOV.	DEC.	JAN.	FEB.	MAR.	APRIL	MAY
CURRENT ASSETS:												
CASH AND DUE FROM FACTOR	203398	181596	159094	122262	119230	124273	116816	100609	109402	114495	130726	125769
MERCHANDISE INVENTORIES	0	0	24375	61875	53750	41250	57500	82500	82500	68688	48750	70000
TOTAL CURRENT ASSETS	203398	181596	183469	184137	172980	165523	174316	183109	191902	183183	179476	195769
FIXED ASSETS—NET	17775	17550	17325	17100	16875	16650	16425	16200	15975	15750	15525	15300
OTHER ASSETS	6800	6800	6800	6800	6800	6800	6800	6800	6800	6800	6800	6800
TOTAL ASSETS	227973	205946	207594	208037	196655	188973	197541	206109	214677	205733	201801	217869

LIABILITIES AND
STOCKHOLDERS'
EQUITY

CURRENT LIABILITIES:

ACCOUNTS PAYABLE	0	0	24375	48750	40625	32500	48750	65000	65000	51188	38688	60000
STOCKHOLDERS' EQUITY	227973	205946	183219	159287	156030	156473	148791	141109	149677	154545	163113	157869
TOTAL LIABILITIES AND STOCKHOLDERS' EQUITY	227973	205946	207594	208037	196655	188973	197541	206109	214677	205733	201801	217869

SEE ACCOMPANYING SUMMARY OF SIGNIFICANT PROJECTION ASSUMPTIONS AND SUMMARY OF SIGNIFICANT ACCOUNTING POLICIES.

PRELIMINARY DRAFT
For discussion purposes only; all exhibits are tentative and subject to change.

EXHIBIT II

EXHIBIT 3 *(continued)*

HEATHER EVANS INCORPORATED

Projected Statements of Cash Flow
Year Ended May 31, 1984

	TOTAL	JUNE	JULY	AUG.	SEPT.	OCT.	NOV.	DEC.	JAN.	FEB.	MAR.	APRIL	MAY
CASH AND DUE FROM FACTOR—BEGINNING	0	0	203398	181596	159094	122262	119230	124273	116816	100609	109402	114495	130726
RECEIPTS:													
INITIAL CAPITALIZATION	250000	250000	0	0	0	0	0	0	0	0	0	0	0
NET SALES	558900	0	0	0	0	69000	69000	46000	46000	92000	92000	92000	52900
TOTAL	808900	250000	203398	181596	159094	191262	188230	170273	162816	192609	201402	206495	183626
CASH DISBURSEMENTS:													
ACCOUNTS PAYABLE—PIECE GOODS & TRIMMINGS	197438	0	0	0	0	24375	24375	16250	16250	32500	32500	32500	18688
CONTRACTORS PAYABLE	116313	0	0	0	13125	13125	8750	8750	17500	17500	17500	10063	10000
OPERATING EXPENSES—NET	344582	21802	21802	22502	23707	34532	30832	28457	28457	33207	36907	33207	29170
SECURITY DEPOSITS	6800	6800	0	0	0	0	0	0	0	0	0	0	0
PURCHASE OF FIXED ASSETS	18000	18000	0	0	0	0	0	0	0	0	0	0	0
TOTAL	683132	46602	21802	22502	36832	72032	63957	53457	62207	83207	86907	75770	57857

| CASH AND DUE FROM FACTOR—ENDING | 125769 | 203398 | 181596 | 159904 | 122262 | 119230 | 124273 | 116816 | 100609 | 109402 | 114495 | 130726 | 125769 |

SEE ACCOMPANYING SUMMARY OF SIGNIFICANT PROJECTION ASSUMPTIONS AND SUMMARY OF SIGNIFICANT ACCOUNTING POLICIES.

PRELIMINARY DRAFT
For discussion purposes only; all exhibits are tentative and subject to change.

EXHIBIT 3 (*continued*)

EXHIBIT III

HEATHER EVANS INCORPORATED

Projected Statement of Income
Year Ended May 31, 1985

	TOTAL	JUNE	JULY	AUG.	SEPT.	OCT.	NOV.	DEC.	JAN.	FEB.	MAR.	APRIL	MAY
TOTAL SALES	1712500	57500	145000	145000	145000	120000	120000	75000	75000	250000	250000	250000	80000
LESS: DISCOUNTS	137000	4600	11600	11600	11600	9600	9600	6000	6000	20000	20000	20000	6400
NET SALES	1575500	52900	133400	133400	133400	110400	110400	69000	69000	230000	230000	230000	73600
COST OF GOODS SOLD:													
INVENTORY—BEGINNING	70000	70000	113750	113750	105625	93125	78500	56000	112875	200375	200375	145125	81250
PIECE GOODS & TRIMMINGS	585000	47125	47125	39000	39000	24375	24375	81250	81250	81250	26000	47125	47125
CONTRACTING COSTS	299625	25375	25375	25375	21000	21000	13125	13125	43750	43750	43750	14000	10000
TOTAL	954625	142500	186250	178125	165625	138500	116000	150375	237875	325375	270125	206250	138375
LESS: INVENTORY—ENDING	98375	113750	113750	105625	93125	78500	56000	112875	200375	200375	145125	81250	98375
COST OF GOODS SOLD	856250	28750	72500	72500	72500	60000	60000	37500	37500	125000	125000	125000	40000
GROSS PROFIT	719250	24150	60900	60900	60900	50400	50400	31500	31500	105000	105000	105000	33600

OPERATING EXPENSES:													
PRODUCTION	153600	12800	12800	12800	12800	12800	12800	12800	12800	12800	12800	12800	12800
SELLING AND SHIPPING	114288	4163	8975	9675	8975	11300	7600	5125	5125	14750	18450	14750	5400
GENERAL AND ADMINISTRATIVE	149524	10132	12672	12672	12672	12672	12672	12672	12672	12672	12672	12672	12672
FACTOR'S CHARGES	63020	2116	5336	5336	5336	4416	4416	2760	2760	9200	9200	9200	2944
TOTAL OPERATING EXPENSES	480432	29211	39783	40483	39783	41188	37488	33357	33357	49422	53122	49422	33816
INCOME BEFORE PROVISION FOR INCOME TAXES	238819	-5061	21117	20417	21117	9212	12912	-1857	-1857	55578	51878	55578	-216
PROVISION FOR INCOME TAXES	71646	-1518	6335	6125	6335	2764	3874	-557	-557	16673	15563	16673	-65
NET INCOME (-LOSS)	167163	-3542	14782	14292	14782	6448	9038	-1300	-1300	38905	36315	38905	-151

SEE ACCOMPANYING SUMMARY OF SIGNIFICANT PROJECTION ASSUMPTIONS AND SUMMARY OF SIGNIFICANT ACCOUNTING POLICIES.

PRELIMINARY DRAFT

For discussion purposes only; all exhibits are tentative and subject to change.

EXHIBIT 3 (*continued*)

EXHIBIT III

HEATHER EVANS INCORPORATED

Projected Schedule of Operating Expenses
Year Ended May 31, 1985

	TOTAL	JUNE	JULY	AUG.	SEPT.	OCT.	NOV.	DEC.	JAN.	FEB.	MAR.	APRIL	MAY
PRODUCTION EXPENSES:													
DESIGNER'S SALARY	30000	2500	2500	2500	2500	2500	2500	2500	2500	2500	2500	2500	2500
ASSISTANT DESIGNER AND SAMPLEHAND'S SALARIES	60000	5000	5000	5000	5000	5000	5000	5000	5000	5000	5000	5000	5000
PATTERN MAKER SALARY	39600	3300	3300	3300	3300	3300	3300	3300	3300	3300	3300	3300	3300
DESIGN ROOM SUPPLIES	24000	2000	2000	2000	2000	2000	2000	2000	2000	2000	2000	2000	2000
TOTAL	153600	12800	12800	12800	12800	12800	12800	12800	12800	12800	12800	12800	12800
SELLING AND SHIPPING:													
SALESMEN'S COMMISSIONS	85625	2875	7250	7250	7250	6000	6000	3750	3750	12500	12500	12500	4000
TRAVEL AND ENTERTAINMENT	20100	1000	1000	1700	1000	4700	1000	1000	1000	1000	4700	1000	1000
FREIGHT OUT	8563	288	725	725	725	600	600	375	375	1250	1250	1250	400
TOTAL	114288	4163	8975	9675	8975	11300	7600	5125	5125	14750	18450	14750	5400

288

-23-

GENERAL AND ADMINISTRATIVE:	Total												
RENT	24000	2000	2000	2000	2000	2000	2000	2000	2000	2000	2000	2000	2000
OFFICE SALARY	31600	800	2800	2800	2800	2800	2800	2800	2800	2800	2800	2800	2800
TELEPHONE	8400	700	700	700	700	700	700	700	700	700	700	700	700
STATIONERY AND OFFICE	12000	1000	1000	1000	1000	1000	1000	1000	1000	1000	1000	1000	1000
LEGAL AND AUDIT	12000	1000	1000	1000	1000	1000	1000	1000	1000	1000	1000	1000	1000
DUES AND SUBSCRIPTIONS	3600	300	300	300	300	300	300	300	300	300	300	300	300
DEPRECIATION AND AMORTIZATION	2700	225	225	225	225	225	225	225	225	225	225	225	225
INSURANCE	7200	600	600	600	600	600	600	600	600	600	600	600	600
BUSINESS AND PAYROLL TAXES	16120	1160	1360	1360	1360	1360	1360	1360	1360	1360	1360	1360	1360
UTILITIES	4500	375	375	375	375	375	375	375	375	375	375	375	375
EMPLOYEE BENEFITS	27404	1972	2312	2312	2312	2312	2312	2312	2312	2312	2312	2312	2312
TOTAL	149524	10132	12672	12672	12672	12672	12672	12672	12672	12672	12672	12672	12672

SEE ACCOMPANYING SUMMARY OF SIGNIFICANT PROJECTION ASSUMPTIONS AND SUMMARY OF SIGNIFICANT ACCOUNTING POLICIES.

PRELIMINARY DRAFT
For discussion purposes only; all exhibits are tentative and subject to change.

EXHIBIT 3 (*continued*)

EXHIBIT III

HEATHER EVANS INCORPORATED

Forecasted Balance Sheets
June 1984 through May 1985

ASSETS	1984							1985				
	JUNE	JULY	AUG.	SEPT.	OCT.	NOV.	DEC.	JAN.	FEB.	MAR.	APRIL	MAY
CURRENT ASSETS:												
CASH AND DUE FROM FACTOR	104309	132776	153418	179135	188572	209584	207952	175695	231498	283601	369154	373163
MERCHANDISE INVENTORIES	113750	113750	105625	93125	78500	56000	112875	200375	200375	145125	81250	98375
TOTAL CURRENT ASSETS	218059	246526	259043	272260	267072	265584	320827	376070	431873	428726	450404	471538
FIXED ASSETS—NET	15075	14850	14625	14400	14175	13950	13725	13500	13275	13050	12825	12600
OTHER ASSETS	6800	6800	6800	6800	6800	6800	6800	6800	6800	6800	6800	6800
TOTAL ASSETS	239934	268176	280468	293460	288047	286334	341352	396370	451948	448576	470029	490938

LIABILITIES AND STOCKHOLDERS' EQUITY												
CURRENT LIABILITIES:												
ACCOUNTS PAYABLE	87125	94250	86125	78000	63375	48750	105625	162500	162500	107250	73125	94250
INCOME TAXES PAYABLE	-1518	4817	10942	17277	20041	23914	23357	22800	39474	53037	71710	71646
TOTAL CURRENT LIABILITIES	85607	99067	97067	95277	83416	72664	128982	185300	201974	162287	144835	165896
STOCKHOLDERS' EQUITY	154327	169109	183400	198182	204631	213669	212369	211069	249974	286289	325193	325042
TOTAL LIABILITIES AND STOCKHOLDERS' EQUITY	239934	268176	280468	293460	288047	286334	341352	396370	451948	448576	470029	490938

SEE ACCOMPANYING SUMMARY OF SIGNIFICANT PROJECTION ASSUMPTIONS AND SUMMARY OF SIGNIFICANT ACCOUNTING POLICIES.

PRELIMINARY DRAFT
For discussion purposes only; all exhibits are tentative and subject to change.

EXHIBIT 3 (continued)

EXHIBIT III

HEATHER EVANS INCORPORATED

Projected Statements of Cash Flow
Year Ended May 31, 1985

	TOTAL	JUNE	JULY	AUG.	SEPT.	OCT.	NOV.	DEC.	JAN.	FEB.	MAR.	APRIL	MAY
CASH AND DUE FROM FACTOR—BEGINNING	125769	125769	104309	132776	153418	179135	188572	209584	207952	175695	231498	283601	369154
RECEIPTS:													
NET SALES	1575500	52900	133400	133400	133400	110400	110400	69000	69000	230000	230000	230000	73600
TOTAL	1701269	178669	237709	266176	286818	289535	298972	278584	276952	405695	461498	513601	442754
CASH DISBURSEMENTS:													
ACCOUNTS PAYABLE—PIECE GOODS & TRIMMINGS	550750	20000	40000	47125	47125	39000	39000	24375	24375	81250	81250	81250	26000
CONTRACTORS PAYABLE	299625	25375	25375	25375	21000	21000	13125	13125	43750	43750	43750	14000	10000
OPERATING EXPENSES—NET	477732	28986	39558	40258	39558	40963	37263	33132	33132	49197	52897	49197	33591
TOTAL	1328107	74361	104933	112758	107683	100963	89388	70632	101257	174197	177897	144447	69591
CASH AND DUE FROM FACTOR—ENDING	373163	104309	132776	153418	179135	188572	209584	207952	175695	231498	283601	369154	373163

SEE ACCOMPANYING SUMMARY OF SIGNIFICANT PROJECTION ASSUMPTIONS AND SUMMARY OF SIGNIFICANT ACCOUNTING POLICIES.

PRELIMINARY DRAFT
For discussion purposes only; all exhibits are tentative and subject to change.

EXHIBIT 3 (*continued*)

EXHIBIT IV

Assumptions for Pro Forma Financial Statements

Income Statement

1. Sales: See Exhibit I, Sales Projections
2. Discount: 8 percent (assume discount taken on all sales)
3. Cost of goods sold:
   —Inventory—see Balance Sheet below
   —Piece goods and trimmings—65 percent of COGS
   —Contracting costs—35 percent of COGS
4. Gross profit: 50 percent of gross sales (42 percent of net sales)
5. Operating expenses—see below
6. Factor's charge—4 percent net of sales (actual charges will be commission equal to a fixed percentage of sales plus interest charge for advances against uncollected receivables)

Operating Expenses

1. Production expenses:
   —Salaries
   >Designer—$2,500 per month, starting June 1983
   >Assistant designer—$2,000 per month, starting June 1983
   >Samplehands—$1,000 each per month, starting June 1983, another starting September 1983
   >Pattern maker—$3,300 per month, starting June 1983
2. Selling and shipping:
   —Salesmen's commission—10 percent on all specialty store sales, based on standard independent representative commission rate
   >—Travel and entertainment—
   >>General travel and entertainment—$1,000 per month
   >>Announcements—$700 each holiday, spring, and fall market period
   >>Trunk shows—$3,000 each spring and fall market period
   —Freight out—0.5 percent of sales
3. General and administrative:
   —Rent—$2,000 per month
   —Office salary—
   >Part-time bookkeeper—2 days per week, at $100 per day, starting June 1983
   >Office manager—$2,000 per month
   —Telephone—$700 per month
   —Stationery and office—$1,000 per month
   —Legal and audit—$1,000 per month
   —Dues and subscriptions—$300 per month
   —Depreciation and amortization—$225 per month, based on $18,000 investment in equipment, furniture, and lease improvements, depreciated on a straight-line basis over an average life of 7 years.
   —Insurance—$600 per month
   —Business and payroll taxes—10 percent of full-time payroll
   —Employee benefits—18 percent of full-time payroll

EXHIBIT 3 *(continued)*

EXHIBIT IV

Assumptions for Pro Forma Financial Statements

Balance Sheets
1. Cash and due from factor—includes 100 percent of invoices for goods shipped in each month
2. Merchandise inventories—includes piece goods and trim received 60 days in advance of sale; finished goods shipped within month
3. Fixed assets—net—depreciated straight-line over 7-year average life, from $18,000 base, as follows:

Sample room equipment	$7,000
Office and showroom furnishing	6,000
Remodelling	5,000
	$18,000

4. Other assets—includes lease deposit of $6,000 (3 months) and telephone deposit of $800
5. Accounts payable—includes piece goods and trimming payable within 60 days; contractors paid within 30 days; all other expenses assumed paid within month
6. Stockholders' equity—$250,000 initial capital

APPENDIXES

APPENDIX A

Resume of
HEATHER H. EVANS

Education

1981–1983

HARVARD GRADUATE SCHOOL
OF BUSINESS ADMINISTRATION
Candidate for the degree of Master of Business Administration in June 1983. Awarded First Year Honors (top 15 percent of class).

Resident Business Tutor, South House, Harvard College: supervised pre-business program and oversaw student activities in residential unit of 350 undergraduate students. Instructor, Economics Department, Harvard College: designed and taught full-credit undergraduate course in managerial economics and decision analysis.

1976–1979

HARVARD COLLEGE
Bachelor of Arts degree, cum laude. Philosophy major. Phi Beta Kappa. Dean's list all semesters. Completed undergraduate course requirements in three years.

Publisher and Executive Committee member, *The Harvard Advocate* magazine. Vice Chairman, South House Committee.

EXHIBIT 3 (*continued*)

Work Experience
Summer 1982
JACKIE HAYMAN, INC.
Assistant to President. Aided president of young firm that manufactures designer clothing under Catherine Hipp label. Involved in all areas of business, including sales, public relations, working capital management, credit, design, production, and shipping.

1979–1981
MORGAN STANLEY & CO. INCORPORATED
Financial Analyst.

Mergers and Acquisitions: Identified possible acquisition targets, recommended prices for those companies, and formulated strategies to locate buyers. Analyzed financial and market data to determine the target's long-range earning potential and the effect of the acquisition on the buyer.

Corporate Finance: Supervised preparation of debt financings for 10 clients. Negotiated terms of security documents and coordinated the activities of teams inside and outside Morgan Stanley.

1975–1979
FASHION MODEL
Managed own career as a fashion model. Represented by Ford Models, Inc., New York, N.Y.; The Model's Group, Boston, Mass.; and L'Agence Pauline, Paris, France. Credits include: *Mademoiselle, Seventeen, GQ, LeMonde, Boston,* and *The Boston Globe.*

Summer 1978
RESOURCE PLANNING ASSOCIATES
Research Associate. Planned and executed study that led RPA to add antitrust economic support work to its services. Worked on projects in oil price forecasting and U.S. mineral reliance.

Personal Background
Attended The Spence School, New York, N.Y. and Lycée Montaigne, Paris, France. Speaks fluent French and conversational Greek.

EXHIBIT 3   *(concluded)*

Background of
Belinda Hughes

Belinda Hughes received her Bachelor of Fine Arts Degree in fashion design from Parsons School of Design in May 1981. After graduation, she worked as Assistant Designer to Kasper at Kasper for J.L. Sports. She designed pants, blouses, and jackets for the Kasper line and prepared sketches and maintained records of fabrication and styles for the company's Japanese licensee. In May 1982, Ms. Hughes became head designer for Creations by Aria, a moderate-price dress house. She covered layout of the dressy dress line, from selection of fabrics to preparation of dresses, and oversaw the sample room staff. Recently, Ms. Hughes has been working as a freelance designer for several lines, including Choo-Chee, Elan Shoe Corp., Roslyn Harte, and College Town, for which she has designed collections ranging from shoes to loungewear.

Ms. Hughes's design talent has been recognized by many academic and industry awards, including: Recognition in Design Citation from Levis (1979), scholarship award from St. John's University (1979), scholarship award from the Switzer Foundation (1980), ILGWU Design Merit Award (1980), ILGWU Design Creativity Award (1981).

EXHIBIT 4 Timing of Cycles in the Garment Industry

	March	April	May	June	July	August	September	October
Holiday line	Order sample fabrics	Sketch and design line		Make samples and order production quantities of fabric		Market weeks—take orders	Contract out cutting and sewing	Deliver garments to stores
Early spring line					Early spring line cycle begins			
Spring line					Spring cycle begins			
Transition line							Transition line begins	
Fall line	Fall line finishes up							

EXHIBIT 5   Heather Evans's Notes on Preliminary Discussions with
Potential Private Investors

---

1. David Ellis, attorney, family friend (excerpt from April 28, 1983, letter):

From an investor's point of view, one would expect at least a 50 percent equity share, and probably substantially more although in nonvoting stock. The investors' stock would be convertible into voting (and indeed, control) stock in case certain minimum standards of solvency and cash flow and performance weren't met. Additional stock would be made available to management if certain performance goals were exceeded. Thus management might start with 25 percent, plus an option on a second 25 percent if the company proves to be a world-beater.

That of course may sound too complicated; but if it's to be an arm's-length minimally attractive proposal, I think you have to offer investors at least 50 percent or 60 percent, albeit in nonvoting shares.

If it were a proposal such as that, I would be thinking in terms of a $20,000 or $25,000 participation for myself (i.e., an investment).

But if you can get 70 percent for yourself, with only 30 percent to investors—take it! If that's the way it goes, I would want to make a gesture of support and encouragement—thus a $5,000 unit.

2. Paul Hood, classmate, HBS:

—Says he is interested in investing for three reasons:
   • Heather Evans: trusts intelligence, dedication, design sense, and business judgment.
   • Concept: gut feel that there is a market need, has spoken with women in business about idea.
   • Upside: mentioned Liz Claiborne deal.
—Key needs in a deal:
   • No limit to upside via forced call on equity.
   • Wants company to own "Heather Evans" name rather than licensing; if Heather Evans can walk after business established, this limits upside.
—Willing to invest $25,000 to $40,000.

3. Herbert Greene, president, Greene Textiles:

—I felt that Greene was a good contact with potential fabric, textile suppliers.
—Name (especially if on board) adds credibility on Seventh Avenue/Garment Business.
—Was in on Liz Claiborne deal, made very big dollars.
—Wants in deal terms:
   • Right to force registration/issue in public market in five to seven years.
   • Low limit on my salary with incentive compensation.
   • Investors get board control until minimum performance criteria met.
—Willing to invest $35,000–$55,000.

EXHIBIT 5   *(concluded)*

4. John Merrill, old friend, HBS classmate:

—Wants company to own name: says if company does very well, main value created will be in name, company should own this.

—Liquidation protection (i.e., if company goes bust, investors get what's left before I get anything).

—Three- to five-year employment contract with three-year noncompete clause at termination of employment contract.

—Right to sell equity, pro rata, on same terms as Heather Evans in any offering.

EXHIBIT 6   Liz Claiborne Prospectus—Excerpts

liz claiborne, inc.
Common Stock
(Par Value $1 Per Share)

Of the shares of Common Stock offered hereby, 345,000 shares are being sold by the Company and 805,000 shares are being sold by certain stockholders. The Company will not receive any proceeds from the sale of shares by the Selling Stockholders. See "Principal and Selling Stockholders."

Prior to this offering there has been no public market for the Company's Common Stock. See "Underwriting" for information relating to the method of determining the initial public offering price.

THESE SECURITIES HAVE NOT BEEN APPROVED OR DISAPPROVED BY THE SECURITIES AND EXCHANGE COMMISSION NOR HAS THE COMMISSION PASSED UPON THE ACCURACY OR ADEQUACY OF THIS PROSPECTUS. ANY REPRESENTATION TO THE CONTRARY IS A CRIMINAL OFFENSE.

	Price to Public	Underwriting Discounts (1)	Proceeds to the Company (2)	Proceeds to the Selling Stockholders (2) (3)
Per Share..................	$19.00	$1.28	$17.72	$17.72
Total.......................	$21,850,000	$1,472,000	$6,113,400	$14,264,600

(1) See "Underwriting" for a description of indemnification and insurance arrangements among the Underwriters, the Company and the Selling Stockholders.

(2) Before deducting expenses estimated at $356,201 payable by the Company and $168,369 payable by the Selling Stockholders.

(3) The Selling Stockholders have granted the Underwriters an option to purchase up to an additional 115,000 shares to cover over-allotments. If all such shares are purchased, the total Price to Public, Underwriting Discounts and Proceeds to the Selling Stockholders will be increased by $2,185,000, $147,200 and $2,037,800, respectively.

The Common Stock is being offered subject to prior sale, when, as and if delivered to and accepted by the several Underwriters and subject to approval of certain legal matters by counsel and to certain other conditions. It is expected that certificates for the shares of Common Stock offered hereby will be available on or about June 16, 1981. The Underwriters reserve the right to withdraw, cancel or modify such offer and to reject orders in whole or in part.

Merrill Lynch White Weld Capital Markets Group
Merrill Lynch, Pierce, Fenner & Smith Incorporated

June 9, 1981

EXHIBIT 6   (*continued*)

PROSPECTUS SUMMARY

The following information is qualified in its entirety by reference to the detailed information and financial statements (including the Notes thereto) appearing elsewhere in the Prospectus.

Liz Claiborne, Inc.

Liz Claiborne, Inc. (the "Company") designs, contracts for the manufacture of and markets an extensive range of women's clothing under the LIZ CLAIBORNE and LIZ trademarks. Since the Company's founding in 1976, it has concentrated on identifying and furnishing the wardrobe requirements of the business and professional woman. Although the Company's products are conceived and marketed as "designer" apparel, they are priced to sell in the "better sportswear" range. The Company's products are sold to over 900 customers operating over 3,000 department and specialty stores throughout the United States. Products are manufactured pursuant to the Company's specifications by independent suppliers in the United States and abroad. See "Business."

The Offering

Common Stock to be sold by:
Company... 345,000 shares
Selling Stockholders .... 805,000 shares (1)
Common Stock to be outstanding after the offering . 3,479,560 shares
Estimated net proceeds to the Company................ $5,757,199
Use of net proceeds by the Company.................... To reduce indebtedness and for certain capital expenditures. See"Use of Proceeds."
Dividends .... None. See "Dividend Policy."
Proposed NASDAQ Symbol .... LIZC

(1) Assumes the Underwriters' 115,000 share over-allotment option is not exercised.

Selected Consolidated Financial Data
(in thousands of dollars except per share amounts)

	Jan. 19, 1976 (Inc.) through Dec. 31, 1976	Fiscal Year Ended				Three Months Ended	
		Dec. 31, 1977	Dec. 31, 1978	Dec. 29, 1979	Dec. 27, 1980	March 29, 1980	March 28, 1981
						(*unaudited*)	
Net Sales..............	$2,060	$7,396	$23,279	$47,630	$79,492	$20,747	$26,523
Net income...........	50	342	1,189	3,497	6,220	1,953	2,687
Earnings per common share (1)	$ .02	$ .12	$ .38	$ 1.12	$ 1.98	$ .62	$ .86

EXHIBIT 6 *(continued)*

	March 28, 1981 (unaudited)	
	Actual	As Adjusted (2)
Working capital...	$11,854	$16,307
Total assets..	27,918	32,613
Long-term debt, including current portion..................	63	—
Short-term debt...	3,884	2,884
Stockholders' equity	13,589	19,346

(1) Adjusted to reflect the issuance of 65 shares of the Company's Common Stock for each share of its predecessor company's common stock pursuant to a merger effected on April 21, 1981. See Notes 1 and 5 of Notes to Consolidated Financial Statements.

(2) Adjusted to reflect the sale of the shares offered by the Company hereby and the anticipated use of the net proceeds therefrom as well as the repayment of long-term debt in April, 1981. See "Use of Proceeds" and "Capitalization."

See "Dilution" and "Shares Eligible for Future Sale" with respect to the availability of shares for sale after this offering and the immediate dilution in net tangible book value per share to be incurred by the public investors.

IN CONNECTION WITH THIS OFFERING, THE UNDERWRITERS MAY OVERALLOT OR EFFECT TRANSACTIONS WHICH STABILIZE OR MAINTAIN THE MARKET PRICE OF THE COMMON STOCK OF THE COMPANY AT A LEVEL ABOVE THAT WHICH MIGHT OTHERWISE PREVAIL IN THE OPEN MARKET. SUCH STABILIZING, IF COMMENCED, MAY BE DISCONTINUED AT ANY TIME.

EXHIBIT 6 *(continued)*

SELECTED FINANCIAL DATA

The following tables set forth information regarding the Company's operating results and financial position and are qualified in their entirety by the more detailed Consolidated Financial Statements included elsewhere in the Prospectus.

SELECTED INCOME STATEMENT DATA:

	Jan. 19, 1976 (inc.) through Dec. 31, 1976	Dec. 1, 1977 (unaudited)	Fiscal Year Ended			Three Months Ended	
			Dec. 31, 1978	Dec. 29, 1979	Dec. 27, 1980	March 29, 1980	March 28, 1981
Net sales	$2,060,118	$7,395,898	$23,279,304	$47,630,227	$79,492,035	$20,747,500	$26,523,023
Net income	49,862	342,489	1,188,857	3,496,575	6,219,592	1,952,998	2,686,670
Earnings per common share (1)	$.02	$ .12	$ .38	$1.12	$1.98	$.62	$.86
Dividends declared per common share (1)(2)	—	$.007	$.023	$.046	$.077	—	—

303

EXHIBIT 6 *(continued)*

SELECTED BALANCE SHEET DATA:

	Dec. 31, 1976	Dec. 31, 1977	Dec. 31, 1978	Dec. 29, 1979	Dec. 27, 1980	March 28, 1981 (unaudited)
Working capital	$246,471	$ 454,196	$1,179,071	$ 4,456,954	$ 9,302,745	$11,854,311
Total assets	674,806	1,901,492	5,144,142	10,786,982	19,281,718	27,918,402
Long-term debt, including current portion (3)	170,000	173,333	173,333	134,815	77,037	62,593
Short-term debt (4)	—	—	—	—	—	3,883,676
Advances from factor (4)	330,696	666,077	2,782,863	—	3,546,098	—
Stockholders' equity	135,029	455,128	1,571,649	4,923,551	10,902,023	13,588,693

(1) Adjusted to reflect the issuance of 65 shares of the Company's Common Stock for each share of its predecessor company's common stock pursuant to a merger effected on April 21, 1981. See Notes 1 and 5 of Notes to Consolidated Financial Statements.

(2) The Company has no present plan to continue to pay dividends. See "Dividend Policy."

(3) The Company repaid its long-term debt in April, 1981.

(4) Factoring advances were replaced by a line of credit in March, 1981. See Notes 2 and 10 of Notes to Consolidated Financial Statements.

EXHIBIT 6   (*continued*)

BUSINESS

Introduction and Background

The Company designs, contracts for the manufacture of and markets an extensive range of women's clothing under the LIZ CLAIBORNE and LIZ trademarks. Organized in 1976 by its present management, the Company has concentrated primarily on identifying and furnishing the wardrobe requirements of the working woman, providing apparel appropriate in a business or professional environment as well as apparel suitable for leisure wear. The Company offers its customers a broad selection of related separates (referred to in the apparel industry as *sportswear*) consisting of blouses, skirts, jackets, sweaters, and tailored pants, as well as more casual apparel such as jeans, knit tops, and shirts. The Company believes that the increasing number of business and professional women has contributed both to the Company's own growth and to the growth of the market for women's sportswear in general.

LIZ CLAIBORNE products are conceived and marketed as designer apparel, employing a consistent approach to design and quality, which is intended to develop and maintain consumer recognition and loyalty across product lines and from season to season. The Company defines its clothing as "updated," combining traditional or classic design with contemporary fashion influences. While the Company maintains a "designer" image, its products are priced in the better sportswear range, which is generally less expensive than many designer lines. Although no comprehensive trade statistics are available, the Company believes, based on its knowledge of the market and such trade information as is available, that measured by sales of women's better sportswear, it is the second largest producer of such merchandise in the United States.

In 1980, LIZ CLAIBORNE products were sold to over 900 customers operating over 3,000 department and specialty stores throughout the United States. Measured by their purchases of LIZ CLAIBORNE apparel, the Company's largest customers during 1980 included Saks Fifth Avenue, Lord & Taylor, Bamberger's, J. L. Hudson, Bloomingdale's and Macy's—New York. A great many retail outlets that carry the Company's products maintain separate LIZ CLAIBORNE areas in which a range of the Company's products are sold. Approximately 25 percent of the Company's 1980 sales was made to the Company's 10 largest customers; approximately 71 percent of 1980 sales was made to the Company's 100 largest customers. Certain of these customers are under common ownership. For example, 16 different department store customers owned by Federated Department Stores, Inc. (which include Bloomingdale's, Abraham & Straus, and Burdine's) accounted for approximately 12 percent of the Company's 1980 sales. The Company believes that each of these department store customers makes its own decisions regarding purchases of the Company's products.

EXHIBIT 6   (*continued*)

Although the Company expects that sales to its 100 largest customers will continue to account for a majority of its sales, increasing emphasis is being placed on sales to local specialty stores and direct-mail catalog companies. The Company began licensing its trademarks in 1978 and presently receives royalties under arrangements with three licensees that sell various products under the LIZ CLAIBORNE and LIZ trademarks.

The Company's products are designed by its own staff and are manufactured in accordance with its specifications by independent suppliers in the United States and abroad. Domestically produced merchandise accounted for approximately 55 percent of the Company's sales during 1980; the remaining approximately 45 percent consisted of merchandise produced abroad, almost entirely in the Far East. Company personnel in the United States and abroad regularly monitor production at facilities that manufacture its products.

PRINCIPAL AND SELLING STOCKHOLDERS

The following table sets forth certain information, as of March 28, 1981, with respect to the number of shares of Common Stock owned, to be offered for sale, and to be beneficially owned after this offering, by all persons who were known by the Company to own beneficially more than 5 percent of the then outstanding Common Stock, all Selling Stockholders, each of the Directors of the Company, and the Company's officers and Directors, as a group:

Name and Address	Ownership of Common Stock prior to Offering (1)		Shares to be Sold (2)	Ownership of Common Stock after Offering (1)(2)	
	Number of Shares	*Percent*		*Number of Shares*	*Percent*
Elisabeth Claiborne Ortenberg (3) 1441 Broadway New York, NY	523,640	16.71	134,478	389,162	11.18
Arthur Ortenberg (3) 1441 Broadway New York, NY	523,640	16.71	134,478	389,162	11.18
Leonard Boxer 4 Emerson Lane Secaucus, NJ	523,640	16.71	134,478	389,162	11.18
Jerome A. Chazen 1441 Broadway New York, NY	523,640	16.71	134,478	389,162	11.18
J. James Gordon	65,000	2.07	16,693	48,307	1.39

EXHIBIT 6   (*concluded*)

Name and Address	Ownership of Common Stock prior to Offering (1)		Shares to be Sold (2)	Ownership of Common Stock after Offering (1)(2)	
	Number of Shares	Percent		Number of Shares	Percent
Joseph Gaumont 200 E. 57th Street New York, NY	227,500	7.26	58,425	169,075	4.86
Charness Family Investments Ltd. (4) 2 St. Clair Avenue, East Toronto, Canada	162,500	5.18	41,733	120,767	3.47
Catway Investments Ltd. (4)	97,500	3.11	25,040	72,460	2.08
Albert Fink Milton (5)	97,500	3.11	25,040	72,460	2.08
Elizabeth Fenner Milton (5)	65,000	2.07	16,693	48,307	1.39
Albert Fenner Milton, Custodian, F/B/O Elizabeth Hunt Milton under the Uniform Gifts to Minors Act (5)	9,750	0.31	8,346	1,404	0.04
Jerome Gold	65,000	2.07	16,693	48,307	1.39
Martin J. Tandler	65,000	2.07	16,693	48,307	1.39
Jacob Rosenbaum (6)	40,625	1.30	10,433	30,192	0.87
Belle Rosenbaum (6)	40,625	1.30	10,433	30,192	0.87
Theodore Brodie (7)	40,625	1.30	10,433	30,192	0.87
Simmi Brodie (7)	40,625	1.30	10,433	30,192	0.87
All ofificers and directors as a group (7 persons)	2,159,560	68.90	554,605	1,604,955	46.13

(1) All shares listed are owned of record and, to the Company's knowledge, beneficially.
(2) Assumes the Underwriters' 115,000 share over-allotment option is not exercised. Percentage is based on total shares to be outstanding after this offering.
(3) Arthur Ortenberg and Elisabeth Claiborne Ortenberg are husband and wife; each disclaims beneficial ownership of all shares owned by the other.

Duncan Field

On Monday morning, September 11, 1978, Duncan Field was continuing his negotiations with Bob Baer, senior vice president of Galaxy Industries. Bob stated:

> Duncan, we're not willing to give you any further information at this time. We still have to be convinced that you and your investors will not have any difficulty handling an acquisition of this size.

Duncan shuddered as Bob continued:

> *You* are the one who came to us and badgered us into considering the sale of our East Valley CATV systems, remember? This is as far as we go—$9 million for the sale of the systems. We are prepared to execute this three-page letter agreement we developed together and accept your $50,000 good faith money. Or, we will simply keep the systems and continue operating them as we had always planned. Which will it be?

Duncan Field knew that he had only a few moments to evaluate his alternatives and respond to Mr. Baer.

BACKGROUND

Duncan Field, 34, had grown up in the suburbs of Pittsburgh where his father was employed by a large national company. His family moved to southern Ohio during Duncan's high school years, then he attended Duke University in North Carolina where he received a Bachelor's degree in mechanical engineering. Engineering had been a struggle and, while Duncan valued the training, he decided he wouldn't be happy as a professional engineer. Duncan had married

This case was prepared by Richard O. von Werssowetz and H. Irving Grousbeck under the direction of Philip H. Thurston.

Harvard Business School case 9–382–137

during his junior year, and his wife agreed to support them while he attended Wharton to study business. (All quoted comments are Duncan's unless otherwise noted.)

> I had taken a lot of business courses at Duke because I wasn't sure if our finances would allow graduate school. Compared to engineering school, business school was a whole lot easier for me, so I used the opportunity to round out my education. I read widely, took some social psychology and communications courses.
>
> My specialty area was investment finance, but my courses were not particularly concentrated.

After receiving an MBA degree in 1968, Duncan and his wife moved to St. Paul where Duncan began work for Paul Russell, vice president of a large commercial bank.

> I was an assistant loan officer and was authorized to make loans, but I really chased Paul's business. He had probably 200 accounts, which were primarily newer high-tech companies and CATV (*community antenna television*, usually known as *cable TV*). Paul was quite a character who didn't delegate well, but was very active, exciting, and stimulating. He had a real interest in the entrepreneur and in start-up ventures.
>
> One of Paul's responsibilities was the bank's venture capital subsidiary. With Paul's style, I ended up acting as the chief operating officer of that subsidiary, without the title, but clearly with those responsibilities. I followed a portfolio of about 50 investments and analyzed new proposals as they came in. I must have looked at over 200 a year, of which we did maybe 5. We made both direct equity investments and also used debt instruments through an SBIC.
>
> Start-ups were flying high then, and there were so many opportunities mixed with so many harebrained schemes that you found yourself looking for reasons not to do the investment. If you couldn't find any reasons not to invest, you did it.
>
> Every person who comes to you *believes* his or her scheme is going to succeed. They've written out why it's going to succeed and are committing their future to it. If you took that at face value, you'd make every investment that came in. Yet clearly, the majority of them don't succeed. So you checked out everything they said. When you found one whose story checked out completely, you did it. Then it became just a question of pricing.

THE MOVE TO CABLE TELEVISION

> Once I had a little money in my pocket, I made several investments in the stock market. I based my choices on stock that was undervalued based on operating results and current position. The results were nearly disastrous, but I finally salvaged about what I would have made in a savings

account. I then recalled some advice a friend's father had passed along: "Don't invest in anything you can't control."

I'd modify that to "something on which you don't have a significant impact or which depends on someone else's opinion for value rather than simply the results of the enterprise." The stock market is two or three iterations removed from how successful a business is. I decided that wasn't the way for me to make my fortune.

After four years with the bank, Duncan attempted to convince the bank to sponsor a separate investment vehicle to raise outside funds to invest in the cable TV industry. Some of the bank's best customers were so successful that they had requirements above the bank's legal loan limit. This was threatening the bank's leadership position on those accounts. The new fund Duncan suggested would provide the bank the means to service those accounts and also the means for bank officers, including himself, to build equity by partial ownership.

It was approved all the way up to the president of the bank, but the chairman thought better of it. My feeling was they just didn't like the idea of doing something that "ritzy."

I then decided that I wanted to pursue the cable TV industry. I had become knowledgeable in it. It was a fun industry and was really a numbers game. There were good rules of thumb to predict value and performance—investors and bankers love that. So I started feeling out people I knew in the industry, looking for a company I could join.

Duncan joined Cosmopolitan Cable Corporation in 1972. Their understanding was that Duncan would go into the field as a general manager as soon as a suitable opportunity arose. Until then, he became director of corporate development and worked as an assistant to Glen Ryan and David Brett, the company's founders.

I did some secondary work on a loan agreement from the other side of the table, chased some franchise opportunities, some possible acquisitions. I analyzed our existing operations to help us predict more closely what we could expect from new systems. It gave me a chance to learn more about the business, and I think they enjoyed having someone to do a lot of the dog work.

It took longer than we expected to find a suitable opportunity for me to get to the field. One early start-up was given to a more experienced person, and then we just didn't start anything up for a while. After a year and a half, we won a big franchise in Texas, our largest project to date. It was clearly more than I could have handled, and they put the head of their largest group of systems in charge of it. I said, "Look, I'm getting nowhere fast, so send me out as a number two man. Let me learn from the ground up. I just want to get out to the field." So I went out as an assistant general manager.

It was a fantastic learning experience, being in on the ground floor. We didn't have our permanent office, we had very few employees, we had made no major decisions on billing systems or electronics or the major suppliers. No marketing had been done. It was a chance to be there right from the beginning and ask at least 10,000 stupid questions. For nine months I acted as the controller, and we also hadn't yet hired a customer service manager or office manager, so I played those roles as well.

The general manager was really good, and our engineer was also excellent. In the cable TV industry, the engineer reports to the general manager, but really runs a separate little empire on the side. Everything in the field—doing installations, repairing things, constructing things— all came under the system engineer. Inside things such as billings, sales, and marketing were under the customer service manager.

After a year and a half in Texas, Cosmopolitan was awarded franchises in several communities in Indiana. Duncan was made regional vice president and was given responsibility for building the systems.

They put me together with an experienced and very capable system engineer. In the four years we were there, we went from a motel room to a system almost 600 miles long with 30,000 customers.

GOING OUT ON HIS OWN

While Duncan had worked at the bank, he had gotten to know another Wharton graduate, Frank Gilmour. Frank had taken over responsibilties for the bank's venture activities when Duncan left and had later joined one of the leading independent venture capital companies, which also had several cable TV investments. For some time, Frank had urged Duncan to start his own cable TV business.

He mentioned it when I went to Texas and mentioned it when I went to Indiana. He brought it up again about a year later, just sort of bugging me to do something. "When are you going to leave and do your own thing? When are you going to learn to make some money off the deal?"

I said I just didn't know. I didn't feel comfortable that I knew enough about the business to go out and be sure I'd succeed. At the bank and at Cosmopolitan I learned the great strength of never missing a projection. I wanted to feel I would do the same.

I also felt that I had accepted a big obligation to Cosmopolitan in Indiana. When I finished that, I'd have earned my spurs, and then we'd talk again.

At Cosmopolitan, Duncan had participated in one of the better stock option plans in the industry. However, he also had seen the value of a larger part of ownership in cable systems. He discussed several plans for managers at Cosmopolitan to gain more personal tax benefits and a better equity ride. One plan would have been for managers to purchase and lease back various real estate properties used by their systems. Cosmopolitan now did this with third parties. Another plan would be for managers to be allowed to purchase other cable systems that were not large enough to be interesting to Cosmopolitan.

Glen Ryan and David Brett decided that these plans would result in too many potential conflicts. They were particularly concerned about what might happen should one of the managers' ventures encounter difficulties.

> So, I decided that if I ever wanted to make any serious money, I'd have to leave and try it on my own.

Duncan reopened his discussions with Frank Gilmour. Gilmour had the right to make investments separately from his venture capital firm. He said his family owned a small firm with an unused $300,000 line of credit which the family was willing to use to fund a cable venture. Frank would use his contacts and experience to help raise the additional financing that would be required. At first, Duncan tried to find an opportunity as a "cast off" from Cosmopolitan. He was spending part of his time trying to find new systems for Cosmopolitan. Duncan felt that this would lead to an opportunity that would be suitable for his own first system, but which would be too small, in a less desirable area (especially one at a distance from their current geographical concentrations), or otherwise unattractive to Cosmopolitan.

> I think it is unusual for someone starting a venture or leaving to take a new job to not have a new job or new venture lined up before they leave the old one. Certainly with the risk involved in starting a new venture, you don't want to get hung up in "no man's land" halfway between two ventures.
>
> It was difficult to reconcile looking for my own system while I was working for Cosmopolitan. I had agreed with Frank Gilmour that Cosmopolitan would get first choice on anything I came up with. I was working there, using their telephones and their time chasing acquisitions that I wanted to make for them. I wasn't going to take the best one and do it on my own. I also had an agreement attached to my stock options not to compete with Cosmopolitan for one year, although I felt I was unlikely to buy any systems they would be interested in.

After several months, Duncan found he wasn't making much progress. He had maintained a very small staff for the Indiana systems and found he simply had very little time to seek any acquisitions.

We had a very tight operation. As a matter of fact, we were already making money—actual profits after depreciation and interest, not only cash flow—which was unheard of. Cable systems usually report losses for some time after they're built. I seemed to be doing 16 different jobs, and if I had any brains, I would have gotten more help.

Then our regional operating manager was moved to help start another franchise. I knew I was on the verge of leaving and felt my successor should have the right to choose the replacement. So it became even more difficult to seek acquisitions for either of us.

Frank Gilmour and his family offered to support Duncan for one year of an independent search for a cable acquisition. Duncan would be paid the same salary and insurance benefits he had at Cosmopolitan. Gilmour would also pay search expenses and hold a $250,000 pool of equity ready for an investment. In return, Duncan and Gilmour's family would split 50/50 the equity they wouldn't have to give away to raise other financing. These resources eliminated most of the risk of the search for Duncan, and he felt the career risks of leaving were also low:

Our industry has such fast growth. I'd done what people thought was a good job. If at the end of that year I had fallen on my nose, I really expected to go back to work for another cable company. It might not be as good as Cosmopolitan or have as good an option plan, but I wasn't going to starve. I could clearly end up with a comfortable position in another operation.

If we managed to buy a system and failed, I still felt the career risk was not too high. I think people forget that if you try to start a new venture, you can fail with grace. But be sure you don't take any bankers down with you—they're not compensated for taking high risks. And it would be nice not to take any venture capitalists down either.

If you're a good manager, you can always go back and get another good job in another firm, probably just as good as you had before. And you can try it again later if you want to *and* if you've gotten the bankers out whole. Venture capitalists understand that some ventures don't make it—that's why they get a bigger rate of return.

After giving 90 days' notice to "pass the baton," Duncan exercised his vested stock options and left Cosmopolitan in February 1978.

BEGINNING THE SEARCH FOR AN ACQUISITION

Duncan and Frank quickly decided they would pursue the purchase of an existing system rather than attempt to win a franchise and build one. Cable systems were sold fairly often and trying to win a franchise normally required a lot of time and effort, at least $10,000–$20,000 in expenses, and involved competing with often 5 to 10 applicants with no certainty of winning. Instead, they would rather acquire a system and try to improve its operations.

They incorporated as Federated Cablevision, Inc. to establish a name and an image of professionalism. To limit overhead expense, Duncan set up an office in his home.

> My wife and I moved into what had been a small study, and I took over our large bedroom downstairs. I bought a used desk and typewriter and some old file cabinets. There was no point in moving because I had no idea where we'd end up.

Duncan used a number of means to try to locate cable systems for sale. Through trade magazines, Duncan had been able to identify 10 business brokers who dealt with broadcasting properties. There were two or three that specialized more in cable and did most of the volume of sales. Glen Ryan and David Brett also referred possible properties to Duncan from time to time as did other Cosmopolitan regional managers.

> I asked the other regional managers to keep their eyes open for me. "Obviously, do what's right for you, but if you're not interested and think I might be, I'd sure appreciate it if you'd steer it in my direction."

Duncan had felt they might easily find a system to buy in three to six months and that it would take about three months to close the purchase. His first real opportunity came during the first month. A local group in a community in California had won rights to a new franchise and was offering to sell the rights rather than build the system. Although this was not quite the established company they had planned to buy, Duncan felt it was a real opportunity.

> The toughest thing to do in the cable business is to build a system from scratch and market it successfully. And that's what I had been doing for the past six years.
>
> But this area was not without risk. The market only needed cable so-so. This would take all our resources, but we could probably make it. You feel that these are the risks of a new venture, so why not get on with it? I wanted to do it.
>
> I went down to look at it on a Wednesday and left at the end of the day Thursday. I was very excited, but wanted to project costs and analyze it. The broker who dropped me off had another meeting scheduled two hours later with some representatives of a large broadcasting group. They came in with their checkbook and bought it. I was back in Indiana sharpening my pencils and they just bought it! I hadn't made an offer! I wanted to make sure it was something we wanted to do.
>
> Looking back, it would have been a great deal. But nonetheless, I wouldn't have done it differently. There are people out there who will buy things without thinking twice, but I'm just not going to compete with that. That particular group had a lot of cash and simply wanted growth.

You just have to realize there's going to be fallout at every stage of the game. You have to look at a lot of deals to see one you want. You're going to see several you want to buy that will be sold before you can reach an agreement. You're going to sign agreements on some that will fall apart before they get closed. You just have to keep banging away. I knew that and so did Frank Gilmour.

Over the next several months, Duncan was disappointed about the quality of deals he was seeing from brokers. He felt this was because of his low financial credibility and because of his insistence on investigating the deals and offering what he considered fair value. Duncan used every device he could think of to build credibility. He sold his background in the industry and pointed to his financial partner who was with a respected venture company that had, in fact, done several cable deals. He had business cards and stationery printed and installed a separate business telephone with an answering service.

The people I called didn't know I was working out of my house. I typed all my own letters and used *ms* for my secretary's initials for *myself*. My friends kidded me about the lousy typewriter, but at least my letters were typed and I didn't make mistakes. I used printed note paper whenever I could so that I could write those out. No one ever had occasion to visit me at my office.

When people asked for our credit references, I'd tell them we'd just gotten started and were looking to acquire our first operation. I resold my background and partners. I didn't try to make them think I had a big operation, but I'm sure many pictured me in a nice office building with a secretary and people helping me analyze the deals.

Duncan realized his insistence on evaluating deals was at odds with most brokers' desires.

I'm hampered by the fact that I'm so cheap. Brokers just want to move the property. They want someone who'll come in and ask two or three dumb questions and say, "I'll buy." In this business, brokers receive about a 1.5 percent commission on the sales price. They don't care if you buy something for $9 million or $8.2 million—it's not much difference to them.

If you want to take time to negotiate and settle on a price and ask every question under the sun; if you then want to go out and line up at least a tentative financing package, and are willing to put up some good faith money—say $10,000—and are willing to sign a letter of intent; if you want to take all that time, they don't want to deal with you. They will deal with you, but they'll spend their time with those who will buy right away.

As a result, I didn't see anything first. I was always down the list. They always profess that they show everyone the deals at the same time, but they don't. I probably never saw some of the better opportunities. At that time, cable systems didn't sell particularly fast, so I still had time to look at some. But I was going to analyze my deals because I didn't want to fail. We could not *afford* to make a mistake our first shot out of the box. That had to be a success.

CONTINUING THE SEARCH

As the weeks went by, Duncan settled into an active search pattern. Although he had an office at home, he would dress respectably and kept standard office hours. Besides pursuing leads from brokers, he searched through the trade magazines for interesting prospects. He would call systems of interest to see if he could open up the possibility of a sale.

Industry fact books provided other leads. These gave statistical summaries of every cable system in the country, with ownership, numbers of subscribers, how many homes they passed, and sizes of the communities they covered.

The fact books were always outdated, but the information was enough to start with. For example, I would plot all the stations owned by large multiple systems operators on a map. If I could find one location remote from the others, I thought that might be an opportunity, so I'd try to find a contact that I could approach or would just "cold call." If I could keep them from hanging up, I'd try to get the chance to talk further.

There were about 2,500 systems in the country, and I read about and considered practically every one during my first six months out.

Duncan visited a number of systems and made offers on several without success.

It's just hard to close a deal. On one system I really wanted, I made an offer and then there were a series of counter-offers, but we got stuck someplace, maybe 10 percent off. We had doubts as to how seriously he wanted to sell it.

The brokers sometimes have conflicting interests, too. You figure in our business that *they'll* end up buying the best ones. They'll let you be the stalking horse for them; then they'll buy it on their own.

Duncan spent a lot of time trying to close one system in Maryland.

I hit one system in Maryland that we agreed on right away. I had gotten enough information from the broker and from talking to the people at the system by telephone that this should be a *good* deal.

So I went down there to confirm that what I was told was true. This time I took *my* checkbook! I made sure from that broker that they wanted a $5,000 deposit and made sure we had that much in our account.

I still liked what I saw, so we negotiated out a price and drafted a three-page agreement. The next day, we took it to his attorney who made a few changes. We signed it, and I gave the broker my $5,000 check. This was the end of April 1978.

The Maryland system was a very small one, serving a population of about 15,000. It had substantial construction left to be done, but Duncan and Frank felt they could build it up and make a good capital gain. They were prepared to do a number of smaller deals to build up a group, and this could be the start.

As Duncan tried to close the deal, problems continued to crop up.

There were a half-dozen stockholders, and while I was negotiating with the president, the others kept changing their minds. First, one shareholder in Delaware decided he didn't want to sell. Then he decided he might but began objecting to the deal. We couldn't get him on the phone, and we couldn't tell what he was objecting to, but he wouldn't agree.

Another shareholder then appeared and said he didn't want to sell; in fact, he wanted to buy it. So he didn't want to go through with this deal, and the president wasn't authorized to act, etc., etc. We put forth that the president was authorized and that we felt they had an obligation.

All this time—it's now July—we're trying to put together a complete purchase agreement that's now running 40–50 pages. We had a big discussion about the form of purchase. It was supposed to be the purchase of assets. This meant the current owner would be liable for ordinary income taxes on part of the depreciated value of assets due to recapture. The first guy finally got us to agree to a stock purchase. In effect *we* ended up paying a higher price.

The second shareholder wanted us to pick up a few other things; then they told us that instead of serving a population of 15,000 they could only serve 13,000.

Figuring the size of the system and the service area had been a continuing problem. Their maps and records were very sketchy, so I had even tried to physically count potential subscribers on a couple of occasions—going out in a car, driving up and down the streets. Now it's hard to follow a cable in the air and count houses at the same time. Besides I would think I saw a single family home, and they would say, no, there's another door to a basement apartment in the back, and it's really a two-family house. So I just gave up.

After a lot of soul-searching, I finally said, "OK. We'll accept the 13,000 people and still buy it at the same price." Finally we got the full agreement signed up in August.

I decided one last time to check their notes. We had demanded they warrant the number of people in their service area as part of the contract. They didn't want to since they hadn't done a count. We had insisted that they do a count, which is where the 13,000 number came from. Now, after it's all signed up, I get their notes, and the notes themselves said only 10,000! Essentially an out-and-out lie!

I said forget it. That's too low. We're backing out. Give us our deposit and expense money back. They said, "Well, it's a nice day, isn't it?"

I don't know how many trips I'd made down there. I'd paid an engineer to check out the system for us. I'd hired an FCC attorney who instructed them on how to clear up *their* FCC legal problems so the system could be transferred. Our corporate attorney had invested I don't know how much time in it, and the bankers were all lined up. We had at least $15,000 cash out plus the $5,000 deposit plus an equal amount of my time. The facts were in our favor, but to get a legal judgment takes so much time and is so futile, most people just chalk it up to experience.

EAST VALLEY CATV

Although the Maryland deal had been Duncan's highest priority during the spring and summer, he had continued to seek other opportunities. In May, he had begun to pursue several cable systems owned by a subsidiary of Galaxy Industries.

Galaxy owned several cable TV systems, but I had heard rumors that they might be unhappy with systems in three towns in East Valley. They had acquired them with some other properties, and several suppliers to the industry and lawyers I knew thought they might be bought.

I called Robert Baer, Galaxy's vice president of finance, who wouldn't give me any information. He said they had no interest in selling. I vacationed in the same region, so I just drove to the towns to see what I could find out. I visited each system as a possible customer to pick up their rates and programming, to talk to their employees, and just to crane my neck around to see what I could see. Their receptionists described the parts of town where their service was and was not available, which helped me gauge undeveloped potential.

Duncan sought other sources of information about the East Valley systems:

The state cable commission had some general financial reports. I also collected all the census data I could find and determined how many occupied year-round housing units there were in each town. I obtained copies of the franchises from the town halls. In no case did I say who I was or why I was interested. I checked reception at TV dealers around town. They don't like cable because it reduces the number of antennas they sell. So you always hear the worst about the systems from them. I could flip channels in their stores to see how well we'd be able to market in each area.

In July, I called Robert Baer again and said I'd like to make an offer. He said, "Well, it's not for sale, but I suppose if you make me an offer I have to listen. Let me think about it and call me back." When I called several days later, Bob said, "No, don't even make me an offer. I don't even want to hear about it."

I said I was going to make an offer anyway. Bob said, "If you call and make an offer, I'd have to pass it along, but it's a waste of time." I said, "Fine."

Duncan felt the East Valley systems were solid opportunities. He was determined to open negotiations even without Galaxy's cooperation.

I spent all my extra time in August trying to come up with an offer without having a single, solitary piece of information from them. I thought about what I knew. Bob had mentioned one reason they couldn't sell the systems was that they were operated together with two other systems. When they later said not to bother to make an offer, I decided that I would have a chance only if I made an offer for the whole group. So I did my research on the two other systems.

I knew I had to make a *serious* offer. Yet I didn't know how good the properties might really be. If they were really good and my offer was too low, I would be left out and would never get another phone call answered.

I also didn't know how bad the properties might be. If I really went in high, I could be badly taken, because the game Baer was playing was not to give me *any* information. But I had to make a real offer or I wouldn't get to first base.

So I went in with an offer I thought he couldn't refuse. I had arranged a meeting, saying I was going to be in their headquarters city on other business. I said I would offer $7 million. He said, "I don't see how we could possibly do something for that, but let me think about it."

Bob called me back on the phone in a few days and said $7 million was not enough, but how about $9 million? I finally knew he was serious. What a great day that was!

THE NEGOTIATIONS

Many phone calls, letters, and discussions followed during the end of August and early days of September as Duncan and Bob Baer tried to establish an agreement on price.

Cable TV systems are normally priced based on multiples of net operating income. Profits don't mean anything in our industry because the capital investment in the system results in high depreciation. Also, most systems are highly leveraged and have interest payments.

For a system that was solid and had some growth potential we expected to pay about seven times net operating income—profits before interest, depreciation, and taxes. However, there can be quite a bit of latitude, depending on the situation. For more mature situations where you expected less growth, you'd expect to pay maybe five times cash flow. In an early situation or for a franchise, you'd then pay about $10 to $20 a home. Down in Maryland we had been talking almost $30 per home in a situation with negative cash flow! You just have to assess what you can build, how long it will take to gain your market, and what you can carry.

Another rule of thumb is that you could expect that 50 percent of the homes you pass by with your cable would subscribe. Yet that varied from 30 percent or less in some sections with good reception to up to 80 percent in others. Those figures are for ultimate market saturation. Of course you also had to forecast the level of saturation each year as you built up to that level.

Other pricing factors included projections of the percentages of customers who would subscribe to additional services such as Home Box Office. You also had to consider the costs of turnover—a lost customer decreased revenues much more than the marginal reduction in expenses.

Because Bob Baer still refused to give me any detailed information about the East Valley systems, our pricing negotiations really involved developing a price backed by a set of formulas of minimum values of various operating factors. Actually, it was more Bob standing fast and me arguing that this town might be worth seven times cash flow but that one was more mature and definitely worth less! It was really a lot of fun arguing back and forth, but no matter what arguments I used, it became apparent that the price was going to be $9 million.

CONSIDERING FINANCING

Duncan was also discussing the price and possible financing with Frank Gilmour. Duncan prepared an operating projection based on his assumptions about the systems. Then he and Frank reviewed the type of financing that might be available and added a target structure of debt and equity. Frank would invest up to $500,000 in equity. All other financing would have to be obtained from other sources.

Duncan's and Frank's projections (Exhibit 1) incorporated a number of assumptions. Some of these follow:

— A purchase price of $9 million cash.

— The requirement to recognize certain recapture income arising from the necessary technical structure of buying the systems.

— The expectation that banks would reliably lend five times current net operating income for cable TV systems. The net operating income for 1978 was estimated to be $1,200,000.

— The current prime rate was 9½ percent.

— An expectation of 6 percent annual inflation consistent with current expectations and built into projected costs and revenues.

— Subordinated debt and equity investors would demand return rates of 15 percent to 30 percent compounded annually, depending on relative position, total leverage, their evaluation of the management and of the system, and skill at negotiation.

— Real population growth of three systems was limited to 1 percent per year and was held at zero for two of the operations.

They expected to raise a total of $9,650,000 to pay the purchase price, closing costs, and provide working capital. The assumed sources of funds were:

$6,500,000	Senior debt from banks at 11 percent.
$1,700,000	Senior subordinated debt with a 14 percent current return and callable warrants. The warrants had a price schedule calculated to give a total compounded return of 18 percent when called.
$1,000,000	Junior subordinated debt with a 10 percent current return and warrants for 20 percent of the equity. If the systems were sold in five years for 7.5 times net operating income plus net current assets (current assets less short-term liabilities), this would provide an additional 17 percent return or "a total return of 27 percent.
$450,000	Equity to be put up mainly by the Gilmours, split 50/50 with Duncan.
$9,650,000	Total financed.

All of these assumptions were made by Duncan and Frank as experienced estimates. They felt they were unlikely to get better ranges of current rates by talking to financing sources unless they were actually negotiating a deal they already controlled. In addition, Galaxy was adamant that all discussions be kept extremely confidential. If Galaxy felt the contemplated sale was the subject of open discussion or even speculation, Duncan and Frank agreed that the deal would probably fall apart.

In addition to maintaining the uncertainty over whether or not financing could be obtained in the amounts needed and for acceptable rates, this lack of financial backing weakened Duncan's negotiating position. Federated Cablevision was hardly a giant in the industry, and Galaxy had expressed concern that they might strike a deal, word would get out, then Federated would not be able to finance the purchase. Nonetheless, Duncan had been able to keep negotiations moving, including preparation of a three-page purchase agreement.

The agreement included a $50,000 good faith deposit, which Federated would pay to Galaxy. If Federated could not close the deal, Frank's $50,000 would be forfeited. However, Duncan knew that Bob Baer and Galaxy Industries had a long-held reputation for the highest business standards and integrity. Therefore, Duncan did feel comfortable that the $50,000 would be returned if Galaxy should back out of the sale. (His Maryland experience had taught him that such sketchy purchase agreements could not guarantee a sale, and their $5,000 deposit there was still tied up.) Yet even with that uncertainty, he and Frank would have to commit a great deal of time and effort to arrange financing once the agreement was made. With interest rates beginning to move upward, financing wouldn't be easy.

A QUESTION OF COMMITMENT

Duncan wanted to buy the East Valley systems but realized that a whole range of risks still remained. He still had been unsuccessful in obtaining actual operating information from Galaxy. Working from limited confirmations by Bob Baer of Duncan's stated assumptions and by considering key operating indicators, Duncan had included important minimums of current operating profit, residential dwellings passed by cable, numbers of current customers, and price rates in the proposed contract. The contract also allowed an engineering inspection of the systems. The price would be $9 million plus net current assets with an adjustment for changes from assumed depreciation. Still every contingency certainly was not covered. Duncan decided to make one more attempt to convince Bob to give him East Valley's operating results.

EXHIBIT 1 East Valley Financial Projections (in thousands of dollars)

	1979	1980	1981	1982	1983	1984	1985	1986
Net operating income	$1,240	$1,360	$1,570	$1,590	$1,800	$1,780	$1,950	$1,910
Interest: Senior 11%	720	710	690	630	530	430	310	190
Senior sub 14%	240	240	240	240	240	240	240	240
Junior sub 10%	100	100	100	100	100	100	100	100
Total interest	1,060	1,050	1,030	970	870	770	650	530
Depreciation	510	1,170	1,600	1,360	1,170	810	680	580
Subtotal	(330)	(860)	(1,060)	(740)	(240)	200	620	800
Recapture income*	—	1,650	1,380	—	—	—	—	—
Profit before taxes	(330)	790	320	(740)	(240)	200	620	800
Taxes	—	150	130	(300)	—	—	200	360
Profit after taxes	(330)	640	190	(440)	(240)	200	420	440
Beginning cash	—	170	160	200	260	220	170	110
Cash from operations	180	1,810	1,790	920	930	1,010	1,100	1,020
Closing costs	(200)	(100)	(300)	(800)	(900)	(1,000)	(1,100)	(2,300)
Senior debt	6,500	—[c]	—	—	—	—	—	—
Senior subordinated debt	1,700	—	—	—	—	—	—	—
Junior subordinated debt	1,000	—	—	—	—	—	—	—
Equity	450	—	—	—	—	—	—	—
Long-term assets	(9,460)	(70)	(70)	(60)	(70)	(60)	(60)	(60)
Ending cash	170	160	200	260	220	170	110	(1,230)

EXHIBIT 1 (concluded)

	1979	1980	1981	1982	1983	1984	1985	1986
Amortization and depreciation								
10-year straight-line (S.L.) closing costs $200k..............	20	20	20	20	20	20	20	20
8-year 150% Alpha Plant write-up to $4,360k.........	350	817	664	539	438	356	289	235
8-year 150% South Plant write-up 1980 to $3,000k.........	100	75	563	457	371	302	245	199
8-year 150% new additions to plant.........	43	85	82	79	76	74	71	69
4-year S.L. Alpha noncompete $500k.........	—	125	125	125	125	—	—	—
3-year South noncompete $250k..	—	—	83	83	83	—	—	—
15-year S.L. Alpha franchises $640k.........	—	43	43	43	43	43	43	43
16-year S.L. South franchises $250k.........	—	—	16	16	16	16	16	16
Total.........	$513	$1,165	$1,596	$1,362	$1,172	$810	$684	$582

*Duncan Field is buying stock, liquidating the company (which makes him show recapture income and thus pay taxes) and then writing up the assets. The recapture income is shown only to compute taxes due; recapture income is not included in the calculation of cash flow.

APPENDIX: BACKGROUND MATERIAL ON THE CATV INDUSTRY IN 1978

Cable television originated in the United States in the early 1950s as a means of importing network (CBS, NBC, and ABC) television by microwave and/or coaxial cable transmission to areas which, for geographical and topographical reasons, could not receive off-air broadcasts. A typical system generally receives broadcast TV signals with an antenna mounted on a tall tower. These signals are then improved through a variety of amplifiers, signal processors, and electronic filters at the head end and then sent through the systems along a network of coaxial cable (trunk line) which is carried on existing telephone poles. A subscriber is then connected to the network with an inexpensive coaxial wire from his TV set (house drops).

The industry has grown enormously since its origins. By the end of 1977, over 3,911 systems served over 12.6 million subscribers with up to 32 channels of program variety, with expectations that as many as 20 million subscribers would be served by 1980. The industry has enjoyed a compounded annual growth rate of over 20 percent during the past 20 years.

FCC regulations, until quite recently, confined the construction of most CATV systems to areas or markets outside the so-called top 100 markets (essentially the areas within a 35-mile radius of the main post office of the 100 largest metropolitan areas in the United States). These systems that lie outside the top 100 markets are generally referred to as *classical systems,* that is, customers are willing to pay to be connected to the cable TV system because they will receive substantially more and better quality TV signals than are obtainable with ordinary household TV antennas. The ratio of paying subscribers to homes passed by cable is called *saturation* or *penetration* and is frequently used as a measure of a system's success as it will determine the revenue used per mile of plant that is generated. Generally, a system with about $200 of revenue per mile per month is barely able to pay its operating expenses, and thus its *operating cash flow* (revenues less direct operating expenses) is said to be zero. Since the incremental cost of serving additional customers is quite nominal, cash flow increases rapidly once saturation exceeds the system's break-even, and frequently systems that are generating $400 of revenue per mile per month are capable of converting half this amount into cash flow, which is largely available for debt service. A typical classical system achieves customer saturation of at least 50 percent within three years of operation and is thought to have the potential of 75 percent or greater saturation after about 7 to 10 years of operation. Because such a great portion of a mature cable system's operating financial inputs are fixed and determinable (subscriber rates, capital plant, and financing costs), classical systems represent credit risks that are probably more quantifiable than in any other industry except, perhaps, utilities.

The financial demands of the rapidly growing CATV industry have traditionally exceeded the industry's ability to fund internally. By 1976, the nation's 3,350 CATV systems supported $1.3 billion in debt, and capital expenditures for new and rebuilt plants are estimated to be $250 million annually. Traditional sources of industry debt financing have been equipment suppliers, commercial banks, and life insurance companies. It is estimated that the life insurance industry has committed approximately $500 million of debt funds to the CATV industry and that commercial banks have committed in excess of $550 million.

A significant recent development in the CATV industry has been the introduction of pay cable. There are two major types of pay cable packages that are in use today. A number of companies including Home Box Office, a subsidiary of Time, Inc., have contracted with film makers for the showing of various movies including many popular first-run movies. "Live" events such as sports are also made available to these companies. The movies and live events are conveyed to satellites from which they may be received by cable systems whose operators have purchased the right to show such premium programming to their subscribers. Once a basic CATV system is in place, the incremental capital equipment required to receive and distribute pay cable consists mainly of a large receiving dish or "earth station" and devices located at each viewer's home that can be programmed to block or allow passage of the pay cable signal (*traps* or *converters*). Earth stations cost roughly $20,000 to $50,000 (if not shared with other systems), and traps cost approximately $5 to $10 per subscriber.

As an alternative to this, many companies distribute Pay TV to their customers on a "stand-alone" basis. In a stand-alone situation, the cable company contracts for films and events through a booking agent. Films are delivered to the company and transmitted to customers directly from the company. Thus, no earth station is needed, and the capital expenditure involved is reduced to approximately $15,000.

HBO, or similar Pay packages, are generally offered to subscribers for a fee of approximately $7 to $9. Fifty percent of these Pay revenues generally flow to the Pay company, with 50 percent flowing to the cable company to cover overhead and profits.

Stand-alone packages are generally less expensive, costing the subscriber anywhere from $3 to $5, although some stand-alone packages offering extensive movies and events do cost more. Generally, 35 percent of Pay revenues flow to the film distributor, leaving the cable operator with 65 percent. There is, however, a monthly fixed cost associated with the mailing of films and the operation of the film transmitter, which must be covered in a stand-alone situation.

Case 2–4

Clarion Optical Co.

It was early September of 1983, and Jerry Stone and Iris Randal were having dinner and discussing their plans to purchase Clarion Optical Co., their current employer. They had decided to attempt to purchase Clarion almost two months ago. Since then, they had spent most of their time talking with potential financial backers and had learned a great deal about potential financing sources.

Now, they needed to make a decision about how to finance and structure the purchase of Clarion. They needed to resolve:

— How to structure the deal for the purchase of Clarion.

— What form(s) of legal organization to use.

— Whom to approach, for how much, and on what terms.

BACKGROUND

Clarion Optical was located outside of Atlanta, Georgia, and had been founded by Cyrus Atkins in 1946. Clarion began as a manufacturer of high-quality glass for optical uses and as a grinder and polisher of lenses for optical instruments. In the early 1970s, Clarion's chief engineer, Jerry Stone, had pushed Atkins, and Clarion, into the custom contact lens business (i.e., lenses for individuals who could not wear standard off-the-shelf products). This business had proved to be so profitable that Clarion had reached the point where it was once again a single-product company, having phased out of the optical instrument market. (See Exhibit 1 for most recent financial statements.)

Since Cyrus' gradual retirement from the business began in the mid-1970s, Stone had been president and had taken over more and more responsibility for the firm's operations.

This case was prepared by Michael J. Roberts under the direction of Howard H. Stevenson.

Harvard Business School case 9–384–120

In early 1983, Clarion's new chief engineer, and one of Stone's early pupils in the lab, Iris Randal, had come to Jerry with an idea for a new product line—implantable lenses for the human eye. The incidence of cataracts was on the rise and new surgical techniques had made the replacement of the human eye lens a commonplace procedure.

Iris had developed a new substance from which to make the lens, which was far less costly and created a better lens than existing technology. Jerry and Iris began developing a business plan to explore and capitalize on the opportunity.

THE SALE OF CLARION

Two months previously, Cyrus Atkins had told Jerry that he had decided that it was time to sell Clarion. Cyrus, a widower, was nearing 80 and had two older children who were successful and well-established professionals. Cyrus had amply provided for them in his large estate, of which his 100 percent ownership of Clarion represented only a part. His interest in Clarion was his last major illiquid holding, and Cyrus was convinced that he should sell the company and tidy up his estate.

Jerry expressed an immediate interest in purchasing the company, and Atkins was pleased at the prospect of Clarion remaining "in the family." He told Jerry that he would give him ample time to try to put together a financing package. Atkins said that he was willing to sell Clarion for 10 times its 1982 earnings of $200,000, or $2 million.

Jerry was convinced that the new implantable lens technology had great potential and was the key to Clarion's future success. He also had a great deal of respect for Iris's engineering and management abilities and decided that she should be part of the management team that attempted the buyout.

Jerry was convinced that the other key staff would remain on. After all, they would not be getting a new boss—he had been managing Clarion for over five years.

Jerry discussed the idea with her, and Iris was thrilled with the prospect of owning a piece of Clarion. She also had a great deal of confidence in the new lens technology and was excited to learn that Jerry planned to make this a keystone of his plan for the business. They raced to put together the money.

VALUING THE ASSETS

On the advice of a friend in the banking industry, Jerry and Iris took Clarion's balance sheet and attempted to determine the fair market value of Clarion's assets. A valuation was performed, and they were pleasantly surprised that this value exceeded book value and Atkins' asking price. (See Exhibit 2.)

— Land and Building: A 20-year-old, fully depreciated structure, the $200,000 figure on the books represented only the cost of the land. The building was in excellent shape and was owned and used exclusively by Clarion. The structure housed all manufacturing, shipping, and management. There was ample space for any contemplated expansion of the business. Jerry and Iris researched the market and determined that the fair market value of the structure was as follows:

- Land $250,000
- Building $750,000

— Equipment: Clarion's equipment was fairly new, but rapid depreciation had decreased its book value to $100,000. Jerry and Iris were convinced that it was worth $500,000.

— Inventory: Because of the custom nature of its work, Clarion kept large stocks of high-quality optical glass on hand. Much of this had been purchased a year or two ago on particularly favorable terms. Now, this $200,000 of book value inventory was worth $500,000.

— Accounts Receivable: Most of Clarion's customers were well established optical shops who paid their bills on time. The $300,000 book value of accounts receivable was an accurate reflection of their true worth.

— Cash: The cash, of course, was worth $200,000, and Jerry and Iris were convinced that $100,000 would give them sufficient working capital.

Having convinced themselves that Clarion's assets were indeed worth $2.5 million, Jerry and Iris set about investigating potential financing sources.

FINANCING THE PURCHASE

Jerry and Iris's business plan indicated that they would need an additional $1 million over the purchase price to fund the research and development effort required to get them into the lens business. This raised their "magic number" to at least $3.0 million. They then began investigating potential sources of this money.

— New England Pension Trust: Jerry and Iris contacted this tax-free pension fund, an extremely conservative financier. The trust indicated that they would be willing to lend up to 80 percent of the value of the land and building—a mortgage at 12 percent.

— Michael Grund: An extremely wealthy acquaintance of Jerry's, Michael had agreed to consider an investment of up to $250,000 if it showed an aftertax IRR of at least 30 percent. Michael was in the 50 percent tax bracket on income, and 20 percent on capital gains.

— Georgia Bank and Trust Co.:   A local bank, Georgia B&T had agreed to lend up to 80 percent of the book value of accounts receivable, and 40 percent of the book value of inventory, at 15 percent.

— Rebel Ventures: This local venture capital firm was excited by the venture and had agreed to give Jerry and Iris up to $3.5 million on any investment that showed a 60 percent pretax IRR. They would, however, require the management team to put up $40,000 of their own funds.

— Bank of Atlanta: The bank had agreed to lend either the company or Jerry and Iris personally up to $300,000 at 17 percent with Jerry and Iris's personal guarantees as security. While they each had little (about $20,000 each) in liquid assets, each had a tangible net worth of close to $250,000 due to their own and their spouses' investments in their separate homes.

— General Insurance Corporate Credit: The credit area of this large insurance company had agreed to purchase the existing equipment from Clarion for $300,000 and lease it back to Clarion for 5 years at $100,000 per year.

With this information in hand, they went to speak with two friends to ask for advice on how to structure the deal:

— Bill Lawrence, an old friend in the real estate business.
— Henry Adams, the trustee at the local bank.

Lawrence's Suggested Structure

Bill Lawrence suggested financing the deal in the following way:

— Have Grund buy the building and land in a separate transaction for $1 million, and then have Clarion rent it back from Grund (transaction described in Exhibit 3). He could:

  • Take an 80 percent mortgage from the bank @ 12 percent.
  • Keep the tax losses and cash flow for an investment of $200,000.
  • Clarion would agree to buy the building and land back at some price at the end of Year 7, in order to give Grund his required 30 percent return.

— Buy the rest of the company for $1 million and finance as follows:

• Excess cash	$100,000
• Borrow on accounts receivable	300,000
• Borrow on inventory	80,000
• Sale/leaseback of equipment	300,000
• Note/personal guarantee	220,000

This would permit Jerry and Iris to retain 100 percent of the equity. It did have its drawbacks though:

— Risk: It seemed as though there would be very little, if any, margin for error in their projections.

— R&D schedule: Without a major influx of venture capital, Jerry and Iris thought it would take three years to generate sufficient cash flow to perform the $1 million worth of R&D required. This would:

  • Delay Clarion's entry into the market.

  • Reduce their share when they did enter.

  • Make the market smaller in the early years because Clarion would not be out developing the market.
    (See Exhibit 4 for relative market scenarios.)

— Cost: Finally, when they did enter the market, they would not have sufficient funds flow to purchase equipment. This would require them to subcontract production and fulfillment (this firm would also finance working capital needs), which would raise COGS to 30 percent (10 points higher than the 20 percent COGS if they manufactured in-house).

— Salaries: Jerry, who was making $60K/year and Iris, making $40K/year would each take a salary cut to $20,000 per year until the business started generating cash.

Adams' Suggested Structure

Adams suggested that they finance the entire purchase with venture capital funds. This would obviously reduce their share of the equity, but would reduce the risk as well. This financing structure would have important implications:

— Investment: They would invest in the plant and equipment necessary to produce the lens, which would:

- Reduce the COGS to 20 percent of sales.
- Increase depreciation charges.

— Fixed charges would drop.

- No rent.
- No lease payments.
- No interest payments.

— Personal stake: They would each invest $20,000 of their own funds in the initial purchase of the company.

THE DECISION

Jerry and Iris knew that these proposals represented the two extreme ends of the financing spectrum, but they thought that running out the numbers would help them get a feel for what the important issues and trade-offs were.

They finished dessert and coffee and went back to the office to lay out all of their assumptions (see Exhibit 4) and crunch through the numbers.

EXHIBIT 1   Clarion Financials

Historical Financial Statements
Year Ended December 31, 1982
(in thousands of dollars)

Income Statement

Sales	$1,010
Cost of goods sold	300
Selling, general and administrative	100
Executive salaries...........	200
Operating income	$ 410
Depreciation.................	10
Net income..................	400
Taxes.......................	200
Profit after tax	$ 200

Balance Sheet

Cash........................	$ 200		
Accounts receivable.........	300		
Inventory....................	200		
Equipment	100		
Land and building	200	Owner's equity..............	$1,000
Total assets.................	$1,000	Total equity	$1,000

EXHIBIT 2   Balance Sheet Comparison (in thousands of dollars)

	Book Value	Appraised Value
Cash...............................	$ 200	$ 200
Accounts receivable...............	300	300
Inventory..........................	200	500
Equipment	100	500
Land and building	200	1,000
Total assets.......................	$1,000	$2,500

EXHIBIT 3   Real Estate Transaction

Assumptions
—Mortgage: 25 years
$800,000
12%
Constant payment of $102,000 per annum

—Amortization schedule: ($000)

Year	1	2	3	4	5	6	7
• Interest payment	96.0	95.3	94.5	93.6	92.6	91.4	90.2
• Principal payment	6.0	6.7	7.5	8.4	9.4	10.6	11.8

—Principal value of mortgage outstanding at end of Year 7 equals $740,000.

Real Estate Cash Flows
(in thousands of dollars)

Year	1	2	3	4	5	6	7
Rent...............	$165.0	$173.0	$182.0	$191.0	$200.0	$211.0	$221.0
Maintenance	40.0	41.0	42.0	44.0	45.0	46.0	48.0
Taxes..............	25.0	25.0	25.0	25.0	25.0	25.0	25.0
Net operating income	100.0	107.0	114.0	122.0	130.0	140.0	148.0
Finance payment...	102.0	102.0	102.0	102.0	102.0	102.0	102.0
Pretax cash flow....	(2.0)	5.0	12.0	20.0	28.0	38.0	46.0
+ Amortization.....	6.0	6.7	7.5	8.4	9.4	10.6	11.8
− Depreciation	150.0	120.0	96.0	76.8	61.4	49.0	39.2
= Taxable income ..	(146.0)	(108.3)	(76.5)	(48.4)	(23.0)	0.5	18.5
+ Tax benefit/(cost)	73.0	54.1	38.2	24.2	11.5	(.2)	(9.2)
= Aftertax cash flow	71.0	59.1	50.2	44.2	39.5	37.8	36.8

Note: Finance payment is a level stream that includes both interest and principal. Amortization (principal repayment) must therefore be added back to pretax cash flow to arrive at a taxable income figure.

EXHIBIT 3   (*concluded*)

Cash Flows on Sale of Building and Land
Sale transaction at assumed prices of $1,000,000 and $1,100,000

Sale	$1,000,000	$1,100,000
− Net book value	407,600	407,600
Gain on sale	$ 592,400	$ 692,400
Accelerated depreciation taken	$ 592,400	$ 592,400
− Straight-line figure	525,000	525,000
Excess depreciation over straight line	$ 67,400	$ 67,400
× 50% tax rate	33,700	33,700

Calcula-tion of tax liabi-lity			
	Gain on sale	$ 592,400	$ 692,400
	− Excess depreciation	67,400	67,400
	Taxable gain	$ 525,000	$ 625,000
	Capital gains tax at 20% rate	$ 105,000	$ 125,000
	+ Excess depreciation tax	33,700	33,700
	Total tax liability	$ 138,700	$ 158,700

Sale price	$1,000,000	$1,100,000
− Tax liability	138,700	158,700
− Mortgage balance	740,000	740,000
Cash out	$ 121,300	$ 201,300

EXHIBIT 4   Scenario Cash Flows

Assumptions
1. *Sales* (see Schedule A, attached)
   —All Debt: They thought that under this scenario, it would take three years to fund the $1 million of R&D required out of cash flow. In this case, Clarion could not enter the implantable lens market until Year 4, at which point they could only attain 40 percent market share; and the market would be smaller, because they would not have been out developing it.
   —All Equity: Clarion could finish the R&D in one year and enter the market in Year 2. They could obtain a larger market share and grow the entire market.
   —Both: In either case, sales of the existing contact lens product line would stagnate at whatever level they were at when implantable lens sales began.
2. *COGS*
   —All Debt: Cost of implantable lens equal to 30 percent sales, due to subcontracting.
   —All Equity: Cost of implantable lens equal to 20 percent of sales.
   —Both: Cost of existing contact lens product equal to 30 percent sales.
3. *SG&A ($000)*

Year:	1	2	3	4	5	6	7
—All Debt	108	120	129	500	600	700	800
—All Equity	107	500	600	700	800	900	1000

4. *Executive Salaries ($000)*

Year:	1	2	3	4	5	6	7
—All Debt	40	40	40	200	300	400	500
—All Equity	100	100	100	200	300	400	500

5. *R&D*
   $1 million required to complete R&D on implantable lens.
   —All Debt: Funded out of cash as available; Jerry and Iris assumed that this could be completed in three years.
   —All Equity: Funded in Year 1 out of venture capital.
6. *Depreciation*
   —All Debt: Equal to zero in all years: No plant, equipment, building to depreciate.
   —All Equity: Depreciation on existing building and equipment equal to $150,000 each year for seven years. Depreciation on new equipment purchased is calculated on a straight-line basis over a five-year life, beginning in the year of actual purchase (i.e., if $1 million worth of equipment purchased in Year 1, then $200,000 taken in Years 1 through 5). (See *Investment*, line 13, for investment required.)

EXHIBIT 4 (continued)
SCHEDULE A
Sales Scenarios (in millions of dollars)

All Debt

| Year | Contact Lens Sales | Implantable Lens Sales | | | Total |
		Market Size	Clarion Share	Resultant Sales	
1	1.10	1.0	0	0	1.10
2	1.28	2.5	0	0	1.28
3	1.60	5.0	0	0	1.60
4	1.60	10.0	40%	4	5.60
5	1.60	20.0	40%	8	9.60
6	1.60	40.0	40%	16	17.60
7	1.60	65.0	40%	26	27.60

All Equity

| Contact Lens Sales | Implantable Lens Sales | | | Total |
	Market Size	Clarion Share	Resultant Sales	
1.1	1.0	0	0	1.1
1.1	5.0	60%	3	4.1
1.1	10.0	60%	6	7.1
1.1	20.0	60%	12	13.1
1.1	40.0	60%	24	25.1
1.1	60.0	60%	36	37.1
1.1	80.0	60%	48	49.1

EXHIBIT 4   (*continued*)

7. *Interest*
   —All Debt:
   - $300,000 borrowed against accounts receivable is outstanding over the entire seven years, at 15 percent per annum. No principal repayments made.
   - $80,000 borrowed against inventory is outstanding over the entire seven years, at 15 percent per annum. No principal repayments made.
   - $220,000 note, personally guaranteed is outstanding over five years, principal and interest paid according to following schedule.

Year	1	2	3	4	5
Interest	38	32	26	19	10
Principal	31	37	43	50	59

   —All Equity: No interest charges.
8. *Lease Payments*
   —All Debt: Lease payments on machinery are $100,000 per annum for five years, at which time ownership reverts to Clarion.
   —All Equity: No lease payments.
9. *Rent*
   —All Debt: As shown in Exhibit 3.
   —All Equity: No rent payments.
10. *Maintenance and Real Estate Taxes*
    —All Debt: No maintenance expenses or taxes.
    —All Equity: As shown in Exhibit 3.
11. *Taxes:*   50 percent of income. Assume that losses are offset against following year's income (i.e., if Clarion has losses of $200,000 in Year 1 and pretax profit of $1 million in Year 2, income tax in Year 2 is calculated on a pretax base of $800,000).
12. *Depreciation:*   (See line 6)
13. *Investment*
    —All Debt: Purchase of building in Year 7 at price required to give 30 percent return.
    —All Equity: Annual investment required in ($000)

Year	1	2	3	4	5	6	7
• Working Capital	63	600	600	1,200	2,400	2,400	2,400
• Equipment	1,000	1,000	2,000	4,000	8,000	12,000	15,000

14. *Principal Repayment*
    —All Debt: On $220,000 personally guaranteed note only; see above under *Interest.*
    —All Equity: None.
15. *Terminal Value:*   Assume that the company is sold at the end of Year 7 for 10 × Year 7 aftertax earnings under both scenarios.

EXHIBIT 4   (*concluded*)

16. *Other:*   In addition, they realized that they needed to make other
    assumptions in order to judge the two scenarios.
    —Assume Jerry and Iris's personal investment in business as follows:
    • All Debt: Investment of 0 in Year 0 plus $60,000 in "lost salary" in
      each of Years 1 through 3.
    • All Equity: Investment of $40,000 in Year 0.
    —Calculate cash flows to Jerry and Iris *jointly* (i.e., do not make any
    assumptions about how equity, investment, or cash flows are divided
    between the two parties).
    —Assume that in the equity scenario, only return occurs via sale of
    equity at end of Year 7—no dividends paid or other distributions
    made.
    —Assume that in the debt scenario, free cash flow is taken out at end of
    each year, including the end of Year 7.
    —Calculate flows and returns to Jerry, Iris, and Rebel Ventures on a
    prepersonal tax basis (i.e., include taxes at the corporate level in your
    calculations, but *do not* include any personal taxes on dividends or
    distributions out of Clarion). Also, do not include Jerry and Iris's
    salaries as part of the cash outflows in calculating returns.
    —Include the price of the building repurchase in Year 7 as an
    investment in that year in the debt scenario.
    —In the all debt scenario, assume that all available cash is spent on
    R&D until the $1 million project is complete; you must "plug" the
    figure for R&D for each year (i.e., free cash flow should equal zero in
    years where R&D project is ongoing).
    —Assume Rebel Ventures will invest whatever cash is required to keep
    Clarion cash positive up to its stated $3.5 million limit.

Viscotech, Inc.

Kenneth Jones, president of Viscotech, walked through the lobby of the Park Tower Building and headed toward a small restaurant near Chicago's business district. He needed some time away from the office, time to ponder the difficult situation in which he found himself. It was March 1984, and only seven months ago, Jones had left his position with a large pharmaceutical firm to become Viscotech's president. Stock, options, and a hefty salary increase had made the future seem bright. Now, all that seemed to be slipping away.

Jones had just come from a meeting with an attorney, Paul Benjamin, who had informed Jones that Viscotech might have committed violations of U.S. securities laws. Jones had to evaluate this information in light of the entire chain of events that had led up to that morning's meeting with Benjamin. As he considered his predicament, he realized that he needed to evaluate both Viscotech's and his own exposure to a potential SEC violation.

VISCOTECH

Viscotech was incorporated in 1977 by Dr. Samuel Evans, a surgeon and professor at the Midwestern Medical School; Louis Brown, a research scientist at the Chicago Institute of Technology; Dr. Harold Stein, a nutritional specialist at the Midwestern Medical School; and Melvin O'Connor, an accountant and attorney in the Chicago area.

This case was prepared by Michael J. Roberts and Richard E. Floor under the direction of Howard H. Stevenson.

The company was founded in order to design, develop, and market a device that could measure the viscosity of saliva. It had long been known that this type of analysis of saliva could help physicians assess nutritional inadequacies in patients.

Between 1977 and 1982, the company had spent almost $500,000 pursuing its research agenda. These funds had been obtained from the company's founders in the form of debt and equity.

By late 1982, Viscotech had succeeded in obtaining several patents that covered the core technology used in the device. Viscotech had focused its efforts on developing its first product, the Doctor's Office Device. This device would be simple, easy to use, and would allow doctors to perform a comprehensive nutritional analysis in their offices. In addition, the technology had broader applications in the feeding and breeding of cattle and swine.

The announcement of the device had received a great deal of favorable attention in the medical press. By the end of 1982, Viscotech had developed a working prototype of the device which was ready for more extensive clinical testing and subsequent submission to the Food and Drug Administration for approval.

1983—THE NEED FOR CAPITAL

In early 1983, it became clear to Viscotech's principals that the company would require another infusion of cash in order to:

— Complete testing and receive FDA approval.
— Develop engineering and manufacturing specifications.
— Research new applications for the technology.

In April of 1983, a group of physicians who were friends of Viscotech's founders indicated that they were interested in investing in the venture. At about the same time, O'Connor had been in touch with the venture capital community seeking funds for Viscotech. At a meeting in late April, the four founders decided to pursue the raising of capital from other acquaintances in the medical community because the venture firms were offering too meager a price for an equity investment.

At this point, O'Connor agreed to proceed with the raising of funds in this manner. In order to protect the founders, he thought it prudent to raise money with a very carefully drawn offering circular. However, because his schedule was quite full with other business commitments, O'Connor knew that he would be unable to prepare such a document for several months.

THE MEDICAL INVESTMENT FUND TRUST

Because of these constraints and the fact that Viscotech needed money quickly, O'Connor suggested that funds be raised through another vehicle—the Medical Investment Fund Trust (MIFT). MIFT could then invest the money in Viscotech, and then Viscotech could spend these funds. Later that year, an offering circular would be presented, and each investor given the option to withdraw and receive his or her funds back. If investors chose to subscribe, they would agree to exchange their investment in MIFT for Viscotech shares.

O'Connor was confident that the trust offered a means of raising money on an interim basis, while avoiding the final commitment until the offering circular was issued. As such, the structure was similar to an arrangement O'Connor and Viscotech had used several years earlier to raise funds.

It was decided that investors who advanced funds through MIFT would receive a certificate representing shares in MIFT. MIFT, in turn, would be granted an option on shares of Viscotech. They would attempt to raise $800,000 in 100 units of $8,000 each. Each unit would represent a claim on 0.1 percent of Viscotech stock.

In May 1983, O'Connor drew up the trust instrument and a brief description of MIFT for potential investors (see Exhibit 1). This package contained information on Viscotech which had previously been made public. Prior to distributing the MIFT package, the company raised $100,000 from six relatives and friends of the principals to meet its needs during the interim.

Beginning in May, and continuing throughout the summer, acquaintances of Viscotech's principals advanced funds to MIFT. The funds were routinely forwarded to O'Connor's office and disbursed by him.

As part of the financing effort, Viscotech conducted a series of informational seminars for friends and acquaintances of the principals. These discussions centered around the technology, the history of the company, and potential markets for the company's devices. No formal offers were made at these seminars, nor were there any discussions of price. Many of the individuals who were present, however, did subsequently invest.

In August, O'Connor began to realize that his schedule was not going to be free for quite some time. Therefore, he contacted a friend of his, Leonard Atkins, an experienced attorney with the Chicago firm of Dewey & White. O'Connor informed Atkins of the MIFT arrangement and told Atkins that he wanted him to draw up an offering circular to close the MIFT financing. Atkins suggested that Viscotech undertake a private offering, but O'Connor said that he would prefer to have the

SEC review any materials. Accordingly, they decided to attempt to raise funds through a Regulation A offering. This plan was approved at the annual shareholders' meeting in mid-August, and Atkins was given instructions to proceed.

KENNETH JONES

Later that August, Viscotech hired Ken Jones as its president. The original principals were able to spend only a portion of their time on Viscotech because of their medical and research responsibilities. In addition, as the product got closer to market, the principals felt the need for an individual with business experience.

Jones had graduated from the U.S. Naval Academy, and subsequent to his sea duty had attended the Midwest Business School. He had worked for a major international pharmaceutical firm as a product manager for four years before joining Viscotech. Jones was given 1,620 shares of Viscotech, options on further shares, and a salary of $65,000 per year.

Jones did not become heavily involved in the financing efforts because most of the potential investors were acquaintances of the founders. He did understand the MIFT arrangement, however, and understood from O'Connor that Atkins had cleared this vehicle for raising funds. Jones did attend and speak at several of the informational seminars, and he was briefed by Atkins on what to say. Specifically, Atkins told him to be wary of making statements that could be interpreted as "promises about Viscotech's future performance."

During the fall, Jones met with Atkins and O'Connor several times regarding the Regulation A offering. Jones edited several drafts of the offering circular. During this process, Atkins was supplied with Viscotech's financial statements prepared by O'Connor, which showed the liability for stock subscriptions through MIFT and detailed the expenditures of funds received. At one point, Jones asked Atkins how MIFT would be treated, and Atkins responded by saying, "We don't need to talk about MIFT."

By early December of 1983, $776,000 had been raised by MIFT from 34 investors. By February, the Regulation A offering circular was in draft form. Atkins had prepared the material for submission to the SEC. The principals decided to send the material off in early March.

THE SEC ISSUE

The last weekend in February, Ken casually mentioned the financing plans to a friend at a neighborhood party. This friend, an attorney with the prestigious local firm of Cole & Eggers, thought that something sounded a bit odd. He suggested that Ken see one of his colleagues, Paul Benjamin, an expert on securities law. Ken made arrangements to see Benjamin during the first week of March and sent him a draft of the circular.

Jones explained the events of the past months to Benjamin, and they reviewed a copy of the circular. The attorney felt that the use of MIFT as a vehicle to insulate Viscotech was not effective, and that both Jones and Viscotech were exposed to SEC charges arising out of the manner in which MIFT had raised its funds. He recommended that Jones "come clean" and go to the SEC. Benjamin felt that this would show Jones's good faith and limit his own personal exposure to SEC charges. In addition, he advocated "freezing" all existing funds in MIFT as a further show of good faith. Viscotech could then raise its funds with a Rule 505 offering that required notifying the SEC but did not require SEC approval. Benjamin drafted a version of this offering, which appears as Exhibit 2, and which gives investors the option of withdrawing their investment. Benjamin also stated that the company would have to hire an individual to prepare the required two years of audited financial statements since O'Connor had had a financial interest in Viscotech while his firm was involved in the company's accounting.

WHAT TO DO

Jones's head was spinning when he left Benjamin's office. He wanted to do what was legal and ethically right. Yet, he also knew how desperately Viscotech needed funds to gear up for manufacturing and marketing of the Doctor's Office Device. Going to the SEC seemed to minimize his personal risk, but could implicate the rest of the company's principals and would surely harm the company's chances of raising money. Viscotech could go ahead with the Rule 505 offering, which merely required notifying the SEC. Benjamin said that there was a low probability that the SEC would request further documentation or the actual offering circular. However, in the event that the SEC did request the offering circular, Benjamin advised that it be very conservatively drafted, like the version excerpted in Exhibit 2. Ken felt, however, that this draft was *so* conservative that many investors would be likely to take recission (i.e., request the return of their investment) if they received this document.

Ken didn't know what to do. Any course that would successfully raise the funds Viscotech needed seemed to involve a good deal of risk.

EXHIBIT 1   MIFT Offering Circular

Confidential Investment Memorandum

Medical Investment Fund Trust

The Medical Investment Fund Trust (MIFT) has been formed as a vehicle to raise funds for Viscotech, Inc. Each $8,000 investment in MIFT will represent a claim on 200 (roughly 0.1 percent) of Viscotech's shares. MIFT seeks to raise $800,000 in this manner.

In the near future, Viscotech, Inc., will distribute an offering memorandum to those individuals who have invested in MIFT. At that time, any investor who desires to do so shall have the right to sell his/her MIFT shares back to the company for the amount of the original investment.

The Business

Viscotech was formed in 1977 by Dr. Samuel Evans, Midwestern Medical School; Louis Brown, Chicago Institute of Technology; Dr. Harold Stein, Midwestern Medical School; and Melvin O'Connor, Esq., O'Connor & O'Connor. The company has spent $500,000 of its founders' funds perfecting a technology that can assess nutritional inadequacies in patients through an analysis of saliva.

Patents

The company has filed and been granted 15 patents, which cover the core aspects of Viscotech's technology. In addition, the company has filed for 63 additional patents, which have yet to be ruled on. These patent applications have been made in 20 countries.

Products

Viscotech plans to produce the following devices:

— Doctor's Office Device: A complex instrument capable of analyzing deficiencies in a patient with respect to vitamins, minerals, blood sugar, amino acids, hormones, and trace elements.
— Home Device: A simpler instrument that will enable individuals to easily assess their own vitamin, mineral, and blood sugar levels.
— Farm Animal Device: A simple instrument that will allow breeders of cattle and swine to determine the optimal feed content for their animals.

With the tremendous increase in individuals' concern with their own nutritional well-being, the company is confident that these instruments will be extraordinarily successful. Imagine being able to take a simple test, using saliva, to determine the adequacy of vitamin and mineral intake, and to make dietary adjustments accordingly.

Markets

The markets for these products offer tremendous potential. In addition to lucrative U.S. markets, incredible potential exists in Third World markets where malnutrition is a problem. Individuals will now be able to test undernourished people to determine the precise therapeutic treatment. The government of India has indicated a strong interest in making a grant of $250,000 to Viscotech for the purpose of developing such

EXHIBIT 1   (*continued*)

an instrument for its use. The company currently plans to introduce the following devices:

The Doctor's Office Device: There is no other product available that performs these tests with the ease, accuracy, speed, and inexpensive price of the Viscotech instrument.

— Projected Potential Market: The potential market is projected to be doctors dealing regularly with patients with nutritional problems:

	Nutritionists	G.P.s	Total
United States	14,000 of 24,000	6,000 of 56,000	20,000 of 80,000
Europe	10,000 of 20,000	5,000 of 70,000	15,000 of 90,000
Rest of world	4,000 (est.)	1,000 (est.)	5,000
Total potential market			40,000

— Average Instrument Usage
  • 6 tests per patient per month, or 75 tests per year.
  • 4 ongoing patients per doctor.
  • 75 × 4 = 300 tests per doctor per year.

— Sales Price
  Instruments $3,000.00 each
  Disposables $ 2.40 per test

Market introduction is projected for the third quarter of 1985 in both the United States and Europe. First year projected sales of 250 instruments represents a less than 1 percent penetration of the potential market, with second year sales of 400 instruments reaching a cumulative penetration of 1.9 percent.

Viscotech plans to initially distribute the doctor's instrument through regional dealers and manufacturers' reps in the major metropolitan areas where the primary market is concentrated. Given the large number of potential customers and the need to demonstrate the instrument to each of these potential customers, economics dictate that Viscotech make use of existing sales and distribution channels into these targeted doctors' offices. Viscotech will have a small, highly qualified in-house sales team to manage this distributor network. Viscotech will also handle all product services directly.

The Home Device: This device will allow individuals to safely and easily sample their own saliva to determine the levels of key nutritional variables: vitamins, minerals, and blood sugar levels.

Viscotech has developed working prototypes of the saliva collection device and the measuring device that comprise the Home Device System. Both components are significantly different from those used with the Doctor's Office Device.

At present the company is having a prototype mold constructed for the saliva collection device with a capability to produce 3,000–5,000 parts. Availability is scheduled for mid-September, after which we will begin the first in-use testing of the Home Device.

EXHIBIT 1   (*continued*)

We estimate that design finalization will take 1–2 years and market introduction 2–3 years.

— Projected Potential Market: the potential market is projected to be men and women in the 15–45 age group that are currently using vitamins, dietary supplements, or have a nutritional problem. This represents an immediate worldwide market of about 100 million individuals:

United States	25 million
Europe	34 million
Japan	12 million
Rest of world	30 million
	101 million

— Average Instrument Usage: Minimum average of 5 tests per month or 70 tests per year.
— Sales Price

Instrument	$45.00
Disposables	$ .90

— Estimated Manufacturing Cost

Instrument	$10.00
Disposables	$ .20

— Total Potential Dollar Market

Annual disposable sales	7 billion tests	@ $ 0.90 = $6.0 billion
One time instruments sales	100 million	@ $45.00 = $4.5 billion

— Sales Projections: Market introduction in the United States is projected for the second quarter of 1987. Projecting sales in such an enormous market is at best difficult. If a 1 percent share of the potential market were achieved during the first five years, end-user purchases of disposables would be $60 million annually, and instrument sales would average $9 million annually. The company feels that it is possible to achieve a 20 percent share of the potential market during the next 5–10 years.

— Marketing and Distribution: An arrangement with a very large multinational consumer marketing company appears to provide the most logical and reasonable path to the marketplace. Such a company could provide both the dollar investment and expertise required to successfully develop sales of the Home Device. Additionally it could provide indemnity for Viscotech against any product liability claims.

Discussions with International Pharmaceutical have taken place over the last six months and have developed to an advanced point. International has the broadest line of any company in the field and is part of a premier, highly successful company in the health care industry. International has made two offers in writing (June 8 and July 12), and Viscotech has made one counterproposal in writing (July 31).

The Farm Animal Device: The instrument system proposed for use by doctors in managing patients is, conceptually, equally applicable for increasing the productivity of food animals such as swine, dairy cattle, and beef cattle.

The objective is to develop an effective instrument system and verify its feasibility for improving the rate of weight addition in swine and

EXHIBIT 1   (*continued*)

cattle. This development process entails empirically modifying the doctor's instrument system to accommodate the saliva of swine and cattle.

Swine and cattle were chosen because they appeared to offer the greatest immediate commercial opportunity.

— Both are maintained and bred primarily in large confined herds, which facilitates management and recordkeeping.
— Both represent large potential markets in terms of numbers of annual breedings.
— Swine represent the largest per capita consumed meat in the world.

Dairy Cattle: Projected Potential Market: The potential market is projected to be only farms with over 50 milk cows, where the payback on an instrument system would be very high.

— Projected Potential Market: Farms with over 50 milk cows.
  United States—50,000 farms out of total 588,000 farms with milk cows
      These farms have 4.8 million of the total 12.5 million milk cows in the United States. Our potential market in the United States is, therefore, 8.5 percent of total farms that have 38.5 percent of total milk cows.
  Europe—estimated 40,000 farms have 5 million of the over 50 million milk cows in Europe.
  Rest of world—conservative estimate 10,000 farms.
  Total market potential—100,000 farms.

— Average Instrument Usage
  • 11 tests per cow per year.
  • 144 cows per farm, which assumes 50 percent of sales will be to farms with 50–100 cows and 50 percent to farms with over 100 cows. This assumption results in penetration of market potential being greater for disposables than instruments.
  • 11 × 144 = 1584 tests per farm per year.

— Sales Price
  Instrument $2,500 each
  Disposables $2 per test

Viscotech is currently funding a research program with dairy cattle at the University of the Midwest.

Market introduction is projected for the third quarter of 1985. First-year sales of 210 instruments represent a less than .5 percent penetration of the potential U.S. market. Second-year sales of 525 instruments brings the cumulative penetration to .7 percent of the total world market.

Distributor arrangements for sale to the dairy industry have not yet been set up.

Swine: Projected Potential Market: The potential market is projected to be only larger operations that average 250 sows. The animals are in a confined controlled environment, and the economic payback of an instrument system would be very high.

— Projected Potential Market
  United States—8,000 operations averaging 250 sows in confinement, which account for 40 percent of total 5 million sows in the United States.

EXHIBIT 1 (*concluded*)

Europe—estimated 4,000 operations accounting for 25 percent of 4 million sows.
Rest of world—estimated 2,000 operations accounting for 10 percent of 5 million sows.
— Average Instrument Usage
1. 19 tests per sow.
2. 250 sows per farm.
3. 19 × 250 = 4,750 tests per farm per year.

Note: This averages 13 tests per day, meaning larger operations of 400–600 sows would definitely need two or three instruments for scheduling purposes. Instrument sales are projected conservatively at one per operation, but with replacement sales beginning after five years of heavy usage.

— Sales Price

Instrument	$2,500 each
Disposables	$1.25 per test

Note: Economics of sow breeding require lower cost per test to provide attractive payback. Competitively, lower disposables' price can be justified based on much higher volume of testing per farm as compared to dairy cattle. Gross margin will be reduced significantly, but still remain attractively above 40 percent.

Viscotech has recently signed a joint R&D/Distribution agreement with National Swine Breeders, Inc. This company is the largest producer of hybrid breeding stock in the United States.

Market introduction is projected for the second quarter of 1985. First-year sales of 100 units represents a 1.25 percent penetration of the potential U.S. market. Second-year sales of 200 instruments brings the cumulative penetration to 2.1 percent of the potential world market.

Projected Income Statements ($000)

	1986	1987	1988
Sales.................................	$2,726	$7,629	$23,400
Commissions (33%)..................	908	2,391	7,722
Cost of goods sold..................	661	1,974	5,850
Gross profit.........................	1,157	3,261	9,828
Research and development.........	352	438	512
Sales and marketing...............	283	441	742
General and administrative........	511	630	803
Interest.............................	77	65	0
Depreciation........................	12	19	28
Profit before tax....................	(78)	1,668	7,743
Tax.................................	—	—*	3,716
Profit after tax.....................	(78)	1,668	4,027

*Due to prior losses and tax credits.

EXHIBIT 2   Viscotech Investment Memorandum

Confidential Investment Memorandum and Recission Offer

20,000 SHARES OF COMMON STOCK

This Confidential Investment Memorandum has been prepared in connection with the offering by Viscotech, Inc. (the "Company") of up to 20,000 shares of its Common Stock, $.10 par value, at $40 per share. The minimum subscription is 100 shares ($4,000).

This memorandum presents background information, has been prepared for the confidential use of private investors, and is not to be reproduced in whole or part. This offering is not made pursuant to any registration statement of Notification under Regulation A filed with the Securities and Exchange Commission, and the securities offered hereby are offered for investment only to qualifying recipients of this offering. The Company claims an exemption from the registration requirements of the Securities Act of 1933, as amended under Section 4(2) of that Act and Rule 505 thereunder.

Nothing set forth herein is intended to represent or in any manner imply that the stock offered hereby has been approved, recommended, or guaranteed by the Government of the United States or of any state, or by any of the agencies of either.

THE SECURITIES OFFERED HEREBY ARE HIGHLY SPECULATIVE AND INVOLVE A HIGH DEGREE OF RISK. PURCHASE OF THESE SECURITIES SHOULD BE CONSIDERED ONLY BY THOSE PERSONS WHO CAN AFFORD TO SUSTAIN A TOTAL LOSS OF THEIR INVESTMENT. SEE "RISK FACTORS."

THIS OFFERING INVOLVES IMMEDIATE SUBSTANTIAL DILUTION FROM THE OFFERING PRICE. FOR FURTHER INFORMATION CONCERNING THIS AND OTHER SPECIAL RISK FACTORS, SEE "RISK FACTORS" AND "DILUTION."

The offering price has been determined arbitrarily, and bears no relationship to the book value per share. Since all such shares must be acquired for investment only, no market for the shares offered hereby will arise, and no sales of such stock will be permitted in the future except pursuant to an effective registration statement or an exemption from registration under the Securities Act of 1933, as amended. Hence, the Company can offer no assurance that the stock will be salable at any time when the subscriber desires, or that the stock will be able to be resold at any time at or near the offering price.

The offering of the common stock is not underwritten. The Company plans to sell shares of common stock by personal solicitation or otherwise, through efforts of its distributors and officers. Such persons will receive no compensation other than reimbursement of out of pocket expenses incurred by them in connection with the sale. Such officers may be deemed "underwriters" as that term is defined in the Securities Act of 1933, as amended.

Unless 50 percent of the shares offered hereby are sold within 90 days from the date hereof, all subscribers' funds will be returned to them without interest or deduction.

–1–

EXHIBIT 2   (*continued*)

TABLE OF CONTENTS

Risk Factors

Viscotech, Inc. (the "Company") was incorporated under the laws of the State of Illinois on December 17, 1977, to do research on, and to develop, instruments and devices to measure precisely and accurately the amount of, and the variations in, elasticity and viscosity (known as viscoelasticity) of saliva in humans and other mammals. It has not yet marketed any such instruments or devices.

Prospective investors should be informed of the following risk factors involved in this offering:

(A) Insolvency:
   1. To date, the Company has been engaged only in research and development, has generated no sales, and is, consequently, currently insolvent.
   2. A substantial portion of this offering has already been raised and the funds have been used to pay current obligations. (See "Use of Proceeds.")
   3. Even if the offering is fully subscribed, unless operations soon become profitable, or the Company raises additional funds elsewhere, investors will stand to lose their entire investment.
(B) Dilution:
   In the event all the shares offered hereby are sold, those persons who purchase these shares will incur an immediate substantial dilution in the book value of $37.34 per share from the offering price of $40 per

EXHIBIT 2   (*continued*)

share while the book value of the presently outstanding shares will increase from minus $2.52 per share to $2.66 per share solely by reason of the proceeds raised through the offering.

(C) No Operating History:
The Company has no operating history, and there is no assurance that it will operate profitably.

(D) No Present Product Market:
The Company has no contracts or commitments from potential users of its products and can give no assurance that the products will be marketed successfully.

(E) Limited Personnel:
The Company has only three full-time employees, a Chief Executive Officer, and two Engineers. The development of the devices it intends to market has been, and will continue to be, of an indeterminate time, dependent upon part-time efforts of its founders, and of outside consultants.

(F) Food and Drug Administration Approval:
The Food and Drug Administration has not approved the Company's complete instrument system for sale, and no assurance can be given that it, or any other governmental agency with jurisdiction, will do so.

(G) Use of Proceeds for Research and Development in Other Areas:
A significant amount of the Company's funds will be used for further research and development in the fields of animal husbandry, consumer products, industrial products, and possibly other areas, and no assurance can be given that this research and development will be successful.

(H) Need for Additional Funding:
The Company believes that it will be necessary to secure funding in addition to that offered pursuant hereto in order to enable the Company to achieve its objectives. The Company will seek to raise such additional funds through any one or more of loans, grants, or additional equity. Should the Company seek to raise additional equity, it may be required to do so at a price per share less than that being offered pursuant hereto, in which case investors will suffer a dilution in the value of their shares. The Company can give no assurance that such additional funding will be available to it on any basis.

(I) Competition:
Many companies with resources far greater than those available to the Company are involved in the field of nutrition and may be able to compete with the Company.

(J) Dividends:
The Company has never paid dividends, and does not expect to do so in the foreseeable future.

(K) No Cumulative Voting:
The common stock of this Company does not have cumulative voting rights. Hence, the holders of more than 50 percent of the shares voting for the election of directors may elect all the directors if they so choose. Since the present management holds more than 50 percent of the shares to be outstanding, it will be in a position to reelect itself as directors.

EXHIBIT 2 (*continued*)

Business

It has long been known that the viscoelasticity of saliva decreases in the event of nutritional deficiency. To date, however, to the knowledge of the Company, there is no instrument or method capable of accurately measuring this decrease at a reasonable cost and evaluating the extent and cause of nutritional inadequacy. Such measurements can be of significant aid to doctors in diagnosing the problems of overweight, obese, or anorexic individuals and to breeders of such animals as cattle and swine. The instruments that the Company has developed are, it believes, capable of making such measurements on minute quantities of saliva, which consists of a variety of nonhomogeneous materials, without homogenizing them or otherwise destroying their integrity. The instruments developed by the Company do not rely on hormonal, chemical, or other ingested material, nor on any implanted devices. Rather, a sample of saliva is extracted and placed on a grid in the instrument, which is capable of determining the exact amount of viscoelasticity present in the sample.

Food and Drug Administration approval is a necessary prerequisite to the marketing of the Company's products for human medical use in the United States. Approval has been granted for the Company's saliva aspirator. Application for approval of the Company's Doctor's Device (the first major product that the Company intends to market) will be submitted subsequent to the completion of clinical trials presently in progress. There can be no assurance that approval will be forthcoming. A delay in the grant of such approval, or the attachment thereto of conditions, or the denial thereof, might have a serious, adverse effect on the Company.

Although the Company has developed prototype machines and other products for use by doctors, clinics, and other medical personnel, such machines have not been distributed, and so their effectiveness in the field remains unproven. The Company has distributed a limited number of its products to users who are not associated with the Company, in order to secure from them reports as to results and other comments. The Company cannot guarantee that such reports or comments will be favorable.

In addition, the Company is planning to contract for the production of several hundred Doctor's Devices to be available for sale to doctors, clinics, and hospitals for delivery commencing in 1984. Although the Company has had negotiations with manufacturers, no commitments or contracts have been made. In consequence, no assurance can be given that the machines can be produced within the projected time and at a favorable price, or that if produced, a sufficient number can be sold to offset the investment.

The Company is presently attempting to develop a device at a commercially reasonable price that would enable a person to sample his own saliva and determine his own nutritional levels. There can be no assurance that its efforts will be successful within a reasonable time and at reasonable cost, or that in any event, Food and Drug Administration approval will be granted, or that such a device would have the degree of consumer acceptance necessary for economic viability.

The Company also has research projects planned to measure bronchial secretions, synovial fluid, spinal fluid, serum, and meconium, any

EXHIBIT 2   *(continued)*

or all of which may be of importance in other branches of medicine. In addition, the Company is supporting research at a university agricultural school to experiment in the application of the Company's concepts in the field of swine production.

All of these activities will take considerable time to complete. No assurance can be given that any will be completed successfully, or within the resources of the company, or that if successfully completed, commercially salable products can be developed and marketed.

Patents

The Company has filed and been granted patents on certain applications of its basic concepts and has filed further patent applications which are presently pending. Patent applications corresponding to certain of the Company's U.S. patents have been filed in twenty or more countries. A schedule setting forth the patent status is included as Appendix A. The Company can offer no assurance that any pending patent application will be granted, that the grant of any patent ensures that the product covered thereby can be marketed successfully, that any patent is valid and enforceable, or that any of its patents cannot be circumvented or attacked by others. Nor can it assure that any of its present or future products will not infringe on patents of others.

Use of Proceeds

The net proceeds of this offering, assuming the sale of the 20,000 shares offered hereby, will be approximately $782,000 after deducting estimated expenses of $18,000. The Company will apply the net proceeds to satisfy its liability on Stock Subscriptions which as of the date hereof totals $776,000 (see Note 8 of Financial Statements), such liability having been created by the receipt by the Company of subscriptions to this offering prior to the issuance of this Confidential Investment Memorandum. The funds creating this liability have been used since June 1983, as follows:

- $200,000 to reduce bank indebtedness.*
- $250,000 to pay current indebtedness to creditors.
- $30,000 to process patent applications.
- $296,000 for working capital, including the salary of the Company's President, other employees, research and development, and other expenses of the Company.

The balance of the proceeds from the offering ($25,000) will be used (approximately $18,000) to pay the estimated expenses of the offering, and the balance added to working capital.

---

*The remaining balance of $65,000 indebtedness to the bank is to be paid, by agreement, $5,000 per month, commencing April 1984. The Company's original indebtedness of $165,000 to the bank was personally guaranteed by certain of the Company's directors. The proceeds of the loan were used in part to repay Company indebtedness to its directors.

EXHIBIT 2 *(continued)*

Since there is no underwriting for the shares being offered, there is no assurance that all of the shares will be sold. As of the date of this offering, the Company has received subscriptions for the purchase of substantially all shares offered hereby, and has accepted funds for the purchase of 19,000 of the shares offered hereby. Such subscriptions cannot be accepted except pursuant hereto. Unless subscriptions pursuant hereto are received within 90 days from the effective date of this Memorandum for at least 16,000 shares offered hereby, all subscribers' money will be returned to them without interest or deductions. In any event, any subscriber who has sent money to the Company for the purchase of the securities offered hereby prior to the receipt of this Confidential Investment Memorandum, who so requests or who fails to complete and return the subscription form attached hereto within such 90-day period will be refunded his or her subscription money in full without interest or deduction.

Certain Transactions

Indebtedness to Affiliates

As of February 28, 1984, the Company was indebted to certain of its officers and other related parties as follows:

Creditor	Amount Due	Date Due	Consideration
Louis J. Brown	$ 7,500	Sept. 1, 1985	Services rendered.
Harold J. Stein	$25,000	Sept. 1, 1985	Services and expenses.
Fredericks Communication	$63,562	$2,000/month commencing Oct. 1, 1984	Expenses; employees' services.
O'Connor & O'Connor	$23,000	Sept. 1, 1985	Expenses; employees' services.
Melvin I. O'Connor	$16,782	Sept. 1, 1985	Cash advanced.

All amounts due bear interest ranging from 8 percent to 12 percent per year.

Mr. Brown and Dr. Stein are consultants to the Company. The debt to Mr. Brown represents accrued consulting fees; and that to Dr. Stein represents approximately $11,000 in accrued consulting fees and approximately $14,000 advanced by him as salary to a nurse engaged to assist him in his research for the Company.

Fredericks Communication, and its subsidiaries, furnished services in fabricating parts, materials, and devices used by the Company, and also conceived, developed, and produced slide shows, display equipment, and audio-visual shows used by the Company at exhibits and medical meetings. The indebtedness to Fredericks consists of services of employees and out of pocket expenses.

The indebtedness to the Company's accountants is produced by services of employees and out of pocket expenses in recordkeeping, statement and tax return preparation, and clerical services.

EXHIBIT 2   (*continued*)

Melvin I. O'Connor advanced funds at various times. The liability to him represents interest on various loans ($4,282) and the remaining balance on these cash loans to the company ($12,500).

The Company intends to continue its arrangements with Mr. Brown for consulting services at a cost to the Company of $1,500 per month, plus out of pocket expenses. In addition, the Company intends to use, as required, the services of Dr. Stein and the staff accounting services of the Company's accountants at the generally applicable rates of each for such services. If the Company deems it advisable it may utilize the services or facilities of other affiliates for compensation to be negotiated in each instance. The Company has negotiated an informal arrangement with Fredericks Communication Co., Inc., whereunder the latter has constructed an office and engineering laboratory in a building owned by Fredericks Communication Co., Inc., and has leased it to the Company on a tenant-at-will basis. Such arrangement has not been formalized by any written agreement.

Fredericks Communication Co., Inc.

Fredericks Communication Co., Inc. ("Fredericks"), originally known as Fredericks Recording Co., Inc., was contacted by the Company in 1981 to supply the Company with disposable grids, then contemplated to be plastic squares with uniform ridges. Thereafter, the Company and a subsidiary of Fredericks known as Fredericks Research & Development, Inc., entered into a joint venture to procure, manufacture, or have manufactured for it the grids required by the Company on an exclusive basis. On November 17, 1983, the Company acquired by merger Fredericks Research & Development Inc. for 10,980 shares of the Company's stock (after giving effect to the August 1983 stock split). At that time Fredericks Research & Development, Inc.'s share of expenses (excluding fixed costs, overhead, and executive salaries) for research and development on Company products was $46,466.34.

The Company has used Fredericks to procure substantially all of the molds, dies, boxes, aspirators, machinery, extruders, and other equipment required by the Company. Fredericks also provided research and development for the grids and other items in connection with the Company's business, and rendered assistance to the Company in conceiving, designing, and producing film strips, slides, and other display material used by the Company in its presentations at trade and other shows. Fredericks principals, Messrs. Smith, Green, and Marvin, in September 1982, purchased 3,960 shares of the Company's stock, after giving effect to the August 1983 stock split, for $120,000 ($30.30 per share). Messrs. Smith, Green, and Marvin loaned the Company $50,000 cash, which was repaid in July 1978, and Mr. Green, along with other Company principals, endorsed a Company Note for $165,000 to a bank in July 1983. Mr. Smith has been at various times Clerk, Assistant Clerk, and Director of the Company, and both he and Mr. Green are currently Directors.

Fredericks has charged the Company for these various services, for its actual costs of materials, services of its staff and special personnel other than executive personnel. The Company intends to continue its ar-

EXHIBIT 2   *(continued)*

rangements with Fredericks respecting procurement and the providing of other services, and to reimburse Fredericks in connection with these activities for Fredericks's expenses and services of its personnel other than executive personnel.

Capital Structure and Description of Common Stock

The capitalization of the Company as of the date of this Offering Circular, and as adjusted to give effect to the sale of the shares offered hereby, is as follows:

	Prior to Offering	Following Offering if All Shares Sold
Notes payable—bank	$ 65,000	$ 65,000
Notes payable— shareholders	135,844	135,844
Accounts payable	47,506	47,506
Stock subscriptions	760,000	–0–
Capital stock	14,412	16,412
Additional paid-in capital	462,028	960,028

The Company's Common Stock, of $.10 par value, is its only authorized class of capital stock. At all meetings of stockholders, holders of Common Stock are entitled to one vote for each share held. The holders of Common Stock have no preemptive or subscription rights. All the outstanding shares of Common Stock are fully paid and nonassessable and are entitled to dividends if and when declared by the Board of Directors.

The Common Stock of the Company does not have cumulative voting rights. Hence, the holders of more than 50 percent of the shares voting for the election of directors may elect all the directors if they so choose. Since the present management holds more than 50 percent of the shares to be outstanding, it will be in a position to reelect itself as directors.

Dividends

Holders of shares of the Company's Common Stock are entitled to receive dividends as may be declared by the Board of Directors out of funds legally available therefore and to share pro rata in any distribution to shareholders. The Company does not contemplate the payment of any dividends in the foreseeable future.

New Financing

The Company believes that it will be necessary to secure funding in addition to that offered pursuant hereto in order to enable the Company to achieve its objectives. By letter dated March 8, 1983, the Indian U.S. International Industrial Research & Development Foundation, a foundation sponsored and funded by the governments of the United States and India, advised the Company that its Board had approved a first year grant of up to $250,000 to be expended on research and development of the Company's products, subject to various conditions and the negotiation of a formal contract. The Company believes that conditions to this grant

EXHIBIT 2   (*continued*)

will include (a) establishment of a joint program with an Indian company for research, development, preproduction, and premarketing of the Company's products, (b) expenditures by the Company and its Indian partners on the program during the first year of the grant of amounts equivalent to those received from the grant during the same time. The Company cannot give assurances that a final contract for the grant will be executed, or that if it is, the Company will be able to satisfy the conditions thereof.

Remuneration

Mr. Jones was engaged as Chief Executive Officer on September 1, 1983, at a salary of $65,000 per year. Mr. Brown is paid consulting fees of $1,500 per month. None of the other officers or directors are compensated. In November 1981, O'Connor & O'Connor, of which Mr. O'Connor is a partner, were issued 900 shares of stock (after giving effect to the 12 for 1 split) in satisfaction of $7,500 of liability to them for cash advances and staff services rendered. The shares were distributed to the partners of O'Connor & O'Connor, other than Mr. O'Connor, who disclaims any benefit therefrom or control thereover. Mr. Jones has devoted full time to his duties as president of the Company since September 1, 1983, and is currently in the process of moving his residence to Illinois.

Applicable Regulations

As indicated above, the products contemplated by the Company for use by doctors and by individuals require approval of the Food and Drug Administration (FDA). There is no assurance that the Company will be able to comply with the FDA regulations or that the necessary approval of the Company's operations and all the products can be achieved. To date it has only received such approval for its aspirators. The Company is in the process of compiling clinical data with respect to the balance of its products, to be supplied to the FDA as required. The Company believes that these contemplated products, however, may be utilized in animal husbandry without FDA approval and, if manufactured abroad, may be utilized outside the United States without FDA approval, although they may require approval by appropriate regulatory agencies in each country. The Company also believes that no government regulations are applicable to any of the contemplated uses in industry, inasmuch as no hazardous procedures are associated with the utilization of the Company's proposed products.

Litigation

The Company is not involved in any litigation and knows of no threatened or contingent liabilities.

The Company, at the request of any subscriber or Adviser (as defined in the Subscription Agreement), will make available for inspection copies of these documents, will provide answers to questions concerning the terms and conditions of this Offering, and will provide such additional information that is necessary to verify the accuracy of the information contained herein or that may otherwise pertain to the Company or to this investment, to the extent the Company has such information or can acquire it without unreasonable effort or expense.

EXHIBIT 2 *(continued)*
Financial Statements

Consolidated Balance Sheet
(Unaudited)

ASSETS	February 28, 1984	June 30, 1983	1982	1981	1980	1979	1978
Current assets:							
Cash	$ 21,110	1,104	$ 6,437	$ 4,745	$ 1,207	$10,331	$12,514
Inventories (Notes 1 and 2)	150,023	18,359	—	—	—	—	—
Subscriptions receivable (Note 3)	131,000	—	73,413	—	—	—	3,000
Prepaid items	1,000	—	—	—	—	—	—
Total current assets	303,133	19,463	79,850	4,745	1,207	10,331	15,514
Fixed assets (Notes 1 and 4)	31,274	26,775	2,074	—	—	—	—
Other assets:							
Patents and patent applications	325,753	183,753	115,467	59,595	3,942	17,637	—
Unamortized organization and other expenses	831	673	279	171	287	403	519
	326,584	184,426	115,746	59,766	34,229	18,040	519
Total assets	$660,991	$230,664	$197,670	$64,511	$35,436	$28,371	$16,033

LIABILITIES AND SHAREHOLDERS' EQUITY/(DEFICIT)

Current liabilities:							
Medway advances (Note 5)	$ —	$ —	$ —	$ —	$43,850	$33,850	$ —
Current maturities of note payable —bank (Note 6)	50,000	—	—	—	—	—	—
Current maturities of amounts due to shareholders (Note 7)	10,000	169,000	2,500	9,000	—	16,000	16,000
Accounts payable and accruals	47,506	196,487	44,075	22,833	6,912	184	1,702
Total current liabilities	107,506	365,487	46,575	31,833	50,762	50,034	17,702
Long-term debt:							
Note payable — bank (Note 6)	15,000	—	—	—	—	—	—
Amounts due to shareholders (Note 7)	125,844	—	—	—	—	—	—
	140,844	—	—	—	—	—	—
Amounts received on stock subscriptions (Note 8)	776,000	20,000					
Shareholders' equity/(deficit) (Note 9):							
Common stock, par value $.10 Authorized 300,000 shares Issued 144,120 shares	14,412	476,440	461,440	103,940	37,940	9,940	9,940
Additional paid-in capital	462,028	—	—	(71,262)	(53,266)	(31,603)	(11,609)
Accumulated deficit	(839,799)	(631,263)	(310,345)	(71,262)	(53,266)	(31,603)	(11,609)
	(363,359)	(154,823)	151,095	32,678	(15,326)	(21,663)	(1,669)
Total liabilities and shareholders' equity/(deficit)	$660,991	$230,664	$197,670	$ 64,511	$35,436	$28,371	$16,033

The accompanying notes are an integral part of the consolidated financial statements.

EXHIBIT 2 (*continued*)
Financial Statements

Consolidated Statement of Operations and Accumulated Deficit
(Unaudited)

	Feb. 28, 1984	1983	1982	June 30, 1981	1980	1979	1978
	$	$	$	$	$	$	$
Sales							
Expenses:							
Rent	1,888						
Office and clerical expenses	11,385	10,853	17,866	6,575			
Meetings expenses	7,741	3,047	5,305	2,959	27	130	
Advertising, shows, public relations	9,482	46,355	26,524	5,499	1,340	681	118
Telephone	3,130	2,021	946				
Taxes	2,276	1,520	948	160	114	184	114
Miscellaneous	1,086	106	142	116	116	116	58
Interest	12,385	8,750					
Depreciation	819						
Payroll and payroll expenses	33,909						
Research and development (Note 11)	124,435	248,047	187,243	2,687	20,066	18,883	11,319
	208,536	320,918	239,083	17,996	21,663	19,994	11,609
Net loss	(208,536)	(320,918)	(239,083)	(17,996)	(21,663)	(19,994)	(11,609)
Accumulated deficit, beginning	(631,263)	(310,345)	(71,262)	(53,266)	(31,603)	(11,609)	—
Accumulated deficit, ending	($839,799)	($631,263)	($310,345)	($71,262)	($53,266)	($31,603)	($11,609)

The accompanying notes are an integral part of the consolidated financial statements.

Consolidated Statement of Changes in Financial Position
(Unaudited)

	8 Mos. Ended Feb. 28, 1984	1983	1982	Years Ended June 30, 1981	1980	1979	1978
Resources provided:							
From operations:							
Net loss	($208,536)	($320,918)	($239,083)	($17,996)	($21,663)	($19,994)	($11,609)
Add items not affecting working capital:							
Depreciation and amortization	904	325	251	116	116	116	58
Working capital applied to operations	(207,632)	(320,593)	(238,832)	(17,880)	(21,547)	(19,878)	(11,551)
Amounts received on stock subscriptions	725,000	20,000	—	—	—	—	—
Proceeds of bank note	165,000	—	—	—	—	—	—
Amounts due shareholders	125,844	—	—	—	—	—	—
Capital investment	—	15,000	357,500	66,000	28,000	—	9,940
	808,212	(285,593)	118,668	48,120	6,453	(19,878)	(1,611)
Resources applied:							
Purchase of fixed assets	5,403	25,026	2,325	—	—	—	—
Reduction of bank note	200,000	—	—	—	—	—	—
Other assets	158	394	108	—	—	—	577
Increase in current maturities of long-term debt	50,000	—	—	—	—	—	—
Patents and patent applications	42,000	68,286	55,872	25,653	16,305	17,637	—
	197,561	93,706	58,305	25,653	16,305	17,637	577
Increase/(decrease) in working capital	$510,651	($379,299)	$60,363	$22,467	($9,852)	($37,515)	($2,188)

EXHIBIT 2 *(continued)*

Consolidated Statement of Changes in Financial Position
(Unaudited)

	8 Mos. Ended Feb. 28, 1984	Years Ended June 30,					
		1983	1982	1981	1980	1979	1978
Changes in the components of working capital:							
Increase/(decrease) in current assets:							
Cash	$ 20,006	($ 5,333)	$ 1,692	$ 3,538	($ 9,124)	($ 2,183)	$12,514
Inventories	131,664	18,359	—	—	—	—	—
Subscriptions receivable	100,000	(73,413)	73,413	—	—	—	—
Prepaid items	1,000	—	—	—	—	(3,000)	3,000
	252,670	(60,387)	75,105	3,538	(9,124)	(5,183)	15,514
Increase/(decrease) in current liabilities:							
Medway advances	—	—	—	(43,850)	10,000	33,850	—
Current maturities of notes payable—bank	50,000	—	—	—	—	—	—
Current maturities of amounts due to shareholders	(159,000)	166,500	(6,500)	9,000	(16,000)	—	16,000
Accounts payable and accruals	(148,981)	152,412	21,242	15,921	6,728	(1,518)	1,702
	(257,981)	318,912	14,742	(18,929)	728	32,332	17,702
Increase/(decrease) in working capital	$510,651	($379,299)	$60,363	$22,467	($ 9,852)	($37,515)	($ 2,188)

The accompanying notes are an integral part of the consolidated financial statements.

EXHIBIT 2   *(continued)*

NOTES TO CONSOLIDATED FINANCIAL STATEMENTS
February 28, 1984
(Unaudited)

Note 1—Summary of Significant Accounting Policies

Principles of Consolidation

The consolidated financial statements include the accounts of Viscotech, Inc. and its wholly owned inactive subsidiaries, Nutrico, Inc. and Animal Technology, Inc. All intercompany balances and transactions have been eliminated in consolidation.

The Company was organized December 29, 1977; and the subsidiaries were organized in December 1980: Nutrico, Inc. for the exploitation of the Company's concepts related to industrial viscometry and Animal Technology, Inc. for the exploitation of the Company's concepts related to animal nutrition.

Inventories

Inventories are valued at the lower of cost (first-in, first-out basis) or market.

Fixed Assets

Fixed assets are carried at cost and depreciated on the straight-line method over estimated useful lives as follows:

Display equipment	Five (5) years
Molds and dies	Seven (7) years
Machinery	Ten (10) years
Office equipment	Ten (10) years

Note 2—Inventories

Inventories consisted of the following:

	February 28, 1984	June 30, 1983
Machines completed awaiting modification	$116,500	$16,500
Machine parts	15,000	—
Aspirators—finished	8,138	500
Grids	3,961	—
Packing materials	5,799	1,121
Instruction booklets, tapes, calibrating fluids, etc.	625	238
	$150,023	$18,359

Note 3—Stock Subscriptions

The Company has offered its shares through the Medical Investment Fund Trust. The Company has not yet received payment for all shares subscribed.

EXHIBIT 2   (*continued*)

Note 4—Fixed Assets

Fixed assets consisted of the following:

	February 28, 1984	June 30, 1983	1982
Display equipment	$2,183	$2,183	$2,183
Molds and dies	23,730	22,163	—
Machinery	5,362	2,758	—
Office furniture	1,141	—	—
	32,421	27,104	2,183
Less accumulated depreciation	1,147	329	109
	$31,274	$26,775	$2,074

Note 5—Medway Advances

In fiscal years 1979 and 1980, the Company received nonrefundable advances from Medway, Inc. to finance research and patent applications. Medway, Inc. was given an exclusive marketing arrangement during this period. Medway's contract for exclusive marketing expired in December 1980.

Note 6—Note Payable—Bank

In July 1983, the Corporation borrowed $265,000 from a bank, unsecured but guaranteed by several shareholders. Of the proceeds, $155,000 was used to repay the shareholders who had loaned that amount to the Corporation. The note, which bears interest at the bank's prime rate plus 2 percent, originally matured in January 1984. At that time, $200,000 was paid. The remaining balance is to be paid in monthly installments of $5,000, commencing in April 1984.

Note 7—Due to Shareholders

In February 1984, several shareholders-creditors accepted term notes for amounts due them as follows:

Shareholder-Creditor	Amount	Interest	Payable	Nature of Debt
Louis Brown	$ 7,500	8%	Sept. 1, 1985	Services rendered
Harold J. Stein	25,000	Prime	Sept. 1, 1985	Research services, out of pocket expenses
Fredericks Communications	63,562	Prime	$2,000/month commencing Oct. 1, 1985	Out of pocket expenses, services of employees
O'Connor & O'Connor	23,000	8%	Sept. 1, 1985	Out of pocket expenses, services of employees
Melvin I. O'Connor	16,782	8%	Sept. 1, 1985	Cash advances
	$135,844			

−16−

EXHIBIT 2   (*continued*)

Louis Brown and Harold J. Stein had been employed as consultants at $1,500 per month each. In addition, Dr. Stein advanced the salary and expenses of a nurse employed by the Company in his office.

Fredericks Communications and its subsidiaries furnished services in fabricating parts, materials and devices used by the Company, and also conceived, developed, and produced slide shows, display equipment, and audiovisual shows used by the Company at exhibits and medical meetings. The indebtedness to Fredericks consists of services of employees and out of pocket expenses.

The indebtedness to O'Connor & O'Connor is produced by services of employees and out of pocket expenses in recordkeeping, statement and tax return preparation, and clerical services.

Melvin I. O'Connor advanced funds at various times. The liability to him represents interest on various loans ($4,282) and the remaining balance on these cash loans to the Company ($12,500).

Note 8—Amount Received on Stock Subscriptions

Funds have been received from subscribers to the stock of the Corporation. Issuance of the stock has been delayed pending approval of a registration under Regulation A of the Securities and Exchange Commission. The registration involves 20,000 shares of $.10 par value stock, to be issued at $40 per share. At June 30, 1983, 800 shares had been subscribed and paid for, and at February 28, 1984, a total of 19,400 shares had been subscribed.

Note 9—Common Stock

On August 31, 1984, the Corporation voted to change its authorized capital stock from 12,500 shares of no par value to 300,000 shares of $.10 par value and to exchange 12 shares of the newly authorized stock for each share of old stock then outstanding. This exchange of shares has been given effect in the accompanying financial statements by transferring from common stock to additional paid-in capital the amounts in excess of par as of February 28, 1984.

Note 10—Merger

On August 31, 1983, the shareholders voted to issue 915 shares of old no par stock (equivalent to 10,980 shares of new $.10 par stock) to Fredericks Research & Development Corporation in exchange for all the outstanding stock of that corporation and to merge Fredericks Research & Development Corporation into the Company. The assets acquired from Fredericks Research & Development Corporation were certain technical procedures in production and the right to limited participation with the Company in certain production profits. No value was recorded for the assets acquired from Fredericks; accordingly, common stock was credited and additional paid-in capital charged for the par value of the shares issued.

EXHIBIT 2   *(continued)*

Note 11—Operations

The Corporation has used most of its resources since its inception in research and development of its concepts for measuring the viscoelasticity of oral mucus in humans and animals and developing instruments for commercial medical application. Expenditures to date are as follows:

Fiscal year June 30, 1978	$ 11,319	
June 30, 1979	18,833	
June 30, 1980	20,066	
June 30, 1981	2,687	($43,850 defrayed by others—Note 5)
June 30, 1982	187,243	
June 30, 1983	248,047	
July 1, 1983 to		
February 28, 1984	124,435	
	$612,680	

Note 12—Taxes on Income

The Company's net operating losses are available to offset future taxable income. Losses through 1980 may be carried forward five (5) years and subsequent losses, seven (7) years.

For tax purposes, the Company has capitalized research and development costs, as discussed in Note 11, which costs will be written off over sixty (60) months from commencement of significant sales.

CONFIDENTIAL OFFEREE QUESTIONNAIRE

NAME _____

ADDRESS _____

BUSINESS ADDRESS _____

The primary purpose of this Questionnaire is to obtain certain information about your present and projected financial position in order to help determine whether you are qualified to receive offers of and participate in the purchase of certain securities.

Any private placements of securities, when and if made, will be made pursuant to the exemption from registration provided for in Section 4 (2) of the Securities Act of 1933, or under Rule 505 which has been adopted by the Securities and Exchange Commission under Section 4 (2). Rule 505 protects investors by providing objective standards in private placements of securities.

One of the requirements of the Rule is that the persons involved in the offering and sale of the securities must have reasonable grounds to believe that each person to whom the offering is made either:

(i) has directly or by access to a "purchaser representative," knowledge and experience in financial and business matters so that he is capable of evaluating the merits and risks of the prospective investment, or

(ii) is an "accredited investor" by virtue of his financial condition.

EXHIBIT 2   (*continued*)

This Questionnaire will assist in compliance with the legal requirements of Section 4 (2) and Rule 505, for the protection of all concerned.

Your answers to this Questionnaire will be kept strictly confidential. Viscotech, Inc. may present this Questionnaire to legal counsel and to other persons legally responsible for an offering, who also will be required to maintain confidentiality. If necessary, this Questionnaire may be presented to appropriate parties in order to establish the availability of an exemption under applicable securities law.

Please complete this Questionnaire as fully as possible in your handwriting and sign, date, and return to Viscotech, Inc.

I. GENERAL
   1. Set forth in the space provided below the state(s) in which you have maintained your principal residence during the past two years and the dates during which you resided in each such state.
   2. What is your present age?
   3. How many dependents do you have; what is their age and relationship to you?

II. OCCUPATION
   1. In the space provided below, please indicate your present occupation; describe the nature of your employment and the length of time you have held this position.
   2. In what other capacities have you been employed in the past five years?

III. FINANCIAL
   1. Income (from all sources) for the calendar year ended 12/31/83:

under $20,000	( )
$20,000–$40,000	( )
40,000–60,000	( )
60,000–80,000	( )
80,000–100,000	( )
over $100,000	( )

   2. Describe briefly all nonsalary sources of income and the amount of income derived from each such source.
   3. Average yearly income (from all sources) anticipated for the three-year period ending 12/31/86:

	1984	1985	1986
under $20,000	( )	( )	( )
$20,000–$40,000	( )	( )	( )
40,000–60,000	( )	( )	( )
60,000–80,000	( )	( )	( )
80,000–100,000	( )	( )	( )
over $100,000	( )	( )	( )

   4. Describe briefly all sources of anticipated income if different from those given in III. 2. and 3.

EXHIBIT 2 (*continued*)

5. Please describe below your present net worth.
   a) Liquid assets (excluding real estate, furniture, automobiles, unmarketable securities) in excess of

Less than $100,000	( )
$100,000	( )
$200,000	( )
$300,000	( )
$400,000	( )
$500,000 or more	( )

   b) Total assets (liquid and nonliquid)

Less than $100,000	( )
$100,000	( )
$200,000	( )
$300,000	( )
$400,000	( )
$500,000	( )

   c) Current liabilities (due within one year)

None	( )
$100,000	( )
$200,000	( )
$300,000	( )
$400,000	( )
$500,000 or more	( )

   d) Total liabilities

None	( )
$100,000	( )
$200,000	( )
$300,000	( )
$400,000	( )
$500,000 or more	( )

   e) Contingent liabilities (include guarantees, endorsements, obligations as co-maker, leases, pending litigation, etc.)

None	( )
$100,000	( )
$200,000	( )
$300,000	( )
$400,000	( )
$500,000 or more	( )

6. Do you have life insurance? If so, in what amounts:

under $100,000	( )
$100,000–$200,000	( )
$200,000–$300,000	( )
$300,000–$400,000	( )
$400,000–$500,000	( )

7. Do you have accident and health insurance?

   Yes _____ No _____

8. Do you have any reason to believe that your future income is likely to be interrupted or substantially diminished in the foreseeable future? If

EXHIBIT 2   *(concluded)*

yes, describe this possibility and probable effect on your financial security.

Yes _____ No _____

9. If you should choose to purchase securities in Viscotech, Inc., is it your opinion that your present financial position is, and is expected to continue to be, such as to enable you:

  a) to bear the economic risk of losing all funds invested in Viscotech, Inc.:

Yes _____ No _____

  b) to bear the economic burden of having all such funds tied up in an essentially illiquid investment for an extended period of time:

Yes _____ No _____

Please provide any additional information which you feel might help Viscotech, Inc. to decide whether or not your financial condition is such that you could afford to lose the entire amount of your investment.

_____   _____
Date   Signature

Case 2–6

Universal Robotics Corporation

Andrew, Robert, and Elliot sat around the kitchen table discussing the plans for their new company—Universal Robotics. It was March 15, 1984, and the group had been actively working toward the start-up for several months. Now, things seemed to be coming together, but there were still many issues to be dealt with; they hoped that tonight's meeting would help them make these important decisions.

BACKGROUND

Andrew Reed, Robert Baker, and Elliot Carlton were all friends who intended to leave their current employment and form a new business. Reed, Baker, and Carlton had been classmates in their undergraduate days at Princeton University. After their graduation, they each took different paths, but met in late 1983 to start a new business. Their business, organized as a Delaware corporation under the name of Universal Robotics Corporation (URC), was formed to design, develop, manufacture, and market industrial robots.

Reed received his MBA in 1978 and had been assistant treasurer and assistant to the chief financial officer of a large manufacturer of computer peripheral equipment. Baker received his doctorate in electrical engineering from MIT and had spent three years in the New Products Division of IBM. After leaving Princeton, Carlton had spent two years as a district salesman for General Electric and then spent three years as vice president of marketing for a manufacturer of factory automation equipment.

Baker had identified three friends at IBM who wanted to leave IBM and join URC. These three individuals were engaged in engineer-

This case was prepared by H. Irving Grousbeck and Paul P. Brountas under the direction of H. Irving Grousbeck.

ing and development work at IBM's Robotics Division. They were well paid and did not want to leave IBM until URC had raised its initial capital and was in a position to compensate them at their existing salary levels.

Since early January 1984, Reed had been actively working (nights and weekends) on the development of a business plan for URC. While Reed's experience in establishing new companies was limited, he had studied that topic in business school and kept up with new venture activities in the business press. As a result of his efforts, he had prepared a preliminary draft of a business plan, contacted two friends in the venture capital business, and spoken with a regional investment banker who was interested in placing an R&D partnership. In addition, he had discussed the proposed business venture with his father-in-law, who was the president of a medium-size bank in Minneapolis. His two venture capital friends were Sebastian Vanderbilt, a general partner of Prestige Ventures Company (Prestige), and Anthony Wallace, a general partner of Beacon Associates (Beacon). The local investment banker was Pincus, Greene & Co.

Baker was an engineering genius and had a well-equipped engineering shop in the basement of his home. For two years Baker worked evenings and weekends on the development of an "intelligent" robot with potentially broad applications in the so-called automated factory. He was able to combine a vision module with a computerized device that was sensitive to touch, and therefore believed that his robot was able both to see and feel components and parts used in the manufacture of products. On January 15, 1984, Baker, after consulting with his personal patent attorney, filed a patent application for his invention.

Carlton had just completed a very successful year with his employer and was awarded a substantial bonus for organizing a new marketing approach for two recently introduced products by his employer. Carlton's immediate boss, however, was 40 years old, and Carlton believed it was unlikely that he would replace his boss in the near future. He wanted to leave and try his hand at running a marketing organization for a high-technology company with an innovative product.

RELATIONSHIP WITH CURRENT EMPLOYERS

After their first meeting in late 1983, Reed, Baker, and Carlton had several meetings at Reed's home to plan the formation and financing of their new venture. At a meeting on March 15, 1984, the preliminary business plan and financing alternatives were reviewed.

Reed reported that he had resigned his position with his former employer effective March 1, 1984. Baker indicated his plans to resign

April 1, 1984. Carlton expressed his desire to remain with his employer until September 1, 1984, at which time he would resign. Carlton's wife was expecting a baby, and he desired both the insurance coverage and his salary during this period.

Reed reported that he met twice with Vanderbilt at Prestige and once with Wallace at Beacon to discuss URC and to determine whether they had any interest in investing in URC. In the meantime, over Christmas, he had several discussions with his father-in-law, who indicated that he and several of his friends and banking clients would like the opportunity to invest in URC. They believed that the robotics business would be the glamour business of the future.

Reed prepared an extensive agenda for the March 15 meeting, including a summary of the tentative financing proposals submitted by Prestige, Beacon, his father-in-law, and Pincus, Greene. The March 15 meeting was held to consider the advantages and disadvantages of the four alternatives and how they might be modified.

It was agreed that Baker's three friends at IBM would join their next meeting to discuss their future roles in URC, although none of them was expected to join URC until the initial financing was completed.

At the March 15 meeting, Baker exhibited considerable uneasiness about leaving IBM. He had heard that IBM had a very formal "exit" procedure, which he would undergo when he announced his resignation. He reported that he had signed a standard IBM form of invention and nondisclosure agreement and there might be some question as to the rights of ownership in his invention and the patent application. Reed reported that he had no contracts with his employer. Carlton, on the other hand, had signed an agreement that prohibited him from soliciting or otherwise inducing any employees of his employer from leaving the company for other employment. After further discussion, it was decided that Reed would select an attorney to represent URC who, as a first order of business, would review each of their obligations to their employers and the possible legal obstacles to the commencement of the new business.

INITIAL "PRE-SEED" CAPITAL

They then discussed the need for some initial funds that would be required to retain an attorney, incorporate the business, and pay the initial start-up expenses, which would be incurred before the financing was consummated. Reed lived frugally and had been able to save a portion of his salary during the past couple of years. In addition, Reed was an astute investor and managed to "hit it big" in a couple of high technology investments. Baker, on the other hand, had no money to contribute to the new venture, but was willing to contribute his invention and patent application to URC. Baker also asked whether it would be proper for him to seek a royalty from URC in exchange for the transfer of all rights to his invention to URC. Carlton indicated that he could only contribute $1,000 to the venture at this time.

At the outset it was decided that each of the three founders would own an equal share in URC. Since neither Baker nor Carlton had excess funds to invest in URC, it was concluded that the initial capital would be $3,000, and each of the founders would pay $1,000 for 100,000 shares of stock (at $.01 per share). Reed agreed to loan URC additional funds which would be required before the first financing was completed.

COMPLETION OF BUSINESS PLAN

Reed had seen a number of business plans used by recent start-ups in the Boston and California areas. He indicated that the business plans varied, depending on the nature of the potential investors and their sophistication. He also briefly discussed the legal aspects of business plans with an attorney and was advised that the plan could be a "liability" document unless properly prepared, in compliance with federal and state securities laws. His preliminary draft of the business plan was 142 pages long, and he was therefore reluctant to show it to his colleagues. However, he did distribute an outline of the format of the business plan (attached as Exhibit 1), and asked Baker and Carlton to draft their respective sections of the business plan; namely, product and technology—Baker; and marketing, distribution, and field services—Carlton. He also asked Baker and Carlton to give thought to the specific risks of the new business so that they could be incorporated in the risks section of the business plan. In the meantime, Reed revised his preliminary draft and tried to cut it back to about 40 pages. He also met with an accountant to review the format of the projections and the assumptions used in developing the projections.

FINANCING ALTERNATIVES

Reed then reviewed the financing alternatives, which differed substantially. Based on the preliminary business plan, it appeared that URC would need $2 million to complete the development and testing of the URC's first prototype robot. The development period was estimated at about 15 months, and therefore at the end of that period a second round of private financing would be required, estimated at approximately $6 million. Both Prestige and Beacon indicated that they could arrange an initial financing of $2 million. Pincus, Greene believed that they could successfully place R&D partnership units sufficient to raise $2 million (after deducting selling commissions of $200,000). However, Reed's father-in-law advised that he and other family members and friends could raise only about $500,000. Thus, if the initial funds were to come from friends and family, URC would run out of money long before the prototype was developed. On the other hand, the $500,000 would be sufficient to test the product concept, at which time it could be easier for URC to raise the additional required funds at a higher per share price. Reed then distributed to Baker and Carlton summaries of each of the four proposals—the father-in-law's proposal (attached as Exhibit 2), the Prestige proposal (attached as Exhibit 3), the Beacon proposal (attached as Exhibit 4), and the Pincus, Greene proposal (attached as Exhibit 5). See Appendix for Glossary defining the terms used in these proposals.

Common Stock

The father-in-law's proposal was attractive because of its simplicity. It provided for the sale of common stock by URC of 100,000 shares of common stock at $5 per share, resulting in a 25 percent equity ownership. Reed's father-in-law wanted to sit on the board of directors, but was not insisting on that right. Reed also indicated that his father-in-law might be willing to personally guarantee a small bank credit line, particularly to bridge the gap between the expenditure of the initial equity funds and the completion of the second round of financing. Reed reported that his father-in-law thought that the $500,000 could be raised from about 25 to 30 friends and relatives, in investments ranging from $10,000 to $50,000.

Subordinated Debt and Common Stock

Reed reported that Prestige was a very conservative investor. While its initial proposal called for $2 million of debt, Vanderbilt indicated that he might be willing to buy $2 million of preferred stock if the preferred stock had a mandatory redemption feature. In any event, whether the $2 million was used for the purchase of notes of URC or preferred stock of URC, Prestige expected to purchase common stock at the same price ($.01 per share) paid by the founders. Prestige wanted the right to purchase 200,000 shares, which would give it a 40 percent equity interest in URC. Prestige's proposal also called for subordination of its loan to bank borrowings, but not to trade creditors.

Convertible Preferred Stock

Beacon's proposal was a straight equity proposal, but Beacon insisted on purchasing convertible preferred stock rather than common stock. The convertible preferred would be convertible into common stock at $4 per share. Thus, if the convertible preferred stock was converted into common stock, Beacon would acquire 500,000 shares of common stock, or approximately 62 percent of the outstanding common stock. Like Prestige, Beacon would require mandatory redemption of the convertible preferred stock, but the redemption would not commence until eight years after the investment was made, as compared with Prestige's proposal, which would commence five years after the date of investment.

Both Prestige and Beacon had excellent reputations and, as "lead investor," each would be able to attract a solid group of investors. Each of them had indicated an initial interest in investing $1 million and raising the additional $1 million from colleagues in the venture capital business. Prestige and Beacon, however, did not like each other and had never invested in the same company. Reed noted that Prestige was generally not a "second round" investor, while Beacon had traditionally come up with second round, and even third round, investments in its portfolio companies.

R&D Partnership

An R&D partnership was attractive because it allowed URC to essentially "pass through" the expenses incurred in the product development phase to private investors, who could use these as tax deductions. These write-offs were more valuable to private investors in high tax brackets, who could use them right away, than they were to URC, who could only accumulate these tax losses and carry them forward against future income.

Pincus, Greene proposed a structure (detailed in Exhibit 5) under which they would raise $2,200,000, deduct $200,000 in selling commissions, and URC would receive $2,000,000. Under this proposal the R&D partnership would be entitled to royalties at the rate of 10 percent per annum in perpetuity. However, URC would have the option to purchase the technology developed by the R&D partnership for $10 million cash or, alternatively, for that number of shares which would give the R&D partnership a 30 percent equity interest in URC.

Weighing the Alternatives

Baker had no financial or investment experience and indicated that he was not in a position to make an informed evaluation of the four proposals. The father-in-law's proposal was attractive because it meant URC would only give up 25 percent of the company initially. On the other hand, the other three proposals would provide URC with the full amount of $2 million which was projected for the development phase. Baker remembered the advice of a colleague of his at IBM who was recently ousted from a company that he founded—"Don't give up control of your company to the venture capitalists." If the Beacon proposal was accepted, the founders would wind up with only 38 percent of the equity. Moreover, Carlton was concerned that additional equity would have to be reserved for future key employees in the range of 10 percent to 20 percent of the equity of URC. This pool of common stock for future employees would further dilute their equity positions. In addition, the business plan called for another $6 million in about 15 months. If the additional $6 million could be raised by giving up only 20 percent of the equity (thereby placing a value of $30 million on the company), significant additional dilution would still result. "I don't know how to cope with this," said Baker. "Reed, you have the MBA, you tell us what we should do."

Reed stated that he would give each of the alternatives careful consideration and come up with a recommendation for an April 6 meeting. In the meantime, Reed also met with the chief executive officers of three or four recently formed high-tech companies in the Boston area and sought their advice.

SWEAT EQUITY

At that point, Carlton shifted the discussion to his own personal arrangements with the new company. He indicated that he wanted a three-year employment contract with fixed minimum salary and an annual bonus award if he met certain agreed-on goals.

Reed stated that he was not interested in an employment agreement, but he wanted to be sure that each founder remained with URC for at least five years. A means of securing that commitment was a "golden handcuff" agreement. He was fearful that one of the founders might leave the company in a year or so and walk away with 100,000 shares of common stock. He therefore suggested that each founder agree that his stock would be forfeited if he did not remain in the employment of URC for five years. Baker disagreed, but was willing to agree on a compromise approach: a portion of the stock (for example— 20 percent) would vest and be nonforfeitable for each year during which a founder remained in the employment of URC. Reed thought that was a reasonable compromise and noted that Beacon's proposal required a founder's agreement which would provide for more rigorous vesting—50 percent of the stock after three years and then 25 percent in each of the fourth and fifth years.

Baker was concerned with the ability of the company to protect its research and development efforts, including inventions and trade secrets, proprietary software, and other proprietary information that URC planned to develop. He suggested that each of the founders, as well as all future employees, sign a patent, invention, and nondisclosure agreement along the lines that he had been required to sign when he joined IBM. Reed also wondered whether each founder should sign a noncompete agreement.

EQUITY FOR FUTURE KEY EMPLOYEES

The founders agreed that at least seven future key employees would be needed by the end of 1984. Reed said, "We have got to get these guys cheap stock. They won't be happy if they have to pay more than the founder's price of $.01 per share. If, however, the investors buy all common stock at $4 or $5 per share, how can we expect to sell stock to these key employees at $.01 per share?" It was concluded that Reed needed professional help to answer this question and that a tax adviser would be consulted to determine whether the sale of cheap stock in the future would create any tax problems. At the same time, Reed agreed to discuss this issue with the investors to ascertain their reaction to the issuance of additional shares at a price significantly less than the investors' price.

BOARD REPRESENTATION

Carlton wondered whether it would be necessary to have any of the investors represented on the board of directors. If so, he favored only one representative from the entire investor group. He wanted a board that was essentially controlled by management. In reviewing the various proposals, Carlton was particularly concerned with the provision that would give the investors the right to elect a majority of the board of directors.

REGISTRATION RIGHTS, ETC.

Baker was totally confused by the requirements for registration of the investors' stock. If the investors obtained registration rights, then what about the founders? Baker also admitted that he had great difficulty in evaluating the four proposals because he simply did not understand the jargon. In particular, he wanted to know what the following provisions meant and how they would affect him and/or URC:

— Standard ratchet antidilution provisions.
— "Take-me-along" agreement.
— "Piggyback" rights.
— Preemptive rights.
— Unlimited S-3s.

THE DECISION

At 1 A.M., Reed, Baker, and Carlton decided that they had had enough. They would each review the specific financing proposals, as well as the other matters discussed during the evening, and would reassemble on April 6 to agree on a final financing proposal and plan for launching URC.

EXHIBIT 1   Outline of Business Plan

---

1. Introduction (or Executive Summary)
   Short description of:
   • Business Objectives
   • Product
   • Technology and Development Program
   • Market and Customers
   • Management Team
   • Financing Requirements
2. Company Description
   • History and Status
   • Background and Industry
   • Company's Objectives
   • Company's Strategies
3. Risk Factors
4. Products
   • Product Description and Comparisons
   • Innovative Features (Patent Coverage)
   • Applications
   • Technology
   • Product Development
   • Product Introduction Schedule and Major Milestones
5. Market
   • Market Summary and Industry Overview
   • Market Analysis and Forecasts
   • Industry Trends
   • Initial Product(s)
6. Competition
7. Marketing Program
   • Objectives
   • Marketing Strategy
   • Sales and Distribution Channels
   • Customers
   • Staffing
8. Management
   • Founders
   • Stock Ownership

EXHIBIT 1   *(concluded)*

- Organization and Personnel
- Future Key Employees and Staffing
- Incentives (Employee Stock Purchase Plan)
9. Manufacturing
10. Service and Field Engineering
11. Future Products (Product Evolution)
- Engineering Development Program
- Future R&D
12. Facilities
13. Capital Required and Use of Proceeds
14. Financial Data and Financial Forecasts
- Assumptions Used
- 3-Year Plan
- 5-Year Plan
15. Appendixes
- Detailed Management Profiles
- References
- Product Descriptions, Sketches, Photos
- Recent Literature on Product, Market, etc.

Note: Use and dissemination should be restricted; document should be treated as confidential; if used as an Offering Memorandum, federal and securities legends should be affixed.

EXHIBIT 2   Summary of Terms—Father-in-Law's Proposal

Number of shares	100,000
Price	$5 per share
Board representation	One seat on the board, but not essential. Right to observe board meetings, if no board seat.
Registration rights	On-demand registration after the company goes public. Piggyback rights for five years after the company goes public.
Preemptive rights	Pro rata participation in future private offerings.
Stock restrictions	Founders will agree to sell their stock back to the company before selling to any third party, and if company elects not to purchase, stock will be offered pro rata to investors on a first refusal basis.
Financial statements	Annual and monthly financial statements.
Other	Possible short-term "bridge" loan.

EXHIBIT 3   Summary of the Principal Terms—Prestige Proposal: Subordinated Notes and Common Stock

Principal amount of notes	$2,000,000
Shares of common stock	(a) 200,000 shares
	(b) $.01 per share (Total $2,000)
	(c) Standard demand registration rights, piggyback registration rights, S-3 registration rights, etc.
	(d) Right to elect one member of the board of directors.
Interest rate on notes	10 percent payable semiannually; no interest payable for the first 24 months after issuance of the Notes.
Repayment of notes	$400,000 annually, commencing at the end of the fifth year after issuance of the Notes. Optional prepayment at any time at par plus accrued interest, provided no default exists and all outstanding Notes are prepaid pro rata.
Subordination	Subordination only to indebtedness for borrowed money from banks and other financial institutions.
Major convenants	
1. Affirmative covenants	(a) Normal covenants regarding continued existence and compliance.
	(b) Covenant to provide current financials monthly/quarterly/annually.
	(c) Permission for noteholders' visitation/examination.
	(d) Permission for noteholders' representative to attend directors' meetings.
	(e) Use of proceeds.
2. Negative covenants	(a) No senior debt above level to be determined; and overall limitation on borrowings at ratio to be determined.
	(b) No liens except those arising in the normal course of business and those securing senior debt.
	(c) No guarantees or similar obligations; no loans or other "investments."
	(d) No dividends; no repurchase or redemption of stock.
	(e) No failure to maintain asset ratios to be determined.
	(f) No merger, business combination, or sale of assets.
	(g) No material litigation.

EXHIBIT 3   (*concluded*)

Events of default	Any failure of material representation; any failure of payment of principal or interest when due; any breach of negative covenant; any breach of affirmative covenant continuing for 30 days after notice from a noteholder; any event allowing acceleration of senior debt; or certain bankruptcy events.
Amendments and waivers	Consent by the holders of two thirds in principal amount of outstanding Notes required, but the obligation to pay principal/interest on any Note can only be affected with the particular holder's consent.

Note: Alternatively, investors would consider purchasing $2 million of noncallable Preferred Stock in lieu of Subordinated Notes, on terms to be determined, provided that company will be required to redeem the Preferred Stock in annual increments commencing five years after date of issuance.

EXHIBIT 4   Summary of Principal Terms—Beacon Proposal: Convertible Preferred Stock

Number of shares	500,000
Price	$4 per share
Dividends	Cumulative dividends of $0.40 per share per annum, payable each July 1. Noncumulative until July 1, 1987.
Liquidation	$4 per share plus all accrued but unpaid dividends, prior to any liquidation payment to Common Stock.
Optional redemption	Redemption at company's option after 5 years at redemption price of $5 per share, plus accrued but unpaid dividends.
Mandatory redemption	Sinking fund redemption at redemption price of $4 per share, plus accrued but unpaid dividends, commencing January 1, 1990, as follows:

Date	Number of Shares Redeemed
January 1, 1990	50,000
January 1, 1991	125,000
January 1, 1992	150,000
January 1, 1993	175,000

EXHIBIT 4   (*continued*)

Conversion feature	Voluntary convention at any time.
Conversion price	$4 per share of Common Stock (one-for-one conversion). (Accrued but unpaid dividends are not payable at time of voluntary conversion but are payable at time of automatic conversion.)
Automatic conversion events	(a) Firm underwritten public offering covering primary sale of Common Stock at public offering price of at least $12 per share with gross proceeds of at least $5 million or more.
	(b) Audited financials for fiscal year reporting at least $25 million in consolidated revenues, and pretax profit (before extraordinary items) of at least 15 percent of revenues for the same period.
Antidilution protection	Proportional adjustments for splits, dividends, recapitalizations, and similar events. Standard "ratchet" formula adjustment for issuances below the Conversion Price (excluding (i) Common Stock issuable upon conversion of Preferred Stock and (ii) 75,000 shares of Common Stock reserved for issuance pursuant to the company's Incentive Stock Option Plan).
Voting rights	(a) *General voting:* Holders of Preferred Stock will have number of votes equal to largest number of full shares of Common Stock into which Preferred Stock may be converted.
	(b) *Election of directors:* Holders of Preferred Stock can elect one third of directors, and holders of Common Stock can elect the remaining two thirds of directors.
	(c) *Contingent voting rights:* Holders of Preferred Stock can elect majority of board in case of certain events:
	(i) $250,000 loss in any quarter after January 1, 1985;
	(ii) consolidated tangible net worth of less than $500,000;
	(iii) material lawsuit;
	(iv) default in payment of dividends; or
	(v) default in sinking fund redemption.
Restrictions and limitations	(a) Two-thirds vote of Preferred Stock required to:
	(i) repurchase any Preferred Stock other than pursuant to redemption provisions;

EXHIBIT 4   (*continued*)

	(ii)	repurchase or redeem any Common Stock (exception for buy-backs under employee stock purchase plans);
	(iii)	authorize or issue any senior equity security;
	(iv)	any merger, consolidation or sale of assets, or certain sales, transfers, and licenses of assets;
	(v)	permit the sale of any subsidiary or any stock of such subsidiary;
	(vi)	increase or decrease authorized Preferred Stock;
	(vii)	amend the Articles so as to adversely affect the rights, preferences, or privileges of the Preferred Stock; or
	(viii)	make any loans or guarantees.
Registration rights	(a)	Covers Common Stock issued upon conversion of Preferred Stock.
	(b)	One demand; 40 percent to request; 20 percent to be sold.
	(c)	Unlimited piggybacks.
	(d)	Unlimited S-3s for $250,000 transactions if company eligible.
	(e)	Company pays for demand and piggybacks; company pays for first four S-3 registrations.
	(f)	Underwriters cutback re: piggybacks.
	(g)	Normal indemnification.
	(h)	Registration rights end 10 years after conversion.
	(i)	Stand-off agreement.
	(j)	Best efforts to make Rule 144 available.
	(k)	Rights transferable to affiliate of company or buyer of 25,000 or more shares.
Sweat equity		Founders forfeit 100 percent of stock if employment terminated prior to three years; 50 percent if terminated after three years; 25 percent if terminated after four years; and no forfeiture (100% vested) if terminated after five years.
Shareholders' agreement		"Take-Me-Along" Agreement and Right of First Offer.
Covenants	(a)	Rights of inspection and access to information.
	(b)	Monthly unaudited financials 21 days after month's end.
	(c)	Audited financials 90 days after fiscal year end.

EXHIBIT 4 *(concluded)*

	(d) Budget 45 days prior to fiscal year end.
	(e) Approval of all subsequent equity financings.
	(f) Approval of single capital expenditures over $50,000.
	(g) Approval of all mergers, acquisitions, diversifications into new businesses, the sale of more than 10 percent of the company's assets (other than in the ordinary course of business), sale of patent rights held by company, or liquidation.
	(h) Approval of Common Stock repurchases or dividends.
	(i) Approval of employee stock ownership plans.
Preemptive rights	Standard pro rata rights in all future private financings.
Key man insurance	So long as Preferred is outstanding, company will maintain key man insurance on founders' lives in the amount of $500,000 each.
Representations and warranties	Standard representations and warranties by company; also individual representations and warranties of founders with respect to patents, proprietary information, conflicts with prior employers, stock ownership, and litigation.
Amendments and waivers	70 percent of outstanding Preferred Stock required.
Expenses	Company will pay all fees and expenses of investors' special counsel if deal is consummated.
Other agreements	Patent Assignment Agreements Stock Restriction Agreements Noncompete Agreements Confidentiality and Proprietary Information Agreements

EXHIBIT 5   Summary of Principal Terms—R&D Partnership

General partner:	Robotics Development Company (RDC) to be formed by Reed, Baker, and Carlton. URC will contribute $22,000 and all of its existing technology relating to robotics to the partnership in exchange for a 1 percent interest in profits, losses, distributions of cash, and distributions upon dissolution.
Limited partners:	Will purchase 100 units of Limited Partnership interests for $22,000 each, which, net of Pincus, Greene selling commissions, will contribute $2,000,000 to the partnership, in exchange for a 99 percent interest in profits, losses, distributions of cash and distributions upon dissolution.
License:	Upon completion of the products the partnership will grant a perpetual license to URC to manufacture and market the products in exchange for a 10 percent royalty (on sales) payable to the partnership.
Option:	The partnership will grant to URC an option to purchase all of its assets (including the license) one year and one day after —The product becomes commercially available, *or* —Development work is abandoned. In exchange for, at URC's option, either —$10 million in cash *or* —A number of shares that would give the partnership a 30 percent interest in URC *after* subdivisions, consolidations, reorganizations, mergers, recapitalizations, reclassification, capital adjustment, and any issuance of common stock as a dividend.

Appendix

GLOSSARY

Registration rights There are generally two types of registration rights—*demand* and *piggyback*.

a. **demand** Demand registration rights entitle the holders of stock to require the Company to register their shares for sale to the public pursuant to a registration statement filed on their behalf with the Securities and Exchange Commission (the SEC) under the Securities Act of 1933.

b. **piggyback** Piggyback rights entitle the holders of the Company's securities to "piggyback" on any registration statement filed by the Company with the SEC for the sale of the Company's securities to the public.

Pre-emptive rights These rights entitle shareholders to purchase their pro rata share of any new securities issued by the Company. The purpose of pre-emptive rights is to allow a shareholder to maintain his percentage equity interest in the Company. For example, if the shareholder owns 10 percent of the equity of the Company and the Company intends to offer an additional 1 million shares, the pre-emptive rights of the shareholder will entitle him to purchase 100,000 shares.

Redemption rights Redemption rights may be either *optional* or *mandatory*.

a. **optional rights** Optional redemption rights entitle the Company to call convertible preferred stock and thereby eliminate the preferred stock from the capitalization. The call price is generally equivalent to the liquidation price, but in some cases may include a premium and/or accrued dividends.

b. **mandatory rights** Mandatory redemption rights benefit the stockholders because they entitle the stockholders to "put" the shares of capital stock to the Company for purchase at the redemption price. These rights are similar to sinking fund provisions of a debenture and are burdensome to the Company because the stock may be put to it at a time when it has insufficient funds to purchase the stock.

Antidilution provisions Antidilution provisions are generally classified either as *ratchet* or *weighted average formula*.

a. **ratchet** The ratchet provision is exactly as the name suggests. It provides for a downward adjustment to the lowest price paid for the stock. If, for example, an investor purchases 100 shares of convertible preferred stock for $100, and the stock is convertible into common at the rate of $10 per share, the investor will receive 10 shares of common at the time of conversion. If the investor has the benefit of the ratchet antidilution provision and a sale of common stock is subsequently made for $1 per share, then the conversion price ratchets down to $1 per share, and therefore the investor will be able to convert the preferred stock into 100 shares of common stock. This is the ultimate in antidilution protection.

b. **weighted average formula**   The weighted average formula antidilution provision is much less severe to the Company. It provides for an adjustment in the conversion price based on the consideration received for the new shares and can be best explained by using the following formula:

X = New conversion price
A = Outstanding shares prior to sale
B = Current conversion price
C = Amount received on sale of new stock
D = Number of new shares sold

$$(X = A \times B + C \div A + D)$$

To illustrate, the original conversion price of $10 is reduced to $9.30 by using the formula, assuming the sale of 300,000 new shares at a $7.00 conversion price, as follows:

A = 1,000,000 shares
B = $10
C = $2,100,000
D = 300,000 shares

In this example, the price paid for the new stock of $7.00 per share results in a new exercise price of $9.30:

(1,000,000 × $10) + (300,000 × $7) ÷ 1,000,000 + 300,000 = $12,100,000 ÷ 1,300,000 shares = $9.30)

Take-me-along agreement   In many venture capital transactions, the venture capital investors want to assure that management will not sell its stock position before the investors sell their shares. In particular, they want to avoid a management bail-out. Accordingly, they insist on the execution and delivery by management of a so-called take-me-along agreement. This agreement generally provides that a management/shareholder who desires to sell a portion of his shares (e.g., 10%) must notify the venture capital investors and "take them along" with him in the sale and thereby allow them to sell 10% of their shares, as well. Obviously, if the purchaser is interested in buying only a specified number of shares, and the management/shareholder desires to sell that number of shares to the purchaser, the take-me-along rights will require the management/shareholder to reduce the number of shares he sells and thereby make room for the other investors who desire to be taken along.

Form S-2 and Form S-3   These are SEC forms used for the registration of securities under the Securities Act of 1933. These forms are so-called short form registrations, particularly Form S-3, which is a very abbreviated form and allows the registration of securities by incorporating information about the Company, which has previously been filed with the SEC pursuant to the Company's Annual Report on Form 10-K, its Annual Report and Quarterly Reports, and its proxy statement for its annual meeting. Companies that have been public companies, have filed reports with the SEC for a specified number of years, have been profitable and meet certain other conditions are entitled to use the short-form registrations.

CVD Incorporated versus A. S. Markham Corporation (A)

It was 2 A.M. on April 10, 1984, and Bob Donadio and Joe Connolly sat in a small Boston coffee house thinking about their trial against A. S. Markham Corporation, a billion-dollar defense contractor. The two founders of CVD Inc. had sued their former employer—Markham—for relief from what they believed to be an onerous licensing contract. Markham, in turn, had sued them and their small company for a series of alleged infractions including breach of employment contracts, misappropriation of trade secrets, and misuse of confidential information.

The testimony in the trial had ended earlier that afternoon and the two men had spent five hours preparing their side's closing arguments with their lawyer. They would make those arguments tomorrow, the trial would end, and the jury would begin its deliberations—a process that was expected to take several days.

As Donadio and Connolly sat in the coffee house, they knew that if they lost the trial, the judgment against them would likely bankrupt the company. On the other hand, if they won, Markham could appeal the decision to a higher court and prolong the dispute even further. Perhaps, they wondered, they should try to settle the case with Markham before the jury returned with its verdict.

This case was prepared by Ennis J. Walton under the direction of Michael J. Roberts.

Copyright © 1987 by the President and Fellows of Harvard College
Harvard Business School case 9-388-042

BACKGROUND

Bob Donadio and Joe Connolly met in 1972, when Donadio recruited Connolly to work for Markham's Advanced Materials Department (AMD). In the seven years that followed, they both had satisfying careers working on Markham's research and development projects sponsored by various agencies of the United States government (see Exhibit 1).

Despite their good feelings about Markham, however, by 1979 both Donadio and Connolly wanted to explore new options. Thinking back, Donadio recalled:

> It wasn't an easy decision to leave Markham. I had put in 20 damn good years with them, and I had obtained all the perks that a person with my seniority could expect to receive. I also had a family to think about: With a wife and three children, two of whom were of college age, I couldn't just leave the company without thinking about the possible impact my decision would have on the rest of my family. In time, I discussed things with my family, and they supported my desire. They weren't completely thrilled at first, but they eventually agreed with me.

Donadio's basic idea for CVD Inc. was to use his knowledge of the chemical vapor deposition (cvd) manufacturing process to become a supplier of infrared materials. Explaining the core technology, Donadio said:

> The cvd process is an extremely useful way to combine different chemical compounds. First, gases or vapors of the compounds are brought together in a specially designed furnace. While in the furnace, the gases will react with one another to form a solid metal-like material that deposits on a substrate and then hardens as it cools. There are many different ways to form these vapors—we simply heat blocks of material in the furnace.
>
> Following this, the solid is polished until it resembles a glasslike material capable of transmitting infrared light and high energy lasers. Once the material reaches this glasslike state, it must be subjected to a battery of tests in order to verify its purity—if it isn't pure, it won't transmit infrared light or lasers properly.
>
> In most cases, materials manufactured by this process have properties that make them better than the same materials produced by another manufacturing process. This is particularly true for zinc selenide (ZnSe/cvd) and zinc sulfide (ZnS/cvd)—the two materials most frequently manufactured in this manner.

Donadio's original plan for the new company was to supply ZnSe/cvd to optical fabricators that used it to make output windows for commercial high energy laser (HEL) applications such as automobile body welding, steel plate cutting, and "bloodless" surgery. "We had suggested these commercial applications to Markham," said Donadio, "but they seemed uninterested." As the company grew, Donadio also expected to manufacture both ZnSe/cvd and ZnS/cvd to create infrared optical lenses used for thermal imaging in military applications that required night vision and thermal sensing in weapons.

Recalling his reasons for joining Donadio, Connolly said:

> Bob first mentioned his idea for a new company to me one day after work in Markham's parking lot. This came as a welcome surprise to me since I was quietly looking around for a new job anyway. I really didn't have much to lose—I knew I could work well with Bob, so I decided to join him instead of joining a different company.

A few days after Donadio and Connolly decided to leave Markham, Donadio advised his supervisor, Dr. Smith, of their decision. During the meeting, Dr. Smith told Donadio that he and Connolly would have to appear before Markham's lawyers if they were serious about starting a cvd processing company. Reflecting on the meeting, Donadio said:

> At the time talking to Smith seemed like the right thing to do. I had consulted with him on many issues before—including this one. At one time, we even entertained the idea of combining our vast knowledge of cvd processes to form the new company. It only seemed right to let him know first.
>
> During that meeting, however, Smith seemed to forget about all that. Instead, he told me that I would have to go before Markham's legal staff if I was serious about leaving to start a cvd processing company. A few hours later, he called Joe in his office to say the same thing.

Connolly added his perspective on being called into Markham's legal department for questioning:

> For a scientist like me, it was quite bizarre to get summoned by Markham's lawyers. The entire atmosphere was different from everything that I knew about the company. Unlike the lab where I worked, the law department seemed cold and impersonal.

After the meeting with Markham's lawyers, it was obvious to Donadio and Connolly that they needed to hire a lawyer to protect their rights. As Donadio recalled:

> We hadn't done anything wrong, but Markham didn't see it that way. Instead, they claimed that we were planning to steal and use its "proprietary information."
>
> We tried to point out that because Markham's cvd research was funded under government contract, it was part of the public domain. I knew this because I'd spent the better part of my career preparing reports for the government that illustrated the cvd process.
>
> From our perspective, Markham didn't have any proprietary information regarding the chemical vapor deposition process. They certainly

didn't have any patents on the process. Moreover, Joe and I had enough expertise with the cvd processes to start a company that purposefully avoided everything that Markham considered "proprietary" or a "trade secret." Had they told us exactly what they considered to be trade secrets, we could have worked around them. But, they just kept claiming that the entire process was proprietary.

After the meetings with Dr. Smith and the lawyers, I worked at Markham for about another month. During that time I was restricted to my desk and no one bothered to talk to me—for a researcher, that's like professional death. In our business, you live off the flow of information between your colleagues. I'm not naive and I'm certainly not a romantic, but I don't understand how stable personal and professional friendships could be lost in one day. I cannot understand why my friends and colleagues decided to ostracize me. Maybe they were under pressure to follow the company line—I don't know.

INITIAL NEGOTIATIONS

Taking Markham's threats seriously, Donadio and Connolly hired Jerry Cohen, an attorney specializing in intellectual property issues, to serve as their lawyer. As their attorney, Cohen maintained a spirited debate with Markham's legal counsel, Len Davis, in an attempt clarify Markham's case.

On one occasion, Cohen, Donadio, and Connolly met with Len Davis to discuss the alleged proprietary information. In that meeting Cohen provided evidence from publicly available government documents to dispute Markham's proprietary claims. However, despite that information, the two sides were unable to reach a mutually acceptable agreement. Instead, Markham threatened to sue Donadio and Connolly for breaching their employment contracts (see excerpts, Exhibit 2) if they formed a new firm that used any of Markham's alleged proprietary information or trade secrets without a license from the company.

In January 1980, Donadio and Connolly formed CVD Incorporated. Without the benefit of salaries and with the threat of a long and costly lawsuit, Donadio and Connolly worked out of their homes during the first few months until they could design the company's manufacturing facility, finish their business plan, and raise capital.

In writing their business plan, Donadio used his knowledge to list 18 different domestic and international commercial companies that might purchase CVD's products. CVD's business plan also included a list of 35 government agencies that might purchase ZnSe/cvd and ZnS/cvd within the next five years. In all, CVD's business plan estimated that its company would generate before-tax profits of approximately $310,000 on sales of $1,400,000 during its third year of manufacturing operations. After that time, the company estimated that its overall sales would increase at an annual rate of 20 percent.

Despite a completed engineering design and optimistic figures, the process of attracting money for their venture was more difficult than they had initially expected. CVD's attempts were mired from the beginning by investors' fears that the company would be caught in an acrimonious and protracted legal fight. Prospective investors were also concerned that Markham would lower its prices and use its established position to maintain its hold on the market.

THE LICENSE

Thus, after many frustrated attempts to raise capital in the spring of 1980, Donadio and Connolly, with advice from Jerry Cohen, decided to sign a licensing agreement with Markham (see Exhibit 3). The terms of the license called for CVD to pay Markham 15 percent and 8 percent on the net selling price for ZnSe/cvd and ZnS/cvd, respectively, for a 10-year period. Once under license, Donadio and Connolly lowered their business plan's projections to reflect the terms of the Markham license.

The license quieted investors' fears, and Donadio and Connolly were successful in raising the funds. The two men received $450,000 by mid-June 1980 from the following sources: $300,000 from a loan from the Small Business Administration; $80,000 from a prospective customer; and the remainder from the men's family and friends.

BEGINNING OPERATIONS

Donadio and Connolly put the firm's money to work immediately purchasing equipment and signing a lease for a 4,500 square foot facility in Woburn. By February 1981, the firm had made significant progress: net sales had reached $751,000. Despite this progress, Donadio and Connolly still worried about the firm's $109,000 licensing fee, which when added to the company's costs and expenses produced net earnings before taxes of negative $99,000. Remembering his thoughts, Donadio said:

> Our revenues and costs were in good shape for a start-up, but it was clear that CVD couldn't survive with the original terms of the license—it was like having a tax on our gross revenues.

Based on an important clause in its license with Markham (see Exhibit 3), CVD informed Markham that it wanted to exercise its right to renegotiate the terms of the license. Markham, however, refused to alter the terms of the contract. In all, the company tried and failed to renegotiate on three separate occasions. Finally, Donadio and Connolly decided not to pay Markham until the company honored CVD's right to renegotiate the terms of the license.

In June 1981, Markham informed CVD that it was in default. Markham also advised CVD that if all obligations were not immediately paid in full, it would cancel the agreement and seek legal action. CVD responded to Markham's notices by seeking new counsel. With little time, Donadio and Connolly, aided by Jerry Cohen, identified Blair L. Perry—a high-technology and antitrust specialist—as a good attorney to handle their case.

THE SUIT

After a short period of negotiations, Perry agreed to handle the case. In exchange, CVD agreed to pay Perry's firm $6,000 on a monthly basis for its legal representation.

In August 1981, CVD filed a complaint against Markham in federal court, arguing that the license was invalid because it represented a violation of the Sherman Antitrust Act, which restricts illegal attempts to maintain a monopoly and restrain competition.

Blair Perry recalled his strategy:

> We filed an antitrust claim for several reasons. First, we wanted to claim the high ground by being the plaintiff. Second, an antitrust violation was the only means of getting the case heard in the federal court system. Here, you can get to trial in two years instead of the five it takes in the state courts. The federal judges are also more used to dealing with the sort of complex issues this case presents.

A few days later, Markham responded with a counterclaim, arguing that the license was valid and enforceable. Markham also claimed that Donadio, Connolly, and CVD Inc. had engaged in unfair and deceptive business practices to obtain Markham's proprietary information. As a result, Markham claimed monetary losses in excess of $4 million as well as other damages. The basis of the dispute was as follows.

CVD argued that the license was invalid because:

— Markham did not have any trade secrets related to the production of ZnSe/cvd and ZnS/cvd.

— Markham acted in bad faith when it compelled CVD to sign the license because they knew that they didn't have any trade secrets.

— The license was signed under duress.

— And, the license was counter to public policy objectives in that it restrained competition and helped sustain Markham's monopoly in this market.

Markham disputed CVD's claims arguing instead that the license was valid and enforceable because:

— Markham had trade secrets and confidential business information related to the production of ZnSe/cvd and ZnS/cvd.

— Donadio and Connolly had learned Markham's trade secrets and confidential business information while employed by Markham.

— Donadio and Connolly had signed employment contracts that prevented any employee from using or disclosing any of Markham's proprietary information unless expressly authorized by Markham.

— The license agreement was a valid legal document—irrespective of whether or not Markham actually had trade secrets or proprietary information—which granted CVD the right to use Markham's knowledge related to the production of ZnSe/cvd and ZnS/cvd.

— Donadio and Connolly signed the license willingly and with a competent attorney protecting their legal rights.

— Donadio and Connolly had breached contracts and duties of good faith outlined in their employment contracts.

— Donadio, Connolly, and CVD had misappropriated Markham's proprietary information relating to the production of ZnSe/cvd and ZnS/cvd.

— And, CVD had breached fiduciary duties mandated by the license.

PRETRIAL ACTIONS

After reviewing the claims of each party, the court urged CVD Inc. and Markham to attempt to settle the matter out of court. In extensive pretrial settlement discussions CVD offered to pay approximately $450,000 to Markham in return for freedom from the royalty obligations and from trade secret claims. Markham refused that offer and in exchange proposed that it would end its legal claims if CVD paid $3 million to Markham. Unable to compromise beyond this point, both sides began the lengthy pretrial preparation process. Recalling some of the reasons why it took so long to make it to court, Blair Perry said:

> The most difficult part of the pretrial process started when we tried to demystify Markham's trade secret claims. No matter what we did, we couldn't get a comprehensive list of what they were claiming as trade secrets. We eventually had to prepare our own list of possible trade secrets in order to be ready for trial—a process that was very time consuming and full of frustrations.
>
> For example, Markham told us that its trade secrets could be found in some of its engineering drawings that we were going to inspect. When I

got to Markham's offices, they took me to a room and showed me stack of about 2,000 drawings. I was simply amazed!

After a cursory look at the evidence, I tried to get the court to force Markham to be more specific. To my dismay, however, the court ruled in Markham's favor, and so I spent a number of days sorting through all those drawings trying to determine which ones were really relevant.

After two years of preparations, the opposing attorneys entered court to empanel a jury. This process was important because each side expected the case to turn on the testimony of the witnesses. In the end, a 12-person jury was selected that featured a chemical engineer as the foreman.

THE TRIAL

On March 5, 1984, the case of *CVD Inc.* v. *Markham* went to trial before Justice Stevenson of the United States District Court, District of Massachusetts. Sparing no expense, Markham appeared in court with five lawyers while Blair Perry alone represented CVD.

After hearing each side's opening statements, Justice Stevenson made two important decisions that affected the way the issues were argued. First, he ruled that Markham could not use the term proprietary because it was unclear and not well grounded in legal precedent. The court also ruled that in order for CVD to obtain relief from the license, they had to show by "clear and convincing" evidence that Markham knew it didn't have trade secrets when it enacted the licensing agreement with CVD.

The information presented during the trial focused on the following topics:

I. The CVD Process.   Markham submitted the following testimony regarding the cvd process:

— The Advanced Materials Division, where Donadio and Connolly were employed, had engaged in the development of unique and sophisticated methods and equipment used to produce ZnSe/cvd and ZnS/cvd since 1959.

— An expert witness testified that there is an art or skill required to produce ZnSe/cvd and ZnS/cvd that could only be obtained through years of skilled experience.

— When asked what he would need to design, build, and operate a cvd furnace to make ZnSe/cvd and ZnS/cvd, an expert witness claimed that he would need "an experienced staff."

— Markham claimed that in 1980, it was the only company with an experienced staff (seven people) capable of producing ZnSe/cvd and ZnS/cvd.

— Markham asserted that Donadio and Connolly had acquired their knowledge of the specific processes, equipment, and methods used by Markham during their employment with Markham.

— Markham argued that no detailed information about the cvd process had been disclosed, and it claimed that CVD had misappropriated the following trade secrets:

a. Passivation Gas Mixture: This gaseous mixture was used by Markham to scrub out the discharge lines from the cvd furnace before it was opened to prevent fires or explosions when fine zinc dust mixed with normal air. Markham's officials testified that the company had had three fires and two explosions before it discovered that a mixture of 97 percent nitrogen and 3 percent oxygen would stabilize the zinc dust and prevent fires and explosions.

One expert witness testified that during the jury's visit to CVD's facilities, he had noticed that CVD had tried to hide its own passivation gas tank (by covering it with brown paper) to prevent Markham and the court from knowing that it used the same passivation gas mixture that Markham employed.

b. Alumina Insert Hydrogen Sulfide Injector: This was an insert that was placed over the tip of the hydrogen sulfide injector to prevent the corrosion of the stainless steel mixing chamber where gases were mixed. By using this, Markham was able to prevent hydrogen sulfide gas from reacting with and corroding the injector tip.

One of Markham's expert witnesses testified that the composition and exact positioning of the alumina insert was critical because corrosion would make it impossible to complete the long furnace phase of the cvd process (usually one to two days) necessary to produce high-quality materials. He also testified that there were other ceramic materials that could be used instead of alumina.

c. Hexagonal Graphite Nut: This piece fit inside Markham's sulfide injector assembly to allow argon gas to be distributed uniformly thereby making it possible for the company to manufacture high-quality zinc sulfide.

— Markham asserted that it always denied public access to its furnace facilities to protect its trade secrets.

The following points regarding the chemical vapor deposition process were made by CVD during the trial:

— The cvd process was well known to scientists in general and chemical engineers in particular.

— The cvd process was taught throughout the education system from grade school to college chemistry courses.

— Donadio and Connolly testified that they acquired knowledge about the process before, after, and during their employment with Markham.

— Donadio and Connolly testified that they returned all documents belonging to Markham at the end of their employment with the company; and, they stressed that their employment contracts did not contain noncompete clauses.

— CVD produced evidence that a U.S. patent on certain aspects of the cvd process had been issued to another individual in 1964 (see Exhibit 4).

— Markham's patent attorney testified (under cross examination) that he had learned of this patent when Markham tried to patent ZnSe/cvd and ZnS/cvd, and therefore, he had stopped the patent process. He explained that Markham had stopped the patent process because Markham believed that there were no commercial applications of the process. Because the government was the only likely customer, and because it already held a royalty-free license on the process, it didn't make sense to proceed with the patent. Moreover, he admitted that he had informed both Donadio and Dr. Smith in a memo that Markham would not seek a patent on these products.

— Markham's patent attorney admitted that Markham had a computer system that listed all information that the company officially protected as trade secrets, and CVD produced evidence which showed the cvd process, ZnSe/cvd and ZnS/cvd, had not been protected by this system.

— Markham's patent attorney testified that Markham had a company policy that required all protected engineering drawings to be marked or stamped secret and placed in a special drawer. And, Connolly testified that he had made hundreds of detailed engineering drawings, and he had never been told to mark them *secret.*

— CVD provided evidence that Markham had disclosed elements of the cvd process in government reports, lectures, and films. These disclosures included information about Markham's hexagonal graphite nut.

— One of Markham's expert witnesses testified (under cross examination) that a "component" engineer could construct Markham's manufacturing process from the information disclosed in the government reports.

— One of Markham's witnesses admitted that many of Markham's alleged trade secrets were known in the industry. For example, the expert witness admitted (under cross examination) that it was well known in the industry that zinc dust would ignite if exposed to oxygen. He also acknowledged that any undergraduate engineer would recognize that a passivation gas containing less oxygen than normal air would slow the rate of oxidation, which caused fires and explosions.

— Another one of Markham's expert witnesses admitted (under cross examination) that it would be obvious to any engineer that a corrosion-resistant material would be needed to prevent the corrosion of the stainless steel injector tip. He further admitted that it made logical sense to use an alumina insert over the stainless steel injector tip because alumina was inert and had a high melting point.

II. The Products: The following points regarding the ZnSe/cvd and ZnS/cvd products were made by CVD:

— Due to their unique light transmission properties ZnSe/cvd and ZnS/cvd were extremely popular among military and commercial customers, and these customers used the products, rather than other infrared materials made by different manufacturing processes.

— Markham's ZnSe/cvd and ZnS/cvd had outstripped Eastman Kodak's ZnSe and ZnS made by the "hot pressing process"; Kodak had discontinued its ZnSe production.

— Before 1980, Markham produced and sold 65 percent and 98 percent of the ZnSe/cvd and ZnS/cvd, respectively.

— Markham had imposed a "price squeeze" by reducing its prices in situations where it knew it was in direct competition with CVD. Markham knew CVD could not reduce its prices, pay exorbitant royalties, and still operate on a profitable basis.

— Markham reduced its prices 20 percent on January 21, 1980, with the intent of preventing CVD from competing.

— Markham had maintained its prices at the January 21, 1980, rate despite inflation and increasing production costs.

— Markham had falsely represented to various potential customers that CVD was in violation of its contract obligations and was thus an unsuitable supplier.

Markham disputed CVD's claims arguing:

— ZnSe and ZnS, irrespective of the manufacturing process, along with 40 other materials can be used for their optical, infrared, and electrical properties.

— Markham only has a 9 percent market share of all 42 infrared materials sold in the United States.

— Donadio admitted that before leaving Markham, he had participated in the formation of the company's prices, which became effective on January 21, 1980.

— Markham claimed that its prices never fell below the average costs necessary to produce ZnSe/cvd and ZnS/cvd.

III. The License: CVD made the following claims about the license:

— Donadio and Connolly testified that Markham threatened to sue them unless they signed a license; this action, they claimed, left them with no other viable alternatives.

— Markham had never listed its "trade secrets" in its negotiations with CVD; therefore no specific information had been granted by the license.

— Jerry Cohen testified that he had tried and failed to get Markham to limit the terms of license.

— Markham's lawyer, Len Davis, acknowledged that he had implied to Donadio, Connolly, and Cohen that the terms of the licensing agreement were less than equitable before they signed the agreement.

Markham took exception to CVD's argument:

— Markham claimed that the processes, methods, and techniques that were used by Markham represented trade secret and confidential business information.

— Donadio and Connolly testified that they had been offered new jobs inside Markham, but they turned them down to start CVD.

— Markham claimed that Donadio and Connolly voluntarily, with aid of a lawyer of their own selection, executed an agreement which recognized the authenticity of Markham's trade secrets and confidential business information.

IV. The Employment Contract: Markham argued that Donadio and Connolly had broken their employment contracts:

— Markham provided evidence that Donadio and Connolly, along with all other Markham employees, had signed employment contracts that prohibited them from using or disclosing any of the information that they had learned or practiced while they were Markham's employees for their own benefit at any time unless they were specifically authorized by Markham.

— Markham provided evidence, described earlier, that Donadio and Connolly had indeed misappropriated proprietary information and were therefore in violation of their employment contracts.

CVD presented evidence, discussed earlier, that the information that Markham claimed to be proprietary was, in fact, well known in the industry.

After 26 days of testimony, each side presented the judge with its own Suggested Instructions to the Jury (see Exhibits 5 and 6).

CONCLUSION

As the two men reviewed the past month of testimony, they were optimistic about the outcome. Yet, they also knew that with a jury, anything could happen. Blair Perry felt good about the way the case was going, but he too had urged caution. As Donadio and Connolly contemplated the future, it was the consequences of this uncertainty that loomed before them. Donadio commented:

> I feel confident, but if we lose, we're out of business. Even if we win, Markham can keep us in court on appeal for years. Perhaps the testimony has convinced Markham that their chances of winning are not very good. Maybe, they'd be willing to settle for a reasonable amount, or even renegotiate the license.

While the possibility of resolving this uncertainty was attractive, the two men were also cognizant of the fact that they had spent tremendous time and nearly a quarter of a million dollars in legal fees ($156,000 of which they had yet to pay). While they felt they could afford some settlement (see Exhibit 7 for financials), to back down now seemed not only wrong, but an admission of guilt that neither man truly felt.

EXHIBIT 1   The Plaintiffs

Name: Robert Donadio

Title: President, CVD Inc.

Education: BS and MS degrees in Mechanical Engineering from Northeastern University 1958 and 1963, respectively.

Work Experience: Served as principal scientist for Markham's Advanced Materials Department (AMD); Managed Markham's domestic and international infrared materials marketing programs.

Special Recognition: Invented Markham's CVD Zinc Selenide and Zinc Sulfo-Selenide with Dr. Smith, B. Henderson, and W. Jung in 1973 (patent was not pursued by Markham); known as an international expert in the area of chemical vapor deposition.

Personal: Married with three children whose ages ranged from 15 to 21.

Name: Joseph Connolly

Title: Vice President, Operations, CVD Inc.

Education: AE degree in Mechanical Engineering from Wentworth Institute in 1969; BS and MS degrees in Mechanical Engineering from Northeastern University in 1972 and 1976, respectively.

Work Experience: Joined Markham's Advanced Materials Department in 1972; eventually served as senior scientist for Markham's AMD and lead engineer on the production of infrared windows for a number of government and commercial contracts.

Personal: Separated with three children whose ages ranged from 3 to 15.

EXHIBIT 2   The Employment Contract Signed by Donadio and Connolly

In consideration of the employment of _____ by the employer, Markham Corporation (Markham), in the course of which employment is contemplated that the Employee may make/create products and/or compose subject inventions and/or proprietary information, and the trust and confidence responded in the Employee by Markham with respect thereto, it is agreed as follows:

1. *Subject Invention* means any invention, improvement, or discovery of the Employee, whether or not patentable, other than those identified below, which during the period of his employment by Markham is (a) conceived by the employer, or (b) first actually reduced to practice by or for Markham, and which arises out of or is related to any of the business activities of Markham or any other company, which is owned or controlled by Markham.

2. *Proprietary Information* means secret or private information concerning Markham's design, manufacture, use, purchase, or sale of its products or materials, such as may be contained in but not limited to, Markham's manu-

EXHIBIT 2   *(concluded)*

facturing methods, processes or techniques, treatment or chemical composition of material, and plant layout or tooling, all to the extent that (a) such
information is not readily disclosed by inspection or analysis of the products
or materials sold, leased or otherwise disposed of by Markham, and (b)
Markham has protected such information from unrestricted use by others.

3. All Subject Inventions and Proprietary Information are and shall remain
   the sole and exclusive property of Markham, subject only to any prior
   encumbrances attaching thereto. The Employee agrees to disclose all
   Subject Inventions, and all Proprietary Information generated by the
   Employee, promptly, completely and in writing to Markham and such
   others and under such conditions as may be designated by Markham.

4. The Employee agrees (a) to execute all documents requested by Markham
   for vesting in Markham the entire right, title and interest in; and to (i) all
   Subject Inventions, (ii) all Proprietary Information generated by the Employee, and (iii) all patent applications filed and all patents issuing on such
   Subject Inventions; (b) to execute all documents requested by Markham for
   filing and prosecutions and such applications for patents as Markham may
   desire covering such Subject Inventions; and (c) to give to Markham all
   assistance it reasonably requires in order to process Markham's rights in its
   Subject Inventions and Proprietary Information.

5. The Employee agrees that his obligation to perform the acts specified in
   paragraph 4 above shall not expire with termination of his employment.
   However, the period during which Markham's rights to Subject Inventions,
   and Proprietary Information generated by the Employee are created shall
   not be extended by virtue of the previous sentence. Markham agrees to pay
   the Employee at a reasonable rate for any time that the Employee actually
   spends in the performance of the acts specified in paragraph 4 above at
   Markham's written request after termination of the Employee's employment and to reimburse the Employee for expenses necessarily incurred by
   him in connection with such acts.

6. All documents, records, models, prototypes, and other tangible evidence of
   Subject Inventions and Proprietary Information, which shall at any time
   come into the possession of the Employee, shall be the sole and exclusive
   property of Markham and shall be surrendered to Markham upon the
   termination of the Employee's employment by Markham, or upon request
   at any other time.

7. The Employee agrees that, unless duly authorized in writing by an Officer
   of Markham, he will not either during his employment by Markham, or
   thereafter as long as the Employee is unable reasonably to demonstrate
   that Markham Proprietary Information has passed into the public domain
   other than as a consequence of the Employee's own acts, divulge, or use for
   his own or another's benefit, any of said Proprietary Information.

8. The Employee represents and warrants that he has not entered and will not
   enter into any agreement inconsistent herewith.

EXHIBIT 3   Excerpts from License Agreement

The license signed between CVD Inc. and Markham had the following important clauses:

1. Markham's cvd process used to manufacture zinc selenide and zinc sulfide, trademarked *Martran,* represents proprietary trade secrets.

2. Markham grants CVD Inc. the nonexclusive right to use its proprietary process for which CVD Inc. agrees to pay Markham royalties of 15 percent and 8 percent on the net selling prices of its ZnSe/cvd and ZnS/cvd products produced pursuant to this agreement.

3. Markham agrees to allow CVD Inc. to renegotiate the terms of this original agreement if they prove inequitable.

4. Markham retains the right to cancel the agreement at any time if CVD Inc. fails to pay the royalties.

5. No termination of the license shall release any party from the royalty obligations that have incurred.

6. This license shall be construed under the laws of the Commonwealth of Massachusetts.

7. This license is effective retroactively from January 1, 1980, until December 31, 1990.

EXHIBIT 4   Vapor Phase Crystallization Patent, Dated February 11, 1964, Granted to H. J. Gould

---

(Excerpts from U.S. Government Patent Filing)

This invention has to do with the crystallization from the vapor phase of crystals at least one component of which is a metal that is solid at normal temperature.

The invention has to do, more particularly, with improved methods and apparatus for supplying to a furnace chamber the vapor of a metallic component that is solid at normal temperature.

This invention is particularly useful in, but is not limited to, the production of semiconductive crystals such, for example, as cadmium and zinc sulphide, selenide, and telluride, and mixtures of such components. It is well known that crystals of that type can be produced in good purity by vapor phase crystallization.

In producing such illustrative crystals, the nonmetallic component is ordinarily supplied to the furnace as a continuous stream of gas, typically as hydrogen sulphide, selenide, or telluride. The rate of supply of such a gaseous component is accurately and conveniently controllable by known methods.

The metallic component is ordinarily supplied by inserting in the furnace in the gas stream a boat containing the metal in solid or liquid form. The metal then evaporates into the gas stream at a rate that is roughly controllable by variation of such factors as temperature, the rate of gas flow, and the area of the exposed metal surface.

EXHIBIT 4 (*continued*)

Such control, however, is less accurate than is often desirable and is unsatisfactory for many other reasons. Even rough control of the vaporizing temperature usually requires a special furnace zone for that purpose. The rate of gas flow that is most suitable for metal vaporization may be undesirable for other reasons. And the area of metal surface usually decreases in an uncontrollable way as the initial charge is exhausted. Moreover, the rate of evaporation from a given surface area is very sensitive to contamination of the surface, which typically increases as the metal charge is consumed.

The present invention avoids all of those difficulties in a remarkably economical and convenient manner. In accordance with one aspect of the invention, the metallic component is supplied in the form of a fine wire, and is fed to the furnace at a definite velocity. The described method has the further great advantage that under equilibrium conditions of operation, the rate of vapor supply is essentially or completely independent of virtually all other variable factors. Hence, those factors may be adjusted arbitrarily as required to meet other conditions.

In accordance with a further aspect of the invention, the metal wire is fed to the furnace chamber through a capillary passage formed of suitable inert material such as quartz, for example. The passage is so arranged that the advancing metal reaches vaporizing temperature at a point spaced from the exit mouth of the passage. Vaporization then occurs within the capillary passage, and the metal leaves the passage mouth as a continuous and uniform stream of vapor. A further advantage of that structure is that, by suitable form and placement of the passage, the metal vapor can be delivered accurately to any desired point of the furnace chamber.

A further aspect of the invention provides means for surface cleaning of the metal wire immediately prior to melting and vaporization. That may be accomplished by passing the wire through a reducing chamber, which is continuously washed by a reducing gas, such as hydrogen, for example. The reducing chamber is preferably maintained at an elevated temperature, which may be only slightly less than the melting point of the metal.

A full understanding of the invention, and of its further objects and advantages, will be had from the following description of certain illustrative manners in which it may be carried out, of which description the accompanying drawings form a part. The particulars of that description are intended only as illustration, and not as a limitation upon the scope of the invention, which is defined in the appended claims.

[Drawings and explanations have been omitted for brevity.]

I Claim the Following as Patented:

1. The method of supplying vapor of a metal at a controlled rate to a furnace for production of a crystal by vapor crystallization, said method comprising providing a capillary passage communicating with the chamber, feeding a wire consisting essentially of the metal into the passage toward the chamber at such a temperature that the wire is vaporized within the passage.

EXHIBIT 4   *(concluded)*

2. The method of supplying vapor of a metal at a controlled rate to a furnace chamber for production of a crystal by vapor phase crystallization, said method comprising providing a capillary passage that opens into the chamber, maintaining in the passage at a point spaced from said opening a longitudinal temperature gradient that is steeper than the gradient in the chamber adjacent to the passage and that embraces the melting temperature and the vaporizing temperature of the metal, and feeding a wire consisting essentially of the metal into the passage toward the chamber at a controlled velocity.

3. The method of supplying vapor of a metal at a controlled rate to a furnace chamber for production of a crystal by vapor phase crystallization, said method comprising providing a passage communicating at one end with the chamber, feeding wire consisting essentially of the metal into the passage toward the chamber at a controlled velocity, maintaining the passage at such temperature that the wire is vaporized therein adjacent said passage end, and contacting the wire in the passage prior to said vaporization with a gas that is substantially inert with respect to the metal and that chemically reacts with impurities carried by the wire.

4. The method of producing a semiconductive crystal comprising a metallic component and containing a substantially uniform relative concentration comprising providing a solid wire which consists essentially of the metallic component and doping agent in said relative concentration, feeding the wire at a controlled velocity into a capillary tube, maintaining a temperature gradient along the tube to vaporize the wire, and crystallizing the resulting vapor to form said semiconductor crystal.

5. The method of producing a semiconductive crystal containing substantially uniformly distributed therein a minor proportion a doping agent, said method comprising providing a solid wire composed primarily of metal selected from the group consisting of cadmium and zinc and containing said doping agent in a concentration corresponding to said propiration, feeding the wire at controlled velocity into a capillary tube, maintaining a temperature gradient along the tube to vaporize the wire, combining the resulting vapors in substantially constant ratio with gas selected from the group consisting of hydrogen sulphide, hydrogen selenide, and hydrogen telluride, and crystallizing said semiconductive crystal from the resulting vapor phase.

EXHIBIT 5 Excerpts from CVD's Suggested Instructions to Jury

[Note: Included in these instructions were legal citations that mentioned specific cases where these points of law were made or reaffirmed. These citations have been omitted in the interest of brevity.]

Donadio and Connolly's Rights as Employees

1. An employee of a company has the right to quit his job and engage in a competing business unless he has a contract of employment that forbids him to do so. In this case there was no evidence that either Mr. Donadio or Mr. Connolly had such a contract with Markham.

2. Mr. Donadio and Mr. Connolly had the right to use the general knowledge, experience, and skill they had acquired while working for Markham for the purpose of engaging in a competing business.

3. If a contract between an employer and an employee or former employee provides that the employee will not use his general knowledge, experience, and skill for the benefit of a new employer, or for the benefit of himself, such a provision is contrary to public policy and is unenforceable.

4. Although an employee has the right to leave his employment and to use his general knowledge, skill, and experience for the benefit of a new employer, he has an obligation not to use trade secrets of the old employer for the benefit of the new one.

No Trade Secrets

5. A *trade secret* may be any information that is used in a business and gives the company that uses it an advantage over competitors who do not know it. For example, a secret manufacturing process or a secret machine of unique design could be a trade secret.

6. However, information that is generally known in an industry cannot be a trade secret.

7. Information cannot qualify for protection as a trade secret unless it is information that gives to the company that knows it an advantage over competitors or potential competitors who do not have the information. Information that would be obvious to a competent engineer experienced in the particular field, or which easily could be determined by a competent engineer by means other than obtaining it from the company which has it, cannot be protected as a trade secret.

8. You must determine in this case whether the information that Markham claims as trade secrets in fact was secret and not generally known outside Markham.

9. A United States patent is a matter of public record and is available for inspection by any member of the public. Information that is disclosed in a United States patent cannot be a trade secret after that patent has been issued, even if it was a trade secret before the patent was issued.

EXHIBIT 5   (*continued*)

10. If you find that information about the chemical vapor deposition process used by Markham was disclosed in reports made to government agencies and other companies, without restriction on the use of such information, then you should find that such information was not trade secret information.

11. An employer who wishes to preserve information as a trade secret must inform the employees who know the information that it is to be treated as secret and must take all proper and reasonable precautions to keep the information secret. If the company fails to do so, it cannot later prevent use of the information on the theory that it is a trade secret.

12. You have heard testimony of Markham's lawyer, Mr. Davis, to the effect that he was unable to deliver a list of the items that Markham claimed to be its trade secrets to Mr. Cohen, the lawyer for the plaintiffs, because it was impossible to make a detailed and complete list of the claimed trade secrets. If you find that as of February 15, 1980, Markham was unable to identify what it claimed to be its trade secrets, then you would be justified in finding that Mr. Donadio and Mr. Connolly had not been put on notice while they were employees of Markham as to what it was that Markham claimed to be its trade secrets, and accordingly that Markham cannot now assert a right to trade secret protection for the information.

The License

13. In *some* circumstances a contract may be binding upon the parties *even if* it later is found that the contract was based on an invalid claim when the person who asserted the claim upon which the contract was based did so in good faith. However, in the case of a contract regarding the use of trade secrets, another principle of law must be considered. Some types of agreements are unenforceable because they are considered to be contrary to public policy, even if they are signed voluntarily by the parties.

14. A contract that is signed under what the law regards as unreasonable coercion or "duress" cannot be enforced by the party responsible for such coercion or duress. If you find that Markham threatened to sue Mr. Donadio and Mr. Connolly and their new company for alleged use of trade secrets, and that Markham made such threats in bad faith, knowing that it had no legitimate basis for the claims that it threatened to assert, and that the plaintiffs signed the license agreement because of such threats, then you should find that the license agreement was signed under what the law calls economic duress and is not enforceable. Also, threats to prevent a person from earning a living or engaging in a lawful business may constitute duress.

15. In deciding whether the license agreement was signed under duress, you may consider the following:
   a. The relative bargaining power of the parties.

EXHIBIT 5   *(concluded)*

---

b. Whether the license required CVD Incorporated to pay royalties at excessive or unreasonable rates.

c. Whether the plaintiffs could have obtained a judicial decision on the Markham trade secrets claims in time to save their proposed new business.

16. Under Section 1 of the Sherman Act, which is part of the antitrust laws of the United States, any contract that unreasonably restrains interstate commerce within the United States or foreign commerce of the United States is illegal.

17. It is also a violation of Section 2 of the Sherman Antitrust Act for a company to use illegal or unreasonable means to preserve or maintain "monopoly power" in a "relevant product market" for a "relevant geographical market," even if that "monopoly power" has been acquired by lawful and proper means or simple historical accident.

18. A company can have monopoly power without having 100 percent of a market, so long as it has the power either to exclude competition or to set its own prices without regard for competitive pricing.

19. A particular type of product may constitute a relevant product market for antitrust purposes if a major customer has specified that the particular material must be used for a particular purpose, and has selected its suppliers accordingly.

20. Even if two products have the same chemical composition, like a diamond and lead in a pencil, they are not the same relevant product market if one of them has physical characteristics and those characteristics lead customers to prefer one over the other for certain purposes.

21. If two companies compete in selling a product to customers located throughout the United States, then the entire country can be the relevant geographical market.

22. You may find that the February 1980 license agreement was a contract that unreasonably restrained trade if you find *either* (1) that the license agreement required CVD Incorporated to pay royalties for the use of information which in fact was not trade secret information, *or* (2) that the license agreement required CVD Incorporated to pay royalties which were unreasonably high in amount and thus unreasonably restrained CVD Incorporated in its ability to compete with Markham.

EXHIBIT 6   Excerpts from Markham's Suggested Instructions to the Jury

[Note: Included in these instructions were legal citations which mentioned specific cases where these points of law were made or reaffirmed. These citations have been omitted in the interest of brevity.]

An Employer's Rights

1. The employee agreements signed by Donadio and Connolly with respect to Markham inventions and proprietary information are valid and binding. These agreements prevent Donadio and Connolly, upon termination of their employment, from using for their own advantage, confidential information gained by them during their employment.

2. An agreement not to use or disclose methods and procedures involved in manufacturing processes is binding on an employee and is a reasonable restraint.

3. Donadio and Connolly, who occupied positions of trust at Markham, owed a duty of loyalty to Markham, a duty which includes not using and disclosing Markham's trade secrets and confidential information even after the termination of employment.

4. The duty of loyalty owned to Markham by Donadio and Connolly preclude them from using, for their advantage, or that of a rival and to the harm of Markham, trade secrets or confidential information gained during the course of their employment at Markham.

5. The confidential information which Donadio and Connolly were under a duty to Markham not to disclose, including not only particular information that Markham told them constituted Markham trade secrets and confidential information, but also any information they knew Markham would not want revealed to others. Their duty of nonuse and nondisclosure applies to unique business information and methods of Markham, trade secrets, customer lists, and the like.

Trade Secrets

6. A trade secret may consist of any formula, pattern, device, or compilation of information that is used in one's business, and that gives him an opportunity to obtain an advantage over competitors who do not know or use it. It may be a formula for a chemical compound, a process of manufacturing, treating or preserving materials, a pattern for a machine or other device. . . . A trade secret is a process or device for use over time in the operation of the business.

7. Manufacturing processes specifically are entitled to protection as trade secrets.

8. Because it is the policy of the law to encourage and protect invention and commercial enterprise, the law protects processes of manufacture invented or discovered by an employer against employees who—in violation of their employment contracts and in breach of the duty of trust and confidence

EXHIBIT 6 *(continued)*

that the law also imposes—seek to apply such processes for their own use or to disclose them to third persons.

9. The fact that Markham's process of manufacturing and producing zinc sulfide and zinc selenide by chemical vapor deposition may to some extent be a combination and adaptation of known principles to new purposes does not prevent that process from being a trade secret, if you find that the process as distilled or parts of it accomplish a result that gives Markham a competitive advantage due to its efforts, ingenuity, research, and development.

10. Even if you determine that general information regarding the technology of chemical vapor deposition and furnaces used in conjunction therewith may be known elsewhere, it does not follow that Markham's detailed engineering drawings, the configuration of its furnaces, apparatus and equipment, the precise materials, techniques and procedures—which Markham claims are trade secrets and confidential information—have been disclosed.

11. General descriptions or explanations of a process or manufacturing apparatus do not constitute disclosures of detailed manufacturing drawings and designs particularly if the equipment cannot be reproduced by others absent such detail.

12. Detailed manufacturing drawings are prima facie trade secrets.

13. Only reasonable steps are required to preserve the secrecy of the information embodied in the process, machinery, and manufacturing techniques for the production of zinc sulfide and zinc selenide by chemical vapor deposition. Although there is no general rule to determine whether the security precautions taken by the possessor of a trade secret are reasonable, the existence or absence of an express agreement restricting disclosure is an important reasonable step.

14. Markham did not have to stamp *confidential* or *proprietary* on its drawings or tell Donadio and Connolly that any component of the furnaces were confidential and proprietary. Such specificity is not required to put employees on notice that their work involves access to trade secrets and confidential information.

Confidential Business Information

15. Confidential information acquired by an employee in the course of his employment is the property of the employer, which the employee holds in trust for the employer and cannot use in violation of his trust.

16. Donadio and Connolly's contractual and fiduciary obligations to Markham also include their agreement and an obligation in law not to use confidential information regarding customer lists and sources of supply to Markham's detriment upon termination of their employment with Markham.

EXHIBIT 6   (*continued*)

17. It does not matter that Donadio and Connolly could have obtained some knowledge of Markham's manufacturing processes and techniques from public treatises or documents. For if you find that they obtained their knowledge through their confidential relationship with Markham, they incurred a duty not to use that information to Markham's detriment.

The License

18. Agreements for the licensing of trade secrets are commonplace and enforceable by courts of law. Through a licensing agreement a company may protect itself from the wrongful use or disclosure of trade secrets and the preservation of confidential information by reaching mutually acceptable terms for payment and confidentiality with a licensee.

19. Payment of royalties for the right to use other parties' trade secrets is consistent with the Massachusetts law of contracts and does not conflict with federal laws and the policy of the patent laws. All agreements, including a licensing agreement, in order to be enforceable must have consideration. That is, for example, a bargained for exchange of rights, promises, or payments. In the license agreement at issue in this case, the defendant granted the plaintiffs a license to use its information to make ZnS/cvd and ZnSe/cvd in exchange for the payment of royalties.

20. In deciding whether the license agreement was premised upon sufficient consideration to be binding and enforceable, you must also consider that our law requires a duty of good faith and fair dealing in business transactions. If you find that Donadio and Connolly occupied positions of trust at Markham and that through their employment they became aware of trade secrets and confidential or proprietary information, then you must find that they had a continuing duty not to use and disclose these secrets and this information after they left the employ of the defendant. The protection of trade secret law is against breaches of trust.

21. In Massachusetts law, duress generally means that one party acted in such a way so as to have made the other party enter an agreement under such fear that would preclude the exercise of his free will and judgment. If the plaintiffs entered this agreement freely and voluntarily, you cannot find that there was duress.

22. In a business context such as the one presented in this case the elements necessary for you to find that the plaintiffs only entered the agreement under duress are that:
    i. The plaintiffs accepted the terms of the defendant involuntarily;
    ii. The circumstances did not permit them any other alternative; and,
    iii. Those circumstances were the result of coercive acts of the defendant.

23. It is not duress sufficient to avoid a contract for a party to threaten that it will exercise its legal rights, because the enforcement of legal rights by legal means is not evidence of duress.

EXHIBIT 6   *(continued)*

24. In considering the circumstances that form the basis of the plaintiffs' claim of duress, you shall also consider whether there can be duress when the plaintiffs consulted with legal counsel throughout their negotiations and that their counsel who negotiated the terms was competent and experienced. You shall also consider the parties themselves and their knowledge and understanding of the terms of agreement and their obligations thereunder.

25. Section 2 of the Sherman Antitrust Act provides: Every person who shall monopolize, or attempt to monopolize, or combine or conspire with any other person or persons, to monopolize any part of the trade or commerce among the several states, or with foreign nations, shall be deemed guilty of a misdemeanor.

26. Monopolization violative of Section 2 of the Sherman Act has two elements: first, the "possession of monopoly power in the relevant market" and, second, the "acquisition or maintenance of the power" by other than such legitimate means as patents, "superior product, business acumen, or historical accident."

27. Monopoly power is the power to control prices or to exclude competition in the relevant market. Your first task, therefore, is to ascertain the relevant product market. The relevant product market is that area of goods in which the product or products offered by Markham effectively compete.

28. There are two related tests for determining whether two products are actually competitive with each other: (1) reasonable interchangeability of use and (2) cross-elasticity of demand. Thus, if the product and its substitutes are reasonably interchangeable by consumers for the same purposes, or if they have a high cross-elasticity of demand in the trade, they are to be included in the same market for the purpose of determining the existence of monopoly power.

29. The test of reasonable interchangeability emphasizes two factors. They are (1) use or uses, and (2) physical characteristics. If the substitutes have essentially the same end uses as the product, they are deemed to be interchangeable with each other and may, therefore, be included in the same product market. Similarly, if the physical characteristics of the substitutes are essentially the same as those of the product, so that customers may practically switch from one commodity to another, they are part of the same market.

30. Once you have ascertained the relevant product market you must decide whether Markham possesses monopoly power in that market (i.e., whether Markham has the power to control prices or exclude competition).

31. The antitrust laws do not prohibit monopoly in and of itself. Thus, it does not condemn one who merely by superior skill and intelligence got the whole business because nobody could do it as well.

EXHIBIT 6 (*concluded*)

32. If Markham's conduct was reasonable in light of its business needs and in accordance with ordinary business dealings and competition, it cannot be found to have used improper means in competing with CVD.

33. If you find that Markham's prices exceeded its total average cost of producing the goods, you must conclude that its pricing practices are lawful and do not constitute an act of monopolization in violation of Section 2. This is because the purpose of the Sherman Act is to encourage a competitive market price and lower prices to consumers.

34. Even if you find that Markham had monopoly power in the relevant market and even if you find that its prices fell below its total average cost, you must determine whether those price reductions by Markham, if any, were in response to price cuts made by CVD. If the prices charged by Markham were made in good faith to meet lower prices charged by CVD, then Markham's prices would be lawful under Section 13(b) of the antitrust laws. That Section provides for the so-called meeting the competition defense. To avail itself of the defense, Markham need not show that its prices were in fact equal to CVD's, but only that facts led Markham, as a reasonable and prudent person, to believe that the granting of the lower prices would meet the equally low prices of another.

EXHIBIT 7   CVD Incorporated Financials

Income Statement
(dollars in thousands)

	1984	1983	1982	1981
Revenues:				
Net sales	$2,840	$2,387	$1,547	$751
Contract research	417	342	160	—
	$3,258	$2,729	$1,707	$751
Costs and expenses:				
Cost of goods sold and cost of contract research	$1,538	$1,451	$ 805	$460
Selling, general, and administrative	835	837	508	229
Research and development	193	52	—	—
Interest	75	89	88	51
Markham royalties (set aside)	—	—	86	109
	$2,642	$2,429	$1,487	$849
Earnings before income taxes and extraordinary items	616	300	220	(99)
Income taxes	252	37	42	—
Income (loss) before extraordinary items	364	264	178	(99)
Extraordinary items	—	—	27[a]	—
Net income (loss)	$ 364	$ 264	$ 205	($ 99)

Note: Figures may not add due to rounding.
[a]Utilization of net operating loss carryforward.

EXHIBIT 7   (concluded)

Balance Sheets

	Feb. 28, 1984	Feb. 28, 1983
Assets		
Current assets:		
Cash	$ 30,334	$ 154,407
Accounts receivable	548,463	379,307
Unbilled progress receivables on contract research	—	26,826
Notes receivable—officers	73,821	—
Inventories	710,189	506,922
Prepaid expenses and deposits	37,127	23,915
Deferred income taxes	—	112,000
Total current assets	$1,399,934	$1,203,377
Equipment and improvements, net	594,701	649,419
Other assets:	—	3,119
	$1,994,635	$1,855,915
Liabilities and Stockholders' Equity		
Current liabilities:		
Notes payable	$ 70,000	$ 80,000
Accounts payable	170,281	249,013
Accrued salaries and related expenses	48,275	48,601
Accrued expenses	159,874	139,719
Accrued royalties	—	194,825
Income taxes	47,761	24,187
Current maturities of long-term debt	111,804	111,804
Deferred revenues	221,100	—
Customers' advances	—	25,000
Total current liabilities	829,095	873,149
Deferred accounts payable	86,340	166,340
Deferred income taxes	199,200	43,500
Long-term debt, less current maturities	182,482	314,286
Stockholders' equity	697,518	458,640
	$1,994,635	$1,855,915

Stratus Computer

In January 1980, it looked as if it really was going to happen. After six months, a false start, and some unexpected blips, Bill Foster had put together the team that he hoped would create Stratus Computer, a new company based on a high-reliability design objective. With the team finally complete, he could turn his full attention to raising the $6.2 million he felt they would need to fund their development efforts.

Bill felt that time was of the essence in obtaining start-up capital. First, he wanted to keep the momentum going with some of the financial contacts he had made and to maintain the enthusiasm of his team. Since there would be almost a two-year development effort before they could sell their first product, he was also anxious to maintain what he saw as a head start in the fast-changing computer market. Finally, after the ups and downs of the past few months, his rapidly depleting checkbook was giving him an extra sense of urgency.

During his six-month odyssey, Bill had identified several possible types of investors. Now he and his team wanted to develop a strategy for obtaining the best possible financing for the new company. Important elements of that strategy would include how they should approach the different possible sources and in what order, how much money they would request, and what financial structure would be best. They also had to decide how much equity they would be prepared to give up and what their bargaining strategy would be. Finally, they needed to set the criteria they would use in making a decision.

This case was prepared by Richard O. von Werssowetz, C. Richard Reese, and H. Irving Grousbeck under the direction of Philip H. Thurston.

PERSONAL BACKGROUND

Bill Foster grew up in California and graduated from San Jose State in 1966 with a BA in math. Following graduation, he went to work for Lockheed, then a small software development company in the San Francisco Bay area. Bill completed a graduate degree in applied math at Santa Clara while working for Lockheed and continued night school until 1973, when he received an MBA from the same institution.

Growing tired of the instability in the aerospace industry, Bill joined Hewlett-Packard's (HP) then fledgling data products division in 1969. During the next seven years, he rose from being a programmer to become engineering manager of the computing systems group. As manager, he was responsible for HP's research and development for computer system hardware and software. About a third of his time was spent talking with prospective customers to assure them that the product being considered was technically sound and able to perform the desired tasks.

In 1976 he was recruited by Data General to become the firm's director of software development. Bill recalled that the opportunity to work for the president of a smaller, but faster growing company appealed to him, as did the chance to sample living on the East Coast. Over the next three years, Bill established a reputation within the company as a good manager and was made a vice president. He explained that his work was rewarding, and a salary of nearly $100,000 a year and stock option benefits had allowed him to accumulate nearly $50,000 in savings.

THE DECISION TO START A COMPANY

Bill talked about his decision to start a company:

I guess I'll never really know exactly why it happened the way it did. I had been thinking for over a year about starting a company. I tried to think about what I could do. I didn't get anywhere. I didn't have any idea. I guess I also didn't have the guts to do it. It didn't seem the smart thing to do to leave this great job I had, making all that money and all that sort of thing.

But I also have known a lot of people who have gone off and started companies and become very successful. All were high-technology related kinds of companies. Most of the founders of Tandem Computer had worked for me when I was at HP. I know many of the founders of Apple. So I was always envious of these people who had gone off and gotten involved with a start-up. I knew I was equal to those people. Yet I had reached the conclusion it just wasn't the right time or maybe never would be to do it, and I didn't have any ideas and didn't know what to do.

I almost feel foolish saying this, but I went on a business trip to Europe in June 1979, and the first night I was there, I woke up about three in the morning and just decided to do it. When I got back home to Massachusetts, I was going to quit my job and try to start a company. It's almost as if I said to myself, "You're really stupid not to have done it a year ago." I must have been thinking about it somewhere in the back of my mind, but I really wasn't aware of it. I called my wife on the phone the next day and told her I was going to do it. She kind of said, "Oh, yeah, I've heard this before." When I got home, I talked some more about it, and then she knew I was going to do it.

I can't really explain why it was, but all of a sudden I started thinking that the worst possible thing that could happen would be to wake up one day when I was 70 years old, look back over my life, and say to myself, "Gee, you never even tried to do it." I was 35, I was not particularly challenged by my job, and I was envious of my friends who had gone off and done something similar. I finally realized that all of the constraints I had were basically artificial constraints. I felt that I would be very disappointed with myself if I didn't at least attempt this—that all of my options would be closed.

Once that happened, it was a very easy decision; I had no qualms about it. Financially, it could have been a tough decision, but it wasn't. I had a lot of stock options that I had to leave behind. I didn't have a lot of money and don't have a lot of money today. At that time, it cost us about $30,000 for the five of us to live for a year. So my wife and I figured if I treated this as an investment in myself, we could withdraw $600 a week; and in a year's time, the business would either be on its way or would have flopped. I would reserve another $20,000 in savings to invest as my share of the equity. The money for my children's college was probably my biggest hangup. But I had worked my way through school; if they had to work their way through, they could do it. It was not reason enough not to do it. Later, when things weren't looking so good, I'd look back and say, "Gee, that was probably a dumb decision!" Then it started to bother me about drawing out of the bank and living off our savings. But for the first three or four months, it was no problem.

In July 1979, within three weeks after returning from Europe, Bill submitted his resignation. Rumors within the company included speculation that he had been fired since "no one in his or her right mind would be crazy enough to walk away from the position and the benefits he had."

EARLY EXPERIENCES

The first step Bill took after leaving his job was to contact a friend who might be able to steer him to a venture capital company. Bill knew nothing about that part of the financial community, but his instincts told him that there was a lot of money available to finance businesses in the computer area. His friend helped him contact Greylock, a prominent Boston-based venture capital company.

Three days after I quit my job, I went to talk to these people. I had no business plan, no partners. I wasn't even sure what I was going to make, but I did know it would have something to do with general-purpose computer systems—that's what I was familiar with. I was selling myself on my reputation as a technical manager: "I've been heavily involved in a very successful HP computer program. I've managed Data General projects."

We spent two or three hours over lunch just basically talking about money being available, what they looked for, what they expected in terms of business planning, and all the rest. I was impressed with the amount of time this partner was spending with me. He was very helpful. When I said that I planned to do this in California since that is where I was from originally, he gave me an introduction to Sutter Hill and Hambrecht & Quist, two West Coast firms. They all owe each other favors: "You let me in this deal, and I may let you in another." They all talk to each other all the time. Besides, to do a large-scale start-up that might require as much as $10 million of venture capital would probably involve several firms working together. Even if they could, they normally would not do a sizable venture all by themselves.

Greylock also mentioned that they normally don't do first round start-ups. I found out later that many venture capital firms are that way. They're not going to invest in three people and a briefcase. There's no track record. They ask, "Can this guy who's worked inside a big company do it on his own? Can he hire the people? Can he meet his schedules? Can he do it without constant changes in direction?" These are big unknowns, and most venture firms aren't going to put money in day one with all those questions. They'd be prepared to pay three or four times the price a year later for the security of having seen some of those milestones. However, although Greylock wouldn't take the lead, they did say they were very interested in what I was doing and that there was a good chance they might come in if Sutter Hill got interested. So now I had an "in" into three of the top venture capital companies in the business.

Bill spent the rest of July and August researching the computer market and trying to find a niche. He went to California in September to visit several of his old friends from HP. As they discussed trying to start a computer company, conversation turned to Tandem Computer. Tandem had focused on those users who had high reliability needs—applications where the computer *couldn't* fail.

These might be banks for automatic tellers or funds transfers. Banks can lose literally tens of thousands of dollars in interest in the time it takes to get a failed computer back up. Other examples are stock exchange applications, airlines or hotel reservations, medical systems. There are quite a few.

Tandem had done very well, with sales of $24 million in the third year and an explosive growth rate.

> They certainly had found a market niche. Yet there still was no competition for them—no one else had come out with a similar product. So I concentrated on what was wrong with their idea, what could be done that was better.

Bill's business plan was to go more or less after the same market, but to have a different technical approach. His concept was for a radically different type of computer architecture that would have two central processing units (CPUs) working together on the same program, doing exactly the same thing at exactly the same time, so that if one CPU failed, the other would keep on operating with no interruption. This would also simplify field maintenance where the costs of repair were growing rapidly even while the cost of hardware itself was declining.

Likely competition would be Tandem, Prime Computer, Digital Equipment, IBM, and HP. However, Bill felt that a new firm had the great advantage of a fresh start on design due to his new architecture. A system's architecture is the pattern by which the basic computer functions are provided by a combination of hardware and software components. This involves many trade-offs between flexibility and capability versus efficiency and cost. Once an architecture is implemented, the pattern of hardware/software interaction becomes relatively fixed. This, in turn, limits the ability of the system to benefit from new hardware advances without severely impacting existing software systems.

A totally new design could take advantage of the latest technological advances. By incorporating these new advances, Stratus could have a truly modular design and could be controlled by a much simpler operating system. Customers of other computer companies with large installed bases had huge investments in software dependent on the original design structure. For them, fundamental changes in architecture were difficult, if not practically impossible. This was already true even of Tandem. Yet Bill's approach would not require applications programmers to add the reliability features into their coding which *was* required by Tandem.

A FALSE START

Bill Foster completed his business plan to use in "prospecting" for venture capital by October 1979. He proceeded to meet with the two San Francisco firms suggested by Greylock. At the same time, he attempted to contact old acquaintances at HP to see if they might be interested in joining him in the venture. By November, Bill was still in California trying to assemble a team and attract interest in the financial community. He explained his frustration at the lack of progress:

I went out to find money, but immediately found myself working for the venture capitalists. They would say, "Do this, do that; go find a marketing person, go find your software person." That wasn't my objective. My objective was to work for myself. I found that I was wasting my time, doing the wrong thing. I was constantly talking to the venture groups, looking for lawyers and CPAs. I should have been putting together my team.

My biggest mistake was to think that they were going to invest in me, Bill Foster—that I was such a great guy they'd give me the money and I'd get the people lined up. But it's just not going to happen. They aren't going to invest $2 million in one individual, it's just too risky.

One group tried to get me to join with another entrepreneur who was also trying to start a company. He had a lot more experience and had already made a lot of money in the computer industry. They got us together, and it was just like oil and water. There was no way I could see myself working *for* that guy, and it would have been hard to work *with* him. Because of his experience, I'm sure he felt he should be my superior.

It was really tough because I *knew* he was going to get his money—with his record, the venturers were going to give him money no matter what he was doing. I didn't know if I was going to get any money at all. I told my wife I'd really be mad if two or three years out he's built a really successful company and I never got off the ground. But she said, "Look, what you want to do is run your own company. Don't start to lessen your goals." She had more confidence in me than I did. So I called him up and told him I wasn't interested. He told me I was making a big mistake.

I had a list of 30 people whom I had been associated with and felt would be good to have involved in the company. I discovered that only two were still with HP. The others had gone on to start their own businesses or work for other entrepreneurs. The start-up activity in California had been going strong from 1976 to 1979 while I was gone. It didn't take me too long to realize that getting a team together in California would be tough.

The venture firms all wanted to talk to everybody I talked to. They were testing me, which I didn't quite realize. They wanted to see if Foster could attract those people. They'd say, "We may invest in Bill Foster. What do you think of the venture? Why would you do this? How would your job function?" They were really conducting job interviews! Remember, I knew nothing about raising money. It appeared that this was the way you do it. I didn't know any better.

After six weeks and two long trips to California, Bill decided to try to start his business in New England. The easy availability of team members in California had not proved to be true, and people in the

Northeast were calling to express an interest in what he was doing. Bill also realized the difficulties of trying to get a business started across a continent. Travel devoured his weekly $600 withdrawals as well as much of his time. In addition, Bill saw that the real estate market had collapsed to the point where selling and buying a house would be a difficult prospect at either end of the country. Added to that was the desire of his family to stay in New England where they had made new friends and enjoyed the change of seasons, which was absent in San Francisco.

The major risk in leaving California as a start-up location was in breaking off discussions with Sutter Hill. They had offered him a spot in their office and support services and had spent time on his venture themselves. Bill was afraid that this might destroy his credibility among such investors. However, it just didn't seem to be coming together. Bill felt Sutter Hill's interest was softening because of the delay in getting started, and the drain on money and time in trying to get started in California would be too great for him to continue on the West Coast.

When Bill discussed his decision with Sutter Hill, they were disappointed, but still had an interest in his venture. They said they wouldn't want to be a lead investor in the East, but might still invest if someone else took the lead. They suggested the New York firms of J. H. Whitney, Venrock, and Bessemer as several fine venture firms that invested in start-up situations. Bill also called several individuals who had been interested in joining him. They had considered his overtures tentative, and none had committed to leaving their companies yet.

TRYING IT AGAIN

Bill decided he would try a different approach in New England. This time he would get his whole team together before really approaching the venture capital firms. He had received a number of calls from people who were curious about his progress to date. Bill contacted one of these, Bob Freiburghouse, an acquaintance whom he had met during a negotiation in the past. In 1974, Bob had started his own software firm which had been very successful. The conversation led to an agreement where Bob would become the vice president of software development for Stratus. In addition, Bob would provide software that he had already developed to the venture on a deferred payment basis—that is, if and when Stratus became profitable, Bob would be paid for the software which was used. Bob began declining all new development business for his company and began to work with Bill on the Stratus plan and on attracting other members of the team. Bill recalled his surprise at being able to attract Bob as part of the management team:

> My original idea when I approached Bob was to buy some of his software for my product. But when he learned what I was trying to do, he said, "Wow! This fits my plans exactly. I've always wanted to get into a manufacturing company instead of just a service company. I'll throw in my resources with you."

Bill went after the other team members. He heard of another individual with experience in hardware who had submitted his resignation from his job with one large computer manufacturer in order to join another large firm. Bill contacted him and convinced him to agree to join the group. The marketing spot was filled by one of the people Bill had contacted in California. He quit his job and began traveling to Boston at his own expense to help with the plan.

Three days before Christmas, the partner who would have handled the hardware engineering called to back out. His original employer had offered him a financial package that was too attractive to turn down. Bill and he had not really discussed specific salaries or stock ownership, so there was no real bargaining or counterproposal. It had just been assumed that if Stratus made it, they would all do very well. Bill remembered his feelings about the setback:

> That was a real blow to me. I had already told J. H. Whitney (one of the firms I was staying in touch with) that my team was set. It was only one phone call, but the word out in the venture community was that Foster had gotten his team together. If you talk to one, it quickly gets around to everybody because they're always talking to each other: "What's going on?"
>
> I was convinced that the whole project was just going to fall through. I was afraid that one of the other partners would drop out. The marketing guy in California was still shaky, wasn't sure he really wanted to come out here. I wasn't sure how Bob would react to it. Things just weren't going that well at all as we moved into 1980. As it turned out, Bob wasn't that concerned. He said, "Well, we'll go out and find somebody else." My marketing fellow apparently wasn't that concerned, so I went after another fellow who had been my top choice, who had an excellent track record, but who I thought would never join us.
>
> Gardner, my new hope for hardware engineering, expressed his skepticism at first: "I'm a very conservative guy. It would really have to be a great deal for me to leave and get involved. It's very unlikely that I'd do that. But I'll talk to you if you want." After our initial conversation, he was intrigued. He wanted to meet my software guy. He felt the real risk was the software—in the computer business when there is a failure or slippage in a program, the problem is generally in the software. So I got Gardner and Bob together, and they hit it off immediately. Each had a fantastic respect for the other, and it would be just a great team. While Gardner would not commit, I felt he would join us if we had success in the financial community.

FINANCING OPTIONS

Now attention was turned to refining the business plan as they went over the schedules and budgets very closely, deciding what they would like to do. Bill had projected growth by considering the Tandem experience. Tandem's first-year sales in 1976 were $581,000. This increased to $7.7 million in 1977, $24 million in 1978, and 1979 sales were running almost double that of 1978. Since Tandem had already blazed the trail and created the market, he felt Stratus could do somewhat better.

After team discussions, the pro formas didn't change very much from those Bill had projected earlier. According to their plan (see Exhibit 1 for summary and financial projections), they would need to raise about $6.2 million to cover the three-year development and market introduction effort. Receivables and inventories for early sales would be financed by increasing notes payable. Then additional financing would be required. They projected that $2 million would be needed to fund the first year during which they would develop a working prototype. This would lend more credibility to their team and their concept. However, the partners could only provide a small amount of the cash equity required, between $50,000 and $75,000.

Even while concentrating on putting together the Stratus team, Bill had been trying to learn more about possible sources of financing:

My mode always was, "It doesn't hurt to talk to anybody. You might learn something." So I was always following up any kind of lead I got, whether it had to do with raising money or finding people or anything. You may run up a phone bill, but people are generally very helpful. I got leads from headhunters and investors, lawyers, and friends. I talked to other people who had started companies. They were probably the most helpful of all—those who had recently done what I was going through. They would reminisce about those exciting times. Of course, if they were successful and got their operation off the ground, they always like to talk about it.

I got many of the new company leads by reading magazines. Some of them have articles about companies that have just started up. I'd just call some of the presidents of the companies that had been interviewed out of the blue, tell them what I was doing, and ask their advice. I met several of the people out in California through those articles.

Bill had found three major options: venture capital firms, private individuals, and other operating corporations. There appeared to be significant differences in the way each of these groups made investments and in the types of deals that might be struck.

Venture Capital Firms

The venture capital firms were the most obvious possibilities. There were a large number of venture firms actively seeking investments. In addition to the best-known, perhaps most prestigious firms such as those mentioned earlier, there was a wide range of other less well-known firms that might be smaller or more recently started or that simply chose to keep low profiles.

Two of these lesser-known firms had also expressed interest in Stratus. These contacts had arisen from Gardner's concern over whether or not they were likely to get funded. When Gardner Hendrie was considering joining the team, he had called an old friend for advice. Burgess Jamieson had worked with Gardner 15 years earlier in an engineering company, then had gone to California to get involved in venture capital and had been very successful. When Gardner explained why he was interested in learning the climate for venture capital, Burgess felt his company, Institutional Venture Associates, might be interested. Bill recalled:

> Before I knew it Burgess hops an airplane and wants to talk to us. Right away he's very interested, partly on the strength of the business plan and partly on his personal association with Gardner. But he felt we should have an East Coast firm in the lead. He'd be very happy with the New York firms we knew, but also suggested we contact Hellman-Gal, a lesser-known Boston company they'd done some business with before. (It seemed that the best-known Boston firms generally preferred second-round financings.) I had heard of Hellman-Gal, but never bothered to call them. I didn't think they did start-ups, and I didn't think they were big enough. But Burgess said they'd be good and also that they felt good about our idea. One of their partners had had some experience in the time-sharing business and knew something about computers himself.

During his early discussions with the venture firms and in talking to the other recently started companies, Bill discovered some apparent ground rules in the venture capital community:

> One rule is that you're not going to raise $7 million day one. No one has put in that much money. The going first round for my kind of deal is around a million and a half. Maybe you can get close to $2 million, but probably not more than $2 million for a team of untried people. That much would get us just past a working prototype.
>
> Number two is that they are going to have control—at least 51 percent. They're going to do it—there's no way you can get around it. At the same time, they won't *commit* to anything on round two. They'll talk about what they'll do if you do a good job, but if they don't like what you've done, you may not get that second-round money.
>
> None of it is cast in concrete. You can talk and you can go through scenarios. They'd sit me down and tell me what other companies did. "In 1974 Tandem gave up 74 percent of their company for $1 million. The investor got 72 percent of Prime Computer for $600,000 in 1972." The new start-ups did a little better—the going rate seemed to be giving up about 60 percent.

I also found that many of the venture capital firms without technical backgrounds used outside consultants to help them evaluate high-technology ventures. The people they relied on were heavily booked and might take weeks to schedule.

Private Individuals

Another possible source of financing was from wealthy individuals. Certain tax provisions could make investments in firms such as Stratus particularly appealing: most of Stratus's early expenses would be for research and development. If the funds for the R&D were provided by a limited partnership, most of the expenditures could be deducted by the individuals against other sources of ordinary income. This would effectively lessen the actual aftertax amount at risk for those individuals substantially. If the research proved successful, the investors would typically receive a royalty (normally 7 percent to 10 percent) on resulting sales. Such royalties would be taxed at long-term capital gains rates.

Bill had been put in contact with a young individual who had taken an idea from an MBA thesis and built it into a very successful company. The company had been recently sold with the entrepreneur's interest worth about $5 to $6 million. Now this person was interested in investing some of the proceeds of the sale and would lead a private placement with about 10 individuals each putting up $300,000 to $400,000.

Because of the tax benefits of this structure and because some of these individuals did not get to see as many good deals as the venture firms, Bill felt that they might have to give up less ownership of Stratus if the money could be raised this way. He felt the best he might do was give away only 40–45 percent of the ownership. On the other hand, this would be more complicated and would probably involve preparation of a private placement memorandum that would essentially be a full-blown prospectus under SEC Rule 242. This might also require review by the state Blue Sky commission. The SEC does not consider even a wealthy lawyer to necessarily be a "sophisticated investor" in terms of a computer start-up.

Other Nonventure Corporations

In another example of how people who had been suggested as sources of advice in dealing with the venture community had become possible sources of financing themselves, Bill had started discussions with a company that had quickly become interested in financing the entire Stratus start-up. Bill's contact, Gary Jameson, had worked for a venture capital firm and was now the vice president of administration of a company that was selling a *product* that depended on reliable computer systems. They bought their computers from major companies, put them in their systems, and sold them to the telephone communications industry. These systems basically required continuous operation.

> They said they were very interested and that they might fund us to the tune of $7 million. Again, this would be set up as a partnership so that this company could get the more immediate tax benefits of expensing the R&D.
> Gary also felt it would be impossible for me to raise money through venture capital sources—that I was wasting my time. Even though I had run R&D teams, I had never been the chief executive officer of a company, had never run the whole show. He said that venture capitalists were really conservative investors, and it would be very unlikely that any venture groups would invest millions of dollars in a company in which the CEO didn't have a proven track record.

Although this was the only nonventure company Bill had contacted, after seeing the interest here, he thought others might have similar interests. He had heard that some of these companies actually had in-house venture groups, but he wasn't sure how their investment strategies differed from traditional venture capital companies.

THE FINANCING DECISION

Striking a deal with any of the financing sources would require detailed negotiations, with no assurances as to how long that might take or whether or not a final agreement might be reached. The risks were increased because the Stratus team was untried in launching a company. One factor in their favor was that there had been a number of recent success stories of computer firms starting up and becoming industry leaders. Those deals also served as a growing database to determine the increased values of the company for each round of financing.

Recent increases in the availability of venture capital also worked to Stratus's advantage. Bill pointed out that more money was chasing roughly the same number of quality deals and that this should give a founding group more leverage in the negotiations. This could extend to a whole range of issues, including the relative percentages of ownership and the relative privileges of the various shareholders through the use of different types of preferred stock or debt instruments with convertible provisions or warrants.

Somewhere in the process, the valuation of the company had to be considered. With ongoing companies, investors could look at the asset bases and price/earnings ratios. With a start-up, the investor had to consider the concept, the projections, and the team and decide on the likely future value.

Another factor for Bill was that more than one round of financing was likely to be needed. How the first round of capital was priced and structured would influence future rounds of investment.

The team members agreed to take smaller salaries than they had earned before. (Bill's would be less than half his former salary and the others would be about 80 percent.) The four founding members of the company would split whatever equity they could retain by dividing the number of shares by 4.2. Each of them would receive a 1/4.2 part except Bill. He would receive 1.2/4.2 or "120 percent" share for putting the team together. However, employee stock ownership and shares for other key employees also had to be taken into account.

Now Bill and the Stratus team faced the difficult task of setting and executing a financing strategy.

EXHIBIT 1   Business Plan Summary and Financial Projections

SUMMARY	I
MARKET	II*
COMPETITION	III*
TECHNOLOGY TRENDS	IV*
PRODUCT	V*
FINANCIALS	A
PRODUCT PRICING	B*
STAFFING PLAN	C*
IMPLEMENTATION PLAN	D*
RESUMES	E*

*Omitted from Exhibit.

I—SUMMARY

(This memorandum, although written in the present tense, discusses a business proposal involving a corporation which is to be organized in the future. The computer systems described herein have not been designed as of the date hereof.)

Stratus Computer, Inc. is a company formed to design, manufacture, and market small computer systems that take advantage of a unique architecture and advances in hardware technology to produce a product that is unequaled in overall reliability. The computer sytems will be priced from $30,000 to $400,000 or more. A wide performance range is offered by using Stratus's multiprocessor architecture, providing system expansion by adding hardware modules to the computer systems. These systems will be sold to Fortune 1000's and system houses. Both markets are growing fast and only require modest software support.

Of the two million U.S. companies that have revenues greater than $100,000, only 6 percent use computers today. This enormous untapped potential leads some to predict that small business systems sales will reach $50 billion over the next decade—a 30 percent sustained annual growth rate for 10 years (*Computerworld*, December 17, 1979).

The competition for this market will be intense. Stratus will achieve its growth objective by focusing its design on reliability issues. High reliability requires a totally new design in order to have good price and performance, but it is unlikely that existing companies will start their design efforts from scratch because they have to be compatible with their current product line in order to protect their existing customer base. Thus, their solutions will be compromises and not totally satisfactory to many customers.

Stratus will require $4.2 million of equity financing; $2.0 million in Year 1 and $2.2 million in Year 2. Prototype systems will be completed in the 18th month, and first customer shipments will occur in the fourth quarter of Year 2. Stratus will become a major computer systems supplier, achieving $75 million in sales by Year 5. Stratus will leverage the technology of semiconductor and peripheral suppliers, and will focus its attention on integrating their hardware with our own unique software to produce computer systems.

EXHIBIT 1 (*continued*)

Stratus takes advantage of the continued decline in hardware costs to achieve high reliability of all key computer components: processors, memory, and peripherals. The result is that the failure of any component will not bring the system down. In many cases, the system will tolerate failure of two or more components. Component failure has zero impact on users. Operators of the computer are not affected by component failure. They do not have to re-enter data, enter special commands, or flip switches. Application programmers do not have to design their programs to react in case of component failure. Therefore, new programs can be designed in straightforward, familiar ways, and existing programs may be transported to Stratus computers with no changes to accommodate the reliability design.

The fact that Stratus achieves nearly 100 percent reliability with no user impact is a significant competitive advantage. Only one other manufacturer, Tandem Computer, provides a high reliability system. However, the Tandem design requires very complex program design by the user, and provides a much lower level of reliability. Also, Stratus provides high reliability at low cost: the average Stratus system will cost less than $100,000, while Tandem systems average more than $200,000.

High reliability of computer components is optional. The user can decide how important reliability is to his application, and then make the appropriate economic trade-offs. He can choose to have highly reliable processors or peripherals, or neither, or both. He can start with a simple system and add extra hardware for high reliability later, with zero impact to his application programs or operational procedures. This flexibility expands the market for Stratus computers—it is not limited only to those who are willing to pay for high reliability. This same flexibility positions Stratus to take advantage of technology trends. As hardware costs drop, the percentage of the computer market that is willing to pay extra for high reliability will increase rapidly because the cost of extra hardware will be small compared with software costs, support costs, and the opportunity costs of system downtime.

As companies and organizations become more dependent on computers, reliability will become a bigger issue. Unlike human beings, computers generally give little, if any, warning that they are about to fail; when they do fail, they are useless until repaired, and sometimes even when fixed they have lost critical information that will never be recovered. Thus, high reliability requires elaborate and expensive safeguards against failure and quick response field service capabilities, and oftentimes will inhibit a company from "computerizing" an application that otherwise would be much more efficient on a computer. Hence, a significant portion of the market will be eager to buy Stratus computers because they eliminate nearly all concerns about interruption in operation due to computer failure or loss of key information, and at a cost much lower than any other alternative.

Stratus computers are expandable. As the user's application grows, he or she can add more processors or peripherals or both to meet the increased demands placed on the system. He or she does not have to throw away or replace old hardware when the system expands—he or she merely adds to it.

EXHIBIT 1   *(continued)*

Stratus computers can be used as a tool to execute applications developed by system houses or end users. Users are supplied with industry standard languages, COBOL, PL/I and BUSINESS BASIC, as well as a source editor and program debugger for program development. A multiprogrammed operating system is provided that permits multiple users to access common system resources, but to be protected from one another.

Stratus computers can coexist in a network with other Stratus computers or with IBM computers. Between Stratus systems basic file access and program communication, support is provided. Stratus provides communication with IBM through emulation of IBM 2780/3780 Remote Job Entry stations and 3270 terminal emulation. Stratus also provides industry standard X.25 packet network support, which means that Stratus computers can communicate across public data networks, such as TELENET (U.S. and international), TYMNET (U.S.), DATAPAC (Canada), TRANSPAC (France), and EURONET (European Common Market).

The major product advantages can be summarized as follows:

1. Reliability
   The design protects against all types of hardware failure. This design is straightforward for operating systems and user software to take advantage of; gains in hardware reliability are not offset by complex, failure-prone software.
2. Expandability
   The system is expandable in terms of processors and peripherals in order to provide for growth of user's applications. Thus the product line is very broad, and the user is less likely to feel constrained at the high end.
3. Flexibility
   The design allows the user to add hardware to increase reliability or performance, or both. This flexibility also reduces Stratus's manufacturing and field support costs.
4. Controlled software costs
   Since software costs are rising, the above three objectives are met with no increase in system or user software complexity. Established, reliable applications are able to take advantage of the Stratus design with no modification to accommodate the architecture.
5. Low cost
   Stratus takes advantage of recent advances in VLSI, memory, and disk technology to provide nearly 100 percent reliability at low cost.
6. Applications development
   The necessary utilities, languages, communications, and operating systems software are provided for users to develop new applications or transport existing programs to Stratus.
7. Field service
   Service costs are not dropping with hardware costs because systems are more complex and few real improvements have been made to service techniques. Stratus reduces the need for expensive, quick response service because the computer will tell the user of a failure, but operation will continue uninterrupted.

EXHIBIT 1   *(continued)*

The president of Stratus is William E. Foster. Mr. Foster has 13 years of industry experience, the last 10 with Hewlett-Packard and, most recently, Data General, two of the leading minicomputer manufacturers. Mr. Foster is one of the few industry people who has been involved with a computer system project from inception through shipment and contributing net profit. He was involved from day one as a designer of the HP3000 from Hewlett-Packard and progressed to have total hardware and software responsibility for the product, which today is one of the leaders in the commercial market.

At Data General, Mr. Foster gained experience building organizations and implementing tight expense controls. He developed a 100-person unstructured group into an organization of more than 400 people with focused managers who were accountable for specific results. He built from scratch DG's Advanced Research Center at Research Triangle Park, Raleigh, North Carolina, building a team from nothing to over 100 engineering and software professionals. Much of DG's success is due to a strong entrepreneurial atmosphere with emphasis on expense control and profit, and Mr. Foster gained from this experience.

The vice president of software is Robert A. Freiburghouse. Mr. Freiburghouse has 18 years of experience in operating a business, software project management, software design, compiler design, computer system design, and software development. He is founder and president of Translation Systems, Inc., a very successful company specializing in the production of compilers. He has designed and built more than eight compilers that are offered as products by various major computer manufacturers. Mr. Freiburghouse designed hardware extensions to several existing computer systems, designed a 32-bit microprocessor, and designed a programming language that has been adopted as an American National Standard (ANSI) and as an International Standard (ISO). Mr. Freiburghouse is a recognized authority on programming languages and compiler design and is a guest lecturer at MIT, Brown University, Bell Laboratories, GE Research Laboratories, and various professional organizations. He has published several papers on compiler design and has written three technical books.

The vice president of engineering has over 20 years of experience in the computer field as a logic designer, a system designer, and as an engineering manager. He has supervised major engineering organizations and has personally executed the detailed design of a successful minicomputer. He is the holder of several patents in computer organization and has a BS and MS in Electrical Engineering.

The vice president of marketing has been with a highly successful manufacturer of computers and computer systems for the past nine years. For eight of those years he has managed increasingly larger sales areas across the country. At present his organization consists of over 70 people with a sales responsibility of over $50 million. In his present responsibility he has designed and implemented numerous marketing plans, which have enabled his organization to successfully sell general purpose small- and medium-scale computer systems to virtually every market. One such plan was aimed at capturing a significant portion of the emerging commercial systems supplier market. The plan called for modifications of the

EXHIBIT 1   (*continued*)

company's credit and contracting procedures as well as a modification of sales commission structures and sales management goal structure. The plan's success has been dramatic. In two years, sales in this market have grown from almost nothing to over $10 million with a dominant market share position. Other activities include successful Major Account campaigns and plans aimed at exploiting most of the emerging computer marketing channels.

In summary, Stratus will be successful for the following reasons:

1. Unique management team that has proven track records in systems development, hardware, software, and marketing.
2. Unique design that is straightforward to implement and takes advantage in the best possible way of the trends in hardware costs.
3. Located in the Boston area, which has an unequaled talent pool of computer hardware and software engineers and few significant start-up opportunities for these people in the last five years.
4. A preexisting set of software products developed by Mr. Freiburghouse that substantially reduces the amount of new development required and allows us to begin implementation sooner.
5. Very large and fast growing market, with a focus on a segment within that market which is growing even faster.

Legal Counsel: Gaston Snow & Ely Bartlett
One Federal Street
Boston, MA 02110

Accountants: Arthur Young & Company
One Boston Place
Boston, MA 02102

A—FINANCIALS
Financial Statements—Fiscal Year 1
(in thousands of dollars)

	Q1	Q2	Q3	Q4	FY
Income Statement					
Revenue	—	—	—	—	—
Cost of goods sold	—	—	—	—	—
Operating expenses:					
Development	121	341	403	447	1,312
Marketing	12	17	22	32	83
G&A	47	40	63	63	213
Total operating expenses	180	398	488	542	1,608
Income (loss) from operations	(180)	(398)	(488)	(542)	(1,608)
Interest expense	—	6	9	8	23
Interest income	—	40	33	21	94
Net interest	—	34	24	13	71
Net income (loss)	(180)	(364)	(464)	(529)	(1,537)

EXHIBIT 1   *(continued)*

	Q1	Q2	Q3	Q4
Balance Sheet				
Cash & cash investments	1,835	1,494	1,033	507
Prepaid expenses	25	25	25	25
Total current assets	1,860	1,519	1,058	532
Electronic test equipment	—	100	200	200
Computer equipment	—	170	170	170
Subtotal	—	270	370	370
Less—accumulated dep.	—	13	31	49
Net plant and equipment	—	257	339	321
Total assets	1,860	1,776	1,397	853
Accounts payable	10	20	20	20
Accrued expenses	30	40	40	40
Total current liabilities	40	60	60	60
Capital lease obligations	—	260	345	330
Stock	2,000	2,000	2,000	2,000
Retained deficit	(180)	(544)	(1,008)	(1,537)
Total stockholders' equity	1,820	1,456	992	463
Total liabilities and equity	1,860	1,776	1,397	853

Cash Flow—Fiscal Year 1 (in thousands of dollars)

	Q1	Q2	Q3	Q4	FY
Cash provided by (used in)					
Operations:					
Net income (loss)	(180)	(364)	(464)	(529)	(1,537)
Add: Depreciation	—	13	18	18	49
Net cash provided by (used in) operations	(180)	(351)	(446)	(511)	(1,488)
Other sources of cash:					
Increase in payables	10	10	—	—	20
Increase in accrued expenses	30	10	—	—	40
Increase in capital leases	—	270	100	—	370
Sale of stock	2,000	—	—	—	2,000
Total sources (uses)	1,860	(61)	(346)	(511)	942
Uses of cash					
Increase in ppd. expenses	25	—	—	—	25
Additions to property, plant, and equipment	—	270	100	—	370
Payments of capital leases	—	10	15	15	40
Total uses	25	280	115	15	435
Increase (decrease) in cash	1,835	(341)	(461)	(526)	507
Cash at start	—	1,835	1,494	1,033	—
Cash at end	1,835	1,494	1,033	507	507

EXHIBIT 1 *(continued)*

Financial Statements—Fiscal Year 2
(in thousands of dollars)

	Q1	Q2	Q3	Q4	FY
Income Statement					
Revenue	—	—	—	400	400
Total cost of goods sold	—	—	—	312	312
Gross margin	—	—	—	88	88
Development	379	362	352	337	1,430
Marketing	42	62	87	112	303
G&A	63	63	63	63	252
Total operating expenses	484	487	502	512	1,985
Income (loss) from operations	(484)	(487)	(502)	(424)	(1,897)
Interest expense	8	10	12	11	41
Interest income	7	51	39	31	128
Net interest	(1)	41	27	20	87
Net income (loss)	(485)	(446)	(475)	(404)	(1,810)
Balance Sheet					
Cash & cash investments	2,228	1,767	1,252	753	
Accounts receivable				300	
Inventories	10	40	150	250	
Prepaid expenses	30	30	30	30	
Total current assets	2,268	1,837	1,432	1,333	
Production and test equipment	25	75	200	200	
Electronic test equipment	200	200	200	200	
Computer equipment	170	170	170	170	
Subtotal	395	445	570	570	
Less—accumulated depreciation	70	85	115	140	
Total plant and equipment	325	360	455	430	
Total assets	2,593	2,197	1,887	1,763	
Accounts payable	30	50	100	400	
Accrued expenses	50	50	60	60	
Total current liabilities	80	100	160	460	
Capital lease obligations	335	365	470	450	
Stock	4,200	4,200	4,200	4,200	
Retained deficit	(2,022)	(2,468)	(2,943)	(3,347)	
Total stockholders' equity	2,178	1,732	1,257	853	
Total liabilities and equity	2,593	2,197	1,887	1,763	

EXHIBIT 1   *(continued)*

Cash Flow—Fiscal Year 2
(in thousands of dollars)

	Q1	Q2	Q3	Q4	FY
Cash provided by (used in)					
Operations:					
Net income (loss)	(485)	(446)	(475)	(404)	(1,810)
Add: charges against income not requiring use of cash:					
Depreciation	21	15	30	25	91
Net cash provided by (used in) operations	(464)	(431)	(445)	(379)	(1,719)
Other sources of cash:					
Increase in accounts payable	10	20	50	300	380
Increase in accrued expenses	10	—	10	—	20
Increase in capital leases	25	50	125	—	200
Sale of stock	2,200	—	—	—	2,200
Total sources (uses)	1,781	(361)	(260)	(79)	1,081
Uses of cash					
Increase in accounts receivable	—	—	—	300	300
Increase in inventories	10	30	110	100	250
Increase in prepaid expenses	5	—	—	—	5
Additions to property, plant, and equipment	25	50	125	—	200
Payments of capital leases	20	20	20	20	80
Total uses	60	100	255	420	835
Increase (decrease) in cash	1,721	(461)	(515)	(499)	246
Cash balance start of period	507	2,228	1,767	1,252	507
Cash balance end of period	2,228	1,767	1,252	753	753

EXHIBIT 1   (*continued*)

Financial Statements—Fiscal Year 3
(in thousands of dollars)

	Q1	Q2	Q3	Q4	FY
Income Statement					
Revenue	1,200	2,100	2,800	3,900	10,000
Total cost of goods sold	600	900	1,100	1,500	4,100
Gross margin	600	1,200	1,700	2,400	5,900
Development	350	330	340	350	1,340
Marketing	200	570	730	900	2,400
G&A	80	100	120	150	450
Total operating expenses	660	1,045	1,230	1,315	4,350
Income (loss) from operations	(60)	155	470	985	1,550
Interest expense	10	10	9	9	38
Interest income	14	40	29	19	102
Net interest	4	30	20	10	64
Income (loss) before taxes	(56)	185	490	995	1,614
Net income (loss)	(56)	170	445	905	1,464
Balance Sheet					
Cash & cash investments	1,852	1,332	882	1,267	
Accounts receivable	800	1,400	1,900	2,800	
System spares	100	200	300	300	
Inventories	500	800	1,500	2,500	
Prepaid expenses	50	50	100	100	
Total current assets	3,302	3,782	4,687	6,967	
Production and test equipment	400	400	400	400	
Electronic test equipment	200	200	200	200	
Computer equipment	170	170	170	170	
Leasehold improvements	25	50	50	75	
Subtotal	795	820	820	845	
Less accumulated depreciation	180	215	255	295	
Net plant and equipment	615	605	565	550	
Total assets	3,917	4,387	5,252	7,517	
Notes payable	—	—	—	1,000	
Accounts payable	600	900	1,200	1,500	
Taxes payable	—	15	60	150	
Accrued expenses	100	100	200	200	
Total current liabilities	700	1,015	1,460	2,850	
Capital lease obligations	420	405	380	350	
Stock	6,200	6,200	6,200	6,200	
Retained deficit	(3,403)	(3,233)	(2,788)	(1,883)	
Total stockholders' equity	2,797	2,967	3,412	4,317	
Total liabilities and equity	3,917	4,387	5,257	7,517	

EXHIBIT 1   *(continued)*

Cash Flow—Fiscal Year 3
(in thousands of dollars)

	Q1	Q2	Q3	Q4	FY
Cash provided by (used in)					
Operations:					
Net income (loss)	(56)	170	445	905	1,464
Add: charges against income not requiring use of cash:					
Depreciation	40	35	40	40	155
Net cash provided by (used in) operations	(16)	205	485	945	1,619
Other sources of cash:					
Increase in notes payable	—	—	—	1,000	1,000
Increase in accounts payable	200	300	300	300	1,100
Increase in taxes payable	—	15	45	90	150
Increase in accrued expenses	40	—	100	—	140
Sale of stock	2,000	—	—	—	2,000
Total sources (uses)	2,224	520	930	2,335	6,009
Uses of cash					
Increase in accounts receivable	500	600	500	900	2,500
Increase in system spares	100	100	100	—	300
Increase in inventories	250	300	700	1,000	2,250
Increase in prepaid expenses	20	—	50	—	70
Additions to property, plant, and equipment	225	25	—	25	275
Payments of capital leases	30	15	25	30	100
Total uses	1,125	1,040	1,375	1,955	5,495
Increase (decrease) in cash	1,099	(520)	(445)	380	514
Cash balance start of period	753	1,852	1,332	887	753
Cash balance end of period	1,852	1,332	887	1,267	1,267

EXHIBIT 1   (*continued*)

Five Year Financial Pro Formas
(in thousands of dollars)

	Y1	Y2	Y3	Y4	Y5
Income Statement					
Revenue	—	400	10,000	30,000	75,000
Total cost of goods sold	—	312	4,100	13,200	33,500
Gross margin	—	88	5,900	16,800	41,500
Development	1,312	1,430	1,340	1,700	4,750
Marketing	83	303	2,400	6,400	16,000
G&A	213	252	450	1,500	2,750
Total operating expenses	1,608	1,985	4,350	9,600	23,500
Income (loss) from operations	(1,608)	(1,897)	1,550	7,200	18,000
Interest expense	23	41	38	75	15
Interest income	94	128	102	50	50
Net interest	71	87	64	(25)	35
Income (loss) before taxes	(1,537)	(1,810)	1,614	7,175	18,035
Net income (loss)	(1,537)	(1,810)	1,464	4,800	9,935
Balance Sheet					
Cash & cash investments	507	753	1,267	1,212	2,127
Accounts receivable	—	300	2,800	8,000	20,000
System spares	—	—	300	900	2,000
Inventories	—	250	2,500	7,000	18,000
Prepaid expenses	25	30	100	300	500
Total current assets	532	1,333	6,967	17,412	42,627
Production and test equipment	—	200	400	900	2,200
Electronic test equipment	200	200	200	300	500
Computer equipment	170	170	170	200	400
Leasehold improvements	—	—	75	100	300
Subtotal	370	570	845	1,500	3,400
Less accumulated depreciation	49	140	295	500	800
Net plant and equipment	321	430	550	1,000	2,600
Total assets	853	1,763	7,517	18,412	45,227
Notes payable	—	—	1,000	—	—
Accounts payable	20	400	1,500	3,500	9,000
Taxes payable	—	—	150	2,375	8,100
Accrued expenses	40	60	200	1,200	3,000
Total current liabilities	60	460	2,850	7,075	20,100
Capital lease obligations	330	450	350	220	75
Stock	2,000	4,200	6,200	6,200	6,200
Retained earnings (deficit)	(1,537)	(3,347)	(1,883)	2,917	12,852
Total stockholders' equity	463	853	4,317	9,117	19,052
Additional debt or equity	—	—	—	2,000	6,000
Total liabilities and equity	853	1,763	7,517	18,412	45,227

EXHIBIT 1 *(continued)*

Five Year Cash Flow
(in thousands of dollars)

	Y1	Y2	Y3	Y4	Y5
Cash provided by (used in)					
Operations:					
Net income (loss)	(1,537)	(1,810)	1,464	4,800	9,935
Add: charges against income not requiring use of cash:					
Depreciation	49	91	155	205	300
Net cash provided by (used in) operations	(1,488)	(1,719)	1,619	5,005	10,235
Other sources of cash:					
Increase in notes payable	—	—	1,000	—	—
Increase in accounts payable	20	380	1,100	2,000	5,500
Increase in taxes payable	—	—	150	2,225	5,725
Increase in accrued expenses	40	20	140	1,000	1,800
Increase in capital leases	370	200	—	—	—
Sale of stock	2,000	2,200	2,000	—	—
Additional cash requirements	—	—	—	2,000	4,000
Total sources (uses)	942	1,081	6,009	12,230	27,260
Uses of cash					
Increase in accounts receivable	—	300	2,500	5,200	12,000
Increase in system spares	—	—	300	600	1,100
Increase in inventories	—	250	2,250	4,500	11,000
Increase in prepaid expenses	25	5	70	200	200
Additions to property, plant, and equipment	370	200	275	655	1,900
Payments of capital leases	40	80	100	130	145
Payments of notes payable	—	—	—	1,000	—
Total uses	435	835	5,495	12,285	26,345
Increase (decrease) in cash	507	246	514	(55)	915
Cash balance start of period	—	507	753	1,267	1,212
Cash balance end of period	507	753	1,267	1,212	2,127

EXHIBIT 1   (*continued*)

Financial Assumptions

1. Revenues
    —Average selling price per system is $80,000.
    —Product will be ready in 18th month; first shipments to occur by 21st month.
    —Service revenues will grow at less than the industry average of 0.6 percent to 0.8 percent of installed base per month, and will account for less than 10 percent of sales though Year 5.
    —Revenue per salesman will be the industry average of $700K to $1,000K per year.
    —Reduced margins from OEM discounts will be offset by reduced marketing expense. Revenue for marketing provides ample margin for competitive discounts.
2. Warranty
    —Because of high system reliability, warranty expense will not be a significant factor.
3. Foreign sales
    —Some sales in Years 4 and 5 will be international.
    —Tax provision does not consider potential benefit of DISC.
4. Marketing expense
    —Higher than average industry rate will be spent on marketing. Combined marketing + G/A for selected companies are: DG 22 percent, Tandem 36 percent, Prime 33 percent, Digital 20 percent, HP 28 percent.
    —Salesperson compensation will be through a very aggressive commission plan.
5. R&D
    —During Years 1 and 2 all technical people will come over at straight salary plus very attractive stock plan.
6. Taxes
    —No loss carryforwards for state purposes; therefore, state provision in Year 3.
    —Assumes 45 percent effective tax rate, which is reasonable in light of:
        —ITC.
        —Jobs tax credit.
        —Surtax exemption.
        —Tax planning.
7. Receivables
    —Assumes 60-day turn cycle.
    —Assumes in Years 4 and 5 that 40 percent of annual sales occur in 4th quarter.
8. Inventories
    —At an annualized run rate, inventory held at 6 to 7 turns per year.
    —Strong manufacturing emphasis on controlling inventory levels.
9. Property, plant, and equipment
    —Early requirements will be financed through leasing. Assumes capital leases from an accounting point of view.
    —Lease terms are $20 per $1,000 of capital equipment per month, full payout in 5 years. Bank receives ITC and depreciation benefits.

EXHIBIT 1   *(concluded)*

10. Accounts payable
    —Assumes 60-day turn cycle.
11. Additional cash requirements
    —Assumes equity infusion and therefore no interest costs.
    —If partial debt financing is assumed at an 18 percent interest cost,
    then a debt to equity ratio of 1:1 yields ROI of 92 percent in Year 4
    and 86 percent in Year 5; debt to equity of .5:1 yields ROI of 67 per-
    cent in Year 4 and 63 percent in Year 5.

	Year 4	Year 5
1:1 ratio		
Debt	5,500	12,500
Equity	5,500	12,500
Interest	495	1,620
Tax	2,100	7,300
Net income	5,075	10,735
ROI	92%	86%
.5:1 ratio		
Debt	3,600	8,300
Equity	7,400	16,700
Interest	324	1,070
Tax	2,210	7,560
Net income	4,965	10,470
ROI	67%	63%

12. Manufacturing
    —No heavy capital equipment required since most of the manufactur-
    ing process consists of integrating vendor hardware. Provisions are
    made for burn-in ovens, wave-solder equipment, electronic and pe-
    ripheral testers. Manufacturing is essentially an assembly and test
    operation.
    —All electronic components will be second-sourced. Where possible,
    peripherals will be second-sourced. The disc will be selected par-
    tially on the availability of a standard interface such as Storage
    Module.

Part III

Acquiring an Existing
Business

In this part of the book, we examine an alternative approach to an entrepreneurial career: purchasing an existing business. This approach has allure for many would-be entrepreneurs who feel they don't have a creative idea for "a better mousetrap," but who nonetheless would like to be in business for themselves.

Chapter 9 describes the search process for a company: potential sources of leads and how to assess, value, and finance the purchase. Unlike the start-up process—which is more or less in control of the entrepreneur—purchasing a business involves a critical relationship with the seller, and that relationship must be managed carefully. Chapter 10 describes the various legal forms of organization a business can choose from. Finally, Chapter 11 describes some of the tax aspects of the purchase process. As in many important transactions, tax consequences can be large and influenced by the handling of the smallest of details.

THE CASES

Berringer Products is a relatively simplified case that focuses on the financial and tax dimensions of the acquisition process.

Allen Lane describes one man's search for a business. After many false starts and close calls, he is left with an opportunity that appears to be attractive. Is it? How should he structure a deal to purchase the company?

The cases Kirk Riedinger and Jamie Turner and Jim Southern both describe recent business school graduates who fund and structure the search for a business and who arrive at very different places wondering whether they have finally found the object of their search and, if so, how they should pursue it.

Chapter Nine

Purchasing a Business: The Search Process

Purchasing an existing business is an excellent alternative for individuals interested in running a small- to medium-sized company. While not usually considered as "entrepreneurial" as developing the next generation of personal computers in a tiny garage, purchasing a company demands making many of the same difficult decisions required of a successful entrepreneur. In addition, it provides an opportunity for the purchaser to leverage his or her financial resources and concentrate sooner on "value adding" issues that are traditionally taught in business school management courses.

Buying a business is an informal process. No one has yet written a book that successfully defines the correct steps and best alternatives for every situation. Hence, there is no substitute for personal commitment, good business sense, and a cautiously optimistic exploration of every opportunity. Success in this process may occur randomly and can often depend on serendipity—being the right person in the right place at the right time. It is a mistake, however, to depend on good luck rather than good work.

This note will provide a framework that outlines many of the steps necessary to identify, evaluate, and negotiate a successful buyout. It is important to note, however, that this framework is not exhaustive. Rather, it provides a starting point that can be tailored to suit the particular nature of your search.

This note was prepared by Ennis J. Walton under the direction of Michael J. Roberts.

The areas discussed in this note are as follows:

— *Self-Assessment:*   Understanding your motives, expectations, risk profile, and financial and professional resources, and determining the seriousness of your search process.

— *Deal Criteria:*   Clarifying the dimensions of the project and characteristics that you find attractive.

— *Deal Sources:*   Learning how to differentiate between the various deal sources in order to find a source that best fits your personal needs and established criteria.

— *Resources:*   Evaluating and garnering the additional cash, credibility, personal and professional contacts, and information necessary to begin the deal process.

— *The Deal Process:*   Recognizing the sequential, often random, search process; establishing a deal timing schedule and work plan that allows you to evaluate deals that do not occur in parallel; understanding how to start the process, keep it moving, and establish initial contact with prospective sellers; and, assessing the sellers' motives, weaknesses, strengths, and special nonfinancial requirements.

— *The Evaluation Process:*   Understanding the various analytical methods used by sellers, requesting or obtaining the key financial indicators, and analyzing the important financial dimensions of the deal.

— *Negotiating the Deal:*   Identifying potential deal killers, learning from the collapsed deal, and pursuing attractive deals.

— *Adding Value:*   Applying your managerial skills to add new value to the enterprise and understanding important harvesting options for the new enterprise.

SELF-ASSESSMENT

The first step in buying an existing business is a personal assessment. This step is crucial because it will help you identify, articulate, and evaluate your hidden motives, expectations, risk profile, and ultimately, the seriousness of your search. Without a good sense of these personal values, the search process can become unfocused and unrewarding, causing you to waste time, resources, and energy.

The problems that could materialize in the absence of a thorough self-evaluation are intensified if you are attempting to purchase a company with another individual. In such cases, it is absolutely essential that all parties understand and agree on their motives and goals. Proceeding with a false sense of those aspirations will more than likely lead to problems—disagreements which impact on the efficiency and effectiveness of the group during the later stages of the process when clear vision and communication are important to make important decisions.

A good self-assessment will probably place you in one of three broad categories.

Serious

The serious and realistic search involves the following:

— A high level of commitment to the search.

— An ambitious set of expectations consistent with the degree of effort and commitment.

— A willingness to:

- Risk at least some personal wealth/security.
- Deeply research the target industry.
- Be patient and wait for the "right" opportunity.
- Move quickly and decisively as needed.
- Pursue the search full time, if needed.

Casual

The casual and realistic search involves:

— A set of expectations that is consistent with this lessened degree of commitment and effort.

— Less willingness to move quickly or decisively on opportunities.

— No specified time horizon for search.

— Not being overly hungry to control one's own firm.

Unrealistic

The unrealistic search involves:

— Objectives that are inconsistent with level of commitment.

— Waiting for a "great deal" to fall in place.

— Looking for bargains and short-cuts.

While there is nothing wrong with either of the first two categories, the number and quality of opportunities discovered is proportional to the intensity of the search. This is not to say, however, that one cannot find excellent deals by "shopping" the market casually, but only that the process may take quite a while.

Another aspect of the self-assessment process that many people deal too lightly with is the listing of any and all business or personal relationships that can be called upon to add credibility or offer advice. Since the search process is lengthy and filled with important decision points, it is of great value to have others whose opinion you trust to call upon for advice.

The most important reason for the self-assessment, however, is tactical. Throughout the search process, you will have to deal with sellers or their intermediaries to get a sense of the deal. Because these individuals are often reluctant to invest their time with individuals unless they sense a degree of rational forethought and commitment, it's important to have a clear and convincing sense of what it is you're looking for. Thus, the better you have assessed yourself, the easier it will be to persuade others to take you seriously or work productively on your behalf.

DEAL CRITERIA

A consistent and thorough screening method is essential for the successful completion of the acquisition process. Consistency is required so that analyses performed on one company are more readily comparable with those of other candidates. Thoroughness is required because all relevant aspects of a potential acquisition must be identified and analyzed. While thoroughness is critical, the screening method should have a clear focus and be kept fairly simple.

There are numerous ways to define the desired target company profile. At a minimum, one should think along such dimensions as:

— Size of deal (purchase price) desired.

— Preferred industry.

— Key factors for success (logistics, marketing, technology, etc.).

— Type of customer base (i.e., industrial versus consumer, national versus regional, etc.).

— Geographic preference.

— Profile of current ownership (i.e., how many, willingness to sell, reputation).

The mechanical dimensions highlighted above establish a preliminary framework for identifying deals that are appropriate for the particular search being undertaken. The screening process must then tackle the issue of distinguishing *good* deals from *bad* deals. Though there are several intangible and intuitive issues involved in this process, as a rule of thumb, an ideal buyout target should include:

— Potential for improving earnings and sales.

— Predictable cash flow.

— Minimum existing debt.

— An asset base to support substantial new borrowings.

When searching for a business, the buyout candidate will most likely not fit in a "nice, neat, little box," so flexibility is important. One must constantly rethink and reassess the criteria developed. Do they fit? Are they appropriate? Is this the best way to examine this company? Will the criteria help to achieve the objective in mind?

DEAL SOURCES

Initiating and sustaining the deal flow is one of the most challenging tasks in buying a business. In general, expect to look at dozens of deals for every one that might appear worth pursuing; there are simply a lot of poor deals out there. A seemingly endless amount of groundwork is often necessary to initiate a deal, and a targeted effort is far more likely to result in a high percentage of attractive candidates. Thus, one of the first orders of business when starting out to locate a company is to know where to look.

Depending on what size deal is sought, there are a number of potential deal sources, and each has its own approach to acquisitions. The chart which follows is a subjective assessment of the various sources of deals and the territory they cover.

Deal Sources by Size (purchase price)

Sources							
Independent brokers	:=======>						
Professional brokers			:==================>				
Venture firms				:=======>			
LBO funds				:===================>			
Personal contacts		:=========================>					
Other professional service firms (banks, CPAs, etc.)		:============>					
Investment banks						:===========>	
	500K	1MM	5MM	10MM	20MM	35MM	>50MM

Deal Size ($)
(not to scale)

The number of deals in the lower ranges—particularly in the $1MM to $50MM category—is on the rise. Geneva Business Services, Inc., a leading national broker of small businesses, estimates that more than 15,000 deals involving companies valued in this range will close in

1987. Mainstream investment banks, on the other hand, are rarely interested in any deal valued less than $10–$20 million. Recognizing the particular niches these players inhabit will help to minimize lost time and unnecessary frustration chasing deals where they are not likely to be found. The paragraphs below will help identify sources according to the size of deal handled.

Business brokers—independent and professional alike—are the most readily available resource; they are listed individually in the Yellow Pages of most phone directories and advertise in the business sections of many newspapers. The broker's primary function is to work on behalf of sellers to find appropriate buyers for their clients' businesses, and he or she is compensated by the seller for closing a deal based on a percentage of the price basis. Occasionally, a broker will work for a buyer to search for a business in return for a retainer fee and/or a percentage of the ultimate purchase price. It should be emphasized, though, that the broker's motivation is to close each transaction; he or she should not necessarily be considered a business consultant in the search process.

Business brokers obtain listings through cold calls and advertising. Because these listings are actively marketed, it is safe to assume that you are probably not the first prospective buyer to see the business. More reputable brokers tend to regulate how "shopped" a business becomes in order to preserve its value and may not even list properties which the seller himself has already tried to market.

At your initial meeting with the broker, you should be prepared to describe your financial constraints and industry preference. It is also valuable to indicate that you have a well-defined time horizon for a search and some knowledge of the target industry. You might want to touch base occasionally with each broker whom you meet, but it is a safe bet that you will be notified if there is an interesting opportunity and if you are a qualified buyer.

Some attention should be focused on the role of independent brokers since they are often the first place people turn for deal flow. Independent brokers are almost entirely unregulated. Because no license is required, and anyone can claim to be one, it is essential to check references (should the broker not supply them) and reputation with other intermediaries and past clients. Fourteen states require brokers to have a real estate broker's license, but, for the most part, anyone with a telephone can call himself or herself a business broker. The largest network of independent brokers is VR Business Brokers, headquartered in Boston, Massachusetts. VR has 10 franchised brokerages operating offices in 500 cities. VR claims to close up to 7,500 deals per annum, 80 percent of which are companies with sales below $800,000. On the other end of the spectrum, one can find a seemingly endless supply of one-person brokerage services in most any city. As such, one must be exceedingly cautious when trying to land a deal via this route. First of all, the deals are going to be small, less than $500,000 in sales. Second, they are most likely to be owned by entrepreneurs who have an unrealistic impression of the value of their businesses, an impression often fueled by the brokers themselves.

As for professional brokers, a few prominent ones are worth noting here:

— Geneva Business Services in Costa Mesa, California.

— W. T. Grimm & Co. in Chicago, Illinois.

— First Main Capital Corp. in Plano, Texas.

— Nation-List Network of Business Brokers, Inc. in Denver, Colorado, is a cooperative exchange of some 50 independent brokers.

These organizations tend to operate on a far more professional basis than the independents, but keep track of the fact that they still represent the seller. Their interest is in getting the highest possible price for the company, thereby ensuring high commission fees (usually around 10 percent to 12 percent at closing). Also, note that deals coming via professional brokers are very likely to be highly "shopped." The deals' legitimacy are often prescreened, but count on paying a premium for businesses carried by professional brokers.

Venture capital firms will most likely be looking for liquidity on investments they made three to five years earlier. Venture-backed companies that have reached this stage are generally beyond many of the risks associated with start-ups and may pose a solid acquisition opportunity. Several points should be noted, however. First, venture capitalists are highly sophisticated investors and will likely extract the highest possible price for the company. Second, they want liquidity for their investment and will be less interested in earn-outs and other creative financing than a deal that is primarily financed with cash. Finally, existing management will likely be highly entrepreneurial and will be wary of the control issues introduced by new owners in the company.

Leveraged buyout (LBO) funds in some sense pose competition to the buyout effort. As a potential deal source, however, there may be opportunity to pick up on deals that are of no interest to the LBO fund. Such deals may still be attractive candidates if they were passed over simply because the deal did not match the particular focus of the LBO fund.

Personal contacts, although often overlooked, may be helpful. Self-initiated contacts with people who have successfully completed the search process for their own businesses may be a good source of both information and moral support. Depending on your specific situation and their area of expertise, they may be able to suggest specific contacts and strategies or allow you to tap their network. Additionally, you may be able to learn some of the common pitfalls they encountered and some rules of thumb they use. These resources may be located through your network or by tracking recently completed deals.

On occasion, combing prominent business periodicals will identify opportunities. Indications that a company will be spinning off subsidiary operations are frequently mentioned in articles in some level of detail. Nationally, *The Wall Street Journal* and publications such as *Inc.* and *Venture* routinely list business opportunities. On the local or regional level, there are business journals, franchise fairs, classified ads, and notices of bankruptcies and deaths. Newspapers and the offices of the county clerk and court clerks are good sources, as are computer databases, available on a time-sharing basis that provide lists of prospective buyers and sellers of businesses. Academic and commercial institutions in some communities sponsor industry forums or trade association meetings. Industry and phone directories (Yellow Pages, Dun & Bradstreet, *Million Dollar Directory,* Thomas' *Register of American Manufacturers,* etc.) may be useful for a cold call or letter writing campaign and as a possible screen for industry, size, and location. You can run this process in reverse by placing your own advertisement in newspapers or journals stating your desire and criteria for purchasing a business.

Local banks represent a broad range of local businesses and have in-depth knowledge of their finances and managerial situations. Like business brokers, the M&A-type departments of banks are primarily interested in closing transactions. Their inventory of deals may include both banking clients that may be for sale or other firms that have engaged the bank to help them find a suitable buyer. A bank may also be amenable to helping you conduct a search on a success-fee basis. A good banker will also be instrumental in structuring the financial arrangements of the newly acquired business. As with lawyers and accountants, the bank may often expect to become the new firm's principal banker.

Trust departments of banks often are the executors of estate business. In cases where there is a need to dispose of such a business, a bank trust officer may serve the same role as an estate lawyer. However, the trust officer has a fiduciary responsibility to the beneficiaries of the estate and will seek the highest price for the business consistent with keeping the transaction clean, fast, and, to the greatest extent, in cash.

Bank work-out departments are another potential source of "bargain" opportunities. While the bank certainly has a strong interest in not disclosing credit problems, it may be a confidential go-between for a potential buyer and the owners of a deeply troubled client if a mutually satisfactory offer were presented. However, bankers indicate that because of pressures within the bank to reschedule the debt and the willingness of owners to personally collateralize additional loans, most troubled loans are in fact worked out.

Traditional, mainline investment banks pose both a problem and an opportunity for buyers seeking a midsized deal. The problem is that investment banks are rarely interested in deals below, say, $20 million. Attracting their attention can be troublesome and getting them to spend time moving on a relatively small deal requires patience and tenacity. The opportunity, for nearly the same grounds, exists because small deals carried by the investment banks are unlikely to have been widely shopped. Owners who rely exclusively on an investment bank to market their company will probably not receive extraordinary service. A buyer who works this route may find a fairly responsive seller on the other end of this inattentive deal pipeline.

No matter where the deal comes from, there will be a seller to contend with. Whether the seller is a single individual, a group of investors, or the shareholders of a small public company one will have to evaluate their motivations. Issues of timing, types of financing, credibility, desire to remain with the company after acquisition, and the like, are all relevant points of thought when approaching the seller. Fairly early on, conversations should focus on the seller's motives for selling the business and his or her expectations as to the value and form of deal. A cautious investor will also use this opportunity to gauge the character and integrity of the seller, as such traits will likely have influenced how the business has been managed in the past.

RESOURCES

Aside from tireless energy and a wealth of patience, resources critical to the buyout project are cash, credibility, and contacts. These three factors, more than anything else, govern the success of the effort. How much will be required is simply a question of deal size. Purchasing a $300,000 business certainly requires fewer resources than putting together a $20 million buyout. As deals get larger, one is competing with a more sophisticated group of potential buyers. Larger deals are more complex, and sellers of larger companies will demand of the potential buyer those credentials they believe are necessary to put the deal together. Lacking the resources necessary to pull off the deal, the potential buyer may not even be successful in establishing an initial meeting with the seller. To get farther than the first phone call with larger deals, one should be prepared to satisfactorily respond to such inquiries as:

— How much cash do you have available?

— Who are your backers?

— What other deals have you done?

— What kind of management talent do you bring?

— What do you plan to do with the company?

Sellers value their time as much as the prospective buyer does. Neither wants to spend fruitless energy on meetings where there is an obvious mismatch between what the buyer brings to the table and what the target company will require. No amount of debt leverage will compensate for a lack of the equity capital and demonstrated personal background needed to purchase and operate the target company. Take stock of the resources available for the buyout project, and then target deals that can be reasonably snared with the resources at hand.

If buyers plan to employ the resources of backers, they must realize the extent to which they are dependent upon the backers and gauge how committed the backers are to the project. All the backers' cash and contacts are absolutely useless if they are unwilling to spend the time and energy needed to pursue the deal. Evaluate the backers' incentives. How important is the project to them? How much time have they agreed to set aside? Do their timing considerations match those of the group? Some backers are quite willing to employ the free efforts of a buyout group simply hoping they will luck into a treasure chest. Be cautious of working like a neglected employee, rather than a respected partner. Such characteristics may prove difficult to evaluate, particularly early on when enthusiasm runs high for the project. Make a critical and even skeptical assessment of the backers' sincerity, interest, and ability to follow through on their part of the bargain before relying on them for the resources critical to the effort's success.

In addition, an experienced lawyer is absolutely essential to the prudent buyer. An attorney's principal role in the search process is usually to review documents with the aim of protecting the client with adequate contractual conditions and to ensure proper disclosure and legal and regulatory compliance. An attorney can also provide tax advice and may be able to identify potential risks and liabilities in a transaction. In many cases, more experienced lawyers turn out to be cheaper because they know the appropriate safeguards and can create good standard documents without extensive new research. In addition, as established members of the local professional community, attorneys may have access to a wider network of contacts than the buyer. For example, they sometimes sit on the boards of local businesses and may have a variety of contacts in the target industry. While tapping into this network might not generate a deal, it may provide you with opportunities to learn about the target industry and to gain credibility therein.

Occasionally, in larger law firms, there may also be an "inventory" of business acquisition opportunities. The buyer must usually compensate the lawyer for time and effort, and if the deal is successful, he or she generally expects to become the newly acquired firm's corporate counsel. As for selecting a business lawyer, there are issues to consider. For instance, you should determine whether or not the lawyer has a potential conflict of interest (e.g., if he is representing the seller). Although no reputable attorney would pursue an engagement while conflict exists without full disclosure, it is still up to you to determine the services she or he might provide. Another issue is the lawyer's reputation. It is wise to do some background or information checks of individual attorneys or their firms. Finally, your choice of lawyer should reflect your perceived legal and other professional needs at various stages of the search and deal process.[1]

THE DEAL PROCESS

Once you have specified the characteristics that you are looking for in a company, understood the best ways to generate deal flow, and have garnered the resources necessary to successfully purchase an existing company, you should prepare to enter the deal market. At this phase, it is important to recognize and prepare for the random nature of the process.

There are two important timing issues to be concerned with when you enter the deal market. First, the sequential nature of the search process makes it difficult to compare deals in parallel. Rarely will you be able to view two deals within a time frame which allows you to evaluate them comparatively. Given that fact, it is important to realize that if you let one deal pass, you will probably encounter another one in the near future. An analytical framework to help you screen businesses (see Figure 9–1) will better equip you to track and compare various deals as you interface with sellers, deal sources, and other active parties at different points throughout the deal process (see also Chapter 2, The Start-up Process).

The second critical issue concerns the timing of the approach: before it hits the market, as soon as it hits the market, or after it has been "shopped." There are advantages and disadvantages to entering at each stage. In some cases, being the first person to see a deal (before it is on the market) may give you the inside track or first right to

---

[1]For example, a lawyer with the technical knowledge to structure the deal from a tax perspective may not be the most skilled negotiator.

refuse. Yet, at this early stage, the seller will not have developed a realistic perspective on his or her demands (asking price, terms, inclination to provide desired information, willingness to actually part with the business, etc.). In such a case, discussions might be futile or you may end up paying a relatively high price. In a later stage, the seller may be more eager to sell, but you should be concerned about the health or the attractiveness of the business that has been on the market for a lengthy period.

Once you understand these basic timing issues and prepare a schedule and work plan, you should begin your search. Most of the search resources are amenable to a free introductory meeting even on the basis of a cold call. A persuasive presentation at this first meeting might include a demonstration of your industry research or experience, a well-thought-out preliminary business plan, a realistic assessment of your financial resources, and suitable dress and demeanor. Academic credentials help your chances of getting in the door, as does the referral of a mutual acquaintance. This meeting should not necessarily result in a commitment; in fact, you might consider meeting with many attorneys, CPAs and bankers, or others you deem helpful before committing to work with anyone in particular. You might also schedule some "warm-up" sessions with some of these professionals before meeting with your highest priority contacts.

The preliminary meeting should serve several purposes: Resources will be interested in qualifying you both as a realistic, potential buyer and as someone they will want to work with. You should attempt to determine their expertise and willingness to help, along with any conditions on your relationship with them. With regard to establishing fees, practice ranges from hourly fees to contingent fees; the arrangement of one lawyer may be substantially different from another. This is another reason to meet with many professionals before committing to work exclusively with any one in particular.

In most of these preliminary discussions, the issue of what to tell and what to hide arises. While this is a personal decision, a perspective on your financial resources, level of commitment, and objectives is probably best expressed frankly. You may want to be more vague if you are dealing with an intermediary who represents a potential seller or if you have reservations about the person with whom you are meeting. The fact that your backers may want their identities shielded will also push you to be somewhat guarded. Checking out the reputations of such individuals before divulging any of your private information is the only prudent course of action.

The average time required to find the right business runs about one year—significantly longer if your search is more casual or if your target is more elusive. Therefore, depending on your degree of commitment, your financial flexibility, and your time schedule, you may elect to manage your own search by calling on the search resources periodically, or you may choose to retain a search resource to conduct the search for you.

An attorney, for instance, could make cold calls and write letters to industry sources on your behalf. While his personal and professional contacts may unearth your dream business, much of the research you pay him for could be easily done yourself from industry directories, Yellow Pages, etc. Thus, if time permits or your budget requires and you are sophisticated enough about basic business and legal issues, you may choose to undertake many of the basic research tasks yourself. This also provides first-hand contact with the marketplace.

The industry-specific knowledge you pick up may be invaluable to you later on, when you need to demonstrate expertise or commitment to financing sources or to a seller. In some industries, acquisition opportunities rarely reach the marketplace because the industry is essentially closed. Therefore, if you are interested in entering such an area, you must "network" your way in. This might include meeting owners or executives of any firms in that industry whether or not they are interested in selling their own businesses. Industry association meetings or trade meetings can be good places to meet people and become more of an insider.

You might consider periodically touching base with some of the individuals in your new network to see if they have any ideas for you and to reiterate your degree of interest. But be sensitive to the demands you are making: A short phone call every three or four weeks is appropriate—more frequent contact may be annoying. You might also update them on your progress, especially because they may be able to help you more at different phases in your search. Keep in mind that they would more likely readily share information or leads with you if you exchange any ideas or intelligence with them.

Once underway, you may come across a potential acquisition candidate. An inexpensive way to obtain financial and operating information on the company and biographical background on the owners or officers is through a Dun & Bradstreet report or by other background checks. Note that the D&B report is based upon information provided by the subject company and is not independently verified.

In addition to doing some preliminary investigative research, it is important to meet the owner(s) and visit the business. An aspect of this evaluation is to understand the "seller's psychology," for it is critical to appreciate the seller's needs—financial and psychological. There are cases in which the owner has no emotional attachment to the business, and he or she would willingly sell to the highest bidder. More likely, especially in small operations, much of the seller's life is tied up in the business, resulting in a high degree of emotional involvement. There may be other significant psychological considerations, you could identify, such as the seller's age, marital situation, illness, or family situation. Usually, a deal structure will need to reflect these factors in the form and terms of the consideration. In these cases you may need to "sell" the seller.

Selling the seller does not simply include a generous financial package (e.g., insurance, providing for his family, etc.), but may require demonstrating your commitment to preserve the character, quality, and spirit of the enterprise he worked long and hard to build. Occasionally, even when an owner indicates a willingness to sell, he or she may in fact be unwilling to part with the firm when it comes to closing the deal and transferring control. Reading the owner's psyche ahead of time may avoid such fruitless discussions or may provide insight into a more mutually satisfying deal structure.

In this respect, your professional resources may be able to provide a great deal of insight and advice because they may either know the seller or have dealt with similar situations previously. It also may be helpful to have your agent negotiate on your behalf for a variety of reasons: to preserve your rapport with the seller, to neutralize personality clashes, and to preserve and improve decision options.

THE EVALUATION PROCESS

After preliminary research and introductory meetings with the prospective seller, you may decide to pursue the opportunity, which would involve reviewing confidential operating and financial statements and interviewing key employees and customers.

"Getting the numbers" can be more easily said than done. Generally, small business owners are reluctant to share any operating and financial data with outsiders, often for tax and competitive reasons. Typically a buyer does not receive any meaningful financials until after signing a purchase agreement and putting down a deposit. Thus, a good understanding of the business and the industry may give you increased credibility and leverage with the seller. A seller with a distressed business may be more willing to provide numbers earlier in the process, and for bankrupt firms, the numbers may be part of the public domain. In most cases, confidentiality agreements must be signed before reviewing any financials.

While not necessary, you are well advised at this point to retain your own counsel to ensure that you are protected and are covering all bases, especially if you are signing any documents or agreements. An accountant might also be very useful depending on the complexity of the situation (financial reports, taxes, inventory, etc.). Other experts may help investigate leases and contracts. To the extent that these are people with whom you have already worked, you will be more comfortable dealing with them and trusting them.

It is often useful to collect a "thumb-nail" sketch of the deal's financial attractiveness prior to performing any detailed analysis. As some preliminary checks, one can screen against company size, profitability, and attractiveness of the balance sheet. Some deals may be thrown out on this basis, while others will merit a more thorough examination of "the numbers."

There are several ways to reasonably estimate the value of a company, and it is most often useful to employ more than one method when performing a valuation analysis. How much to pay, how much debt and from what source, and potential harvest values are going to be valued differently. Each plays an important role in the assessment of the opportunity at hand. Below are types of analysis that can prove useful in establishing an estimate of the deal's price (see Chapter 3, Valuation Techniques):

Method Used	What the Results Indicate
Discounted cash flow	Underlying operating value of the business and ability to service debt.
Asset valuation	Liquidation value and/or adjusted book value of assets.
Multiples	Multiples of cash flow, P/E, sales, or EBIT are useful to establish some sense for market value relative to other firms in the same industry and offer some indication of harvest potential. Each type of multiple has its own merit; what is critical is that one be consistent in applying them.

Both cash flow analysis and multiples analysis estimate the opportunity's value based upon future events, either operating results or market reaction to public offering. When trying to place a value on a business in this manner, there are a multitude of assumptions that must be made. Some of the most prominent include:

— Level of risk: How volatile are the company's cash flows?

— Competition: How fiercely contested is the market for the company's products?

— Industry: Is this a growing or declining industry, and what profitability trends exist?

— Organizational stability: How well established is this company in the intended line of business?

— Management: Is a competent and complete team in place?

— Company growth: Historically, has the company been growing or shrinking, and how fast?

— General desirability: To what degree does the marketplace find this line of business attractive?

A cautionary note on valuations: Many deal proposals are put together with "recast financial statements." In theory, such a practice is legitimate and endeavors to reflect true operating results possible in the business. In reality, assumptions implicit in the recast are not always reasonably attainable and can be downright misleading. Always ask whether or not the financials shown have been recast, and, if so, understand all adjustments that have been made to the statements. No assumption should be left unchallenged. This will be particularly true for smaller companies whose owners will often have previously operated with numerous adjustments to minimize their tax burden.

Once a general idea on price is established, the deal will have to be structured with attractive returns to one's equity investment. There are two fundamental considerations. First, is the overall financeability of the deal, which includes:

— Assets to secure bank financing.

— Cash flow to support further debt instruments (i.e., company-issued debentures).

— Personal collateral, if any.

Second, one must consider (possibly in conjunction with the above analysis) the actual structure of the financing. What is desired here is a structure which caters to the interest of all parties involved. The buyer might, for example, establish financing "strips" of debt and equity to provide both secured fixed income and participation in potential capital appreciation. Tax losses may be scrutinized and sold to investors who will find such items attractive (see Chapter 6, Deal Structure).

NEGOTIATING THE DEAL

When you discover a company whose purchase is financially feasible and meets your other criteria, it is important to recognize any situations that could prevent you from closing the deal successfully. The following represent a few important obstacles:

— Forcing the deal: One must be responsive to timing issues inherent in a less than perfect process. This may be the area of greatest difficulty due to the lack of control associated in timing the buying of a company. Patience and persistence go a long way toward managing one's expectations in this area. One's attitude plays a role here, as well. While the deal should not be forced, one must recognize there are always reasons *not* to do a deal. Buying a company is an emotional as well as intellectual process, and there are times when the cynical outlook should be tempered with a bit of positive thinking.

— Competition: One should expect to run into competition from other buyout firms or larger companies in the same industry, perhaps with greater resources. A professional buyout firm will typically have the resources, capital, time, and sophistication to move quickly and expertly on a deal. In particular, with the great mergers and acquisitions activity of the mid- to late-1980s, many buyout firms who in the past would have sought relatively larger deals have begun searching for small- and medium-sized deals ($10–$20 million). Larger companies in the same industry may be willing to pay a higher premium due to operating synergies in common with the target acquisition candidate. This makes for a challenging search process and means that if deals can be found that have not been shopped around, then one's chances of success improve dramatically.

— Poor communication: This pertains to all parties involved— backer, target company, project team, and the many professionals required to complete a deal. There is plenty of opportunity for communications to either drag out or break down entirely. Demonstration of commitment is again prominent, as frequent and regular discussion will sustain each party's involvement and better move a deal to completion.

Such obstacles do not necessarily have to get in the way, but one should be prepared to meet them if they do appear. Indeed, you may have to walk away from your share of deals. While having to walk away from a business you wanted can be disappointing, you should learn several important lessons. For example, you should become a better judge of character and business situations. This is knowledge that will be invaluable to you as you continue the deal process. Also, the first-hand experience and knowledge you gain about the industry in the collapsed deal may result in greater credibility in the future with sellers or their intermediaries.

ADDING VALUE

Before you purchase a company, you can begin to concentrate on ways to improve the firm's performance. Indeed, such plans are a vital component of understanding a business's potential and your willingness to pay. Adding value to a new firm can be accomplished in many ways:

— Making operational changes: You should give a good deal of thought up front as to what you plan to do with the company after the acquisition. You may recognize opportunity to broaden distribution, open new markets, and otherwise make operational changes that boost sales and/or margins. In evaluating such possibilities, be realistic. Chances are the easy things have already been tried, so exercise some creative thought in defining positive operating improvements. This also requires an assessment of the management team and personnel in place. In short, are they reliable, competent, honest, and are they the right people for the challenge that lies ahead for the business?

— Changing the financial structure of the business: In many small businesses, the very essence of the company can be improved if the underlying financial structure is modified. For example, negotiating a longer payment schedule with your creditors, creating incentives for your customers to pay bills sooner, and obtaining lines of credit from commercial banks can help change the dynamics of the business and improve cash flow.

CONCLUSION

Searching for a small business to buy can be difficult; not only is there no established marketplace for these firms, but you are trying to purchase an entity created and cultivated by another individual, and you are attempting to meld it with your own style, character, and interests. This process can be extremely time-consuming, expensive, and frustrating. And although available research indicates the good acquisition candidates are few and far between, sound search techniques and a realistic personal assessment can significantly improve your chances of success and allow you to achieve some measure of control over some of the more random elements of the process.

Finally, remember that this process is also an investment decision. Even a superb company is of little value to an investor if nobody is willing to pay for it. Identifying an appropriate "exit" strategy to make one's investment liquid will define the project's monetary returns. This can include running the company in perpetuity, getting out in a secondary public offering, liquidating the assets, or selling out to another organization.

FIGURE 9–1   Purchasing a Business: The Search Process

Business Screening Analyses

1. General
   Company, business strategy, age and history, trends.
2. Product
   Description/technical specifications, function, volume, prices, value added/commodity, patents.
3. Management Team
   Key employees—names, positions, education, track record, skills.
   Organization chart.
   Is management team complete? Efforts/ability to hire new management?
   Willingness to remain after purchase?
   Characterization of management team (i.e., aggressive/passive, young/old, etc.).
4. Market Position
   Market size ($, units).
   Market growth and growth drivers.
   Segmentation of the market (geographic, functional).
   Who, how, and why does the buyer buy (id of buyer)?
   Relationship with customers (number, loyalty, concentration).
   Distribution channels (types, support/training required, advertisement strategy).
   Market share of major players.
   Company's major differentiating factors (price, quality, service, features, brand identity).
5. Competition
   Barriers to entry/exit—economies of scale, proprietary technology, switching cost, capital requirements, access to distribution, cost advantages, government policy, expected retaliation, brand identity, exit cost.
   Competitive factors—number, strength, characterization, product differences, concentration, diversity, management, financials/ration analysis, industry capacity, competitive advantages, corporate stakes.
   Substitution threat—relative price/performance of substitutes, switching cost, buyer propensity to substitute.
   Suppliers' power—relationship, concentration, manufacturing/marketing process, presence of substitute inputs, importance of volume to supplier, switching cost of supplier, cost relative to total purchases, impact of inputs on cost or differentiation, threat of forward integration, supplier profitability.
   Buyers' power—bargaining leverage, buying patterns, concentration, volume, switching cost, ability to backward integrate, substitute products, price sensitivity, price/total purchases, product differences, brand identity, impact on quality/performance, buyer profitability, decision-making units' incentives and complexity.
   Trends—technology, economic, changes in tax law.

FIGURE 9–1   (*continued*)

6. Operations

Work force—seize, union/nonunion, work rules, contract expiration, age and skill level, match with developing technology, attrition, attitude, manufacturing engineering staff competence.

Manufacturing flow and scheduling—job shop/batch continuous, systems, process flow, material handling, multiplant strategy/logistics, cost accounting, work discipline, work order tracking, percent dead time.

Capacity—percent of total capacity, bottlenecks current and projected.

Purchasing—opportunities for redesign, fewer parts, add/subtract vendors, larger discounts, incoming material sampling, out-sourcing policies.

Quality control—attitude/priority, problem areas, methodology.

Capital equipment—age/maintenance, sophistication, general versus special purpose, level of automation, trends.

R&D—percent of sales compared to industry, type, technical strengths/weaknesses, organization, importance, trends.

Information systems—importance, competitive advantage, level of sophistication, systems under development.

7. Financials

Sales/profitability

Income statement.

Historical and two-, three-, five-year pro formas.

Growth—sales, costs, profits, EPS, sustainable growth rates.

Quality of earnings—accounting, pension funding, depreciation, write-offs, earnings segments, earnings patterns, earnings sensitivity.

Ratio analysis—compared to competitors and industry averages, gross margins, ROS, ROE, P/E comparables.

Leverage and liquidity

Balance sheet.

Historical and pro formas.

Examination of equity and debt composition.

Ratio analysis—current and quick ratios, debt as percentage of total capitalization, assets/equity, days receivable, days payable, days inventory.

Funds flow

Statement of changes.

Historical and pro formas.

Analysis of sources and uses of cash.

Assets

Composition and type, quality, bankability, book and market values, obsolescence, age.

FIGURE 9–1 *(concluded)*

8. Valuation
   Terminal value—FCF perpetuity/annuity, book value, liquidation value, P/E value.
   Components of value (i.e., investment tax credits, depreciation, energy cost savings, etc.).
   Sensitivity analysis.
   Expected returns analysis.
9. Risk/Reality Check
   Industry.
   Technology.
   Financial.
   Product/company liability.
   Employee/supplier/customer response.
   Seller's desire to do the deal.
   Is value appropriate?
   Prohibitive terms?
   Value to be added.

Chapter Ten

The Legal Forms of
Organization

One of the key issues an entrepreneur must resolve when considering a new venture is what legal form of organization the enterprise should adopt. The most prevalent forms are:

— The individual proprietorship.

— The partnership.

- • General partnership.
- • Limited partnership.

— The corporation.

- • The S corporation (formerly Subchapter S).
- • The "regular" corporation.

Each of these forms of organization differs from the others along several dimensions. The characteristics of the business entity will determine its tax status. It is important to note that merely claiming partnership or corporate status *will not* result in the tax treatment accorded that form of organization. The IRS (see Internal Revenue Code Sec. 7701 (a) (3)) has elaborated four factors which determine the classification and resulting tax status of an organization:

1. Continuity of Life—An organization possesses continuity of life when the death, insanity, or retirement of an owner will not cause the organization's dissolution.

This note was prepared by Michael J. Roberts under the direction of Howard H. Stevenson.

2. Centralized Management—Management is centralized when continuing, exclusive authority to make managerial decisions is constituted in some subgroup of the organization's ownership.

3. Limited Liability—The liability of an organization is limited when no member of the organization is personally liable for debts or claims against the business.

4. Free Transferability of Interest—Interest can be freely transferred only when each member of the organization can transfer all attributes and benefits of ownership without the consent of other members.

As the table below indicates, the proprietorship and partnership occupy one end of the spectrum with regard to each of these criteria while the corporation occupies the other; the limited partnership form falls in the middle.

	Corporation, including S Corporation	Limited Partnership	Proprietorship/ Partnership
Continuity of life	Yes	No	No
Centralized management	Yes	Yes	No
Limited liability	Yes	Yes/No	No
Free transferability of interest	Yes	No	No

It is also important to note that *any* business which seeks tax treatment under any of the legal forms of organization *must* have as its objective the carrying on of a trade or business *for profit*. An individual cannot engage in a hobby, such as travel or purchasing books or stamps, and then claim tax deductions for expenses involved in pursuing these activities.

In most cases, the IRS has an incentive to tax as corporations entities which have claimed *not* to be corporations, but which, in fact, possess the characteristics of corporations.

In general, tax courts have found that:

— If the organization claims to be a corporation, and it possesses at least two of the four characteristics, it will be taxed as a corporation.

— If an organization claims to be a partnership, but in fact possesses three of the four characteristics of a corporation, it will be taxed as a corporation.

The remainder of this chapter will discuss each of the forms of organization mentioned above. Figure 10–1 lists several important aspects of the various legal forms of organization.

INDIVIDUAL PROPRIETORSHIP

The individual or sole proprietorship is the oldest form of organization: a person who undertakes a business without any of the formalities associated with other forms of organization. The individual and the business are one and the same.

Classification

A proprietorship is legally defined as follows:

— Continuity of life: The proprietorship ceases to exist upon the death, insanity, or retirement of the proprietor.
— Centralized management: A proprietorship is deemed not to have centralized management because the proprietor is viewed as the legal decision-making authority. Therefore, management is not centralized in any subgroup of the ownership.
— Limited liability: The individual proprietor is personally liable for all liabilities of the business.
— Free transferability of interest: The proprieter cannot freely transfer his interest; once she or he does, the proprietorship is dissolved.

Tax Status

The proprietorship does not pay taxes as a separate entity. The individual reports all income and deductible expenses from both the business and any other sources on the personal income tax return. Note that the earnings (as reported on the company's income statement) of the business are taxed at the individual level whether or not they are actually distributed in cash. There is no vehicle for sheltering income. Moreover, the sole proprietor cannot deduct as a business expense the costs of medical or life insurance.

THE PARTNERSHIP

The General Partnership

A partnership is defined as "a voluntary association of two or more persons to carry on as co-owners of a business for profit." A partnership is more complicated than merely a collection of individuals. The partners must resolve and should set down in writing their agreement on a number of issues:

— The amount and nature of their respective capital contributions. One partner might contribute cash, another a patent, and a third property and cash.

— The allocation of the business's profits and losses.

— Salaries and drawings against profits.

— Management responsibilities.

— Consequences of withdrawal, retirement, disability, or death of a partner.

— Means of dissolution and liquidation of the partnership.

The Limited Partnership

A limited partnership is a partnership which has both limited *and* general partners.

— The general partner assumes the management responsibility *and* unlimited liability for the obligations of the business, and must have at least a 1 percent interest in profits and losses.

— The limited partner has no voice in management and is legally liable only for the amount of the capital contribution plus any other debt specifically accepted.

In a limited partnership, the general partner may be a corporation (a corporate general partner). In situations where a corporation is the sole general partner, in order to ensure that there are sufficient assets to cover the unlimited liability which the general partner must assume, the corporate general partner must have a net worth equal to $250,000 or 10 percent of the total capitalization of the partnership, whichever is less.

Classification

A partnership is treated much like a proprietorship.

— Continuity of life: The partnership will cease to exist upon the death, insanity, or retirement of any of the partners, unless specifically reconstituted according to the governing law and documents of the partnership.

— Centralized management:

  • In a general partnership, management is not centralized because *all* of the partners have decision-making authority.

  • In a limited partnership, a subgroup of the owners—the general partners—has decision-making authority, and therefore, management is centralized.

— Limited liability: The nature of a partnership is such that someone, or some group, must accept unlimited liability.

   • In a general partnership, all of the partners have full, unlimited liability.

   • In a limited partnership, the limited partner's liability is limited to the capital contributed plus any other liability the limited partner agrees to accept. The general partners in a limited partnership *still* have full, unlimited liability.

— Free transferability of interest: Partnership interests are generally not freely transferable.

Tax Status

For tax purposes neither a general nor a limited partnership is considered a separate tax entity (although the partnership does file a return) but is merely a conduit through which income (or losses) is passed to the partners.

— Profit and losses are allocated to individuals in accordance with the partnership agreement, as long as that distribution has some basis in economic reality.

— Cash distributions are allocated in a manner which may or may not parallel profits and losses.

   Generally, the following tax rules apply:

— The apportionment of profits and losses must have some economic substance; it may not be designed solely to avoid taxes.

— Generally, the amount of losses which a partner may deduct is limited to the amount of capital at risk (i.e., equity contributed plus debt assumed). (Note: Real estate partnerships are an exception to this "at risk" rule.)

— The income of the partnership is taxed at the personal level of the individual whether or not any cash is actually distributed.

— The distribution of cash out of income or retained earnings is not itself a taxable event. The only time when cash distributions are a taxable event is when the cash distribution exceeds the partners' basis in the partnership.

— The basis is equal to the amount of capital originally contributed, plus the amount of income on which tax is paid, less any cash distributions. (Example: An individual invests $100 in a partnership, and his share of income in Year 1 equals $30. He must pay tax on this $30 at the personal rate. His basis is now $130. If he receives a $20 cash distribution, his basis drops to $110.)

THE CORPORATION

Both the "regular" corporation and the S corporation are creatures of the law. The S corporation technically refers to an election which corporate shareholders may make to receive "Subchapter S tax treatment."

Classification

A corporation is defined according to the following criteria:

— Continuity of life: The death or divestiture of interest by any shareholder, or group, will not cause a dissolution of the corporation.
— Centralized management: The decision-making authority of a corporation is legally constituted in the corporation's board of directors, rather than in the shareholders.
— Limited liability: The "corporate veil" protects the shareholder from personal liability (exception: owners and managers of a corporation may be personally liable for certain liabilities which result from fraud or violations of the tax code or securities laws).
— Free transferability of interest: Shareholders are usually free to sell their interest in the corporation without the consent of other shareholders. They may bargain this right away in the original shareholders' agreement. In the case of an S corporation, however, the sale of shares to any entity *except* an individual U.S. citizen or testamentary trust will automatically trigger the loss of S corporation status.

Legally, the organization of a corporation requires a charter, bylaws, a board of directors, and corporate officers (president, treasurer, clerk). The precise legal requirements are a function of the specific state law where the firm is incorporated.

Tax Status: S Corporation

The S corporation is a vehicle of Congress specifically targeted to give certain advantages to the small business. Essentially, an S corporation is treated like a partnership for tax purposes (i.e., it functions as a conduit through which income is allocated). However, the S corporation owners are afforded the same protection from unlimited liability as the owners of a corporation.

In order to qualify for S corporation status, the organization must meet a number of rather restrictive conditions. It must:

— Have only one class of stock, although differences in voting rights are allowed.

— Be a domestic corporation, owned wholly by U.S. citizens and derive no more than 80 percent of its revenues from non-U.S. sources.

— Have 35 or fewer stockholders.

— Derive no more than 25 percent of revenues from passive sources (i.e., interest, dividends, rents, and royalties).

— Have only individuals, estates, and certain trusts as shareholders (i.e., no corporations).

The election of S corporation tax status requires the unanimous, timely consent of all shareholders. This status may be terminated by unanimous election, or if one of the above-mentioned conditions is broken.

Tax Status: Regular Corporation

Corporations do not receive a deduction for dividends paid to shareholders. Further, shareholders are taxed on the receipt of dividend income. Hence, shareholders are taxed twice on the same earnings. This "double taxation" is the main disadvantage of a corporation. (The exceptions to this rule are qualified investment companies and real estate investment trusts which qualify under Sections 856–858 of the tax code.)

In order to avoid this double taxation, the principals of closely held corporations (especially wholly owned companies) often resort to the tactic of attempting to structure the return of earnings in a form that is deductible to the corporation (i.e., interest or salary). The IRS has a number of rules which deal explicitly with these issues.

— Salary: By raising his salary to a very high level, the owner of a corporation could effectively reduce earnings to zero and pay tax only once, at a personal level, on salary received.

   • Federal Tax Code Section 162, paragraph (A) states that the IRS will permit ". . . a reasonable allowance for salaries or other compensation for personal services actually rendered."

   • The IRS can, upon audit, reclassify a portion of salary as dividends, and thus create both a corporate and a personal tax liability.

— Interest: By initially capitalizing the business with debt (rather than equity) the owners can receive some of their cash distributions in the form of interest rather than dividends. Interest expense is deductible by the corporation and is therefore a "cheaper" way to get money out of the business.

- Federal Tax Code Section 385 deals with the issue of "thinly capitalized" corporations (i.e., where the IRS believes that the capital structure of the business is too heavily weighted in favor of debt).
- In essence, the IRS can, upon audit, reclassify debt as equity and reclassify interest as dividends when:
  - The debt does not have the characteristics of debt (i.e., is held in proportion to stock, payment of interest is contingent upon certain conditions, or interest is unreasonable).
  - The corporation has "excessive" debt (i.e., a debt to equity ratio of greater than 10:1).

Another disadvantage of the corporate form of organization is the inability to flow through losses. In a proprietorship, partnership, or Sub S corporation, losses will flow through to the owners of the firm for deduction that year on their personal tax return. A corporation accumulates tax losses for its own use in later years.

One exception in this area involves "Section 1244 stock." This is a special creature of the tax code. If a new business is formed and elects 1244 treatment rather than regular treatment, and if the business goes bankrupt, owners of the stock can claim an ordinary income loss up to the amount of their investment. Had the company been formed with regular shares, the loss would have been a capital loss.

There are, however, several tax advantages to the corporate form of organization. These include:

— Deductibility of certain personal fringe benefits, such as medical and health insurance.
— The ability to shelter earnings (i.e., keep earnings within the company and transfer them out, as dividends, at a later date when the recipients may be in a more tax advantageous situation).

SUMMARY

Each of the various legal forms of organization is distinguished from the others in a variety of ways. Often the decision about which legal form to elect is made solely in an attempt to minimize taxes. While this is a legitimate economic aim, the forms of organization differ along many other important dimensions. It is important to have a full understanding of *all* of these differences before electing the legal form. The counsel of a competent attorney is usually called for.

FIGURE 10–1 Comparison of Various Legal Forms of Organization

	Proprietorship	Partnership	Regular Corporation	Subchapter S Corporation
Taxable year	Usually calendar year	Usually calendar year; however, September, October, or November can be elected	Any year-end is permissible	Calendar year, unless a valid business purpose can be demonstrated for another choice
Expensing of depreciable business assets	Limited to $10,000 in 1986	Limited to $10,000 in 1986		Limited to $10,000 in 1986
Ordinary distributions to owners	Drawings from the business are not taxable; the net profits are taxable; and the proprietor is subject to the tax on self-employment income	Generally not taxable	Payments of salaries are deductible by corporation and taxable to recipient; payments of dividends are not deductible by corporation and generally are taxable to recipient shareholders	Same as regular corporation
Limitations on losses deductible by owners	Amount "at risk," except with respect to real estate activities	Partner's investment plus his or her share of the partnership recourse liabilities except for real estate partnerships	No losses allowed to individual except upon sale of stock or liquidation of corporation	The shareholder's investment plus his or her loans to the corporation; basis of loans reduced by losses and distributions
Dividends received	$100 dividend exclusion ($200 on joint tax return)	Conduit	70% dividend-received deduction	Treated as ordinary income; no exclusion or deduction

Formal election required	No	No	Must incorporate under state law	Yes
Capital gain	Taxed at individual level; 28%, except 33% on certain amounts	Conduit	Taxed at corporate level, 34%	Amounts flow through to extent of shareholder's portion of corporation's taxable income, but (unlike partnership) ordinary losses and capital gains are netted at corporate level
Capital losses	Carried forward indefinitely	Conduit	Carry back three years and carry over five years as short-term capital loss offsetting only capital gains	Carry over five years as short-term capital loss, offsetting only capital gains
Section 1231 gains and losses	Taxed at individual level, combined with other Section 1231 gains or losses of individual; net gains are capital gains for individual; net losses are ordinary losses for individual	Conduit	Taxable, or deductible at the corporate level	Net gain is a capital gain to the shareholder; net loss is an ordinary loss to the shareholder; however, corporation's Section 1231 losses are not netted with shareholder's Section 1231 gains
Basis of allocating income to owners	All income and deductible expense picked up on owner's return	Profit and loss agreement (may have "special allocations" of income and deductions if they reflect economic reality)	No income allocated to stockholders	Number of shares owned on the last day of the corporation's tax year

475

FIGURE 10-1 (continued)

	Proprietorship	Partnership	Regular Corporation	Subchapter S Corporation
Basis for allocating a net operating loss	All losses flow through to owner's return	Profit and loss agreement (may have "special allocations" of income and deductions if they reflect economic reality)	No losses allocated to stockholders	Prorated among shareholders on a daily basis, based on actual ownership
Group hospitalization and life insurance premiums and medical reimbursement plans	Itemized deductions: for medical expenses, half of insurance premiums up to $150, medicine and drugs in excess of 1% of adjusted gross income, other bills over 3% of AGI; no deduction for life insurance premiums	Cost of partners' benefits are not deductible as a business expense; may be treated as distribution to individual partners, eligible for some possible deduction as if paid by individual	Cost of shareholder-employee's coverage is generally deductible as a business expense if plan is "for the benefit of employees"	Same as regular corporation
Retirement benefits	Limited to H.R.-10 plan benefits, normally 15% of income up to $15,000; however, some defined-benefit H.R.-10 plans may provide more. Limitation increases to essentially same as regular corporation	Same as individual	Normal corporate employee benefits up to $115,000 after which a 5% excise tax is owed	Corporation can deduct normal corporate employee contribution; however, owner-employee must add income contribution in excess of $15,000 to taxable income. Limitation increases to essentially same as regular corporation

Organization costs	Not amortizable	Amortizable over 60 months	Amortizable over 60 months	Same as regular corporation
Partner's or shareholder's "reasonable" salary	Not applicable	Treated as an allocation of partnership profits and a conduit	Expense to the corporation taxable to the shareholder-employee, subject to FICA	Same as regular corporation
Charitable contribution	Subject to limits for individual; gifts for the use of private foundation, 20% of AGI; gifts to public charity, cash 50% of AGI; appreciated property, 30% of AGI. Other limitations for specific items contributed	Conduit	Limited to 10% of taxable income before special deductions	Same as regular corporation
Liability	Individually liable on all liabilities of business	General partners individually liable on partnership's liabilities; limited partner liable only up to amount of his or her capital contribution	Capital contribution is limit of liability of shareholder	Same as regular corporation
Qualified owners	Individual ownership	No limitation	No limitation	Only individuals, estates, and certain trusts may be shareholders
Type of ownership interests	Individual ownership	More than one class of partner permitted	More than one class of stock permitted	Only one class of stock permitted

FIGURE 10-1 (continued)

	Proprietorship	Partnership	Regular Corporation	Subchapter S Corporation
Transfer of ownership	Assets of business transferable rather than business itself	New partnership usually created; consent of other partners normally required if partnership interest is to be transferred	Ready transfer of ownership through the use of stock certificates; restrictions may be imposed by shareholders' agreement	Shares can be transferred only to individuals, certain types of trusts, or estates; no consent by new shareholders to Subchapter S election is needed
Capital requirements	Capital raised only by loan or increased contribution by proprietor	Loans or contributions from partners (original, or newly created by remaking partnership)	Met by sale of stock or bonds or other corporate debt	Met by sale of stock or bonds, but corporation has only one class of stock and is limited to 35 shareholders
Business action	Sole proprietor makes decisions and can act immediately	Action usually dependent upon the unanimous agreement of partners or general partners	Unity of action based on authority of board of directors	Same as regular corporation except unanimous consent is required to elect or revoke Subchapter S status

Management	Proprietor responsible and receives all profits or losses	Except for limited or silent partners, investment in partnership involves responsibility for management decisions	Shareholder can receive income without sharing in responsibility for management	Same as regular corporation
Flexibility	No restrictions	Partnership is contractual arrangement, within which members can do in business what individuals can, subject to the partnership agreement and applicable state laws	Corporation is a creature of the state functioning within powers granted explicitly or necessarily implied and subject to judicial construction and decision	Same as regular corporation
Investment credit	None	Conduit	None	Conduit
Tax preferences (minimum tax)	All preference items are subject to an expanded alternative minimum tax	Conduit	Taxed at corporate level; 20% on preferences in excess of either $10,000 or tax liability, whichever is greater. Certain other items based on complex calculation for which professional guidance is needed	Conduit

FIGURE 10–1 (concluded)

	Proprietorship	Partnership	Regular Corporation	Subchapter S Corporation
Character of income and deductions	Taxed at individual level; long-term capital gains deduction; limitation on investment interest deductions	Conduit	Taxed at corporate level	Except as to long-term capital gains, income and profits are computed at corporate level, so that characteristics are determined at corporate level and do not flow to shareholder

SOURCE: S. Jones and M. B. Cohen, *The Emerging Business* (New York: Coopers & Lybrand, 1983).

Chapter Eleven

The Tax Aspects of Acquiring a Business

For the entrepreneur, one alternative to starting a new enterprise is to purchase a going concern. There are both advantages and disadvantages to this approach. On one hand, it is not necessary to have a creative idea around which to start a business; you simply need the money to buy a company. On the other hand, the huge entrepreneurial returns that come from starting a successful company are harder to earn; as a going concern, much of the risk has been eliminated. Consequently, the costs of getting into business—the purchase price—will most likely be higher, implying a lower financial return for the purchaser and investor. However, by purchasing a going concern, many risks are also reduced or eliminated.

There are many issues to be considered in purchasing a firm, from its competitive position to the quality of the company's assets and its people. This note will focus explicitly on one issue: the structuring of the actual purchase of the business. With the advent of the 1986 Tax Act (taking effect in 1987), many of the regulations that impact the structuring of the purchase have changed. This note will discuss some of the most important tax issues that must be addressed in the acquisition of a company.

Essentially, there are three parties to any transaction: the purchaser, the seller, and the taxing authorities. If the seller wishes to obtain a particular aftertax dollar amount, the purchaser can most cheaply meet this objective by minimizing the tax consequences of the transaction.

This note was prepared by Michael J. Roberts.

Note that some transactions are tax-free; that is, the taxing authorities do not view certain transactions as taxable events. For instance, purchases of stock for stock, and certain mergers, are treated as tax-free reorganizations. Strict rules apply because it is naturally in the IRS's interest to find that a taxable event has occurred. This note will only address taxable transactions. Apart from price, there are two critical tax-related issues that the purchaser must address in consummating the acquisition:

— Whether the purchase should involve the acquisition of stock or assets.

— If assets are acquired, whether their basis should be written up (also termed *stepped-up*).

PURCHASE OF STOCK OR ASSETS

One key issue is whether the purchase should involve the acquisition of stock or assets. First it is important to define these terms:

— The purchase of stock is also termed *a purchase of equity*. The actual equity shares—literally paper stock certificates—of the firm are purchased from their owner.

— The *purchase of assets* refers to the acquisition of particular assets and the assumption of specified liabilities from the balance sheet. Note that the term "asset purchase" is a short-hand term used to describe the purchase of assets and the assumption of liabilities.

One of the fundamental principles that affects the tax paid in a transaction is that an asset purchase is a two-step transaction, and thus, taxes are levied twice; an equity or stock purchase, however, involves only a single step and is thus taxed once.

This is because, in an asset transaction, the *firm* sells the assets and pays tax—usually at the corporate rate for long-term capital gains[1]—on any gain arising from the sale of those assets. Then, in order to return any funds to the individual seller, the firm must make a distribution to the seller, and this "liquidating" distribution is taxed at the individual capital gains rate.

In a stock transaction, the individual owner of the shares simply sells this stock, and tax is paid *once* on any gain, which is computed as the difference between purchase price and basis in the stock. This tax

---

[1]This is complicated by "recapture"; the firm pays tax at ordinary income rates on recapture income.

treatment will be described in more detail below. Barring unusual circumstances, however, if assets are purchased, the seller will pay more tax on the transaction and therefore, will require a higher purchase price in order to generate the same aftertax funds to the seller from the sale. Thus, the purchaser will often be required to pay a higher price in an asset transaction.

There is, however, a benefit to the purchaser that occurs in an asset purchase. If *stock* is purchased (absent any special elections described below), the company does not change for tax purposes; that is, its depreciable basis in its assets remains the same. The purchase price paid becomes the buyer's basis in his *stock* rather than changing the basis of the company's assets.

If, however, the transaction is an asset purchase, the seller may "write up" (or step-up) the basis of these assets to their fair market value. This fair market value is set by an appraisal of the assets and may not be more than the purchase price, but may be less. This increase in basis raises depreciation charges and thus raises the aftertax cash flow of the business by sheltering more profit via this increased depreciation tax shield. If the purchase price exceeds the fair market value of the assets, this excess amount is simply "goodwill," which is worthless for tax purposes: the amortization of goodwill is *not* generally deductible against taxable income.

There are several more points that bear mentioning before moving on to a more detailed discussion of these tax issues.

First, there is one nontax issue that is also raised by the stock versus asset purchase question; this concerns legal liability. The obligation and liability for corporate wrong-doing remains attached to the *equity* of the business. Thus, if the buyer purchases equity, the ongoing entity continues to have the legal liability for any act that may have occurred in the past, prior to the buyer's actual purchase of the business. These are typically referred to as contingent liabilities. (Note: These obligations—when their potential is known to the buyer—can be somewhat mitigated by a carefully crafted purchase contract including warranties, representations, and offsets.)

If assets are purchased, the selling entity—the company—retains the legal liability for any wrongful acts that occurred prior to the sale. Note that the purchaser is responsible for any *financial* liabilities specifically assumed in the transaction.

Another point concerns the use of the term *book value*. Typically, we think of the value we see on the balance sheet when we think of book value. This will cause problems as we begin to discuss the tax treatment of certain transactions, because firms can legally keep a second set of books for tax purposes. For instance, an asset with a value of $100,000 on the "financial reporting books" may have a basis on the "tax books" of only $50,000. This is because financial statements are prepared to give shareholders—and others—a fair perspective on the operations of the business. The tax books, on the other hand, are typically prepared with another objective entirely—the minimization of taxes. (These two sets of books are reconciled on schedule M of the tax form.) Thus, accelerated depreciation schedules will be used to minimize earnings—and hence, taxes. Because we are interested in tax consequences, it is the number on the tax books—the tax basis of the asset—that will be of concern to us.

Finally, note that in an asset sale, any financial liabilities assumed in the purchase are considered part of the sales proceeds to the seller and are included in the purchase price. Note also, however, that the basis of what is sold in an asset sale is the book value of the assets, *not* the net book value of the equity in those assets.

STOCK VERSUS ASSETS: THE SELLER'S PERSPECTIVE

If the seller sells his or her stock in the firm, she or he will pay tax *once* (at the personal capital gains rate) on the difference between the basis in the stock and the purchase price. If the seller sells the firm in an asset transaction, tax must be paid on income from the sale, as described below.

The taxation of income upon a sale of assets by a corporation in liquidation changed dramatically with the advent of the 1986 Tax Act. Prior to the 1986 act—and the repeal of the General Utilities Doctrine—the taxable gain was defined to include only the amount of "recapture." *Recapture* refers to a certain class of income that is generated when an asset is sold for more than its tax basis. The taxing authorities allow depreciation to be charged against income under the theory that depreciation represents a cost of "using up" the asset. If, however, an asset is then sold for more than its depreciated value (i.e., tax basis) then the taxing authorities argue that it was "over-depreciated," and that they have the right to recapture the taxes that excess depreciation had earlier eliminated. Recapture income is generally the lesser of total tax depreciation taken *or* gain realized.[2] If the asset is sold for its tax basis there is no recapture. If, however, the asset is sold for more than its depreciated value, then tax must be paid. Under pre-1986 law, the tax paid at the corporate level was based only on recapture income, *not* on any increase in purchase price of the asset over its original undepreciated book value. For most classes of assets—

---

[2]Note that recapture is calculated differently for real estate assets.

real estate is an exception—recapture is limited to the total amount of depreciation taken on the asset. Thus, if an asset was sold for more than its original purchase price this excess was not taxed at the corporate level; the tax on the excess was paid only by the holders of the stock when they received the liquidating distribution from the firm.

For example, if an asset was purchased for $50, depreciated to a net value of $10, and then sold for $100, the pre-1986 law demanded that tax be paid *only* on $40 of recaptured income. Appreciation (the difference between the original purchase price of $50 and the sale price of $100) was sheltered from the tax at the corporate level. Note that this treatment applied only to liquidating sales of assets. The 1986 act (effective 1987) changed this treatment such that tax is paid on the *entire* gain at the corporate level. This is part of the repeal of the General Utilities Doctrine. Thus, the tax liability is computed as follows:

— The firm pays tax once as a corporation on the income generated by the sale. The tax on the recapture portion of the gain is paid at ordinary income rates and the remainder is paid at capital gain rates. Note that the calculation of recapture and capital gain must be done on an asset-by-asset basis. That is, the "fair market value" of each asset is compared with its tax basis, and the gain calculated. This gain is classified as recapture income if it is less than the total tax depreciation taken on the asset. Any amount in excess of this recapture portion is classified as a capital gain under the 1986 act, but escaped taxation under the "old" law.

— The cash left over after the corporate tax has been paid is distributed to the stockholder, who pays a personal income tax on the difference between these proceeds and his or her personal basis in the stock.

Thus, from the seller's perspective, a stock transaction would generally be preferred because only one level of tax would be collected. In addition, a sale of stock removes the responsibility for potential legal liability from the seller (except in the case of fraud or specific warranties).

STOCK VERSUS ASSETS: THE PURCHASER'S PERSPECTIVE

If the purchaser buys the stock of a company, the company for all intents and purposes remains unchanged; it merely has different shareholders. Therefore, the basis of its assets remains the same. That is, if a piece of equipment was largely depreciated, it will have that same low basis in the company. And, the tax shield from depreciation on those assets will remain relatively low.

Of course, the purchaser may prefer an asset acquisition, in order to garner both a higher basis in the assets and avoid the responsibility for some potential legal liability. From the seller's perspective, such a transaction is less attractive, and the buyer will often have to pay a higher price in order to entice the seller to participate in a transaction on these terms.

Note that the purchaser may purchase stock, but treat the transaction *as if* it were an asset purchase. An election under Section 338 allows the purchaser of the stock of a corporation to treat the transaction *as if* the transaction was an asset purchase and write up the value of assets. Under pre-1986 law, a Section 338 election caused a tax to be paid by the company based on income generated *to the extent of recapture items only.* The 1986 act requires that tax be paid on the full amount of the write-up. Thus, the popularity of such elections had decreased markedly.

Note also that a Section 338 election does not cause potential legal liability to simply disappear. In this case, it is as if the purchaser bought the stock of the company and then resold it to himself or herself in an asset transaction; the responsibility for legal liability remains with the equity.

SUMMARY

Thus, the issue of how to structure the transaction must consider the question of taxes. If the seller needs to receive a certain dollar figure after tax, the purchaser has a choice:

— Pay a higher price in an asset transaction in order to gather the higher depreciation tax shield in future years.

— Pay a lower price in stock transaction and then either write up the assets (and pay the associated taxes) or not, depending on the tax impact of that decision.

Actual liabilities and warranties are specific items that should be the subject of a written agreement in all cases.

Berringer Products

Berringer Products (BP) was a manufacturer and distributor of electronic flow control valves for the chemical industry. Specifically, the firm sold valves which regulated the flow of all sorts of gases and liquids through complex production processes. The firm also manufactured a line of valves that was used in nuclear power cooling systems.

The firm was founded in 1948 in Bridgeport, Connecticut, by Thomas Berringer, an engineer. Berringer had developed valves for use on submarines during World War II and applied some of this expertise to the chemical industry following the end of the war. The firm grew from a small job shop to become a concern of over 30 employees; in 1986, the firm's revenues approximated $1.5 million.

Thomas Berringer died in 1978, and the business passed through his estate to his son William. William had little interest in the business, but ran it in a "caretaker" mode for several years.

Because Thomas's wife had died some years earlier, William received the entirety of his father's estate, worth about $3 million. When his father died, the company—Berringer Products—had passed through Mr. Berringer's estate, and its basis had been stepped-up to its 1978 book value of $500,000. William had one daughter, Wendy, who was not interested in the family business. Thus, when—in September of 1986—William Berringer heard of the impending tax law change which would eliminate preferential treatment for capital gains, it

This case was prepared by Michael J. Roberts.

seemed to him to be an opportune moment to sell the business.[1] He mentioned this fact to his banker and accountant, who agreed that this would be a good time to sell the company, and who said that they often heard from individuals interested in purchasing businesses.

Several weeks later, William Berringer received a call from Richard West, who indicated that he had been referred to Berringer by Berringer's banker. West said he and two associates were searching for a business to acquire and were interested in speaking with Berringer. The two agreed to meet in mid-October.

THE PURCHASERS

Richard West, Scott Becker, and Barry Schraft were three class-mates from Harvard Business School, who had graduated in 1981. The three had kept in touch and, as students, had often discussed the possibility of running their own company. At their fifth reunion, they resolved to try.

— Richard came from a wealthy New York family and had gone to work on Wall Street as a manager of pension fund money.

— Scott had worked for a medical products company in the manufacturing area, developing manufacturing and inventory control systems.

— Barry had worked for a small distributor of office equipment as the assistant to the chief financial officer.

While Scott and Barry thought they could contribute $200,000 and $75,000, respectively, to a venture, Richard was in a position to invest up to $600,000 personally.

Richard West's family was quite wealthy, and they had indicated their willingness to back him and his friends in the venture by contributing up to $500,000. However, his father had said that if the family invested money in the venture, their equity security would need to give them liquidation preference, superior voting rights, and preferential distribution of gains.

---

[1]In 1986, ordinary income was taxed at a sliding rate up to 50 percent, and long-term capital gains were taxed at ordinary rates after excluding 60 percent of the gain. The effect was a maximum tax of 20 percent on long-term capital gains. Under the proposed new tax law, capital gains and ordinary income would each be taxed according to the same rate schedule, with a maximum 34% marginal rate. In the top marginal bracket, this equality in rates would phase in over two years, but the immediate impact was to raise long-term capital gains rates to 28 percent and to drop short-term capital gains rates and taxes on ordinary income to 38.5 percent. Other changes affected allowable deductions. (See Appendix for detailed tax rate schedules.)

THE MEETING

At their October 14 meeting, Richard, Barry, and Scott learned of Berringer's motivations for selling the business, and of his desire for a transaction by year-end. The three purchasers were attracted by what they saw as the improvement potential in the business, and Berringer was interested in the three because of their apparent ability to finance the purchase without raising outside equity capital.

Berringer stated that he wanted to net $1.25 million in cash after taxes from the sale of the business and was willing to structure the transaction in any one of a number of ways to achieve that result.

The three men also examined Berringer's financial statements (see Exhibit 1) and, in addition, learned that:

— Berringer's wife was on the payroll for $25,000 per year, although she only came in one day a week and, from what the three could surmise, performed mostly personal business—phone calls, bill-paying, etc.—when she was in the office.

— Berringer's daughter Wendy was on the payroll for $10,000 per year, and she typically worked two or three days per week for 10 weeks during her summer vacation from school.

During the rest of October, and on into early November, the three men examined Berringer Products and learned the following:

Product Line

BP sold a product line of over 500 different flow control valves. These valves differed along a number of dimensions including size, volume of flow, and nature of materials from which they were manufactured. Valves used with corrosive chemicals, hot liquids, or highly pressurized gases, for instance, needed to have certain physical properties to perform well. In addition to this standard line, BP also manufactured custom valves. This custom work represented approximately 20 percent of sales.

The line of flow control valves for nuclear power plant cooling systems had been introduced in 1980 and had been incorporated into the design of several plants currently under construction. These valves, while representing less than 5 percent of BP's unit volume, represented 15 percent of its dollar volume. The replacement rate for installed valves was unknown.

BP's business was concentrated *primarily* in the Northeast, where Berringer maintained its own direct sales force. The firm had three main competitors, who all split this regional market fairly evenly, although each had its strong and weak niches of the market. Eighty-five percent of BP's sales were generated in the New England region. Outside of New England, the firm generated sales via a catalog and took orders over the phone. Its manufacturer's representative network was almost nonexistent.

Management and Personnel

Apart from William Berringer, there were two vice presidents in the company, both of whom had originally been hired by Thomas Berringer.

The vice president of sales was 59 years old, and the vice president of engineering and manufacturing was 60. Apart from these two officers, the company had 26 employees: 14 hourly workers, many of whom were affiliated with the AFL-CIO machinists union, and 12 salaried employees.

The functions were generally well, if unimaginatively, run. Receivables and payables were in poor shape because of a recent health problem affecting the bookkeeper.

Manufacturing Plant and Equipment

BP's plant of 18,000 square feet had been built in 1960, and was in excellent repair. Offices occupied 4,000 square feet, the factory itself 10,000 feet, and warehouse space the remainder. There was no room available for expanding the facility, but the building had the capacity to support additional activity. The building was largely depreciated, but the men estimated that its market value was about $400,000. The machinery and equipment had been well maintained and modernized, and was worth approximately $400,000. Furniture and fixtures were worth about $30,000. The plant's safety record was excellent.

Financing

The company had been financed over the years primarily with retained earnings and with the occasional use of bank debt.

Liabilities

The one outstanding financial liability was a $119,000 industrial revenue bond, payable at 6.25 percent interest. Principal was payable at the rate of $25,000 annually. The note was secured by a first mortgage on the facility.

A pro forma balance sheet for a closing at the end of 1986 is presented in Exhibit 2. This exhibit also presents recapture calculations for the business's assets. The business had an excellent product liability reputation, and one or two minor suits had been settled out of court. The company's line of valves for nuclear power plant cooling systems had only recently been marketed, and while the valves had been installed in several plants, none of these plants was yet operational.

PLANS FOR IMPROVEMENT

Richard, Scott, and Barry believed that they could improve operations in a number of ways:

— eliminate excess overhead (i.e., family members on payroll, company cars, some top management).

— expand geographically to regions outside New England.

— introduce financial controls in order to improve inventory turns, control expenses, and improve margins.

Based on these plans the three men generated the pro forma financials presented in Exhibit 3.

THE DECISION

Richard, Barry, and Scott knew they had to resolve several issues, including:

— Price: what they were willing to pay for the business.

— Form of organization: should the firm be organized as a corporation, a partnership, or a Subchapter S corporation? This decision, in turn, might affect the value of the business.

— Financing and ownership: through what specific instruments should the business be financed, and how should the ownership be divided among the three, given their financial positions? The men also felt that the business could support roughly $500,000 in debt financing, should their equity resources prove insufficient.

— Structure of the transaction: should they purchase assets or equity? If they purchased equity, should they write up the assets to fair market value to get the increased depreciation tax shield?

The men would meet the following morning to resolve these issues.

EXHIBIT 1 Historical Financials

Berringer Products
Operating Statements of Berringer Products, Inc., 1980–1985
and Six Months Ending June 30, 1986
(in thousands)

	1980	1981	1982	1983	1984	1985	Six Months Ending June 30, 1986
Sales	$1,031	$1,217	$1,484	$1,623	$1,526	$1,419	$807
Cost of goods sold	661	770	922	1,038	1,048	1,027	563
Gross income	$ 370	$ 447	$ 562	$ 585	$ 478	$ 392	$244
Selling expenses	$ 154	$ 188	$ 220	$ 243	$ 247	$ 195	$ 93
General and administrative expenses	148	179	161	168	138	142	82
Operating income	$ 68	$ 80	$ 181	$ 174	$ 93	$ 55	$ 69
Other income (expense)	(4)	6	6	(1)	—	(9)	(4)
Net income before federal income taxes	$ 64	$ 86	$ 187	$ 173	$ 93	$ 46	$ 65
Provision for federal income taxes	34	43	84	69	38	2	29
Net income after federal income taxes	$ 30	$ 43	$ 103	$ 104	$ 55	$ 44	$ 36
Retained earnings, beginning of year	$ 540	$ 553	$ 571	$ 725	$ 790	$ 813	$851
Add: Net income	30	43	103	104	55	44	36
Net proceeds on officers' life insurance	—	—	90	—	—	—	—
Other adjustments	—	1	—	—	—	—	—
Total	$ 570	$ 597	$ 764	$ 829	$ 845	$ 857	$877
Less: Dividends paid	13	26	39	39	32	6	13
Other adjustments	4	—	—	—	—	—	—
Retained earnings, end of year	$ 553	$ 571	$ 725	$ 790	$ 813	$ 851	$874

Balance Sheets of Berringer Products, Inc., as of December 31, 1980–85 and as of June 30, 1986
(in thousands)

	1980	1981	1982	1983	1984	1985	June 30, 1986
Cash	$217	$229	$ 293	$ 60	$ 58	$ 64	$ 98
Accounts receivables (net)	86	134	148	197	142	180	193
Inventories	197	196	266	331	405	371	327
Prepaid expenses	15	14	16	19	28	34	29
Total current assets	$515	$573	$ 723	$ 607	$ 633	$ 649	$ 647
Land improvements	$ 13	$ 14	$ 15	$ 16	$ 22	$ 22	$ 22
Buildings	245	245	245	289	294	297	311
Machinery and equipment	324	324	326	416	613	700	709
Furniture, fixtures, and other	39	37	38	44	44	48	48
	$621	$620	$ 624	$ 765	$ 973	$1,067	$1,090
Less: Accumulated depreciation	427	429	445	466	495	545	573
Net fixed assets	$194	$191	$ 179	$ 299	$ 478	$ 522	$ 517
Investments	$ 57	$ 56	$ 160	$ 160	$ 16	$ 16	$ 46
Prepaid federal income tax	—	—	—	—	—	23	23
Cash surrender value of officers' life insurance	11	17	12	17	21	24	26
Other	26	17	—	—	—	—	—
Total assets	$803	$854	$1,074	$1,083	$1,148	$1,234	$1,259

EXHIBIT 1 *(concluded)*

Balance Sheets of Berringer Products, Inc.,
as of December 31, 1980–85 and as of June 30, 1986
(in thousands)

	1980	1981	1982	1983	1984	1985	June 30, 1986
Accounts payable	$ 45	$ 63	$ 70	$ 42	$ 67	$ 42	$ 50
Accrued payroll and expenses	19	28	47	58	51	31	47
Accrued general taxes	11	10	13	19	25	34	22
Accrued federal income taxes	36	43	85	71	39	29	38
Other	5	5	20	—	—	—	—
Total current liabilities	$116	$149	$ 235	$ 190	$ 182	$ 136	$ 157
Notes payable[a]	$ —	$ —	$ —	$ —	$ 50	$ 144	$ 125
Due to officers and stockholders	31	31	11	—	—	—	—
Total liabilities	$147	$180	$ 246	$ 190	$ 232	$ 280	$ 281
Common stock	$103	$103	$ 103	$ 103	$ 103	$ 103	$ 103
Retained earnings	553	571	725	790	813	851	874
Total net worth	$656	$674	$ 828	$ 893	$ 916	$ 954	$ 977
Total liabilities and net worth	$803	$854	$1,074	$1,083	$1,148	$1,234	$1,259

[a] A 6 ½% industrial revenue bond payable, balance will be $119,000 at December 31, 1986.

Operating Statements of Berringer Products, Inc., 1980–1985 and Six Months Ended June 30, 1986

(expressed as percentage of sales)

	1980	1981	1982	1983	1984	1985	Six Months Ending June 30, 1986
Sales	100.0%	100.0%	100.0%	100.0%	100.0%	100.0%	100.0%
Cost of goods sold	64.1	63.3	62.1	64.0	68.7	72.4	69.8
Gross income	35.9%	36.7%	37.9%	36.0%	31.3%	27.6%	30.2%
Selling expenses	14.9%	15.5%	14.8%	15.0%	16.2%	13.7%	11.5%
General and administrative expenses	14.4	14.7	10.9	10.3	9.0	10.0	10.2
Total selling, general, and administrative expenses	29.3%	30.2%	25.7%	25.3%	25.2%	23.7%	21.7%
Operating income	6.6%	6.5%	12.2%	10.7%	6.1%	3.9%	8.5%
Other income (expense)	(0.4)	0.5	0.4	0.0	0.0	(0.7)	(0.4)
Net income before federal income taxes	6.2%	7.0%	12.6%	10.7%	6.1%	3.2%	8.1%
Provisions for federal income taxes	3.3	3.5	5.7	4.3	2.5	0.1	3.6
Net income after federal income taxes	2.9%	3.5%	6.9%	6.4%	3.6%	3.1%	4.5%

EXHIBIT 2   Acquisition Financials

Berringer Products
Assumed Balance Sheet at Closing, December 31, 1986
(in thousands of dollars)

Cash	$ 120	Accounts payable	$ 84
Accounts receivable	200	Accrued expenses	100
Inventory	440	Notes payable	119
Net current assets	760	Total liabilities	303
Land and building*	340	Common stock	103
Less: depreciation	215	Retained earnings	874
Net	125	Total net worth	977
Machines, equipment,			
furniture, and fixtures*	760		
Less: depreciation	365		
Net	395		
		Total liabilities and net	
Total assets	$1,280	worth	$1,280

*See detail of cost, depreciation, tax basis, and recapture calculations below.

Recapture Calculations

	Total Fixed Assets	Land	Building	Machinery and Equipment	Furniture and Fixtures
Cost basis	$1,100	$25	$315	$710	$50
Book depreciation	580	—	215	340	25
Excess tax depreciation	305	—	90	200	15
Net tax basis	215	25	10	170	10
Fair market value	830	30	370	400	30
Realized gain (fair market value—net tax basis)	615	5	360	230	20
Recapture[a]	383	0	133[b]	230[c]	20[d]
Depreciable life	—	—	20 yrs.	7 yrs.	5 yrs.

[a]Recapture is the additional base amount on which tax is calculated, *not* the amount of tax itself.
[b]Recapture on building is equal to excess of tax depreciation over book (90) *plus* 20% of the straight-line amount (20% × 215 = 43).
[c]Recapture equal to lesser of total (tax + book) depreciation claimed (540) *or* gain realized (230).
[d]Recapture equal to lesser of total (tax + book) depreciation (40) or gain realized (20).

EXHIBIT 3   Financial Projections

Berringer Products
Pro Forma Income Statements
(in thousands of dollars)

	1987	1988	1989	1990	1991
Sales	$1,680.0	$1,765.0	$1,858.0	$1,950.0	$2,050.0
COGS	1,126.0	1,147.0	1,184.0	1,248.0	1,312.0
Gross margin	554.0	618.0	666.0	702.0	738.0
Selling expenses	161.0	168.0	173.0	177.0	181.0
G&A[a]	155.0	162.0	167.0	170.0	174.0
Operating income	238.0	288.0	326.0	355.0	383.0
Interest 6.25%					
Outstanding note	7.4	5.9	4.3	2.7	1.2
Profit before taxes	230.6	282.1	321.7	352.3	381.8

Schedule of Interest and Principal Repayments
(in thousands of dollars)

	1987	1988	1989	1990	1991
$119,000 note assumed:					
Interest	$ 7.4	$ 5.9	$ 4.3	$ 2.7	$ 1.2
Principal	25.0	25.0	25.0	25.0	19.0

[a]Assumes $30,000 salary for each of the three principals.

Appendix

Berringer Products
Tax Rates[a]

Personal Income Tax Rates (married, joint filer)

1986		1987		1988 and On	
Income	Tax	Income	Tax	Income	Tax
$ 0–4,000	$ 0	$ 0–3,000	11%	$ 0–30,000	15%
4–6,000	11%				
6–8,000	250 + 12%	3–28,000	330 + 15%	30–72,000	$ 4,500 + 28%
8–13,000	530 + 14%				
13–17,000	1,175 + 16%	28–45,000	4,080 + 28%	72–149,000	16,260 + 33%
17–22,000	1,880 + 18%				
22–27,000	2,700 + 22%	45–90,000	8,840 + 35%	149–up	41,670 + 28%
27–32,000	3,740 + 25%				
32–38,000	5,170 + 28%	90–up	24,590 + 38.5%		
38–49,000	6,770 + 33%				
49–65,000	10,550 + 38%				
65–92,000	16,370 + 42%				
92–118,000	27,970 + 45%				
118–175,000	39,525 + 49%				
175 and up	67,555 + 50%				

Corporate Income Tax Rates[b]

Income	1986	1987	1988 and On
$ 0–25,000	15%	15%	15%
25–50,000	$ 3,750 + 18%	$ 3,750 + 16.5%	15%
50–75,000	8,250 + 30%	7,825 + 22.5%	$ 7,500 + 25%
75–100,000	15,750 + 40%	14,250 + 37%	13,750 + 34%
100,000–up	25,750 + 46%	24,000 + 40%	22,250 + 34%

Capital Gains Tax Rates

	1986	1987	1988 and On
Personal	20%	28%	Same as income
Corporate	28%	34%	Same as income

[a]Taxes given as flat sum on base income plus percentage rate on incremental income over base.
[b]For calendar year corporations. Transition rules for fiscal year payers are complex. Also, corporations with incomes exceeding $100,000 lose the tax saving on the first $75,000, starting in 1988. The amount lost is a function of the level of income and when the tax year ends.

Case 3–2

Allen Lane

It was March 1982, and Allen Lane sat at his desk pondering a confusing array of issues relative to his bid for Plas-Tek Industries (PTI). Allen had been trying to buy a company for almost two years. On a number of occasions he had come quite close, only to have one circumstance or another block his way. Would his bid for PTI meet the same fate, or would his search for a business finally be over?

BACKGROUND

Allen Lane, 45, had had a variety of experience since his graduation from business school in 1965 (see Exhibit 1 for resume). He spent several years with Wagner Electric Co. in Springfield, Massachusetts, eventually filling the role of vice president of operations for this relatively small manufacturer of electronic parts.

Allen left the firm in 1972 to become an independent consultant to industry. He focused primarily on operations-oriented work: inventory control systems, manufacturing methods, material control, etc.

After three years of relative success, Allen disbanded his efforts in order to join James & Co. in New York.

> I enjoyed working for myself and was making a comfortable living. I grew tired, however, of working on the same kind of problems. James offered the opportunity to get involved with more general management issues and strategic problems. I was also excited about working with some people whom I considered to be extremely bright and interesting.

This case was prepared by Michael J. Roberts under the direction of Howard H. Stevenson.

Copyright © 1983 by the President and Fellows of Harvard College
Harvard Business School case 9–384–077

Allen joined James in January of 1975 and worked with a varied roster of clients and industries. By 1980, however, Allen reached the conclusion that it was time to leave.

> I was becoming frustrated with the cumbersome and generally bureaucratic processes at the very large companies that are the base of James's clientele. James really did expand my horizons and my point of view. My experience there built a lot of general management perspective and honed important general management skills (I thought) that I was eager to use. I wanted to run my own company.

In June 1980, Allen informed James of his intentions to leave. It was important to Allen that James was generous enough to offer the continued resources of the firm, including office space and secretarial services, while he looked for an opportunity. Allen began thinking about how to get into his own business.

LAYING THE GROUNDWORK

Allen had once before thought about buying a company but had no idea where to begin and did not have any close friends who had tried. His experience at James had given him numerous contacts and some credibility, as well as modest financial resources (i.e., roughly $100,000 in liquid assets that he felt he could afford to invest in a company). He described the thought process behind his plan of action and his progress.

> First, I was sure that I wanted to purchase a going concern rather than start up a business:
>
> —The start-up process is a lot riskier, takes longer to pay out, and requires a more single-minded commitment to the process than does purchasing a going concern.
>
> —I never felt I had a "better mousetrap" around which to start a business.
>
> —I enjoy being a fixer, a consultant, more than being a creator.
>
> —Finally, I had the time and resources to wait until I found a good deal.
>
> Next, I decided that in order to have a shot at finding something you needed to have a *focus:* "If you don't know where you're going, any path will get you there." Even if you change your focus later on, at least people have a sense that you know what you want. I decided to look for an industrial distribution business.
>
> —I specifically excluded high-tech and software-type businesses:
> • There is a lot of growth, which makes these businesses attractive, but they are "faddish" and as a result there is an incredible amount of competition for deals from large corporations with very deep pockets.

- I felt that I had to understand and be able to manage the key aspects of the technology in order to minimize risk and successfully run the business.
- I wanted it to be a business where the decisions *I* would make would have a major influence and make the difference—not the research engineer down the hall.

—I decided to focus on a distribution business:

- I had done a lot of work in the industry as a consultant.
- Distribution businesses are typically very undermanaged.
- One of the key factors for success is excellent systems—a good fit for my skills.
- In any given segment (like electronics components distribution) the firms are typically spread over a wide range in terms of their profitability. If you can buy a company in the bottom third of that range, and manage its margin up into the upper third, you can make *a lot* of money. And, the skills required to do this are all basic general management skills.
- These businesses lend themselves to asset-based financing (i.e., they have heavy current assets).
- There are lots of small, owner-managed distributors around, and the competition for deals is less (to a large extent because they are not, historically, favored corporate acquisition targets).

About this time, I started talking with contacts who were in the deal flow, who encouraged me and suggested I look into electronics distribution. They also told me that I wouldn't *really* understand the acquisition process until I actually went through the process of trying to buy a company.

Early that fall (1980), I spoke with another guy, Dan Ray, who was also leaving James, and who had some experience in the electronics distribution business. We decided to work together.

We had just started making contacts in an attempt to look at deals when we heard through an accounting firm that Spectronics might be for sale. We called the president, Bert Spec, and sure enough, it was for real.

We had only been at it for only a short time, and we were ready to chase our first deal.

SPECTRONICS

Spectronics was a $165 million (sales) distributor of electronic components, located in Newark, New Jersey. It was a publicly traded company, but Burt Spec owned a controlling interest of about 55 percent.

We looked at the numbers and, in the price range he was talking, about $20/share or $15 million, the deal made good economic sense. Spectronics also seemed to offer the potential for improvement in rate of return that we were looking for. (See Exhibit 2.) We put together a 200-page business plan that outlined the industry, our credentials, the company, our plans for it—the works. After six or eight weeks, we managed to pull together an $11 million package of financing that included $1 million in equity, $8 million in secured debt, and $2 million of "mezzanine debt" (i.e., a higher risk unsecured loan with a higher return to the lender). We offered $21.50 a share. By now, it was the middle of December, and we had been working on the deal for about three months.

We found out a week later that the company was sold for $2/share *less* than our offer. The other group had offered $19.50 plus a huge "consulting contract" for Bert Spec. We were livid and wanted to sue, but this would have required revealing our equity backer who was anxious to protect his anonymity. So—there went our first deal.

A Reflection

Looking back two years later, it was probably a good thing that we didn't get the first deal that came down the pike. We learned an incredible amount, and it cost us nothing but our time. The valuable lessons included:

—Don't go after a public company unless you have a backer willing to underwrite the process. The lawyers and accounting fees required to put a public deal together are far higher than for a private company. This is a sunk cost, and if the deal falls apart—as they often do—you've lost these fees.

—The acquisition business is a rough-and-tumble one. We were advised not to tell potential investors the name of a company until we absolutely had to. We heard horror stories about guys like us getting squeezed out by the people who had the money and who went around the entrepreneurs and bought the company themselves.

—It is a lucrative business. If you find a deal, *and* hold on to it, you can extract 10–20 percent just for finding it and packaging the deal. If you put some money in or are actually going to manage the venture, your share can go up to 50 percent or so with a limited investment in even a large deal.

Back to the Drawing Board

So, Dan and I put our heads together to decide where to go. We came to the conclusion that all of our initial thoughts on the industry were correct. Moreover, we knew a lot more about the industry, had some contacts, and we thought we could keep our backers together. So, we decided to maintain our focus on the electronics distribution industry.

We called every company—about 60 or so—that met our criteria:

—Northeast corridor location.

—Sales of $5 to $50 million.

We looked for any way in other than a cold call—a lawyer, accountant, friend, anything. We talked to industry observers, customers, suppliers, and banks in an attempt to plug into the grapevine.

We had heard that 5 percent of *all* businesses are "for sale" and that 2 percent are *very actively* for sale. Well, out of our 60 calls, we found 8 that seemed interested enough to warrant a meeting. Of these, we had second meetings with 4, a third meeting with 2, and pursued 1, Ace Electronics, very aggressively.

ACE ELECTRONICS

By now it was March of 1981, and we had been looking at the industry for about six months. Ace was a little different—it focused on very low-tech and together with current inventories had a large stock of almost obsolete parts. Ace was owned by Abe Fox, who had started the business 25 years ago, and was now retiring. He was typically one of the only sources in the *country* for some old condensers, vacuum tubes, and electromechanical parts. You can imagine that his margins were *very* good.

We spent two months haggling and finally shook on a deal. He went away to California for a vacation, and when he came back, he declared that the deal was off.

Another Reflection

Ace really opened my eyes to the world of small business. Most small businesses that we looked at, and of which Ace was the first, have "undervalued inventory." Ace, for instance, had its inventory on the books for $600,000, although the owner claimed (and after some careful checking we concurred) that it was worth at least $4 million. (See Exhibit 3 for two sets of financial statements.)

This understatement is done because of *taxes.* If you overstate your cost of goods sold, you reduce your stated profit, and hence your taxes. Over time the stated book value of inventory becomes small relative to the actual value.

This is not a problem to the buyer, of course, if you are going to continue this practice. However, I had decided early on that I did not want to play such games.

This can create a problem in a small company acquisition. If you keep the inventory on the books at its understated amount, the IRS is very unlikely to see any potential issue. However, if you mark the inventory up to its "fair market value," the IRS may catch on and can (fairly) claim that the company had been underpaying its taxes all along.

So, then you come up against two issues:

—Sale of Stock versus Assets: The liabilities of a company always remain attached to the stock. If you buy the assets of a firm, the seller maintains the potential tax liability. However, if you buy the stock, as most sellers prefer, then *you* are stuck with the potential liability.

—Tax on "Discovered Inventory":   Once the inventory is discovered, of course, this item has to be run through the income statement and shows up as profit, which must be taxed. My view, of course, was that Ace should pay this tax since it had been underpaying all along, and that it had, in effect, accrued taxes. Naturally, Ace would think that if I am "stupid enough" to be honest and declare this to the IRS, I should pay the tax.

Perhaps at this point, I should comment on what I perceive as my own style. There is a large gray area between what is ethically right and wrong. There are many opportunities to "play games" in the process of looking for a deal: exaggerating net worth, experience, the numbers on a deal, and so forth. These things may be ethically "wrong," or perhaps they are borderline. Whatever the case, I had decided early on that they just didn't make good business sense for me. One of the critical things I had going for me was my reputation. People "calibrate you" based on the veracity of your total presentation. If they detect that you are being less than totally honest about *anything,* then they discount *everything* that you say—I couldn't afford to let that happen. Thus, I decided that the right style for me was to be very open and straightforward with sellers, financial sources, and others.

GARDENPRO

Gardenpro was a distributor of garden products, hardware, and paint, located in New Jersey. I heard about the deal from a business broker who showed me financials (with the name of the company deleted) and I was interested. He set us up to meet Chuck Stamen, Gardenpro's owner/manager.

It was an attractive business in a good location and was a distributor—just the kind of company I was looking for.

I met Chuck, and after the preliminary chat and tour, we started talking price. Pretty soon, Chuck mentioned that "the financials didn't fairly reflect the earning power of the business." Why was that so? Well, it seems that Chuck had a little scheme going where he pulled about $500,000 in cash out of the business—off the books and tax free.

It worked roughly like this: he would take an order for products from one of his "friendly" customers and give the order to his employees to load in the truck. Then Chuck would announce that he had to do some business with the fellow anyway, and he would drive the truck over. His friend would pay about 80 cents on the dollar—in cash—for the goods, and then Chuck would just rip up the order. No one would ever know.

Of course, he wanted me to value this off-the-books amount in making my bid. My position was that I wasn't going to play these games, and further, I was likely to lose these customers altogether, because I wasn't going to accept 80 cents on the dollar for my products if I was selling them.

I did submit a bid and knew that I could obtain financing. By this point, I was familiar with the approximate formula that secured lenders use to calculate the "financibility" of a company.

—85 percent of the receivables under 90 days old (to solid accounts), plus

—40 percent to 60 percent of the inventory, depending on its salability, and to some extent on how good the deal is.

In addition, you can usually also borrow one quarter to one third of the appraised value of the plant and equipment; real estate assets can be mortgaged up to 80 percent or 90 percent. This is a very straightforward approach to calculate how much you can borrow on an asset-financed deal.

As you might expect, I lost Gardenpro to someone with a higher bid. But I later found out that the company was never sold.

HYDRAPRESS

A few months later, in October of 1981, I came across Hydrapress, a manufacturer of hydraulic presses for making refractories and special bricks for use in high-temperature processes, such as furnaces for molten metal and glass. I heard about this deal from another business broker. He was hesitant to refer me to Morris Golden, president of Hydrapress, because I did not have the $3 or $4 million in hard cash required to do the deal. But he did set me up with an investment banker who had appraised Hydrapress and who was representing the seller.

We got together, and I learned that it was a fairly typical selling situation. Golden was 68 and had decided it was "time to retire and enjoy life." His wife wanted to go to Florida, and all his friends were telling him to sell the company and tidy up his estate.

The investment banker told me that there were two very serious buyers lined up who clearly had the cash and were interested in purchasing the company as an investment. They would need a management team; perhaps I could work a joint deal with one of them. I did speak with each of these groups, but told them I was also working to raise the capital to make a bid on my own. In any event, under the banker's auspices, I was able to visit Hydrapress and meet with its principals.

After visiting numerous banks, I finally did get an oral commitment for the money from the Fiduciary Bank and wrote my proposal letter. I bid $3.4 million, but lost out by a small margin to a NYSE company.

Six months later, the investment banker called to ask if I was still interested. It seems that when push came to shove, Golden had balked at selling the company. According to the banker, he kept finding little nits with the deal until the buyer got so exasperated that he finally walked away.

By this time, I was chasing Plas-Tek and didn't have the time to get involved. More importantly, I had learned a lesson about buying a company from the founding owner: It's *tough*. No one wants to sell "his or her baby."

A PERSPECTIVE

Allen commented on a few other aspects of the deal business he had learned about over the past several years.

"Ham and Egging"

One of the real "arts" to the process of trying to buy a company is called *ham and egging*. It refers to the delicate process of trying to get the financing secured before you have the company locked up and trying to get the company committed before you have the financing.

Naturally, potential backers don't want to spend the time evaluating the deal or commit to financing unless they are fairly certain that you have an acceptable deal worked out with the company. The company, on the other hand, feels it is wasting its time talking to you unless you have the money.

I was always very straightforward with companies; I would describe the deal to different financial backers, get an oral commitment of interest, and tell the company that I had this oral commitment. Naturally, I projected the attitude that I was sure that financing would be available.

The process does get much easier as you go along. The first time is always the hardest. On subsequent deals, even if the previous deals have fallen apart, you can talk about having raised money before, and you have a portfolio of backers to deal with. After people know you, and have seen you in action on one deal and have come to trust you, they are far quicker to make a commitment on financing.

A Hierarchy of Buyers

All this leads one to talk about what I call "a hierarchy of buyers." None of the companies would even be talking to me if they could have sold to a NYSE company in an all-cash deal, or a tax-free exchange of stock. From a seller's perspective it appears that there are several classes of buyers doing deals:

—Class A: Another company who views the seller as a business with "strategic fit." They are willing to pay cash, and pay a premium price for the company.

—Class B: Investment bankers representing some company looking for a deal, often a conglomerate. Generally they won't pay the premiums that a strategic buyer will, but in either case, as a seller you don't have to worry about the money being there.

—Class C_1: A leveraged buy-out specialist who will in all probability pay even less, but who has done deals before and who has a track record in raising the cash.

—Class C_2: An individual who doesn't have the cash, hasn't done a deal, but knows what he's doing and can probably raise the money. I felt that I was a C_2 given my contacts and experience.

—Class C_3: An individual with nothing but desire; this was me when I started out, before the Spectronics deal.

PLAS-TEK

In March of 1982, I ran into Jeff Brewster, an accountant with a Big 8 firm, with whom I had spoken around the time of the Spectronics deal. He thought he might have a few companies I'd be interested in, and we scheduled a lunch for the following week. One of the companies was Plas-Tek.

Background

Harry Elson had founded Plas-Tek, a manufacturer of specialty plastic components, in 1954. When he died in November of 1981, he left an estate that was valued at $7 million or so to a half-dozen well-known charities. Plas-Tek was part of the estate, and the trustee/executor, a big New York bank, had decided to sell it. In fact, PTI was actually two companies: HE Manufacturing and its sister company, Plas-Tek Sales Company. PTI refers to both companies.

The bank had a valuation of the business performed (see Exhibit 4 for a description of PTI's business and the valuation report) and then contacted customers, suppliers, and competitors to see if any were interested in purchasing Plas-Tek. When none expressed interest, the bank quietly put Plas-Tek on the market.

By the time I heard about the business, it had been on the market for a month or so, and the bank told me that unless I were going to bid $600,000 or more not to bother. They told me that they wanted to close off bidding later that week, but I figured that I could stall them for a little while. When Elson died, all of his estate went into a charitable trust. The bank's trust and estate department had a fiduciary obligation to get the highest price for the business. They would not look good if they refused to let me submit a bid.

So, during the next few days, I raced around trying to put together a deal and submit my bid. I had the valuation and the banks' ". . . beat $600,000" as a starting point.

Strategy

My strategy was to first *value* the business, and then *price* it. They are two different things. Obviously, I wanted my price to be lower than the business's value but high enough for the bid to get *me* to the bargaining table with the bank.

The Business: Fit with Allen Lane

First, I had to evaluate the business and how it fit with my skills and objectives. Clearly, it wasn't in the distribution area, but they did have some things in common, including the importance of customer service. Further, it was *definitely* going to require a lot of hands-on management. With Elson dead, there was really a management vacuum at Plas-Tek.

The Business Itself

Obviously, a crucial issue was the business itself. I was amazed to see that Plas-Tek had gross margins in excess of 50 percent for a nonproprietary product. Harry was pulling down over half a million a year from a business with a million dollars in sales! Was this a legitimate profit, and, more important, would it continue if I bought the business?

Key Employees

Plas-Tek had the equivalent of eight full-time shop workers as well as a bookkeeper and a customer service/order entry clerk. I spent a day walking around the shop and was convinced that I could learn the manufacturing end of the business. As an engineer, I felt comfortable with the basic molding and machining operations. Still, there were several key employees whose efforts would be crucial to getting off to a good start.

—Bernie, the shop foreman, had been with PTI for 18 years. I talked with him and was convinced of his desire to stay on. He was about 55 and was making almost $50,000 a year, so he seemed to have little incentive to move. Unfortunately, he was in failing health, and if something did happen, we would be in tough shape.

—Sarah, the bookkeeper, knew the financial side of the business as well as Harry's pricing policies.

—Eleanor, the customer service/order entry clerk, knew a little bookkeeping as well as who the key customers were, what they ordered, and how it was priced. She also knew where all of the finished goods inventory was stored.

Harry had been clever in having a lot of part-time people on board, so there were often two people who knew the same job.

A Partner

Since the Spectronics deal, I had looked at doing things both on my own and with a variety of partners. Generally, I am the verbal type and do my best thinking in a teamlike atmosphere. I also wanted someone to mind the store while I was away and vice versa. I didn't want to be tied to the business night and day, every day.

I thought it was important that a partner and I each be able to handle key aspects of the business, but still have a clear enough division of responsibilities that we not get in each other's way. I was also looking for someone with flexibility and a set of values, goals, and expectations that was compatible with mine.

I also knew that if I brought in a partner, I wanted it to be a full 50 percent partner. I had been involved with some less-than-equal partnerships before, and such a partner feels that he is doing more than his share of the work. The individual I chose as a partner was capable of matching my $100,000 equity contribution in order to buy his half of the equity. Dan Ray had joined a semiconductor firm after the Spectronics deal fell through, but we had kept in touch. I knew he was still interested in doing something with me, and I still thought he would make a good partner.

Financing

Because I had the experience of putting together the described deals (and others), I had a portfolio of equity backers, asset-secured financiers, and other lenders to draw on for financing.

I did have about $100,000 in equity, and ideally, I hoped to finance the remainder so that my partner and I could control 100 percent of the equity.

I thought we might be able to get the estate (represented by the bank) to take back a note if we could get a reputable bank to guarantee this debt. I did have excellent relationships with a few banks that I had worked with on other deals, and they seemed eager to work with me.

I also knew that if we borrowed on the business itself, that we would have to personally guarantee at least a portion of the note, and that the interest rate would be about 2 percent over prime (i.e., in the 17 percent to 19 percent range).

A Lawyer

I had worked with a variety of lawyers. Some were good negotiators, others good on tax or securities issues. I had developed a list of criteria to aid in the selection of an attorney (see Exhibit 5). We had to pick one and get him up to speed fast.

Stock versus Assets

The purchase of stock versus the purchase of assets was a major issue in the deal structure, and we knew we had to make a decision on this point early on. I would have preferred a simple purchase of assets. In this way, we would not have to assume *any* of the liabilities associated with the old company.

The bank, however, wanted to clean up and settle the estate. They were strongly in favor of a purchase of stock, which would saddle me with all liabilities, including contingent liabilities.

Contingent Liabilities

Contingent liabilities are real or potential liabilities that do not exist on the balance sheet. For instance, if an employee had lost an arm in an industrial accident, but had not sued the company, there was a contingent liability in that he *might* sue later and *might* win some *unknown* amount of money. We thought that the following contingent liabilities might exist for Plas-Tek and checked them out thoroughly:

—Existing lawsuit.

—Potential lawsuit.

—Potential tax liability.

We interviewed employees in an attempt to discover any potential problems (i.e., injuries or customer problems). As best we could determine, there were no existing lawsuits against the company, and we checked the literature to unearth the possibility of potential product liability suits. We made a list of all the major substances the company used and ran computer searches to determine whether any of these was suspected of causing cancer or other diseases. Fortunately, they checked OK.

On the tax issue, however, we were not so lucky. There were two areas of potential liability:

—Unreasonable compensation: Harry had been pulling out *a lot* of money as salary, and hence deducting it on the corporate tax return. If the IRS stepped in, they could declare that some amount of this "salary" was excessive compensation, and reclassify it as a dividend. (See Exhibit 6 for tax code and explanation.) Then, the company would be liable for an income tax on this amount. This issue was complicated by the fact that Harry was operating PTI as two separate companies: HE Manufacturing was a straight corporation, and Plas-Tek Sales was a Sub S. If the IRS questioned the transfer-pricing policies of the company, the potential tax liability could increase to an even greater amount. (See Exhibit 7 for a full explanation of the potential tax liabilities.)

—Accumulated earnings: HE Manufacturing, the straight corporation, had a substantial amount of interest-earning current assets on its books. (See Exhibit 4 for balance sheet.) The IRS could, on examination, claim that these assets were earnings that Elson had accumulated in HE Manufacturing rather than distributing them as dividends. (Again, see Exhibit 7 for full explanation.)

THE DECISION

Allen and his partner put a pot of coffee on the stove and prepared themselves for a long evening. They knew that it would not be easy to resolve these issues and value the business, but they had to submit their bid the following morning.

EXHIBIT 1   Resume of Allen Lane

Allen Lane

Experience
1975 to 1980
JAMES & COMPANY, INC.   NEW YORK, NEW YORK
Engagement Manager. As consultant to top management of large
manufacturing and distribution companies, led teams of several consultants and up to 50 client personnel to formulate strategies, and to
identify and implement opportunities to increase profitability and improve functional performance.

Served clients in electronics (telecommunications equipment, computers, components), machinery (business equipment), consumer products
(sanitary paper, pharmaceuticals) and process (paper, packaging) industries ranging in annual revenues from $150 million to $9 billion.

Developed and presented consultant training in techniques for assist-
ing manufacturers and distributors to reduce costs and improve delivery performance.

1972 to 1975
LANE AND ASSOCIATES   CAMBRIDGE, MASSACHUSETTS
As Principal, designed and implemented management systems to enhance competitive performance and improve profitability of manufacturing and distribution clients. Applications included inventory management, order entry, billing, accounts receivable, sales analysis,
purchasing, accounts payable. Industries served included automotive
parts and pharmaceuticals.

1965 to 1972
WAGNER ELECTRIC CO.   SPRINGFIELD, MASSACHUSETTS
As Vice President, Operations, for this $30 million manufacturer, re-
sponsible for planning and scheduling factory operations and managing inventories (raw material, work in process, finished goods). As
Manager, System and Planning, responsible for developing capacity
plans to support company's rapid growth. Also developed production
planning and scheduling, labor control, budgeting, and other operational and accounting systems.

1958 to 1963
ACME STEEL FABRICATORS, INC.   BOSTON, MASSACHUSETTS
Purchasing Agent and Assistant to Vice President, Manufacturing, for
this $5 million manufacturer of steel tanks, pressure vessels, and
other weldments.

Education
1965
EASTERN BUSINESS SCHOOL   BOSTON, MASSACHUSETTS
MBA; concentrated in manufacturing and control.

1958
RENSSELAER POLYTECHNIC INSTITUTE   TROY, NEW YORK
Bachelor in Mechancial Engineering; elected member of Tau Beta Pi,
Pi Tau Sigma honorary societies.

EXHIBIT 2   Profitability of 15 Largest Publicly Held Electronic Components Distributors

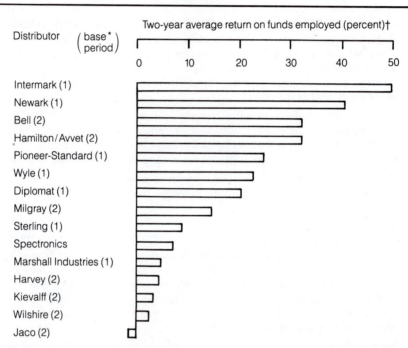

*Base period: (1) = 1978 and 1979; (2) = 1977 and 1978.
†[Profit before interest and taxes] / [(Assets) - (Accounts payable and accrued expenses)].
Corporate expenses, corporate assets and all accounts payable and accrued expenses
have been allocated to electronics distribution business on basis of sales.

SOURCE: Annual Reports (line of business data for electronics distribution).

EXHIBIT 3   Two Sets of Ace Financial Statements, Fiscal 1979 (in thousands of dollars)

	Income Statement #1 (as reported to IRS)	Income Statement #2 (as "estimated" by Fox)
Sales	$4,000	$4,000
Cost of goods sold	3,050	2,250
Gross margin	950	1,750
Expenses	750	750
EBIT	200	1,000
Interest	0	0
Taxes	100	100
Net profit	$ 100	$ 900

EXHIBIT 3   (*concluded*)

	Balance Sheet #1 (as reported to IRS)	Balance Sheet #2 (as "estimated" by Fox)
Assets		
Cash	$ 30	$ 30
Accounts receivable	500	500
Inventory	600	600
Fixed/other	20	20
Additional inventories	—	4,900
Total	$1,150	$6,050
Liabilities and Net Worth		
Accounts payable	$ 250	$ 250
Accrued expenses	50	50
Accrued taxes	25	25
Bank loan	100	100
Net worth	725	725
Additional net worth	—	4,900
Total net worth	725	$5,625
Total	$1,150	$6,050

EXHIBIT 4   Introductory Letter and Valuation Report

March 16, 1982

Dear Mr. Lane:

Enclosed is the evaluation report that we had prepared to guide us in the sale of Plas-Tek, Inc. Based on this report and our own preliminary analysis, we have now set the asking price for the sale of the companies at $750,000, and are so advising all of the parties who have met our preliminary requirements for establishing serious interest in the acquisition.

Please let us know within the next ten (10) days (*a*) if you are willing to pay our asking price, (*b*) the terms of your proposal, and (*c*) if you wish to make a counterproposal.

At this time we will only give serious consideration to offers to purchase at a price in excess of $600,000.

As you were previously advised, we intend to sell the corporation's entire stock (after removal of cash and marketable securities). We will only consider offers on terms if the purchase price is adequately secured by satisfactory collateral security other than the assets of the business itself.

Our plan is to proceed as follows: We will immediately enter into negotiations with qualified buyers in order of the magnitude of their initial offer. We anticipate, based on the interest expressed to date by a number of apparently serious and qualified prospective purchasers, that we can settle within our proposed price range. If we find that we are unable to do so,

EXHIBIT 4   *(continued)*

we intend to broaden the base of prospective purchasers by announcing the availability of the companies to a wide variety of customary sources of prospective purchasers.

We trust that it will be apparent to you that we consider this to be the most expeditious way for us to attain the highest price we can, consistent with our responsibilities as executors of the estate of Harold Elson.

Accordingly, if you wish to be the successful purchaser, it will certainly be in your interest to make the highest offer in response to this request as soon as you can do so, as we intend to complete this transaction as quickly as we can.

Sincerely yours,

Senior Trust Officer
New York Bank

PLAS-TEK INDUSTRIES (PTI)

We have been asked to determine the fair market value of PTI. All of the outstanding common stock of the company is presently held in the estate of Harold Elson. The purpose of this appraisal is to assist the executors of the estate in determining the value of the business in order to sell it.

Conclusion

Based on our analysis of the relevant facts, it is our opinion that the current fair market value, in an all-cash transaction, of the operating assets and business of PTI is $600,000.

Description of Business

The business will be referred to in this report as PTI. HE Manufacturing is a corporation, and Plas-Tek Sales is a Subchapter S company; PTI refers to both companies.

The business was founded some 25 or more years ago by Harold Elson and was operated by Mr. Elson until his death on November 20, 1981, at age 72.

PTI, located in Patterson, New Jersey, is in the business of manufacturing and distributing gaskets, washers, "O" rings, and similar items made of plastic. PTI makes parts out of fluoroplastic resins as well as other materials, including nylon, polyethylene, and acrylic resins.

Products are generally made to industry standards or customer specifications. Approximately 90 percent of sales are made to distributors and original equipment manufacturers (OEM) with the balance sold to end users. PTI's customers come from a variety of industries, the most important being the food and chemical industries.

Sales are made primarily in response to requests for quotations and to repeat customers. PTI has no salesmen. Advertising is confined primarily to a small listing in *Thomas' Register*. The company has about 300 active customer accounts. Listed below are the sales figures for the five largest customers, which accounted, in the aggregate, for 35.3 percent of 1981 sales.

EXHIBIT 4   (*continued*)

	1981 Sales	Percent of Total Sales
Customer A	$98,487	10.5%
Customer B	72,377	7.7
Customer C	61,615	6.5
Customer D	51,599	5.5
Customer E	48,362	5.1
		35.3%

Income Statements

Shown following is a summary of income statements of the company for the five-year period ended August 31, 1981.

PTI Income Statement (in thousands of dollars)

	Fiscal Years Ended August 31				
	1981	1980	1979	1978	1977
Net sales	$942	$1,050	$894	$709	$652
Gross profit................	551	640	495	427	369
Operating and overhead expense	97	92	78	76	67
Profit before officer salary, investment income and income taxes	454	548	417	351	302
Investment income*	93	92	65	66	18
Profit before officer salary and income taxes	547	640	482	407	320
Officer salary...............	480	505	415	360	280
New Jersey sales tax........	20	23	18	19	6
Profit before federal income tax	$ 47	$ 12	$ 49	$ 28	$ 34

*Interest and dividends on cash and securities.

Manufacturing

Gaskets and washers are machined principally from cylinders or other shapes molded by PTI itself and also from plastic purchased from outside vendors. The company's facilities occupy a 3,700 square foot building owned by it in Patterson, New Jersey. Principal items of production equipment include a press, a sintering oven, and a number of lathes and other machine tools. The company has five full-time production employees and four part-time employees. The company is nonunion. Hourly wage rates range from $5 to $9. The office staff consists of a manager and a bookkeeper-secretary-receptionist.

Management

The success of PTI has essentially been based on, and dependent on, the management efforts of Harold Elson. The company built a reputa-

EXHIBIT 4   (*continued*)

___

tion of fulfilling orders quickly. Mr. Elson put a great deal of personal effort into providing responsive service to his customers, often working on weekends to do so.

Approach to Value
The definition of *fair market value* employed in this appraisal is the price at which the property would change hands between a willing buyer and a willing seller when the former is not under any compulsion to buy and the latter is not under any compulsion to sell, both having reasonable knowledge of relevant facts.

In establishing a value for PTI, we have taken into account a variety of factors, including the nature and history of the company, the economic outlook, the book value, financial condition and earnings capacity of the company, its dividend capacity and intangible values, past sales of securities of the company, and comparisons with public companies in the same or similar industry.

It is assumed for the purpose of this valuation that PTI will be purchased exclusive of its excess cash or investment assets. The excess cash and investments would either be removed from the company prior to sale or would be compensated for with an additional dollar-for-dollar payment by the purchaser of the business.

Balance Sheet
Exhibit A shows a combined balance sheet for the business with the excess cash and investments set forth.

It can be seen that, with the excess cash investments removed, the net worth of the operating assets of the business is $200,000. If the land and buildings were carried at their current appraised value of $92,000, the adjusted net worth of the company would be $292,000.

Earnings Capability
In 1981 PTI earned $454,000 before officer salary, investment income, and income tax. Clearly, a buyer would be attracted to the acquisition of PTI for its earnings capability rather than for its asset base. The estimate of fair market value, then, must begin with an analysis of the earnings history and capability of the company.

Set forth below is a summary of the earnings of the company.

Year	Operating Profit* before Officer Salary ($000)
1981	$454
1980	548
1979	417
1978	351
1977	302

*Before investment income and federal and New Jersey income taxes.

EXHIBIT 4   (*continued*)

A key question is how much of the earnings ability of the company was
due to the personal efforts of Mr. Elson and, accordingly, how much of
such earnings ability is likely to remain in the future in his absence. The
months since his death, in November 1981, have seen a decline in sales
as illustrated below. It is the feeling of those presently running the business, however, that a good part of this decline is attributable to softness
in the economy in general rather than to the absence of Mr. Elson. Some
of the softness had already begun to make itself felt in the months prior to
Mr. Elson's death. No customer is known to have ceased doing business
with the company because of Mr. Elson's death. We understand that the
executors have communicated with all the major customers and these customers have assured the executors of their satisfaction and that they anticipate continuing to do business with PTI.

PTI Sales
(in thousands of dollars)

	3 Months Sept.–Nov.		2 Months Dec.–Jan.*		5 Months Sept.–Jan.*	
	Amount	*% Chg. from Prev. Yr.*	*Amount*	*% Chg. from Prev. Yr.*	*Amount*	*% Chg. from Prev. Yr.*
1981....	$214	− 3.2%	$111	−24.0%	$325	−11.4%
1980....	211	+ .5	146	−17.0	367	− 7.3
1979....	220	+25.0	176	0.0	396	+12.5
1978....	176	+10.0	176	+58.6	352	+29.9
1977....	160	+ 3.2	111	+ 6.7	271	+ 4.6
1976....	155		104		259	

*Of following year.

We have taken the view that the current decline in sales volume is temporary, being related to the currrent soft economy and possibly to the uncertainty related to a prospective change in ownership of the company. With
new capable ownership in place, there is no reason that the business
should not be able to continue at least in the levels of the recent past. Accordingly, we have elected to employ the 1981 levels of profit before taxes
and owner compensation as the best available indication of future profitability, and the one on which buyer and seller might be most likely to
base a sale price.

Staffing
      In view of Mr. Elson's heavy personal involvement in the business
and the long hours that he put in, a new owner might well be required to
staff the company with more than one person to replace Mr. Elson.
      We have assumed that the functions formerly performed by Mr. El-
son could be replaced at a cost of $150,000.

EXHIBIT 4 (*continued*)

Future Earnings Capability

Using this estimate of management cost, and the 1981 level of pre-tax income before owner compensation, produces the following estimate of the earnings capability of PTI.

Pro Forma Earnings (in thousands of dollars)

Profit before owner compensation and increased taxes $454
Management compensation 150
Profit before income taxes.. 304
New Jersey income tax (10%)... 30
Profit before federal income tax.. 274
Federal income tax (1982 rates).. 106
Net income after taxes...$168

We have concluded, then, that a party acquiring PTI and staffing it at the annual cost shown above, would be buying a business capable of generating net income after taxes at the annual rate of $168,000.

Capitalization Rate

The capitalized earnings approach to value is based on the premise that a potential investor in a going concern will base the purchase price he is willing to pay on some multiple of the earnings power of the company. The approach consists of applying an appropriate price/earnings multiple (P/E) to the earnings of the company in question. It becomes necessary, then, to determine the appropriate P/E. The most reasonable way to do so is to determine what earnings multiple investors have been willing to pay for stocks of other companies engaged in similar lines of business.

Ideally, in selecting comparable companies, we look for companies not only in the same general line of business, but with a similarity that extends as far as possible into all areas of corporate circumstances, including capital structure, specific services performed, areas and intensity of competition, growth rates, and, if possible, size in terms of assets held, and the volume of sales. Only in the most unusual circumstances, however, will there be available even one publicly-traded company that would begin to satisfy these multifarious requirements.

Since PTI is a fabricator of plastic products, we have conducted our search for comparable companies from the industry group of plastic products manufacturers. After examining a large number of companies, we have selected four as comprising a respresentative group for purposes of this appraisal. Key facts on the companies in this group are set forth in Exhibit B.

Exhibit B shows a range of price/earnings ratios for plastic parts fabricators of from 3.6X to 6.4X with an average of 5.4X. The comparable companies are, of course, considerably larger than PTI. In the case of some of the companies, there is a proprietary element to their product offerings, which is lacking with PTI. They are also possessed of more management depth.

For the above reasons, we have selected a price/earnings ratio of 4.5X for PTI, which is below the average of the group.

EXHIBIT 4   *(continued)*

Applying the 4.5X multiplier to the previously calculated earnings level of PTI produces a preliminary value for PTI of $750,000.

$$168,000 \times 4.5 = \$756,000, \text{ say } \$750,000.$$

This, in effect, represents the hypothetical value at which PTI would trade if it were a public company. It is acknowledged that it is unlikely that a company as small as PTI would trade as a public company. Nonetheless, this approach to value corresponds with that which would be taken by many prospective buyers.

Adjustment for Illiquidity and Control

The valuation procedure above compares PTI to a group of companies whose securities are traded in the public market. The result produced, then, is the hypothetical price at which shares of PTI would trade if it were a public company. Since PTI is not a public company, it is necessary to make an adjustment in the price to reflect the fact that a holder of stock in PTI would not be able to sell his shares without considerable effort or delay. This adjustment is normally made by applying a discount to the price, called a discount for illiquidity.

A further adjustment must be made to reflect the fact that we are valuing PTI as a whole, rather than valuing a minority holding in the company. The market prices that we used to establish value were based upon transactions in minority interests in companies. It is necessary to reflect this difference. This is normally done by applying a premium called a control premium to the price paid on minority transactions.

It is our opinion that in the case of PTI, the appropriate discount for illiquidity and premium for control would approximately cancel each other out, leaving the value, based upon market prices, at what it would be without such adjustment, $750,000.

Dividends

With the exception of Subchapter S distributions, PTI does not have a history of paying dividends to its shareholders. For this reason, the dividend approach to value is not apposite in this case.

Prior Transactions

There are no known prior transactions in the stock of PTI. Therefore, this approach to value is not relevant.

Book Value

As stated earlier, the book value of the operating assets of PTI is $200,000, or $292,000, if the current appraised value of the real estate is taken into account. Since this value is considerably below the value based on earnings, it has little relevance in this case.

Adjustment for Cash Sale

The executors of the estate that owns PTI wish to sell the company in a transaction that will permit a winding up of the estate shortly thereafter. Accordingly, they are not in a position to offer extended payment terms to prospective buyers.

EXHIBIT 4   *(continued)*

Ordinarily, if a business of this size were sold, particularly to an individual, it would be customary for the seller to permit the payment of a significant portion of the purchase price over time.

Since an extended payment sale is not possible in this case, two effects will be produced, (i) the number of willing buyers with means available to consummate a purchase will be reduced, and (ii) the remaining buyers, in the absence of the availability of seller financing, will not be willing to pay as much for the company.

Because of these two effects, we have adjusted downward our assessment of the value of PTI by 20 percent, producing a value of $600,000.

Contingent Liabilities

The value determined in this appraisal presumes that a buyer of PTI would, in purchasing the business, assume no liabilities, real or contingent, other than the trade payables and other similar accrued liabilities arising from operations in the ordinary course of business. To the extent that the form of the transaction would require him to become actually or potentially obligated for other liabilities, the appraised value would have to be correspondingly adjusted.

Conclusion

Based on our analysis of the relevant facts, it is our opinion that the current fair market value, in a cash transaction, of the operating assets and business of PTI is $600,000.

EXHIBIT 4 (continued)

Exhibit A
Combined Balance Sheets
(in thousands of dollars)

	HE Manufacturing	PLAS-TEK Sales	Eliminations	Combined	Investment Assets and Liabilities	Operating Assets and Liabilities
Assets						
Cash........................	$170	$133		$ 303	$ 290	
Securities.................	507	234		741	750	
Accounts receivable.....	41*	150	$41*	150		$148
Inventory..................	60			60		60
Loans receivable.........	19	20		39	45	
Prepaid expenses........	6	—		6		6
Total current assets......	803	537	41	1,299	1,085	214
Fixed assets—net						
Equipment.................	5	6		11		11
Building....................	10	—		10		10
Land........................	10	—		10		10
Total assets...............	$828	$543	$41	$1,330	$1,085	$245
Liabilities and Capital						
Accounts payable........	$ 36	$ 50	$41	$ 45		$ 45
Taxes payable............	10	7		17	17	
Accrued salary—officers....	164	218		482	482	
Accrued expenses	10	—		10	10	
Total liabilities...........	220	375	41	554	509	45
Capital.....................	608	168		776	576	200
Total liabilities and capital.	$828	$543	$41	$1,330	$1,085	$245

*All HE accounts receivable are due from Plas-Tek sales.

EXHIBIT 4 (concluded)

Exhibit B

Company (market)	Fiscal Year	Revenues ($millions—1980 FY)	Earnings per Share Latest 12 Months		Book Value per Share (1980 FY)	Stock Price 2/18/82	Price/ Earnings Ratio
			Amount	Period Ended			
Kleer-Vu Industries, Inc. (ASE)	Dec.	$13.5	$1.48	9/81	$5.16	5¼	3.5
Liqui-Box Corp. (OTC)	Dec.	43.8	1.28	9/81	9.64	8¼	6.4
Plymouth Rubber Co. C1.B (ASE)	Nov.	63.8	.38*	11/81	6.75	2	5.3
Star-Glo Industries, Inc. (OTC)	Dec.	8.3	.57*	9/81	2.73	3⅝	6.4
Average							5.4
Range							3.5–6.4

*Excluding extraordinary items.

EXHIBIT 5   Criteria for Selection of Attorney

1. Strong professional orientation—possess strong character, high degree of integrity and honesty, and general business competence.
2. Creative deal maker—ability to spot opportunities for mutual benefit in structuring deal terms.
3. Interest in working with entrepreneurs on a relatively small deal—enthusiasm for working on interesting issues with substantial creativity rather than mega-deal.
4. Caliber of corporate and tax skills—ability to integrate full range of corporate and tax issues into deal structure.
5. Strength as "hands-on" negotiator—ability to achieve goals at the bargaining table; good speaker, fast on feet.
6. Understanding of business issues—ability to craft deal in light of overall business goals, not merely tax and financing considerations.

EXHIBIT 6   Business Expenses—Unreasonable Compensation

TAX CODE SEC. 162. TRADE OR BUSINESS EXPENSES (paragraph a)
(a) In general, business expenses deductible from gross income include the ordinary and necessary expenditures, paid or incurred during the taxable year, directly connected with or pertaining to the taxpayer's trade or business, including
—cost of goods sold, including a proper adjustment for opening and closing inventories,
—a reasonable allowance for salaries or other compensation for personal services actually rendered,
—traveling expenses (including amounts expended for meals and lodging other than amounts which are lavish or extravagant under the circumstances) while away from home in the pursuit of a trade or business; and
—rentals or other payments made as a condition of the use or possession, for purposes of the trade or business, of property to which the taxpayer has not taken or is not taking title or in which he has no equity.

Explanation: Unreasonable Compensation

Compensation deductions are usually questioned by the IRS only in closely held corporations. The usual reason for disallowance is that the compensation paid is "unreasonable." Factors that are generally considered in establishing reasonableness include: the work actually performed by the individuals; their training and experience; the time and effort devoted to the work; the results that have been achieved; the requirement for ability and skill; the inadequacy of compensation in earlier years; and compensation paid for comparable services by similar businesses.

Compensation payments which are based on profits are subject to the same rules as amounts paid as straight salary. Thus, a legitimate bonus arrangement is recognized as an allowable deduction, even though in years of high profits, the amounts paid may be larger than would ordinarily be paid on a straight salary basis.

In all cases, the IRS carefully checks any compensation arrangement which distributes compensation in a way which is proportional to stockholdings. The IRS may reclassify some or all of such compensation payments as dividends.

The wrongful deduction of business expenses, including unreasonable compensation, may be grounds for criminal action.

EXHIBIT 7   Letter from Accountants on Contingent Liabilities

April 14, 1982

Dear Mr. Lane:

A review has been made of the federal income tax returns and financial statements of HE Manufacturing Corporation and its related company, Plas-Tek Sales Company, for their fiscal years ending in 1979, 1980, and 1981. The purpose of the review was to estimate the magnitude of tax deficiencies from certain adjustments which may result from an examination of their federal returns by the Internal Revenue Service. Our findings were made taking into account certain assumptions regarding reasonable compensation and other matters which were discussed at a meeting last week among ourselves and counsel.

Background

The capital stock of each of the companies was owned entirely by Harold Elson, who died in late 1981. Plas-Tek Sales is a Subchapter S corporation which reports on a fiscal year ended August 31. HE Manufacturing Corporation reports its income on a June 30 fiscal year. The business consists of the manufacture of gaskets, washers, and other plastic products.

Operations over the years have been quite profitable. In each of the three years prior to his death Mr. Elson's salary from both companies amounted to more than $400,000. The balance sheet of HE Manufacturing discloses substantial amounts of cash and investments and relatively small liabilities. For these reasons, concern has been expressed that the Internal Revenue Service could assert an unreasonable compensation and/or accumulated earnings issue if the tax returns of the companies were to be examined.

Since Plas-Tek Sales has a Subchapter S election in effect, the accumulated earnings issue would not result in a tax deficiency unless the company's Subchapter S status could be involuntarily terminated. We believe the prospect of that situation to be extremely remote. While unreasonable compensation is not generally considered in a Subchapter S situation because all earnings are taxed currently to the shareholders, a net deficiency could result if compensation, taxed at a minimum rate of 50 percent, were converted to dividend income taxable (before 1982) at a maximum rate of 70 percent by changing its character to passive income. Since such an assessment would be at the individual level it has not been considered in our review of corporate matters.

Unreasonable Compensation

Based upon our discussions and the valuation appraisal it is believed that compensation of $150,000 per year for PTI could be sustained if the issue were to be challenged by Internal Revenue Service. Using that number as a bench mark, we have calculated the deficiency to HE Manufacturing which would result using three different approaches:

EXHIBIT 7   (*continued*)

1. Disallow amounts in excess of $75,000 per company.
2. Disallow compensation in excess of $75,000 and allocate the taxable income earned between the companies on an equal basis. This results in allocating income from Plas-Tek Sales to HE Manufacturing.
3. Disallow compensation in excess of $75,000 per company and allow Plas-Tek Sales a return of 5 percent on sales plus its reported expenses. Allocate excess income to HE Manufacturing.

The federal income tax deficiency before interest which would result from adjustments described above, as summarized on Exhibit A, would be as follows:

> Alternative 1—$ 86,768
> Alternative 2—$196,280
> Alternative 3—$369,773

We are not aware that Internal Revenue Service has ever challenged the intercompany pricing of products sold by HE to Plas-Tek. However, considering the structure of the related companies, i.e., HE being taxable but Plas-Tek electing Subchapter S status, the Service could maximize the tax revenue by allocating income back to HE Manufacturing. The fact that the cash ultimately resides in Plas-Tek may be reconciled by the Service by claiming that HE paid a dividend of the excess income to Elson which was then reinvested by him in Plas-Tek, a common position when dealing with related corporations. The result would then be additional income tax to HE with no corresponding reduction of tax at the individual level.

We are not in a position to conclude as to the reasonableness of the profit rate that should be realized by each of the companies, i.e., manufacturing by HE and sales by Plas-Tek. The gross profit reported by Plas-Tek for each of the three years was exactly 40 percent, whereas the gross profit realized by HE ranged from 27 percent to 35 percent. Accordingly, Alternative 2 was predicated upon an equal splitting of the combined net profit between the two companies. It is conceivable, however, that the Service may take the position that Plas-Tek is nothing more than an agency and is entitled only to a reasonable commission on sales plus its actual selling expenses and officer's compensation of $75,000. If the Service were to take such a position, substantial income would be allocated to HE.

Accumulated Earnings Tax

If it were to be assessed, the accumulated earnings tax would be imposed only upon HE since all of the taxable income of Plas-Tek is taxed currently to its shareholder under the provisions of Subchapter S. The balance sheet of HE at June 30, 1981, included $507,000 of securities on total assets of $828,000 and shows a ratio of current assets to current liabilities after excluding unpaid salary to shareholder of more than 12 to 1. Based upon those statistics, it is reasonable to assume that an accumulated earnings question would be raised upon examination.

EXHIBIT 7   (*concluded*)

If assessed, the accumulated earnings tax is calculated on an annual basis on the "accumulated taxable income" of the corporation. In simplified terms, the tax base is equal to the taxable income for the year less federal income taxes on income and any dividends paid for the year. Because HE paid out substantial salaries to its shareholder, the reported taxable income in the three years in question was relatively modest. Thus, tax for all three years would only amount to approximately $20,000. Of course, the Service could attempt to impose the tax on the income of the corporation after a substantial increase due to disallowed compensation deductions. If that were to happen, however, we believe a successful argument could be made that the excessive compensation should be treated as a constructive dividend to the shareholder, thus reducing the "accumulated income" tax base back to an amount approximately equal to the taxable income reported on the returns. Accordingly, the accumulated earnings tax issue does not appear to be especially troublesome.

Statute of Limitations

It was represented to us that the Internal Revenue Service has examined the returns of PTI through fiscal 1978. While it was stated that the examination resulted in a "no change" report, we have yet to see a copy of the letter. Returns for the three fiscal years since 1978 remain open under the statute of limitations.

While specific representations have not been made, we believe the companies followed the practice of filing returns on or before the original due date, without extension. On that basis, the normal three-year statute of limitations would run as follows:

	Fiscal Year Ending		
	1979	1980	1981
HE	9/15/82	9/15/83	9/15/84
Plas-Tek	11/15/82	11/15/83	11/15/84

Normally the statute of limitations is not a major consideration to a Subchapter S corporation, unless it has capital gains taxable at the corporate level or loses its qualification, since an adjustment to the corporation's income would be reflected as an assessment to its shareholders. While the matter is somewhat unclear, one case has held that an assessment may be made by reference to the statute as it applies to the shareholders, a point which should be considered in the case of fiscal year corporations.

We will be pleased to provide further services in this area if required.

Sincerely,

Case 3–3

Kirk Riedinger and Jamie Turner

Time had truly run out for Kirk Riedinger and Jamie Turner. They had spent almost two years pursuing acquisition opportunities, each time coming up short. Having now run out of money and investor patience, they finally had a deal they felt they could close. They wondered, however, if their excitement and the time pressures they faced were pushing them into an ill-considered decision.

It was April of 1987, and Kirk and Jamie were attempting to purchase the St. Louis Institute of Technology, a career training center. However, their search effort was out of money and more would be needed immediately to fund expenses prior to a closing. Furthermore, it was not clear that they could develop a proposal that would both attract investors and leave them with a meaningful equity interest.

While they wanted desperately to fulfill their dream of becoming owners of a business, Kirk and Jamie worried that the pressure of knowing that this might be their last chance was forcing them into an expensive deal that would not fit the objectives they had outlined for themselves two years ago.

BACKGROUND

Kirk Riedinger and Jamie Turner met during their fraternity days at Stanford University. Upon graduation in 1980, Kirk went to work for Burroughs Computer as an account manager while Jamie, who graduated in 1981, joined Lehman Brothers as a corporate analyst. In

---

This case was prepared by David M. Dodson under the supervision of H. I. Grousbeck, Lecturer, Stanford University Graduate School of Business.

1983, their paths crossed again at the Harvard Business School (Exhibit 1).

During the second year of the MBA program, Kirk became frustrated with the notion of going to work for a large, traditional company. He had always wanted to run his own business and had dreamed of building a network of companies. At Harvard, he became acquainted with Professor Forbes, a lecturer in the New Ventures class, who encouraged Kirk to look into buying an existing company.

In April 1985, Kirk and his roommate Jamie began talking about joining forces and looking for a business to buy. They both wanted to find a company that would serve as a base from which to launch other ventures. Kirk explained to Jamie, "We just need to get our foot in the door. If we can get one company off and running, nothing can stop us!" Kirk's infectious enthusiasm persuaded Jamie to join the adventure. The next day they ceremoniously called all the companies they had offers from and declined the opportunities. There would be no turning back now.

Their first step was to obtain financing to fund a search process, since neither had any appreciable assets. Kirk and Jamie estimated that a search would take between one and six months; however, Professor Forbes warned them that it might take a year or longer. While they remained convinced that they would have a deal within a few months, they set out to raise $80,000 for a search fund by selling $10,000 units in a search company.

GALENA CORPORATION

Jamie contacted Bill Briggs, a former Stanford rugby teammate and recent graduate of Harvard Law School, to draft a private placement memorandum. According to its terms, investors in Galena Corporation could purchase $10,000 units that would given them a proportionate right of first refusal on whatever deal Galena eventually undertook. For instance, if someone purchased one unit for $10,000, that investor would hold a right of first refusal on 12.5 percent ($10,000 ÷ $80,000) of the eventual equity available to outside investors.

In addition, investors would receive, for no further consideration, an equity position in the acquired company equal to the amount invested in Galena. This would occur regardless of whether or not an investor decided to make a further commitment to the eventual deal. Jamie and Kirk told each investor that they expected the eventual acquisition would require $800,000 to $1 million in investor funds. They were careful only to accept individuals capable of eventually investing at least $100,000 apiece.

Kirk and Jamie set up Galena as the general partner of a limited partnership, providing the limited partners with immediate tax write-offs. Galena would conduct a search for 12 months, after which, if no deal had been consumated, Kirk and Jamie would be free to pursue alternative careers or fund a new search effort.

To fund Galena, Kirk and Jamie made a list of all the potential investors they knew. Jamie suggested that they list the names in order of each investor's likelihood of investing and start with the least likely. In this way, "We can crawl up the learning curve on the investors we probably won't get anyway, then hit the heavy hitters with both guns loaded." Kirk disagreed, arguing that they should conserve time by going after the most promising investors first. They both had doubts as to the likelihood of raising money for a search fund, and by starting at the top they could find out quickly if they might reasonably hope to raise the funds. In the end, they agreed upon this strategy.

The prospect list contained a wide variety of personal contacts including entrepreneurs, venture capital firms, classmates, and relatives. Initially they found the process slow, with no one willing to write the first check. "It seemed as if everyone was waiting for the other person to commit first," Jamie recalled.

Eventually, they persuaded a classmate from HBS, Bill Roberts, to act as the lead investor. "Having a lead investor made all the difference—from that point on the other investors felt comfortable with the deal," observed Kirk.

With Roberts' lead, they attracted an additional $70,000 by selling seven units to six additional investors:

- *Don Bolden*—Father of a classmate from Stanford and owner of a Portland, Oregon, advertising firm.
- *Rajiv Singh*—A venture capitalist Jamie knew from Montreal who specialized in financial institutions.
- *Charles Donovan*—An entrepreneur and friend of Jamie's who owned a Montreal manufacturing company.
- *Mike Foster*—A real estate developer in the Boston area whom Kirk and Jamie had met via the network they set up.
- *Millard Alexander*—An entrepreneur and friend of Kirk's who owned an airplane leasing company in the Boston area.
- *William Turner*—Jamie's father.

Originally Jamie and Kirk felt that they both should work in part-time jobs. However, through the counseling of Professor Forbes, they realized that the search process would require at least one of them to devote a full-time effort to the search. Thus, Kirk worked exclusively for Galena while Jamie took a job as a casewriter at Harvard and remained off the Galena payroll. To supplement his income, Kirk planned to do some outside consulting.

Next, they put together a brief introduction to Galena and a statement of the criteria they intended to use in the search (Exhibit 2). The criteria specified a manufacturer or distributor in a low/no-tech industry with a dominant share of a niche market. The company would have to exhibit the potential for significant growth either through an increase in sales of the core business or as a base for future acquisitions. They preferred an undermanaged situation that would offer opportunities to improve upon the existing business. They looked for a profitable company with about $5 to $40 million in sales. They would not consider start-up businesses, turnarounds, ones in the oil and gas exploration business, real estate, highly regulated industries, or financial institutions.

To enhance their image in the eyes of investors and potential sellers, they rented shared office space in the Boston area and printed stationery and cards. Finally, to get into the deal flow, Kirk and Jamie created lists of business and professional people they knew. They believed that deals would come from the following: the Galena investor group; business brokers; professionals who had access to business opportunities (e.g., attorneys, CPAs, bankers); and personal contacts acquired and cultivated over time.

Generally, it proved unrealistic to expect business brokers to take the initiative of calling back with a deal, so Kirk and Jamie periodically contacted them by telephone. Each week they would set a goal of calling a specific number of brokers. They always tried to offer some information that they felt the brokers could use in order to improve the chances of receiving good leads. In spite of frequent follow-up, it became apparent early in the process that brokers reserved the best opportunities for their prior customers or cronies, while passing the "dirt deals" on to Kirk and Jamie.

MAXIM'S SCHOOLS

By fall, they had evaluated approximately 30 companies; however, none had yet met their criteria. Then, through one of Jamie's contacts, they heard about a chain of cosmetology schools in San Diego called Maxim's Schools. Such cosmetology schools taught hair design, manicure, skin care, and makeup application. Instruction occurred primarily in clinics where students practiced on actual patrons and in labs where they worked with mannequins.

While Kirk and Jamie had no interest in cosmetology, they went to have a look—principally as a courtesy to Jamie's friend. To their surprise the deal appeared much more attractive than anticipated. The industry met many of their criteria: an undermanaged situation, profitable results, and high growth potential in a no-tech industry.

Kirk called Professor Forbes and told him that they found "The Deal" and to expect preliminary documentation within a few weeks. However, as the negotiations wore on, the Galena partners soon confronted the harsh reality of deal making. "We really had no idea how long it would take nor how difficult it would be to reach the point of signing a letter of intent," Jamie noted. By December, the transaction had fallen through due to the sellers' inflexibility on price and Jamie and Kirk's growing skepticism regarding the seller's integrity. With the holidays approaching and the two men in need of a break, Kirk went off to Seattle, and Jamie returned to Montreal.

MORE DEALS

While the San Diego deal proved disappointing, Kirk and Jamie had "smelled blood." They now knew that getting into business would take longer than they had anticipated, however, and would require considerably more work. They rekindled many of the contacts they had abandoned while looking at Maxim's Schools and attempted to reactivate previous leads. During this time they examined a number of potential opportunities:

— SportsPro, Inc. consisted of a chain of running apparel stores located in the New England area. While the company had the potential for profitable growth, Kirk and Jamie questioned whether they had the "eye" needed for a fashion-dependent industry.

— Photo Supplies distributed photocopy supplies through telemarketing. Despite being the best-priced deal they saw, they were concerned over the ethics of the seller and industry practices.

— Weston Awning manufactured awnings for commercial storefronts. Unlike the previous companies, Kirk and Jamie found the manufacturing process simple, and the product attractive. However, the process was best suited to regional production, and they wondered whether they could expand the business on a national scale. In addition, the seller wanted a very high price for the company.

— Cohen Industries manufactured electric and gas stoves in New York. The company competed with corporations such as Frigidaire and Magic Chef. As Kirk and Jamie looked more closely at the opportunity, they found that profitability depended on cost shaving, at which the owner, Elon Cohen, was a master. They questioned whether they could improve on Cohen's cost controls, and the company currently scratched out only a modest profit.

Although Kirk and Jamie evaluated each of these opportunities carefully, their growing frustration and their experience with Maxim's led them back to the proprietary schools area.

THE PROPRIETARY SCHOOL INDUSTRY

The vocational school industry included all schools that provided postsecondary education for training in a specific trade or profession, both public (supported through tax dollars) and private—proprietary—schools. Of the 1.7 million students enrolled in vocational schools in 1985, 72 percent attended proprietary schools. Programs offered at the schools fell into three main categories: trade programs (41 percent), cosmetology and barber programs (36 percent), and business and secretarial programs (21 percent). Typically, a large percentage of students at such schools was financed by various government grants and loans.

In 1985 over 6,000 resident (noncorrespondent) schools existed in the United States. The average enrollment of a school was 200; however, it varied dramatically according to the program. Business and secretarial programs maintained the highest average enrollment with 314, followed by trade schools with 157, and cosmetology and barber schools with only 62. While the industry in general remained highly fragmented, several companies had grown through acquisition and internal growth (Exhibit 3). CareerCom, for instance, grew substantially from 1983 to 1986 by acquiring 10 sites and opening 25 new sites. During this time the company's revenues grew from $15.4 million to $37.7 million. The larger companies generally followed one of two possible growth strategies. The first, used by MacMillan, was to purchase strong, well-run schools and rely on the existing management to incrementally improve earnings. The second strategy involved purchasing single-program schools exhibiting marginal or poor performance. New management would then build a "super-school" by expanding the programs offered and improving the performance of the existing program.

On average, the industry earned an aftertax return on book assets of 14 percent, with pretax margins of 10–20 percent. However, many of the larger companies achieved margins of 20 percent (Exhibit 3). Still, roughly one school in four lost money in 1986.

Most observers felt that private vocational (proprietary) education compared favorably to that at public vocational schools. A common benchmark used to rate programs was the completion rate, which referred to the percentage of entering students who actually graduated from the program. While public schools had an average completion rate of 40 percent, proprietary schools enjoyed a 60 percent completion rate. This occurred despite the fact that proprietary schools charged significantly more for tuition. Tuition at proprietary schools ranged from $1,000 up to $9,000, while many public programs were offered at little or no charge to the student. Additionally, studies indicated that proprietary schools educated students at a lower cost per student than did public schools. As a result, some observers believed that state and local governments would encourage the future growth of proprietary schools over public schools.

Among proprietary schools, the competition for students could be very intense. As a fixed-cost business, small changes in student enrollments greatly influenced the bottom line. As one executive put it, "It's simple; I have three priorities: marketing, marketing, and more marketing."

BRADLEY'S ACADEMIES OF BEAUTY

While Jamie and Kirk continued to look at a wide variety of businesses, they found themselves concentrating on cosmetology. In an effort to uncover opportunities in that industry, during January of 1986 they assembled a list of 30 cosmetology schools that met their basic criteria for acquisition (size, geography, programs offered). They then proceeded to write to each company, introducing Galena and promising to follow up by telephone (Exhibit 4). One such letter was sent to a promising company in St. Louis, Missouri, called Bradley's Academies. Marilyn Bradley, CEO of Bradley's, had founded the first academy in 1977 in St. Louis. Since that time she had expanded the company to 19 schools in St. Louis and Tucson having combined revenues of $3.5 million (Exhibit 5).

Since they had previously evaluated Maxim's Schools, Jamie and Kirk were able to analyze this opportunity quickly and confidently. By late February they had signed an initial letter of intent to acquire Bradley's Academies. They moved into an apartment in St. Louis, cut off contact with other leads they had been pursuing, and began the difficult task of putting together a purchase and sale agreement.

However, while Kirk and Jamie could analyze the company quickly, they lacked experience in closing a deal, and by June 1 they had still not signed a definitive purchase agreement. During this period, Ms. Bradley, who was prone to irrational behavior, grew impatient with Galena's "analysis paralysis." When Jamie and Kirk finally presented her with a 30-page purchase document steeped in legalese, it "hit her like a sledgehammer." However, in spite of Bradley's shock, they eventually reached agreement to purchase the company (Exhibit 6).

On June 9, 1986, Kirk and Jamie circulated a private offering memorandum to the investors in Galena. They calculated that $1.4

million would be needed: $1 million for a down payment and $400,000 for working capital. They offered eight investment units, each consisting of $50,000 of equity and $125,000 of five-year, 12 percent subordinated debt. Each original share in Galena had afforded the investor a right to purchase an equal share of the equity and debt that Kirk and Jamie were offering investors. Kirk and Jamie were offering 60 percent of the equity to investors on the terms outlined above; each unit in Galena carried the right to purchase 7.5 percent of the equity in Bradley's (60% ÷ 8 units). If a Galena investor chose not to invest, he automatically received .405 percent[1] of the total stock in Bradley's.

Kirk and Jamie then devised a formula to increase the attractiveness of the subordinated debt by agreeing to tie the vesting of their own stock to the repayment of the subordinated debentures. If all the notes were paid off in five years, Jamie and Kirk would own 40 percent, and the investors 60 percent, of the company. If the subordinated debt was not fully repaid in five years, Kirk and Jamie's ownership would be reduced proportionately; however, 12 percent of their stock would be vested at the time of the transaction.

While the Galena investors had not anticipated the acquisition of a cosmetology school, Kirk and Jamie convinced all but one of them to invest. They ended up with commitments for full units from four of the investors and for partial units from two of the investors. This left them roughly $375,000 short. As a result, they attempted to attract two additional individuals on the same terms as the Galena investors. Within a few weeks Kirk and Jamie were able to obtain verbal commitments from a Boston venture capitalist and from a friend.

After searching for a full year, and examining almost 150 companies, things had finally come together.

ACCREDITATION PROBLEMS

On the morning of July 17, 1986, just two weeks before the scheduled closing, Kirk received a call from Marilyn Bradley informing him that Bradley's Academies's accreditation had been suspended, leaving the company ineligible for federal financial student aid—its lifeblood. Without accreditation the company had little value, since more than 90 percent of the students received federal aid.

Kirk and Jamie had known that Bradley had responded earlier in the year to an inquiry by NACCAS (National Accrediting Commission of Cosmetology Arts & Sciences) regarding an incident in 1984. During

---

[1]$10,000 investment in Galena, divided by the total money raised ($80,000 for Galena + $1,400,000 for Bradley's = $1,480,000), multiplied by the amount of equity available to investors in the Bradley's deal (60 percent).

that incident, the FBI had entered Bradley's office and confiscated records suggesting that Bradley's Inc. had defrauded the federal government (Exhibit 7). Kirk and Jamie had previously assumed that the inquiry was routine, since Bradley had corrected the problem and the Department of Education (the overseer of NACCAS) had accepted those changes.

July 17 became "the worst day of our lives," Kirk and Jamie recalled. They had accumulated over $20,000 in unpaid bills (mostly legal, accounting, and travel), and the $80,000 search pool was completely exhausted. Only the week before, they had given themselves a going-away party in Boston attended by many of their friends and investors. Now they were forced to contemplate the tarnish to their credibility that would result from telling their investors that the deal had caved in.

At this point they considered three options: (1) to walk away from the transaction and return to traditional careers; (2) to raise a second fund to search for a new opportunity while helping Bradley with an appeal, in consideration for a purchase option on her company at a lesser price; (3) to work for Bradley's Inc. until approval of the appeal, at which time they would complete the deal. Ultimately, they decided upon the second option.

CHELAN CORPORATION

Since Kirk and Jamie would now be attempting to raise money in part from investors who had not invested in Galena, they chose to form a new corporation, Chelan. Chelan consisted of nine $7,000 units under terms identical to Galena; however, the search commitment for Chelan would last only 9 months as opposed to Galena's 12-month term. Since the 12-month obligation to Galena had expired, Kirk and Jamie had no legal requirement to include the units invested in Galena in a Chelan deal. However, they felt a moral obligation to their original investors, and therefore extended the terms of their commitment to Galena investors for an additional nine months, leaving Jamie and Kirk with obligations to both Galena and Chelan investors.

Kirk and Jamie had far less trouble obtaining the commitments to Chelan than they had anticipated. Within three days they raised the full $63,000. Every one of the investors who had committed to investing in Bradley's had agreed to invest in Chelan.

After reviewing the documentation that Bradley had assembled for the NACCAS hearing, Kirk and Jamie felt confident that a solidly prepared appeal could restore Bradley's accreditation. Following several meetings with legal counsel, they completed the 104-page appeal on August 22, just in time for Federal Express to deliver it by overnight mail. Now they could only wait for the NACCAS oral hearing date. They expected a final decision before the end of 1986. While feeling confident about the outcome of the appeal, Jamie and Kirk nevertheless continued to search for other acquisitions from their original Boston base.

On December 13, NACCAS informed Bradley that it would be continuing the appeal process for an additional six months. With the limited cash position in Chelan, Jamie and Kirk could not afford to wait for the appeal decision; they had to look for an alternate deal.

"That began what Jamie and I called the 'Bleak Winter Months,' " Kirk recalled. With only $38,000 left and few leads, they had to resume the search process from scratch. They decided to reevaluate their search strategy, which had focused on proprietary schools, and to consider a more opportunistic approach. Jamie investigated a model airplane manufacturer while Kirk looked into franchise opportunities such as fast foods and quick lube automotive shops. Reflecting on the broad range of deals they began considering, Jamie commented, "We had a 'deal-at-all-costs' mentality—anything was fair game—because in five months we would run out of money."

Several months later, pursuing a contact they had cultivated since the Bradley's transaction, they had lunch with Mr. Joe Miles, part owner and vice president of the St. Louis Institute of Technology (SIT). Miles had served as an informal advisor to Kirk and Jamie while they had pursued Bradley's. They explained to Miles how things with Bradley had developed and asked Miles if he might offer some suggestions about getting back into the proprietary school deal flow. Miles listened carefully but offered few suggestions or comments; Kirk and Jamie felt that a dead end was developing.

As they got up to leave, Miles put his arm on Kirk's shoulder and said, "Why don't you buy our company?"

Kirk and Jamie were ecstatic. They recalled that during the negotiations with Bradley's they had commented to each other on how someday they would like Bradley's to operate as smoothly as SIT. Now they had a chance to own SIT. Analyzing their situation, they knew that they had only 12 weeks before Chelan would run out of funds. After several rounds of negotiations with Joe Miles and his partner, Chelan signed a letter of intent to purchase SIT. Kirk and Jamie packed their bags and moved back to St. Louis, leasing an apartment in the same complex they had lived in when they were evaluating the Bradley's opportunity.

THE ST. LOUIS INSTITUTE OF TECHNOLOGY

St. Louis Institute of Technology operated a proprietary career training center. The school offered five comprehensive programs:

Electronics Technology; Automotive Technology; Drafting; Surveying and Mapping; and Heating, Air Conditioning, and Refrigeration Technology. The school emphasized hands-on training and practical applications. SIT offered two curriculum choices in each specialty. Associate degree programs required 18 months to complete, and tuition averaged $9,645. SIT enrolled 420 students in degree programs.

SIT also offered diploma programs lasting from six to nine months, with tuition averaging $4,425, in which about 180 students were registered. In addition to tuition, students paid for books, tools, supplies, lab fees, and a registration fee. The total cost for these items ranged from $350 to $1,000, depending on the particular course of study. For various reasons, some students who enrolled in a program did not complete the program. SIT's completion rate averaged about 70 percent.

Over the past 18 years, there had been a substantial increase in the amount of financial aid available under various federal programs for students attending college. These programs funded almost 70 percent of the tuition for a majority of SIT's students. Accordingly, like many colleges and other career schools, SIT was heavily dependent on the continued availability of federal educational monies.

The company provided unsecured tuition loans to students who were not eligible to receive government student financial aid sufficient to cover the full cost of attendance. Historically, about 80 percent of the students received some funds from this source. However, scheduled increases in the availability of federal funds were expected to reduce this proportion to 30–35 percent. SIT successfully collected 99 percent of its loans prior to graduation. The school was accredited through the National Association of Trade and Technical Schools (NATTS) and enjoyed good standing. The accreditation process occurred every five years, and SIT's license would not be up for renewal until 1990 (although a change in ownership would trigger a review process).

Classes were scheduled between the hours of 6 A.M. and 10 P.M. Monday through Thursday, and between 7 A.M. and 5 P.M. on Saturday. Laboratories and classrooms were open for extra assistance on Friday from 8 A.M. to 12 noon. Individual class sizes ranged from 10 to 50 students, depending on the nature of the class and the subject being offered. Supervised laboratories operated with an approximate ratio of one instructor per 20 students.

In addition to Joe Miles, SIT employed three key people (Exhibit 8): Ross Wilkens, co-owner and president; Spence Kendrick, executive director; and Nathan Stevenson, vice president of administration and controller. Both Wilkens and Miles had been absentee owners, with Miles spending half his time in Fiji. Kirk and Jamie anticipated that Wilkens and Miles would retire as employees of SIT, but perhaps remain active as advisors or board members. Kendrick, however, was a key individual in the organization, and Jamie and Kirk considered his retention critical to the success of the deal. SIT employed 52 other full-time employees and 21 part-time personnel. No one at SIT belonged to a labor union, and Kirk and Jamie believed that labor relations were favorable.

Successful student recruitment at proprietary schools depended on a number of factors: a school's educational reputation, its job placement record, the frequency and scheduling of classes, its location, and the availability of governmental student financial aid. SIT divided responsibility for student recruitment between outside and inside sales forces. Outside sales people were responsible for recruiting students throughout the state of Missouri. Generally, they contacted prospective students through presentations made at high schools. The inside sales force was located at the school and focused on recruiting students through telephone marketing programs as well as local television, radio, and newspaper advertising. All sales representatives were paid a commission based on successful student enrollment and the subsequent retention of the student.

Total revenues had grown consistently, increasing from $3.1 million in 1984 to $3.5 million in the fiscal year ending September 30, 1986. Pretax income had varied considerably over the last three and a half years, and a loss was recorded in 1985 (Exhibit 9). Kirk and Jamie anticipated purchasing the assets and assuming the liabilities of SIT, with some minor adjustments (Exhibit 9). They believed that management had depressed income in order to reduce tax liability. Looking at industry margins, they felt that SIT should have attained pretax margins of 15–20 percent. One way that SIT had reduced its reported income was by paying management fees to a company owned by Miles and Wilkens. Jamie and Kirk also noticed that loans to School Management Inc. and Tool Box Inc. (companies owned by Miles and Wilkens) had been "written off" as bad debts.

By adding back noncash charges, plus other items believed to be structured solely to reduce income, Jamie and Kirk arrived at a more realistic view of the company's cash flow. They were able to show an average of almost $500,000 of pretax cash flow over the past three years and to project $800,000 for fiscal 1987 (Exhibit 10). However, this cash flow still left historical margins below industry benchmarks. Had Kirk and Jamie continued to underestimate income? Was something else embedded in the numbers that they were missing?

Using both the historical data from SIT and the industry data they could assemble, Kirk and Jamie projected the finances of the company over the next eight years (Exhibit 11). Beyond the attractiveness of the financial forecast, they believed that this venture had enormous growth potential. Many of the schools in this highly fragmented industry were undermanaged. Thus, the prospects for expansion by acquisition were good. Ten companies they identified as having gone public currently traded at aftertax price-earnings multiples of up to 88, with many trading in the low 20s (Exhibit 3). Kirk and Jamie felt that these companies were trading at multiples that were unrealistically high. They felt that an EBIT multiple of 8 was a fairer estimate of value over the longer term, but felt comfortable paying a somewhat higher multiple for SIT because of what they believed to be its superior growth prospects.

Still, there were problems. They worried about the dependence they would have on government funds; after all, they noted in their initial strategy that they were not interested in highly-regulated industries. They also would have to re-apply for accreditation, due to the proposed change in ownership. While prospects for accreditation were excellent (SIT had an exemplary reputation and Wilkins sat on the NATTS Accreditation Board), their experience with Bradley's had left them apprehensive.

The two had found negotiations with Miles and Wilkens frustrating. The sellers exacerbated the process by establishing different sets of demands as preconditions to an agreement. Kirk and Jamie would negotiate specific terms with Miles, only to find some of these terms unacceptable to Williams. This technique ratcheted up the concessions Kirk and Jamie were forced to make. Ultimately, however, they agreed on the following terms (see Exhibit 12):

— $1 million cash at closing.

— A seven-year term loan of $1,838,000 with an interest rate of 10 percent.

— A noncompete payment of $265,000 (total to both sellers) for the seven year term of the loan. Kirk and Jamie calculated that the noncompete payments had a present value at 15 percent of $1.1 million.

Therefore, they believed that they were paying $3,595,000 for the business.

The pace of negotiations had left them little time to raise the required equity from their investors. Kirk and Jamie calculated that they would need roughly $1.6 million: $1 million to pay the sellers at closing, and $600,000 for working capital and closing costs. They had developed a preliminary cut at a deal they would offer their investors:

— The $1,600,000 would be raised by selling 9 units for $177,777 each.

— Each unit would consist of $111,111 of debt and $66,666 of equity.

— In total then, they would raise $1 million in debt and $600,000 in equity.

— The debt would carry a 12 percent interest rate, but no principal payments would be due during the first eight years of operations.

Kirk and Jamie had run a set of pro forma financials that reflected these assumptions regarding both seller and investor financing (Exhibit 11). They had not yet decided, however, on what portion of the total equity they should offer to each investor. Kirk and Jamie also wondered how to approach investors with a request for twice the amount of funds they had indicated to investors that they would require. They also needed to assume an existing $170,000 bank loan, and they were having trouble interesting banks in lending these funds. After making eight bank presentations, they had not been able to obtain a loan commitment.

Kirk and Jamie had other problems as well. The Chelan bank balance stood at $342, and they had run up unpaid bills of about $18,000. Further, they calculated that it should cost them $25,000 to $30,000 in additional expenses to get to the point of closing. Where would they get the $45,000 they needed? As they contemplated the work that remained, they had several concerns:

— Were they burdening the business with an unreasonable amount of debt? What would happen if enrollments fell by 10 percent or more?

— Their original plans had been to purchase a firm that would become the vehicle for creating a large network of companies. Would SIT form a suitable base for attaining those goals?

Kirk and Jamie looked at each other asking the same question: "Is this really what we set out to accomplish two years ago?"

EXHIBIT 1   Résumés

JAMES Z. TURNER

Business Address: Home Address:
Galena Corporation   37 Worcester Street
55 Wheeler Street   Apartment 3
Boston, Massachusetts 02138   Boston, Massachusetts 02118
(617) 492-2978   (617) 266-1084

*business
experience*

1985–Present   GALENA CORPORATION   CAMBRIDGE, MA
Treasurer and Co-Founder. Raised a blind pool of equity
capital. Designed and executed a search strategy to locate
an acquisition candidate.

summer 1984   SOLAR TURBINES INCORPORATED   SAN DIEGO, CA
First Line Supervisor. Supervised hourly workers in a
metal structures plant. Scheduled work assignments and
coordinated work flow with production control. Handled
plant shipping and receiving responsibilities. Extensively
involved with customer inspectors and in-house
engineering. Counseled workers on discipline, productivity,
safety, and quality issues. Worked continuously on union
relations and actively participated in the selling of a new
general labor agreement.

1981–1983   LEHMAN BROTHERS
KUHN LOEB INCORPORATED   NEW YORK, NY
1982–1983   **Corporate Analyst, Financing Department.** Member of
new capital markets group linking Corporate Finance with
trading floor operations. Actively involved in new product
development, advised clients on debt and equity market
movements and transactions, helped form shelf registration
bids, automated and performed financial analysis for debt
and equity offerings, and specialized in selling Lehman's
services to the banking industry.

1981–1982   **Corporate Analyst, Corporate Finance.** Generalist on
debt and equity offerings. Assisted in merger fairness
opinions, performed dividend and stock repurchase
analyses, and developed an export finance model.

summer 1980   J. HENRY SCHROEDER
BANK AND TRUST COMPANY   NEW YORK, NY
Summer intern in Stock Transfer department. Analyzed
automation needs and recommended computer equipment
purchases. Redesigned existing work and information flow
patterns to yield higher worker productivity.

EXHIBIT 1   *(continued)*

1977–1979	Summer jobs included cannery work and logging in Alaska, and engine room and deck positions on Great Lakes freighters.

education
1983–1985   HARVARD GRADUATE SCHOOL
OF BUSINESS ADMINISTRATION   BOSTON, MA
Received Master in Business Administration in June 1985. Awarded First-Year Honors. General management curriculum with second-year electives in production and finance. Selected to tutor Human Resource Management and Business, Government, and The International Economy. Member of Canadian, Venture Capital, Finance, and Small Business Clubs. Captain of Rugby Club.

1977–1981   STANFORD UNIVERSITY   STANFORD, CA
Received Bachelor of Science degree in Industrial Engineering. Member of Stanford Rugby Club. Freshman crew. Represented Zeta Psi on Inter-Fraternity Council.

personal
background   Raised in Montreal. Fluent in French with good knowledge of German and Spanish. Have traveled extensively in Europe, Africa, and North America. Interests include squash, tennis, skiing, hiking, theatre, and reading. Single, willing to relocate.

references   Available upon request.

October 1985

EXHIBIT 1   (*continued*)

KIRK THOMAS RIEDINGER

Business Address:	Home Address:
Galena Corporation	37 Worcester Street
55 Wheeler Street	Apartment 3
Boston, Massachusetts 02138	Boston, Massachusetts 02118
(617) 492-2978	(617) 266-1084

business experience

1985–Present GALENA CORPORATION   CAMBRIDGE, MA
President and Co-Founder. Raised a blind pool of equity capital. Designed and executed a search strategy to locate an acquisition candidate.

summer 1984 MENTOR GRAPHICS CORPORATION   BEAVERTON, OR
Project Manager. Managed a cross-functional task force. Developed a process to implement direct sourcing and integration of computer peripheral devices. This project will increase margins 5–10 percent.

Researched shipping alternatives and handling requirements for computer equipment. Identified the optimum transport mode and carrier to minimize cost at different volumes.

Planned office layout for a new building under construction. Supervised the production of architectural, electrical, and facility blueprints.

1981–1983 CRESAP, MCCORMICK & PAGET SAN FRANCISCO, CA
SYDNEY, AUSTRALIA

1982–1983 **Management Consultant.** Evaluated the station operations of a major international airline. Formulated comprehensive recommendations to improve the efficiency and effectiveness of the operations. Planned and managed the implementation of these recommendations which resulted in annual savings of $1 million.

1981–1982 Developed and implemented an integrated management system for a small regional airline. Prepared a follow-up report detailing the marketing and operational impact of this system and presented the findings to top management.

Assessed the financial and organizational implications of relocating the Nevada School of Medicine. Prepared statistical models to quantify the effects of relocations and summarized findings in a report to the Board of Regents.

Developed sales force incentive compensation plan for a start-up firm in the construction industry.

EXHIBIT 1 *(concluded)*

1980–1981   BURROUGHS CORPORATION   SAN FRANCISCO, CA
Account Manager. Sold computer systems to distributors.
Developed sales proposals, performed equipment
demonstrations, and coordinated computer installations.

education
1983–1985   HARVARD GRADUATE SCHOOL
OF BUSINESS ADMINISTRATION   BOSTON, MA
Received Master in Business Administration in June 1985.
General management curriculum with second year
electives in marketing and operations. Member of
Marketing and Small Business Clubs.

1977–1980   STANFORD UNIVERSITY   STANFORD, CA
Received Bachelor of Arts degree With Distinction
International Relations. Member of Zeta Psi fraternity.
Participated in Overseas Studies Program, Tours, France.

1976–1977   CLAREMONT MEN'S COLLEGE   CLAREMONT, CA

personal   Have traveled extensively in Europe, East Asia, and
Australia. Interest include skiing, hiking, squash, film, and
literature.

references   Available upon request.

October 1985

EXHIBIT 2   Acquisition Specifications

Galena Corporation
November 1985

Galena Corporation, a Massachusetts corporation, has been formed
to conduct an active search for an ongoing business to acquire and operate. The principal officers of Galena Corporation are Kirk Riedinger and
James Turner, president and treasurer, respectively.

Galena Corporation represents a significant pool of equity capital
(low seven figures) to be used in acquiring an existing business. The Corporation is located in the Boston area, and the search will be
concentrated in the northeastern United States. However, acquisition candidates that are located outside that geographic region will be considered.

The ideal acquisition candidate is a manufacturer of a product with
little or no technical content. The company has a significant share of a
small market, unrealized growth potential, and leverageable assets. It is
profitable. A more complete list of acquisition criteria is presented on the
attached Specification Sheet.

EXHIBIT 2 *(concluded)*

SPECIFICATIONS FOR PURCHASING A BUSINESS

The Galena Corporation: James Turner and Kirk Riedinger wish to acquire and operate an ongoing business that includes but is not limited to the criteria listed below. Turner and Riedinger will purchase the company outright or buy a controlling interest, and will provide management.

GENERAL CRITERIA

— Manufacturer.
— Product with little or no technical content.
— Dominant share of a small market niche.
— Unrealized growth potential.
— Breaking even or profitable.
— Leverageable assets.

SIZE

— $5 to $40 million in sales.

GEOGRAPHIC PREFERENCE

— None.

WILL ALSO CONSIDER

— Distribution and service businesses that:

  • offer growth potential.
  • serve distinct market segments.

WILL NOT CONSIDER

— Start-up businesses.
— Highly regulated industries.
— Oil and gas exploration.
— Real estate.
— Financial institutions.

EXHIBIT 3   Financial Statistics on Publicly Held Proprietary Schools

Rapidly Growing Firms in the Proprietary Schools Industry

	Revenue *(in thousands of dollars)*			
	1983	*1984*	*1985*	*1986*
National Education Corp.	$158,000	$174,000	$183,000	$247,000
DeVry	132,000	147,000	148,000	154,000
MacMillan	90,000	106,000	116,000	159,000
CareerCom Corp.	15,000	23,000	32,000	38,000
United Educational & Software	14,000	19,000	23,000	25,000

Publicly Held Proprietary Schools

	Exchange	*Symbol*	*P/E*	*EBIT Multiple*
Bell & Howell Co. (DeVry division)	NYSE	BHW	15	9.2
MacMillan Inc. (instruction division)	NYSE	MLL	22	11.8
National Education Corp.	NYSE	NEC	23	12.4
Wilfred American Educational Corp.	NYSE	WAE	10	6.8
CareerCom Corp.	OTC	CRCM	28	17.4
National Technical Systems	OTC	NTSC	6	4.0
United Education & Software	OTC	UESS	19	11.8
Programming & Systems, Inc.	OTC	PSYS	16	9.9
Sandy Corp.	AMEX	D.SXS	88	50.2
Advanced Systems, Inc.	NYSE	ASY	35	20.4

Pretax Profit Margins of Publicly Traded Proprietary Schools

	Pretax Margins	
	1986	*1985*
Advanced Systems, Inc.	19%	20%
Wilfred American Educational Corp.	20	25
Programming & Systems, Inc.	21	21
National Education Corp.	10	10
DeVry	10	10
Katherine Gibbs	11	11

EXHIBIT 4   Search Letter

February 22, 1986

CONFIDENTIAL

Ms. Lisbeth Massei
President
Massei School
1810-A Ludeman Lane
Fontana, California 93030

Dear Ms. Massei:

Prior to calling you within the next few days, I would like to briefly profile our investment group. It is my intent to explore with you the possible acquisition of Massei School by our company. Our preliminary research indicates the possibility of structuring a transaction beneficial to the ongoing corporation, the company's shareholders, and management.

Galena Corporation represents a significant pool of equity capital to be used in a single acquisition. The principal officers of Galena are James Turner and myself. Since we are interested in acquiring only successful operations, it is our policy to maintain the company's identity, basic management team, and method of operation. Key managers will be encouraged to remain with the company and participate in the ongoing organization.

I plan to call you in the near future to discuss the pros and cons of a possible sale. I look forward to talking with you soon.

Sincerely,

Kirk Riedinger

KTR:hig

EXHIBIT 5   Bradley's Financials

Bradley's Academies
Summary Profit & Loss Statements
(\$US thousands)

	1986*	1985	1984	1983†
Sales				
Tuition	2,126	2,019	2,069	2,081
Clinic	1,150	1,208	1,284	1,362
Other	118	82	93	97
Total sales	3,394	3,309	3,446	3,540
Operating costs				
Cost retail sales	20	61	80	70
Cost services	114	104	94	161
Kit costs	54	125	85	30
Salaries and benefits	836	760	743	733
Marketing	88	101	115	71
Rent, property taxes	586	484	398	357
Utilities	128	132	134	137
Other	316	289	281	424
Total operating costs	2,142	2,056	1,930	1,983
Depreciation/amortization	110	136	108	99
Operating income	1,142	1,117	1,408	1,458
Overhead (est. @ 22%)	747	728	758	779
EBIT	395	389	650	679

*The current fiscal year ends 9/30. The 1986 numbers are annualized from half year data. Seasonality is minimal.
†The 1983 numbers are annualized from seven-month numbers because the Tucson acquisition was effective 03/01/83.

EXHIBIT 6   Bradley's Acquisition Financial Structure

Bradley's Academies
Proposed Purchase Price Structure

Year	Down Payment	Principal Repayment	Noncompetition Agreement	Seller's Salary
0	$1,000,000	$ 0	$ 0	$60,000
1	0	0	120,000	0
2	0	80,000	120,000	0
3	0	130,000	120,000	0
4	0	280,000	120,000	0
5	0	330,000	120,000	0
6	0	380,000	120,000	0
7	0	500,000	60,000	0
Total	1,000,000	1,700,000*	780,000	60,000

*This figure assumes a downward adjustment for an estimated tax recapture of $200,000. The actual tax recapture figure will be determined prior to the sale by an independent auditor and the amount of principal repayment will be adjusted downward accordingly.

EXHIBIT 7   Bradley's Accreditation Notice

National Accrediting Commission of Cosmetology Arts & Sciences

Ms. Marilyn Bradley
Bradley's Academies of Beauty
4785 Venturi Lane, Suite 27
St. Louis, MO 62734

CERTIFIED MAIL
RETURN RECEIPT REQUESTED

March 5, 1986

CONFIDENTIAL

Dear Ms. Bradley:

Please be advised that the National Accrediting Commission of Cosmetology Arts and Sciences ("NACCAS") has reviewed certain information concerning the guilty plea to a felony which Bradley's Inc. entered on October 7, 1985, on a charge concerning misconduct relating to federal student financial aid programs. After considering such information, an order has been issued directing Bradley's Inc. to show cause why the accreditation for the above referenced schools should not be withdrawn for:

1. Violation of Standard II Ownership, Management and Ethical Operation, Criteria 6 which states, "Management personnel are knowledgeable about applicable federal, state, and local laws and regulations which apply to the school."

EXHIBIT 7   (*concluded*)

2. Violation of Standard II Ownership, Management and Ethical Operation, Criteria 9a which states, "The management achieves its announced objectives through techniques that are ethical."
3. Violation of the NACCAS Ethics of Accreditation and Commission Membership which states:
   a. "Clear evidence of intent to deceive to misrepresent to the public, to students, to other institutions, or to the Commission and its representatives is cause for denial or withdrawal of candidacy or accreditation."
   b. "Institutions are required to be open and forthright on all matters in their relationships with the Commission and its representatives. Withholding of negative information is a serious matter and may jeopardize the institution's status with the Commission."
   c. "It is the obligation of every institution applying for accreditation, or reaccreditation, to provide the Commission with access to all parts of its operations, with due regard for the rights of individual privacy, and with complete and accurate information with respect to the institution's affairs, including reports of other accrediting, licensing, and auditing agencies. Failure to do so, or to make complete, accurate, and honest disclosure, is sufficient reason in and of itself to deny or revoke accreditation."

A response to this show cause order must be submitted to NACCAS within thirty (30) working days of your receipt of this letter. The Commission will review the response at its June 1986 meeting and may take any action it may deem necessary. You will be afforded an opportunity to appear before the Commission at that time to present oral arguments in response to the show cause order. If the school does not respond within thirty (30) days of receipt of this letter the Commission could act to withdraw the school's accreditation.

Very truly yours,

M. D. Lee, President NACCAS

MDL/kah

EXHIBIT 8   St. Louis Institute of Technology Employee Profile

---

Ross B. Wilkens is an owner and president of the St. Louis Institute of Technology. He has been in the private school business for 21 years. He is a current member of the National Association of Trade and Technical Schools (NATTS) and sits on the NATTS Accrediting Commission. He is a former president and board member of NATTS. He is also a former president, and has been twice selected as Outstanding Member, of the St. Louis Private School Association. It is anticipated that he will provide consulting and advisory services to the new owners on a part-time basis.

Joe E. Miles is an owner, vice president, and treasurer of the St. Louis Institute of Technology. He has been associated with a private school of business for 21 years. He served as part owner and president of Outlook College, Inc. until its sale in 1982. Prior to that he served as vice president of Westrend's Education Division. He also served as chairman of Irving Systems, Inc. (a chain of nine schools) until its sale in 1986. He is a past president and member of both the Association of Independent Colleges and Schools (AICS) and the St. Louis Private School Association. It is anticipated that he will provide consulting and advisory services to the new owners on a part-time basis.

Spence H. Kendrick has served as executive director of the St. Louis Institute of Technology since 1985. He has been associated with the private school business for 15 years. Prior to his current position he worked as midwest regional director for National Education Corporation. In this position, he had complete P&L responsibility for five multidiscipline schools located in three states. It is anticipated that he will remain as executive director of SIT.

Nathan R. Stevenson has served as vice president of administration and controller of the St. Louis Institute of Technology since 1982. He has been associated with the private school industry for seven years. He graduated from the University of St. Louis with a BS in accounting. He has also received a certificate in financial management from the University of St. Louis Graduate School of Public Management. It is anticipated that he will remain in his position as vice president of administration and controller of SIT.

EXHIBIT 9   St. Louis Institute of Technology Financials

St. Louis Institute of Technology
Summary Profit and Loss Statements
(in thousands of dollars)

	Audited			6 mo.	Annual
	1984	*1985*	*1986*	*1987*	*1987**
Total revenues	3,066	3,388	3,491	2,040	3,955
Operating expenses					
Administrative	819	857	956	520	1,032
Occupancy	353	399	566	286	566
Recruiting	578	744	768	340	774
Interest	10	22	56	28	62
Instructional expenses					
Automotive	106	119	91	47	94
Heating, A/C, and					
refrigeration	78	91	100	52	117
Drafting	124	131	133	73	156
Electronics	327	325	279	165	341
Mapping and surveying	66	76	79	38	81
Video cassette recorder	0	16	34	0	0
Communication					
equipment repair	0	13	27	0	0
General education	95	107	81	33	76
Total operating costs	2,556	2,900	3,170	1,582	3,299
Gross income from					
operations	510	488	321	458	656
Minus:					
Management fees	438	472	0	0	0
Write-off bad debt	0	0	164	92	172
Loss on sale	0	93	0	0	0
Other loss (income)	38	(8)	(3)	18	38
Reported pretax income	34	(69)	160	348	446
Taxes (35%)	12	0	$32†	122	156
Reported profit aftertax	22	(69)	128	226	290

* The current fiscal year ends 9/30. The 1987 numbers are annualized using half year
data and the most recent internal budget projections.
†Reduced by tax loss carryforward from previous year.

EXHIBIT 9   *(concluded)*

St. Louis Institute of Technology
Projected Balance Sheet at Closing
(in thousands of dollars)

Current assets		Current liabilities	
Cash	5	A/P	95
A/R students	1,800	Payroll taxes	34
A/R other	19	Other payables	212
Prepaid expenses	74	Short-term debt	170
Inventory	124	Total current liabilities	511
Total current assets	2,022		
A/R intercompany*	305	Long-term debt†	316
Fixed assets		Prepaid tuition	1,902
Furniture and fixtures	126		
Equipment	994	Total liabilities	2,729
Leasehold improvements	259		
Library	34		
Less: accumulated depreciation	(958)		
Net fixed assets	455		
Other assets			
Deposits	20	Stockholders' equity	
Notes receivable (NDSL)	111	Common stock	145
Officer insurance premium	36	Retained earnings	75
Total other assets	167	Total stockholders' equity	220
		Total liabilities and	
Total assets	2,949	stockholders' equity	2,949

*This is an intercompany loan that is currently being written off. It will not be assumed by the buyer.
†This is bank debt that will be paid off by the seller at closing. It will not be assumed by the buyer.

EXHIBIT 10   St. Louis Institute of Technology Adjusted Financials

St. Louis Institute of Technology
Adjusted Financial Statements
(in thousands of dollars)

	Audited			6 mo.	Annual
	1984	1985	1986	1987	1987 est.
Adjusted aftertax income					
Reported pretax income (from Exhibit 9)	34	(69)	160	348	446
Adjustments					
+ Management fees	218*	252*	0	0	0
+ Write-off of bad debt	0	0	164	92	172
Adjusted pretax income	252	183	324	440	618
Taxes (35%)	88	64	113	154	216
Adjusted aftertax income	164	119	211	286	402
Adjusted cash flow					
Reported pretax income (from Exhibit 9)	34	(69)	160	348	446
Adjustments					
+ Management fees	$218*	$252*	0	0	0
+ Write-off of bad debt	0	0	164	92	172
+ Depreciation	137	170	186	93	186
Adjusted pretax cash flow	389	353	510	533	804
Adjusted taxes (from above)	88	64	113	154	216
Adjusted aftertax cash flow	301	289	397	379	588

*Jamie and Kirk added back only the portion of the management fee (charged by Miles and Wilkens' company), which they felt to be excessive.

EXHIBIT 11   St. Louis Institute of Technology Projected Financials

St. Louis Institute of Technology
Preliminary Financial Projections
(in thousands of dollars)

	Year 1	Year 2	Year 3	Year 4	Year 5	Year 6	Year 7	Year 8
School sales	4,300	4,945	5,687	6,255	6,818	7,432	8,101	8,830
Gross profit before depreciation	1,763	2,027	2,332	2,690	3,000	3,344	3,645	3,974
Depreciation	180	180	180	180	180	180	180	180
Gross profit	1,583	1,847	2,152	2,510	2,820	3,164	3,465	3,794
Recruiting expense	903	1,038	1,195	1,314	1,432	1,560	1,701	1,855
EBIT	680	809	957	1,196	1,388	1,604	1,764	1,939
Noncompete agreement	265	265	265	265	265	265	265	0
Interest								
Bank	20	20	20	20	20	20	20	20
Seller	184	184	174	164	152	140	126	0
Investor	120	120	120	120	120	120	120	120
Total interest	324	324	314	304	292	280	266	140

PBT	91	220	378	627	831	1,059	1,233	1,799
Taxes (35%)	32	77	132	219	291	371	432	630
PAT	59	143	246	408	540	688	801	1,169
Beginning cash	550*	669	695	810	1,085	1,471	1,990	1,498
+ PAT	59	143	246	408	540	688	801	1,169
+ depreciation	180	180	180	180	180	180	180	180
	789	992	1,121	1,398	1,805	2,339	2,971	2,847
− Working capital and capital expenditure	120	202	207	198	208	211	213	216
Cash available for debt	669	790	914	1,200	1,597	2,128	2,758	2,631
Repayment of seller debt†	0	95	104	115	126	138	1,260	0
Ending cash	669	695	810	1,085	1,471	1,990	1,498	2,631

*$1,600,000 of investor financing reduced by $1 million payment to seller and $50,000 closing costs.
†Only debt to seller would be repaid. $170,000 of bank financing and $1 million of investor debt assumed to remain outstanding.

EXHIBIT 12   Acquisition Terms

ST. LOUIS INSTITUTE OF TECHNOLOGY

1014 E. WHEELER STREET
ST. LOUIS, MISSOURI 62726
TELEPHONE: (314) 788-5130

April 9, 1987

Dear Sirs:

This letter is to set out the broad terms of the transaction we have been discussing. If and when countersigned by you (herein called the "Buyers"), the terms will be binding in principle on the parties. It is anticipated that this letter will be entirely superseded by a Purchase and Sale Agreement as soon as possible.

Galena Corporation will organize a new corporation (herein called the "Buyer") which will purchase from the Sellers the operating assets of The St. Louis Institute of Technology, Inc. (herein called "SIT") and will assume certain of the liabilities of SIT, as noted.

1. At the closing, Buyers will convey to Sellers the following assets.

   Cash
   Accounts receivable students, other
   Prepaid expenses
   Inventories
   Furniture and fixtures
   Equipment
   Leasehold improvements
   Library
   All intangibles such as accreditations, contract rights, customer lists, leases, trademarks, trade names, patents, rights in inventions, licenses, fire and casualty insurance policies, group life insurance policies, and the like.
   Deposits
   Officer insurance premium
   Bonding
   Notes receivable, NDSL

2. Buyer will assume the following liabilities of Sellers as of the opening of business on the day of closing:

   —Accounts payable, payroll taxes, other payables.
   —Note payable—St. Louis National Bank (estimated to be $170,000 as of 7/1/87).
   —Prepaid tuition

3. Other taxes, rent, and utilities will be prorated to the date of closing.

4. Cash distributions of profits prorated to close date to current Subchapter S shareholders shall be permitted.

5. Consideration for the purchase will be according to the attached Schedule A. The Buyer will assume entire responsibility for tax recap-

EXHIBIT 12 (*continued*)

ture, if any, due to a step up in the asset valuations. The Sellers will be responsible for taxes due for past Investment Tax Credits. Final determination of the actual values paid for individual assets and liabilities assumed as noted above will be determined as of the opening of business on the closing day or by audited figures within 90 days thereof updated to the day of closing with unaudited figures.

6. The Sellers note shall be secured by a pledge of 75 percent of the stock on terms such that the Sellers gain control of Buyer on any default of Buyer's notes to Sellers.

7. The Buyer and the Sellers agree to enter into a Noncompetition, Consulting, and Employment Agreement, as outlined below. Payments will commence in the first year and will be paid quarterly over a seven year period according to the following schedule:

Years 1 through 7 $66,250 $\times$ 4 = $265,000/year

The Noncompetition, Consulting, and Employment Agreement will contain geographic restrictions, and will not restrict the Sellers' current school operations or those filed by 7/15/87.

8. The Purchase and Sale Agreement between the Buyer and the Sellers will embody the terms of this letter and contain representations, warranties, and covenants commonly found in such agreements including without limitation, no known or anticipated liabilities or claims not disclosed on the financial statements and no known or anticipated circumstances which would tend to frustrate the successful operation of the business.

9. Each party will represent that no broker's fee is due and will hold the other harmless from claims of any person through it.

10. The Sellers agree not to discuss the sale of the business or the corporation with any other person for a period of three months from the countersigning of this letter, notwithstanding Sellers shall have the right to make a due diligence investigation of Buyers.

11. Buyer's entering into a binding arrangement is conditioned on its obtaining financing on terms satisfactory to it. Buyer anticipates that financing will be in place before the execution of the Purchase and Sale Agreement so that Closing may be simultaneous with the execution of the Purchase and Sale agreement for the assets and the above mentioned Noncompetition, Consulting, and Employment Agreement. Performance by any party under any of the agreements described herein is contingent on all agreements being executed as described.

12. Buyer's entering into a binding Purchase and Sale Agreement is further conditioned on:

a. Arrangements satisfactory to all parties being reached with key employees.

EXHIBIT 12   (*continued*)

---

b. Verification that the leases of real and personal property can be assigned to the Buyer, or that Sellers are willing to remain a guarantor of existing leases so that lease terms are not materially altered.

c. Verification that accreditation is in good standing and will be transferred to the Buyer.

d. Verification that all licenses and permits for operation of the business will be transferred to the Buyer.

13. Upon execution of this letter by both parties, Buyer will undertake a due diligence investigation, and the Sellers will furnish reasonable information and allow Buyer's representatives on the premises at mutually agreeable times with access to such books and records as may be appropriate. The investigation of the business may include, without limitation, an appraisal of the machinery and equipment and an accounting investigation, both at Buyer's expense.

14. Buyer's counsel will initiate the drafting of the Purchase and Sale Agreement, the Note, the Employment and Noncompetition Agreements and the other substantive closing documents.

15. From the execution of this letter until closing, the Sellers will exert their best efforts to operate the business in the normal course, to continue present salary and wage levels, and to institute no material change in any aspects of the business. Buyer will be kept informed as to daily operations, including any material changes in working capital.

16. The parties hereto will exert their best efforts to keep the contents of this letter and subsequent negotiations confidential, discussing the subject matter only to further the negotiations and accomplish the execution and performance of the transactions described.

If the foregoing terms and conditions are satisfactory to you, and accurately and fairly represent our discussions to date, please so indicate by accepting this letter as a binding commitment by both parties. Please sign in the space below.

Very truly yours,

Joe E. Miles

Ross B. Wilkens

Agreed:

By: Kirk Riedinger

By: James Turner
Date

EXHIBIT 12   *(concluded)*

SCHEDULE A

St. Louis Institute of Technology Purchase Structure

Year	Cash Payment	Note Principal	Note Interest	Total
0	$1,000	$ 0	$ 0	$1,000
1		0	184	184
2		95	184	279
3		104	174	278
4		115	164	279
5		126	152	278
6		138	114	278
7		152	126	278
Balloon				
End of Year 7		1,108	0	1,108
Total Payments		1,838		$3,962

Jim Southern

There was no reason to feel this way, Jim Southern told himself. Here he was on the brink of doing his first big deal, yet at a time when he should have been filled with excitement and a sense of pride, every instinct was telling him to cut and run.

It was June 28, 1984, and Southern was within 48 hours of signing a Purchase and Sale Agreement to buy from American Printing, Inc., its business forms division, which had 1983 sales of $43 million. To Jim the acquisition looked attractive, and he was to be its chairman, CEO, and a 42 percent stockholder. Both debt and equity financing were conditionally in place. But an 11th-hour demand by the seller that Jim personally guarantee $4 million of Accounts Payable was the immediate cause for concern.

Maybe the late request was a red herring and would go away, Jim thought, or perhaps it could be traded for a less onerous provision. On the other hand, was it a blessing in disguise that would force him to address some of the issues that had been swept aside during the acquisition negotiations? Among Southern's concerns were questions about his own ability to run a company of this magnitude, about how much more he should investigate the division being bought, about the special risks and opportunities inherent in the highly leveraged proposed capitalization, and about the wisdom of personally guaranteeing $4 million of Accounts Payable in light of his net worth of less than $100,000.

This case was prepared by H. Irving Grousbeck under the direction of Howard H. Stevenson.

BACKGROUND

Jim Southern entered the Harvard Business School in 1981 at the age of 30. After having graduated from Southwestern University in 1973, he had spent two years in operations and MIS systems with a privately held trucking company, four years selling life insurance and developing a successful estate planning practice, and two years structuring oil and gas partnerships as a general partner. (See Exhibit 1 for resume.)

Upon receiving his MBA, he spent a few months looking for an entrepreneurial business opportunity. In September of 1983 he joined forces with a robotics engineer in a small company that had been formed to manufacture and market high precision robotic work stations designed for electronic and mechanical assembly. Though the company's principal product was reasonably well perfected and annual sales approximated $400,000, Jim and his partner had no success attempting to raise the $4 million of equity capital they felt would be required to capture a significant market share. In December of 1983 Jim resigned and began to look for a more established, lower technology entrepreneurial venture.

His first step was to approach Richard Tucker and his son, Dick Tucker, Jr. The Tuckers were a substantial Texas family involved in various business activities and investments. Jim Southern and Dick Tucker were contemporaries who had become business acquaintances eight years earlier.

At their first meeting Jim described to the Tuckers his desire to acquire and manage a "low-tech" company. Though he had prepared nothing in writing, Jim set forth in some detail a set of specifications. These included a Boston or Dallas location, sales of $4 million to $40 million, significant market share, leverageable assets, and break-even or profitable operations. The Tuckers registered initial interest and encouraged Jim to prepare a memorandum for their review. Though no discussion took place at that meeting as to how the equity would be divided, the Tuckers expressed a willingness to invest up to $250,000 in a venture they found attractive. Jim had accumulated $50,000, which he was prepared to invest.

Jim drafted a nine-page memo dated February 10, 1984, which appears as Exhibit 2. After further discussion based on this memo, the Tuckers and Southern reached agreement as follows: A new S Corporation named Nova Capital Corp. would be formed to conduct the search for an acquisition. Dick Tucker and another investor still to be found would each contribute $25,000 of capital, and each would receive 50 percent of the common stock. The $50,000 of paid-in capital plus $30,000 of consulting fees to be generated by Southern would fund a 12 to 15 month search at an aftertax cost to each of the two investors of about $12,500. Southern also thought it possible that Nova could generate some additional fee income from performing M&A or corporate financial services for consulting clients.

In late February, Jim set out on a three-pronged mission: to find a second Nova investor, to generate consulting clients, and to begin a systematic search for a business to acquire. Though the first two objectives were pursued in an ad hoc manner, Jim followed the four specific strategies for finding a corporate acquisition, which he had outlined in his February 10th memo.

His computer search of the Dun & Bradstreet *Million Dollar Directory* uncovered between 75 and 100 Dallas or Boston companies in various industries that met Jim's preliminary tests. In discussing some of these with Tom Silver, a business school professor and friend, Jim learned that Tom was a director of a publicly held printing company based in Ft. Worth, American Printing, Inc., that had considered selling its business forms division. However, Tom was reluctant to introduce Jim to the CEO of that company until Jim was in control of more resources than the $300,000 that Dick Tucker and he were prepared to invest, since it was thought that the division in question would be valued in the $12 to $16 million range.

Putting thoughts of American Printing temporarily aside, Jim began pursuing a manufacturer of vacuum heaters with about $40 million in sales, which was mentioned to him by the partner of a Boston public accounting firm. Despite repeated attempts to schedule a meeting with management, Jim was unsuccessful and concluded that either the company was not for sale or management was in serious negotiations with others.

An industrial battery company with $10 million in sales next came to Jim's attention, together with two different distributors of hydraulic and pneumatic valves. After visiting both distributors and meeting with their managements, Jim decided against entering negotiations with either company because he preferred to buy a manufacturing entity rather than a distributor.

As he began to analyze preliminary data from the industrial battery company, Jim and Dick Tucker decided to circulate Jim's February 10 memo to six or eight investors known to them in Texas. Firm commitments were neither sought nor offered, but responses were such that Southern and Tucker believed that up to $2 million of equity would be available to Nova on reasonable terms for the right acquisition. Though only $20,000 of Dick's agreed $25,000 had actually been paid in to Nova, the search for further capital was temporarily suspended.

Jim apprised Tom Silver of these encouraging events and requested an introduction to John O'Leary, chairman and CEO of

American Printing, Inc. At Silver's suggestion, O'Leary agreed to meet with Southern early in March. Though O'Leary, a man in his late 50s, was initially somewhat put off by Southern's youth and relative lack of experience, the two men had a warm conversation. O'Leary stated that American Printing might be willing to sell its business forms division in an all-cash transaction in order to enter areas of the printing industry offering greater growth potential. The session ended with O'Leary agreeing to provide Southern with recent financial statements and related information on American's forms division. In preparation for the receipt of this data, Jim assembled certain historical information on the forms industry, which appears in Exhibits 3 and 4.

THE COMPANY

American Printing's business forms division had 1983 sales of about $43 million, representing 35 percent of American's overall revenues. (See Exhibits 5 through 7 for summary financial statements.) The division was engaged in three lines of business. The first was the manufacture of authentic insurance documents for the property and casualty industry. The second was general forms manufacturing on a job-shop basis. The third was the warehousing and distribution of insurance documents and business forms printed by the company. The 1983 sales of each of its business segments are shown in Exhibit 8.

Authentic Insurance Documents

The Company held a 50 percent share of the authentic insurance document market in the United States. *Authentic insurance documents* refers to policies and endorsements for property and casualty insurance companies. In this market, the Company assumed the responsibility for (*a*) the authenticity (legality) of policy language, (*b*) changes in state laws and regulations, (*c*) the manufacture and printing of new policies and endorsements in a timely fashion, and (*d*) the distribution of the policies and endorsements in small quantities to a given insurance company's branch offices throughout the United States. These services represented substantial value to the insurance companies and, as a result, commanded a 35 percent gross margin, which was two times greater than the forms business as a whole.

In order to make its product line available to its entire force of independent agents, an insurance company had two choices. It could either print its own policies and distribute them as called for by the agents, or it could contract with a company such as the Company to make its policies available to its agency system.

The latter method was preferable for two reasons. First, it relieved the insurance company of the legal and economic burden of policing its policy language. Second, it permitted it to make its products available to a very large number of agents without bearing enormous printing and warehousing costs.

Authentic insurance documents fell into two categories: snap-out forms and continuous forms. The Company printed both kinds. The high volume, low premium policies such as homeowners and automobile policies were usually produced via computer. Thirty percent of the Company's insurance business was continuous forms manufacture for computer-generated policies. The remaining 70 percent was snap-out forms for low volume, high premium policies such as inland marine, jewelers' block, commercial auto, and workers' compensation policies.

To facilitate the sales process, the Company maintained a catalog service for its customers. The service consisted of six binders of facsimile policy pages for each of the following categories of insurance coverage: homeowners, automobile, workers' compensation, inland marine, crime and glass, and general liability. The catalog service cost the customer $85 per year. The Company maintained a supply of standard policies for these participating customers. Customers could order any policy in the catalog in quantities of 50 or more for next day shipment. Upon receipt of the customer's order, the company pulled the appropriate form from inventory, imprinted it with the insurance company's name and logo, and shipped the order via UPS the next day.

The market for authentic insurance documents tended to follow a seven year underwriting cycle, which was currently in a trough. However, 1984 interim results at the Company indicated that orders were running 10 percent ahead of last year in this business segment. Furthermore, two changes in policy language scheduled for 1985 and 1986 were projected to boost sales in this segment by $800,000 to $1,600,000. In addition, the insurance industry had just gone through a three year period of relatively few policy revisions.

The following table shows the primary competitors and their estimated share of this $26 million market.

The 1983 Authentic Insurance Document Market (in millions of dollars)

Company	Sales	Share
American Printing	$12.9	50%
Recording & Statistics Inc.	6.1	23
Various Insurance Bureaus	6.0	23
Moore Business Forms	1.0	4
	$26.0	100%

General Forms Manufacture

In addition to the authentic policy documents described in the above section, the Company also printed general business forms for its insurance company customers as well as for the business community at large. This market was a $12 billion market served by thousands of printers ranging from the $1 billion Moore Business Forms to the local print shop and photocopy store. Margins were thin, typically 10 percent to 20 percent. The Company's cost accounting system permitted management to monitor low margin business by customer and by job so that no unprofitable bids would go out. This entailed monthly revisions of standard costs on a timely basis.

The Company used its general forms business to balance out its plant capacity. By combining a general printing job with warehouse and distribution services, it was able to command higher margins than competitors who lacked its distribution capabilities. The Company's customer base in this segment included some of the best-known financial institutions in the country. Among them were Fireman's Fund, Bank of America, Aetna, Dun & Bradstreet, C.I.T., Manufacturers Hanover, General Motors, and Continental Insurance.

Plants and Warehouses

The Company employed 750 people in total and operated five plants and 12 warehouses around the country. Four of the plants and most of the warehouses were located east of the Rocky Mountains. Each warehouse was equipped to provide certain value-added services such as crash imprinting and offset imprinting to further customize a buyer's order. These services played a big role in the authentic insurance document business.

Sales Force

The Company sold through 55 captive salespeople located in 18 district sales offices around the country. Fourteen of these offices were east of the Mississippi River. Five regional sales managers oversaw this sales force from regional offices in New York, Boston, Chicago, San Francisco, and Dallas. Sales salaries ranged from a low of $20,000 to a high of $60,000, half of which, on average, was commission. The Company did not have a centralized marketing department nor a vice president of marketing.

Sales by Product Line

Exhibit 9 shows sales by product line for the past three years. The trends portrayed in this table must be evaluated in light of many variables such as wage inflation, paper prices, the severe recession of 1981–82, and the loss of a major customer. However, the most conservative analysis of these trends suggested that the Company was somewhat insulated from shocks of the general economy.

Customers

The Company's target customer for the future was the firm with $100,000 to $300,000 of annual manufacturing, warehousing, and distribution business. However, the Company did not intend to give up any of its larger high margin accounts. At the current time, no customer accounted for over 6 percent of total sales. Furthermore, most of these large customers were on multi-year contracts. Where appropriate, the Company tied certain warehouse leases to the expiration dates of major distribution contracts. This meant that the nonrenewal of a major customer contract would have no adverse affect on profits other than the loss of the gross margin on that particular piece of business.

THE SEARCH FOR FINANCING

Though prior to March 1984, Jim had received introductions to half a dozen commercial banks in Boston, Dallas, and New York, he had found time to visit only one institution in each city. He had neither sought nor received any more than preliminary indications of interest from the middle-level loan officers to whom he had spoken.

Following his early March meeting with O'Leary, however, Jim realized that he had found a potentially attractive company to acquire but had been unable to spend the time necessary to properly cultivate sources of debt capital. As he hastily made the rounds of all six banks, he quickly learned that each bank had a different group of people specializing in fixed asset loans and current asset loans. Often they were located on different floors or even in separate buildings. Jim spent the rest of March preparing pro forma projections and meeting with lenders.

On April 10th Professor Silver told Jim that Mr. O'Leary had called him to inquire about the financial capabilities of Jim and his investor group. Though O'Leary had seemed reasonably satisfied with

Silver's somewhat evasive reply, Jim realized that acquisition negotiations could not proceed without some indications from potential lenders of their willingness to extend substantial credit. After some prodding from Jim, Southwest Bank and Consolidated Bank mailed written indications of interest to Jim dated April 18, 1984 (Exhibits 10 and 11). Though Jim was pleased to receive them, he recognized that they represented very preliminary and highly conditional commitments, and he wondered whether or not he should show them to Mr. O'Leary.

Both of the banks stated that the next step in the loan approval process would be an appraisal of fixed assets to be conducted by Joseph Pettus & Co. The cost of this audit was estimated at $7,000–$10,000, to be advanced by the potential borrower. Jim also realized that he needed to enlist the help of a good lawyer and competent auditors. The funds in Nova Capital Corp. were insufficient to compensate these professionals for the work that would soon be required in order to keep the deal from foundering.

NEGOTIATIONS

Jim reviewed the information that had previously been provided by O'Leary: recent audited financial statements, a list of fixed assets, and internal projections for the next two years. A closer look at the latter document revealed that management planned to close two manufacturing plants in 1985 at a total cost of $1,050,000 in order to increase efficiency and reduce unneeded overhead.

Southern decided on a strategy of seeking a reduction in purchase price based on this information. He asked Dick Tucker to accompany him to a meeting scheduled with O'Leary for April 25th. A few minutes into the session, after exchanging pleasantries, Southern told O'Leary that the Tucker family was prepared to help him spearhead the acquisition of the forms division, and that preliminary commitments had been obtained from two banks to provide substantial debt financing. However, and here Jim tried to keep his composure, the buyers were prepared to offer a price of book value less the $1,050,000 of plant closing costs set forth in the division's internal planning document. The offer was subject to the usual condition of reasonable satisfaction following a "due diligence" inspection of the assets to be sold. No sooner was the proposal on the table than Mr. O'Leary extended his hand to Jim and said, "Fine, you've got a deal." The meeting ended on a friendly note, with both sides agreeing to contact their respective lawyers so that the documentation process could begin.

Jim and Dick were stunned that their offer had been so quickly accepted. They immediately began to worry that, in their inexperience, they had missed something major and thus had agreed to overpay for American's forms division.

Over the next two weeks Jim immersed himself in analyzing the company and visiting with the general manager and the controller of the forms division, both of whom were based in American's home office. Presumably they were the only American Printing officials other than O'Leary who knew that negotiations with Southern were taking place. Both division officials were in their 30s and appeared bright and energetic. The general manager held an engineering degree and had graduated from Harvard Business School near the top of his class as a Baker Scholar. The controller was a CPA who had spent eight years in public accounting. Both men had been with American Printing for the past five years. Jim decided that they would make valuable additions to his management team. He wondered about the wisdom of offering them a stock interest in the new company before having reached formal agreement to acquire it.

Feeling that O'Leary had seemed unusually eager to accept his offer instead of proposing a counter-offer, Jim decided on a bold step: He rather hastily drafted and mailed to O'Leary a letter stating that he was lowering his offer another one million dollars because of the need to close one additional plant, and because of the cost of maintaining and then discontinuing certain duplicative MIS systems.

Three days later a hand-delivered letter from O'Leary arrived. It contained a flat rejection of Jim's offer, but restated a willingness to proceed on the earlier basis. Jim was disappointed but not totally surprised. He and O'Leary met for lunch, and Southern attempted to sell the older man on the need for at least half of the million-dollar concession. After two glasses of wine and some spirited discussion, O'Leary agreed to a reduction of $250,000. The two men shook hands on the revised deal.

FURTHER DEVELOPMENTS

Throughout the rest of May Jim found himself fully taxed trying to manage his lawyers, bring the two competing banks to the point of loan commitments, conduct his own due diligence (principally by refining his projections for the division), and attempt to pin down the equity sources for the venture. Early in June Jim's lawyer reported that negotiations were proceeding extremely slowly, possibly because lawyers for the seller questioned the buyer's financial capability. In response to this glitch Jim was able to generate letters addressed to

John O'Leary from both competing banks (Exhibits 12 and 13). Thereafter negotiations returned to their more normal prior pace.

Jim was mildly encouraged that the structure of the transaction was taking shape. Assets with a book value of $16.3 million were to be purchased for $15.0 million, reflecting the agreed discount of $1.3 million (Exhibit 14). Payment would consist of $11.0 million cash and the assumption of $4 million of Accounts Payable. No other liabilities were to be assumed. The seller had offered to guarantee any Accounts Receivable greater than 90 days old. Though assuring the value of all the other assets to be assumed thus became the obligation of the buyer, Jim took some comfort from the $1.3 million discount he had negotiated.

Southern visualized that he could assemble the following sources of cash:

From Southwest Bank or Consolidated Bank:	
Senior revolving loan at Prime plus 2% for 85% of A/R less than 90 days old plus 45% of inventory	$ 8,500,000
Ten-year fixed asset loan at Prime plus 2% with equal quarterly repayments of principal starting at the beginning of Year 2	3,500,000
Equity	800,000
Total	$12,800,000

After applying $11.0 million cash to the asset acquisition as described above, Jim would have $1.8 million left for working capital.

The $800,000 equity figure had been arrived at in a curious fashion. In a preliminary discussion with a banker, Southern had been asked how much equity he would cause to be invested in the venture. Being somewhat unsure how to respond, he offered an estimate of "about 5 percent." Since approximately $16 million of assets were to be purchased, the equity amount became established at $800,000. Based largely on Jim's five-year projections (Exhibit 15), the Tuckers together agreed to take $375,000. Professor Silver and two of his friends spoke for $250,000. Jim himself planned to take $65,000. Another former professor of Jim's took $35,000, and Southern penciled in the last $75,000 for the two key employees of the division to be acquired.

The $800,000 would buy 50 percent of the equity and would take the form of $100,000 of common stock and $700,000 of 10 percent subordinated debentures. Interest would accrue annually and become due and payable, together with principal in full, on December 31, 1989; prepayment would be permitted without penalty at any time. Upon the repayment of these debentures in full by the Company, the other 50 percent equity interest would be issued. Three fourths of that "carried interest" would go to Southern, and one fourth would be allocated by him to other key employees on a five-year vesting schedule from date of employment.

All parties were pointing toward the signing of a Purchase and Sale Agreement by the end of June, with the final closing scheduled for July 31, 1984. Though daily problems arose, which demanded seemingly endless amounts of Jim's time to resolve, measurable progress was being made. To Jim the most troubling element of the situation was O'Leary's steadfast refusal to permit Jim and his agents to conduct any due diligence investigations of the Forms Division plants, warehouses, or sales offices. Mr. O'Leary took the position that he did not want any contact between a prospective buyer and his employees to occur until a written agreement had been signed. Jim wondered to what extent this put him in the position of agreeing to buy a "pig in a poke" and left him open to criticism from his investors and lenders. He also worried that he might find unpleasant surprises sufficient to make him unwilling to complete the transaction but insufficient to allow him to withdraw from it without incurring substantial liability and the loss of his investors' $200,000 good-faith deposit. That deposit was to be made upon the signing of the Purchase and Sale Agreement, scheduled for June 30, 1984.

On June 28 Jim received a hand-delivered letter from Mr. O'Leary stating that he and his lawyers had concluded that they were uncomfortable with the assumption of $4 million of Accounts Payable by such a highly leveraged new company under inexperienced management. Their specific concern was the possibility that the buying entity might voluntarily or involuntarily become bankrupt prior to discharging all of the assumed payables, thus leaving American Printing legally liable therefor. The letter stated that American would be willing to keep those liabilities and discharge them with an additional $4 million cash to be provided by the new company at closing. In the alternative, American would accept Jim's personal guarantee of timely payment.

EXHIBIT 1   Résumé

James L. Southern

business
experience
1979–1983   OIL AND GAS

Summer 1982, with Brock Petroleum Corporation of Houston, Texas. Conducted a study for the president to determine the feasibility of production acquisition in the Texas and Louisiana Gulf coast region. Initiated contact with several insurance companies for the purpose of raising equity for production acquisition.

Consultant to independent producer, 1981. Developed oil and gas accounting system fully integrated with month-end financials and joint interest billing.

Partner, Soma Investments, Amarillo, Texas, since 1979. Formed this partnership with an Amarillo businessman to buy nonoperating working interests in exploratory oil and gas prospects. Soma currently has one gas prospect drilling and four producing properties.

1976–1982   INSURANCE   AMARILLO, TEXAS

Agent for Prudential Insurance Company of America. Developed a life insurance and estate planning practice catering to individuals and owners of closely held businesses. Revenues were substantial by Prudential and industry standards. Member, Million Dollar Round Table since 1977; a Chartered Life Underwriter (CLU) since 1980.

1973–1975   SNEAD MANAGEMENT SYSTEMS   HOUSTON, TEXAS

Programmer, 1973. Designed computerized cost accounting systems for construction and mining companies and a billing system for a municipal water, gas, and electric utility. Later promoted to new business development.

President of Kilo-Wate Inc., a subsidiary of Snead Management Systems, 1974. Developed the national marketing effort for a line of conveyor belt scales and truck weighing systems for mines and quarries. Traveled extensively in the United States developing a distributor network and selling directly to the end user.

1972–1973   TEXAS CRUSHED STONE   AUSTIN, TEXAS

Night-shift computer operator during senior year in college for this producer of crushed aggregate products.

EXHIBIT 1   (*concluded*)

1969–1972   MISCELLANEOUS WORK EXPERIENCE
Various summer and part-time jobs during college: bank
teller, truck driver, and route salesman for Royal Crown
Cola; delivery truck driver for a warehouser of paper and
industrial goods; vending machine concession in fraternity
house; on-campus representative for fraternity sportswear
distributor; laboratory assistant to chairman of physics
department.

education
1981–1983   HARVARD GRADUATE SCHOOL OF
BUSINESS ADMINISTRATION   BOSTON, MA
Master in Business Administration in June 1983. General
management curriculum with emphasis on finance and
new venture syndication.

1969–1973   SOUTHWESTERN
UNIVERSITY   GEORGETOWN, TEXAS
Received Bachelor of Arts degree. Major in economics with
emphasis on mathematics and physics. Member, Phi Delta
Theta, a social fraternity.

personal   Married, two children. Hold private pilot license. Special
interests include running and snow skiing. References
available upon request.

EXHIBIT 2   Acquisition Agreement

Plan for Acquiring a Business
February 10, 1984

Dick Tucker and Jim Southern wish to acquire and operate an ongoing business that meets certain criteria. The purpose of this document is to discuss the acquisition criteria, the method of searching for the acquisition, and the likely financial structure of a successful acquisition.

Tucker and Southern will commit a total of $300,000 to this endeavor, $250,000 by Tucker and $50,000 by Southern, and seek to add one additional investor who will commit $250,000.

Profile of Potential Acquisition Candidates

We seek to acquire a going concern with sales in the $2 to $40 million range. The ideal company is a manufacturer of a product with little or no technical content. It has a dominant share of a small market, unrealized growth potential, leverageable assets, little or no debt, and a single owner over age 65. It is profitable.

We will also consider distribution companies that handle products that feed emerging technologies, that serve special market niches, or that have potential for expanding their trade territories geographically.

The following is a list of products that may be of interest to us:

DC electric motors.

Electric power supplies.

Fiber optic cable.

Vacuum heaters.

Precision aluminum casting.

Optical encoders.

Electrical switches.

Certain building materials.

Heating and air-conditioning supplies.

Plumbing supplies.

Hydraulic and pneumatic valves.

Specialty business forms.

Medical and surgical supplies.

Certain businesses will not be considered for acquisition: highly regulated industries, oil and gas exploration and production, real estate, service businesses, retailing, and financial institutions.

Although we prefer an industrial product, certain consumer products may be of interest to us due to the population changes that favor consumption by two age groups: the 30- to 40-year-olds and the elderly.

The search will concentrate in Boston and Dallas. This is an arbitrary decision and is subject to change.

EXHIBIT 2   (*continued*)

Nova Capital Corp: A Search Corporation

In February of 1984, Dick Tucker and Jim Southern will form Nova Capital Corp., a Massachusetts corporation, to conduct the formal search. Nova will, in turn, hire Southern to conduct the search in the most expeditious manner possible and within certain budget limitations.

Others who have done this before advise us that a search and successful acquisition could take from 12 to 18 months. Search expenses will be covered mainly by capital contributions from shareholders. However, since the search activity does not require a full-time effort, Southern will be expected to generate consulting revenue from time to time throughout the year.

Capital Structure: Nova will be organized with $50,000 of paid-in-capital from Tucker and one other investor, each of whom will own 50 percent of Nova's common stock.

Operating Expenses: Operating expenses are estimated to be around $80,000 for one year:

Operating Expenses for One Year

Office space (200 feet)	$ 4,000
Telephone	4,000
Direct mail expense	4,000
Travel	6,000
Southern's salary	48,000
Miscellaneous	$14,000
Total annual expenses	$80,000

Tax Issues: Assuming Southern generates $30,000 in consulting fees during the year (60 days at $500 per day), Nova will have a loss of $50,000. Nova has been set up as an S Corporation so that this loss may be passed on to the shareholders.

The IRS may take the position that these expenses should be capitalized as part of the cost of acquiring a business. Our argument will be that we are in the trade or business of consulting and business brokering. Although this venture could be conducted as a partnership, the corporate form of business carries with it the presumption of a trade or business and further strengthens our position on the deductibility of losses. The tax department of Arthur Young & Co. in Boston is advising me in these matters.

Consulting Fees: Nova has two consulting clients at this time. The first is an interior landscape company in Boston. The second is a regional airline in Austin. Consulting revenues from these two clients are projected to be $16,000 over a three-month period. Approximately 25 percent of this work has been performed and billed.

Commissions: There is the possibility that the search corporation could earn a substantial commission. One source of commission income is the consulting clients. For example, the regional airline in Austin has retained Nova to help it raise venture capital. This could result in a $120,000 commission. A second source of commissions is the deals the search uncovers. Once Nova rejects a company for its own purposes, there is no reason why Nova should not farm out the information to any one of several leveraged buyout firms in the Boston area on a commission basis.

EXHIBIT 2   *(continued)*

Commissions range from 2 percent to 5 percent of the total value of the transaction.

Commissions will be paid directly to Nova Capital Corp. In order for Southern, who is not a stockholder in Nova, to share in the commissions, he will be entitled to a bonus of one third of any commission generated by Nova. His bonus will take the same form as Nova's commission. That is, if the Nova commission is cash, the bonus will be cash; if the Nova commission is a carried interest, the bonus will be a carried interest, etc.

The likelihood of Nova receiving commission income is fairly low. Furthermore, the amount of Southern's effort required to close a venture capital or acquisition deal for someone else is fairly high and would be a poor allocation of his time.

Search Strategy: There are many players currently searching for acquisitions. In addition to the large leveraged buyout funds that have received so much publicity lately, there are numerous individuals and smaller funds also involved. The result has been to bid up acquisition prices to a cyclical high. Nova's strategy is to identify acquisition candidates outside of these channels.

There are three reasons why Nova should be successful in finding such companies. First, the leveraged buyout funds have so much capital to invest that they do not have the time or staff to go looking for deals. Instead, they must rely on deals that are brought to them by brokers, other leveraged buyout funds, and the candidates themselves. Second, not all companies shop around for the highest bidder. Amarillo Coca-Cola Bottling Company is an example of a profitable company that quietly sold to the first and only bidder. Nova should be able to locate similar situations through an aggressive search. Third, not all companies make good acquisitions for leveraged buyout funds. The funds must invest in management. They cannot provide management for each deal they participate in. That means that smaller companies whose owners are retiring, for example, are less desirable to the fund than a corporate divestiture where the management team goes with the acquisition.

Search Methods: There are four sources, in order of importance, of prospects that Nova expects to cultivate: personal contacts, business brokers, direct mail, and professional contacts.

Personal contacts will probably be the most valuable source of acquisition candidates. Getting the word out to these contacts that we are actively looking for a business to buy will result in bona fide prospects being revealed to us.

Business brokers will also be a fairly good source of deals. Although they typically charge a commission based on the Lehman formula (5 percent of the first million, 4 percent of the second million, and so on), they will be bringing us deals where the owners are definitely interested in selling. Nova does not intend to engage any brokers on a retainer basis but will contact selected brokers in the Boston and Dallas areas to alert them of our criteria. Reputable brokers generally show a deal to only one buyer at a time and can be helpful in negotiating with the company's management.

Direct mail is a useful and proven method of identifying smaller companies interested in selling. Nova will conduct a computer search of

EXHIBIT 2   (*continued*)

---

the Dun & Bradstreet *Million Dollar Directory* to identify companies within our targeted zip codes, product lines, and sales volumes. This search will produce a list of companies, their names, addresses, and CEOs, which will become the basis for a direct mailing. A brief letter to the CEO expressing interest in buying his company will generate a response of roughly 10 percent. At that point, Southern will follow up with a phone call to determine whether or not Nova has further interest.

Professional contacts such as lawyers, CPAs, and bankers will also be cultivated. Others who have done this before claim that this is the least useful source of deals. One reason for this is that these people pass along information to their own friends, clients, and business associates first. The implication to Nova is that the lawyers, CPAs, and bankers who are personal acquaintances of Nova principals should prove to be good sources of leads. However, to spend a great deal of time trying to meet people on a wholesale basis will probably not be fruitful.

Screening Criteria: It is useful to have formal criteria for the type of business we are seeking for two reasons. First, we do not have the time or money to search all over the United States. Second, by having formal criteria, which are relatively narrow in scope, we increase the likelihood of a third-party referral.

The following criteria apply to both public and private companies:

Screening Criteria

Sales: $5 to $40 million
Manufacturer or distributor
Industrial product (see list on page 1)
Profitable
Little or no long-term debt
High current assets
Fixed assets that are currently carried
    at low book values
Boston or Dallas headquarters

Further Analysis: Once a company has been called to our attention, we will do further analysis to determine our level of interest. The following is a general discussion of what we are looking for.

The company should have a mature product with a clearly defined niche in a small market. It should have growth potential from either geographic or product line expansion. We should avoid rapidly growing markets with very large potential because they tend to attract big competitors and high acquisition prices. Examples of these markets are computers, software, telecommunications, and robotics.

The company should be large enough to have in place a layer of reasonably capable middle management that will remain after the acquisition.

Acquisition debt must be serviceable from existing cash flow. We are not looking for situations that require increases in market share to service the debt.

The purchase price should enable us to realize at least a 4 to 1 return, cash on cash, after tax, over five years (approximately 30 percent compounded annually).

EXHIBIT 2 *(continued)*

We will also look for tax benefits from writing up fixed assets and inventories. This results in higher depreciation and higher cost of goods sold for tax purposes and has the effect of lowering the amount of income tax the company pays. Distribution companies typically have high inventories and low fixed assets. Manufacturing companies typically have high fixed assets and relatively low inventories.

<u>Postacquisition Management Plans:</u>   After the acquisition, Southern will be installed as on-site management. He will be expected to relocate his family. We do not contemplate absentee management.

Furthermore, we do not intend to disrupt the normal operations of the business for a period of at least six months after the acquisition. Any changes in marketing or production will be deferred until we are comfortable with the performance of both Southern and the new business.

Financial Structure of the Acquisition

<u>The Nova Group:</u>   We anticipate borrowing 80 percent or more of the total purchase price. The original Nova group will consist of Tucker, Southern, and one additional investor. It will provide the initial equity for the purchase. Any additional equity will be brought in at a much higher price than the Nova group pays for its equity.

By adding one additional investor to our group, we will have an initial equity base of $550,000. The following four exercises are useful to illustrate the size company the Nova group can expect to buy with $550,000.

First, assume the Nova group desires to own 100 percent of the common stock. Assuming the company will support a debt to equity ratio of 7 to 1, $550,000 of equity will buy a company selling for $4.4 million (8 × $550,000). Further assume that the $4.4 million purchase price represents 8 times profit after tax and that profit after tax represents 5 percent of gross sales. This hypothetical company would have gross sales of around $11 million ($4.4 million / 8 / 5% = $11 million).

Second, assume that the Nova group is willing to raise an additional $550,000 from outsiders in exchange for 30 percent of the equity. This is a very realistic assumption given the number of funds and individuals seeking acquisitions. This effectively doubles the size of the company we can buy. In this example, the Nova group would end up with 70 percent of a company with $22 million in sales. Theoretically, this is much more desirable than owning 100 percent of a $11 million company.

Third, assume that the additional $550,000 equity can be raised in the form of preferred stock bearing a high coupon rate. This would enable the Nova group to own 100 percent of the common in the $22 million business.

Fourth, some companies may be purchased with little or no cash. For example, Jim Stone arranged the purchase of the Robert Williams Company (a manufacturer of plastic film) on a no cash basis. Gross sales were $16 million, and the company was very profitable. Later, and for tax purposes only, he injected $400,000 of equity into the deal.

<u>Unanimous Consent:</u>   All three members of the Nova group must agree on the acquisition before negotiations begin. In this respect, a commitment to the Nova group is very much different from a blind pool over which the investor has no control.

EXHIBIT 2 *(concluded)*

Board Participation: All three members of the Nova group are expected to hold board seats.

Jim Southern's Participation: Southern is expected to commit 100 percent of his efforts to the Nova search. He agrees not to engage in any other business activities for the duration of the search. In order to defray the search expenses, he is expected to generate consulting revenues of approximately $30,000 over the next 12 months. This represents 60 days at $500 per day.

Southern is prepared to make a capital contribution to the acquisition of up to $50,000. He is also expected to manage the acquired corporation.

In return, Southern expects to receive a carried interest in whatever business is ultimately acquired. The size of the carried interest has not yet been determined but is in the range of 30 percent to 50 percent of the total equity retained by the Nova group.

In dealing with this issue, there are two scenarios that need to be addressed. The first is the acquisition that requires a substantial equity infusion. Southern's carried interest, if negotiated in advance, might turn out to be so large that the deal does not make sense to the other two Nova investors. The second scenario is the acquisition that requires no cash and no personal guarantees. Because the search is viewed by all parties as a joint effort, the other investors would expect to participate in such a cash-free acquisition even though Southern would not need their participation.

Holding Period: The holding period will be dictated by events over which we have little control such as the stock market, overall business climate, and the cyclical nature of the business we acquire. By planning for a three- to seven-year holding period, we should give ourselves ample opportunity to sell the company in a favorable market.

Summary of Offer

Nova is seeking one investor who will commit $250,000 to the search and acquisition of a business as described above. In order to fund the search expenses, the investor will purchase $25,000 of Nova stock from Nova. His ownership in Nova for purposes of allocating profits and losses will be based solely on the ratio of his capital contribution to the total capital contributions.

Pro Forma Nova Capital Structure

Tucker	$25,000	50%
New investor	25,000	50%
Total paid-in-capital	$50,000	100%

For voting purposes, Tucker and the new investor will share voting rights 50/50.

We do not anticipate that Nova will be the acquiring corporation. Instead, a separate holding company will be established for this purpose. Capital contributions and ownership in the holding company will be based on the same 50/50 ratio between Tucker and the new investor. Southern's capital contribution and ownership percentage will be negotiated.

EXHIBIT 3   The Business Forms Industry (selected historical sales statistics)

Year	Reported Sales (in millions of dollars)
1958	374.0
1963	598.4
1967	895.8
1970	1,199.1
1971	1,242.3
1972	1,381.9
1973	1,705.8
1974	2,253.3
1975	2,218.5
1976	2,425.3
1977	2,702.6
1978	3,078.1
1979	3,761.2
1980	4,186.8
1981	4,603.1
1982	4,689.6
1983	4,834.7

EXHIBIT 4   Publicly Traded Business Forms Companies (1983 results)

Company	Net Sales ($ millions)	Net Income as percent of Sales	P/E	Debt to Equity	EBIT Multiple
1. Nodaway Valley Corp.	20	14.6%	3	0.0	1.7
2. Deluxe Check Printers Inc.	682	12.9	18	0.3	9.4
3. John H. Harland Co.	217	11.5	10	0.2	5.0
4. NEBS inc.	137	9.5	22	0.6	13.1
5. NCR Corp.	4,070	8.4	9	0.6	5.1
6. Ennis Business Forms Inc.	95	8.3	16	0.4	8.9
7. Wallace Computer Serv. Inc.	243	7.7	17	0.3	9.2
8. Safeguard Bus. Systems Inc.	168	6.5	18	0.7	10.9
9. Moore Corp. Ltd. (Canada)	2,000	6.3	12	0.4	6.9
10. Std. Register Co.	412	6.0	15	0.4	8.5
11. Reynolds & Reynolds	289	5.9	10	0.4	5.6
12. Burroughs Corp.	4,400	5.6	11	0.9	6.9
13. Scanforms Inc.	12	4.4	14	0.0	7.2
14. Duplex Products Inc.	241	4.1	12	0.5	6.8
15. American Bus. Products Inc.	280	3.5	15	0.5	8.2
16. SCM Corp.	1,960	2.1	11	0.9	6.5
17. R. L. Crain Ltd. (Canada)	94	2.0	9	0.7	5.5
18. Ruddick Corp.	730	1.8	11	0.0	6.9
19. Cybermatics Inc.	28	1.1	6	0.0	3.8
Averages:	846	6.2%	12	0.4	7.2

EXHIBIT 5   Balance Sheets

American Printing, Inc.
Forms Division
Summary Balance Sheets
(in millions of dollars)

	1983	1982	1981
Assets			
Current assets:			
Cash	0.2	0.2	0.2
A/R	6.4	6.55	7.6
Inventory	5.8	6.1	6.03
Total current assets	12.4	12.85	13.83
Fixed assets:			
Plant & equipment	9.9	9.5	9.4
Less depreciation	6.0	5.1	4.2
Net P & E	3.9	4.4	5.2
Other	.4	.52	.53
Total fixed assets	4.3	4.92	5.73
Total Assets	16.7	17.77	19.56
Liabilities and Net Worth			
Current liabilities:			
A/P (trade)	1.5	1.7	1.4
Accruals	2.5	2.5	2.6
Total current liabilities	4.0	4.2	4.0
Net worth:			
Retained earnings	12.7	13.57	15.56
Total liabilities and net worth	16.7	17.77	19.56

EXHIBIT 6   Income Statements

American Printing, Inc.
Forms Division
Statements of Income*
(000s omitted)

	For the Years Ended		
	December 13, 1983	December 31, 1982	December 31, 1981
Net sales	$43,154	$44,675	$42,656
Cost of sales	34,092	36,678	35,319
Gross profit	9,062	7,997	7,337
Selling and administrative expense	5,296	6,045	5,674
Income before taxes	3,766	1,952	1,663
Provision for income taxes	1,853	964	651
Net income	$ 1,913	$ 988	$ 1,012

*Audited.

EXHIBIT 7   Cash Flow Statements

American Printing, Inc.
Forms Division
Cash Flow Statements*
(000s omitted)

	For the Years Ended		
	December 31, 1983	December 31, 1982	December 31, 1981
Net income	$1,913	$ 988	$1,012
Depreciation	991	917	830
Cash provided from operations	2,904	1,905	1,842
Capital expenditures	(373)	(111)	(1,896)
(Increase) decrease in working capital	250	1,182	(415)
Cash advanced to (from) parent	$2,781	$2,976	($ 469)

*Audited.

EXHIBIT 8   Sales Breakdown by Business Segment

American Printing, Inc.
Forms Division
1983 Sales by Business Segment
(in millions of dollars)

Segment	Sales	Market Share
Insurance documents	$12.9	50%
General forms manufacture	24.8	1
Warehouse and distribution	5.5	
	$43.2	

EXHIBIT 9   Sales Breakdown by Product Line

American Printing, Inc.
Forms Division
Sales by Product Line
(000s omitted)

	Annual Sales			Percent of Change from Prior Year	
	1981	1982	1983	1981–82	1982–83
Authentic insurance documents					
Policies	7,480	6,420	6,158	−14.2%	−4.1%
Endorsements	4,950	6,050	5,879	22.2	−2.8
Catalog service and manuals	390	430	816	10.3	89.8
	12,820	12,900	12,853	0.6	−0.4
General forms manufacture					
Imprinting	2,450	2,320	2,595	−5.3	11.9
General use printing	14,540	16,430	15,847	13.0	−3.5
Letterheads & envelopes	1,400	1,350	1,319	−3.6	−2.3
Checks and drafts	1,650	1,970	1,264	19.4	−35.8
Small-run forms	2,620	2,090	1,505	−20.2	−28.0
Office supplies	810	700	641	−13.6	−8.4
Other	1,166	1,395	1,630	19.6	16.1
	24,636	26,255	24,801	6.6	−5.5
Warehouse and distribution	5,200	5,520	5,500	6.2	−0.4
Total sales	42,656	44,675	43,154	4.7%	−3.4%

EXHIBIT 10   Correspondence

SOUTHWEST BANK

Dallas, Texas

April 18, 1984

Mr. James L. Southern, III
President
Nova Capital Corp.
One Post Office Square
Suite 3840
Boston, MA 02109

Dear Jim:

I am pleased to inform you that the Southwest Bank is sincerely interested in financing your acquisition of the Forms Division of American Printing, Inc.

The financing package will be subject to the bank's security interest in all the company's assets. Availability will be determined based upon a commercial finance audit of the company's books and records, and a Joseph Pettus & Co. detailed appraisal of machinery and equipment.

I suggest that you set up a large revolving credit for the first year. This would encompass the availability created by accounts receivable, inventory, and machinery and equipment. This would serve to reduce your required cash outflow in the early stages following the acquisition.

It is anticipated that the asset availability plus money infused by Nova Capital should equal approximately $13 million. Additionally, the total line of credit will be in excess of this amount to provide for future expansion.

Final approval of this loan package is subject to our bank's Loan Approval Committee, a detailed Joseph Pettus & Co. appraisal, and a satisfactory commercial finance audit.

Sincerely,

James R. Snodgrass
Assistant Vice President

JRS/syg

EXHIBIT 11 Correspondence

CONSOLIDATED BANK

NEW YORK, NEW YORK

April 18, 1984

Mr. James L. Southern, III
President
Nova Capital Corp.
One Post Office Square
Suite 3840
Boston, MA 02109

Dear Jim:

Based upon the information reviewed to date regarding the proposed acquisition of American Printing's Forms Division, we are pleased to offer the following financing proposal:

Line of Credit:	$13,000,000.
Terms:	$10.5M revolving line secured by current assets. $2.5M 7 year term note against fixed assets.
Advance Rates:	80% of accounts receivable less than 60 days past due. 50% of raw material and finished goods inventory. 75% of fixed asset auction value.

As discussed, we will need to review monthly cash flows to determine if an overadvance facility will be required. It is also true that the above quoted advance rates may vary slightly depending upon the results of a review of our examiners.

We suggest that the term portion of this facility incorporate a fixed rate or interest cap feature.

Also, as we discussed, no firm pricing will be quoted on this package until we have reviewed the monthlys and you have received a letter of intent to sell from American Printing.

As always, the terms and conditions of this offer are subject to the results of our audit report, final approval of senior management, and any substantial changes in government regulations and monetary policy.

It has been a pleasure working with you and we look forward to hearing from you soon.

Sincerely,

Robert X. Broadbent
Vice President

EXHIBIT 12   Correspondence

SOUTHWEST BANK

Dallas, Texas

June 6, 1984

John F. O'Leary, Chairman
American Printing, Inc.
Ft. Worth, Texas

Dear Mr. O'Leary:

We understand that Nova Capital Corporation ("Nova") is negotiating for the purchase by a corporation to be formed by Nova ("Purchaser") of the assets of the Forms Division ("Division Assets") of American Printing, Inc. This is to advise you that we have indicated in our letter to Nova of April 18 our interest in financing the acquisition of the Division Assets and providing the working capital needs of the Purchaser. Subject to the evaluation of the Division Assets being to our sole satisfaction, it is our present feeling that our initial loan and the equity investment contemplated by the Purchaser is sufficient to enable the Purchaser to acquire the Division Assets.

Very truly yours,

Terence Kugo
Vice President

EXHIBIT 13   Correspondence

CONSOLIDATED BANK

New York, New York

June 5, 1984

Mr. John F. O'Leary
Chairman and Chief Executive Officer
American Printing, Inc.
Ft. Worth, Texas

Dear Mr. O'Leary:

We have reviewed certain financial statements and equipment listings of American Printing's Forms Division provided to us by Mr. James Southern of Nova Capital Corporation.

Based on such review, we have issued a letter of intent to Nova Capital Corporation offering to make a secured loan, under certain conditions, for the purpose of partially financing the acquisition of the Forms Division by Nova Capital Corporation or related entity.

We believe that the said loan together with equity contributed by Nova Capital Corporation would be sufficient to fully finance the proposed acquisition of the Forms Division.

If you have any further questions please contact me directly.

Very truly yours,

Allan A. Lane
Divisional Vice President

EXHIBIT 14   Acquisition Balance Sheet

American Printing, Inc.
Forms Division
Assets and Liabilities Being Acquired
December 31, 1983*
(in millions of dollars)

Assets		Liabilities	
A/R	$ 7.4	A/P	$4.0
Inventory	5.0		
Plant and equipment (net)	3.9		
Total	$16.3		

*Audited.

EXHIBIT 15   Southern's "Best Guess" Projections for the Forms Division
(in millions of dollars)

	Last five months	Calendar Years			
	1984	1985	1986	1987	1988
Sales	17.5	47.0	47.0	47.0	47.0
EBIT	1.6	4.6	4.6	4.6	4.6
Add depreciation	.2	.5	.7	.7	.8
Pretax operating cash flow	1.8	5.1	5.3	5.3	5.4
Bank interest @ 12%	.8*	1.4	1.4	1.3	1.3
Depreciation	.2	.5	.7	.7	.8
Pretax profit	.8	3.2	3.2	3.3	3.3

*Includes closing costs.

Part IV

Managing the Enterprise and Harvesting Value

In this final section, we look at what happens after the start-up. Managing a venture in an entrepreneurial manner involves a constant search for new opportunities. Yet, growth and wealth often create bureaucracy, specialization, and a desire to protect assets rather than to seek growth. This last part provides a good opportunity to review Chapter 1; the ideas therein are useful for existing companies that want to remain entrepreneurial. Chapter 12, "Managing Growth," describes the administrative challenges that growth engenders and how they can be successfully managed.

Sometimes, the period after the start-up brings not growth and success, but problems. Chapter 13, "Bankruptcy: A Debtor's Perspective," describes how to deal with the unhappy and final stage in the life of some businesses.

Chapter 14 looks at a firm's decision to become a public company. "Securities Law and Public Offerings" describes the legal and business considerations in going public.

THE CASES

Michael Bregman looks at a business with pleasant problems. How should Michael manage his business's growth? What strategy is appropriate, and what resources will be required?

Spinnaker Software Corporation examines an extremely successful company that is now experiencing difficulties. Does it bet on its ability to return to its lofty position, or retrench?

Dragonfly Corporation looks at a business with grave financial and legal problems. Is bankruptcy the answer?

SSS examines a company that has decided to become a public entity. Is this the right course of action? What are the criteria for selecting an underwriter? What are the key items to negotiate? Which investment banker should SSS choose?

Valerie Morgan examines a woman and her growing publishing business, and the administrative challenges that growth has caused. How should Valerie deal with these issues? What should her role in the company be?

The Johnsonville Sausage Co. describes how one entrepreneur has dealt with the challenges of growth, and how his role—and his organization—has evolved.

Finally, Howard Head and Prince Racquets provides insight into the life of a famous entrepreneur and the companies he has started. The case looks at the issue of when, if, and how value should be harvested.

Chapter Twelve

Managing Growth

The set of changes that smaller, younger firms need to make as they grow is often termed *the transition from entrepreneurial to professional management*. This note addresses the issues that firms must deal with in making the transition:

— What is entrepreneurial management and how does it differ from professional management?
— What pressures force the firm to make the transition?
— How can entrepreneurs and their firms make the transition with a greater chance of success?

ENTREPRENEURIAL AND PROFESSIONAL MANAGEMENT

The terms *entrepreneurial* and *professional management* mean very different things to different people. To some, *entrepreneurial management* suggests creative people and an innovative and successful organization, while *professional management* implies a stifling bureaucracy. To others, entrepreneurs are associated with disorganization, and professional management offers efficiency and effective-

---

This note was prepared by Michael J. Roberts.

ness. For the sake of this note, however, *entrepreneurial and professional management* are merely descriptive terms and imply nothing about the creativity, innovation, or success of the organization.

Entrepreneurial Management

Entrepreneurial management is a style of management that is typically used when the firm is young and small. It is characterized by a number of features, including:

— *Centralized decision making:*   In a small organization, the general manager can usually make most of the decisions required to manage the firm. The business is sufficiently small and simple enough that one person can comprehend all the information required for decision making.

— *Informal control:*   The entrepreneurial firm is typically informal. There is little need for formal procedures, systems, and structures because the firm is small enough that activity can be monitored via the personal supervision of the entrepreneur. Moreover, the firm is young and inexperienced and has not yet learned the routines required for success.

The entrepreneur's own ability to collect information, make decisions, and monitor their implementation reduces the need for formal structure, policies, and procedures.

Professional Management

Professional management is characterized by:

— *Delegation of decision-making responsibility:*   Larger firms are sufficiently complex that one individual cannot make all of the decisions required to manage the firm. Therefore, the general manager must delegate responsibility to a hierarchy of middle managers. This pattern of delegation both determines and is determined by the firm's structure.

— *Use of formal control systems:*   In response to the delegation of decision-making responsibility, formal systems are introduced. Because the general manager does not *personally* make all of the firm's decisions, there is a need for systems to guide and evaluate the performance of those who *are* making those decisions. These systems usually include a mechanism for setting objectives, monitoring performance against those objectives, and rewarding desired performance. In addition, general managers also develop policies and standard procedures to guide the actions of those below.

THE "STRATEGY OF COORDINATION"

Just as the firm has an (explicit or implicit) strategy for its actions in the competitive marketplace, it also has an internal strategy for coordinating its efforts. Essentially, the dimensions of organization that we have been discussing are all elements of the way in which the firm chooses to coordinate its efforts.

There are two key dimensions to the strategy of coordination:

— The delegation of responsibility: whether the general manager makes the day-to-day operating decisions personally or delegates that decision-making responsibility to a hierarchy of middle managers.

— The use of formal control systems: whether the firm uses formal systems to set objectives, monitor performance, and control the activities of organization members.

These two dimensions describe a broad range of approaches to coordinating the firm's efforts. If we simply think in terms of the two-by-two matrix defined by these two dimensions, we can see that there are four archetypical strategies of coordination:

— Entrepreneurial management, which relies on centralized decision making and informal, personal control.

— Professional management, which utilizes the delegation of responsibility and extensive formal controls.

— Laissez-faire management, in which responsibilities are delegated, but control remains informal.

— Bureaucratic management, in which centralized decision making is supplemented with formal control.

| | | Use of Formal Control Mechanisms | |
		Low	High
Delegation of responsibility	High	Laissez-faire management	Professional management
	Low	Entrepreneurial management	Bureaucratic management

A *fundamental proposition* that underlies these ideas is that decisions regarding delegation and control have a strong influence on the firm's performance along two critical dimensions:

— Efficiency: the firm's ability to achieve its goals with a minimum of resources.

— Effectiveness: the firm's ability to adapt its goals and innovate to meet the changing needs of its environment.

Moreover, these two performance dimensions—and the decisions regarding delegation and control that underlie them—are *fundamentally in opposition.* Broadly speaking, choices that favor delegation have the potential to increase effectiveness, but simultaneously decrease efficiency; and the use of formal controls increases efficiency while reducing effectiveness. *Thus, the general manager's choices regarding delegation and control determine how these critical trade-offs are made.*

MAKING THE TRANSITION TO PROFESSIONAL MANAGEMENT

When properly implemented, professional management offers an approach to coordinating the activities of a larger, more complex organization while avoiding the problems inherent in laissez-faire or bureaucratic management. There are several steps required for a successful transition to professional management.

Recognizing the Need for Change

The first step in the transition process is a recognition of the need for change. This is often extremely difficult because it is a by-product of success. Success reinforces beliefs and behavior that are appropriate to the entrepreneurial mode but that may not fit the needs of a larger, more complex firm.

Frequently, it is a crisis of some sort that highlights the need for change. Fortunately, knowledgeable outsiders can often help the entrepreneur see the need for such change before a crisis. Experienced board members or consultants can spot the early warning signs: lack of follow-up on details, incredible stress on the individual entrepreneur, and a sense of organizational disarray.

Once the entrepreneur has recognized the need for change, it is often difficult to know what to change *to.* Those who have successfully made the transition report that it requires a fundamental change in orientation: the manager must shift from getting personal satisfaction from direct action to a mode where that sense of accomplishment comes from achieving results *through others.*

Developing the Human Resources

Given this change of personal role in the organization, the entrepreneur needs to develop the human resources required to implement that model. Often, individuals who can accept and execute responsibility are not present in the entrepreneurial organization. The entrepreneur's style has made it difficult for aggressive, independent, employees to survive. Moreover, many young firms simply lack the resources to attract and hire managerial talent.

In order to develop a competent managerial team, the entrepreneur must overcome personal loyalties that threaten the organization. In virtually every firm, the entrepreneur has a "right-hand person" without whom the business would not have survived in the early years. Unfortunately, many of these employees are unable to develop the more specialized skills needed to grow with the company. Entrepreneurs must overcome their personal loyalties and find more suitable employees for critical positions.

Delegating Responsibility

Once the entrepreneur has perceived the need for change and developed a management team, real delegation of responsibility can begin. The power of professional management lies in placing the responsibility close to the source of information required for sound decision making. Typically, this means delegating responsibility to managers who are close to customers, suppliers, and competitors. In the process of delegating, the general manager must be careful *not* to give up responsibility for key policy issues that require personal perspective. Moreover, delegation does not mean that the entrepreneur loses the opportunity to have *input* into the decision-making process; surely, the benefit of that experience should not be lost.

Developing Formal Controls

A final step in the transition process is the development of formal control mechanisms. Successful entrepreneurs realize that, with the onset of delegation, they can no longer control the behavior of individuals in the organization. It is important that the focus of the control system shifts to performance rather than behavior. In addition, successful firms realize the danger in simply adapting policies and procedures that are used at other firms. Firms that customize policies ensure that the practice makes sense for the organization. The process of devoting time and effort often inspires creative solutions, and builds commitment.

CONCLUSION

The reason why the transition to professional management is often so difficult is that it requires *far more* than changes in organizational systems and structures. It requires a *fundamental change in the attitudes and behaviors of the entrepreneur.* Merely creating organizational structures and systems accomplishes little if the entrepreneur is unwilling to truly delegate. Control systems are meaningless if the entrepreneur fails to use them. It is this need to fundamentally change the individual general manager's self-concept behavior that makes the transition process so difficult.

Chapter Thirteen

Bankruptcy: A Debtor's Perspective

For the most part, government in America treats the private sector with cautious noninterference. Direct public participation in the economic affairs of an individual or a corporation is limited to a monitoring function through such bodies as the Internal Revenue Service, the Securities and Exchange Commission, and the Federal Trade Commission. Only when things go wrong does the government step in to take action. In the case of financial failure, public policy has dictated that the legal system act as a buffer between debtors and creditors, seeking to maximize both economic efficiency and equity. Thus, bankruptcy laws have been passed to help ensure that resolutions to situations of financial adversity maximize the present and future value of the "estate" and deal fairly with all debtors and creditors.

Bankruptcy is by no means the obvious result of financial trouble. There are many types of financial adversity and many solutions other than resorting to bankruptcy proceedings. An individual or a firm that becomes insolvent, without cash to pay the bills, may simply stall creditors until the situation improves. They may also default on loan payments, negotiate reduced schedules, or liquidate inventory to generate funds. The notion of bankruptcy implies a sense of direct cause. Someone, either debtor or creditor, decides that the individual or firm should not continue in its present financial incarnation. Then,

This note was prepared by Martha Gershun under the direction of Howard H. Stevenson.

Copyright © 1983 by the President and Fellows of Harvard College
Harvard Business School note 9–384–119

bankruptcy becomes an option for either the debtors or creditors to utilize the law to amend the situation.

For the debtor, bankruptcy provides a chance to bail out from under an impossible burden of debts, to wipe the slate clean and start again. Often it provides an alternative to years of struggling to pay off angry and impatient creditors with an income—personal or corporate—that is insufficient to meet all obligations as they come due. For creditors, bankruptcy provides a chance to get back some portion of their claims on an equitable basis with all other creditors. Often it provides an alternative to continuously postponed payments and the fear of being treated unfairly vis-à-vis other creditors. No one wants to see his debt go unpaid while another creditor is paid in full. Bankruptcy provides a means for creditors to hedge their bets: it gives them a guarantee of partial payment, rather than a gamble for full payment at a cost of entering into the timing uncertainty inherent in the legal system.

This chapter will discuss bankruptcy from the point of view of the individual or corporate debtor. First, it will describe the new Bankruptcy Reform Act of 1978 and the legal jurisdiction for bankruptcy law in the United States today. Then, it will examine bankruptcy in general and three forms of bankruptcy in particular: liquidation, corporation reorganization, and the adjustment of debts of an individual with a regular income. Finally, it will talk about some of the ways debtors can protect themselves before taking this final step and will discuss what actions are prohibited under the new law.

THE NEW LAW

Until a few years ago, the prevailing code for bankruptcy law in the United States was the Bankruptcy Act of 1898, also known as the Nelson Act. While this act was amended some 50 times, including a major overhaul under the Chandler Act of 1938, it remained in effect for 80 years until Congress passed the Bankruptcy Reform Act of 1978. The new code, Public Law 95-958, has eight odd-numbered substantive chapters. The first three are administrative rules which are relevant to *all* bankruptcy proceedings, and the remainder deal with specific types of bankruptcy. Note that the election of any type of bankruptcy triggers an automatic stop of all lawsuits against the company:

— Chapter 1 sets forth general definitions and rules.

— Chapter 3 deals with case administration.

— Chapter 5 deals with such issues as creditors' claims, debtors' duties and advantages, exemptions, and trustees' powers.

— Chapter 7 deals with liquidations.

— Chapter 9 deals with municipal debts.

— Chapter 11 deals with reorganizations for businesses including railroads.

— Chapter 13 deals with debts of a person with a regular income.

— Chapter 15 contains the necessary provisions to set up a new United States Trustee Pilot Program.

Under the new act, bankruptcy courts are established as adjuncts of each U.S. District Court. Bankruptcy judges are appointed by the president, with the advice and consent of the Senate. This situation prevailed until early 1983 when the Supreme Court determined that bankruptcy judges were members of the judicial branch of the government just like all other judges and, as such, had to be given certain guarantees of independence, including lifetime tenure.

Total bankruptcy proceedings of all types increased from slightly more than 10,000 cases commenced in the fiscal year ending June 30, 1946 to more than 254,000 in fiscal 1975. They declined during the next three years to just under 203,000 in fiscal 1978 before soaring to approximately 298,500 for the fiscal year ending September 30, 1980, the first year of operations under the Bankruptcy Code of 1978, and then continuing to soar to reach 561,000 in fiscal 1987.

A final note: not all companies can elect to go bankrupt. Banks, including savings and loans, insurance companies, and all foreign companies are prohibited from doing so.

GETTING INTO TROUBLE

For an individual, the path to bankruptcy is often clearly discernible in retrospect; through hindsight, it is easy to see where a person made a bad decision, when they became overextended, how they misjudged their financial situation. There are two ways individuals accumulate sufficient unpaid debts to contemplate bankruptcy. The first is painfully simple: they purchase more on credit than they can afford to buy. This happens because they underestimate the amount of money they will have to pay for their accumulated credit purchases or because they overestimate the amount of income they will earn. Thus, the incidence of individual bankruptcies has increased with rises of easy consumer credit and in periods of unemployment, when people may lose their jobs unexpectedly or be unable to find new work if they are laid off. The second road to individual bankruptcy is more complex. It occurs when an individual's personal finances are in order, but he or she chooses to act as guarantor for a business or for another individual whose situation may not be as fortunate. When an individual agrees to accept the burden of another's debts (either for an individual or a corporation), then that person becomes legally responsible if the first entity defaults on payments. Sometimes, this additional financial requirement is more than the individual's personal budget can accommodate. Bankruptcy then becomes a way of eliminating these added debts, leaving the individual free to begin again.

For corporations, the path to bankruptcy is considerably more complicated. Ray Barrickman outlines 18 potential causes of business failure: excessive competition, the general business cycle, changes in public demand, governmental acts, adverse acts of labor, acts of God, poor overall management, unwise promotion, unwise expansion, inefficient selling, overextension of inventories, poor financial management, excessive fixed charges, excessive funded debt, excessive floating debt, overextension of credit, unwise dividend policies, and inadequate maintenance and depreciation.[1]

John Argenti, studying corporate failures in Great Britain, posits a chain of events, beginning with poor management, which usually precipitates a firm's slide into bankruptcy:

> If the management of a company is poor then two things will be neglected: the system of accountancy information will be deficient, and the company will not respond to change. (Some companies, even well-managed ones, may be damaged because powerful constraints prevent the managers making the responses they wish to make.) Poor managers will also make at least one of three other mistakes: they will overtrade; or they will launch a big project that goes wrong; or they will allow the company's gearing [financial leverage] to rise so that even normal business hazards become constant threats. These are the chief causes, neither fraud nor bad luck deserve more than a passing mention. The following symptoms will appear: certain financial ratios will deteriorate but, as soon as they do, the managers will start creative accounting that reduces the predictive value of these ratios and so lends greater importance to nonfinancial symptoms. Finally the company enters a characteristic period in its last few months.[2]

These are not all root causes of bankruptcy, of course. The direct catalyst for bankruptcy proceedings is a person or company's inability to pay debts on time. When this situation occurs, the individual or company may begin voluntary bankruptcy proceedings or their creditors may try to force them into involuntary bankruptcy. Any person, partnership, or corporation can file for voluntary relief under the bankruptcy code. Even solvent entities can file for bankruptcy as long as there is no intent to defraud.

---

[1]Ray E. Barrickman, *Business Failure, Causes, Remedies, and Cures* (Washington, D.C.: University Press of America, 1979), p. 28.

[2]John Argenti, *Corporate Collapse: The Causes and Symptoms* (London: McGraw-Hill, 1976), p. 108.

For example, Manville Corporation filed for bankruptcy in late 1982, even though the company had a book net worth of nearly $1.2 billion. The manufacturer was seeking protection from an anticipated 32,000 lawsuits relating to the injury or death of workers who used Manville's asbestos products. Assuming an average settlement of $40,000 per lawsuit, Manville calculated that it could not afford to stay in business and sought bankruptcy relief from these "creditors."

Sometimes, the resort to bankruptcy is motivated more by strategic than financial issues. Wilson Foods, a producer of meat and food products, recently sought Chapter 11 protection in order to force union officials to reduce labor wages. Wilson's chairman announced publicly that the firm did not intend to close any of its plants or lay off any workers. He further stated that Wilson had sufficient cash, receivables, and available credit to meet its short-term obligations. The bankrupt can apply to the court to nullify a union contract that would otherwise have lasted until 1985. The court must decide such cases based upon what is in the best interest of the estate. Thus, the move allowed Wilson to put in place sharply reduced hourly wages. A similar case—Bildisco—has been decided by the Supreme Court. The outcome of this case, involving the issue of whether or not bankruptcy allows a firm to change contract terms with union employees, determined that firms may use Chapter 11 protection in this manner. Unions are currently lobbying for congressional relief from this decision.

In order to seek relief from their debts, a person or corporation must file in the office of the Clerk of the United States District Court in which the domicile, residence, principal place of business, or principal assets of the entity have been located for the preceding 180 days. The filing fee is $60 for parties commencing a bankruptcy case under Chapter 7 (liquidation) or Chapter 13 (adjustment of debts for an individual with regular income). The filing fee for businesses seeking relief under Chapter 11 (business reorganizations) is $200; railroads must pay a filing fee of $500. *A person or corporation can only file for bankruptcy protection once every six years.*

In certain situations, creditors can force debtors to go bankrupt. An involuntary bankruptcy case can be commenced by:

— Three or more creditors whose aggregated claims amount to more than $5,000 over the value of any assets securing those claims; or

— One or more such creditors if there are less than 12 claim holders; or

— Fewer than all the general partners in a limited partnership.

Creditors do not have to prove that the debtor is unable to pay his or her bills; mere failure to pay on time, regardless of ability to pay, is sufficient grounds for creditors to seek involuntary bankruptcy. However, in an involuntary bankruptcy proceeding, the court can require petitioners to post a bond to cover the debtor's costs if the court finds in the debtor's favor. Furthermore, if the creditors are found to have petitioned in bad faith, the court may award the debtor any damages caused by the proceedings, including punitive compensation. In practice, involuntary bankruptcy is uncommon. For the year ending June 30, 1979, only 926 involuntary bankuptcy cases were filed out of a total of 226,476 cases.[3]

CHOOSING YOUR POISON: WHICH CHAPTER?

There are three distinct chapters of the bankruptcy code that can shape the outcome of the bankruptcy proceedings: Chapter 7 (liquidation), Chapter 11 (reorganization), and Chapter 13 (adjustment of an individual's debts).

In theory, bankruptcy procedures can be concluded very quickly. In practice, however, they are often long, drawn-out affairs. Corporate reorganizations, in particular, can take many years to reach completion. Speaking before the 94th Congress, Representative Elizabeth Holtzman noted that "it is reported that the average corporate reorganization case in the Seventh District of New York takes eight years to resolve."[4]

In a Chapter 7 bankruptcy the assets of the individual or corporation are liquidated and distributed to creditors. In a Chapter 11 or Chapter 13 bankruptcy the debtors keep their assets with some arrangement to pay off their debts over time. Since the outcomes of these types of bankruptcy are radically different, affecting the form of the assets that the debtor keeps as well as the timing and amount of payments that the creditors receive, both groups have some ability to influence the choice of prevailing chapters.

When the creditor files for an involuntary bankruptcy case under Chapter 7 or 11, the debtor can convert the case to a bankruptcy under any of the other chapters. When a debtor files for voluntary bankruptcy under any chapter, the creditors can request that the trustee convert the case to a Chapter 7 or a Chapter 11 bankruptcy. Only a Chapter 13 bankruptcy cannot be commenced without the debtor's consent. Before choosing a chapter for bankruptcy, debtors should carefully consider whether they would prefer to liquidate their assets

---

[3]Table of Bankruptcy Statistics with reference to bankruptcy cases commenced and terminated in the United States District Courts during the period July 1, 1978, through June 30, 1979. Administrative Office of the United States Courts.

[4]House Report #686, p. 56.

or continue their business with personal finances, attempting with reorganization or adjustment to pay off their debts over time.

Chapter 7: Liquidation

Chapter 7 of the Bankruptcy Act provides for either voluntary or involuntary liquidation of the assets of the debtor or distribution to the creditors. When a petition is filed under Chapter 7 it constitutes an Order for Relief. The debtor now has a legal obligation to:

1. File a list of creditors, assets and liabilities, and a statement of financial affairs.
2. Cooperate with the trustee appointed to the case.
3. Give the trustee all property of the estate and all records relating to the property.
4. Appear at any hearing dealing with a discharge.
5. Attend all meetings of creditors.

As soon as possible after the Order for Relief, an interim trustee will be appointed. If creditors holding at least 30 percent of the specified claims request one, an election will be held to choose one person to serve as trustee in the case. This can be the debtor serving as trustee while debtor in possession. If no trustee is elected in this manner, the interim trustee will continue to serve. The duties of the trustee include:

1. Reducing the property of the debtor's estate to cash and closing up the estate as expeditiously as possible.
2. Accounting for all property received.
3. Investigating the financial affairs of the debtor and examining all claims for validity.
4. Providing information about the estate to any interested party, furnishing reports on the debtor's business if it is authorized to be operated, and filing a final report of the disposition of the estate with the court.

Portions of the debtor's estate will be exempt from liquidation; that is, they may not be distributed to the creditors. In many states, the debtor can choose between the federal exemptions or the relevant state exemptions. However, states can require their residents to adhere to the state exemptions; Florida and Virginia have passed such laws, and South Carolina, Delaware, and Ohio are considering similar statutes. Under the current federal exemptions, a debtor gets to keep:

1. The debtor's interest, not to exceed $7,500, in the debtor's (or a dependent's) residence; in a cooperative that owns property used by the debtor (or a dependent) as a residence; and in a burial plot for the debtor or a dependent.

2. The debtor's interest, not to exceed $1,200, in a motor vehicle.

3. The debtor's interest, not to exceed $200 in value for any particular item, in household furnishings, clothing, appliances, books, animals, crops, or musical instruments, that are kept for the personal, family, or household use of the debtor or a dependent.

4. The debtor's interest, not to exceed $500, in jewelry held for personal, family, or household use of the debtor or a dependent.

5. The debtor's interest, not to exceed $400, in any property in addition to Item 1 exemptions.

6. The debtor's interest, not to exceed $750, in any implements, professional books, or tools of the trade of the debtor or a dependent.

7. Any insurance contract that is not mature other than a credit contract.

8. The debtor's interest, not to exceed $4,000, in any accrued dividends or interest or loan value or any nonmature life insurance contract under which the debtor or a dependent is insured.

9. Prescribed health aids for the debtor or a dependent.

10. The debtor's right to receive social security benefits, unemployment compensation benefits, local public assistance benefits, veterans' benefits, and illness or disability benefits.

11. The debtor's right to receive alimony, support, or separate maintenance.

12. The debtor's right to receive a payment, stock bonus, pension, profit sharing annuity, or similar plan on account of illness, disability, debt, age, or want of service.

13. The debtor's right to receive an award under a crime victim's reparation law; a payment on account of a wrongful death of an individual of whom the debtor was a dependent; a payment under a life insurance contract that insured the life of an individual of whom the debtor was a dependent; a payment not to exceed $7,500 on account of personal bodily injury, not including pain and suffering or compensation for actual pecuniary loss, of the debtor or an individual of whom the debtor is a dependent; or a payment in compensation of loss of future earnings of the debtor or an individual of whom the debtor is or was a dependent.

The rest of the debtor's estate is distributed first to secured creditors and then to priority claimants. These claims include, in order: administrative expenses and filing fees assessed against the debtor's estate; certain unsecured claims arising before the appointment of a trustee in involuntary cases; wages, salaries, or commissions, including vacation, severance, and sick leave pay to the extent of $2,000 per individual earned within 90 days of the date of filing or the date of cessation of business, whichever occurred first; contributions to employee benefit plans up to $2,000 per employee earned within 180 days; claims of individuals, up to $900 each, arising from the deposit of money in connection with purchases of property or services that are not delivered; claims of governmental units of taxes and custom duties.

Next come the general unsecured creditors and the general unsecured creditors who filed late claims. Punitive penalties are next in distribution, followed by claims for interest accruing during the bankruptcy case. Interest is paid at the legal rate on the date the petition was filed. If there is any surplus after these six classes are paid, it goes to the debtor. If there aren't enough funds to pay a class in full, claims within the class are paid pro rata. The table below shows how assets are distributed in cases closed during 1977. It is interesting to note that fully 22.9 percent of the assets in bankruptcy cases were used to pay administrative expenses. (Note: These figures were the results of bankruptcies under the Bankruptcy Act, *not* the current code.)

Distibution of Assets in Cases Closed in 1977

	Payment	*Percent of Total*
Paid priority creditors	$ 27,799,506	12.1
Paid secured creditors	77,479,621	33.8
Paid unsecured creditors	61,109,352	26.6
Other payments	10,612,376	4.6
All administrative expenses	52,534,678	22.9
Total distribution	$229,535,533	100.0

Source: Table of Bankruptcy Statistics with reference to bankruptcy cases commenced and terminated in the United States District Courts during the period July 1, 1976 through June 30, 1977. Administrative Office of the United States Courts.

When the debtor is an individual, the court will usually grant *discharge.* **This means the debtor is discharged from all past debts except certain debts arising from alimony, child support, and taxes, or debts that were not listed on the debtor's financial statements when bankruptcy was filed.**

Chapter 11: Reorganization

The purpose of Chapter 11 of the new Bankruptcy Code is to provide a mechanism of reorganizing a firm's finances so it can continue to operate, pay its creditors, provide jobs, and produce a return to its investors. Usually debtors and creditors will opt for this form of bankruptcy if they think a business or estate has more value as a going concern than as a pile of liquidated assets. The objective of the reorganization is to develop a plan that determines how much creditors will be paid and in what form the business will continue. Any individual, partnership, or corporation that can file for liquidation under Chapter 7 can file for reorganization under Chapter 11, except stockbrokers and commodity brokers. Furthermore, railroads can proceed under Chapter 11, while they are prohibited from seeking liquidation.

Like a Chapter 7 case, a reorganization can be either voluntary or involuntary. After the entry for an Order for Relief, the creditors and debtor must meet within 30 days to discuss the organization of the business. Under the new Bankruptcy Code, the court may not attend a creditor's meeting. Rather, the interim trustee or the U.S. trustee will preside. This follows from the new code's attempt to correct previous problems caused by having bankruptcy judges serve as both judge and administrator in bankruptcy cases.

After the Order for Relief, the court will appoint a committee of general unsecured creditors. This committee is usually comprised of those creditors holding the seven largest claims; however the court has great latitude in composing the committee to make it representative of the different kinds of interests in the case. This committee is primarily responsible for formulating a plan for the business and collecting and filing with the court acceptances of the plan. The debtor keeps possession of the business unless any of the creditors can show the debtor is guilty of fraud, dishonesty, incompetence, or gross mismanagement, or otherwise proves such an arrangement is not in the interests of the creditors. If the court upholds that either of these conditions exists, a trustee will be appointed. Unlike a Chapter 7 trustee, a Chapter 11 trustee is not elected and cannot be a creditor or an equity holder of the debtor or the debtor's business. The duties of a Chapter 11 trustee include being accountable for all of the information and records necessary to formulate the reorganization plan and filing the plan with the court or recommending conversion to a Chapter 7 or a Chapter 13 case or dismissing the case altogether.

If a trustee is not appointed, the debtor possesses these powers. No court order is necessary for the debtor to continue to run the firm;

rather, the business is to remain in operation unless the court orders otherwise.

The debtor has 120 days to file the reorganization plan and 60 more days to obtain acceptances. The plan must designate the various classes of creditors and show how they will be treated. The plan can be a liquidation. Thus, a business could be liquidated under Chapter 11 rather than Chapter 7. The plan must be accepted by half of the creditors in number who are affected by the plan and two thirds of the creditors in dollar amount. Creditors must vote to accept or reject the plan, and the plan must obtain the endorsement of a simple majority of those who vote. If the court confirms a reorganization plan, the debtor is discharged from any past debts except as they are handled under the new plan.

Chapter 13: Adjustment of Debts of an Individual with Regular Income

Chapter 13 of the new Bankruptcy Code covers individuals with regular income whose unsecured debts are less than $100,000 and whose secured debts are less than $350,000. This includes individuals who own or operate businesses. It does not include partnerships or corporations. There cannot be an involuntary Chapter 13 bankruptcy case.

The purpose of Chapter 13 is to allow an individual to pay off debts with future earnings while the court protects him or her from harassment by creditors. Furthermore, it allows the debtor to continue to own and operate a business while Chapter 13 is pending. A plan under Chapter 13 can be an extension—creditors paid in full—or a composition—creditors paid in part—and is payable over three years, with a two-year extension allowed for cause.

In a Chapter 13 case the property of the estate includes property and earnings acquired after the commencement of the case but before it is closed. The court will appoint a Chapter 13 trustee to administer the case but not to take possession of the estate.

Chapter 13 has several major advantages for the debtor:

1. Once it is filed, all of the debtor's property and future income are under the court's jurisdiction. An automatic stay order is issued against litigation and collection efforts.

2. Unlike Chapter 7, the trustee does not take possession of the debtor's property. The debtor can increase his or her estate while on the plan.

3. Chapter 13 can help preserve the debtor's credit. Also, the six-year ban on filing for bankruptcy can be avoided in an extension plan and some compensation plans.

4. Since only the debtor can file a plan, there are no competing proposals.

5. The court can still convert a Chapter 13 case to a Chapter 11 case or a Chapter 7 case if it determines it is in the best interests of the creditors or the estate.

The court will hold a confirmation hearing on the plan. Secured creditors can stop confirmation if one of the following is violated: (*a*) they keep the lien securing their claims or (*b*) they receive the property securing their claims. Unsecured creditors have no voice in the confirmation process. The court will grant the debtor a discharge after all payments under the plans are completed.

POWERS OF TRUSTEE

In addition to the responsibilities enumerated in Chapters 7, 11, and 13, the trustee in a bankruptcy case has a great deal of power that can determine how assets are allocated and debt restructured. Note that in some instances, the debtor himself (debtor-in-possession) is functioning as the trustee. Chapters 3 and 5 of the Bankruptcy Code set forth such powers as the ability to employ professionals to help carry out the duties of trustee; the power to use, sell, or lease property; the power to obtain credits secured by priority claims and new liens; the power to reject or assume contracts and unexpired leases; and the power to avoid preferences and fraudulent transfers, known as *the avoiding powers*. These powers can change the status of certain classes of creditors, depending on how they are applied. For instance, by rejecting an unexpired lease, the trustee can convert a long-term leaseholder into just another unsecured creditor. If a trustee is not appointed, then the debtor in possession of the estate assumes these powers.

NEGOTIATIONS AND SETTLEMENTS

While they may feel persecuted and helpless, debtors actually have a great deal of power to negotiate with their creditors for arrangements that will leave the firm intact, either before or after bankruptcy is declared. This power stems from several sources: the incentive for all creditors to reach a speedy and workable solution to the debtor's financial problems; the differing interests of various classes of creditors; and the ultimate protection of the bankruptcy laws.

A debtor in serious financial shape may find he or she has a lot of leverage with creditors who fear the recourse of bankruptcy. These creditors may be willing to undertake voluntary arrangements to restructure loans, postpone payments, relinquish lease obligations, or ignore accrued interest, as a way of helping the debtor avoid bankruptcy. Creditors have several motivations for such voluntary arrangements. If the debtor is threatening to seek bankruptcy relief under Chapter 7, the creditors might determine they have a better long-run chance of repayment if the firm continues to exist than if it is dissolved and the assets are sold at low liquidation values. Creditors might also fear the high administrative and legal costs of bankruptcy proceedings, particularly in a complicated case. These costs might be incurred by the creditors directly or they might be incurred by the debtor's estate, thus reducing the amount of money for distribution to creditors. When Itel Corp., the computer leasing company, filed for bankruptcy in January 1981, it took two years for the company to be reorganized under Chapter 11. The first four months of administrative and legal expenses cost the estate $6.7 million. Creditors might also prefer a voluntary arrangement because it avoids the adverse publicity of a liquidation; they want the prospect of future business with the debtor; or such an arrangement appears faster than a court-supervised settlement. Sometimes creditors who want a voluntary arrangement will pay off the debtor's liabilities to other creditors just to avoid legal proceedings.

Debtors also derive power from the differing interests of creditors. As noted above, a creditor for whom speed of settlement is more important than full payment might negotiate with another creditor whose interest lies in full payment rather than a quick solution. In such an instance, both groups of creditors can be satisfied if the first pays the second's claims in order to expedite a settlement. Trade creditors and money creditors might have varying interests too, with trade creditors preferring a settlement that leaves the firm intact to do business in the future, and money creditors preferring a liquidation that provides as much cash as possible. Debtors can use this dichotomy to their advantage, using available cash to pay off money creditors while asking trade creditors to forbear in the hope of putting the firm back on solid financial ground rather than driving it into bankruptcy.

Of course, creditors do not have to be conciliatory. In 1978, Food Fair, Inc., ran into cash shortages, and its suppliers refused to extend credit beyond their normal terms. Angered by what they perceived as preferential treatment to suppliers with family connections to Food

Fair's management, the supermarket's other suppliers refused to extend trade credit terms, even after the company significantly reduced its outstanding obligations. The firm was forced to seek bankrutpcy protection under Chapter 11.

In his book, *Corporations in Crisis,* Philip Nelson notes that the measures available to debtors and creditors short of filing for bankruptcy can lead to economic inefficiencies on the macro level:

> Focusing for the moment on the triggering decision, it appears that, because bankruptcy is only triggered when economic actors perceive that bankruptcy promotes their interests, social losses may easily accumulate as a firm struggles on outside the court's protection. In most sample cases, no economic actor had the incentive and the knowledge to trigger bankruptcy when it was needed. Executive preference for continued salaries, the distaste for the stigma of bankruptcy, inadequate information flows, and ignorance of the advantages offered by bankruptcy combine to encourage delays. Only at the few firms where the controlling executives associated relatively little stigma with bankruptcy and understood its advantages was bankruptcy triggered promptly. As a result, bankruptcy often comes after the resources of the firm are largely expended.

Despite this point of view, the debtor in each individual case certainly has the right and considerable power to cut the best possible deal.

Debtors also derive power within the framework of formal bankruptcy proceedings. Removed from a position of turmoil and harassment, where every unpaid creditor can hound the individual or corporation for immediate payment, the debtor who has filed for bankruptcy is suddenly in a position to bargain with creditors. Further, the automatic stay against all lawsuits that is provided by the bankruptcy law is an additional incentive for creditors to work out an acceptable plan. As with settlements that occur short of the bankruptcy proceeding, the debtor's leverage lies in the creditor's wish for a speedy, efficient plan that maximizes the wealth of the debtor for distribution or future payment. If the creditors retain some faith in the firm, there is usually a strong incentive to seek Chapter 11 relief. The debtor in this position can often negotiate a deal that will get the firm back on its feet. When Itel Corp. filed for bankruptcy, the firm received four 60-day extensions from the Bankruptcy Court to work out a reorganization package that would be acceptable to creditors. In the final deal, Itel's Eurobond holders were allowed $110 million of claims, although that class of creditors only had $91 million in principal and accrued interest outstanding when Itel filed for reorganization.

The distribution to Eurobond holders per $10,000 of claim was estimated by Itel's reorganization plan as follows:

Security	Face Amount	Market Value
Cash	$3,690	$3,690
14% secured notes	2,035	1,689–1,780
10% notes	1,032	443– 501
New preferred stock	11.5 shares	259– 305
New common stock	124.3 shares	186– 311

Itel said one of the main reasons for increasing the amount of these creditors' claims was to avoid possible delays in the reorganization plan from pending litigation involving the Eurobonds.

The Bankruptcy Code was not intended to shift the balance of power away from creditors; it was designed to give both debtors and creditors motivation for seeking a solution that will maximize the settlement for both parties.

DEBTOR'S OPTIONS

While the new Bankruptcy Code deals generously with debtors, providing a chance to discharge debts and begin again, no debtor wants to be thrown into bankruptcy proceedings against his or her will. There are several steps a debtor can take to ensure against involuntary bankruptcy. These include being sure that the number of creditors exceeds 12 and that no 3 creditors' claims amount to more than $5,000. Sometimes, this could mean paying off some creditors in full while not paying others all that they are due. If there are more than 12 creditors in a case, 1 or 2 claimants cannot force an individual or a corporation into involuntary bankruptcy.

There are many steps a debtor can take to maximize the amount of exempt assets that can be retained in a bankruptcy case. In contemplating bankruptcy, the debtor should examine exemptions closely and arrange his or her affairs in such a way as to give the best possible start following declaration. These measures should not be considered cheating or violating the law. The regulations were set to give debtors the best possible chance of regaining financial stability, while treating all creditors fairly.

There are also many actions a debtor *cannot* take under the law. Besides the obvious violation of hiding assets or hiding liabilities, the most important prohibition placed on debtors is that of preferential treatment. Once a debtor has filed for bankruptcy, the trustee has the power to disallow any payment to a creditor that enables that creditor to receive more than others in the same class. A preferential payment is one made 90 days prior to the bankruptcy. If the creditor was an insider, this limit extends to one year if the insider has cause to believe the debtor was insolvent. This provision ensures the bankruptcy policy of equality of distribution among creditors. Any creditor who manages to extort a larger share than others of the same class prior to the bankruptcy is forced to return it to the general pot for fair allocation. This provision also limits the debtor's ability to play one creditor off against others in an attempt to avoid bankruptcy, since creditors know such settlements could be disallowed if bankruptcy is declared within three months.

There are many avenues available for the savvy debtor to pursue, either before filing for bankruptcy or after such proceedings have been initiated. Debtors in financial trouble would be wise to seek competent legal counsel early so as to carve the best path out of their predicament.

REFERENCES

Argenti, John. *Corporate Collapse: The Causes and Symptoms.* London: McGraw-Hill, 1976.

"Asbestosis: Manville Seeks Chapter 11." *Fortune,* September 20, 1982.

"Bankruptcy." Harvard Business School 9-376-221, prepared by Laurence H. Stone, copyright 1976.

Bankruptcy Reform. Washington, D.C.: American Enterprise Institute for Public Policy Research, 1978.

Barrickman, Ray E. *Business Failure: Causes, Remedies, and Cures.* Washington, D.C.: University Press of America, 1979.

Bluestein, Paul. "A $2.5 Billion Tale of Woe." *Forbes,* October 30, 1978, p. 51.

"A Brief Note on Arrangements, Bankruptcy, and Reorganization in Bankruptcy." Harvard Business School 9-272-148, rev. 7/75, written by Jasper H. Arnold, Research Assistant, under the supervision of Associate Professor Michael L. Tennican.

Disclosure Statement for Itel Corporation's Amended Plan of Reorganization, Case No. 3-81-00111, December 8, 1982.

Drinkhall, Jim. "Fees Charged by Itel's Overseers Suggest Bankruptcy Can Be Enriching Experience." *The Wall Street Journal,* June 5, 1981, p. 27.

"Food Fair Inc. Seeks Protection under Chapter 11." *The Wall Street Journal,* October 3, 1978, p. 2.

"Itel Corp. Plans to Amend Plan for Reorganization." *The Wall Street Journal,* January 20, 1982, p. 33.

"Itel Corp. Receives More Time to Submit Reorganization Plan." *The Wall Street Journal,* November 16, 1981, p. 23.

"Itel Files Petition for Protection of Chapter 11." *The Wall Street Journal*, January 20, 1981, p. 4.

"Manville's Costs Could Exceed $5 Billion in Asbestos Suits, Study It Ordered Shows." *The Wall Street Journal*, September 15, 1982, p. 7.

Nelson, Philip B. *Corporations in Crisis: Behavioral Observations for Bankrupt Policy.* New York: Praeger Publishers, 1981.

Quittner, Arnold M. *Current Developments in Bankruptcy and Reorganization.* Practicing Law Institute, 1980.

Schnepper, Jeff A. *The New Bankruptcy Law: A Professional's Handbook.* New York: Addison-Wesley Publishing, 1981.

Table of Bankruptcy Statistics with reference to bankruptcy cases commenced and terminated in the United States District Courts during the period July 1, 1978 through June 30, 1979. Administrative Office of the United States Courts. See also July 1, 1976 through June 30, 1977.

"Unpaid Bills: Itel Goes Bust." *Fortune*, February 23, 1981, p. 19.

"Wilson Foods Seeks Chapter 11 Protection Citing Labor Costs, Cuts Wages Up to 50%." *The Wall Street Journal*, April 24, 1983, p. 16.

Chapter Fourteen

Securities Law and Public Offerings

In "Securities Law and Private Financing," we looked at the process and laws that affected private financings. In this piece, we will look at similar issues as they relate to public offerings.

WHY "GO PUBLIC"?

For many companies, the decision on whether or not to become a public company is a difficult one. For some, the "glamour and prestige" of becoming a public company are the deciding factors. For others, the scrutiny and lack of privacy that go along with being publicly held clearly outweigh the advantages.

The Advantages

There are some significant advantages that go along with being a public company. They include,

— A Vast Continuing Source of Capital: The public equity markets do represent a vast pool of capital. A healthy, growing firm can often tap this source more cheaply than other private sources of equity. And, as the company continues to grow, the public equity market

This note was prepared by Michael J. Roberts under the direction of Howard H. Stevenson.

will be available as long as investors have confidence in the company's prospects.

— Liquidity: A public market for the company's securities makes them far more liquid. The company can give employees stock or options as an incentive to lure talented individuals. And the principals of the firm can (subject to certain SEC regulations) sell their stock as they desire.

— Wealth Creation: Taking a company public establishes its value in the market. In addition, through a "secondary offering" of securities, the principals can often sell a portion of their interest at the time of the initial public offering. This creates wealth for both the founders and the financial backers—such as venture capital firms—who invested in the business.

— Glamour and Prestige: For many individuals, "taking their company public" is an important goal. It certainly is one measure of success, as a certain minimum size is generally required in order to take a firm public. Being a public concern may also enhance the company's image with customers, suppliers, and employees.

For some entrepreneurs, these advantages are outweighed by the disadvantages of being a public concern.

The Disadvantages

The disadvantages include:

— Cost: Going public is expensive; estimates run from $100,000 to over $300,000 for an "average" public offering. In addition, there is an underwriters' commission of 7–10 percent, which goes to compensate the investment bank for selling the securities. Finally, there is an annual expense associated with the added accounting and record-keeping required for a public company.

— Public Scrutiny: A public company must file, and make available to the public, its financial statements, as well as certain information about stockholders, customers, business plans, and officers. A company might prefer that its suppliers, customers, and competitors not know how profitable it is, or be aware of some aspect of its business. Finally, certain business practices, such as officers' salaries and business expenses, also come under public scrutiny.

— Pressures on Management: Being a public concern also puts certain pressures on top management. The stock market likes to see constant earnings growth, and the faster the better. There has been a great deal of publicity lately that this "short-term earnings focus" is the cause of serious longer-term competitive problems for many American industries. Finally, management must spend a good deal of time dealing with the financial community, keeping bankers and analysts up to date and interested in the stock.

— Loss of Independence: As a sole owner or small group of principals, management could feel securely in control. But public ownership brings with it a larger constituency. Managers must now manage the company for the good of all the shareholders. Previously borderline "business expenses" may now be totally inappropriate. In addition, there is always the possibility that some outside group may actually try to take over the company. As a public concern, management is far more vulnerable.

These disadvantages are accentuated by the close relationship that usually exists between ownership and management in the entrepreneurial concern. In large public companies, these "disadvantages" have been accepted as a way of life by a management team, which typically controls very little of the stock. In entrepreneurial firms, where the founder(s) may still hold a majority of the shares, the distinction between management and ownership may easily blur. This can lead to management that manages for itself rather than the entire group of stockholders. While this can happen in large companies, minority shareholders in small firms have less chance of successfully combating this practice.

The Decision

The decision to go public is an important one and should be made with the counsel of experienced accountants, lawyers, and bankers. Remember, though, that these people have their own stakes: the investment banker stands to gain a good deal on the sale of the company's securities; a local accountant often loses out to a "Big 8" firm when a company goes public and seeks an accounting firm with a national reputation.

In general, it does seem that many entrepreneurs overestimate some of the benefits of being a public company. Liquidity, for instance, is often seen as a major advantage. But, it is a very difficult task indeed for a president to explain at an analysts meeting why he "dumped" some of his holdings in the market.

Clearly, the need for equity capital must be at the heart of the firm's decision to go public. And, before wandering down this path, the firm would be well-advised to consider other options, such as a private placement of debt or equity.

SELECTING AN UNDERWRITER

Once a company has made a decision to seriously consider going public, it is time to choose an underwriter. Underwriters, or investment bankers, are required both to sell the securities and lead the company through this complex process.

Choosing an Underwriter

The process of selecting an underwriter is not easy. Many investment banks will be anxious to serve the company and will make convincing arguments about why their firms are well suited to execute the company's public offering. When choosing a firm, the following criteria are important.

— Reputation: The underwriter's name will appear at the bottom of the prospectus, often in letters as large as the company's name. The underwriter's reputation will affect its ability to sell the stock both to other investment banks and to institutional and retail customers.

— Distribution: Investment banks have certain strengths and weaknesses in terms of their ability to distribute the stock. Some have a strong institutional network selling to large pension funds and money managers. Others sell primarily to retail accounts—private investors.

— It is often desirable to have a mix of stockholders. Institutions have deep pockets, but can be unfaithful, deserting and selling a stock on the first sign of bad news. Retail accounts tend to be more stable, but are not as big a force in the stock market.

— After-Market Support: It is important that a bank support a company after the public offering. This support includes:

  • Research—to sustain interest in the stock on the part of investors.

  • Market-making—committing capital to buying and selling the stock, to provide investors with liquidity.

  • Financial advice—bankers can provide valuable advice on the subject of dividends, new financing, or mergers and acquisitions.

Recently, underwriters have become more competitive, and investment banking is not the "gentlemanly business" it was considered to be years ago. The entrepreneur would be wise to consider and negotiate with a variety of firms.

What about Stock Price?

Note that we have not mentioned price as one of the criteria. Clearly, you would prefer to sell stock in your company to the underwriters who thought it was worth the most in the market. During the negotiation process, underwriters will often "estimate" the price at which the stock will be sold in the public offering.

— First, they make projections of the company's earnings per share.

— Then, they attempt to place a price/earnings multiple on this figure to arrive at a per share value.

In theory, this approach should work just fine. But, the price/earnings multiple is a very subjective judgment, based on an assessment of what multiples "similar" companies are trading at.

The night before the offering, after many months of work and after spending a good deal of money, the market will in all likelihood appear quite different than it did at the time of the initial negotiations. The underwriter may suggest an offering price that is substantially different from the price discussed during negotiations. The company has little choice save to cancel the offering entirely.

This fact is *not* lost on the underwriters.

Other Issues

Once a company has decided to go public, and chosen an underwriter, several other important issues remain.

— Listing: The company must decide where its shares will be listed and traded. The New York and American Stock Exchanges, as well as other exchanges, all have certain requirements that must be met in order for the firm to obtain a listing.

— Amount of Primary Offering: The firm must decide how much money it wishes to raise.

— Amount of Secondary Offering: In addition to selling its "own shares"—the primary offering—the principals of the firm may sell some of their own stock. This is called a *secondary offering,* and the owners of the stock, *not* the company, get to keep the money that is raised from sale of secondary stock.

REGISTERED OFFERINGS

All public offerings must be registered with the SEC under the Securities Act of 1933.

The Registration Process

The registration process for a company that is not yet publicly traded involves the preparation by management of a carefully worded and organized disclosure document called a *registration statement*. This includes a "prospectus," which will be provided to the potential investor. The registration statement is filed with the appropriate securities agency, which, for federal registrations, is the SEC. The various items of disclosure that must be discussed in a registration statement are fixed by law. In addition, there must be set forth any other material matter that affects or may affect the company.

The SEC staff reviews the disclosure documents and (unless a special "cursory review" procedure is used) makes detailed comments on the disclosure, and the documents are revised as a result of these comments. If the staff is satisfied with the revisions, the SEC enters an order declaring the registration statement "effective," and sale of the offering may commence. The SEC order in no way constitutes an approval by the SEC of the accuracy of the disclosures or the merits of the offering, and any representation to that effect violates the securities laws. At the time of the effectiveness of the registration statement, the underwriters will usually place a "tombstone" advertisement in the financial press announcing the offering. A copy of the final prospectus in an initial public offering must be distributed to persons purchasing company securities of the type sold in the offering for 25 days after the effective date, or until the offering is sold or terminated, whichever last occurs. During this period, if any material event affecting the company occurs, it must be disclosed by a sticker "supplement" to the prospectus. In general, the disclosure documents become outdated after approximately nine months from the effective date and may not be used thereafter unless updated by posteffective amendment to the registration statement.

Cost

Federal registration is expensive and time-consuming. An initial public offering using an underwriter frequently takes four months to accomplish and costs from $150,000 to $250,000, exclusive of underwriting commissions. A typical cost breakdown is as follows: printing

$75,000, legal fees $75,000, accounting fees $50,000, and Blue Sky and miscellaneous costs $25,000. (These figures are rough and may vary considerably from offering to offering.) In view of the amount of the costs involved, federal registration of a first offering using an underwriter is generally not feasible unless in excess of $2 million dollars is involved in the financing.

The cost of a public offering depends as much upon whether or not an underwriter is used as upon whether or not federal registration is required. This is true because the agreement between the company and the underwriter usually requires the company's attorneys and accountants to undertake at the company's expense detailed and costly verification of the disclosures in the prospectus. Underwriting commissions typically run from 7½ percent to 10 percent of the gross amount of the offering in first equity offerings. The underwriter may also require warrants to purchase an amount of stock equal to 10 percent of the shares sold at the offering at a small premium over the offering price as additional compensation. Because placement of a large amount of securities often involves market price stabilization and other sophisticated and highly regulated techniques, an attempt by a company to place a large amount of securities without a professional underwriter or selling agent usually involves an unacceptable amount of risk. Also, it may be extremely difficult for a large amount of securities to be placed without the assistance of a professional underwriter or selling agent with a number of investor customers that rely upon his or her investment advice.

Underwriters

Underwriters essentially agree to sell the company's securities for a fixed percentage of the underwriting. Underwritings are of two types—"firm-commitment" underwritings in which the sale of the entire offering at an established price is guaranteed by the underwriters and "best-efforts" underwritings in which the underwriter uses his best efforts to sell as much as he can of the offering at the offering price. Best efforts underwritings may also include a provision requiring that either all or a minimum amount of the securities must be sold as a condition of any of the securities being sold. The type of underwriting used is usually determined by the size and strength of the company and of the underwriter.

The first step in an underwritten offering is usually the execution of a nonbinding "letter of intent" between the company (or selling stockholder) and the managing underwriter. Although not a legally binding document, the letter of intent is one of the most important documents in the offering, as it establishes the basic terms of the underwriting, usually including the price range—perhaps as a range of multiples of the company's most recent earnings. (If multiples of per share earnings are used, it should be made clear whether the per share figures are to be calculated using the number of outstanding shares before or those after the offering.) After the letter of intent has been signed, the disclosure documents (including the prospectus) are prepared for filing with the SEC.

From the outset of an underwritten offering, the managing underwriter and the company (or selling stockholder) commence subtle negotiation of the price of the offering, which is usually culminated by the setting of the price on the evening before the offering. During the course of the registration, the company incurs substantial offering expenses, which (as both parties well realize) will be to a large extent unrecoverable if the financing is postponed or aborted. In addition to the problems a firm-commitment underwriter has in guaranteeing sale of the entire offering when the price is at a high level, a managing underwriter has an incentive to negotiate a low price for his or her own customers and for those of the members of his or her underwriting and selling syndicate, with which she or he usually has an established business relationship. (A broker with unhappy customers soon has no customers.) She or he often does this by subtly threatening to abandon the deal after the company has expended substantial unrecoverable funds in preparation for the offering and after it has terminated negotiations with competing underwriters. It is thus important for the company, if possible, to require the underwriter to bear his or her own expenses (including attorneys' fees) so that any abandonment will result in some loss (although a lesser one) for the underwriter. This arrangement should be set forth in the letter of intent. On the other hand, the offering price should not be set too high or the price of the securities may suffer in the aftermarket, thereby reducing the value of the remaining securities holdings of the principal owners and diminishing the company's ability to raise capital in the future.

Throughout the period of registration, including the prospectus delivery period following the effective date, the company must carefully monitor the public statements of its management, its public relations advisors, and its advertising program to assure that no optimistic disclosures concerning the company's condition or prospects are disseminated to the investing public. If, for example, an article on the company appears in *Forbes* or *Business Week* during registration, it may be deemed to be part of the company's selling effort (to the extent it is based upon information supplied by management) and thus subject to the rigid standards of the securities laws. Disclosure during the period preceding the initial filing of the registration statement with the SEC (the "prefiling period") is particularly sensitive, as such disclosure might be considered to be an attempt to precondition the market ("gun-jumping"). Even the information to be contained in an announcement of the filing of the registration statement is regulated by SEC rule. After the effective date, however, certain types of supplementary selling literature may be used if preceded or accompanied by a final prospectus.

The registration statement as initially filed contains a preliminary prospectus with a "red herring" legend printed in red sideways on the cover page. While the SEC staff is reviewing the registration statement and preparing its comments (the "waiting period"), the preliminary prospectus will be used by the underwriter in the formation of its underwriting and selling syndicate. Although the various members of the underwriting and selling syndicate often have an established business relationship with the managing underwriter, a new syndicate is formed for each deal. The preliminary prospectus will be used by syndicate members during the waiting period to solicit "indications of interest" from the investing public. The reception of the investing public to the preliminary prospectus will affect the price of the offering, which, as noted above, is usually established immediately prior to the effective date.

As a result of registration with the SEC, a company becomes subject to the periodic reporting requirements of the SEC. In the case of a first public offering, the company must report the actual use of proceeds to the SEC three months after the offering so the SEC can compare this with the disclosures in the prospectus. If there is a discrepancy, the company can expect SEC inquiry.

Offerings registered with the SEC generally must also be registered with the securities administrators of each of the states in which the offering is to be made. A simplified registration by "coordination" with the federal registration is usually allowed under state law. Many states do exempt from registration offerings of securities that will be listed on the New York or American Stock Exchange. If an underwriter or selling agent that is a member of the NASD is used, the terms of the underwriters' or sales agents' compensation must be reviewed by the NASD.

Form S-18

In 1979, the SEC adopted a new form and filing procedure to simplify and expedite initial public offerings for smaller companies. The principal features of this new approach are (a) the filing is made in the local SEC regional office (nine offices around the country) rather than in Washington; (b) audited financial statements are required for only the two most recent years (rather than three fiscal years generally in other forms); (c) the general disclosures are somewhat simpler and are tailored for less mature companies. The primary advantage of Form S-18 is dealing with the lighter workloads and geographical proximity of the regional offices. These, coupled with the reduced financial statement requirements, could be expected to reduce by 25 percent or more both the amount of time and the expenses involved in an offering.

The use of Form S-18 is limited to offerings (a) not in excess of $7.5 million; (b) by domestic or Canadian issuers; (c) which are not insurance companies, investment companies, or already publicly held companies, or the subsidiary of any such company. Within 10 days after the first full-month period following the effective date of the registration statement, the company must report the use of the offering proceeds to the SEC.

Regulation A Offerings

If the financing involves a public offering on behalf of the company of $1.5 million or less, and if the company's management, principal equity owners, and other persons whose securities require registration before resale seek to publicly offer not more than $300,000 as part of that offering (with a maximum of $100,000 for each person), the offering may be made under SEC Regulation A rather than pursuant to full registration. When considering such an offering, an issuer must be aware of several potential obstacles. For example, a company may not issue more than $1.5 million of its securities under Regulation A during any 12-month period, and for purposes of calculating that limitation, any offerings made pursuant to an exemption or in violation of the registration requirements are included. Further, companies that are less than one year old or that have not had profitable operations during one of their last two fiscal years (and any affiliates of such companies) must include the value of securities issued to insiders and securities issued for noncash consideration when calculating the dollar limitation unless assurances are given that such securities will not be publicly sold within a year. Also they may not use Regulation A for secondary sales (i.e., shares sold by existing shareholders rather than the company itself). Finally, the exemption is totally unavailable to issuers that have been *inter alia,* convicted of violating the securities laws or subjected to an SEC refusal or stop order, post office fraud order or injunction within the previous five years, or whose directors, officers, principal security holders or underwriters have been convicted of violating the securities laws within the previous 10 years or enjoined from violating the same.

Assuming availability of the exemption, the Regulation A offering procedure is similar to that used with Form S-18 and is similarly less complex. The primary difference between Form S-18 and the use of Regulation A is that the latter has no requirement for audited financials. A 90-day prospectus delivery period exists for Regulation A offerings. Within 30 days after each period following the date of the original offering circular the company must report the status of the offering and the use of proceeds to the SEC.

Like fully registered offerings, Regulation A offerings must be registered (usually by "coordination") with the securities administrators for the states in which the offering is to be made. Use of an underwriter that is a member of the NASD requires NASD review. In practice, the "Reg. A" offering is little used.

State-Registered (Intrastate) Offerings (Rule 147)

If a local business seeks local financing exclusively, registration under the federal securities laws is not required. More accurately, if all of the "offerees" and purchasers in the offering are bona fide residents of the state under the laws of which the company is organized (e.g., the state of incorporation, if the company is a corporation), if the company's business is principally conducted and the company's properties principally located in that state, and if the proceeds of the offering are to be used in the state, the issuer may avail itself of exemption under SEC Rule 147. In such instances, the financing may be made pursuant to a long form ("qualification") registration under the state securities laws.

As a matter of practice, exclusive reliance upon the Rule 147 exemption is a somewhat perilous course. In order to satisfy Rule 147, the issuer must meet various technical requirements as to "residence," some of which are included in Rule 147 and some of which relate to common law standards. At the time of sale, for example, the issuer must obtain from the purchaser a written representation of his residence. Yet, there is no provision in the rule that will protect the issuer from a good faith mistake in determining the residence of a purchaser. Moreover, should even a single purchaser resell to a nonresident within nine months of the offering, the exemption will be lost. To prevent this latter problem, certificates evidencing the securities offered under Rule 147 must bear a legend reflecting these transfer restrictions and a "stop transfer" order must be entered.

Rule 147 also provides a means for segregating an intrastate offering from other discrete offerings pursuant to other exemptive provisions of the act. In order to have Rule 147 available, an issuer must not have sold any similar securities to purchasers outside the state in the prior six months, and may not make any such sales in the subsequent six months. Rule 147 does not require the filing of any documents.

Because registration-by-qualification requirements vary widely from state to state, it is impossible to estimate the costs of a Rule 147 offering. Such costs are generally somewhat less than are those for Regulation A offerings, however. As in the case of other offerings, NASD review is required if a NASD member serves as underwriter or sales agent.

ACQUISITIONS

Like any other securities, securities issued by a company in the acquisition of another company must be registered under federal and state securities laws unless an exemption from registration applies. Most state securities laws provide registration exemptions for acquisitions by statutory merger or stock for assets. Under federal law, however, full registration is required unless either the intrastate or private offering exemption is available. Thus, regardless of the form of the transaction and the number of separate steps it may involve, the company must consider its overall effect and the identity of ultimate recipients of the securities in determining the availability of an exemption.

Under present law, solicitation of the target company's shareholders requesting the execution of proxies to vote on the acquisition is deemed to constitute an offering of the acquirer's securities. If the private or intrastate offering exemptions are unavailable, the acquirer must therefore register. A somewhat simplified registration procedure is available under SEC Form S-14, pursuant to which SEC staff review is less strict than for registration under the more conventional Form S-1. Additionally, in some cases involving acquisitions by very substantial companies, a Form S-15 may be available. Form S-15, like Form S-16, is a simple and streamlined form that relies principally on an issuer's obligation to file periodic reports on its business and operations with the SEC. The prospectus under a Form S-14 registration statement is made up of a proxy statement conforming to SEC rules, to which a cover sheet setting forth the terms of the offering has been added—the combination sometimes being referred to as a "wrap-around" prospectus. Form S-14 may not be used in a stock-for-stock acquisition. As with other offerings, the various state securities laws must also be reviewed.

Securities received by the acquired company's management or principal equity owners as a result of an acquisition are restricted and can be resold only if the resale is registered, exempt, or permitted under Rule 145 (which is similar to Rule 144 but without a holding period or filing requirement). Resales pursuant to a registration statement are particularly hazardous, however, because management may be held personally liable for misstatements in the prospectus concerning the acquiring company as well as any concerning their own company. The risk of liability in this situation is great, as the target company's management rarely has access to information concerning the sometimes unfriendly acquirer.

Acquisitions of equity securities of public companies for either cash or securities is further discussed below in connection with tender offers and takeover bids. See also "Investment Companies" for regulation under certain circumstances.

DISCLOSURE OF MATERIAL INSIDE INFORMATION

In any purchase or sale of a security, whether public or private, if one of the parties has any nonpublic material inside information that relates to the present or future condition of the company's business or its properties, he must disclose it to the person on the opposite side of the transaction or be personally liable under the antifraud provisions of the securities laws for any damages that may result. Similar liability will accrue to any person who aids and abets the misuse of inside information by tipping others or otherwise even if that person does not actually trade. In this regard, both "tippers" and "tippees" are liable under the law.

This simple principle is at the heart of all securities laws and yet is perhaps the most abused. The courts' necessarily amorphous definition of *materiality* is partially responsible for this abuse: any fact which, under the circumstances, would likely have assumed actual significance to a reasonable investor is deemed material. The liabilities can be enormous in scope, and prudent companies and their management should either disclose significant information or, if such information is particularly sensitive, refrain from trading.

One emerging area of securities law deserves special mention because of the magnitude of the exposure involved and the ease in which violations may occur. If any public pronouncement by a public company (whether by press release, report to stockholders or otherwise) contains a statement concerning the company's condition or prospects that is erroneous or misleading in a way that is material to an investor, so that the price of the company's securities in the securities markets is affected (either up or down), the company, its management, and its principal owners may be personally liable for any ensuing loss to *all* persons who trade in the company's securities to their disadvantage in the open market, regardless of whether or not management, the company's owners, or the company are concurrently trading in the company's securities in the market. Cases decided in this area so far indicate that management must have some ulterior purpose for the misinformation in order to be held liable; however, this purpose need not include any intention to violate the securities laws.

MANIPULATION

The securities laws broadly prohibit use of fraudulent or manipulative devices of any type in the purchase or sale of securities, whether in private transactions or in the securities markets. Specifically, market manipulation of securities prices up or down or at any level (except in connection with stabilization in a public offering, as to which special rules apply) or falsely creating the appearance of security trading activity—by the use of fictitious orders, wash sales, or other devices—is prohibited. Again, violation can lead to substantial personal as well as company liability.

REGULATION OF PUBLIC COMPANIES

Companies of significant size that have a larger number of security holders, and companies that are listed on a national securities exchange, are regulated under the Securities Exchange Act of 1934. The filing reporting requirements of this statute attach when the company files a registration statement under the Exchange Act as a result of being listed on a national securities exchange or of having in excess of $1 million in total assets and in excess of 500 holders of a class of its equity securities at the end of one of its fiscal years, or following the effectiveness of a Securities Act Registration statement. (A registration statement under the Securities Exchange Act of 1934 should not be confused with a public offering registration statement under the Securities Act of 1933.) Registration under the Exchange Act submits the company to the periodic reporting, proxy, tender offer, and insider trading provisions of that act. Once registered, the number of equity security holders must drop below 300 before the company may be deregistered.

Periodic Reports

In order to maintain a constant flow of reliable information to the SEC and the financial community, companies registered under the Exchange Act and those that have previously undertaken full registration under the Securities Act are subject to the periodic reporting requirements of the SEC. Under these requirements, the company must file with the SEC annual reports (containing audited financial statements) on Form 10-K, quarterly reports on Form 10-Q, and current reports on Form 8-K. These reports are generally available to the public through the SEC.

Proxy Solicitations

To ensure that security holders of companies registered under the Exchange Act are advised of proposals (including the election of directors) to be acted upon at meetings of security holders, such companies must use proxy or information statements that conform to SEC rules. Such proxy statements are reviewed by the SEC staff prior to distribution to security holders. They must be transmitted at least annually and upon each proxy solicitation to the company's voting security holders. The form of the proxy itself is also regulated.

Tender Offers and Takeover Bids

Tender offers to acquire the securities of a company whose securities registered under the Exchange Act (other than offers by a company to repurchase its own shares, which are regulated separately) must conform to the SEC tender offer rules. These require the filing of certain information with the target company and the SEC not later than the date the tender offer is first made. Securities tendered are recoverable by the tenderer within the first 15 business days of the commencement of the tender offer and for 10 business days following any tender by a competing bidder, as well as after 60 days from the initial offer. Acceptance of less than all of the shares in a tender offer must be on a pro rata basis. Of course, if the tender is being made using securities of the acquiring company rather than cash, they must be registered under the Securities Act prior to the offering.

In order to alert the SEC and the management of a target company to an acquisition of securities that could lead to a change of control, any person acquiring any equity security of an Exchange Act–registered company, which results in his owning in excess of 5 percent of the outstanding securities of that class, must file with the SEC within 10 days after the acquisition. He must also transmit to the company certain information concerning the acquiring person, his purpose in making the acquisition, and his method of financing the acquisition. This requirement applies even if the shares were received as a result of an acquisition in which the acquirer exchanged some of its equity securities in return for securities of the acquired company. If two or more persons who together own in excess of 5 percent of a class of equity securities of an Exchange Act–registered company enter into a mutual arrangement to acquire control of the company, they too must file Form 13 D within 10 days after entering of the arrangement.

If either of the above transactions results in an appointment of directors for the company other than by vote of security holders, there must be transmitted to all security holders eligible to vote for the election of such directors if elected at a meeting of security holders, at least 10 days prior to the appointment, information equivalent to that contained in a proxy or information statement under the proxy rules.

The securities laws of some states contain tender offer provisions designed to discourage takeover of corporations based in those states or whose principal business and substantial assets are within the state. The federal laws, however, do not purport to discourage tender offers directly but rather seek to ensure full disclosure of information concerning such offers.

Insider Reporting and Trading

Management and 10 percent equity security holders are deemed *insiders* of an Exchange Act–registered company and must report their transactions in the company's equity securities to the SEC on forms 3 and 4. The SEC publishes these transactions quarterly.

The insider trading provisions of the Exchange Act contain a section, 16 b(5), which includes an absolute six-month trading rule designed to preclude any incentive for insiders to make use of insider information to gain for themselves short-term profits by trading in the company's securities.

If both a purchase and a sale or a sale and purchase of such securities by an insider falls within any six-month period, any security holder of the company may sue on behalf of the company to recover for the company the "profits" thereby obtained. The word *profits* has a technical meaning in this context and does not necessarily refer to any benefit obtained by the insider—in fact, the insider may have incurred a net overall loss in a series of such transactions and still be liable to the company for substantial sums. The formula used by the courts in measuring the recovery is to match the highest sale with the lowest purchase in any six-month period, then to match the next highest sale with the next lowest purchase, and so on, so that the largest possible amount of profits from any given set of trades is thereby computed. Since theoretical losses incurred are not offset against theoretical profits, the liability to the insider can be substantial even though he sustains an overall loss.

That an insider, in fact, is not trading on inside information is no defense to an insider trading suit. In fact, if an insider purchase and sale have both occurred within six months, there is virtually no defense to a timely and properly prosecuted insider trading suit, and the best course of action is usually to pay the profits to the company as quickly as possible to minimize the ample legal fees that are usually awarded by the courts to plaintiff's counsel in such actions. These suits may be brought by anyone with standing.

Investment Companies

A company whose principal business is investing or trading in securities is subject to regulation under the Investment Company Act of 1940, unless it has not made and is not making a public offering and has fewer than 100 security holders. Although this act is primarily directed toward mutual funds, it also regulates companies that inadvertently fall within the statutory definition of *investment company*. Thus, if a public company sells a major portion of its assets, and, rather than distributing the proceeds to its security holders, holds and invests the proceeds in other than government or commercial paper while exploring alternate business activities, it may be deemed to have become an investment company. "Hedge funds" and investment clubs that rely upon the private offering exemption become investment companies when the exemption is lost and the offering becomes public, or when they have more than 100 participants.

SUMMARY

We have attempted to describe the factors that influence an entrepreneur's decision on whether or not to take a company public. We have also tried to describe the complex process of raising equity through the public markets.

Our placement of this piece in the section on "Managing and Harvesting the Venture" bears explaining. We do not mean to imply that going public is a clean exit route for the entrepreneur to take his or her money and move on. While the entrepreneur can often get some money out of the business in a public offering, a large portion of his or her equity will undoubtedly still be tied up in the venture. Rather, we mean to imply that the decision relative to going public is one that is made after the business's start-up. It is a decision about where to obtain capital for growth.

Case 4–1

Michael Bregman

In July 1980, Michael Bregman was preparing a strategy to expand his fledgling Canadian restaurant business. During the last eight months, he had started pilot locations for two different restaurant concepts. The first was Mmmuffins (as in, "Mmm, good!"). This was a take-out bakery operation offering a wide variety of fresh, hot muffins (baked on the premises) together with accompanying beverages. The second was Michel's Baguette, a more elaborate French bakery cafe. Baguette offered a take-out counter for a variety of french croissants and breads (also baked in the restaurant) as well as an on-premises cafe with soups, salads, sandwiches on fresh bread, an omelette bar, and fresh croissants.

Michael hoped to build a substantial restaurant chain with one or both of these concepts. Even though the two pilots were just underway, a flurry of construction of new shopping centers across Canada appeared to offer a unique opportunity for rapid growth. In fact, one major developer was negotiating with Michael for a package of locations right now. The package included some locations Michael felt would be good, but the developer also wanted commitment to some locations Michael felt would do poorly. Such a deal would be a major undertaking for his young company. It would heavily influence the company's direction during the crucial formative years.

Michael was still considering the merits of franchising versus internal growth and evaluating the relative attractiveness of the two restaurant concepts. He wanted to make conscious strategic decisions in these areas before he committed to any course of action.

This case was prepared by Richard O. von Werssowetz under the direction of Howard H. Stevenson.

BACKGROUND

Michael Bregman was a native of Canada. After earning a degree in finance from Wharton at the University of Pennsylvania, he entered directly into the MBA program at Harvard from which he graduated in 1977. Michael sought a job in the food business because of an interest he had developed due to his family's long association with that industry.

Michael's grandfather had built a successful bakery as had Michael's father, Lou Bregman. In 1971, Lou Bregman had purchased Hunt's and Woman's Bakery (Hunt's) division from the Kellogg Company which Lou had been supplying. The division had been losing money on annual sales of about $20 million, but under Lou Bregman's guidance soon prospered. Hunt's sold bakery products to 130 company-owned retail stores and to 370 supermarkets. Michael had worked after school and in summer jobs in various restaurants and bakeries.

> I joined Loblaws, a Canadian chain that was perceived as being a very stodgy supermarket company. Everybody thought I was crazy because I had offers from some of the big consulting companies and investment banks, places where I should be going. But at Loblaws I had the chance to work for a new president with no experience in supermarketing right in the midst of a turnaround. I would call him a marketing genius and really went to work for him rather than the company.

Michael worked on corporate development projects including the launch of NO-NAME [unbranded] products in Canada which was very successful.

Things were not going as smoothly at Hunt's. Lou Bregman was having disagreements with his majority partners (who were in the real estate business) as the result of some difficult financial times. The company was in a turmoil and Lou asked Michael to join Hunt's to see if he could help out. Michael agreed in June of 1978 and was put in charge of the retail division. Lou concentrated on the central bakery operations, and the other partners attempted to provide overall direction. Michael quickly found himself at odds with the other managers and strongly disagreed with what he thought were stupid decisions. He stayed at his father's urging until December 1978, then resigned.

> I must say that I felt pretty defeated at the time. I'd worked so hard and had accomplished so little. I'd fought a lot, and I've never been much of a fighter, but I also can't do anything unless I believe in it. It was a difficult time.
>
> I didn't know what I was going to do. I'd always planned all along to start my own business at some time. I didn't know what or when, but I did know I wanted to do it quickly because I think it gets harder and harder as life goes on and you have all sorts of commitments.

I went out for lunch one day with my old boss from Loblaws who suggested I go back to them again. I really hadn't thought of that but had simply been keeping in touch. I told him I couldn't really make a long-term commitment because my heart was in starting my own business. He said that would be all right, that he could put me on a short-term assignment. It took about five minutes worth of convincing for me to agree.

EVOLUTION OF A START-UP

As his first project, Michael was asked to recommend a strategy for Loblaws' in-store bakeries. Should Loblaws have them? If so, what should they be: bake-off stores of frozen products (baking prefrozen doughs) or scratch bakeries? He prepared a similar study of the deli department. Michael was then asked to implement his recommendations in the bakery area and became Director of Bakery Operations, a new position. He worked closely with the Manager of Bakery Operations, who was oriented to the day-to-day management more than to strategy and planning for the department. Bakeries became important to Loblaws new super stores, which were designed to provide greater variety and savings than traditional supermarkets. Bakery products were successful in drawing customers to the stores with fresh-baked crusty bread and rolls.

> Somewhere along the way, a small businessman visited me. He thought we should sell his muffins in our stores. We had taken muffins for granted: they'd been around forever and were sort of stable and unexciting—what do you do with a muffin? All of a sudden this fellow comes in with these giant muffins, much larger than any we'd ever seen. We sold our small muffins for 15 cents each; we'd have to retail his at 45 cents.
>
> Naturally everybody was against them just on price. But I decided to test them in two of the most affluent stores. They went like crazy; it was wild. We kept upping the orders, and we could never keep them in stock. We didn't promote them, just put them on the counter, but there was immediate appeal. That triggered something in me. Seeing that you could take a very drab product and make it exciting. And I thought you could do more with it than I saw him do.

Despite Michael's interest in the food industry and fascination with the performance of the large muffins, he really didn't like the bakery business:

> It always seemed to be an old man's game, a tired industry that was declining and very production-oriented, very unexciting. Over 75 percent of the retail bakeries in North America had closed between the early 60s and mid-70s. Before that, the retail baking industry was comprised of hundreds of independent skilled bakers who had come over from Europe

and opened up shops and carried on as they had in Europe. The little shops handled two or three hundred items, mostly—if not all—made by hand. You needed skilled bakers to continue, who became very expensive and in short supply.

"Mom and Pop" were willing to work crazy hours and take low salaries because they wanted their own bakery. But by the mid-70s those same skilled people could get jobs in any supermarket in the country, earn $25,000, work 40 hours, have terrific benefits and no headaches. That, together with the shift of customers to the shopping centers, really put an end to most of that business.

The pressure really began with the bakery chains, like my father's, that were serviced from central plants. But then the supermarkets started doing in-store baking, selling a fresher product at a lower price. Gas had gone crazy, and it had become prohibitive to deliver fresh products from a central facility to many small shops daily or twice a day. And the supermarket had a different view of the baking business. They were very price conscious. They weren't in the baking business to make money, but to draw customers to buy other things. The last thing they wanted to do was to draw a customer into the store to see a bakery that had prices that were too high. Their cost systems were often really rather silly and ignored investment and overhead and value of the space used by any individual area. Some supermarket departments, like the bakeries, were really much more expensive marketing tools than they thought. But the supermarkets tended to just look at the total bottom line as a contribution number. Looking at these things, it was easy to be negative about the industry.

Then I started to feel there was a massive opportunity out there! People still liked baked goods, and they hadn't been supplied with them in the right fashion. As I thought in general terms of what was going to happen to the retail baking industry, I felt that the stores were going to get smaller, and the industry would have to specialize in one or two lines of products. Also, you'd surely have to bake on the premises to create the freshness that no one else could duplicate. That's really the key component of quality in our industry. I also reminded myself that the retail baking business is primarily based on impulse sales and location is extremely important.

I guess I had all of this in mind in May 1979 while my father and I were driving to a restaurant show in Chicago. For the first time it really occurred to me: Why don't we open a muffin shop? We sort of chuckled—what a stupid idea. Later I began to think, why not? There's not a lot of money to lose and a lot to gain if it worked. It was totally different from anything we'd seen in North America.

During the summer, I began investigating some space in the Eaton Centre. This was Toronto's principal downtown shopping complex with over 3.7 million square feet of space. The Eaton Centre was directly connnected to three subway terminals and had 200,000 office workers within easy walking distance. It was anchored by two major department stores and two office towers. There were over 300 retail shops and restaurants in the complex. Their leasing agent was pretty skeptical, but was willing to lease some space. In August, I committed to lease 350 square feet at $15,000 a year or 8 percent of sales, whichever was greater, beginning December 1. Now I needed to develop my shop.

In the meantime, Lou Bregman had sold his interest in Hunt's and had considered retirement. But, when he had the chance to buy a downtown bagel store that had gone bankrupt, he decided to develop a new full-service restaurant and bakery called Bregman's. Michael was helping his father get started with that, and Lou Bregman coguaranteed the lease obligations with Michael for the muffin shop.

In addition to his duties at Loblaws, helping his father's new venture, and planning his muffin shop, Michael found himself drawn into yet another start-up:

> My wife and I had honeymooned in France when we were married in May 1978. I really fell in love with their croissants. I couldn't believe how great they were. I'd never tasted a decent croissant in North America. They were all poor imitations and I thought this would be a great product to bring over here. I had seen a few French bakery stores in Chicago and New York, but very few. I knew that this would be something to pursue in the future.
>
> As we were settling our lease deal for the muffin shop in the Eaton Centre, I mentioned to the leasing agent that I had heard that a French bakery chain, Au Bon Pain, was coming to the center. He was surprised I'd heard of it, but said they had some problems with them. I said I was planning to get in the same business and he got very excited. He called his boss and very quickly offered to negotiate with us. Space in the Eaton Centre was very difficult to obtain and seemed to me to be one of the best possible locations. So we leased the space and decided to do our French bakery, too. Again, we personally guaranteed the leases.

Despite the serendipitous opening at the Eaton Centre, Michael's commitment to the French bakery restaurant was not a spur-of-the-moment decision. He had been actively investigating the possibilities of both the muffin shop and the French bakery since the Chicago show in May. Because the French bakery would require much more capital, Michael had prepared a short business plan that he circulated to three or four people he thought might invest. One was Ralph Scurfield of Calgary, president of the NuWest Group, the largest homebuilder in North America. Michael had met him while Ralph was enrolled in an executive program at Harvard. Michael had done a field study for NuWest and had kept in touch with Ralph. Ralph said that he knew very little about the restaurant business, but that he did know Michael Bregman and would be willing to bet some money on him. A long negotiation ensued as Michael sought locations for the muffin shop or for the French bakery. They reached agreement in the fall:

We capitalized the company with $450,000. My father and I each put in $62,500 in common stock, and Ralph put in $125,000 in common stock and an additional $200,000 in preferred shares. I had a net worth of about $8,000 and got a loan for my share. I had to get my wife, mother, and father to cosign and my parents to put their house up. It scared the daylights out of me. If things went wrong, it wouldn't sink them, but I didn't know how I could live with it.

I would take a salary cut to $25,000 a year, which together with my wife's income would just about let us live and cover the loan. The contract ended up 60 pages long with 5 pages of basics and the rest disaster clauses. I would have tie-breaking power unless things went wrong and would also have to get Ralph's approval for capital expenditures over $5,000. The initial spending requirements were approved as part of the agreement. There was also a complex redemption plan for the preferred which included penalties for not making the five-year schedule.

The fall of 1979 was frantic as Michael managed to get both of his projects underway. Although he and his father had been in the baking business, neither of them was familiar with the special processes needed for muffins of this type nor with French baking. At the same time Michael was working to design the stores, he had to find and test muffin recipes and learn to operate the specialized French baking equipment. Part of his strategy was to use the very best help he could find. For design, he employed Don Watt & Associates, one of Canada's premier designers. The equipment suppliers were also very helpful in the strenuous task of laying out all of the necessary customer service and baking equipment in 350 square feet for the muffin shop. Michael also found a French baker who lived in Washington who agreed to come up just before the bakery opened to teach several bakers how to bake French bakery products.

Somehow they got underway. Michael left Loblaws at the end of November 1979 and Mmmuffins opened December 15. Michel's Baguette began construction at that point and opened in April 1980. It was not a time Michael would like to repeat.

EVALUATING THE FIRST EFFORTS

By July 1980, the two stores were beginning to stabilize and Michael was preparing to expand. He reviewed the state of each operation to help him decide what directions he might take.

He was pleased with both store designs and concepts. The extra expense and effort he had put in store planning had been well worth the investment. Both facilities were attractive and inviting. As for product selections, they had developed recipes for over 15 varieties of muffins which could be made from four different base mixtures. About 10 would be offered at any point in time. At Baguette, the menu appeared workable and proved to offer a popular range of choices (Exhibit 1).

Sales for both stores had been encouraging and costs were beginning to steady. He now had seven months of experience with Mmmuffins and three months with Baguette. (Exhibit 2 is a record of sales and variable costs for the two stores. Exhibit 3 is a year-to-date financial statement showing the total performance and financial position.)

After hectic start-up periods, the operations of each store were now satisfactory. As expected, they were very different from each other. The Mmmuffins store had only 350 square feet of space; this small area had to contain supplies' storage, preparation of raw materials and mixes, baking, clean-up, and the retail service counters. Michael described how this worked:

> I think our design was one of the very most important reasons behind our early success. Don Watt, our designer, was able to create the magnet to draw customers in the first time. If they liked our service, they'd come back. They came in first because of the color, the lighting, the photography—it's just a different showcase.
>
> The design also worked well functionally. There's just enough space to do everything, but no extra space to become cluttered or dirty and not be corrected. The customer cannot see the preparation area, but the manager can easily keep track of all activities. The total staff complement for the store runs between 6 and 12 people including part-timers, depending on the part-time mix. You need one manager and one assistant to cover the shifts. There are salespeople at the counter and bakers in the back; the employees can trade off some during slack buying periods. Service at the counter is fairly simple, and you can train a baker in two days from start to finish. You could almost get this down to two hours for most of the functions.
>
> Although we didn't really know what we were doing when we opened, we soon learned better ways to do things. We got better at finding and selecting specialized preparation equipment that fit our particular needs. Since we bake from scratch using no commercial mixes, every extra efficiency helped. We learned what items we could make ahead of time and better ways to store them. This is really important when you begin baking early in the morning before opening and continue throughout the day.
>
> I knew that if we were going to grow, we'd have to systematize the operation, so during the first months I wrote an operating manual with everything from opening procedures, to how to clean the store, to recipes, to baking procedures, to how to greet customers and work the counter— everything. I found it one of the most grueling experiences I had ever been through in my life. I was working behind the counter myself during those opening months and was learning how important those controls and procedures were.
>
> I also learned how important the manager was. As Baguette opened and I left the Mmmuffins store under the supervision of a manager I had

hired, little problems started to arise—fighting among the staff, quality being a little less consistent than it should have been. I'm sure there was fault on both sides, but I found that the manager constantly needed attention.

But all in all, I was very pleased.

As a much larger and more complete bakery and restaurant, Michel's Baguette was much more complex:

Baguette had 2,500 square feet of space, which was really a bit too tight. This had a larger food preparation, baking, and storage area, a take-out bakery counter, the cafeteria-style serving line, and an on-premises eating area with seats for 35. Once again, our physical design was an important asset. Our store helped attract customers at the same time that it worked well functionally in a very tight space.

With a larger menu, there were many more tasks to perform. There was a total staff of 55 to 60 people, including part-timers. You really need a very qualified head manager to be the general manager of the overall business, as well as two assistant managers who have the capability to be the acting general manager when the general manager isn't there. You need a head baker who is quite skilled and who can guide the whole production area of the store. There are kitchen prep people, two kinds of service people, cafeteria counter people who actually prepare the portions, the salads, and sandwiches. Most of these jobs are more complex than those at Mmmuffins, and the baking is particularly difficult. It takes 20 steps to make croissants, and the breads also have more steps and are more demanding than making muffins. There are many delicate areas where you can ruin the product, but I must say that we brought in the right equipment from France and, with care, can consistently make excellent products. All of the baked goods and other items are made from scratch and are baked continuously throughout the day.

I began to spend most of my time at Baguette once it opened and again had to learn as we went. This would take more effort to systematize, and I hadn't written a manual here yet. I was lucky in hiring some good bakers and restaurant managers to help me out. I went after managers that I had heard did a good job for other restaurants in the city and was able to get two to join me. They both worked out very well.

The primary appeal of each concept was absolute freshness and quality of baked goods. As Michael looked at the two operations, he was satisfied that they each properly reflected the key conceptual definitions he felt were critical to their success: hard-to-replicate standards of quality with costs kept to acceptable levels by careful specialization, organization, and store design. Michael described how these worked together:

For superior quality our recipes are based on using fresh eggs, buttermilk, and other very perishable items—very expensive, very hard-to-handle items. Bakeries don't use fresh eggs; they use powered or frozen. But we had decided we would use fresh: we didn't care about any of the rules; we would be better than anybody. But this created very difficult production problems. You can't make too much at once, and you can't make too little because it's a waste of time. The mixes and products aren't very storable, you can't freeze them, and you can't keep them for more than one day.

Besides ingredients, we control our quality by specializing. This means making limited types of baked goods in the best possible way and then providing only those menu items needed to support the specialized baking operation. With Mmmuffins this is practically absolute: there are only muffins and beverages. The bakery for Baguette is simply too capital intensive for the menu to remain that simple. So we combine the bakery with a restaurant. Having the fresh croissants and fresh bread to make sandwiches helps the restaurant, and the sampling that goes on in the restaurant spills over and helps the bakery. The restaurant and bakery counters also have different peak times, so you have better distribution for the bakery equipment and your service people can sway back and forth. But other than the baking, we do no cooking! It's just an assembly operation. We assemble salads, cut meat, cut cheese. But except for omelettes, we don't fry anything, we don't boil anything, we don't cook. Other than the baking, in terms of the back-of-the-house, it's a very simple restaurant.

The stores' layouts and service delivery systems are designed to efficiently support each menu concept. Both provide efficient preparation areas. Both have ovens prominently situated in view of shoppers and passers-by—the sight and aroma of fresh baking are major merchandising tools. At Mmmuffins, we have very efficient customer handling along with some innovative packaging for quantity purchases. At Baguette, we selected a cafeteria line for the restaurant to go along with the counter service for the take-out bakery. This is one step up from the fast food joint where you have to fight for a seat and eat from a tray with disposables. We use better dinnerware, metal utensils, and glasses. This is a step down from the full-service restaurant where you are served by waitresses. We selected this because I felt strongly that in the mall environment, people want to eat quickly but in some comfort.

CONSIDERING FRANCHISING

With both Mmmuffins and Baguette well started, Michael began to consider expansion. He felt there should be many opportunities for good restaurants and specialty food stores despite competition ranging from retail bakeries and supermarkets, to fast food operations, to full-service restaurants. Almost all of these types of competitors would be clustered in large shopping areas and malls. Yet both had held their own in the very competitive and highly visible Eaton Centre. The question was how to expand. Michael had two concepts, limited experience, and limited resources. How could he best capitalize on his work to date to build a significant restaurant business?

One avenue of growth he could pursue was franchising. Certainly enough others had chosen this method to make franchising a very important factor in the Canadian and U.S. economies. A *Foodservice & Hospitality Magazine* survey estimated that franchising represented 16.5 percent of the total Canadian foodservice and lodging industry in 1979. This market share was increasing. Survey respondents reported a 29 percent increase in total food service franchise sales resulting from a 10.5 percent increase in total units operating and a 17 percent increase in average sales per unit (to $381,443).

For U.S. firms, franchised units accounted for approximately one quarter of all food service sales. Exhibit 4 lists several characteristics of U.S.–owned restaurant franchisors for 1978 with projections for 1979 and 1980. About 40 percent of all U.S. franchised restaurants were located in California, Texas, Ohio, Illinois, Michigan, and Florida. A January 1980 study by the U.S. Department of Commerce noted that:

> The entry into the restaurant franchising system mostly by small companies continued in 1978 with a net gain of 38 franchisors, bringing the total to 388. During 1979, 17 franchisors with a total of 227 restaurants, 198 franchisee-owned, went out of business while 13 franchisors with a total of 168 restaurants, 84 franchisee-owned, decided to abandon franchising as a method of marketing.
>
> Big franchisors with over 1,000 units each increased to 11 in 1978 from 8 a year earlier. These 11 franchisors had 27,750 restaurants, 50.2 percent of all franchised restaurants, and accounted for $11.4 billion in sales, 54 percent of the total. Compared with 1977, the 8 franchisors with over 1,000 units each had 45 percent of the total units and 47 percent of the sales.
>
> Menu expansion and diversification continues on the increase to meet the mounting competition from other chains and to enlarge customer counts that have been adversely affected by higher food costs and periodic gasoline shortages. The higher costs of cosmetic and structural construction changes are forcing fast food franchisors to reevaluate their investment in design, and cast their decor changes more and more in marketing terms.

Growth statistics of the 25 largest U.S. franchised restaurant systems are shown in Exhibit 5.

While franchising was one means to achieve growth for either Mmmuffins or Baguette, it would impose additional complexities in doing business. A franchisee is an independent businessperson with personal capital at risk and a fair amount of management flexibility. In addition to the demands inherent in such relationships, there was increasing government regulation of franchise offerings and operations. On October 21, 1979, a new U.S. Federal Trade Commission rule requiring comprehensive disclosure statements for prospective franchisees became effective. Sixteen separate states also required various types of disclosures (although some states accepted a uniform format). Canada had no such comprehensive disclosure requirement, but many felt there was a need for one and expected such a rule in Canada in the future. Some pressure for such regulation came from established franchisors who were worried about the effect that a few incapable, overconfident, or unscrupulous franchisors might have on the industry.

The areas of disclosure required by the new U.S. law illustrate the many aspects of the business and the relationship that must be considered in franchising. These include:

— Specific background information about the identity, financial position, and business experience of the franchisor company and its key directors and executives.

— Detail of the financial relationship including initial and continuing fees and expenses payable to the franchisor.

— Requirements for doing business with the franchisor or affiliates (such as purchase of supplies from a franchisor source), and any realty fees, financing arrangements, or other financial requirements.

— Restrictions and requirements for methods of operation placed on the franchisee.

— Termination, cancellation, and renewal terms.

— Control over future sites.

— Statistical information about the number of franchises and their rates of termination.

— Franchisor-provided training programs and other support.

Even without disclosure requirements, it was considered a good idea to develop policies and practices for dealing with franchisees for the long term before opening the first operation. One reason for this was a general desire for consistent treatment of franchisees. Some examples of current practices of Canadian franchisors are summarized in Exhibit 6.

Increased regulation was not the only area of change in franchising. There was ever-increasing competition in Canada as more U.S. franchisors sought new markets in other countries. The need for better communication with franchisees had started a trend in the development of franchisee advisory councils by franchisors. The ultimate roles of these councils was still evolving. There was also a fairly constant trade back and forth between franchisors repurchasing franchised units for company ownership and company-owned units being franchised.

A QUESTION OF STRATEGY

The question of using franchising as a means of expansion was only one aspect Michael needed to consider in planning for growth for his restaurant business. A fundamental question was how suitable were his concepts for wide use? He had started and managed both current units personally. How well would they "travel"? Both concepts depended on fresh baking which made them more demanding than many franchises. Other stores offering similar baked goods (donuts, cookies, or other items) used premixed ingredients, premade frozen products to be baked in the units, or simply distributed centrally baked products.

Michael also had to include the capital requirements and likely performance of additional units of either type in his planning. His estimates of capital requirements for new locations are shown in Exhibit 7. His estimates of stand-alone operating results if operated by a franchisee are shown in Exhibit 8.

Finally, no matter what methods of growth he might choose, his location strategy would be critical. Where would his concepts best fit? One aspect was the type of location and surrounding demographics. Another would be geographic—how far away, and Canada versus the United States. Even within Canada, there were very different demands between the more stable eastern portion and the rapidly growing western area. Should he concentrate on finding more established and stable locations in the East? Or should he take advantage of the many openings in new centers that a construction boom in the West was creating? What differences were there between good locations for Mmmuffins and good locations for Baguette?

AN OFFER OF LOCATIONS

To help learn about possible locations that might be available, Michael began talking with major Canadian development companies. One important firm was Real Estate Canada (REC) which developed and controlled a large number of shopping malls across Canada. After preliminary discussions, REC offered Michael locations for Mmmuffins stores in one new mall and one mall expansion, both in Toronto suburbs. This was an important developer and Michael felt the locations would be good for Mmmuffins, so he agreed and they shook hands on the deal.

Later, while lawyers were completing the legal paper work, things changed. REC came back and said they wanted to include another location in Manitoba in central Canada in the agreement:

They said they were creating a package for me: the two Toronto locations and Manitoba in the West or nothing. And being the naive kid that I was, I got extremely upset. But we had a deal! I'd already told my partner about my plans for Toronto and that was OK, but the town in Manitoba had only about 50,000 people and was a thousand miles away. It was a rural environment and difficult to reach.

So I told them that we were just a young chain, and we just wanted to do a few stores at a time. They said no; that's the way it has to be. They had a brand new mall and needed to fill the space.

In the excitement of the offer of the initial two locations, Michael had been somewhat swept away with events. Now he was confronted with a more difficult situation than he had anticipated and felt he should pause to rethink his overall company strategy before reacting to this new offer. How should he make his company grow? How fast? How should he divide his efforts between the two concepts? Now he realized he should answer these questions before he went ahead with any expansion deal.

EXHIBIT 1   Michel's Baguette Product Line Highlights

BAKERY		CAFE	
Bread:	Baguette	Salads:	Julienne
	Boule		Niçoise
	Alpine		Spinach
	Mini-Baguette		Side Salad
	Whole Wheat Baguette		Salade du Jour
Croissants:	Butter	Soups:	Yellow Pea with Ham
	Almond		Soup du Jour
	Petit Pain Au Chocolat	Quiches:	Bacon
	Raisin-Custard		Spinach
	Cream Cheese		Mushroom
	Cheddar Cheese	Omelette Bar:	Cheddar Cheese
	Ham and Cheese		Ham
	Apple Cinnamon		Swiss Cheese
	Blueberry		Green Pepper
	Cherry		Onion
			etc. . . .
		Sandwiches:	Ham and Cheese
			Roast Beef
			Tuna
			Chicken Salad
			Egg Salad
			Cream Cheese
			Swiss Cheese
			Le Hero
			Le Jardin
			Roast Beef and Herb Cheese
			etc. . . .
		Beverages:	Coffee
			Tea
			Milk
			Soft Drinks
			Juices
			Perrier
		Croissants:	(as in Bakery)

EXHIBIT 2   Initial Store Level Operating Results

Period Ending	No Wks.	$ Sales	Avg. $ Sales per Week	Food, Supplies	Labour	Food, Supplies, and Labour
				Percent of Sales		
Mmmuffins:						
Jan. 19, 1980	5	9,010	1,802	38.2	38.8	77.0
Feb. 16	4	10,866	2,716	36.3	29.8	66.1
March 15	4	14,901	3,725	24.5	23.9	48.4
April 12	4	17,250	4,312	28.0	22.5	50.5
May 10	4	16,696	4,174	34.6	25.6	60.2
June 7	4	17,346	4,337	38.5	25.4	63.9
July 5	4	20,602	5,150	31.1	21.0	52.1
Highest week's sales June 21—$5,574						51.4%
Michel's Baguette:						
May 10	4	44,470	11,118	37.7	33.5	68.2
June 7	4	52,921	13,230	27.4	25.4	52.8
July 5	4	65,487	16,372	25.9	23.1	49.0
Highest week's sales June 21—$17,289						48.7%

EXHIBIT 3 Financial Statements

BALANCE SHEET
June 30, 1980
(unaudited)

Assets

Current assets:

Term deposit	$120,000
Receivables	1,525
Inventory	6,669
Prepaid expenses	15,345
Deferred charges	1,062
Deferred income taxes	7,250
Total current assets	151,851
Equipment and leasehold improvements	400,741
Incorporation expense—at cost	7,151
Total assets	$559,743

Liabilities and Shareholders' Equity

Current liabilities:

Bankers' advances	$ 1,436
Payables and accruals	124,736
Dividend payable	4,500
Total current liabilities	130,672

Shareholders' equity:

Share capital	450,000
Deficit	(20,929)
Total liabilities and shareholders' equity	$559,743

STATEMENT OF LOSS AND DEFICIT
Period from Inception, December 4, 1979, to June 30, 1980
(unaudited)

Sales	$269,428
Cost of sales	169,919
Gross operating profit	99,509
Store expenses	78,473
Income from store operations	21,036
Other income—interest	14,972
	36,008
Administration expenses	55,187
Net loss before income taxes	19,179
Deferred income taxes	7,250
Net loss	11,929
Dividends	9,000
Deficit, end of period	$ 20,929

EXHIBIT 3   *(concluded)*

INTERNAL STATEMENTS OF OPERATIONS
STORE LEVEL
Inception to July 5, 1980

	Mmmuffins	*Michel's Baguette*
Sales	$106,404	$162,745
Food costs	35,090	44,861
Gross profit............................	71,314	117,884
Operating expenses:		
Supplies............................	6,083	7,259
Labour	29,249	52,333
	35,332	59,592
Gross operating profit..................	35,982	58,292
General expenses.......................	2,228	1,992
Occupancy costs........................	19,411	35,609
Administrative costs	5,442	8,137
Total expenses	27,081	45,738
Net profit from operations	8,901	12,554
Add depreciation and amortization	5,367	9,005
Cash flow from operations	$ 14,268	$ 21,559

Note: Slightly different period than prior statements.

EXHIBIT 4   Statistics of U.S.–Owned Restaurant Franchises

				Percent Changes	
Item	1978	1979†	1980†	1978–79	1979–80
Restaurants (all types)*					
Total number of establishments	55,312	59,928	66,672	8.3	11.3
Company-owned	15,510	16,781	18,549	8.2	10.5
Franchisee-owned	39,802	43,147	48,123	8.4	11.5
Total sales of products and services: ($000)	21,100,788	24,591,880	28,990,499	16.5	17.9
Company-owned	6,733,545	7,816,198	9,111,129	16.1	16.6
Franchisee-owned	14,367,243	16,775,682	19,879,370	16.8	18.5
Total sales of products and services by franchisors to franchisees: ($000)					
Merchandise (non-food) for resale	33,013	37,534	48,656	13.7	29.6
Supplies (such as paper goods, etc.)	170,889	231,017	287,379	35.2	24.4
Food ingredients	298,063	383,774	481,004	28.8	25.3
Other	46,817	53,728	40,771	14.8	−24.1
Total	548,782	706,053	857,810	28.7	21.5

*See tables that follow.
†Data estimated by respondents.

		Establishments		Sales	
Size Groups	Franchising Companies Number	Number	Percent	($000)	Percent
Restaurants (all types)*					
Distribution by Number of Establishments—1978					
Total	388	55,312	100.0	21,100,788	100.0
1,001 and greater	11	27,750	50.2	11,400,272	54.0
501–1,000	11	8,925	16.1	3,513,637	16.7
151–500	34	8,833	16.0	2,928,603	13.9
51–150	59	5,580	10.1	1,712,930	8.1
11–50	153	3,642	6.6	1,360,850	6.4
0–10	120	582	1.0	184,496	0.9

*See tables that follow.

Source: U.S. Department of Commerce, "Franchising in the Economy 1978–1980," January 1980.

EXHIBIT 4 (*continued*) Restaurants: 1978–1980 Distribution by Major Activity

Number of Establishments

Major Activity	Firms	1978			1979			1980		
		Total	Company-Owned	Franchisee-Owned	Total	Company-Owned	Franchisee-Owned	Total	Company-Owned	Franchisee-Owned
Total	388	55,312	15,510	39,802	59,928	16,781	43,147	66,672	18,549	48,123
Chicken	31	6,708	1,870	4,838	7,193	2,011	5,182	7,826	2,197	5,629
Hamburgers, franks, roast beef, etc.	117	26,038	4,648	21,390	27,833	5,077	22,756	30,651	5,695	24,956
Pizza	66	7,542	3,042	4,500	8,355	3,288	5,067	9,434	3,577	5,857
Mexican (taco, etc.)	29	2,329	993	1,336	2,527	1,044	1,483	2,913	1,183	1,730
Seafood	11	2,297	899	1,398	2,444	901	1,543	2,704	966	1,738
Pancakes, waffles	15	1,441	363	1,078	1,577	418	1,159	1,770	491	1,279
Steak, full menu	86	7,924	3,479	4,445	8,756	3,813	4,943	9,771	4,180	5,591
Sandwich and other	33	1,033	216	817	1,243	229	1,014	1,603	260	1,343

EXHIBIT 4 (*concluded*) Restaurants: 1978–80 Distribution by Major Activity

Sales (in thousands of dollars)

Major Activity	Firms	1978			1979			1980		
		Total	Company-Owned	Franchisee-Owned	Total	Company-Owned	Franchisee-Owned	Total	Company-Owned	Franchisee-Owned
Total	388	$21,100,788	6,733,545	14,367,243	$24,591,880	7,816,198	16,775,682	$28,990,499	9,111,129	19,879,370
Chicken	31	2,034,012	653,977	1,380,035	2,247,838	765,738	1,482,100	2,563,755	899,485	1,664,270
Hamburgers, franks, roast beef, etc.	117	10,862,837	2,589,465	8,273,372	12,961,887	3,038,923	9,922,964	15,521,446	3,595,801	11,925,645
Pizza	66	1,735,279	696,364	1,038,915	2,007,066	776,902	1,230,164	2,364,317	903,182	1,461,135
Mexican (taco, etc.)	29	602,376	304,697	297,679	648,100	315,922	332,178	766,692	377,652	389,040
Seafood	11	563,827	216,486	347,341	667,098	260,633	406,465	772,794	299,624	473,170
Pancakes, waffles	15	601,029	139,899	461,130	681,728	164,023	517,705	834,135	216,290	617,845
Steak, full menu	86	4,531,709	2,104,623	2,427,086	5,170,218	2,461,797	2,708,421	5,883,140	2,779,340	3,103,800
Sandwich and other	33	169,719	28,034	141,685	207,945	32,260	175,885	284,220	39,755	244,465

EXHIBIT 5   Top 25 U.S. Franchise Restaurant Systems

Growth in System-Wide Sales 1974–1979 (in millions of dollars)

Franchise System	1974	1978	1979	'74–'79 % Change	'78–'79 % Change
McDonald's	$1,943	$4,575	$5,385	177%	17.7%
Kentucky Fried Chicken†	925.5	1,393.4	1,669	80	19.8
Burger King†	467	1,168	1,463	213	25.3
Wendy's	24.2	783	1,000*	4,032	27.8
International Dairy Queen†	590	823.2	926	57	12.5
Pizza Hut	232	702	829	257	18.1
Big Boy	484*	660*	750*	55	13.6
Hardee's†	280	564.6	750	168	32.8
Arby's	120	353	430	258	21.8
Ho Jo's	300*	425*	425*	42	0.0
Ponderosa†	183	328.5	406.9	122	23.9
Church's	126.9	345	405.7*	220	17.6
Bonanza	190	346	378	99	9.2
Tastee Freez†	267.9*	353.8*	350*	31	(1.1)
Long John Silver's†	45.5	283.4	342	652	20.7
Sonic Drive-ins†	52.1	291.7	336	545	15.2
Burger Chef†	250	301	335	34	11.3
Taco Bell†	71.1*	212*	320*	350	50.9
Western Sizzlin†	100	217.3	278.1	178	28.0
Dunkin Donuts	163.3	249.4	283.8	74	14.0
A & W	174.4	247.5	255 ·	46	3.0
Arthur Treacher's	48.3	191.5	226.3	369	18.2
Sizzler†	85.5	181.8	225.9	164	24.3
Perkins Cake 'n Steak	75*	200*	223*	197	11.5
Pizza Inn	58.6	165.8	189*	223	14.0

*Estimated
†Fiscal year-end figures (remaining figures are calendar year-end)

EXHIBIT 5   *(concluded)*

Growth in Number of Units 1974–1979

Franchise System	*1974*	*1978*	*1979*	*'74–'79* % Change	*'78–'79* % Change
McDonald's	3,232	5,185	5,747	78%	10.8%
Kentucky Fried Chicken†	4,627	5,355	5,444	18	1.7
Burger King†	1,199	2,153	2,439	103	13.3
Wendy's	93	1,407	1,818	1,855	29.2
International Dairy Queen†	4,504	820	4,860	8	0.8
Pizza Hut	1,668	3,541	3,846	131	8.6
Big Boy	881	1,041	1,100	25	5.7
Hardee's†	924	1,125	1,231	33	9.4
Arby's	439	818	928	111	13.4
Ho Jo's	922	882	867	(6)	(1.7)
Ponderosa†	389	588	636	63	8.2
Church's	565	970	1,125	99	16.0
Bonanza	550	700	675	23	(3.6)
Tastee Freez†	2,215	2,022	2,000*	(10)	(1.1)
Long John Silver's†	208	1,001	1,007	384	0.6
Sonic Drive-ins†	220	1,061	1,182	437	11.4
Burger Chef†	950	853	831	(13)	(2.6)
Taco Bell†	562	877	1,100	96	25.4
Western Sizzlin†	140	319	400	186	25.4
Dunkin' Donuts	780	956	1,007	29	5.3
A & W	1,899	1,500	1,306	(31)	(12.9)
Arthur Treacher's	250	730	777	211	6.4
Sizzler†	256	352	402	57	14.2
Perkins Cake 'n Steak	183	342	400*	119	17.0
Pizza Inn	336	743	760	126	2.3

Note: Includes U.S. and foreign sales and units.
*Estimated.
†Fiscal year-end figures (remainder are calendar year-end figures).

Source: *Restaurant Business,* March 1, 1980.

EXHIBIT 6   Sample Canadian Franchisor Terms (February 1980)

Franchisor (Franchise)	History, Current Status, and Expansion Plans	Franchise Requirements and Costs	Services Offered to Franchisee
Mister Donut of Canada Ltd. (Mister Donut)	—Established 1955 —55 franchised units in Canada. 715 franchised units in U.S., Japan —Locations: Ont. 43, Que. 9, B.C. 2, Alberta 1 —Canadian sales $10m. —10 operations to open in 1980	—Initial fee $10,000 —Royalty fee 4.9% of gross sales —Advertising fee .5% —Current equipment package $50,000	—Opening supervision —Field supervision —Classroom training —Newsletter —Site selection —Lease negotiation
McDonald's Restaurants of Canada Ltd. (McDonald's Restaurants)	—Established 1967 in Canada —156 franchised; 168 company owned —Total Canadian sales $500m —45 new units planned across Canada	—Franchise fee $10,000; initial investment $190,000; total cost is around $400,000 —Percentage rent plus royalty fee —Total commitment by sole operator to run operation —4% advertising fee	—Continual consultation on operation —Marketing —Training —Personnel —Real estate
The Harvest Inn, Inc. (The Pantry Family Restaurant)	—Established 1975 —5 units company owned, 2 franchised, all in B.C. —Full service restaurant for breakfast, lunch, and dinner —4 additional units are planned for B.C.	—$20,000 initial fee —Royalty fee 4% gross —Advertising fee 2%	—Full turnkey service includes site selection, interior design —Accounting, training, and personnel selection

EXHIBIT 6   (*concluded*)

Burger King Canada Ltd. (Burger King)	—Established 1976 —27 franchised units and 10 company owned. 2,650 worldwide; B.C. 2, Alta. 2, Ont. 30, P.E.I. 1, N.B. 1, N.S. 4 —26 franchised units planned for Ont., N.B., B.C., N.S., Alta. —Menu includes hamburgers and specialty sandwiches	—Initial fee $40,000 —4% royalty fee —4% advertising fee	—Complete service package
Smitty's Pancake Houses Ltd.	—Established 1959 —86 franchised and 6 company owned; 3 in Hawaii —Total sales $59m —16 units planned for 1980	—Initial fee $25,000 over 70 seats; $25,000 under 70 seats	
Country Style Donuts Ltd.	—Established 1962 —66 franchised, 4 company owned, 4 in U.S., Alta. 4, Sask. 1, Man. 3, Ont. 55, Que. 5, N.S. 1 —Total sales $15m —14 new units planned for Alta., Ont. and Sask. —Menu incl. coffee and donuts	—Initial fee $85,000 ($2,500 deposit, $27,500 for construction, $50,000 equipment contract, $5,000 inventory) —Royalty fee 4.5% of gross —2% advertising fee	—Turnkey operation —4-week training course —Supervisory assistance on opening —20-year franchise term

EXHIBIT 7   Estimated Capital Requirements of Additional Stores

Mmmuffins:

Equipment package	$15,000
General construction (including fixtures and leasehold improvements)	40,000–60,000
Opening supplies and inventories	5,000
Miscellaneous (design, insurance, permits, pre-opening salaries, opening promotion, landlord chargebacks, working capital)	10,000
	$70,000–$90,000*

Michel's Baguette:

Equipment package	$145,000
General construction (including fixtures and leasehold improvements)	170,000–235,000
Furniture and supplies	35,000–45,000
Miscellaneous (working capital, design, permits, opening promotion, pre-opening salaries, advance rent)	20,000–40,000
	$370,000–$465,000*

*These are stand-alone estimates. If franchised, any franchise fee would be an additional requirement.

EXHIBIT 8 Estimated Earnings Potential

Mmmuffins Potential Annual Cash Flow*
350-Square-Foot Mall Location

	$3,000		$4,000		$5,000	
Weekly sales	Dollars	Percent	Dollars	Percent	Dollars	Percent
Annual sales	$156,000		$208,000		$260,000	
Food cost (1)..........	48,360	31.0	62,400	30.0	78,000	30.0
Selling supplies	7,020	4.5	9,360	4.5	11,700	4.5
Labour (incl. benefits) (2)	31,200	20.0	37,440	18.0	41,600	16.0
Gross operating profit....	69,420	44.5	98,800	47.5	128,700	49.5
Operating expenses:						
Royalties	9,360	6.0	12,480	6.0	15,600	6.0
Telephone	500	.3	500	.2	500	.2
Utilities	3,500	2.2	3,800	1.8	4,000	1.5
Uniforms and laundry	600	.4	600	.3	650	.3
Advertising	3,120	2.0	4,160	2.0	5,200	2.0
Repairs and maintenance....	800	.5	800	.4	800	.3
Insurance	900	.6	900	.4	900	.3
Total occupancy (rent) (3)	16,800	10.8	17,500	8.4	21,000	8.1
Depreciation and amortization (4)	7,000	4.5	7,000	3.4	7,000	2.7
Miscellaneous (5)	1,560	1.0	2,080	1.0	2,600	1.0
Total operating expenses	44,140	28.3	49,820	24.0	58,250	22.4
Earnings before interest and tax (6)	25,280	16.2	48,980	23.5	70,450	27.1
Add: Depreciation and amortization (7)....	7,000	4.5	7,000	3.4	7,000	2.7
Cash flow before interest, tax, and franchisee compensation....	$ 32,280	20.7%	$ 55,980	26.9%	$ 77,450	29.8%

Note: See notes on next page.
*Post start-up; no operator/franchisee compensation is included.

EXHIBIT 8   (*continued*)

NOTES TO MMMUFFINS CASH FLOW PROJECTIONS

1. Based on prices of 60–65¢ per muffin, $3.45 for 6, and 40¢ per cup of coffee.
2. Based on 70-hour weekly selling period with hourly wages of $3.75–$4.75 for baking staff, $3.50–$4 for full-time selling staff, and $3–$3.50 for part-time staff. OWNER-OPERATOR'S COMPENSATION IS NOT INCLUDED.
3. Total occupancy includes all services for which landlord invoices including rent, merchants' association fees, common area charges, heating, ventilating and air conditioning, realty taxes, etc. Total occupancy may vary depending on location. We have assumed base rent of $40 per square foot for a 350-square-foot store or 7 percent of sales (whichever is greater) plus $8 per square foot in "extras."
4. Depreciation and amortization is calculated by applying the straight-line method on $70,000 over 10 years.
5. Miscellaneous expenses may include cash shortages, licenses and permits, office supplies, professional fees, etc.
6. Earnings before interest, tax, and franchisee's compensation is expressed as such due to wide variances in compensations paid, amount of debt to service, individual's accounting treatment of expenses, etc.
7. Depreciation, being a noncash expense, is added back to illustrate total cash generated before interest, tax, and franchisee compensation.

EXHIBIT 8 (continued)

Baguette Potential Annual Cash Flow*
3,000-Square-Foot Mall Location

	$14,000		$18,000		$22,000	
Weekly sales	Dollars	Percent	Dollars	Percent	Dollars	Percent
Annual sales	$728,000		$936,000		$1,144,000	
Food cost	232,960	32.0	299,520	32.0	354,640	31.0
Selling supplies	21,840	3.0	28,080	3.0	34,320	3.0
Labour (incl. benefits) (1)	203,840	28.0	243,360	26.0	286,000	25.0
Gross operating profit	269,360	37.0	365,040	39.0	469,040	41.0
Operating expenses:						
Royalties	43,680	6.0	56,160	6.0	68,640	6.0
Utilities (2)	14,000	1.9	15,000	1.6	17,000	1.5
Telephone	700	.1	700	.1	700	.1
Uniforms and laundry	2,200	.3	2,600	.3	3,000	.3
Advertising (3)	7,280	1.0	9,360	1.0	11,500	1.0
Repairs and maintenance (4)	5,000	.7	6,000	.6	7,000	.6
Replacements (5)	3,500	.5	4,500	.5	5,500	.5
Insurance	3,000	.4	3,000	.3	3,000	.3
Total occupancy (rent) (6)	75,000	10.3	77,000	8.2	89,500	7.8
Depreciation (7)	30,000	4.1	30,000	3.2	30,000	2.6
Miscellaneous (8)	7,280	1.0	9,360	1.0	11,500	1.0
Total operating expenses	191,640	26.3	213,680	22.8	247,340	21.6
Earnings before interest and tax	77,720	10.7	151,360	16.2	221,700	19.4
Add: Depreciation (9)	30,000	4.1	30,000	3.2	30,000	2.6
Cash flow before interest, tax, and franchisee compensation	$107,720	14.8%	$181,360	19.4%	$ 251,700	22.0%

Note: See notes on next page.
*After 6 month start-up period; no operator/franchisee compensation is included.

EXHIBIT 8   (*concluded*)

NOTES TO BAGUETTE CASH FLOW PROJECTIONS

1. Based on 70-hour weekly selling period with hourly wages of $4–$5 for baking staff, $3.50–$4.50 for full-time service, food preparation, and bussing staff and $3.25–$3.75 for part-time staff. Management salaries include: assistant store manager at $14,500 per year, head baker at $15,600 per year. OWNER-OPERATOR'S SALARY IS NOT INCLUDED.
2. Based on actual experience in Toronto store. Utility expenses may vary widely depending on location, use of gas versus electric oven, hours of operation, etc.
3. One percent allocation is for local advertising and promotion. At this time the franchisor does not maintain a national advertising fund.
4. As most equipment is under warranty, first year repair expenses should be lower than projections. Actual cost in future years will vary considerably due to periodic breakdowns, preventive maintenance program, use of equipment, etc.
5. Replacements include costs of replenishing supplies of utensils, dishware, cutlery, trays, etc.
6. Total occupancy includes all services for which landlord invoices: rent, merchants' association fees, common area charges, heating, ventilation and air conditioning, realty taxes, etc. We have assumed a base rent of $18-per-square-foot for a 3,000-square-foot store or 6 percent of sales (whichever is greater) plus $7 per square foot in nonrent "extras." Actual total occupancy costs will vary for each location and should be evaluated individually.
7. Depreciation is calculated by applying the straight-line method on $360,000 over 12 years.
8. Miscellaneous expenses may include professional fees, licenses and permits, cash shortages, office supplies, etc.
9. Depreciation, being a noncash expense, is added back to illustrate total cash generated before interest, tax, and franchisee's compensation.

Spinnaker Software Corporation

The big strategic issue we face in 1985 is whether we want to pursue our policy of taking aggressive action in key long-term areas, or cut back and live more comfortably. Taking the aggressive road implies, of course, keeping a structure that is dimensioned for a much larger volume of sales than the current one. But we have to decide whether there is a business, a large market, here or not. If we think there isn't, we should sell the company and quit. But if we think there is, as we do, we shouldn't cut any more.

With these words, Bill Bowman, chairman and cofounder of Spinnaker Software Corporation, set forth the key issue for the fourth year of his company. In 1982, Spinnaker sold about $750,000 worth of four microcomputer programs. In 1984, sales went well over $15 million, with a product line of 60 titles.

BACKGROUND

Spinnaker was formed in April 1982 by two former colleagues from the Boston Consulting Group, Bill Bowman and David Seuss. Bill had had work experience in computers, first as a programmer and later as a manager for the U.S. government. He went to the Harvard Business School with the idea of returning to his government job, since his record there had been very positive; but when the time came, no

This case was prepared by José-Carlos Jarillo-Mossi under the direction of Howard H. Stevenson.

suitable position was available for him. He had to change his plans and, upon graduation, joined the Boston Consulting Group.

I had been invited to their presentation at a fancy country club on Cape Cod and was very impressed by it. I joined them in June 1978. What attracted me was the possibility of a fast-track career, being involved in strategic decisions, and the opportunity to see many different industries, since all my experience had been on the mainframe computer side of things.

I spent my time at BCG involved in marketing cases, mostly on pretty boring, 2- or 3-percent–growth industries. The last case I had was toilet bowl deodorizers: a strategy case for a company that made them. In fact, this was a 6-percent-decline-a-year industry. When I finished, I just quit. I was 29 years old and had four children by then. But I couldn't take it any more.

An important reason for my decision was that I was seeing microcomputers come into the scene, and I did not want to be left out. BCG did not even have a high-tech case by then. But my "entrepreneurial spirit" had been there all the way, too. I had formed three teams of friends to look for ways to start something on our own, although I soon realized that, as people got promotions and pay raises, their risk profiles changed quite radically.

I left with no job in sight, but with the intention of learning as much as I could about the computer industry. After almost five years out of it, I had missed many very important changes. For instance, when I started my MBA, microcomputers did not exist at all. In fact, Dan Fylstra (founder of Visicorp, the first successful personal computer software company) was a section mate of mine. At BCG I was reading all about his success and all the fantastic things they were doing on those wild and new Apples. I felt frustrated not to know more about those machines.

Three months later I got a job with a high-tech data communications company in Cambridge. They worked mainly for the military in very sophisticated data and communications networks. At that point they wanted to start selling something in the open market through a subsidiary, and I was hired as director of planning to help sell a sophisticated minicomputer they had designed. They were not very marketing-driven, although they were very good technically. I gained an awful lot of experience there and learned about the high-tech, micros world.

While at BCG I had studied, on my own, the economics of the minicomputer software business (turnkey systems). I continued with this in my new job. I came to the conclusion that it was an attractive business, for which up-front capital wasn't needed. The only catch is that it is almost impossible to grow beyond $25 million, but they make nice little companies.

David Seuss had also been a student at the Harvard Business School, where he first met Bill. After his MBA he went to work at the Boston Consulting Group. According to his recollections of that period,

When I left business school, there was nothing more remote from my mind than starting my own company. I had absolutely no interest in entrepreneurial activities, and for the first two years at BCG this didn't change. I really liked BCG. It was great. It was a terrific experience, I met great people, I did interesting things, and learned an enormous amount. But by the third year there I decided I wanted to be a manager, rather than a consultant. I got tired of giving advice—I wanted to do things. I then looked at my alternatives. The typical way out of BCG is to convince one of your clients to offer you a line job. This didn't work for me. You could also go to work for a client in a staff position and wait a couple of years to get into the line. I couldn't take this. I could not go on doing for two years something I don't like, with the idea of eventually achieving what I wanted. Besides, I had the best staff job in the world. I only worked on the biggest problems, with the most money at stake, and at the highest level of the largest organizations. My ability to influence the decisions in those companies was far superior to what I would have as an internal planner. I concluded that, if I wanted to get a line management job, my only alternative was to start my own company.

One day, at the beginning of April 1981, Bill was working at his new job when David asked to see him. He was preparing a study for a European manufacturer of minicomputers and was interested in Bill's views on the industry. Over lunch, Bill reported on his research on the minicomputer software business, and how it was a relatively easy business to get into. According to Bill,

By the end of the meal we agreed that all you needed to succeed was a little luck and a lot of hard work. We looked at each other, and I said, "Do you want to do that?" We then shook hands and decided to do it.

STARTING A NEW COMPANY

They agreed to meet every week to prepare the business plan and eventually came up with three business ideas in the minicomputer software area. In the course of interviewing people to develop those ideas further, Bill met an old friend who was working for a venture capital company in San Francisco. His friend told Bill to talk to a person he knew at TA Association—another venture capital firm—in Boston. According to Bill,

I didn't call him for several months, for I wasn't too interested. We didn't need capital, only good ideas. At that time, we kept changing our ideas of what the business should be about. The problem, I guess, was that nobody or nothing was forcing us to act, our salaries and reputations in our companies were going up, and, therefore, we were in fact becoming more risk averse. As a result, nothing was happening. One day I was cleaning my briefcase and saw the little slip of paper with the venture capitalist's name and phone number. I decided to throw it away, but when I had already crumpled the paper and was going to throw it to the trash can, I thought, "If I don't call this guy my friend in San Francisco will eventually ask about it, and I won't know what to say." So I called and got an appointment for lunch.

When I arrived at his office, on December 1, 1981, his secretary told me he was sorry, but some last minute problems in closing a deal had detained him out of the office, and he wouldn't be able to have lunch with me. To be honest, I was relieved: I had fulfilled the social obligation, and I could go back to work. I was about to leave, when his secretary told me that someone called Jacqui Morby would have lunch with me instead. I was down again. I didn't know who he or she was, and what he or she might want. As it turned out, she was one of the most important investors in the microcomputer software industry: she had done Digital Research, Sierra On-Line, and some more. In that lunch I didn't have to "impress," since I wasn't looking for money, so I was pretty relaxed. While talking about microcomputers, we both agreed that as prices went down, the channels of distribution would change radically. They would go from specialized stores to mass retailers. There were no marketing skills in the companies already in the market. That was a clear opportunity for two marketing types, trained at BCG.

Jacqui takes a somewhat different approach to judging ventures. She does not spend most of her time over financial projections, but tries to find out whether the would-be entrepreneurs will be capable of making it or not. If her gut feeling is that they will, she goes ahead. Neither David nor I had P&L experience, or for that matter any management experience at all. In this sense, we had all the wrong background, including consulting, which makes you the lowest level of human being in the eyes of a venture capitalist, perhaps justifiably. Over coffee she suggested that David and I rethink our ideas and come up with a business plan in the microcomputer industry. TA would look at it and, possibly, provide the funds. I couldn't believe it, but we went back to her office to discuss some more points, and by December 21 we got funding for a three-week study of the microcomputing industry.

David and Bill set out to do a preliminary study of the market. Their first idea was to get into business software, but, according to Bill,

We went to the retailer and asked them, "What is the software that people ask you for and you don't have?" And the answer was always "Educational software." So we didn't arrive at our strategy through any brilliant analytical technique. We just asked retailers what the public wanted.

Bill had bought a PC for himself and knew the fascination it had for his kids. These two pieces of information convinced them to start in the educational software area. They also knew that Lotus Corporation was about to enter the business software market aggressively. Some other companies like Visicorp and Microsoft were becoming more and more involved in business software; at the same time, nobody with business sophistication was in the educational segment. David and Bill saw a clear void and thought they could dominate the segment before it started growing too much. They believed that being first really pays off. According to the first paragraph of their business plan,

> The company will publish software in the home educational and sophisticated games segment of the microcomputer industry. It will assemble a portfolio of software that it will market through its own sales force to software retail stores and schools, and through software distributors to microcomputer hardware stores. Software will initially be purchased from outside authors, and the company will add value in documentation, packaging, distribution, and retailer support. The company expects to invest heavily in advertising and a direct sales force in order to establish a brand franchise, build strong retailer support, and create a competitive barrier in marketing.

On February 15 they presented the business plan to TA; on March 15 the funding was approved, and on April 1st they started the company. David had some studies to finish at BCG, and he stayed there until June. Bill resigned from his job and started working full time on April 8, 1982.

The company was valued at $1.6 million after the funding, and TA provided $800,000. The rest of the shares were divided between the founders and a large pool reserved for future key managers and employees.

The final decision wasn't easy for David. He recalled:

> Studying business alternatives with Bill was easy and a lot of fun. But making the decision to actually jump ship was very difficult. When TA offered funding, I panicked and said, "Wait a minute. I'm leaving a job that's paying me $125,000 a year, just three years out of business school, at which I'm very good and headed for the top, to go off into a wild scheme that will be bankrupt probably in six months. Then, when I go looking for a job, I won't be a manager at the Boston Consulting Group, but a failed entrepreneur." I started looking carefully at family budgets, mortgages, and things like that, which I thought I had behind me forever. My wife had quit her job to get an MBA, and we had lost her $50,000 salary. So we were going to go from a family income of $175,000 to one of $50,000 in a week. That's a hard adjustment. I couldn't sleep for a couple of weeks. I would go home and start working on things like "OK, if the company goes bankrupt, Priscilla could drop out of school and this would save us the tuition, we have this much in savings, I have this long to get a job." I went from a mind-set of jetting around the world in first class advising corporate leaders on issues of major importance to figuring out if I could meet my monthly bills. It's quite a change. TA was putting pressure on us,

asking for an answer. Finally, on a Monday morning I summoned up all my courage and quit.

A very important factor in my decision, besides my desire to be in line management, was that I had spent all my life alienating the people I worked for. I have a very hard time in organizational settings, with my superiors. When I worked as an engineer, every plant manager I worked for was mad at me. At the business school I used to irritate my professors and my classmates a lot. When you take aggressiveness and make it boisterous, I think it is hard to take. At BCG it was the same. More than one VP said, "I wish David wasn't so hard to work with sometimes." I think I irritated every VP there, but the great thing at BCG is that if you do good work for your client, you are OK. Good work really counts for an awful lot. But at some point I said to myself, "I'd be better off if there was nobody above me. Since I cannot work with hierarchies, let's get rid of them."

The business plan called for the new company to do the development, packaging, and launching of the product by February 1983. But then they learned that the crucial time in the industry was the Christmas season, so they decided to shorten an already very tight schedule. To sell in the Christmas season they had to ship on September 1; that was slashing in half the time they had. They put together a PERT chart that included everything—they didn't even have a name. It called for shipping on August 27, 1982 (see Exhibit 1). They had to work seven days a week during those months to that date, and all the activities were in the "critical path." They couldn't afford any delay.

The transition from consultants to operating managers wasn't an easy one. Priscilla, David's wife, took charge of shipping. She recalls the conversation she had with David when he offered her that job:

Priscilla: When did you tell the distributor we will ship to him?

David: Three weeks from now.

Priscilla: What do we have to do to ship?

David: Not much. Reproduce the disks, put the disk and documentation in the box. Shrink-wrap the box, pack the boxes into shipping cartons, and call UPS.

Priscilla: Do we have the equipment and software for disk reproduction?

David: No. Maybe we should start looking into it.

Priscilla: Is the documentation being printed yet?

David: No. I haven't gotten around to writing it yet.

Priscilla: What about the shrink-wrapping machine? Is there a lead time on getting one?

David: Lead time? Gee, I never thought of that!

Priscilla (with rising alarm): Do we have a shipping scale on order, have you bought cartons, sealing tape, and gotten a UPS account?

David: Well, no.

Priscilla: Where the heck are we going to do all this?

David: Maybe we should rent some space.

In spite of their lack of operating experience, they managed to keep up with their plan. On August 27 they were operating the packaging machine for the first time when the UPS man came two hours earlier than expected, and they didn't have the product finished. It was shipped the following Monday. "It seems incredible," Bill said, "but we only missed the deadline by two hours."

> Jacqui had provided the contact with Tom Snyder, an independent programmer who wrote that first two products (Snooper Troops 1 and Snooper Troops 2). Two more programs came from a small company on the West Coast, and that was the product line. I think that the packaging was a breakthrough, compared with the usual standards. Our advertising agency worked for us as though we were a large corporation. I was very impressed by their interest.

Spinnaker sold slightly over $750,000 in the year ending January 31, 1983. A new home computer, the Commodore 64, had been launched for that Christmas season, and they thought it was going to be a winner. But it operated with cartridges instead of disks, and no one at Spinnaker had any knowledge of the technology to produce cartridges. Bill and David suddenly had to learn about things like chip-on-board technology. But getting into cartridges was very important. According to Bill,

> We knew that if we did that, we would get into the mass merchandisers' channel, riding on Commodore's coattails. Getting into mass merchandisers was our main objective since the beginning. I remember two years' worth of business school professors telling me that the most important decisions you make in a company are the channel decisions. That has been my experience, too.

UNEXPECTED GROWTH

Again, they had to work against the clock. The main industry trade show was the Consumer Electronics Show in Chicago in June. If they wanted to introduce the Commodore line in time for the 1983 Christmas season, they had to have it ready by then. Bill recalled:

> We could only find rooms in a very classy, starchy private club in downtown Chicago through a friend of mine. There we were, trying to put together tiny chips of ROMs to introduce the software the next morning. Again, it worked, and we met many purchasers of mass merchandisers who were desperately looking for software in cartridges for the Commodore 64. We had a nice booth and a full line of cartridge software. In the Christmas season of 1983 the sales of that machine exploded. We did $11.3 million in sales in the year ending January 31, 1984.

That explosive growth caught the company by surprise. The original business plan had called for sales of only $3,440,000 in 1983. Even more surprising, according to David, was:

> . . . how quickly we were able to establish ourselves at the forefront of the industry, in terms of visibility, distribution, etc. I think the secret was aggressiveness. We thought that way. A vice president at the Boston Consulting Group used to say, "Big boys play with big boys, and little boys play with little boys." And we acted like and dealt with the big boys. We immediately went after the largest retailers, looking for the best market share. Our background really helped in this thinking big. Also, our marketing orientation was very important. Now it's been matched by our competitors, and it's no longer a competitive advantage, but it helped us to get out in front.

This rapid expansion demanded a constant effort, particularly from Bill, who had responsibility for building the organization. They were always behind in hiring, expanding, finding room. The experts were predicting growth for the following year on the order of 100 percent, with triple the number of machines sold. Management at Spinnaker looked at its market share and saw that just by keeping it they would be a much, much larger company one year later.

And they acted on those estimates. They had been conservative in hiring in their first year: The day they shipped their first product in August 1982, they were only five people in the company, including Bill, David, and Priscilla. By the end of the year there were up to 15 people. One year later they were at 50, and then they got rolling and went from 50 to 100 in about five months. Bill did not find hiring all those people as difficult as he thought it would be. Spinnaker had the policy that everybody in the company should have equity, and that proved to be important for many people in making the decision to work there. Besides Lotus, Spinnaker was the only venture-capital-backed microcomputer software company in the Cambridge area.

Both founders believed that their system of "split management" was one of the critical factors that made it possible to cope with that hypergrowth. David and Bill had decided to split the responsibilities completely. Bill would take charge of internal affairs like hiring, engineering, financing, and control, while David took charge of sales and marketing. Bill described it this way:

> From our time at BCG, we were used to being completely responsible for a part of a team's work and to knowing that the whole team depended on each individual's effort. Dependability is absolutely necessary to work in such a way. At Spinnaker, this management style allowed us to devote twice as much time to each issue as the typical entrepreneur can devote.

Each one makes every tactical and operational decision in his own area without bothering the other. Strategic matters are decided in common. People said this could not work, and the venture capital people forced us to decide on who would be chairman, so that someone would be in charge. But our system works wonderfully.

In David's view:

The common background Bill and I have, through HBS and BCG; has really helped us to work out our two-man show. The habits of teamwork and individual dependability have been very useful. We are able to discuss everything and, at the same time, to detach our own egos from the ideas we may be pushing.

To sustain its fast growth, the company needed more funds. In December 1982, $1.5 million was raised from NEA; Harvard Trust; Alex Brown; and L. F. Rothschild, Unterberg, Tobin. The valuation was $9.5 million. Nine months later in October 1983, $5 million more was raised at a valuation of $50 million, in what was supposed to be a mezzanine round. This was probably the highest valuation ever given to a company of Spinnaker's characteristics. Investors from all over the world participated in the financing (General Electric's pension fund, the previous investors, private investors from Europe, and so on). The valuation of the company had gone up from $9.5 to $50 million in 10 months.

To round up that expansion, Spinnaker started opening the European market. Bill and David had observed that, in most consumer industries, foreign sales reach some 40 percent of corporate sales when the market matures. Therefore, they decided to start working abroad, although foreign markets lagged the United States by two years. The investment had been important relative to the size of the business, which was only 5 percent of sales at that point. Bill commented,

We have started in out typical fashion, in partnership with important companies in each national market. We are trying to bring high quality and a fully "localized product"; we don't sell anything that is not in the local language of the country. We even revise the programs to be sold in the United Kingdom, to conform to British spelling. When those markets pick up, we are going to be the only experienced company there.

CHARACTER OF THE COMPANY

The most fun thing for me in these two years has been to shape the character of the company, to have the opportunity to have an impact in the tone of a group of 100 people. David and I are very different in our characters. He is flamboyant, fast judgments, no kids, while I'm more orderly, more people-oriented, have seven kids. But we have identical views on how to treat employees, and my views on the importance of the family have had an impact on our software, on our company, on how we do things around here. We already have lots of traditions in the company that haven't started artificially, but rather as a projection of our personalities. The most conspicuous of those traditions is probably the Friday evening party. Every Friday, at 5:45 P.M., we have a party at which David and I inform everybody about how things are going, and we socialize together for a while. All employees are strongly urged to bring in their spouses and kids. All this started in the first months when we still worked in three small offices near my house in Belmont. My wife, Leigh, didn't like my arriving home too late on Fridays, so she would bring the kids and some beer and cheese to the office. Obviously, we couldn't possibly work with five kids around in three offices no bigger than 300 square feet, and so we had to have a little party. That tradition keeps going. We enjoy getting together as a company with our families. This is an intense environment, where people work very hard. We think that getting their spouses to feel like part of the company helps to deal with the demands of time and all those business problems. We really work hard on this although, of course, some people avail themselves of it, and some people don't. The other day, one of our top engineers told me, "The day those things stop is the day I'm leaving." I would never have forecast the importance of things like that, nor would I have forecast the personal impact I could have in a company by creating the tone for a group of very disparate individuals.

There are many other small traditions of that kind, like giving employees their birthday off or running the Employee Appreciation Day: once a year, during the summer, the whole company would go to the beach and have a good party with lobster and steaks. In previous years, they had given shares of the company at this party to every single employee, according to the number of months of employment. They did not do that anymore, but the party was still something everybody looked forward to.

The 1984 Christmas party had been at the Fogg Museum at Harvard. Bill felt that

> It was very elegant, and our employees really like that. We try to play our East Coast versus West Coast image. A small example is that the music you hear in the phone system when put on hold is always classical music. That's not what you normally find in a small high-tech company in California.

Another tradition was the Spinnaker breakfast at the Consumer Electronics Show in Chicago. Normally, the important vendors there offered parties for their customers and the press. Instead, Spinnaker offered its "breakfast," with a talk by David, on the second day of the show, and it invariably attracted practically every important person in the industry.

Bill summarized,

In a word, we try to have a very comfortable, familiar atmosphere, with an important element of class—conservative class, if you like.

STRUCTURE OF THE INDUSTRY

The microcomputer software market could be divided in two major categories, business and home software. Business software was normally sold through specialized computer retail outlets and varied in price in the $200–$600 range. It worked only on the so-called business microcomputers, like the IBM-PC (and compatibles) and Apple's Macintosh. These machines sold in 1984 for between $3,000 and $5,000, once the necessary peripherals such as printers and modems were added.

The home software was sold in versions for practically every machine (including the ones mentioned above) but its "natural" marker was the low-priced computers, in the range of $100–$1,000. These machines—Commodore and Atari were the main contenders—were sold through mass-merchandise retailers, like Sears, K mart, Toys "R" Us. The software for those machines was sold mainly through those stores, although specialized computer stores also carried it if there were versions for the computers they sold. It was relatively easy for software manufacturers to obtain distribution in the computer specialty stores. They only had to reach an agreement with one of the major software distributors, who would carry the inventory for the dealers. These distributors normally were given a discount of 60 percent from retail price.

The sale of home software through the mass-merchandising channels was not unlike the sale of packaged goods. The critical variable was shelf space. An average retailer carried around 100 titles. That space was fought for by the manufacturers of computers, who also sold software, and all the independent—or third-party—software companies. Of those 100 slots, 40 would usually go to the first-party vendors, or computer manufacturers. Of the remaining 60, only 30 percent were educational, which was the main area of Spinnaker's business.

Software publishing had been compared to the book industry, but the cost structure of programs was different from that of book production. A program in a diskette could not possibly be produced for less than $2.50. This resulted in higher wholesale prices and, thus, in higher inventory carrying costs. This made it impossible for the retailer to carry many programs, which was the reason for the reduced shelf space discussed above. It also made carrying inventory a risky activity. The intrinsic value is high, the success of given programs could not be predicted at all, and each diskette only ran in a particular brand or model of computer, thus compounding the initial uncertainty.

The most important characteristic of the home software industry was its volatility. For a small company like Spinnaker, the actions of the computer manufacturers could be devastating. According to David, in charge of marketing and sales,

> Our worst threat is first-party manufacturers. For instance, Commodore decides to go ahead with a promotion that consists of giving away two pieces of software with each new machine sold. But 50 percent of our business in the Commodore market was the couple of programs that the new buyers take with the computer. So, suddenly, a big chunk of our business is seriously threatened by a promotion that doesn't want to sell software, but hardware: they can destroy us without trying, or even without noticing. Another thing that first-party manufacturers do is, when they want to lower the price of their machines to the retailer, they just give him free software. They are not interested in the software business; they only want to sell machines and don't look at software as a profit center. They are a terrible threat.

But the hardware market itself was extremely volatile. This posed more risks for the software manufacturers since their sales were necessarily tied to those of the computer manufacturers: "They sell the razors and we sell the blades," commented Bill. David summarized that volatility:

> If IBM prices the PC jr too high, it doesn't sell, and we get stuck with the inventory we had prepared for it. The Commodore 64 is replaced by a new model with a slightly different disk-drive protocol, so that 20 percent of the old programs don't work. If one of my important products happens to be in that 20 percent, I get stuck with a large field inventory that is suddenly obsolete. If Atari cuts its prices and gains market share rapidly, my business is affected: this year, Atari did cut prices, and sales in its price category went from almost nothing to 50 percent, while Commodore plummeted. I happened to have fantastic Commodore distribution and lousy distribution of Atari software. And these things are happening constantly, with no possibility whatsoever of predicting most of them. In October, Atari was dead. In November, it rides the crest of the wave. Apple seemed finished in 1983. In 1984, they look like the only survivor, besides IBM, in the higher-priced segment. IBM's PC jr was going to get the whole home market. And it flops. And when almost everybody has written it off, then it comes back and is a best seller. Two months later, IBM discontinues it. We are constantly kicked around by these things.
>
> On the other hand, it's terribly exciting. For people like Bill and me, with a strong tendency to look at the environment, the competition, the markets, etc., this is fantastic. Again, this is probably a plus from BCG. And we get instant feedback from our decisions. If you work in the paper business and decide whether you want to buy woodlands, it will take 50

years to know if you made the right move. In this business, it will take less than six weeks. Our joke is that long-term planning is next month. I don't have any idea right now of what Commodore is going to be doing in three months' time. And all my strategy has to depend on that.

1984

In December of 1983, Spinnaker sold $2.3 million, out of a total of $11 million for the whole fiscal year. All the experts in the industry were predicting an industry growth of some 200 percent to 300 percent for the coming year. Thus, 1984 was poised to be the year in which Spinnaker was to grow to over $50 million and establish itself as a mature, fully grown company. Of course, one of the goals of the founders for that year was to take the company public. According to Bill, in charge of internal development, the big strategic issue for 1984 was how to cope with that growth and secure the resources needed to sustain it.

To achieve that growth and reaffirm its dominating position in the industry, Spinnaker developed what they called the branding strategy. According to Bill,

> There are four ways you can market home software. The first is title specific. That's how hit games are advertised. The problem with that approach is that the money you spend does not extend beyond the life of the specific program. The second way is promoting the authors. Some companies have tried that, but it has not really worked, and all it achieved was a rise in that author's royalties. The third way is licensing characters. The problem with licenses is that there aren't many of them, they are very narrow in terms of the age group and, again, the money you invest works mainly for the benefit of the licensor, not the licensee. The fourth one is branding. You recognize that consumers are not homogeneous, but they form some groups that share interests, and you try to tailor make brands to address those groups. Currently, we have four segments and six brands.

The four segments were educational, adventure games, home productivity, and arcade games. The educational segment had the top-of-the-line Spinnaker brand. By the end of 1983, that brand had achieved outstanding prestige and was the undisputed number one in educational software. There was much speculation in the industry that large, established companies in related fields were seriously thinking of entering the market. David explained,

> We asked ourselves, "What company represents a serious threat to our marketing position?" We decided that Fisher-Price could enter this market from a very strong position, so we offered them a deal in which we

would use their name. If turned out that this is exactly what they were looking for since they had been badly burned in video games, and they didn't want to go into educational software on their own. They did want their name to be present in this market. Fisher-Price is now our second brand in the educational segment. All Fisher-Price does is let us use their name, with its tremendous prestige, and give us access to their fantastic testing facilities. We have to get the distribution by ourselves since the buyer of software products for a large retailer is normally a different person from the buyer of Fisher-Price toys. The brand was launched in July 1984, and it's doing very well. A problem was that their name competes with our own Spinnaker line, and the contract had to be very carefully negotiated. One of the most important points in the contract is that Fisher-Price programs have to be always cheaper than comparable Spinnaker programs.

The third brand was Telarium, which represented their first diversification outside educational programs. It consisted of what was known as *adventure games*. They were able to sign the best authors in the science-fiction community—like Ray Bradbury, Arthur C. Clark, and others—who wrote the scripts used to produce the games, often based on best-seller novels. Unlike other adventure games in the market, Telarium programs had good text, from the literary point of view, and outstanding music. This was relatively unusual. To introduce the line, Spinnaker made a deal with Waldenbooks to be in every one of their 850 stores by October 15, 1984. Once again, time pressures were high, since Spinnaker couldn't start working before September 15. Bill recalled that effort:

> We had people working 24 hours a day for a month. We converted the board room into a dormitory with sleeping bags and pillows. People would work until they couldn't go on anymore, and then they would go upstairs, sleep for a few hours, come down, and start working again. We had a caterer bringing in meals for a month, weekdays, Saturdays, and Sundays. It was . . . ridiculous, that's what it was. But we had to have the product in a month. We did meet the deadline, but we won't do it again. It was extremely painful, although when it was finished, the camaraderie that existed in the team was fantastic. This involved some 30 percent of the people in the company. I think this is going to be our biggest line next year.

The fourth line, Windham Classics, was also an adventure line, but based on children's books like *Robinson Crusoe, The Wizard of Oz,* and other classics. Although it had been in the shops only a few months, it looked promising. It was introduced with very little advertising, and, therefore, getting distribution had been much more difficult than with the other lines. Where it did have distribution, the sell-through had been very good. According to David,

It's really helped us to understand the role of advertising: It's extremely important in order to get distribution, but word-of-mouth is crucial for selling. These games are very good, and this has been said in user groups, magazine reviews, etc. In some places, the sell-through is much higher than that of the Spinnaker line. It's been a lot of fun.

The fifth brand was called Maxion. It was, simply, a dumping ground. It sold for $9.95 at retail, compared to a normal price of $20 to $40 for other programs, and it was carefully cost-engineered. Bill's brother, a Harvard MBA student, had launched it during the summer of 1984. Bill explained,

We hired him for the summer and gave him $12,000 to launch the project. He was able to do everything with that money. This brand works this way. When products become outmoded in the Spinnaker brand, you have three choices: destroy the inventory, as Atari did, putting millions of cartridges of a flop game in a hole in New Mexico and pouring concrete all over; the second approach is to cut the price and sell it, but this undermines the value of the brand name; the third approach is to create a new brand, put the products in that brand, and blow them out at $9.95. The retailers love it: They get cheap stuff to sell, and, at the same time, the consumers don't see Spinnaker in dump bins so it also protects our customers' inventories. We don't promote these games as educational, and we emphasize the game aspect of the programs. This has been a very interesting approach, and I don't know of any company that has done something like it. It's working well, and it's the top selling brand in some mass retailers.

Finally, the line called *Better-Working* was positioned in the so-called home productivity segment. It consisted of a few programs used for serious work at home, like word processing, filing, financial planning, and so on. In January 1985 the programs were not in the shops yet, but the reception by the industry had been outstanding in Bill's opinion. Their quality was good, and the price of $49.95 compared well with normal prices of $75–$200 for competing programs. That was the only new line that had the name Spinnaker on it too since it was not competing with educational games, and the Spinnaker brand could lend it prestige.

THE BIG DISAPPOINTMENT

Consistent with the forecast growth in sales, Spinnaker had laid down an aggressive expansion policy for 1984. At the beginning of the year, the break-even point was about $12 million in sales. Since the gross margin was normally 50 percent, that meant expenditures in the $6 million range. With the expansion plan, the planned break-even went up to a level of $40 million in sales (i.e., expenditures of $20 million). In July 1984, however, management realized that sales were not growing that fast, and that it was necessary to put the brakes on expansion plans. When they stopped committing expenditures, the level of sales needed to break even was $19 million, which represented $9.5 million in expenditures. Of this, $3.5 million was personnel, and the rest was advertising, sales, and depreciation. Since sales only reached $15 million that year, Spinnaker closed its books with a loss of almost $2 million for the year ended January 31, 1985 (see Exhibit 2).

The poor performance in sales, compared to the ambitious plans, was not attributable to particular problems at Spinnaker, but to the poor performance of the industry overall. In fact, Spinnaker's market share turned out to be as expected. According to company estimates, the market was divided as follows:

Education	20%	Stable
Adventure	10%	Going up
Home productivity	25%	Going up
Arcade games	35%	Going down
Utilities and others	10%	Stable
Total home software	100%	

Of the education segment, the company estimated it had a 30 to 40 percent market share. Overall, its market share was set at 10 percent.

The main reason for the low level of sales was the collapse of the home computer market. Here are some estimates of sales for the years 1983 and 1984:

	Simple Machines	Serious Machines	Total
1983	5.0	0.5	5.5
1984	0.6	3.6	4.2

Commenting on those figures, Bill said,

> If you look at the total figures, it seems that the market has shrunk. But if you focus on "serious machines" (defined as those with at least a disk drive), it's gone up enormously. Another point that most people have not realized is that 4 million out of the 5 million "simple machines" sold in 1983 were sold at dumping prices by companies abandoning the market, like Texas Instruments and Timex. People bought those machines "to find out what a computer is."

Figures on sales for home software companies were extremely hard to come by, since no public companies were in the field except for the first-party manufacturers, which did not disclose sales by product. According to a knowledgeable industry observer, sales of home software for 1983 and 1984 were estimated as follows:

Software Sales *(in millions of dollars)*		
	1983	1984
Commodore (hardware manufacturer)	$ 60	$ 50
Atari (hardware manufacturer)	25	15
Spinnaker (independent)	11	15
Broderbund (independent)	12	15
CBS Software (a subsidiary of CBS Communications)	0	7
Scarborough (independent)	2	6
Sierra On-Line (independent)	8	9
Electronic Arts (independent)	2	5
Other 10 firms	20	30
Total	140	152

Commenting on this, Bill said,

This is a growth of 8.5 percent, but remember that prices have gone down some 30 percent overall, and in many cases even more. For instance, we have grown 35 percent in dollar volume, but more than 80 percent in unit volume since we are very aggressive in pricing. We have a complex pricing model that reflects the actual consumer behavior. It shows that the market is very price sensitive. We are the first of the independent companies and the fastest growing of the top five.

David, though, found little consolation in the fact that everybody in the industry had shared the same expectations. (See Exhibit 3 for a graph representing forecasts given by experts in the industry.)

The main mistake we've made was to believe that we would grow to $50 million this past year. Sure, everybody thought that way. For instance, CBS had an internal commitment to make $20 million, and they are going to make $6. But, on the other hand, Bill and I pride ourselves on our ability to look at conventional wisdom and see what's wrong with it. We've always taken the contrary view. The reason we succeeded was that other people looked at the educational software market and said, "There is no market there," and we said, "There will be if we do it right." It is the same with the way we distributed. We should have seen last year that the market could not grow as much as everybody was saying. With conventional wisdom you can only get average returns.

The customary thing to do for companies facing such a slow-down in the industry was to lay off people in order to cut expenditures. But Spinnaker decided against it because management felt that it was essential to maintain the credibility of the company. Many companies were formed and disappeared every month in the microcomputer software market. Everybody was worried about dealing with a company that might not be around in six months' time. According to Spinnaker's management, layoffs were a self-fulfilling prophecy: Customers would smell problems and stop buying, forcing even more layoffs. On the other hand, the company desperately needed to cut expenses. In fact, one of the alternatives they had considered was to reduce the number of employees down to 30. They couldn't wait for people to leave without replacing them since the turnover at Spinnaker was low compared to the rest of the industry. At the peak, in July 1984, Spinnaker had 112 employees. Through a policy of aggressive performance reviews and not hiring new people to replace those who left, Spinnaker reduced its work force to 82 people by January 1985. In part, this was made possible by a sophisticated new computer system for internal accounting and shipping. With that move, the payroll would stabilize at 82 people, without sending any wrong signal of impending disaster for the company. According to Bill,

> That strategy has paid off, and everybody in the industry knows now that in January 1985 Spinnaker is as strong a competitor as ever, probably even more so, because many people have left the market and nobody is entering.

In fact, the shakeout during 1984 had been impressive: There were only 5 companies in the educational segment in June 1983; in June 1984 the number had grown to 75. In December 1984 the figure was back down to 20.

For David, the worst experience in all the time at Spinnaker had been the disappointment of 1984. He had really believed that they could sell $50 million. He said that the most difficult things he had done at Spinnaker were that year's constant adjustments to lower expectations, like cutting budgets, not replacing people who left, freezing product plans, canceling contracts, having little liquidity.

Bill put it this way:

> David and I have had to readjust to reality twice in a year. First, we were always behind in selling, recruiting, renting space, and so on. And suddenly, we realize that we have vastly overestimated the rate of growth, and we have far too little money, too much space, and a heavy personnel structure. This false sense of failure—we are growing very fast, anyway—

hasn't affected us very much, though, Entrepreneurs either tie their egos to their business or they don't. Business, to many entrepreneurs, is an extension of themselves, and it's their whole life, and when the business goes down, they have to value themselves less as a person. David and I are different. We have other goals in life. We could close down tomorrow, take a week off in Aruba, come back, and start something else. It's that ability that keeps you sane and able to see things in perspective. This year has been very rough for everybody, and we have seen some of our competitors personally devastated. It's very sad to see. You have to keep your ego out of the business. I sleep very well: Going home and changing diapers is a great break. For the same reasons, David and I had never had a problem in my being chairman and he president. I don't tell him what to do in his areas, and he doesn't tell me either. In the joint, strategic areas, we try to reach agreements and, when it's not possible, someone yields, because our relationship is more important than any particular issue.

CURRENT SITUATION

The current structure of the company is its strongest strategic asset, and we don't want to cut it. These 82 people form the core of a series of strengths that put Spinnaker in a very good situation for a market that starts growing again at its previous pace. Furthermore, we have compared our sales per employee with other companies, and we have one of the best ratios in the industry.

Bill Bowman summarized the current structure of the company and its main strengths as of January 1985:

- *Direct sales force.*   Although the rule of thumb is that below $50 million in sales it does not pay to have a direct sales force, we've discovered that this is not true. If we had to pay the customary 5 percent commission, we would be paying more. But, more important, this is one of our most important assets. The fact that we sell directly to large retailers—something nobody of our size does—explains a large part of our success obtaining the fantastic distribution we have.

- *Branding.*   We have a brand manager for each brand. This is obviously "too much," at the current level of sales. But if we believe that branding is a real strategic alternative, we have to put our resources where our mouth is.

- *International sales.*   We have only two people working full time in this area, and they have achieved incredible success, compared to anyone else. Besides, the international operation pays for itself.

- *Manufacturing.*   We have a manufacturing operation that works very well. Only 13 people work here full time. For the

Christmas season, we've had up to 140 workers. The cost overrun was only $75,000. Not bad, if you think that many of those workers didn't even speak English, being mostly Portuguese immigrants. I don't think any independent company has lower manufacturing costs than we do.

- *General administrative infrastructure.* It's now very efficient, with the introduction of the central computer, and provides us with the best order-tracking system in the industry.

- *Product development system (SAS).* It has been an important investment and gives us a competitive advantage nobody else has. It cost well over $1 million, but it enables us to take a script from an author and some art work, and a secretary can translate it into SAL (Spinnaker Adventure Language) that we created here. It is a very complex computer program and a sophisticated graphics tool. The result is that we put the new game on the machine once and automatically get versions for each of the different microcomputers we support. This cuts the development costs dramatically, because normally you have to rewrite the program for each version for a different computer. Another important advantage is that we have all versions ready for sale at the same time, and we can profit from advertising, and not lose sales. SAL is a part of SAS (Spinnaker Adventure System). The second part of SAS is a graphics tool that takes a normal picture on paper and prepares programs for all the different computers that display it. We have something similar for music: Our musician plays some music in a special organlike machine, and in less than an hour we have the computer code that will play the music, optimized for each microcomputer. Another very important saving is that we have to "play test" the programs only once. Testing is a very important cost; it can take between 200 and 400 hours to test all the options that one of these programs offers. We would have to do it for each version of the same program if they were programmed independently, as almost everybody else in the industry does. Thanks to the system, our production costs are now about a third of what they were one year ago. It is an enormous asset for us. Two or three companies, at most, have something similar for text, but nobody has anything like it for graphics and music in the whole industry, and these features are becoming more and more important.

Spinnaker's founders insisted that there was no fat in the company, giving as an example the fact that there were only three secretaries for all 82 people employed. They also insisted that they had always tried to substitute technology for people, as in their accounting system and product development. The current structure put the break-even point for 1985 at $19 million in sales.

Commenting on Spinnaker's current competitive position, David Seuss said,

> Today, I think that our brand franchises constitute a terrific competitive advantage, especially Fisher-Price and Spinnaker. Brands are nice barriers. Another advantage is the distribution in the mass channel. These two things don't change fast. We really provide consulting to the mass merchandisers, and they see us as a company they ought to work with. We see lots of different retailers and can therefore advise any of them on what they are doing incorrectly. We sell directly to Toys "Я" Us, Child's World, Target, etc., and through rack jobbers to Sears, Montgomery Ward and K mart. They won't take any other approach. But we keep very close contact with the large mass merchandisers anyway. Very few software companies can say this.

At the beginning of 1985 there was no more venture capital available to the industry. According to *Business Week,*

> Now, when even greater innovation is needed to expand personal software into a truly mass market, entrepreneurs with bright ideas for software products may be in trouble. When they go hunting for venture capital, they're bound to find that the well has run dry.
>
> Venture capitalists have come full circle from the heady days of 1983 when they raced to invest in the personal software boom.[1]

For Bill, this had the advantage that no new competitors would enter and that some would fail. He thought, therefore, that Spinnaker might increase its market share in 1985:

> In the Consumer Electronics Show in Chicago two weeks ago, it was very clear that Spinnaker is number one. All the major retailers came to talk to us first, and the presentation given by David on the state of the industry was attended by everybody. Our prestige is just going up. We are also developing a lot of product because lead times are long and we can't cut immediately. In this moment, I don't think anyone else is doing serious product development, and that is also going to have a positive impact. On the other hand, we are in one of the most unpredictable markets there is, so you never know.
>
> Last year, there was a shift in consumers from mass retailers to computer stores because IBM and Apple (who only sell through specialized stores) drastically cut their prices. In those stores, we have no particular advantages since anybody can put their product in them. But next year we are going to see very powerful new machines sold by Atari

---

[1] *Business Week,* March 8, 1985, p. 100.

and Commodore through mass merchants. We are dominant there thanks to our direct sales force. I think our predictions of 25–30 percent growth are very conservative.

Summarizing the strategic dilemma the company was facing for 1985, Bill said,

I think that the answer is clear. If the market is really going to be small, we should sell the company. But, in that case, the cash flow doesn't matter much since what we would sell are the strategic assets I talked about before, particularly the sales force and the product development system. If the market is going to pick up again, then we want to increase our market share and be an important player. For that, we need our strategic assets. During the summer, the board decided to go ahead with this strategy. I hope they are going to stick to it now. But then we'll need cash.

The company had what they considered to be a very good financial agreement with their bank. They had a line of credit of $6 million that was unsecured at prime rate. The only restriction was that it was limited to 80 percent of their accounts receivable. According to the financial forecasts for fiscal 1986, the company would not be able to live with that 80 percent constraint by October. Although the bank was prepared to discuss relaxing that point, everybody agreed that Spinnaker needed more equity to pursue its aggressive strategy. Bill hoped to have it raised by July and was starting to work almost full time on it. He wanted between $3 million and $5 million, depending on the price he could get. They did not think they could go public, given the situation of the market. In their opinion, their best chance was to sell a small percentage of the company to a large corporation. Bill pointed out that in the last few months there had been some interesting deals of this kind with small high-tech companies and larger firms, although none of those deals had been in their segment of the industry.

Bill summarized his views on the future of the industry:

I think 1986 is when the home computer industry will take off, as VCRs have in 1984. In fact, this industry follows VCRs by a couple of years. It also follows microwave ovens and other consumer technology businesses. The cycle is always the same. First, someone invents something and starts selling it. The technology yuppies jump to buy it, and the manufacturers get an incredible growth. Venture capital is poured into the industry, and a lot of product hits the market. But the average consumer does not know why he or she needs the product, so growth stops and there is a shakeout. Technology keeps improving, however, and some pioneers start figuring out what the product is really for and provide the right mix of product, service, price, etc. In the home computer case, we've been through the first two phases, and I think we are now starting the last one. Education and entertainment won't achieve more than a 30–35 percent penetration in U.S. homes. Computers in education are best with very young kids (there is emerging plenty of well-researched evidence on this), but there are many single people in the United States. What's going to push penetration is communications, really simple and useful communications with databases, consumer services, etc. The economics of a bank change when a third of its customers have home computers: It can afford to penalty-price manual delivery of services and can start subsidizing electronic services. That pricing advantage of electronic communications will attract reluctant people to computers. You can see that happening right now with electronic mail, which is already much cheaper than normal mail. I think this explosion at the consumer level is four or five years away, and our strategy is to invest in R&D in communications and try to get into partnerships with companies like AT&T that are going to dominate the industry. We can provide the front-end software for the customers of a bank, for instance.

DEVELOPMENT BUSINESS

A recent issue also had potential strategic importance to the future of Spinnaker. They were thinking about launching a third-party development business. David explained,

We have a terrific product development capability, but at the same time we have a limit on the number of products we can get on the shelves. So, why not make programs for other people and have more of the shelf? This is changing radically what Spinnaker has always been all about. We have right now a proposal in front of Commodore to develop four programs to learn foreign languages for $350,000, and 12 educational products for $1 million. They would also pay a royalty. Another proposal is going to Atari to develop 47 products for $8.3 million. Both companies are introducing new machines this year, and they know they need software if they are to succeed.

There was little competition in this side of the business. One other company that produced software for companies like Atari, CBS Software, and Radio Shack had grown out of traditional educational materials and got into software later. According to David, they were not good suppliers, in the sense that they were mainly educators and did not understand the business needs of their customers. In fact, they were down to 20 people from a peak of 90. In contrast, David said,

We are a publisher and understand the market. We also have a great development system, which nobody else in the industry has. And this can be a source of competitive advantage. We have the scale and the expertise to defend a position in the industry. There is a definite advantage in having lots of people with experience in the industry, with the ability to pursue several different projects at the same time. We have that. We are also developing expertise in the educational side, along with the technical aspects. There is an important knowledge gap in how you use computers in education, and as we pour money into it, we can get a great competitive advantage there. If we get the Commodore and Atari contracts, together with our Fisher-Price brand and the new curriculum programs, we'll have four teams trying to develop educational software taking four different new approaches. Nobody else is doing this. And we could do the same with Apple and IBM.

In a related development, Atari had asked Spinnaker to handle its whole software business, including program development, packaging design, advertising, and store display. Atari would just manufacture, which it could do offshore at very low cost, and take care of sales and distribution since it was already selling the hardware to the stores.

David summarized all these issues this way:

I think we have the right strategy and the right approach. But we could run out of cash, and this is a terrible environment to raise money in.

EXHIBIT 1   Product Schedule

General Data Sheet #3

CRITICAL PATH

6-22-82
BCG #19

	LOGO	Position Concepts	Layout, Copy	Art & Mechanical	Seps & Print	Box making	Booklet	Layout, Copy	Art & Mechanical	Space	MASTER DISK	DISK PROD'N	ASSEMBLY SHIP
MAY FRI 14	Begin												
21	Review												
MON 28 / 31	Approve Begin				Begin Tool								
IUNE FRI 4		Review											
11		Approve Begin											
18			Review		Tool Ready	Begin							
MON 21			Approve Begin			Begin Edit Review							
FRI 25					Appr. Tool	Begin TM To Cabot Approve Begin		Art & Mechanical Begin					
MON 28													
JULY FRI 2				Approve Begin									
9									Order				
TUES 16 / 20					Receive	Receive Printing Begin box	Begin Mech			Program Ready / Cut Disk / Appr. Prog. / Rec. Master			
FRI 23													
MON 26 / 30						Begin Print							
AUG 6					Boxes Ready	Books Ready		Approve	Send Subtbel / Begin Prog				
13						Books Ready			Sats. app.				
20													
MON 23										Disks Ready	Begin Assembly	
FRI 27											Ship Subtbel / Rec. Subtbel	
MON 30												
SEPT FRI 6 / 10												Ship Shoes
17												**In Stores / On Shelf**

EXHIBIT 2 Spinnaker Software Financials (year ending January 31, 1985, in thousands of dollars)

Cash Flow	Feb.	Mar.	Apr.	May	Jun.	July	Aug.	Sept.	Oct.	Nov.	Dec.	Jan.	Total
Net income	($ 136)	($ 158)	($ 147)	($ 223)	($ 295)	($ 140)	($ 339)	($ 903)	($ 298)	$ 110	$ 143	($ 265)	($2,651)
Deprec. & Amor.	$ 4	$ 4	$ 5	$ 6	$ 6	$ 7	$ 7	$ 8	$ 8	$ 9	$ 9	$ 10	$ 83
Royalty amor.	$ 0	$ 88	$ 17	($ 244)	($ 45)	($ 192)	($ 22)	($ 7)	($ 12)	($ 24)	($ 34)	($ 8)	($ 483)
Inventory	($ 157)	($ 153)	($ 204)	($ 193)	($ 377)	($ 400)	($ 482)	$ 94	($ 228)	$ 318	$ 413	($ 112)	($1,025)
Receivables	$ 850	$ 499	$ 399	$ 226	$ 96	$ 52	($ 428)	($ 604)	($ 449)	($ 123)	($ 655)	$ 168	($ 373)
Payables	($ 150)	($ 245)	$ 236	($ 419)	($ 109)	($ 71)	$ 85	$ 237	$ 180	$ 385	$ 328	$ 348	$ 805
Bank debt	$ 0	$ 0	$ 0	$ 0	$ 0	$ 0	$1,570	$ 483	$ 359	$ 338	$ 524	$ 134	$3,141
Investment	($ 85)	($ 92)	($ 103)	($ 96)	($ 102)	($ 45)	($ 57)	$ 62	($ 112)	($ 64)	($ 84)	($ 72)	($ 974)
Prod. devel. cap.	($ 187)	($ 197)	($ 214)	($ 225)	($ 125)	($ 119)	($ 131)	$ 645	($ 112)	($ 119)	($ 121)	($ 114)	($1,019)
Misc W.C. changes	$ 17	($ 8)	($ 30)	($ 19)	($ 1)	($ 96)	($ 12)	$ 43	$ 1	($ 18)	$ 11	($ 66)	($ 178)
													$ 0
Net cash flow	$ 156	($ 262)	($ 41)	($1,187)	($ 952)	($1,108)	$ 192	($ 66)	($ 207)	$ 512	$ 534	($ 246)	($2,674)
Balance Sheet													
Cash & equivalents	$3,389	$3,127	$3,086	$1,899	$ 948	($ 160)	$ 31	($ 35)	($ 242)	$ 270	$ 804	$ 559	
Acct. receivable	$2,703	$2,204	$1,805	$1,579	$1,483	$1,535	$1,963	$2,567	$3,016	$3,439	$4,094	$3,926	
Inventory	$1,160	$1,313	$1,517	$1,710	$2,087	$2,487	$2,969	$2,875	$2,647	$2,329	$1,916	$2,028	
Net fixed assets	$ 638	$ 726	$ 824	$ 914	$1,009	$1,047	$1,097	$1,152	$1,256	$1,311	$1,386	$1,448	
Product develop.	$ 328	$ 525	$ 739	$ 964	$1,089	$1,208	$1,339	$ 694	$ 806	$ 925	$1,046	$1,160	
Other	$ 262	$ 271	$ 302	$ 326	$ 320	$ 412	$ 436	$ 395	$ 399	$ 422	$ 415	$ 477	
Total assets	$8,480	$8,166	$8,273	$7,392	$6,936	$6,529	$7,835	$7,648	$7,882	$8,696	$9,661	$9,598	
Royalty payable	$ 638	$ 726	$ 743	$ 499	$ 454	$ 262	$ 240	$ 233	$ 221	$ 197	$ 163	$ 155	
Accts. payable	$1,980	$1,735	$1,971	$1,552	$1,443	$1,372	$1,457	$1,694	$1,874	$2,259	$2,587	$2,935	
Taxes payable	$ 37	$ 38	$ 39	$ 44	$ 37	$ 33	$ 45	$ 47	$ 52	$ 57	$ 61	$ 57	
Bank debt.	$ 0	$ 0	$ 0	$ 0	$ 0	$ 0	$1,570	$2,054	$2,413	$2,751	$3,275	$3,141	
Total liabilities	$2,655	$2,499	$2,753	$2,095	$1,934	$1,667	$3,312	$4,028	$4,560	$5,264	$6,086	$6,288	
Equity	$5,825	$5,667	$5,520	$5,297	$5,002	$4,862	$4,523	$3,620	$3,322	$3,432	$3,575	$3,310	
Total	$8,480	$8,166	$8,273	$7,392	$6,936	$6,529	$7,835	$7,648	$7,882	$8,696	$9,661	$9,598	

The figures in this exhibit have been disguised, while maintaining relevant relationships.

EXHIBIT 3   Home Software Forecasts

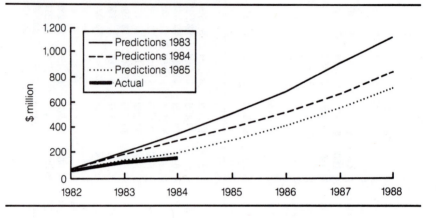

Case 4–3

Dragonfly Corporation

On December 20, 1982, with the close of the Christmas season just a week away, Janet and Michael Thompson received yet another call from their attorney: It was time to make some difficult decisions about their fledgling business. For the past three and one-half years, the couple had been operating their Dragonfly teenage clothing stores in Seattle, trying to earn a living and keep the business alive despite continuing losses. Now their angry landlord was threatening legal action if Dragonfly did not deliver on its overdue lease payments. The Thompsons' attorney was pushing them for an answer: What did they want to do?

The financial picture was not rosy. Dragonfly had lost money since it opened, with the accumulated deficit from both stores near the end of 1982 reaching over $100,000. (See Exhibits 1 and 2.) While the owners believed the business had gone more smoothly over the past year, the numbers were ambiguous. The Thompsons' best calculation to date still showed Dragonfly losing money (Exhibit 3). But the couple believed they were managing the business more wisely and felt they had corrected many of their early operating problems. They weren't sure why their dream child still wasn't profitable. Was it the serious recession, which had hit Seattle worse than most U.S. cities? Or was there still something wrong with the way they were running the business?

The Thompsons felt they had several possible courses of action. They could try to buy time with the landlord and hope the economy and their business turned around. They could turn to Janet's parents for

This case was prepared by Martha Gershun under the direction of Howard H. Stevenson.

additional financial help to see them through this crisis. Or they could admit the project wasn't working and begin bankruptcy proceedings.

The Thompsons felt their decision was complicated by the substantial investment Janet's parents had already made in the business. Could they admit defeat to their family and close up the stores? Even worse, could they ask the family to increase their investment in an endeavor that might fail sooner or later?

There was also the problem of timing. While the Thompsons knew that Christmas was the peak sales season for retail operations, they also knew that January was the peak season for refunds. How should they interpret their recent financial figures in the face of such unevenness? Janet and Michael were inclined to think the entire situation was somehow unfair. Just when they felt the stores were turning around, the issue of the lease payments was raising the specter of bankruptcy and forcing them to make a decision about Dragonfly before all the facts were in.

BACKGROUND

Janet Hepburn and Michael Thompson met in Seattle as assistant buyers for Bon Marché, a full-line department store chain, and were married in 1970. Three years later, they quit their jobs at Bon Marché—Michael took a job as store manager for the Lerner's chain, and Janet decided to stay at home in anticipation of the birth of their first child. In 1975, the couple moved to Arizona where Michael took a job working for Kidder Peabody in commercial sales. He hated the environment and found the work boring. He quit in 1976 to return to retailing with a job for a local women's clothing store. Meanwhile, the couple's second child was born. In 1979, the Thompsons returned to Seattle and began looking into franchising a store with the Lady Madonna chain, a successful group of stores offering maternity clothes at the upper end of the pricing scale. Janet was tired of staying home and wanted to get back into the work force. Both the Thompsons liked the lifestyle of retailing. They enjoyed going on buying trips, choosing inventory, and serving customers. With their combined experience in retailing, the couple believed they could make a serious attempt to run their own business.

In the process of investigating the Lady Madonna operation, the Thompsons became intrigued with what they perceived to be an obvious market niche for an upscale store serving Seattle's teenage market. When vigorous research turned up few competitors in the local area, the Thompsons decided to abandon the Lady Madonna franchise idea and pursue opening their own store instead, selling teenage clothes and accessories at fairly high price points. They developed pro forma cash flows which showed that the business would just break even in the first year of operation (Exhibit 4).

Janet and Michael had friends who were successfully operating a chain of T-shirt shops. They liked the idea of opening one store now and using it later to leverage the venture into a thriving chain. Since they believed that most of the expenses involved in running retail stores were fixed on the corporate level, the Thompsons saw the long-term opportunity to generate a sizable income for themselves and a generous profit for their company. (See Exhibit 5.)

DRAGONFLY

The Thompsons were not particularly worried about financing their new venture. Janet's parents had expressed willingness earlier to finance their entry into the Lady Madonna enterprise, and the couple did not think starting up their own store would take a great deal more capital. They approached Janet's older brother, Charles, who was a corporate attorney in Chicago, and asked him to help them develop a plan to use in approaching the Hepburns for money. Based on Charles's knowledge of business and the Thompsons' retail experience, it was determined that $120,000 would be sufficient to start up the new operation, which by now had been dubbed *Dragonfly*.

Janet called her parents to discuss the prospect of underwriting the new store. She asked them for $90,000. The Hepburns offered little resistance to the idea. They were happy to see Janet so excited about the new business and felt that $90,000 was a small investment to help their daughter reach financial independence. Mr. Hepburn had recently retired from a successful career in real estate and preferred to give his children money now, rather than having them wait until after his death for an inheritance. He had only two concerns. First, the deal must be structured so that Michael was as responsible as Janet for the financial success of the venture and any obligations to the Hepburns. Second, the Hepburns must receive the tax benefits from any start-up losses.

With those caveats in mind, the family met on June 1, 1979, with Janet and Michael's attorney to set up the Dragonfly Corporation.

THE BEGINNING

The Thompsons thought it seemed like a very informal way to begin such a serious venture. Here they were, serving coffee in their living room to Janet's parents, her older brother, and their attorney, Jeff Lawrence. When the meeting was over and the papers were signed, they would be the owners and managers of the Dragonfly Corporation. The family decided to give the company authorization to issue 50,000 shares of stock with a par value of $1. Initially, 20,000 shares were issued: 15,000 shares to the Hepburns for $15,000 in cash and 5,000 shares to Janet and Michael for their 1977 Volvo, which had a fair market value of $5,000. Jeff Lawrence explained that they would designate Dragonfly as a Subchapter S corporation for income tax purposes and allow the Hepburns to take their proportionate tax benefits that might accrue from early losses. Later, when the corporation began to make money, this could be changed so that either Janet and Michael or the company paid any tax liabilities.

The remaining capitalization was undertaken in the form of debt. In order to be sure that Michael was financially tied into the project, the Hepburns loaned the young couple $75,000 at an annual interest rate of 7.75 percent. The Thompsons, in return, loaned this money to Dragonfly, payable beginning July 1, 1979, in quarterly installments of $1,677.51, including the 7.75 annual interest. Charles felt this capital structure had the additional advantage of giving the couple leverage in any financial adversity, because they would be the store's primary debt holders. The corporation also borrowed $30,000 from Seattle Trust for leasehold improvements, payable in monthly installments of $1,000, with interest at 21 percent per year. (The debt was guaranteed personally and secured by the leasehold improvement.)

Confident that they had enough money to set up shop properly, the Thompsons began looking for a site for their store. They decided to lease a site at the Woodscross Shopping Center, near the major north/south road in that part of Seattle. Woodscross was in an old, open mall, which had recently been renovated. The Thompsons believed that the emerging character of the shopping center would appeal to their upscale customer base. Also, because the renovation made it a slightly risky location, the rents at Woodscross were roughly half (i.e., $7.50 per foot versus $15 to $17 per foot) those in the more fashionable parts of town. Janet and Michael signed a lease on behalf of Dragonfly for 3,000 square feet at $1,875/month or 6 percent of monthly sales, whichever was greater. The lease was for slightly over four and one-half years, ending March 1, 1984. They also agreed to pay some portion of common area maintenance costs, averaging about $425/month. (See Exhibit 6 for sample lease clauses.)

With the signing of the lease, the Thompsons went to work in earnest. Michael supervised the store setup while Janet went off to buy their beginning merchandise. One month later, on August 1, 1979, they were ready to open for business.

EARLY RESULTS

The results for Dragonfly's first full year in business were not very good. Sales had been lower than expected, and much of the merchandise had been marked down significantly before it was sold. Thus, gross margins were considerably lower than the industry average. In addition, operating expenses were way out of line, bringing the annual loss at December 31, 1980, to $42,253. (Exhibit 7 gives financial and operating data for the industry. Exhibit 8 itemizes Dragonfly's expenses.) Faced with cash shortages, the Thompsons fell behind in their rent payments on the store.

The second year brought problems, too. While sales were up slightly and gross margins were up, Janet had clearly overbought, and inventory levels were up to $80,000. Also, the Thompsons had managed to reduce Dragonfly's expenses but had primarily done so by missing more payments to their Woodscross landlord and by reducing the amount of money they were taking out of the store. They were forced to borrow $15,000 from Janet's parents to make ends meet at home. In addition, the Hepburns lent Dragonfly $30,000.

1982: A TOUGH YEAR

Thus, the Thompsons began 1982 in a precarious position. Their personal financial situation was very tight (Exhibit 9). Janet had cut back on all the extras at home; the family was eating meat only twice a week. Dragonfly was saddled with $80,000 of inventory, and it looked as though only heavy markdowns would move the clothes. To make matters worse, the Woodscross mall was deteriorating rapidly. Already, 10 of the 60 tenants in the new part of the shopping center where Dragonfly was located had begun preparations to move out. It didn't look as though the renovated shopping center was going to make it.

Furthermore, the economic recession, which was clearly hurting retail operations nationwide, was particularly evident in Seattle. Both Boeing and Weyerhaeuser, the two major employers in the area, had hit upon hard times. Boeing was actually laying off workers, while Weyerhaeuser was trying to make do with reduced capital spending, pay freezes, and shorter work weeks. Overall, unemployment in Seattle was up from 5–7 percent in 1975 to 10–12 percent in 1982.[1]

---

[1]Seattle First National Bank, "Pacific Northwest Industries: Quarterly Summary, February 1983," p. 3.

To counter the problems posed by the deterioration of the Woods-cross Mall, the Thompsons decided to open a second Dragonfly store in one of the more prosperous sections of Seattle. The new location, in the Bellevue Strip Mall, was 1,450 square feet. The lease, beginning on July 1, 1982, was for two years at $910/month for the first year and $970/month for the second, or 7 percent of gross sales, whichever was greater. Janet and Michael believed there were a number of reasons for opening a second store, despite their precarious financial condition.

First, they hoped to recycle merchandise between the two stores, selling the clothing faster and increasing gross margins by avoiding mark-downs. Opening a second store provided other merchandising advantages, too. With a larger customer base, Janet felt there was a better chance of approaching a normal curve in the distribution of sizes; she hoped this would lead to greater sales as customers began to rely on Dragonfly to have the sizes they needed. Janet also felt it was a good idea to send sale merchandise to a second location. She knew customers felt bad if they purchased an item at the regular price and then saw it on sale later. Dragonfly also had potential economies of scale in advertising. The Thompsons had developed a large mailing list of existing customers and felt they could spread this advertising cost among the possible revenues from two locations instead of just one. They were also looking for protection in case the situation at Woods-cross did not improve. In a worst case scenario, the Thompsons thought they could fold the first Dragonfly store on March 1, 1984, when the lease was up, and move the merchandise to the Bellevue location. In the four months then remaining on the Bellevue lease, they could either try to make the second store successful or use it to liquidate the inventory from both stores. Most important, with many of their significant expenses fixed, the Thompsons saw the second store as a chance to generate excess revenues for the incremental cost of the second set of lease payments. Despite the problems with the Woods-cross store, they were pursuing their vision of a profitable multisite operation.

Finally, near the end of 1982, the precarious financial situation forced the Hepburns to reclassify the $30,000 of debt they held as equity.

THE WOODSCROSS SITUATION

In the meantime, faced with increasing cash flow problems, the Thompsons fell further behind on their lease payments for the Woods-cross Dragonfly store. In February, they made arrangements with the landlord to begin paying off their previous balance at the rate of $875/month. But this expense left little cash for regular monthly rental payments; these dropped off to $500/month. Thus the balance owed to Woodscross was still increasing at $925/month.

In late June, the Thompsons talked with the Woodscross landlord again and offered to pay rent of 6 percent of gross revenues, which at the time was considerably less than the $1,875/month base fee. They would spend the differential in advertising for the store, in the hope of increasing Dragonfly's sales, as well as the shopping center's traffic. In addition, they would still be obligated for the common area maintenance charges of about $425/month. At the same time, the payments on the overdue balance would drop to $650/month (Exhibit 10). The landlord agreed, but the Thompsons did not receive any documentation confirming the transaction.

By early October, the Thompsons believed they had spent as much money on advertising as they could reasonably expect to be effective. Michael met with the Woodscross landlord and proposed that Dragonfly begin paying the full $2,300/month toward the rent again, with the payments on the overdue balance remaining at $650/month. He felt that the meeting went well and believed that his proposal had been accepted. Thus, the Thompsons were extremely surprised when Jeff Lawrence called on October 25, 1982, to say that he had received a very inflammatory note from the Woodscross lawyers. The letter (Exhibit 11) threatened to pursue further legal action if the Thompsons did not sign a confessed judgment for the entire amount overdue of $21,576.79. Jeff Lawrence responded immediately with another letter explaining the situation as the Thompsons understood it (Exhibit 12), and also suggested to the Thompsons that they consider signing the note.

BATTENING DOWN THE HATCHES

Jeff cautioned the Thompsons that this kind of angry response from a creditor often preceded the initiation of bankruptcy proceedings. He told them to be prepared for the worst possibility. Janet was extremely upset by this news. She had known Dragonfly was in trouble, but it did not seem possible that the landlord had suddenly decided to close up their entire operation.

During this time, another distressing piece of news came to light; about six months earlier, one of Janet's vendors had insisted on subordinated credit. Lawrence had gotten the Thompsons to sign a general subordination agreement, which subordinated their debt to that of all trade creditors. While the account had been paid off, this agreement was still in the contract with that vendor. Janet spoke with her brother, and Charles was very anxious that this subordination agreement be terminated before the issue of bankruptcy was discussed further. He did not want this small creditor to destroy the careful chain he had set up, in case bankruptcy was actually triggered. As far as Charles was concerned, this was a further example of incompetence on the part of Jeff Lawrence. He should have known better than to allow Janet to sign such a contract. Thus, Charles proposed that the Thompsons make arrangements with this creditor to change the agreement immediately. As well, he suggested they start to think about the real prospects for Dragonfly and frame their response to the Woodscross landlord in this light. Perhaps there was a way to negotiate their way out of the lease, using bankruptcy as their own threat.

THE DECISION

By December, the Thompsons still hadn't heard from the Woodscross landlord again. Jeff cautioned them that it was unlikely the incident had been dropped. Rather, he suggested, Woodscross might be waiting to see how Dragonfly fared through the Christmas season before determining what action to take. While Woodscross had earlier mentioned bankruptcy as a final recourse, Lawrence now confirmed Charles's earlier opinion that one creditor did not have the power to force involuntary bankruptcy on either a business or an individual. Rather, bankruptcy should be viewed by the Thompsons as a way out, if they decided that the Dragonfly stores were not financially viable.

Now, on December 20, Jeff Lawrence had called again. He felt Woodscross would not wait any longer for an answer about the overdue lease payments. Did Janet and Michael want to stall and hope the after-Christmas season bore out their optimism about Dragonfly's improved performance? Did they want to strike a deal and get out of the lease? Did they want to seek more money from Janet's parents? Or did they want to file for bankruptcy and put the entire disappointing experience behind them?

The Thompsons were very torn. They believed the stores were doing better. Inventory levels were down. Existing merchandise was moving rapidly, with little or no markdowns. Their accounts payable appeared to be good. And the economy finally seemed to be turning around. Just when the situation should be at its brightest, the Woodscross mess was threatening to blow out their light. The Thompsons were resentful and confused: Was it really time to quit?

EXHIBIT 1

DRAGONFLY CORPORATION
Income Statement
(unaudited)
For the Years Ending December 31

	1980	1981
Net sales	$246,236	$261,336
Cost of goods sold	160,148	155,562
Gross margin....................................	86,088	105,774
Operating expenses	117,918	106,951
Interest expense................................	10,423	8,899
Net profit (loss)................................	$ (42,253)	$ (10,076)

EXHIBIT 2

DRAGONFLY CORPORATION
Balance Sheets
(unaudited)

	December 31, 1980	December 31, 1981	December 20, 1982 (est.)
Assets			
Current assets:			
Cash	$ 2,560	$ 4,821	$ 4,930
Inventory	61,432	81,846	84,977
Prepaid insurance........	408	0	0
Total current assets ..	64,400	86,667	89,907
Fixed assets:			
Furniture and fixtures....	25,682	26,278	46,429
Office and shop			
equipment	2,802	2,908	2,805
Leasehold improvements .	22,540	22,540	32,321
Less accumulated			
depreciation............	(11,319)	(15,441)	(19,206)
Total fixed assets	39,705	36,285	62,349
Other assets:			
Deposits..................	1,970	1,970	1,970
Organization costs, net of			
accumulated			
amortization	2,023	1,463	903
Total other assets	3,993	3,433	2,873
Total assets.................	$108,098	$126,385	$155,129

EXHIBIT 2 *(concluded)*

DRAGONFLY CORPORATION
Balance Sheets
(unaudited)

	December 31, 1980	December 31, 1981	December 20, 1982 (est.)
Liabilities and Stockholders' Equity			
Current liabilities:			
Notes payable—bank	$ 30,116	$ 33,574	$ 33,201
Notes payable— stockholders	4,776	9,901	8,623
Accounts payable—trade..	55,514	48,230	90,045*
Gift certificates outstanding.............	284	163	210
Accrued liabilities	7,296	5,520	5,264
Deposits..................	0	82	0
Long-term debt due within one year.........	1,053	1,053	1,053
Total current liabilities...........	99,039	98,523	138,396
Long-term debt due after one year..................	71,272	70,151	69,098
Debt due Hepburns	0	30,000	0
Stockholders' equity.........	20,000	20,000	50,000
Accumulated deficit.......	(82,213)	(92,289)	(102,365)
Total liabilities and equity..	$108,098	$126,385	$155,129

*Includes:

Trade payables	$68,468
Woodscross rent	21,577
	$90,045

Does *not* include remaining balance of lease payments due:

Woodscross, January 1983 through March 1984	$32,200
Bellevue, January 1983 through July, 1984	17,100
	$49,300

EXHIBIT 3   December 20, 1982, Financials

DRAGONFLY CORPORATION
Estimated Financial Condition
As of December 20, 1982
Accrual Basis

Sales—gross............................	$247,000
Sales tax (6.5%).........................	16,055
Sales—net.............................	230,945
Cost of goods sold	143,186
Gross margin...........................	87,759
Expenses:	
Rent*................................	31,360
Payroll†	36,000
Advertising	9,000
FICA................................	8,400
Medical insurance	1,800
Miscellaneous........................	1,400
Interest	10,640
Net loss	$ (10,841)

*Rent breakdown:

Woodscross	$24,100
Bellevue rent	5,460
Bellevue common area payments	1,800

†Does not include $21,000 salary to Thompsons not accrued or paid.

EXHIBIT 4 Pro Forma Cash Flows, March 1979–February 1980

	March	April	May	June	July	Aug.	Sept.	Oct.	Nov.	Dec.	Jan.	Feb.	TOTAL
Projected sales	$20,000	$13,000	$18,000	$20,000	$25,000	$27,000	$20,000	$16,000	$20,000	$30,000	$16,000	$17,000	$247,000
Cost of merchandise	10,000	9,000	9,000	10,000	12,500	13,500	10,000	8,000	10,000	15,000	8,000	8,500	123,500
Cost of markdowns	1,500	1,500	1,100	1,100	2,500	1,000	1,000	1,000	1,100	1,300	2,000	1,000	16,100
Totals	11,500	10,500	10,100	11,100	15,000	14,500	11,000	9,000	11,100	16,300	10,000	9,500	139,600
Gross profit	3,500	7,500	7,900	8,900	10,000	12,500	9,000	7,000	8,900	13,700	6,000	7,500	107,400
Selling expenses:													
Sales salaries	1,700	1,700	1,700	1,800	1,900	2,100	1,800	1,600	1,700	2,200	1,600	1,650	21,450
Advertising	600	500	400	500	600	600	400	400	500	400	600	500	6,000
Buying trips	500	—	—	—	—	500	—	—	500	—	—	—	1,500
Selling supplies	100	1,400	100	100	100	1,400	100	100	200	200	100	100	4,000
Other	50	50	50	50	50	50	50	50	50	50	50	50	600
Total	2,950	3,650	2,250	2,450	2,650	4,650	2,350	2,150	2,950	2,850	2,350	2,300	33,550
Occupancy expenses:													
Depreciation	400	400	400	400	400	400	400	400	400	400	400	400	4,800
Insurance	90	90	90	90	90	90	90	90	90	90	90	90	1,080
Maintenance	265	265	265	265	265	265	265	265	265	265	265	265	3,180
Rent	1,875	1,875	1,875	1,875	1,875	1,875	1,875	1,875	1,875	1,875	1,875	1,875	22,500
Other (merch. assn.)	150	150	150	150	150	150	150	150	150	150	150	150	1,800
Total	2,750	2,750	2,750	2,750	2,750	2,750	2,750	2,750	2,750	2,750	2,750	2,750	33,000

Administrative:													Total
Officer's salary	1,200	1,200	1,200	1,200	1,200	1,200	1,200	1,200	1,200	1,200	1,200	1,200	14,400
Bad debt	20	20	20	20	20	20	20	20	20	20	20	20	240
Bank discount	120	110	110	120	150	162	120	100	120	130	100	110	1,502
Dues, etc.	30	30	30	30	30	40	30	30	30	30	30	30	370
Employee benefits	75	75	75	75	75	75	75	75	75	75	75	75	900
Life insurance	50	50	50	50	50	50	50	50	50	50	50	50	600
Loan interest and repayment	253	253	660	660	660	660	660	660	660	660	660	660	7,106
Office supplies	10	20	20	20	20	20	20	20	20	20	20	20	230
Professional services	100	300	100	100	300	100	100	300	100	100	300	100	2,000
Taxes (payroll)	750	730	730	750	780	810	750	705	750	830	705	705	8,995
Taxes (excise)	250	250	250	250	300	325	250	225	250	350	225	225	3,150
Telephone	75	70	70	70	75	75	70	70	70	70	70	70	855
Total	$2,933	$3,108	$3,315	$3,345	$3,660	$3,537	$3,345	$3,455	$3,345	$3,585	$3,455	$3,265	$40,348
Profit (loss)	$(133)	$(2,008)	$(415)	$353	$940	$1,563	$555	$(1,355)	$(145)	$4,515	$(2,555)	$(815)	$500

EXHIBIT 5   Pro Forma Income Statements for the Years Ending
February 28

	1980	1981	1982	1983	1984
Revenues:					
Gross sales—Store 1	$247,000	$300,000	$350,000	$350,000	$ 350,000
Gross sales—Store 2	-0-	-0-	250,000	350,000	350,000
Gross sales—Store 3	-0-	-0-	-0-	250,000	350,000
Total gross sales	$247,000	$300,000	$600,000	$950,000	$1,050,000
Expenses:					
Cost of goods sold	$139,600	$165,000	$330,000	$522,500	$ 577,500
Selling expenses	33,550	35,000	40,000	40,000	40,000
Administrative expenses*	25,948	30,000	75,000	100,000	100,000
Officers' salaries	14,400	20,000	40,000	60,000	60,000
Rent	22,500	22,500	47,000	71,500	73,500
Common area maintenance	3,180	4,000	8,000	12,000	12,000
Other occupancy expenses	7,320	8,000	9,000	10,000	10,000
Total expenses	$246,498	$284,500	$549,000	$816,000	$ 873,000
Profit before taxes	$ 502	$ 15,500	$ 51,000	$134,000	$ 177,000

*Includes repayments and interest; assumes new bank loans to finance opening Store 2 and Store 3.

EXHIBIT 6   Lease Excerpts

Section	Lease Index
1	Premises
2	Construction of Premises
3	Lease Term
4	Delayed Possession and Options to Terminate
5	Rent
6	Taxes and Insurance Premiums
7	Utilities
8	Common Areas
9	Common Area and Mall Maintenance
10	Conduct of Business on the Premises
11	Alterations
12	Maintenance and Repair
13	Quiet Enjoyment
14	Assignment or Sublease
15	Indemnification; Liability Insurance
16	Signs and Advertising
17	Entry by Lessor
18	Eminent Domain
19	Fire or Other Casualty

EXHIBIT 6   (*continued*)

Section	Lease Index
20	Waiver of Subrogation
21	Insolvency
22	Defaults
23	Liens and Encumbrances
24	Advances by Lessor for Lessee
25	Attorneys' Fees
26	Waiver
27	Other Stores
28	Notice
29	Successors or Assigns
30	Lease Consideration
31	Merchants Association
32	Change of Location
33	Subordination; Notice to Mortgagee; Attornment
34	Holding Over
35	Memorandum of Lease
36	Sale of Premises by Lessor

Selected Excerpts from Lease

SECTION 14
ASSIGNMENT OR SUBLEASE

Lessee shall not assign, sublease or transfer this lease or any interest therein or in the premises, nor shall this lease or any interest thereunder be assignable or transferable by operation of law or by any process or proceeding of any court, or otherwise, without first obtaining the written consent of Lessor. No assignment of this lease by Lessee shall relieve Lessee of any of its duties or obligations thereunder. If Lessee is a corporation, then any merger, consolidation or liquidation to which it may be a party or any change in the ownership of or power to vote the majority of its outstanding voting stock shall constitute an assignment or transfer of this lease for the purposes of this section.

SECTION 15
INDEMNIFICATION; LIABILITY INSURANCE

Lessor shall not be liable to Lessee or to any other person, firm or corporation whatsoever for any injury to, or death of any person, or for any loss of, or damages to, property (including property of Lessee) occurring in or about the Shopping Center or the premises from any cause whatsoever. Lessee agrees to indemnify and save Lessor harmless from all loss, damage, liability, suit claim, or expense (in-

EXHIBIT 6   *(continued)*

cluding expense of litigation) arising out of or resulting from any actual or alleged injury to, or death of, any person, or from any actual or alleged loss of, or damage to, property caused by, or resulting from, any occurrence on or about the premises, or caused by, or resulting from, any act or omission, whether negligent or otherwise, of Lessee, or any officer, agent, employee, contractor, guest, invitee, customer, or visitor of Lessee, in or about the Shopping Center or the premises. Lessee shall, at its own expense, maintain at all times during the lease term proper liability insurance with a reputable insurance company or companies satisfactory to Lessor in the minimum limit of One Hundred Thousand Dollars ($100,000) (per accident) for property damage, and in the minimum limits of Five Hundred Thousand Dollars ($500,000) (per person) and One Million Dollars ($1,000,000) (per accident or occurrence) for bodily injuries and death, to indemnify both Lessor and Lessee against such claims, demands, losses, damages, liabilities, and expense as against which Lessee has herein agreed to indemnify and hold Lessor harmless. Such policy or policies shall name Lessor, its ground lessor and lenders as insureds, be issued by companies noted A+, AAA or better in Best's insurance guide, and shall be noncancellable as to such named insureds except upon at least ten (10) days prior written notice. Lessee shall furnish Lessor with a copy of said policy or policies or other acceptable evidence that said insurance is in effect.

SECTION 21

INSOLVENCY

Lessee agrees that it will not cause or give cause for the institution of legal proceedings seeking to have Lessee adjudicated bankrupt, reorganized or rearranged under the bankruptcy laws of the United States, or for relief under any other law for the relief of debtors, and will not cause or give cause for the appointment of a trustee or receiver for Lessee's assets, and will not cause or give cause for the commencement of proceedings to foreclose any mortgage or any other lien on Lessee's interest in the premises or on any personal property kept or maintained on the premises by Lessee; and Lessee further agrees that it will not make an assignment for the benefit of creditors, or become or be adjudicated insolvent. The allowance of any petition under the bankruptcy law, or the appointment of a trustee or receiver of Lessee's assets, or the entry of judgment of foreclosure in any proceedings to foreclose any such mortgage or other lien, or an adjudication that Lessee is insolvent shall be conclusive evidence that Lessee has violated the provisions of this sec-

EXHIBIT 6   (*continued*)

tion if said allowance, appointment, judgment, or adjudication or similar order or ruling remains in force or unstayed for a period of thirty (30) days. Upon the happening of any of such events, Lessor may, if it so elects, elect to terminate this lease and all rights of Lessee hereunder without prior notice to Lessee.

SECTION 22
DEFAULTS

Time is the essence hereof, and if Lessee violates or breaches or fails to keep or perform any covenant, agreement, term or condition of this lease, and if such default or violation shall continue or shall not be remedied within ten (10) days (three (3) days in the case of non-payment of rent or other payments due hereunder) after notice in writing thereof given by Lessor to Lessee specifying the matter claimed to be in default, Lessor, at its option, may immediately declare Lessee's right under this lease terminated, and reenter the premises, using such force as may be necessary, and repossess itself thereof, as of its former estate, removing all persons and effects therefrom. If upon the reentry of Lessor, there remains any personal property of Lessee or of any other person, firm or corporation upon the premises, Lessor may, but without the obligation to do so, remove said personal property and place the same in a public warehouse or garage, as may be reasonable, at the expense and risk of the owners thereof, and Lessee shall reimburse Lessor for any expense incurred by Lessor in connection with said removal and/or storage. Notwithstanding any such reentry, the liability of Lessee for the full rent provided for herein shall not be extinguished for the balance of the term of this lease, and Lessee shall make good to Lessor each month during the balance of said term any deficiency arising from a reletting of the premises at a lesser rental than that herein agreed upon as the Minimum Rent, plus the cost of renovating the premises for the new tenant and reletting it.

SECTION 23
LIENS AND ENCUMBRANCES

Lessee shall keep the premises free and clear of any liens and encumbrances arising or growing out of the use and occupancy of the premises by Lessee hereunder. At Lessor's request, Lessee shall furnish Lessor with written proof of payment of any item which would or might constitute the basis for a lien on the premises if not paid.

EXHIBIT 6   *(continued)*

SECTION 24
ADVANCES BY LESSOR FOR LESSEE

If Lessee fails to do anything required to be done by it under the terms of this lease, except to pay rent, Lessor may, at its sole option, do such act or thing on behalf of Lessee, and upon notification to Lessee of the cost thereof to the Lessor, Lessee shall promptly pay the Lessor the amount of that cost, plus interest at the rate of twelve percent (12%) per annum from the date that the cost was incurred by Lessor to the date of Lessee's payment.

SECTION 25
ATTORNEYS' FEES

Lessee agrees to pay, in addition to all other sums due hereunder, such expenses and attorneys' fees as Lessor may incur in enforcing all obligations under terms of this lease, including those fees and expenses incurred at trial and on appeal, all of which shall be included in any judgment entered therein. Such covered fees and expenses shall include those incurred in suits instituted by third parties in which Lessor must participate to protect its rights hereunder and those incurred in suits to establish and enforce rights of indemnity hereunder.

SECTION 27
OTHER STORES

Lessee agrees that neither it, nor any subsidiary or affiliate of it, nor any other person, firm or corporation using any store or business name licensed or controlled by Lessee, shall, during the term of this lease, operate a store or business which is the same as or similar to that to be conducted on the premises, or which merchandises or sells the same or similar products, merchandise or services as that to be sold or furnished from the premises, at any location within a radius of four (4) miles from the Shopping Center without the written permission of Lessor. Lessee further agrees that it will not promote or encourage the operation of any such store or business within said radius by any person, firm or corporation. In addition to any and all other remedies otherwise available to Lessor for breach of this covenant, it is agreed that Lessor may at its election either (a) terminate this lease or (b) require that any and all sales made at, in, on or from any such other store be included in the computation of the percentage rent due hereunder with the same force and effect as though such sales had actually been made at, in, on or from the premises.

EXHIBIT 6 (*concluded*)

SECTION 32
CHANGE OF LOCATION

Lessee shall move from the premises at Lessor's written request to any other premises and location in the Shopping Center, in which event such new location and premises shall be substituted for the premises described herein, but all other terms of this lease shall remain the same, with the exception that the Minimum Rent provided for herein shall be abated during the period that Lessee is closed for business as a result of the move to the new location; provided, however, that Lessee shall not be moved to premises of less square footage than those herein leased, and that Lessor shall bear all actual cash expenses incurred by Lessee in so moving. It is further understood and agreed, however, that in the event that Lessee shall move to any other premises and location within the Shopping Center for any reason other than to comply with a request from Lessor, then this paragraph shall be inapplicable and the Lessee shall bear all expenses of moving.

EXHIBIT 7   Industry Operating Results 1980 Specialty Stores—Sales under $1 Million (percent figures unless otherwise noted)

	Average	Middle Range
Sales data		
Credit sales	20.87	11.70 – 36.68
Sales per square foot—selling space ($)	114.90	42.61 – 137.94
Sales per square foot—total space ($)	85.68	37.60 – 126.00
Returns—% gross sales	1.82	1.00 – 3.60
Sales per employee ($)	50,643	41,194 – 68,270
Markdowns	12.15	0.90 – 15.23
Employee discounts	1.09	0.00 – 2.12
Shortages	1.90	0.96 – 2.94
Gross margin	41.47	39.66 – 43.83
Net operating expenses		
Earnings from operations	3.57	1.59 – 5.00
Other income	0.62	0.18 – 1.72
Pretax earnings	4.19	2.52 – 5.31
Management payroll	8.43	6.57 – 10.54
Selling payroll	9.13	7.48 – 9.87
Payroll total	17.56	16.30 – 20.33
Supplementary fringe benefits	0.73	0.41 – 0.99
Media costs	3.09	2.21 – 3.33
Taxes	2.11	1.80 – 2.23
Supplies	2.99	2.00 – 3.78
Credit services	0.83	0.43 – 1.84
Other	1.05	0.81 – 1.37
Travel	0.85	0.13 – 1.40
Postage and phone	0.88	0.50 – 1.20
Insurance	1.29	0.74 – 1.66
Depreciation	0.97	0.29 – 1.56
Professional services	0.53	0.18 – 0.68
Bad debts	0.41	0.09 – 0.67
Outside maintenance and equipment service	0.26	0.18 – 0.30
Real property rentals	4.35	3.09 – 4.97
Total:	37.90	36.29 – 40.60

Adapted from National Retail Merchants Assn., *Financial and Operating Results of Department and Specialty Stores 1980*, pp. 104–5.

EXHIBIT 8   Dragonfly Expenses

DRAGONFLY CORPORATION
Statement of Operating Expenses
For the Years Ending December 31

	1980	1981
Operating expenses:		
Sales salaries	$22,607	$30,445
Advertising	9,317	10,726
Alteration costs	204	0
Bank card discounts	2,014	2,343
Buying trips	2,648	2,056
Delivery....................................	149	0
Display.....................................	330	0
Selling supplies	5,559	5,864
Over/short.................................	45	(629)
	42,873	51,172
Occupancy expenses:		
Depreciation/amortization	8,964	4,683
Insurance	742	742
Maintenance...............................	542	151
Property taxes	0	542
Rent..	20,128	16,942
Utilities....................................	101	95
	30,477	23,137
Administrative expenses:		
Officer's salary............................	23,447	13,542
Employee benefits..........................	874	2,169
Bank charges	187	223
Donations.................................	25	40
Dues and subscriptions	101	50
Officer's life insurance.....................	2,231	1,780
Bad debts	367	0
Office expense.............................	1,645	104
Professional services.......................	6,794	5,080
Business taxes	1,216	1,024
Payroll taxes..............................	5,661	5,232
Telephone	854	1,172
Postage....................................	787	712
Temporary help............................	154	79
Travel and entertainment	225	0
Miscellaneous.............................	0	1,435
	$44,568	$32,642

EXHIBIT 9   Janet and Michael Thompson—Personal Balance Sheet,
January 1, 1982

Assets	
1972 VW	$ 1,000
House	140,000
Marketable securities*	20,000
Equity in Dragonfly	5,000
Note receivable—Dragonfly	75,000
	$241,000
Liabilities	
First mortgage on house—Bank	$ 47,000
Second mortgage—Hepburns	35,000
Note payable—Hepburns	75,000
Note payable—Hepburns	15,000
Total liabilities	172,000
Net worth	69,000
Total liabilities and net worth	$241,000

*While these stocks were in Janet's name, Washington is a community property state.

EXHIBIT 10   History of Lease Obligations and Payments for
Woodscross Store

Time Period	Rent Incurred* (approx.)	Rent Paid	Payment on Old Balance	Total Remaining Unpaid Obligation†
July–Dec., 1979	$13,800	$13,800	$ 0	$ 0
Jan.–Dec., 1980	$27,600	$20,128	0	7,472
Jan.–Dec., 1981	27,600	16,942	0	18,130
Jan. 1982	2,300	878	0	19,552
Feb. 1982	2,300	500	875	20,477
March 1982	2,300	500	875	21,402
April 1982	2,300	500	875	22,327
May 1982	2,300	500	875	23,252
June 1982	2,300	500	875	24,177
July 1982‡	1,425	1,425	650	23,527
Aug. 1982	1,425	1,425	650	22,877
Sept. 1982	1,425	1,425	650	22,227
Oct. 1982	1,425	1,425	650	21,577
Nov. 1982	2,300	2,300	0	21,577
Dec. 1982	2,300	2,300	0	21,577

*Including common area maintenance assessments.
†Does not include future obligations under lease, which runs through March 1984.
‡Thompsons negotiate with landlord to pay rent of 6 percent of gross sales or $2,300 per month, *whichever is less.*

EXHIBIT 11   Correspondence from Attorney

October 25, 1982

Jeff Lawrence, Esq.
Attorney at Law
600 Seattle Trust Building
10655 NE Fourth
Bellevue, WA 98004

Re: Woodscross Properties
Janet and Michael Thompson Lease Default

Dear Mr. Lawrence:

As we have discussed recently by telephone, your clients, Janet and Michael Thompson, are currently in substantial default under the terms of their lease with Woodscross Properties. Any prior understanding which may have existed with respect to payment of this default was mutually rescinded by request of your clients on or about June 1, 1982. A subsequent arrangement, which was conditioned upon execution and delivery of an installment note and deed of trust, was proffered to Mr. Thompson on or about July 14, 1982, but he never executed a note and he failed to provide a legal description for his residence so that the deed of

EXHIBIT 11   (*continued*)

trust could be prepared, notwithstanding his repeated assurances that it would be forthcoming. As indicated in our prior correspondence to your clients, that offer has long since lapsed.

You now indicate that the Thompsons cannot further encumber their residence, that they own no other property on which a deed of trust might be placed, that they have no other security to offer in any form, and that they are even fighting to hold off lien foreclosures on their new store. In spite of all this, you propose that Woodscross Properties should be content without even a promissory note evidencing the indebtedness or the installment terms. You further suggest that no interest should accrue on the lease indebtedness. Moreover, although you acknowledge that the Thompsons' family members are helping them financially, they are reportedly unwilling to provide a guarantee of payment for this debt.

The fact that the Thompsons desire to avoid signing a note evidencing the terms of payment suggests that they have no intention of paying the lease default. Your suggestion that Woodscross Properties should rely solely on the Thompsons' good faith is completely unrealistic and unacceptable, both as a general business practice and as a result of your clients' past failures to perform as promised. We have enclosed a promissory note, bearing interest at 15% per annum, and requiring payments of $800 per month, which you have indicated are within the Thompsons' means. We have also enclosed a confession of judgment, which is to be entered in the event of default by the Thompsons in their payments due under the note.

Kindly arrange for Mr. and Mrs. Thompson to sign the note and confession of judgment and return the fully executed documents to us by no later than 5 o'clock p.m., November 5, 1982. If we do not receive them by that date and time, Woodscross Properties reserves all rights to collect the amounts due, without further notice to you.

Very truly yours,

PELLETT & CRUTT

Andrew A. Savage

Enclosures
CC: Woodscross properties

EXHIBIT 11   *(continued)*

PROMISSORY NOTE

$21,576.79

Seattle, Washington
_____ , 1982

FOR VALUE RECEIVED, the undersigned ("Maker") promises to pay to the order of Woodscross Properties, a Washington corporation limited partnership, the principal sum of Twenty-One Thousand Five Hundred Seventy-Six and 79/100 Dollars ($21,576.79), together with interest thereon, all as hereinafter provided and upon the following agreements, terms, and conditions:

Interest. All sums which are and which may become owing hereon shall bear interest from the date hereof until paid, at the rate of fifteen percent (15%) per annum.

Payment. Maker shall pay principal and interest in consecutive monthly installments of Eight Hundred Dollars ($800.00), or more, commencing on the fifteenth day of November 1, 1982, and continuing on the fifteenth day of each succeeding calendar month thereafter until the total indebtedness herein is paid in full. Each payment shall be applied first to interest accrued to the installment payment date and then to principal. All payments shall be payable in lawful money of the United States of America which shall be the legal tender for public and private debts at the time of payments. All payments shall be made to the holder hereof at Suite D–9, Woodscross Mall, Bellevue, Washington 98008, or at such other place as the holder hereof may specify in writing from time to time.

Prepayment. All or any part of the sums now or hereafter owing hereon may be prepaid at any time or times. Any such prepayment may be made without prior notice to the holder and shall be without premium or discount. All partial prepayments shall be applied first to interest accrued to the date or prepayment and the balance, if any, shall be credited to the last due installments of principal in the inverse order of their maturity without deferral or limitation of the intervening installments of principal or interest.

Late Payment Charge. If any installment of principal or interest shall not be paid within five (5) days commencing with the date such installment becomes due, Maker agrees to pay a later charge equal to three percent (3%) of the delinquent installment to cover the extra expense involved in handling delinquent payments. This late payment charge is in addition to and not in lieu of any other rights or remedies the holder may have by virtue of any breach or default hereunder.

Default; Attorneys' Fees and Other Costs and Expenses. Upon the occurrence of any Event of Default, at the option of the holder, all sums owing and to become owing hereon shall become immediately due and payable. The occurrence of any of the following shall constitute an "Event of Default": (i) Maker fails to pay any installment or other sum owing hereon when due; (ii) Maker admits in writing its inability to pay its debts, or makes a general assignment for the benefit of creditors; (iii) any proceeding is instituted by or against Maker seeking to adjudicate it a bankrupt or insolvent, or seeking reorganization, arrangement, adjustment, or composition of it or its debts under any law relating to bankruptcy, insolvency or reorganization or relief of debtors, or seeking

EXHIBIT 11   (*continued*)

appointment of a receiver trustee or other similar official for it or for any substantial part of its property; or (iv) any dissolution or liquidation proceeding is instituted by or against Maker, and if instituted against Maker, is consented to or acquiesced in by Maker or remains for thirty (30) days undismissed or unstayed or remains for thirty (30) days undismissed after such proceeding is no longer stayed. Maker agrees to pay all costs and expenses which the holder may incur by reason of any Event of Default, including without limitation reasonable attorneys' fees with respect to legal services relating to any Event of Default and to a determination of any rights or remedies of the holder under this note, and reasonable attorneys' fees relating to any actions or proceedings which the holder may institute or in which the holder may appear or participate and in any reviews of and appeals therefrom, and all such sums shall be secured hereby. Any judgment recovered by the holder hereon shall bear interest at the rate of eighteen percent (18%) per annum, not to exceed, however, the highest rate then permitted by law on such judgment. The venue of any action hereon may be laid in the County of King, State of Washington, at the option of the holder.

No Waiver. The holder's acceptance of partial or delinquent payments or the failure of the holder to exercise any right hereunder shall not waive any obligation of Maker or right of the holder or modify this note, or waive any other similar default.

Liability. All persons signing this note as Maker thereby agree that they shall be liable hereon jointly and severally, and they hereby waive demand, presentment for payment, protest, and notice of protest and of nonpayment. Each such person agrees that any modification or extension of the terms of payment made by the holder with or without notice, at the request of any person liable hereon, or a release of any party liable for his obligation shall not diminish or impair his or their liability for the payment hereof.

Maximum Interest. Notwithstanding any other provisions of this note, interest, fees, and charges payable by reason of the indebtedness evidenced hereby shall not exceed the maximum, if any, permitted by governing law.

Applicable Law. This note shall be governed by, and construed in accordance with, the laws of the State of Washington.

_____

Michael Thompson

_____

Janet Thompson

_____

DRAGONFLY CORPORATION

BY _____

    Its _____

EXHIBIT 11   (*continued*)

IN THE SUPERIOR COURT OF THE STATE OF WASHINGTON FOR KING
COUNTY WOODSCROSS PROPERITES, a)
limited partnership consisting of DICK)
MALLET and GEORGE VALE, as general)
partners, and other persons or entities)
as limited partners,)
)
          Plaintiff,)   No.
)
      v.   (CONFESSION OF JUDGMENT
)
MICHAEL THOMPSON and JANET THOMPSON)
husband and wife, the marital)
community thereof, and DRAGONFLY)
CORPORATION, a Washington)
corporation,)
)
          Defendants.)

Michael Thompson, Janet Thompson, husband and wife, the marital community thereof, and Dragonfly Corporation, defendants, do hereby confess judgment in favor of Woodscross Properties, plaintiff, on the terms and conditions and for the sums set forth below, and do hereby authorize the above Court to enter judgment for said sum and on said terms and conditions against defendants and in favor of plaintiff.

1. Defendants agree and confess that this confession of judgment and judgment based thereon may be entered immediately herein if, at any time hereafter, an Event of Default occurs, as defined in that certain promissory note (the "Promissory Note") executed by defendants and dated _____ , 1982, a copy of which is attached hereto as Exhibit A and incorporated herein by this reference.

2. In proof of the occurrence of an Event of Default as specified above, it shall be necessary and sufficient proof for plaintiff to present to the Court a writing certified by the then current holder of the Promissory Note that an Event of Default has occurred as defined in the Promissory Note.

3. Judgment may be entered in the principal amount of $21,576.79, together with interest in accordance with the terms of the Promissory Note, save and except the following: (a) any amount paid to plaintiff pursuant to the Promissory Note by defendants shall be deducted from the amount of said principal and interest specified in the Promissory Note; and (b) plaintiff's court costs, disbursements, and attorneys' fees incurred in connection with defendants' default in making payments due under the Promissory Note shall be added thereto.

4. Defendants specifically waive their right to a hearing on the merits of any issues that may arise in connection with the execution or enforcement of, or otherwise relating to, the Promissory Note, and confess and admit that the above-entitled court has full and exclusive jurisdiction

EXHIBIT 11   (*continued*)

over the parties and over the subject matter of any action arising from or relating to the Promissory Note, and defendants, for themselves and for all parties claiming under, by, or through them, hereby waive any and all claims or defenses, whether substantive or procedural, to entry of judgment in accordance with the terms and conditions of this confession of judgment.

   5. Defendants state, agree, and admit that this confession of judgment is a completely voluntary and knowing act of defendants. Defendants have been fully advised by their counsel of the effects and scope of the judgment confessed herein.

   6. Defendants hereby expressly waive notice of presentation of this confession of judgment to the court. If, notwithstanding defendants' waiver of any notice requirements, plaintiff elects to notify defendants of the time and place for presentation of the judgment, defendants shall have a right to be heard on the following questions only: (a) whether plaintiff has complied with the requirements set forth in paragraph 2 regarding proof that an Event of Default has occurred; and (b) the reasonableness of the attorneys' fees and costs to be included in the judgment.

   7. Defendants state, admit, and believe that this confession of judgment is for money justly due and owing to plaintiff under the terms of the Promissory Note, which was executed by defendants, as their free and voluntary act, to evidence indebtedness owing by defendants to plaintiff for delinquent lease payments arising under a commercial lease between the parties.

   DATED this _____ day of _____ , 1982.

_____
Michael Thompson

_____
Janet Thompson

_____
DRAGONFLY CORPORATION

BY _____

    Its _____

EXHIBIT 11   *(continued)*

STATE OF WASHINGTON)
)   ss.
COUNTY OF _____)

MICHAEL THOMPSON, being first duly sworn, states: I am the defendant in the above-entitled action, and I am authorized to make this verification on its behalf. I have read the foregoing Confession of Judgment, know the contents thereof, and that the same is true in all respects; I verify that the Confesson of Judgment herein contained has been voluntarily made by Michael Thompson with full knowledge.

_____

SUBSCRIBED AND SWORN TO before me this ____ day of _____ , 1982.

_____
NOTARY PUBLIC in and for the State
of Washington, residing at

_____

STATE OF WASHINGTON)
)   ss.
COUNTY OF _____)

JANET THOMPSON, being first duly sworn, states that I am a defendant in the above-entitled action, and I am authorized to make this verfication. I have read the foregoing Confession of Judgment, know the contents thereof, and that the same is true in all respects; I verify that the Confession of Judgment therein contained has been voluntarily made by Janet Thompson with full knowledge.

_____

SUBSCRIBED AND SWORN TO before me this ____ day of _____ , 1982.

_____
NOTARY PUBLIC in and for the State
of Washington, residing at

_____

EXHIBIT 11   *(continued)*

STATE OF WASHINGTON)
)   ss.
COUNTY OF _____)

_____ , being first duly sworn, states: I am the _____ of Dragonfly Corporation, the defendant in the above-entitled action, and I am authorized to make this verfication on its behalf. I have read the foregoing Confession of Judgment, know the contents thereof, and that the same is true in all respects; I verify that the Confession of Judgment therein contained has been voluntarily made by Dragonfly Corporation with full knowledge.

_____

SUBSCRIBED AND SWORN TO before me this _____ day of _____ , 1982.

_____
NOTARY PUBLIC in and for the State
of Washington, residing at

_____

STATE OF WASHINGTON)
)   ss.
COUNTY OF _____)

On this _____ day of _____ , 1982, before me, the undersigned, a Notary Public in and for the State of Washington, duly commissioned and sworn, personally appeared MICHAEL THOMPSON known to me to be the party that executed the foregoing Confession of Judgment, and acknowledged the said Confession of Judgment to be his free and voluntary act and deed for the uses and purposes therein mentioned, and on oath stated that he was authorized to execute this said Confession of Judgment.
        WITNESS my hand and official seal hereto affixed the day and year in this certificate first above written.

_____
NOTARY PUBLIC in and for the State
of Washington, residing at

_____

EXHIBIT 11   *(concluded)*

STATE OF WASHINGTON)
)   ss.
COUNTY OF _____)

On this ____ day of _____ , 1982, before, me, the undersigned, a Notary Public in and for the State of Washington, duly commissioned and sworn, personally appeared JANET THOMPSON known to me to be the party that executed the foregoing Confession of Judgment, and acknowledged the said Confession of Judgment to be her free and voluntary act and deed for the uses and purposes therein mentioned, and on oath stated that she was authorized to execute the said Confession of Judgment. WITNESS my hand and official seal hereto affixed the day and year in this certificate first above written.

NOTARY PUBLIC in and for the State of Washington, residing at

STATE OF WASHINGTON)
)   ss.
COUNTY OF _____)

On this ____ day of _____ , 1982, before me, the undersigned, a Notary Public in and for the State of Washington, duly commissioned and sworn, personally appeared _____ , known to me to be the _____ of DRAGONFLY CORPORATION, the corporation that executed the foregoing Confession of Judgment, and acknowledged the said Confession of Judgment to be the free and voluntary act and deed of said corporation, for the uses and purposes therein mentioned, and on oath stated that he was authorized to execute the said Confession of Judgment and that the seal affixed (if any) is the corporate seal of said corporation.

WITNESS my hand and official seal hereto affixed the day and year in this certificate first above written.

NOTARY PUBLIC in and for the State of Washington, residing at

EXHIBIT 12   Correspondence from Attorney

October 27, 1982

Mr. Andrew A. Savage, Esq.
2300 The Bank of California Center
Seattle, WA 98164

RE: DRAGONFLY CORPORATION
    Woodscross Shopping Center

Dear Andrew:

On October 8, 1982, we discussed Michael Thompson's and my meeting
with Frank Murdock, Manager of Woodscross Properties. On that date, we
proposed that the Dragonfly Corporation continue to pay the accrued
lease balance in monthly payments of $649.95 with the current lease pay-
ments to revert to the pre-percentage rent amount of approximately $2,300
per month.

As you are aware, the Thompsons have paid $875 a month on the past-due
balance from February through July, at which time it was reduced to the
$649.95 monthly installment. Payments were made without a note and
without security.

As I informed you, my clients do not have property which they can pledge
to secure the unpaid lease amounts accrued and I have advised them that
no note should be necessary where all parties are basically going back to
their pre-July agreement.

Mr. and Mrs. Thompson have access to additional financial support from
their relatives and fully intend to weather the current economic downturn.
They have made a great investment in their Dragonfly stores and are excellent managers. They will be around to complete payment of the Woodscross Properties lease obligations.

On October 8, 1982, you informed me that you would be consulting with
Frank Murdock and return to me with your response to our offer or alternative proposal. Please inform me of Mr. Murdock's response.

Very truly yours,

JEFF LAWRENCE

Case 4–4

SSS

In January of 1983, Vincent Lamb, Jr., president of Scientific Systems Services (SSS), was attempting to choose an investment bank to underwrite the initial public offering of SSS stock (see Exhibit 1 for recent financials). SSS had recently decided to become a publicly held corporation, and Lamb had mentioned this fact during a presentation at a financial conference for high-tech firms. In response, several firms had forwarded underwriting proposals to SSS. In addition, Lamb had solicited proposals from additional underwriters and had narrowed the choice down to the four that appear as exhibits in this case. (See Exhibits 2 through 5.)

SSS

SSS designed, marketed, and serviced integrated computer systems for monitoring and controlling industrial processes. These systems combined commercially available hardware and custom software configured to meet customer requirements. The company's principal customers were large electric utilities and automated industrial facilities.

RECENT FINANCING HISTORY

SSS was founded in 1965 by two engineers, and the initial financing was obtained from their personal funds. One of the founders left SSS in 1971, and the other left the company in 1978; Lamb was

This case was prepared by Michael J. Roberts under the direction of Howard H. Stevenson.

Copyright © 1983 by the President and Fellows of Harvard College
Harvard Business School case 9–384–129

then installed as chief executive. Lamb and a small group of officers and key employees purchased 152,000 shares from the former president, and SSS entered a period of rapid growth.

In late 1980, two vice presidents left SSS and an option was obtained to purchase their combined holdings, 500,000 shares for $500,000. SSS decided that the most appropriate way to handle this transaction was to arrange for a venture capital firm to purchase this block of stock as well as some additional shares to provide much needed working capital.

The Charles River Partnership purchased the 645,000-share block[1] for $750,000, and later that year purchased an additional 60,760 shares for $3.30 per share. With a major venture capital firm as the largest single owner of SSS, the stage was clearly set for SSS to become a public corporation.

Eleven months later, in November of 1982, SSS was in need of funds to finance its efforts to enter the business of systems integration, (i.e., packaging hardware and software). SSS sold 422,640 shares of stock for $7 per share via a private placement, which was arranged by the firm J. C. Bradford. At the time of this private placement, Bradford had also attempted to negotiate for the public offering. Lamb had been very careful to keep the two transactions separate, so that SSS would have maximum flexibility in choosing an underwriter.

In early 1983, SSS had decided that it was an appropriate time to consider the option of going public.

— SSS needed a great deal of capital to fund the expansion program (primarily via acquisitions, which it had chartered).

— The increased capitalization would help SSS gain credibility for bidding on large contracts with major utilities.

— SSS's ability to attract and hold onto high-caliber employees would be enhanced by a stock option plan and a publicly traded security.

A SECONDARY OFFERING

One issue, which had to be resolved, centered around a secondary offering of stock. All of the current institutional owners of SSS stock had the right to sell, on a pro rata basis, their own shares ("piggy-back rights"). (In a primary offering, only the company sells its own authorized but as yet unissued shares of stock—no individuals actually

---

[1]Note: All share figures and per share amounts have been adjusted to reflect a 5:1 stock split which occurred in February of 1983.

sell stock even though their ownership position is diluted.) Lamb and the board had to decide what portion, if any, of the total offering could be of secondary stock.

THE SELECTION OF AN UNDERWRITER

Lamb was very concerned that the chosen underwriter have the commitment not only to sell the stock, but to support it strongly as a public issue. Lamb reasoned that, as a low capitalization stock, SSS would be unlikely to develop a strong following with large institutions. Therefore, strong research and market support would be crucial to developing a following of individual investors and eventually, to develop an institutional following as the stock became more widely traded.

Lamb was concerned with several other issues:

— Should SSS use one or two underwriters? If they used two, what additional qualities should they seek in an underwriting team?

— How important was a strong retail brokerage network?

Lamb was charged with recommending a plan of action to the board of directors at a special meeting which would be held the following week. This decision was complicated by the fact that the overall market had improved dramatically over the past several months (see Exhibit 6), and this made comparison of the underwriting offers more difficult.

As he looked over the proposals, Lamb knew that he needed to prepare an agenda for the board discussion and his recommendations as to the priorities of the various considerations.

EXHIBIT 1   Scientific Systems Services Financials

SCIENTIFIC SYSTEMS SERVICES, INC.
Balance Sheets
December 31

	1981	1982
Assets		
Current assets:		
Cash and temporary cash investments	$ 816,766	$2,244,504
Certificates of deposit..........................	100,067	308,067
Contract receivables	1,195,169	2,189,444
Income taxes receivable.......................	—	247,363
Costs and estimated earnings in excess of		
related billings on uncompleted contracts...	345,366	994,550
Assets held in trust (current portion)..........	137,669	53,740
Prepaid expenses and other....................	45,346	37,556
Total current assets	2,640,383	6,075,224
Assets held in trust	1,162,331	228,836
Property:		
Land	355,385	355,385
Building.......................................	—	1,147,637
Laboratory equipment	317,783	1,025,687
Furniture and fixtures.........................	312,917	756,705
Leasehold improvements	45,808	85,345
Equipment held under capitalized leases......	44,474	276,837
Total..	1,076,367	3,647,596
Less accumulated depreciation and		
amortization	275,297	478,872
Property—net.................................	801,070	3,168,724
Other assets....................................	74,895	88,461
Total...	$4,678,679	$9,561,245

EXHIBIT 1   *(continued)*

	1981	1982
Liabilities and Stockholders' Equity		
Current liabilities:		
Current portion of long-term debt	$ 152,635	$ 180,660
Accounts payable	181,733	490,138
Billings in excess of related costs and estimated earnings on uncompleted contacts......................................	348,547	323,456
Accrued payroll and related taxes	90,698	376,599
Accrued employee benefit plan	—	74,467
Income taxes payable	199,857	—
Deferred income taxes (current portion).......	329,356	778,591
Accrued vacation benefits.....................	107,588	172,880
Other...	14,993	10,877
Total current liabilities....................	1,425,407	2,407,668
Long-term liabilities:		
Long-term debt	1,425,293	1,470,659
Deferred income taxes	30,536	114,723
Total long-term liabilities	1,455,829	1,585,382
Stockholders' equity:		
Commitments		
Common stock—$.01 par value; authorized 10,000,000 shares;* issued 575,332 shares in 1981 and 3,337,925 in 1982; outstanding 466,532 in 1981 and 2,773,425 in 1982........................	115,066	33,379
Paid-in capital	977,703	3,987,420
Retained earnings	1,239,074	2,176,446
Total.....................................	2,331,843	6,197,245
Treasury stock—at cost 108,800 shares in 1981 and 564,500 in 1982	(534,400)	(629,050)
Stockholders' equity—net.....................	1,797,443	5,568,195
Total..	$4,678,679	$9,561,245

*Reflects 5:1 split.

EXHIBIT 1   (*concluded*)

SCIENTIFIC SYSTEMS SERVICES, INC.
Statements of Income and Retained Earnings
For the Years Ended December 31

	1980	1981	1982
Revenues.............................	$4,992,559	$7,920,386	$15,523,134
Cost of revenues	3,244,496	4,830,694	10,314,390
Gross profit	1,748,063	3,089,692	5,208,744
Selling, general, and administrative expenses......	1,174,415	2,132,373	3,798,272
Operating income	573,648	957,319	1,410,472
Interest income	1,764	24,896	212,370
Interest expense	(47,699)	(42,910)	(134,022)
Income before income taxes.....	527,713	939,305	1,487,820
Provision for income taxes......	238,266	408,047	550,448
Net income......................	289,447	531,258	937,372
Retained earnings, beginning of year...........................	474,428	733,846	1,239,074
Dividends paid..................	(30,029)	(26,030)	—
Retained earnings, beginning of year............................	$ 733,846	$1,239,074	$ 2,176,446
Earnings per share:			
Earnings per common and common equivalent share	$ .13	$ .23	$ .37
Earnings per common share assuming full dilution........	$ .13	$ .22	$ .36

EXHIBIT 2 J. C. Bradford Proposal (entire proposal attached)

May 7, 1982

Mr. Vincent Lamb
Chairman of the Board and President
Scientific Systems Services, Inc.
Box 610
Melbourne, Florida 32901

Dear Vincent:

J. C. Bradford & Co. is prepared to assist Scientific Systems Services, Inc. in its efforts to increase the firm's equity capital under either of the following options.

OPTION I: A PRIVATE PLACEMENT OF COMMON STOCK TO INSTITUTIONAL INVESTORS. Under this option, we would act as agent to assist SSS in raising $3,200,000 in new equity for the company, and as agent to assist certain shareholders in selling common stock valued at $800,000. We would propose to value the stock at around 23 times the trailing 12 months' earnings per share for the quarter ending June 30, 1982. We are prepared to act in this capacity immediately upon notification by you, and would anticipate closing such a transaction within 45 to 60 days after you have given us your approval to proceed. Our fee for this transaction would be 3 percent of the proceeds raised, payable at closing.

OPTION II: A PUBLIC OFFERING OF COMMON STOCK. We are prepared to act as manager or co-manager of a public offering of SSS common stock. We understand that you want to raise about $4,000,000 in new equity for the company and $2,000,000 for selling shareholders. We believe that the Company can justify a valuation in such an offering of between 19 times and 23 times the trailing 12 months' earnings per share for the quarter ending June 30, 1982. We would suggest an underwriting discount of no less than 7 percent under this option. This offering could take place around September 1, 1982.

Under either option, we would recommend that you have a minimum of a 2.5-for-one stock split prior to undertaking the applicable transaction.

Attached to this letter are several tables which show what could conceivably be done in a public offering at several different pricing levels ranging from a low of 18 times earnings to a high of 23 times earnings. To keep the number of total shares offered at a constant level, we have decreased the number of shares sold by the Company and increased the number of shares offered by selling shareholders at each higher price level. About 45 days prior to the offering date, the Company would fix the number of shares offered by the Company and the selling shareholders, based upon prevailing market conditions at that time. This event would occur upon entering registration with the SEC.

We look forward to further discussions with you and your board on this. Thank you so much for the fine meeting we had this week.

Yours very truly,

J. Robert Philpott, Jr.
Vice President
Corporate Finance Department

EXHIBIT 2 (*continued*)

Historical and Projected Quarterly Earnings per Share, Assuming 510,000 Shares

	1981				1982				1983			
	Q_1	Q_2	Q_3	Q_4	Q_1	Q_2	Q_3	Q_4	Q_1	Q_2	Q_3	Q_4
Quarterly earnings per share	$.225	$.247	$.273	$.296	$ .47	$ .47	$ .50	$ .49	$ .70	$ .74	$ .82	$ .78
Trailing 12 months EPS				$1.04	$1.29	$1.51	$1.74	$1.93	$ 2.16	$ 2.43	$ 2.75	$ 3.04
Trailing 12 months net income ($000)				$ 531	$ 658	$ 770	$ 887	$ 984	$1,102	$1,239	$1,402	$1,550

Assuming 510,000 Shares Outstanding

	1977	1978	1979	1980	1981	1982$^{(P)}$	1983$^{(P)}$
Annual revenues ($000)	$1,299	$2,637	$3,531	$4,992	$7,945	$16,400	$21,300
Aftertax profit ($000)	$ 72	$ 271	$ 181	$ 289	$ 531	$ 984	$ 1,550
EPS	$ .14	$ .53	$ .35	$ .57	$ 1.04	$ 1.93	$ 3.04
Increase in revenues		103%	34%	41%	59%	106%	30%
Increase in aftertax profit		276%	(33%)	60%	84%	85%	58%
Increase in EPS		278%	(34%)	63%	82%	85%	58%

P = projected

Historical and Projected Quarterly Earnings per Share, Assuming 1,275,000 Shares

	1981				1982				1983			
	Q_1	Q_2	Q_3	Q_4	Q_1	Q_2	Q_3	Q_4	Q_1	Q_2	Q_3	Q_4
Quarterly earnings per share	$.09	$.10	$.11	$ .12	$ .19	$ .19	$ .20	$ .19	$ .28	$ .30	$ .33	$ .31
Trailing 12 months EPS				$ .42	$ .52	$ .61	$ .70	$ .77	$ .86	$ .97	$ 1.10	$ 1.22
Trailing 12 months net income ($000)				$531	$658	$770	$887	$984	$1,102	$1,239	$1,402	$1,550

Assuming 1,275,000 Shares Outstanding

	1977	1978	1979	1980	1981	1982(P)	1983(P)
Annual revenues ($000)	$1,299	$2,637	$3,531	$4,994	$7,945	$16,400	$21,300
Aftertax profit ($000)	$ 72	$ 271	$ 181	$ 289	$ 531	$ 984	$ 1,550
EPS	$ .06	$ .21	$ .14	$ .23	$ .42	$ .77	$ 1.22
Increase in revenues		103%	34%	41%	59%	106%	30%
Increase in aftertax profit		276%	(33%)	60%	84%	85%	58%
Increase in EPS		250%	(33%)	64%	83%	83%	58%

EXHIBIT 2 (*continued*)

Scientific Systems Services, Inc.

Assumptions: Offering 9/1/82, off trailing 12 months' figures to 6/30/82 of $770,000 net income (or $.61 per share). At P/E multiple of 18, Company worth $13,860,000. 1,275,00 shares outstanding before offering.

$$\frac{\$13,860,000}{1,275,000} \text{ shares} = \$10.87 \text{ per share} \qquad \text{Offer at \$11 per share} \qquad 7\% \text{ spread}$$

Number of shares outstanding before offering	1,275,000
Number of new shares issued by Company	370,000
Number of shares sold by selling shareholders	180,000
Total shares offered for sale	550,000
Number of shares outstanding after offering	1,645,000

$$\text{Dilution} \qquad \frac{1,645,000}{1,275,000} = 1.29 = 29\%$$

Offering P/E Multiple	Per Share	New Shares by Company	Gross Proceeds to Company	Net Proceeds to Company	Shares Sold by Selling Shareholders	Gross Proceeds to Selling Shareholders	Net Proceeds to Selling Shareholders	Gross Proceeds of Offering
18	$11	370,000	$4,070,000	$3,785,100	180,000	$1,980,000	$1,841,400	$6,050,000

Projected earnings for the Company for 12 months through 6/30/83 are $1,239,300.

$$\frac{\$1,239,300}{1,275,000} = \$.97 \qquad \frac{1,239,300}{1,645,000} = \$.75$$

If 10% pretax, 5% aftertax, earned for 10 months on net proceeds to Company, add $157,712 to 6/30/83 net income and earn $1,397,012 for 12 months ending 6/30/83.

$$\frac{\$1,239,300 + \$157,712}{2/12\,(1,275,000) + 10/12\,(1,645,000)} = \frac{\$1,379,012}{212,500 + 1,370,833} = \frac{\$1,397,012}{1,583,333}$$

$$= \$.88 \text{ or } 44\% \text{ over } 6/30/82.$$

Assumptions: Offering 9/1/82, off trailing 12 months' figures to 6/30/82 of $770,000 net income (or $.61 per share). At P/E multiple of 20, Company worth $15,400,000. 1,275,00 shares outstanding before offering.

$$\frac{\$15,400,000}{1,275,000 \text{ shares}} = \$12.08 \text{ per share} \qquad \text{Offer at \$12 per share} \qquad 7\% \text{ spread}$$

Number of shares outstanding before offering	1,275,000
Number of new shares issued by Company	340,000
Number of shares sold by selling shareholders	210,000
Total shares offered for sale	550,000
Number of shares outstanding after offering	1,615,000

$$\text{Dilution} \qquad \frac{1,615,000}{1,275,000} = 1.27 = 27\%$$

Offering P/E Multiple	New Shares by Company	Per Share	Gross Proceeds to Company	Net Proceeds to Company	Shares Sold by Selling Shareholders	Gross Proceeds to Selling Shareholders	Net Proceeds to Selling Shareholders	Gross Proceeds of Offering
20	340,000	$12	$4,080,000	$3,794,400	210,000	$2,520,000	$2,343,600	$6,600,000

Projected earnings for the Company for 12 months through 6/30/83 are $1,239,300.

$$\frac{\$1,239,300}{1,275,000} = \$.97 \qquad \frac{1,239,300}{1,615,000} = \$.77$$

If 10% pretax, 5% aftertax, earned for 10 months on net proceeds to Company, add $158,100 to 6/30/83 net income and earn $1,397,400 for 12 months ending 6/30/83.

$$\frac{\$1,397,400}{2/12\,(1,275,000) + 10/12\,(1,615,000)} = \frac{\$1,379,400}{1,558,333} = \$.90 \text{ or } 48\% \text{ over } 6/30/82.$$

EXHIBIT 2 (concluded)

Scientific Systems Services, Inc.

Assumptions: Offering 9/1/82, off trailing 12 months' figures to 6/30/82 of $770,000 net income (or $.61 per share). At P/E multiple of 22, Company worth $16,940,000. 1,275,00 shares outstanding before offering.

$$\frac{\$16{,}940{,}000}{1{,}275{,}000 \text{ shares}} = \$13.29 \text{ per share} \qquad \text{Offer at } \$13.25 \text{ per share} \qquad 7\% \text{ spread}$$

Number of shares outstanding before offering	1,275,000
Number of new shares issued by Company	310,000
Number of shares sold by selling shareholders	240,000
Total shares offered for sale	550,000
Number of shares outstanding after offering	1,585,000

$$\text{Dilution} \quad \frac{1{,}585{,}000}{1{,}275{,}000} = 1.24 = 24\%$$

Offering P/E Multiple	Per Share	New Shares by Company	Gross Proceeds to Company	Net Proceeds to Company	Shares Sold by Selling Shareholders	Gross Proceeds to Selling Shareholders	Net Proceeds to Selling Shareholders	Gross Proceeds of Offering
22	$13.25	310,000	$4,107,500	$3,819,975	240,000	$3,180,000	$2,957,400	$7,287,500

Projected earnings for the Company for 12 months through 6/30/83 are $1,239,300.

$$\frac{\$1{,}239{,}300}{1{,}275{,}000} = \$.97 \qquad \frac{1{,}239{,}300}{1{,}585{,}000} = \$.78$$

If 10% pretax, 5% aftertax, earned for 10 months on net proceeds to Company, add $159,166 to 6/30/83 net income and earn $1,398,466 for 12 months ending 6/30/83.

$$\frac{\$1{,}398{,}466}{2/12\,(1{,}275{,}000) + 10/12\,(1{,}585{,}000)} = \frac{\$1{,}398{,}466}{1{,}533{,}333} = \$.91 \text{ or } 49\% \text{ over } 6/30/82.$$

Assumptions: Offering 9/1/82, off trailing 12 months' figures to 6/30/82 of $770,000 net income (or $.61 per share). At P/E multiple of 23, Company worth $17,710,000. 1,275,000 shares outstanding before offering.

$$\frac{\$17,710,000}{1,275,000 \text{ shares}} = \$13.89 \text{ per share} \qquad \text{Offer at } \$13.75 \text{ per share} \qquad 7\% \text{ spread}$$

Number of shares outstanding before offering	1,275,000
Number of new shares issued by Company	290,000
Number of shares sold by selling shareholders	260,000
Total shares offered for sale	550,000
Number of shares outstanding after offering	1,565,000

$$\text{Dilution} \quad \frac{1,565,000}{1,275,000} = 1.23 = 23\%$$

Offering P/E Multiple	Per Share	New Shares by Company	Gross Proceeds to Company	Net Proceeds to Company	Shares Sold by Selling Shareholders	Gross Proceeds to Selling Shareholders	Net Proceeds to Selling Shareholders	Gross Proceeds of Offering
23	$13.75	290,000	$3,987,700	$3,708,561	260,000	$3,575,000	$3,324,750	$7,562,500

Projected earnings for the Company for 12 months through 6/30/83 are $1,239,300.

$$\frac{\$1,239,300}{1,275,000} = \$.97 \qquad \frac{1,239,300}{1,565,000} = \$.79$$

If 10% pretax, 5% aftertax, earned for 10 months on net proceeds to Company, add $167,000 to 6/30/83 net income and earn $1,405,466 for 12 months ending 6/30/83.

$$\frac{\$1,239,300 + \$154,523}{2/12\,(1,275,000) + 10/12\,(1,565,000)} = \frac{\$1,393,823}{1,516,667} = \$.92 \text{ or } 51\% \text{ over } 6/30/82.$$

EXHIBIT 3   Dean Witter Proposal (entire proposal)

DEAN WITTER REYNOLDS INC.
100 Peachtree St., N.W., Suite 800
Atlanta, GA 30303 Telephone (404) 658-5800

January 17, 1983

Mr. Vincent S. Lamb, Jr.
Chairman
Scientific Systems Services, Inc.
1135 John Rodes Boulevard
Melbourne, Florida 32901

Dear Vince:
As we discussed, this letter is written to summarize why Dean Witter Reynolds ("DWR") is best qualified to become Scientific Systems Services' investment banker. In your evaluation of potential investment bankers, we believe that you should consider the capabilities of each firm in light of the services you will require; of equal importance are the people in those firms who will be working with and be committed to Scientific Systems Services. The combination of the people, their degree of commitment, and the firm's resources will ultimately determine the quality of services that your Company receives, and the anticipated quality of these services could well serve as criteria for choosing your investment banker.
A key Dean Witter Reynolds strength lies in managing and co-managing public offerings. The firm's performance during 1980 and 1981 represented approximately 13 percent of all public domestic offerings of debt and equity, totaling approximately $15 billion of capital. DWR also ranks as one of the leading major bracket investment banking firms in terms of dollar volume of initial public offerings. Since January 1980, the firm has managed 17 such offerings with an aggregate dollar amount of $440.75 million. The firm offers not only outstanding syndication abilities as the lead manager, but also unexcelled distribution power. DWR has often shared this distribution strength when acting as the book-running co-manager with a specialty or regional firm as a co-manager. In the southeastern Unitied States, we have long been the leading originator of initial public offerings among major bracket investment banking firms for companies across a wide spectrum, including technology companies.
Dean Witter Reynolds has substantial experience servicing software and related companies. Recently, DWR was the sole lead underwriter of the intitial public offering of On-Line Software International, Inc. DWR sold 70.9 percent of the offering and placed a substantial percentage of the shares in 100–200 share trades. The offering was priced at $15 on September 29, 1982, and the opening bid and ask were $15.75–$16.25. Buoyed by recent interest in high-technology stocks, On-Line's common stock closed on January 14 at $26 bid.
Perhaps more impressive was our lead co-management on Friday, January 14, 1983, of the initial public offering of Quality Micro-Systems (QMS), which was offered at $17 per share and is now trading at $23 bid per share. This offering was brought to fruition in less than two months from our initial involvement, and has received tremendous national retail and institutional interest. QMS, based in Mobile, Alabama, designs, man-

EXHIBIT 3 *(continued)*

ufactures and markets intelligent graphics processors used primarily in dot-matrix and other printing systems. These processors feature extensive use of "PROM", or applications firmware which, as you know, is essentially software on a circuit board.

In addition, DWR recently completed a private placement of $8 million of convertible subordinated debentures of Applied Data Research, Inc. We will soon be filing as a manager of the initial public offering of American Software, Inc., an Atlanta-based applications software firm. All of these offerings have featured primary involvement by our Atlanta staff, as discussed below.

We believe that DWR's strengths include the following:

Distribution—DWR has long been known for its outstanding retail sales force representing approximately 9 percent of all registered sales personnel working for New York Stock Exchange member firms. More than 4,600 account executives in 338 offices worldwide are in contact with over 1 million active investors making DWR the second largest retail-distribution power with similar strengths in institutional distribution.

Syndication—Your investment banker must be able to distribute securities under all market conditions. DWR's syndicate department provides effective coordination, working with the client to determine the desired distribution pattern for the security, and assembling an underwriting group to achieve this distribution. DWR's distribution strength means more than simply an outlet for the sale of securities. Sales professionals maintain close contact with investment banking officers, advising on the factors affecting the market. This close cooperation helps to ensure an effective distribution and optimal pricing in even volatile markets. As a result of our exceptional retail and institutional placement capabilities, DWR, as your book-running manager, can tailor the distribution to be placed with any desired mix of institutional and retail investors and in any geographic location to meet your objectives.

Equity Trading—DWR is one of the largest factors in equity trading in the United States. Our large capital position allows the trading department to take a leading role in the marketplace and exert market-making power even in unfavorable markets. The firm's block trading capabilities are currently considered among the best on Wall Street. In surveys of institutional investors, DWR consistently places among the top firms for research, execution of orders, block trading, and overall service. DWR's Over-the-Counter Trading Department makes markets in approximately 1,000 stocks through 42 traders, representing one of the largest such commitments.

Sensitivity—Pricing new securities requires not only an analysis of comparable companies' trading patterns but also sensitivity to the supply and demand factors of the marketplace. As one of the largest managing underwriters, DWR has consistently demonstrated intelligent pricing resulting in satisfied sellers and investors.

EXHIBIT 3   (*continued*)

Technology Orientation—DWR has placed a priority on developing high-technology business and made a substantial commitment to this business. DWR's technology group is staffed with corporate finance professionals in Atlanta, New York and San Francisco, who work primarily with science and technology clients, including the undersigned. This group, which would be available to you at all times, provides a full range of investment banking services and coordinates support and sponsorship from research, trading, and syndication/distribution.

Research Coverage—DWR's research effort is recognized by independent polls as one of the top four in Wall Street. Our research group of some 50 analysts features a technology group of 8 analysts, including 3 analysts who specialize in software and software-related issues. Terry Quinn of our staff covers the leading software companies in the southeast, and has indicated a strong interest to follow your Company. Terry is also a coauthor of our Emerging Growth Stock publication, in which your Company would be included for monthly distribution to our customers and account executives.

Southeastern Presence—DWR is unique among major investment banking firms in that we have a historic commitment to regionalization. Here in Atlanta, we are the successor to Courts & Co. with a 50-year investment banking heritage, and have the largest investment banking staff of any major firm, including three technology specialists. Bill Green and John Williams would be your key account officers in Atlanta, assisted by other staff members in Atlanta and New York. These officers have extensive experience with technology issuers, including Lanier Business Products, Microdyne Corporation, On-Line Software, Quality Micro Systems, SCI Systems, and numerous others. Should you choose to work with us, we would recommend processing the transaction here in Atlanta. We would use the Atlanta law firm of Hansell, Post as underwriters' counsel. If you choose to print here, we believe you would save considerable expense versus most alternative locations. We have worked in the past with many of the leading SEC corporate lawyers in the South, and could be of assistance in your selection process in this respect if requested. In any event, we could facilitate early implementation of your SEC filing and assure that we would at no time cause you delay in the financing.

Valuation and Capitalization—In valuing your Company, we seek to be aggressive and competitive with offers you may receive from other firms of stature, but also realistic. We have reviewed certain relatively comparable software companies, including Ask Computer Systems, Tera Corporation, and others. These two companies, in particular, currently trade at price/earnings ratios (on trailing 12 months earnings) of $46.8\times$ and $37.3\times$, respectively. Factors favoring SSS relative to these larger companies include your greater margin expansion potential, your evolving product mix, and other factors. We believe that Scientific Systems Services can be marketed on a basis similar to or perhaps higher than Tera, but perhaps at a discount to Ask. We would currently propose a

EXHIBIT 3 *(continued)*

valuation range for the offering of 37.0× possibly to 42× trailing 12 months earnings. Based on your current 1983 earnings forecast of $1.5 million in profits after tax, this range would provide 24.5× and up to 27.5× forecast 1983 earnings of $1.5 million, or a total current value for the Company prior to the offering of about $37 million to $41.5 million.

We understand that you desire to raise approximately $8 million in new equity funds and $4 million in funds for selling shareholders, for a total offering of about $12 million. This could appropriately be accomplished by undertaking a 5 for 1 or similar split of the current shares, providing about 2,750,000 shares prior to the financing. The offering could then be composed of, say, 800,000 shares, consisting of 535,000 shares for the Company and 265,000 shares for selling shareholders, and a filing price range of perhaps $13 to $16 per share. We would suggest establishing a maximum filing price of perhaps $17 to provide initial flexibility to exceed this range if demand allows. We would also request an over-allotment option of 10 percent of the basic amount of the offering (here 80,000 shares) which could be provided by the Company, by the selling shareholders, or by both.

The above concepts would, of course, be refined more carefully in the context of an implementation.

Underwriters' Compensation—Based on present market conditions, and assuming that your shares were priced in the mid-teens, we would expect to recommend a gross spread of approximately 7 to 7.25 percent. We would be pleased to discuss the components and rationale for this spread level should you desire.

Marketing—If selected as your managing underwriter, we would undertake with you immediately the preparation of a well-written prospectus and target an early filing with the SEC as soon as your year-end numbers are available, perhaps by mid or late February. We would then orchestrate a series of institutional and retail information meetings in Atlanta, Boston, New York, Chicago, San Francisco, and other major cities.

Depending on the success of these meetings and demand for your shares, we may be able to increase the filing price range of the offering above the level set forth above. We would be delighted to do this if market conditions allow. In the Quality Micro Systems offering last week, we were in fact able to achieve a price $2 above the high end of the initial filing range and still produce a significant premium in after market trading. Without question, the intensive marketing effort conducted for that company played an important role in this price improvement.

Currently our system is highly attuned to quality offerings of emerging technology companies. We are most eager to demonstrate our marketing capabilities to serve your Company.

EXHIBIT 3 *(concluded)*

We sincerely hope that this presentation will lead you to select DWR as your investment banker. Let us emphasize that we would view this selection as only the first step in building a relationship. We would consider this to be a commitment to work with you over a long period of time, and we hope you would view it in the same way. We are anxious to begin working with you at an early date and feel that such a relationship will be mutually rewarding. If there are any questions, please do not hesitate to call.

Sincerely yours,

DEAN WITTER REYNOLDS, INC.

William S. Green
Managing Director

John Williams
Vice President

EXHIBIT 4   E.F. Hutton Proposal (excerpts from proposal)

* = Included in Exhibit 4.

EXHIBIT 4 *(continued)*

E.F. Hutton
E.F. Hutton & Company Inc. One Battery Park Plaza, New York, N.Y. 10004
(212) 742-5336

Thomas G. Greig III
Senior Vice President

December 13, 1982

Mr. Vincent S. Lamb
Chairman and President
Scientific Systems Services, Inc.
2000 Commerce Drive, P.O. Box 610
Melbourne, FL 32901

Dear Mr. Lamb:
This letter will outline the terms of an underwritten public offering
for Scientific Systems Services, Inc. ("SSS") for which E.F. Hutton & Company Inc. ("Hutton") proposes to act as managing underwriter.
Size of Offering: Hutton has assumed that SSS intends to raise a
minimum of $9 million in a primary offering of common stock. We have
assumed $9 million based on forecasts supplied to us and assume net
proceeds to SSS of $8.025 million. Hutton believes that SSS could success-
fully market a larger issue of $12 million, combining both primary shares
and shares owned by existing shareholders ("secondary stock"). Hutton
recommends that no member of management be allowed to sell more than
20 percent of his holdings and that the secondary portion should amount
to no more than 35 percent of the offering. It is presumed that the
proceeds from the primary portion of the offering would be used for working capital.
Recapitalization: Hutton recommends SSS effect a 6.1 for 1 stock
split prior to the initial filing of the registration statement, resulting in
3,642,675 shares outstanding.
Pricing: Hutton believes that initial public offerings are priced principally on future earnings and how they relate to current earnings trends,
and not on the basis of current earnings. Based upon information
provided by SSS to date, Hutton believes that SSS's common stock will
sell at a multiple range of forecast 1983 and 1984 earnings (fully diluted,
from continuing operations, before extraordinary items) of $31 \times - 36 \times$ and
$24 \times - 27 \times$, respectively. This forecast is based on estimated growth for
the markets in which SSS competes, the current condition of the equity
market and the new issue market, the future financial prospects for SSS
and its historical financial record which will be included in the prospectus. Given a capitalization of 3,642,675 shares (after effecting a 6.1 for 1
stock split), Hutton recommends an initial filing price range of $14–$16 per
share. This is based upon a calculation of 1983 and 1984 earnings per
share presented in a price/earnings analysis included in Section II, resulting in 1983 earnings per share of $0.45 and $0.59 for 1984. Hutton feels that
pricing of the offering should be such that there is a reasonable expectation for the stock to trade initially at a 10 percent to 15 percent premium to

EXHIBIT 4   (*continued*)

the offering price. Hutton's final pricing recommendation would be based on this immediate aftermarket premium philosophy, general market conditions, initial public offering market conditions and condition of the managing underwriter's "book". An analysis of price/earnings valuations of companies perceived as comparable to SSS, in terms of either their line of business or their future prospects for growth and profitability, is included in Section II. Given the assumptions as to 1983 and 1984 earnings per share and Hutton's pricing ideas, the offering would consist of approximately 650,000 primary shares, and 200,000 secondary shares, resulting in approximately a $12 million offering. Given 4,292,675 (primary) shares outstanding after the offering, SSS would have a market value of at least $60 million ($14 per share). Moreover, if earnings are substantially above the current forecast as a result of the award of a multiplant utility contract in 1983, Hutton believes that a market valuation of approximately $80 million ($18 per share) can be supported.

Over-Allotment Option: Hutton recommends that SSS extend to the underwriters an over-allotment option for up to 10 percent of the size of the offering. These shares would be purchased by the underwriters to cover the underwriters' short-sale position, if any, resulting from the offering, only if, in Hutton's judgment, the after market performance of SSS stock would not be adversely affected.

Gross Spread: Based on an offering of 850,000 shares, Hutton's present anticipation is that the gross spread (underwriting discount) will range from 6.75 percent to 7.3 percent of the offering price for an offering range of $14–$16 per share. Section IV sets forth the gross spread information for initial public offerings of common stock in 1982. Hutton's final gross spread recommendation will depend on the condition of the general market, the new issue market, and the managing underwriter's "book" at the time of the offering.

Co-Manager: Hutton is prepared to co-manage the offering with another firm or firms of SSS's choosing. Hutton believes those firms should be selected in view of Hutton's strengths of retail distribution capability, recognition by institutions of Hutton's knowledge of the computer industry and the profitable experience of Hutton's customer base in investing in the stocks of such companies. If selected as a co-manager, Hutton believes that it should be the lead manager in order for it to effectively organize and execute a retail and institutional market distribution plan.

Timing: Hutton recommends that SSS proceed with an initial public offering during the first quarter of 1983. We believe an SSS offering based on December 31, 1982, financial statements would be readily marketable based on recent market conditions. Hutton personnel would be pleased to begin working with SSS immediately to gain in-depth knowledge of SSS and ensure that SSS is optimally postured for its initial public offering.

Syndication: Hutton recommends that a syndicate of approximately 65 underwriters be formed to distribute the offering. This syndicate would include the "major bracket" national securities firms, the larger regional underwriting firms, selected smaller regional firms, and selected foreign underwriters and would be determined according to the desired distribution mix for the offering chosen by SSS. Hutton as managing underwriter

EXHIBIT 4 *(continued)*

will underwrite approximately 25 percent of the offering, retain for sale through its own distribution network approximately 40 percent to 50 percent of the offering, and distribute the balance of the stock to the other syndicate members based upon SSS's choice of retail versus institutional and geographic distributional goals. After release of the stock for sale, Hutton as managing underwriter will stablize the market for SSS's stock, if necessary, by making purchases of the stock in the open market to assure an orderly distribution and after market for the stock. When, in Hutton's determination, such has been achieved, Hutton will terminate the syndicate thereby releasing the syndicate members to make a market in SSS's stock and begin normal trading activities.

Distribution Mix: Hutton recommends a specific retail/institutional mix as well as a broad geographic distribution for SSS's common stock offering. Hutton believes that the goal for the offering should be a 65 percent retail, 35 percent institutional distribution for the following reasons:

> Retail: The high percentage of retail distribution would place the stock in a large number of relatively small lots of approximately 300–500 shares each. New York Stock Exchange statistics indicate that retail investors hold twice the dollar amount of equities, and account for only one-half the trading volume as compared to institutions, thereby suggesting retail investors are better long-term holders of securities and are less likely to sell a stock after a short-term price upswing, or in the event of intermittent growth or profitability. Hutton believes that a broad shareholder base gives a company the greatest likelihood of less volatile after market trading and a better forum from which to raise future equity to support rapid growth.
>
> Institutional: Institutional distribution is desirable since (i) it is a finite audience of approximately 150 addressable institutions who over the past several years have been the consistent purchasers of emerging growth stocks; (ii) these institutions have been price leaders in supporting high valuations through purchase in the offering and in the after market; (iii) institutional holders can also cause additional research coverage. Institutional demand for the offering will be more than 35 percent. Institutions would have their orders only partially filled and would be encouraged to purchase up to their desired holding levels through buying in the open market after the offering, thereby supporting the issue in the after market.

In order to achieve this distribution mix, Hutton believes that SSS must engage managing underwriters who will address both retail and institutional securities purchasers. Section I contains charts which describe the roles of different investment banks in distributing securities. E.F. Hutton, with its 5,172 account executives managing over 800,000 accounts, is particularly well qualified to provide SSS with the retail distribution necessary for consummating a successful offering, especially in highly volatile markets.

EXHIBIT 4 *(continued)*

___

Hutton also recommends broad geographic distribution for the offering. Hutton would tailor its own internal distribution and that of the underwriting syndicate to obtain this goal.

Marketing Program: As manager of SSS's initial public offering, Hutton will conduct a coordinated, national marketing program to educate the investment community on SSS and its business, and to generate purchase orders for the issue. This program would begin with producing a marketing oriented prospectus, the principal sales document in the offering. During the SEC review of the offering documents, Hutton will orchestrate both an institutional marketing program to expose SSS to buyers in major domestic and European financial centers, as well as an internal marketing program to generate interest in the offering within Hutton's own distribution system.

- The prospectus in the registration statement will be the most important marketing document for the offering; therefore, it must contain a detailed business description of SSS, organized to present SSS's major selling points for use by the retail sales force as well as by the institutional analyst community. Hutton will assist SSS in the final drafting of the prospectus so as to accomplish this marketing objective.
- In marketing the SSS offering to institutional purchasers, sales information meetings and "one on one" discussions will be held in various cities, the most likely being Boston, New York, Chicago, San Francisco, and Los Angeles. Similar meetings in the major European financial centers of London, Edinburgh, Geneva and Zurich we feel is also desirable. Hutton will assist SSS in preparing a presentation geared to the needs and interests of this institutional audience. A proposed timetable for these meetings is included in Section V.
- Hutton will aggressively market the SSS offering to its 4,872 retail and 300 institutional account executives who serve over 800,000 retail and 1,500 major institutional accounts from 335 domestic and foreign offices. This program would include:
  — A wire to branch managers describing the offering and key marketing points, followed by a four-page sales memorandum to each account executive and an article in *Products and Markets,* an internal publication.
  — Interaction between corporate finance and equity research personnel and retail syndicate coordinators to explain the offering and field questions.
  — Daily communication with the 10 Hutton regions to monitor national demand during the offering.
  — Hutton's institutional sales force is kept abreast of the offering through conference calls twice daily, one of which is taped and available for replay on a toll-free 800 number. Hutton's corporate finance team will sponsor SSS management in these broadcasts to the institutional sales force.
  — Hutton corporate finance and equity research personnel on the SSS team will make themselves available to the entire sales force to answer questions about SSS or the offering.

Section VI of this presentation contains a more detailed description of the internal marketing program.

EXHIBIT 4   (*continued*)

After Market Sponsorship: Given SSS's importance to E.F. Hutton as a potential client and the involvement of the other senior officers in developing a relationship between the two firms, SSS will become a cornerstone in the continuing evolution of Hutton as the major factor in investment banking for technology based companies. SSS would be a client of E.F. Hutton, not of specific individuals, and would enjoy the visibility and sponsorship of the senior management of the firm. However, individuals must take responsibility for the execution of proper after market sponsorship. That responsibility would belong to Tom Greig from Hutton's New York headquarters. Hutton believes that the client services provided by an investment banker between transactions are at least as important as the execution of the offering itself. Consequently, Hutton strives to offer its corporate finance clients after market sponsorship unequalled by its competitors. This sponsorship will include:

- Research Coverage: E.F. Hutton will provide regular research coverage on SSS through its equity research department. Coverage will include comprehensive annual research reports on SSS, its prospects and its industry, "all-wires" releases which outline fast-breaking events concerning SSS, and an up-to-date research comment database which brokers can access through their desk-top quote machines.
- Exposure to Financial Community: Hutton will ensure that the financial community keeps current with SSS by providing in-depth research coverage and arranging securities analyst meetings, institutional forums and investor conferences. In particular, Hutton will sponsor SSS at forums such as the New York Society of Securities Analysts and assure that SSS be given the opportunity to participate in events staged by groups such as the American Electronics Association.
- Management Follow-Up: When not working directly with SSS on a specific transaction, Hutton's corporate finance team will keep abreast of SSS's financial progress, monitor developments in its industry, keep it informed with reports on market conditions and provide it with financing alternatives to capitalize on specific market opportunities.
- Market Making: E.F. Hutton is the primary market maker for the securities of its investment banking clients and, in this role, will assure SSS of a liquid and stable market for its securities. Following SSS's initial public offering, Hutton will become the lead market maker for its stock.
- Special Services: As an investment banking client, SSS will receive special attention by functional areas of Hutton other than those thus far mentioned. Special services available to SSS would include cash management consulting, lease financing, tax shelter assistance and distribution of "Rule 144" stock.
- Long-Term Commitment: E.F. Hutton, through its Technology Group, aspires to become the preeminent investment banker to computer and electronics companies among the national securities firms. To attain this goal, Hutton must secure as clients today the industry leaders of tomorrow and then strengthen these relationships by continuing to provide the best possible service. E.F. Hutton wishes to initiate such a long-term relationship with SSS.

Financial Statements and Accountants: Hutton understands that SSS will provide annual financial statements, which will be audited by

EXHIBIT 4   *(continued)*

Deloitte Haskins & Sells and will meet the SEC requirements for the form S-1 Registration Statement. SSS will also provide additional financial data Hutton believes is necessary for marketing purposes. The underwriters will request Deloitte Haskins & Sells to provide "cold comfort" review of information included in the registration statement which can be traced back to the financial records of the company.

Printing: Hutton recommends that SSS select a qualified financial printer to print the registration statement, prospectus, underwriting agreement and underwriting syndication papers. Hutton will request that 40,000 preliminary prospectuses and 30,000 final prospectuses be printed. SSS will assume all printing costs.

"Blue Sky" Law Qualification: The underwriters will request that SSS register varying amounts of the shares in the offering in all states in order for the stock to be sold to retail investors over a broad geographic area. The cost of registration and fees of counsel in completing the applications and in clearing the offering through the various state "Blue Sky" commissions will be paid by SSS.

Underwriters' Counsel: It is Hutton's intention to use as underwriters' counsel, a law firm experienced in securities law and in offerings for technology based companies. The underwriters will request that this counsel handle all matters as to "Blue Sky" law qualification. The fees of such counsel, other than the fees incurred for "Blue Sky" qualification, will be paid by the underwriters.

Underwriting Agreement: Neither SSS nor Hutton will be obligated to proceed with the offering unless and until the underwriting agreement is executed. Such agreement will contain Hutton's usual provisions including an agreement that neither SSS nor its officers, nor directors will, without prior written consent of Hutton, sell, transfer or otherwise dispose of any shares of common stock for a period of 90 days from the date of the offering. The execution of the underwriting agreement is subject to SSS and Hutton being satisfied with the form and substance of the preliminary, amended, and final registration statements and propectuses, and with all items and conditions of the underwriting agreement.

The following presentation contains additional information on an initial public offering of SSS common stock, as well as on Hutton's ability to manage this offering. Specifically included are financial and market data on companies in SSS's industry, a price/earnings and recapitalization analysis of SSS, a proposed underwriting syndicate, an offering timetable, and information on recent initial public offerings.

Hutton is most interested in developing a long-term investment banking relationship with SSS. We are enthusiastic about the prospects for the continued growth of SSS and will marshall Hutton's resources to help SSS meet its goals.

I look forward to discussing Hutton's interest in SSS with you at greater length.

Yours truly,

Thomas G. Greig III
Senior Vice President

EXHIBIT 4   *(continued)*

Segmentation of Managing Underwriters

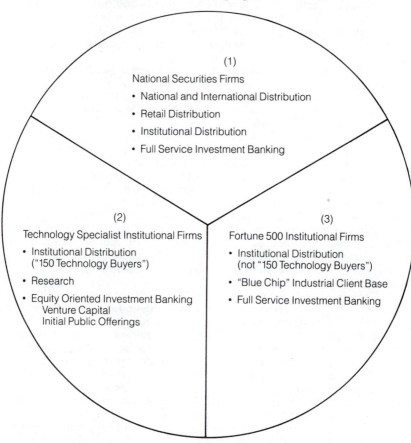

(1)
National Securities Firms

- National and International Distribution
- Retail Distribution
- Institutional Distribution
- Full Service Investment Banking

(2)
Technology Specialist Institutional Firms

- Institutional Distribution
  ("150 Technology Buyers")
- Research
- Equity Oriented Investment Banking
  Venture Capital
  Initial Public Offerings

(3)
Fortune 500 Institutional Firms

- Institutional Distribution
  (not "150 Technology Buyers")
- "Blue Chip" Industrial Client Base
- Full Service Investment Banking

(1) National Securities
    Firms

- E.F. Hutton
- Merrill Lynch
- Dean Witter
- Shearson/Amer. Express
- Blyth, Paine Webber
- Smith Barney
- Bache

(2) Technology Specialist
    Institutional Firms

- Hambrecht & Quist
- L. F. Rothschild
- Alex Brown
- Robertson, Colman
- Montgomery Securities

(3) Fortune 500
    Institutional Firms

- Morgan Stanley
- First Boston
- Goldman Sachs
- Kidder Peabody
- Lehman Brothers
- Salomon Brothers

EXHIBIT 4   *(continued)*

Price/Earnings and Recapitalization Analysis

This analysis sets forth the effect on earnings per share and the resulting
range of price/earnings multiples resulting from an initial public offering of
shares by Scientific Systems Services, Inc.

Assumptions:

1. SSS becomes public in the first quarter of 1983 off year end 1982 financial statements.
2. The filing range for the offering price would be $85.71 to $97.95. For computational purposes we assumed an offering of 105,000 primary shares at $85.71 per share.
3. Net proceeds to SSS from the primary portion of the offering are $8,025,000. This consists of gross proceeds of $9,000,000 less a gross spread of $630,000 (7%) and issuance expenses of $345,000.
4. 1983 revenues and net earnings from operations will be $24,000,000 and $1,680,000 (7% after tax), respectively. 1984 revenues and net earnings from operations will be $36,000,000 and $2,520,000, respectively. In addition, the valuation study (see next pages of this Section) also considers the scenario in which the Company's 1983 revenues are $30 million, with $2.1 million earnings, and its 1984 revenues are $45 million with $3.15 million earnings.
5. Net proceeds of $8,025,000 are received April 1, 1983. As a result, the Company earns additional interest income, at 5 percent after tax, on an average of $5 million during the last nine months of 1983.

SSS Forecast Operating Results

| | *Year Ended December 31,* | | |
	1982	*1983*	*1984*
Net sales	$16,800,000	$24,000,000	$36,000,000
Net income before			
extraordinary items	1,000,000	1,867,500	2,520,000
Earnings per share	1.98	2.77	3.60
Weighted average shares			
outstanding	505,000	673,750	700,000

Price/Earnings Impact

Filing price range per share		$85.71–$97.95	
Earnings per share	$ 1.98	$ 2.77	$ 3.60
Price/earnings range	44x–50x	31x–36x	24x–27x
Market value of SSS			
Post offering (millions)		$ 60–69	

EXHIBIT 4   (*continued*)

For discussion purposes we have not incorporated any stock split in the above analysis. Prior to the initial public offering Hutton recommends SSS split its stock 6.1 for 1 so as to target an initial filing range of $14–$16 which would broaden retail investor participation in the offering.

Recapitalization Analysis Assuming a 6.1 for 1 Stock Split

	1982	*1983*	*1984*
	Year Ended December 31,		
Net income before extraordinary items	$1,000,000	$1,867,500	$2,520,000
Earnings per share	$ 0.32	$ 0.45	$ 0.59
Weighted average shares outstanding	3,091,682	4,124,794	4,285,500

Price/Earnings Impact

	1982	*1983*	*1984*
Filing price range per share		$ 14–$16	
Earnings per share	$ 0.32	$ 0.45	$ 0.59
Price/earnings range	44x–50x	31x–36x	24x–27x
Market value of SSS Post offering (millions)		$ 60–69	

Increased 1983 Earnings

Management has informed Hutton that the forecast 1983 operating results could be dramatically higher ($2.1 million versus $1.68 million) if the company secures a multiplant utility contract in the first quarter of 1983. Hutton's valuation study (please see the next pages of this section) indicates that the postoffering market value of the Company could approach $80 million (approximately $18 per share) in such a case.

EXHIBIT 4   (*continued*)

Comparative Market Analysis
Index of Five SSS Comparable versus the NASDAQ Industrials Index

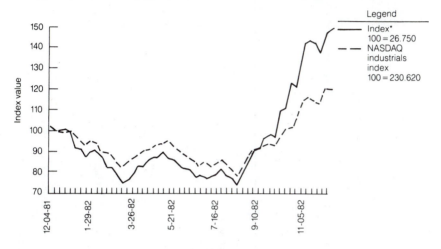

Weekly — 12-04-81 to 12-09-82

*Index includes: Shared Medical Sys. Corp., Systematics Inc., Policy Mgmt. Sys. Corp., Triad Sys. Corp., and SEI Corp.

EXHIBIT 4 *(continued)*
Valuation Study (in millions of dollars)

E.F. Hutton & Company Inc.
Corporate Finance Department
December 10, 1982

	Scientific Systems Services			*On-Line Software International*	*Systems & Computer Technology Corporation*	*Par Technology*	*ARGOSystems*	*Dionex Corporation*	*Quantum Corporation*
Current market value (12-10-82)	$60.00	$70.00	$80.00 (1)	$77.66	$290.61	$186.88	$96.52	$98.78	$199.60
Current market price (12-10-82)	14.00	16.00	18.00	21.875	22.75	25.00	31.50	24.50	22.50
Market value/projected revenues (dollars in millions)									
Calendar 1983 revenues-ratio	$24.00-2.5x	$24.00-2.9x	$30.00-2.7x	$24.00-3.2x	$49.00-5.9x	$44.00-4.2x	$42.00-2.3x	$22.00-4.5x	$63.00-3.2x
Calendar 1984 revenues-ratio	$36.00-1.7x	$36.00-1.9x	$45.00-1.8x	37.00-2.1x	74.00-3.9x	59.00-3.2x	53.00-1.8x	28.00-3.5x	78.00-2.6x

Market value/projected net income

Calendar 1983 net income-ratio	1.87-32.1x	1.87-37.4x	2.29-34.9x	3.5-22.2x	5.9-49.3x	6.6-28.3x	3.5-27.6x	2.8-35.3x	10.0-20.0x
Calendar 1984 net income-ratio	2.52-23.8x	2.52-27.8x	3.15-25.4x	5.3-14.7x	8.9-32.7x	8.9-21.0x	4.6-21.0x	3.5-28.2x	12.5-16.0x

Growth rate valuation

Five year projected compound growth rate	50%	50%		50%	50%	35%	30%	25%	25%
Indicated P/E (.65x) (2)	32.5x	32.5x		32.5x	32.5x	22.75x	19.50x	16.25x	16.25x
Market valuation on 1983 net income	$60.78	$60.78	$74.43	$113.75	$191.75	$150.15	$68.25	$45.50	$162.50

(1) If SSS is awarded the contract for eight power plants in the first quarter of 1983, Hutton believes a $75–$80 million valuation can be defended assuming 1983 revenues and earnings (after entered income from an April 4 offering) of $30 million and $2.29 million, respectively.

(2) Under current market conditions, Hutton believes that investors capitalize common stocks at a P/E based upon forecasted earnings of 65% of a company's expected sustainable growth rate.

EXHIBIT 4 *(continued)*

Comparative Pricing Analysis: Selected Technology Company Initial Public Offerings

Company	Lee Data Corporation	PAR Technology	ARGOSystems	Dionex Corporation	Quantum Corporation	Mogem Systems, Inc.
Shares filed (000)	2,207	750	606	1,200	1,700	1,290
Shares offered (000)	2,607	900	801	1,400	2,500	1,500
IPO filing date	10-18-82	10-29-82	10-27-82	11-02-82	11-09-82	11-05-82
IPO effective date	11-18-82	12-03-82	12-02-82	12-07-82	12-10-82	12-10-82
Fiscal year end	03-31-82	12-31-81	06-30-82	06-30-82	03-31-82	03-31-82
Latest 12 months for IPO	09-30-82	09-30-82	10-01-82	09-30-82	10-02-82	09-30-82
Size data: ($000)						
Revenues (LTM)	$ 29,380	$ 27,574	$ 32,187	$ 16,888	$ 29,769	$ 12,896
Pretax income—margin	9,068-30.9%	7,148-25.9%	4,329-13.4%	3,648-21.6%	6,509-21.9%	3,358-26.0%
Net income (a)—margin	5,725-19.5%	4,162-15.1%	2,462- 7.6%	1,934-11.5%	4,114-13.8%	2,316-18.0%
EPS (LTM)	$ .47	$ .59	$ 1.08	$ .55	$ 1.02	$ .49
Projected EPS (next fiscal yr.)	1.40	1.00	1.40	.65	1.00	.75

R&D expenses—% of revenues	$ 1,606-5.5%	$ 749-2.9%	$ 1,146-3.6% (c)	$ 1,078-6.4%	$ 2,345-7.9%	$ 944-7.3%
Tangible book value	13,736	7,392	9,442	7,752	13,981	1,731

Market Data:

Pro forma shares outstanding (000)	12,332	7,475	3,064	4,032	8,871	5,601
Filing price range	$14.00-16.00	$ 14-17	$ 16-18	$ 14-16	$ 15-17	$ 15-18
P/E range—LTM EPS	30.0x-34.0x	23.7x-28.8x	14.8x-16.7x	25.5x-29.1x	14.7x-16.7x	30.6x-36.7x
P/E range—projected EPS	10.0x-11.4x	14.0x-17.0x	11.4x-12.9x	21.5x-24.6x	15.0x-17.0x	20.0x-24.0x
Pro forma market value ($MM)	$167.0-190.9	$104.7-127.1	$49.0-55.2	$56.4-64.5	$133.1-150.8	$94.0-100.8
Offering price	$ 19.00	$ 20.00	$ 21.50	$ 19.00	$ 20.50	$ 21.00
P/E—LTM EPS	40.4x	33.9x	19.9x	34.5x	20.1x	42.9x
P/E—projected EPS	13.6x	20.0x	15.4x	29.2x	20.5x	28.0x
Pro forma market value ($MM)	$ 234.3	$ 149.5	$ 65.9	$ 76.6	$ 181.9	$ 117.6

NASDAQ Industrial Index:

On filing date	233.26	242.89	243.12	250.00	265.43	261.88
On pricing date	262.34	276.28	274.92	279.19	277.45	277.45
Percent change	12.47%	13.75%	13.08%	11.68%	4.53%	5.95%

EXHIBIT 4 (continued)
Comparative Pricing Analysis: Selected Technology Company Initial Public Offerings

Company	Lee Data Corporation	PAR Technology	ARGOSystems	Dionex Corporation	Quantum Corporation	Mogem Systems, Inc.
Growth Data:						
Earnings per share (a)						
LTM	$ .47	$ .59	$ 1.08	$ .55	$ 1.02	$ .49
1 year prior	.14	.41	.85	.58	.03	.24
2 years prior	(.07)	.10	.63	.43	(1.50)	.22
3 years prior	(.25)	.07	.46	.36	—	(.21)
4 years prior	—	.04	.55	.27	—	—
Compound growth rate	NMF	105.0%	22.9%	24.3%	NMF	NMF
Revenue/net income ($MM) (a)						
LTM	$ 29.4/$5.7	$ 27.6/4.2	$ 32.2/2.5	$ 16.9/1.9	$ 29.8/4.1	$ 12.9/2.3
1 year prior	13.7/ 2.0	21.4/2.9	28.1/1.9	16.0/2.0	13.7/0.2	8.3/1.1
2 years prior	6.7/(0.4)	10.3/0.7	20.9/1.3	12.0/1.4	—/—	3.4/0.6
3 years prior	0.6/(1.4)	7.6/0.4	19.2/0.9	10.7/1.2	—/—	0.6/(0.6)
4 years prior	—/—	6.1/0.2	17.0/1.0	8.7/0.9	—/—	—/(0.8)
Compound growth rate	NMF	49.8%/112.6%	21.6%/32.3%	22.5%/25.7%	235.0%/NMF	220.0%/NMF

Line of Business:

Designs, manufactures, markets and services multifunction interactive terminal systems.	Point-of-sale systems for restaurants, software systems for gov't/ military.	Electronic reconnaissance systems which acquire and analyze radar and military communications signals.	Develops, manufactures and markets ion chromatography.	Designs, manufactures and markets rigid disk drives based on Winchester technology.	Integrated line of standard banking applications software programs.

(E)—Estimate
(a)—From continuing operations before extraordinary items.
(b)—Eight month financial figures.
(c)—Excludes $8,000,000 of customer-funded research and development.
LTM = Last twelve months.
NMF = Not meaningful figure.

755

EXHIBIT 4   *(continued)* 1982 Initial Public Offerings*: Growth and Business Information *(July–December)*

Date	Issuer	Shares (000s)	Offering Price	Total Dollar Amount (000s)	Latest 12 Months Net Sales (000s)	Net Income (000s)(1)
07-08	Tera Corp.	2,500	$16.00	$ 40,000	$ 31,015	$5,258
07-13	Ryan's Family Steak Houses	475	9.25	4,394	8,157	718
07-20	Super Sky International	640	13.00	8,320	27,088	3,199
07-21	Atlantic Southeast Airlines	860	6.50	5,590	9,743	1,531
07-29	CPI Corp.	750	14.00	10,500	108,899	5,302
08-05	Foster Medical	2,300	13.75	31,625	122,814	(1,376)
08-11	Environmental Testing	1,000	5.00	5,000	556(9)	867(9)
08-17	Electronic Mail Corp.	800	6.25	5,000	–(8)	–(8)
08-20	Universal Money Centers	600	5.00	3,000	NA	NA
08-26	Vicorp Restaurants	900	10.25	9,225	37,571	2,021
09-01	Family Entertainment Centers	475	10.50	4,988	5,212	(296)
09-02	North Fork Bancorp.	500	17.50	8,750	6,437	1,655
09-09	Electronic Theatre Rest.	610	8.25	5,033	5,935	(1,929)
09-15	Electronics Corp. of Israel	720	11.25	8,100	11,669	1,936
09-23	Psych Systems	700	5.00	3,500	3,429	199
09-29	Genex Corp.	2,000	9.50	19,000	5,154	(2.38)
09-29	On-Line Software	800	15.00	12,000	14,859	2,034
09-29	Rodime	1,000	8.00	8,000	4,294(10)	611(10)
10-07	TANO	515	9.25	4,764	29,888	947
10-13	Pacific Express Holding	1,300	5.00	6,500	12,291	(10,251)
10-14	University Federal Savings	400	12.00	4,800	31,376	(2,059)
10-15	Gott	635	10.75	6,826	28,623	1,633
10-18	InteCom Inc.	2,500	20.00	50,000	17,652	(3,504)
10-26	Sizzler Restaurants	900	17.00	15,300	120,927	3,376
10-27	Fidelity Federal S&L	2,798	10.00	27,976	189,321	(30,198)
10-29	Merrimac Industries	550	7.00	3,850	10,376	927
11-02	Systems & Computer Technology	2,580	16.50	42,570	26,792	3,225
11-04	Aaron Rents	1,000	15.50	15,500	52,724	4,030
11-04	Altos Computer Systems	3,300	21.00	69,300	57,351	6,360
11-04	Americana Hotels & Realty Trust	5,000	20.00	100,000	83,692	7,372
11-09	Washington Federal S&L	954	11.75	11,208	82,465	(26,701)
11-16	Taco Viva	400	9.00	3,600	12,736	605
11-18	Lee Data	2,607	19.00	49,535	29,380	5,040
11-26	Triangle Microwave, Inc.	696	6.25	4,350	4,474	799
12-01	Patient Technology, Inc.	575	6.75	3,881	676(11)	17(11)
12-01	Quality Systems, Inc.	600	17.00	10,200	8,919	948
12-02	ARGOSystems	801	21.50	17,213	32,187	2,462
12-03	PAR Technology Corp.	900	20.00	18,000	27,574	4,162

*Value of $3.0 million or more, offering price of $5.00 or more.
(1) From continuing operations before extraordinary items.
(2) Percentage difference between latest interim figure and the corresponding figure one year earlier.
(3) Based on historical E.P.S. figures. Latest 12 months.
(4) Actual book value prior to offer.
(5) Based on data for four years.
(6) Based on data for three years.
(7) Based on data for two years.
(8) Insufficient or no prior operating history.

EXHIBIT 4   (*continued*) 1982 Initial Public Offerings*: Growth and
Business Information (*July–December*)

Five Year Growth Rates				Latest 12 Mos.			
Sales		Net Income (1)				Price/	
Fiscal Year	Latest Interim (2)	Fiscal Year	Latest Interim (2)	EPS	P/E (3)	Book (4)	Business Lines
57.2(5)	42.5	58.8	43.4	$ 0.66	24.2x	8.5x	Computer software/sys.
51.4(6)	5.9	50.7(6)	41.9	0.90	10.3x	4.7x	Operates restaurants
50.0	37.0	69.0	58.7	1.10	11.8x	3.8x	Designs & installs skylights
352.2(7)	187.7	44.2(7)	274.4	0.99	6.6x	5.2x	Regional airline
33.7(7)	31.6	102.1	52.5	1.62	8.6x	4.4x	Portrait photo studios, cleaning
11.5(6)	21.6	NA	NMF	(0.69)	NMF	NMF	Distributes medical supplies
NA	NA	NA	NA	(0.43)	NMF	6.7x	Management of chemical wastes
–(8)	–(8)	–(8)	–(8)	–(8)	NMF	NMF	Communications mgt. & special info. processing
NA	NA	NA	NA	NA	NA	NA	Markets automatic tellers
14.0	18.2	49.0	89.7	1.01	10.1x	4.6x	Operates & franchises restaurants
NMF	311.5	NMF	NMF	(0.29)	NMF	3.7x	Operates restaurants
17.4	50.5	33.0	55.0	3.93	4.5x	1.0x	Bank holding company
NMF	449.5	NMF	NMF	(0.55)	NMF	7.8x	Operates restaurants
57.0	36.8	149.2	103.0	1.09	10.3x	3.0x	Telecommunications equip.
NMF	225.0	NMF	NMF	0.29	17.2x	2.4x	Patient test equip.
495.8	104.3	NMF	NMF	(0.25)	NMF	3.7x	Genetic engineering
52.9	42.3	149.8	72.6	.67	22.4x	6.4x	IBM-compatible software
NMF	NMF	NMF	NMF	.16	50.0x	4.4x	5¼" Winchester disk drives
26.6	47.0	34.7	140.3	1.11	8.3x	1.7x	Process control systems
135.0	438.7	NMF	NMF	(22.99)	NMF	NMF	Jet service between S.F. & L.A.
20.0	9.3	NMF	NMF	(2.92)	NMF	0.4x	Savings & loan
28.5	29.2	40.5	17.0	1.42	7.6x	3.0x	Consumer plastic products
NMF	NMF	NMF	NMF	(0.32)	NMF	42.6x	Large PBX phone systems
19.5	25.9	3.3	178.2	1.55	10.9x	1.0x	Steakhouse restaurants
28.1	6.5	NMF	NMF	(7.02)	NMF	.3x	Savings & loan
25.2	.8	28.8	367.8	.81	8.6x	2.2x	Signal processing systems-for defense
33.3	54.0	39.9	170.5	.29	55.0x	22.6x	Software for gov't./universities
32.3	14.7	24.2	40.9	1.21	12.8x	1.3x	MFG/rent/sell furniture
428.7	59.7	396.0	53.0	.55	38.2x	16.5x	Multiterminal microcomputer system
8.5	NMF	29.0	NMF	3.08	8.6x	1.1x	Real estate investment trust
9.7	8.3	NMF	NMF	(7.08)	NMF	.6x	Savings & loan
37.6	17.9	31.9	111.0	.52	17.3x	4.1x	Fast-service Mexican restaurants
365.4(6)	326.7	NMF	1,984.4	.47	40.4x	12.8x	Multifunct. interactive term. systems
NA	94.4	NA	286.0	.53	11.8x	7.2x	Microwave components
NA	NA	NA	NA	.02	NMF	21.8x	Electronic medical instruments
85.2	66.9	80.7	175.5	.52	32.7x	15.9x	Information systems for dentists
24.1	79.2	61.3	207.9	1.08	19.9x	4.8x	Electronic reconnaisance systems
53.3	42.5	106.9	68.9	.58	34.5x	18.9x	P.O.S. systems: defense/ software

NA = Not applicable.
NMF = Not meaningful figure.

(9) For the period from 12-27-81 through 4-24-82.
(10) Operating data for the 40 weeks ended July 3, 1982.
(11) For eight months ended Aug. 31, 1982.

EXHIBIT 4 (continued)

Date	Issuer	Shares (000s)	Offering Price	Total Dollar Amount (000s)	Gross Spread $	Gross Spread %	Management	Under-writing	Selling	EFH Commission (100 shares)	Selling Concession EFH Comm.	Aggregate Underwriting (100 shares)
07-08	Tera Corp.	2,500	16.00	40,000	1.04	6.50	.20	.19	.65	.47	1.38x	475
07-13	Ryan's Family Steak Houses	475	9.25	4,394	.79	8.50	.18	.16	.45	.35	1.29x	76
07-20	Super Sky International	640	13.00	8,320	.98	7.50	.20	.205	.57	.42	1.36x	131
07-21	Atlantic Southeast Airlines	860	6.50	5,590	.52	8.00	.08	.11	.33	.29	1.14x	95
07-29	CPI Corp.	750	14.00	10,500	1.00	7.14	.20	.25	.55	.43	1.28x	188
08-05	Foster Medical	2,300	13.75	31,625	.98	7.13	.20	.20	.58	.43	1.35x	460
08-11	Environmental Testing	1,000	5.00	5,000	.42	8.40	.08	.08	.26	.25	1.04x	80
08-17	Electronic Mail Corp.	800	6.25	5,000	.63	10.00	NA	NA	NA	.28	NA	NA
08-20	Universal Money Centers	600	5.00	3,000	.50	10.00	NA	NA	NA	.25	NA	NA
08-26	Vicorp Restaurants	900	10.25	9,225	.70	6.83	.14	.14	.42	.37	1.14x	126
09-01	Family Entertainment Centers	475	10.50	4,988	.84	8.00	.17	.17	.50	.37	1.35x	81
09-02	North Fork Bancorp.	500	17.50	8,750	1.23	7.03	NA	NA	.75	.50	1.50x	NA
09-09	Electronic Theatre Rest.	610	8.25	5,033	.70	8.49	.14	.19	.37	.31	1.19x	116
09-15	Electronics Corp. of Israel	720	11.25	8,100	.82	7.29	.22	.18	.42	.37	1.14x	130
09-23	Psych Systems	700	5.00	3,500	.50	10.00	.27	(1)	.23	.25	0.92x	189
09-29	Genex Corp.	2,000	9.50	19,000	.75	7.89	.15	.15	.45	.37	1.20x	300
09-29	On-Line Software	800	15.00	12,000	1.08	7.20	.22	.28	.58	.44	1.33x	224
09-29	Rodime	1,000	8.00	8,000	.56	7.00	.11	.15	.30	.31	0.97x	150

Date	Company										
10-07	TANO	515	9.25	4,764	.74	8.00	.14	.20	.40	.37	1.07x	103
10-13	Pacific Express Holding	1,300	5.00	6,500	.43	8.50	.09	.085	.25	.25	1.00x	111
10-14	University Federal Savings	400	12.00	4,800	.96	8.00	.36	(1)	.60	.37	1.60x	76
10-15	Gott	635	10.75	6,826	.86	8.00	.19	.17	.50	.37	1.33x	108
10-18	InteCom Inc.	2,500	20.00	50,000	1.35	6.80	.30	.35	.70	.55	1.27x	875
10-26	Sizzler Restaurants	900	17.00	15,300	1.19	7.00	.24	.30	.65	.50	1.30x	270
10-27	Fidelity Federal S&L	2,798	10.00	27,976	.72	7.20	.14	.18	.40	.37	1.07x	504
10-29	Merrimac Industries	550	7.00	3,850	.56	8.00	.12	.16	.28	.31	.90x	88
11-02	Systems & Computers Technology	2,580	16.50	42,570	1.16	7.03	.23	.30	.63	.50	1.26x	774
11-04	Aaron Rents	1,000	15.50	15,500	1.08	6.97	.22	.26	.60	.44	1.36x	260
11-04	Altos Computer Systems	3,300	21.00	69,300	1.47	7.00	.30	.37	.80	.56	1.43x	1,221
11-04	Americana Hotels & Realty Trust	5,000	20.00	100,000	1.60	8.00	.40	.20	1.00	.56	1.79x	1,000
11-09	Washington Federal S&L	954	11.75	11,208	.82	6.98	.17	.20	.45	.37	1.20x	191
11-16	Taco Viva	400	9.00	3,600	.76	8.44	.15	.17	.44	.31	1.42x	124
11-18	Lee Data	2,607	19.00	49,535	1.33	7.00	.27	.31	.75	.50	1.50x	808
11-26	Triangle Microwave, Inc.	696	6.25	4,350	.63	10.00	.25	(1)	.37	.25	1.48x	NA
12-01	Patient Technology, Inc.	575	6.75	3,881	.68	10.00	.37	(1)	.30	.25	1.20x	NA
12-01	Quality Systems, Inc.	600	17.00	10,200	1.25	7.35	.25	.30	.70	.50	1.40x	180
12-02	ARGOSystems	801	21.50	17,213	1.52	7.07	.30	.32	.90	.56	1.61x	256
12-03	PAR Technology Corp.	900	20.00	18,000	1.45	7.25	.29	.29	.87	.56	1.55x	261

*Value of $3 million or more, offering price of $5 or more.
(1) Combined with management fee because issue was not syndicated.

EXHIBIT 4 (concluded)

1982 Initial Public Offerings*: Gross Spread Information (July–December)

Date	Issuer	Shares (000s)	Offering Price	Total Dollar Amount (000's)	Primary as % of Shares Offered	Dilution (%)(1)	1 Day after Offer(2)	% Change	1 Week after Offer(2)	% Change	Stock Symbol
07-09	Tera Corp.	2,500	16.00	40,000	50.0	13.6	16.00	—	16.13	0.8	TRRA
07-13	Ryan's Family Steak Houses	475	9.25	4,394	86.6	33.9	10.00	8.1	10.25	10.8	RYAN
07-20	Super Sky International	640	13.00	8,320	0.0	0.0	13.00	—	13.25	1.9	SSKY
07-21	Atlantic Southeast Airlines	860	6.50	5,590	92.5	32.7	6.25	(3.8)	6.00	(7.7)	ASAI
07-29	CPI Corp.	750	14.00	10,500	56.7	11.5	13.75	(1.8)	13.75	(1.8)	CPIC
08-05	Foster Medical	2,300	13.75	31,625	100.0	45.6	13.25	(*3.6)	13.00	(5.5)	FMED
08-11	Environmental Testing	1,000	5.00	5,000	100.0	33.3	4.75	(5.0)	4.50	(10.0)	ETCC
08-17	Electronic Mail Corp.	800	6.25	5,000	100.0	50.0	6.25	—	6.25	—	EMCA
08-20	Universal Money Centers	600	5.00	3,000	100.0	NA	NA	NA	5.00	—	UMCI
08-26	Vicorp Restaurants	900	10.25	9,225	44.4	16.7	10.88	6.1	10.63	3.7	VRES
09-01	Family Entertainment Centers	475	10.50	4,988	70.6	21.5	10.75	2.4	9.75	(7.1)	FMLY
09-02	North Fork Bancorp.	500	17.50	8,750	100.0	54.3	17.50	—	17.50	—	NFBC
09-09	Electronic Theatre Rest.	610	8.25	5,033	100.0	21.7	8.25	—	8.00	(3.0)	ETRC
09-15	Electronics Corp. of Israel	720	11.25	8,100	93.1	23.5	12.00	6.7	13.25	17.8	ECILF
09-23	Psych Systems	700	5.00	3,500	100.0	49.8	6.25	25.0	6.25	25.0	PSYC
09-29	Genex Corp.	2,000	9.50	19,000	100.0	17.3	8.88	(6.6)	8.00	(5.8)	GNEX
09-29	On-Line Software	800	15.00	12,000	62.5	14.1	15.25	1.7	16.13	7.5	OSII
09-29	Rodime	1,000	8.00	8,000	100.0	20.2	7.75	(3.1)	8.25	3.1	RODMY
10-07	TANO	515	9.25	4,764	77.7	30.2	9.25	—	9.62	4.0	TANO

Date	Company		Shares (000)	%					%	Symbol
10-13	Pacific Express Holding	5.00	1,300	100.0	41.6	NA	NA	3.75	(25.0)	PXXP
10-14	University Federal Savings	12.00	400	100.0	77.1	13.50	12.5	13.00	8.3	UFSL
10-15	Gott	10.75	635	86.6	29.9	13.00	21.0	13.75	27.9	GOTT
10-18	InteCom Inc.	20.00	2,500	66.4	12.1	22.00	10.0	25.63	28.1	INCM
10-26	Sizzler Restaurants	17.00	900	100.0	27.3	17.00	—	20.00	17.6	SIZZ
10-27	Fidelity Federal S&L	10.00	2,798	100.0	0.0	11.00	10.0	12.75	27.5	FFED
10-29	Merrimac Industries	7.00	550	63.0	23.2	8.75	25.0	8.25	17.9	MMAC
11-02	Systems & Computers Technology	16.50	2,580	71.4	14.4	NA	NA	20.88	26.5	SCTC
11-04	Aaron Rents	15.50	1,000	15.0	4.0	20.75	33.9	21.50	38.7	ARON
11-04	Altos Computer Systems	21.00	3,300	82.0	19.1	29.75	41.7	31.75	51.9	ALTO
11-04	Americana Hotels & Realty Trust	20.00	5,000	100.0	0.0	21.25	6.3	21.00	5.0	AHRC
11-09	Washington Federal S&L	11.75	954	100.0	0.0	19.00	61.7	18.00	53.2	WFSL
11-16	Taco Viva	9.00	400	56.3	15.8	10.75	19.4	9.50	5.6	TVIV
11-18	Lee Data	19.00	2,607	69.0	14.6	28.25	48.7	28.00	47.4	LEDA
11-26	Triangle Microwave, Inc.	6.25	696	93.1	30.0	8.50	36.0	11.00	76.0	TRMW
12-01	Patient Technology, Inc.	6.75	575	100.0	35.9	8.75	29.6	9.00	33.3	PTIX
12-01	Quality Systems, Inc.	17.00	600	51.7	14.5	18.25	7.4	20.75	22.1	QSII
12-02	ARGOSystems	21.50	801	81.1	21.2	33.25	54.7	32.50	51.2	ARGI
12-03	PAR Technology Corp.	20.00	900	53.1	6.5	27.50	37.5	—	—	PARR

*Value of $3.0 million or more, offering price of $5.00 or more.
NA Not available
(1) Primary shares as a percent of shares outstanding after the offer.
(2) OTC stocks show bid price.

EXHIBIT 5   Alex Brown Proposal (entire proposal attached)

January 13, 1983

Mr. Vincent S. Lamb, Jr.
President
Scientific Systems Services, Inc.
2000 Commerce Drive
Melbourne, Florida 32901

Dear Vince:
    It was a pleasure to meet with you and Mike at your office. Don and Al very much enjoyed meeting with you, Pat, and Howard in Boston. We continue to be impressed by the Scientific Systems Services, Inc. (Triple S) story and are convinced that a public offering of Triple S securities will be well received by the investment community.
    To assist you in finalizing decisions regarding the offering, we have outlined below our preliminary conclusions regarding the offering, structure and timing, and Triple S's valuation.

Structure
    We understand that an offering of $12 million is being contemplated, and that the offering will consist of $8 million of primary stock and $4 million of secondary stock. Such an offering could be readily accomplished.

Valuation
    Our valuation of Triple S is based upon our understanding of its business, current market environment, and our assumption of projected Triple S's financial performance. Currently, we believe that your 1982 performance when finalized will show revenues of $15.7 million and net income of just under $1 million. We believe that 1983 projections call for approximately 60 percent revenue growth to a total of $25 million in revenues and $1.5 million of net income. We believe that this net income figure should be increased to reflect the net income received from the proceeds of the offering. Conservatively, we feel that the Company could estimate receiving net proceeds of $7.2 million after all deal costs and that an 8 percent pretax return could be realized on these funds for nine months of the year. Hence, we believe the offering would add at least $250,000 to net income for 1983. We estimate Triple S's market value in the initial public offering to be approximately $45 million. This valuation represents a multiple of approximately 26 times expected 1983 net income. Initial public offerings in today's market are generally being priced at a modest discount to market, although the market is currently particularly receptive to new issues even to the point of some buyers saying that "new is better." Therefore, for your planning purposes, we would estimate that the initial public offering would be priced at approximately 25 × 1983 expected earnings and would trade at approximately 26 × expected 1983 net income. The 25–26 × valuation range is one which we consider to be very supportable. It is possible, however, that Triple S could attain an even higher market value if the market remains strong and if the road show marketing effort is particularly well received.

EXHIBIT 5   *(continued)*

In our phone conversation, Vince, you asked about the methodology which we use to determine valuations. As we have discussed, Alex. Brown looks at market conditions, your business, and overlays these factors on prices received by publicly-traded comparable companies. These comparable companies include a large number of software and systems companies as well as turnkey systems companies. On average, this group of companies, which includes ASK, MSA, Cullinane, Computer Associates, Pansophic, Tera, and PMS, is trading at approximately 26× expected 1983 net income.

Timing
Work on the offering should begin as soon as possible. Prompt action is desirable in order to capitalize on the existing strong market and to achieve maximum visibility for Triple S by entering the market ahead of the numerous filings that are expected to occur when year-end results are available.

Prospectus preparation and all legal work can be accomplished within a 4–5 week period. The first step of the process should be an all hands meeting (including underwriters and their counsel, Triple S and its counsel and auditors) during which a time and responsibility schedule is agreed upon. Alex. Brown's involvement should facilitate this entire process as a result of our considerable experience in writing computer service prospectuses and our knowledge of your Company.

Expenses
If Triple S's initial public offering is in the $12 million range, we estimate that the underwriting spread will not exceed 7.5 percent. Other expenses, consisting of printing costs, Company counsel and filing fees should total approximately $175,000. Expenses of the underwriters, including underwriters' counsel fees and their travel expenses, are borne by the underwriters.

Selection of Managing Underwriter
Alex. Brown is uniquely qualified to serve as investment banker and lead underwriter to Triple S. Our firm's emphasis has always been to concentrate our resources on after-market support and sponsorship, particularly in the areas of research, market-making and knowledgeable institutional and retail sales support. This emphasis, combined with our strategy of focusing on specific markets within the high technology sector, has allowed Alex. Brown to achieve the leading position within its chosen markets. As you know, Alex. Brown is considered to be the leading investment banker to the computer services industry.

The cornerstone of our work in the computer services industry is our monthly research product, published by a team headed by Al Berkeley. This monthly research, sent out to over 6,000 investors, serves to educate the financial community regarding computer services, industry trends, and individual companies. Further, Alex. Brown sponsors the annual Computer Services Seminar where you spoke. In 1982 over 50 companies spoke at the seminar, addressing an audience of over 500 institutional investors.

EXHIBIT 5   *(continued)*

You have mentioned that you might utilize two managing underwriters for Triple S's initial public offering. Alex. Brown would be pleased to work jointly with any of the underwriters which you have mentioned. Given our considerable knowledge of the Company and our leadership position in computer services, we are uniquely qualified to serve as Triple S's lead or book-running manager.

We hope that this letter addresses all of your questions plus conveys our enthusiasm for Triple S. Please feel free to call me, Don Hebb, or Al Berkeley if there are additional questions which we may answer. We look forward to hearing from you.

Very truly yours,

Beverly L. Wright

Schedule for Public Offering of Shares of Common Stock

January 1983							February 1983							March 1983						
S	M	T	W	T	F	S	S	M	T	W	T	F	S	S	M	T	W	T	F	S
						1			1	2	3	4	5			1	2	3	4	5
2	3	4	5	6	7	8	6	7	8	9	10	11	12	6	7	8	9	10	11	12
9	10	11	12	13	14	15	13	14	15	16	17	18	19	13	14	15	16	17	18	19
16	17	18	19	20	21	22	20	21	22	23	24	25	26	20	21	22	23	24	25	26
23	24	25	26	27	28	29	27	28						27	28	29	30	31		
30	31																			

CO	Scientific Systems Services, Inc.
U	Alex. Brown & Sons
CC	Peirsol, Boroughs, Grimm & Bennett
UC	Piper & Marbury
CA	Deloitte, Haskins & Sells
P	Printer

EXHIBIT 5 *(concluded)*

Date	Undertaking	Responsibility
January 24, 1983	Prepare and distribute time schedule and team list.	U
	Commence preparation of registration statement and O & D questionnaries; consult SEC.	CC
	Select printer.	CO
	Prepare necessary board of directors resolutions.	CC
	Commence preparation of underwriting documents and Blue Sky filings.	UC
	Deliver draft of registration statement to all parties.	CC
February 2 and 3	Meeting of team to revise draft.	All
February 5	Send out draft to team.	CC
February 9 and 10	Team meets to revise draft and review underwriting agreements, syndicate list, comfort letter.	All
February 11	Draft of all documents to printer.	CC
February 14	Printed draft to team.	P
February 16 and 17	Meet at printer's for final review of drafts.	All
February 18	File registration statement with SEC and NASD.	All
	Press release.	CO
	Syndicate invitations.	U
	Blue Sky filings.	UC
Week of March 7	Road show; due diligence meetings.	CO, U
March 16	Receive SEC comments. Team available to draft response to SEC comments.	CC
March 17 and 18	Meet at printer's to review SEC comments, revise registration statement and refile.	All
March 21	Negotiate price and spread.	CO, U
March 22	Underwriting agreement signed.	CO, U
	Price amendment filed.	CO
	Registration statement declared effective.	CO, U
	Comfort letter delivered.	CA
	Blue Sky clearances received.	UC
	Stock released for sale.	U
	Tombstone released for publication.	U
	Press release.	CO
March 28	Preclosing.	CO, U, CC, UC
March 29	Closing.	CO, U, CC, UC

EXHIBIT 6 1982 Stock Market Performance

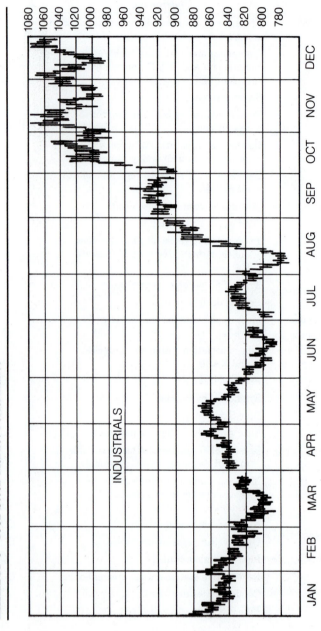

Valerie Morgan

Valerie Morgan hung up the phone with a sigh.

> This issue comes up regularly. We have to decide on whether or not to close the magazine for the month. The salespeople in advertising have sold 30 pages of ads for the month and have four more pages "on the fence." If we could wait until tomorrow, they think they could bring more ad revenues in. Editorial needs to know *now*, because we have a strict 60–40 split between editorial and ads. If there are more ad pages, then they need more articles. Production has only a few days to lay out, typeset, and produce the entire publication. If we make a change after we've started, it will involve a full day of work to change everything around again.
>
> I'm really torn when these issues come up. I feel as though I should be doing other things in the organization. I don't like being in the middle of this kind of conflict. I don't have time for the creative, big-picture issues I'm good at. I should be working on developing new product concepts, but I just don't have the time. Yet, I *like* being involved. Isn't that my job?

BACKGROUND

Morgan Publications (MP) was founded by Valerie Morgan in 1979 to publish *Human Resource News,* aimed at informing human resource professionals of the wide variety of courses and seminars available in all aspects of corporate training for human resource professionals. In

This case was prepared by James Z. Turner under the direction of Howard H. Stevenson.

1981, Morgan began *Computer Training,* a similar publication aimed specifically at personnel managers. Then in 1985, the firm began publishing *End-User Computing,* aimed at all information processing professionals. In addition, Morgan sponsored conferences for professionals in these various fields. By 1986, the firm had $3.2 million in revenues and a healthy profit of nearly $500,000.

VALERIE MORGAN

Valerie described the events that led up to her founding of Morgan Publications. (In addition, see Exhibit 1 for chronological outline.)

> I received my BA in Russian from Barnard College and a master's in education from Harvard. At the age of 21, I was teaching Russian, French, and some German back at my old high school. Why did I study Russian in college? I read *War and Peace* and thought it was romantic. I loved teaching, and I did it for five years. I learned about the bureaucracy of the school system. Bureaucracy is a major force in this world. For example, I tried to eliminate grades. You can imagine how that went over.

In a few years, Valerie became disillusioned with teaching:

> I was 25 and I realized that I was getting a year older every September, but the kids were the same age. After five years of teaching, they gave me two coffee cups as a reward—I had had enough.
>
> My family was upset. "Why do you want to quit your job when you have tenure?" they asked. Well, that's *exactly* why I wanted to quit—tenure had boxed me in even more and my desire to get out became stronger.

For the next year, Valerie decided to have some fun. She cashed in her teacher's pension fund and her old savings bonds. She took a few courses at Harvard and Boston University, but she soon began to run out of money.

> I decided to start a business. I paid $125 to incorporate and started with two guys who soon dropped out. I was going to teach languages to business people. I had never done this before; but providing the actual service is the least of the problems. Selling, getting money, and so forth is more important and harder to do. A great product is irrelevant if you can't support it with the other functions. Selling a service was painful. It hurt. What did I know? I was 25 years old. My late father was an attorney, and he would give me a name to get me in the door. But it was still awful. The closest thing to selling I had done was pushing Girl Scout cookies. If you can't do it, then you stop. But I found out I could do it.

Valerie got her first contract to teach languages at Raytheon. She dropped everything to teach this course, but when it ended she had nothing again and, she said, she "was starving."

That's how I learned. I had no formal training. I followed each spider web thread. I learned that teaching in business is called training. I learned that it's the largest industry in the world—training is needed by clients in all areas of business, from the smallest manufacturing firms to the largest corporate clients. I joined the local chapter of the American Society for Training and Development (AST&D) and discovered I was a consultant, so I doubled my fees. I volunteered for everything and got extremely involved. It gave me credibility, and I could also find people to sell to. I had no credentials, so this was important for me.

From 1974 to 1977, management training was a glamorous field. Soft "people" skills were all the rage. I thought, why not be a management trainer? But who would hire me? I had never been a manager or a management trainer. So, I made a deal with an experienced management trainer. I apprenticed myself. I was good in curriculum design, and he was good in management training and had the contacts. I made the deal and worked for two years. I also kept my language stuff going so that I could eat. Suddenly, I was well known. I had made something out of nothing—I had discovered the secret of marketing!

Toward the end of this period, I stopped teaching languages altogether. I learned that U.S. businessmen didn't really want to learn French so as to be able to conduct business in French, and that the French were perfectly willing to conduct business in English anyway. So, I taught the cultural aspects—teaching them to do something right. You know, the United States thinks it owns the world and that the rest of humanity proceeds as dictated by the United States. I had to get people to recognize that their prejudices have a huge effect on how they do business. Good salespeople don't assume that every customer is the same. I guess a lot of people don't want to hear that, because I was not rehired in a number of cases.

By 1979, Valerie was restless. Her father had warned her against "just selling time and not building any value," and she agreed that this was exactly what she was doing. She was also tired of having to put on a performance every time she sold.

I got together with a fellow trainer, Ken Dryden, and we went into his office and covered the walls with chart paper. Then we fantasized about what we wanted to do. I put down *figure skating rink* because I liked figure skating. He put down *sailboat marina* because he liked sailing. Then we thought of buying the Mariott hotel and converting it into a management training center. On the second day, we returned to the office and said, "What's feasible?" Someone had put newspapers/publishing up there. . . . So we did that for all the wrong reasons. We knew a lot about training so we thought we could apprentice on a training newspaper and then start ones on figure skating and sailboat marinas—our real loves.

I knew nothing about publishing, but ignorance should never be a reason for not doing something. There was a magazine out then called *AD EAST*. I thought it was good, so I called them up to find out how they did it. I didn't know that publishing is in the top five for start-up failures—95 percent of publishing companies fail in their first 18 months. It was good that I didn't know. It's okay to fail, but it only would have made me worry more. Basically, I copied *AD EAST*. I got their printer and editor.

Then all I needed was money. We were going to sell ads and give the paper away for free. I was going to be the saleswoman. I did the income statement, the balance sheet, and the cash flows using nothing but common sense—I had never done it before.

We were undercapitalized, and I quickly learned what it means to be in hock all the time. Before that, I thought it was criminal to be in debt. When I was studying at Harvard for my master's, I really squeaked by to save on government loans. They were at 3 percent, and half of them were forgiven anyway because I went and taught! I had a huge shift in thinking when I went into business.

We decided that we needed $40,000 to start, so I went to the banks. My partner was not a businessman and simply didn't want to get involved. He didn't like cash flows. In those days, I thought good clothes were pressed cords and a jacket. No one would talk to me. My father finally got me into a bank, and this old loan officer looked at me and said, "Are you sure you want to do this, dear?" But I had the presentation printed up, and it looked very official. He looked at it and said, "Maybe you should talk to one of the younger guys." Finally, after three months of talking, the bank gave me the full amount unsecured.

We were in business.

A BRIEF HISTORY

Following the firm's founding in 1979, growth was slow and MP was a relatively unprofitable company. They had only one publication, *Human Resource News*. Advertisers viewed *HRN* as a small, regional, and unproven advertising vehicle, so they were unwilling to pay rates sufficient to cover costs. Valerie described the situation:

I didn't understand the notion of *break-even*. I had run the cash flows before starting the company. I had spent a lot of time understanding the costs in detail, but when it came to income, I just made up the sales numbers I needed to make money. Then, I set my rates at a level I thought was sufficient to generate that income. I was way off. I was naive enough to think that people would automatically want to buy ads in my magazine.

Originally, this was just a publishing company. At first, that was all I was going to do, but it didn't turn out that way.

By 1980, I had a newspaper on my hands that wasn't working. The decision to hold the first conference was strictly a cash flow move. I was talking to some friends of mine in the Boston area who were involved with the computer industry and high tech. I had helped organize a couple of conferences before, so when they suggested that I hold a computer conference, I said why not? A conference has one big advantage over a magazine. Planning for a conference involves a one-time, up front investment so you know exactly how much you are going to lose even if no one comes to it. A publication is far more uncertain—you might have to wait a year before you known how it will turn out financially, how much money you stand to lose.

In December of 1980, I decided to hold the first conference hoping that it would turn the company around. It was very successful. I didn't know it before the fact, but in retrospect, I found out that conferences make a very good business for two reasons. First is the contained risk, contained loss reason. And the second thing that makes this such a good business is that by doing a conference, you are really in essence getting paid for doing market research. When the first conference was successful, I discovered that there would be a market for a magazine on computer training. So, after the 1980 conference, not only had I made a profit; I had gotten my next idea in the process.

Valerie decided that she would try to launch *Computer Training* to coincide with the annual computer conference to be held in December of 1981. The only problem was that she didn't have any capital to get the publication off the ground. *HRN* was losing money, and the shot in the arm from the conference wasn't enough to finance the new publication.

I clearly needed more money from the bank, and they wouldn't give it to me. The banker told me to try to keep working with *HRN* to get it on its feet. I kept trying to explain what a good opportunity this was, but he wouldn't listen. So, to start the magazine, I had to stretch myself really thin. I was essentially borrowing from my suppliers. I kept cajoling and begging and pleading with them to wait a little while longer for payment on the bills. It's easy to say now that I was undercapitalized and that there was no way I should have done this. But what the hell was I going to do? I had to do something to get the business going again. I'll tell you one thing, I owe a lot to my printer and my suppliers—these are the people who helped me succeed and since then, I have made sure to pay all my bills on time.

So, at this point, we had *HRN* losing money, we had a start-up that seemed very promising, but start-ups always lose money at first, and we had just come off of one small but encouraging shot in the arm from the conference. To say the least, 1982 was a crisis year. (See Exhibits 2 and 3 for summary financials.)

I was very much over my head that year—one successful conference didn't make us an overnight success. Interest rates went to 22 percent on our loan. I had never before missed a payment, but as luck would have it, our account was assigned to a new loan officer that year, and he wanted that money yesterday even though we were stretched.

That's when I learned that the banks are people too. They are not a religion—some fail just like businesses. I had previously thought, "Oh my

God, these are the guys that tie you to the railroad tracks." I thought that bankers were sort of above it all, holier than thou types. Then I realized that all kinds of horrible things go on inside banks—there's nothing sacred about them at all. The way I began to look at it, banks were my partners; by lending me money, they were in this thing with me. I said to them, "Do you want me to fail or to succeed?"

They wanted to secure their loans, and I said no. They threatened to call the note, and I said go ahead. It was a great Mexican standoff. Then they realized that they would get nothing because their loan was unsecured. This young account officer kept on calling, and I said no in every tone of voice possible. Finally, I turned around and complained of harassment and of either antifeminism or anti-Semitism. I don't remember which, but their knuckles turned white. After all, I was the press. What I learned then was that you've got to use everything you can. If they'd called the note, we would have been out of business.

If they were stupid enough not to get collateral the first time, I was not going to give it to them later on. Banks are not any smarter than their dumbest loan officers. They have quotas like everyone else. They considered the government of Argentina a better credit risk than me! It taught me that pressure is hard to take. I had sleepless nights, but they did too. This situation lasted for five months, and it was actually a good thing because it sharpened my wits. Each step of the way through these rough times, I just tried to make the best out of the hand I was dealt.

The November 1982 conference was coming up, and MP desperately needed the cash. So they made 5,000 calls thinking they would be lucky to get 200 people. They got 800. As Valerie explained:

> The conference really helped us stay alive. It gave us an infusion of cash and a new focus for our energies.

That year, 1983, was a year to solidify our position and to put a few dollars away in the bank. We decided to sponsor a second conference just like the first one, only in the springtime. It also went off well. Then, in 1984, we actually employed the upside down philosophy that had worked so well with *Computer Training*. We decided to hold a conference first and then find out if a magazine could come out of it. That conference did very, very well—over 1,200 people came the first time out. We had stumbled into a hot little niche, and *End-User Computing* was born. *EUC* did so well, we launched it as a monthly publication. Now, we've been racing for two years to catch up and assimilate the growth.

THE BUSINESS

Essentially, MP operated in two distinct lines of business:

Publishing: MP published three magazines, which were primarily "controlled subscriptions." That is, they were sent free of charge to qualified readers—those readers whom advertisers would find attractive. Valerie explained:

> Each of the publications was targeted at functional roles in the organization—that's the niche I chose. We're not McGraw-Hill, but we're not looking to be. It would be dumb to try to tackle a giant area. After the first $40,000 loan, I have never had to borrow any more money, and the return on my investment has been enormous. Ninety percent of the people who read my magazines are in large companies. These publications are aimed at job functions, and I really don't compete with anybody. The biggies—like *Computer World, Datamation,* and *P.C. Week*—are giant publications, but they organize themselves around hardware and software, and we organize around job functions. We sort out all of the options they offer—we make sense out of the new stuff on the market and all the goings on in the industry and try to provide information for those whose job it is to train people in various functions. This is what gives us focus—we are able to succeed within a small niche.
>
> We don't have to compete editorially with the giants. In fact, our editorial department is organized differently because we're trying to amortize our resources—we have six editors including our editorial director. Everyone writes for each of the publications, and we also use contributed material from field practitioners. We are not a news magazine, so we take stuff from outside people. It's a fluid, creative process here. We don't have much turnover. I have a suspicion that this way of operating is stimulating to people—we want to maintain this small company feel. Our editorial staff is not using this company as a stepping-stone to the bigger firms. In fact, they're more likely to come to us *from* a larger firm. When you don't have many resources, you have to be creative, and we'd like to stay that way.
>
> The only problem is that sometimes it's not easy to explain this to ad agencies because they work on commissions, and the commission from a little magazine like ours is going to be tiny compared to the commissions from something like *P.C. Week.* But at the same time, our costs are less—we're like little mammals running around the feet of dinosaurs.

MP published three magazines:

— *Human Resource News:* Begun in September 1979, *HRN* was a newspaper that now had a 10,000-person base of qualified subscribers. *HRN* targeted training directors and staff in business and industry and covered all aspects of training—sales, technical, and management.

— *Computer Training:* Begun in December 1981, *CT* was targeted at data processing trainers. The magazine had a base of 13,000 qualified subscribers and 7,000 paid subscribers (at $24 per year). Valerie's goal was to transform as many as possible of *CT*'s qualified subscribers into paid subscribers.

— *End-User Computing:* Begun in January of 1985, *EUC* had a base of 75,000 qualified subscribers by mid-1986. This publication was aimed at all information processing professionals in charge of nontechnical, nondata processing computing.

Based on this group of subscribers, MP sold advertising space in its publications, which accounted for the bulk of its publishing revenues.

Conferences: The second area of MP's business involved industry conferences. *Computer Training* sponsored two industry conferences per year, and *End-User Computing,* one per year. These conferences were week-long affairs, typically featuring 75 presentations and several days of exhibits by vendors. In 1986, approximately 3,000 industry professionals paid $500 to $600 to attend the various conferences, and vendors paid to exhibit their products.

ORGANIZATION

MP was organized as shown in Exhibit 4. The company employed 42 persons in all, with the breakdown as follows:

Conferences: The conference department was managed by Lynn Williams. She supervised five individuals who coordinated and executed all of the arrangements required for the three annual conferences, each of which had 1,500 to 2,500 attendees.

Sales: David Metcalf managed the sales area. He supervised six employees who sold advertising and conference exhibition space; one was in charge of telemarketing for conferences, each of three people was responsible for one of the publications, and two helped support the overall sales effort.

Editorial: Each publication had its own editor-in-chief who was responsible for the nonadvertising content of the publications. Frank Kendall oversaw all of the publications and also served as editor-in-chief of *End-User Computing.* In addition, there was a pool of editorial assistants who supported the writing efforts on all of the publications. The editorial staff also used free-lance writers and practicing managers/professionals in the field as a source of articles.

Production: The production department was managed by Margaret Rapp. She supervised two typesetters, three production assistants, an art director, and a graphic artist. In addition to producing the magazines themselves, the production department was also responsible for producing brochures and conference materials.

Circulation: Jane Silbert managed six individuals in the circulation department. They were responsible for obtaining and qualifying subscribers and maintaining the mailing lists.

THE EVOLUTION OF THE ORGANIZATION

Valerie described how the organization, and her job, had evolved over time:

In the beginning, it was just my partner—Ken Dryden—an editor and I. He kept a full-time job, so he wasn't around much. I sold ads and helped out whenever I could. The editor coordinated a team of free-lance writers. We subcontracted all of the layout printing and subscription fulfillment.

Gradually, we hired people for these jobs: someone to sell ads, someone to coordinate the editorial side, someone else for circulation. I would fill in at different points, sell ads, help edit during that crunch, typeset and proof during the production part of the cycle. We didn't have any janitorial service, so I'd vacuum every week.

I also did the bookkeeping on ledger sheets up until 1985 when we decided we needed a computer.

We do most everything ourselves now. We have gradually brought many of the services we used to buy from outside back in-house. For instance, we bought a Digital VAX computer to do our own subscription fulfillment work—keeping tabs on the mailing lists. We have six data entry clerks who run the machines. We bought a big Xerox machine to print the handouts for our conferences—we found that we were printing over a million sheets of paper for each conference.

By bringing these functions in-house, we are able to achieve a far greater degree of control over what we are doing. No one ever cares like I care. Dealing with sloppy people just infuriates me. On the other hand, when the computer breaks down, it is now *my* problem.

The partnership with Dryden never worked out. He wanted complete responsibility for some segments of the business, but he was only around one day a week. If I tried to step in when he wasn't here, he would get upset. Six months into it, it was obvious our 50/50 split of the equity was not fair. We had each put in $10,000, and I told him, "Let me buy you out, or I'm leaving." It was clear that he really couldn't run the business, and in 1984 I bought him out. It was a complicated arrangement—part of the deal involved income and part stock—overall, he was bought out for approximately $300,000.

I don't have the same kind of knowledge about what goes on here that I used to have. In 1982, we had 10 employees—two in sales, two in editorial, one in conferences, and three in circulation. I could step into any job and do it well. Today, with 42 employees, things have gotten more specialized, and people have figured out better ways to do things. If I try to do something, I'm likely to mess it up.

I never *do* any of these jobs anymore. I try to create an atmosphere where others enjoy working and will value doing a quality job, though. When I want something done, I cajole others into doing it. It is a real bitch sometimes, and I'd much rather just do it myself, but I can't. The company has just gotten too big.

I have also learned to keep my mouth shut. I was walking through production a while back and saw a cover proof for one of the publications. I mentioned, in an off-hand way, that I thought it was an odd cover. Apparently, they raced around for two days getting a new cover. I never intended that!

I really give everyone a lot of autonomy. My only control system is to get upset after the fact, which really doesn't help much. It is hard to build in controls—the managers that work for me think it implies that I don't trust them. Even when I try to get information just to stay informed of what's going on, it's tough to do.

I've been talking about trying to make things more formal, more structured, and people say, "I really love it here; I'd hate to see things change."

We do have a budgeting system, and I can get people to commit to an annual set of numbers—say a sales increase or a cost number. But, when I try to go a level deeper, to get some sort of operating plan to back up a sales or cost increase, people say, "That takes so much time. Wouldn't you rather we spent that time working and making money?"

What am I supposed to say to that, or to another common rejoinder— "Either you trust my judgment or you don't, and if you don't, I shouldn't be working for you." I understand what people are saying, but I really think that we have gone about as far as we can go with this informal approach.

VALERIE MORGAN: A TYPICAL DAY

Valerie described how she viewed her role in the organization:

My job is hard to describe. One dimension involves the overall management of operations—coordinating the different functions. At another level, I help the department heads out with their jobs—some of them more than others. They each have different styles, and that's fine with me. Probably one of the most important aspects of the job is one I only recently became aware of—a figurehead. I realized that—even unconsciously—I have provided a sense of leadership, imbued this institution with certain values. Morgan is a company, not just a person.

She described some of her activities on a typical day:

Every day it seems I'm doing both big picture and very detailed things. On one hand, I try to stay involved with decisions that affect the basic content of the publications. These decisions influence how the public perceives us.

At the other end of the spectrum, I get involved with a good many details. Today, for instance, a big advertiser requested that we break our rate card (i.e., lower our advertising price) in exchange for a long-term contract. Most other publishers will do this, but we don't. Also, I was involved in a big discussion over whether we should buy a new bookcase for the sales department. I just can't keep myself from getting involved.

Fires come up all the time. Someone feels really overworked and wants to hire some part-time help for a few days. An advertiser will be furious because we made a mistake in an ad we ran and not want to pay. The salesman comes in and can't think of anything except keeping the customer happy.

I also get involved in a lot of little things that come up every day. I wander around constantly and just can't stand it when I see something being done less efficiently than is possible. Then, I just get involved in things I *like* to do and think I'm good at: brainstorming sessions for ad programs, hospitality parties at the conferences.

Finally, there are always conflicts between the departments to be resolved. A salesman promises special space at a conference to one vendor, and the conference department is furious because this compromises their position with all of the other exhibitors.

It seems as though the publishing business consumes far more of my time. Our conference business really seems to run pretty smoothly under Lynn.

My biggest problem is in deciding how to spend my own time and how to effectively manage the organization. When we were small, I did everything: managing the office, answering the phones, bookkeeping, selling ads, proofreading articles, managing the free-lancers, writing and producing marketing material.

Now, there are so many more demands on my time, and I don't know what to do. For instance, should I focus my energies on where we are making money and try to get everything out of these opportunities that I possibly can, or should I focus on where we may be losing money?

We have also developed new systems. For instance, I now get my department managers to set goals for the coming year in the form of budgets. We began this process in January 1985. The problem is accountability: How do you get people to stick to them? They want to operate as though there were endless resources. Now, if they get an idea in the middle of the year, and it is not in the budget, I don't want to hear about it. (For an example of monthly budget results, for each magazine, see Exhibit 5. For an example of a specific budget for a department see Exhibit 6.)

We also have a performance appraisal system in place for everyone except the department managers. I try to build in a 15–20 percent upside in compensation for people who perform really well. For employees below the department-manager level, each department manager was given a pool of dollars to divide as he or she saw fit.

We have a policy of not letting people run ads who haven't paid their bills. Our terms are net 30, but that is really a joke. We will stop advertising after about three months. The accounting department runs a list, and our delinquent accounts get letters informing them that their ads are being pulled. The accounts scream at the salesmen, and the salesmen call me. What am I supposed to do?

THE ISSUES MORGAN FACED

At this point in the development of her company, Valerie was taking a good hard look at the future:

> People don't believe me when I tell them that I like what I'm doing because of the quality of life it affords me. I never expected this to work. I think I'm unemployable, and this job allows me to call my own shots. But there certainly have been suggestions that I give it all up.
>
> For example, in early 1985, I was wooed by a large conglomerate publishing company in New York. They invited me down to the city, wined and dined me, and introduced me to all the bigwigs who kept telling me about what a great "window of opportunity" this was. At the end of the day, and by this time I was exhausted, they whisked me into the president's office (which was bigger and more lavish then my entire house), and they really tried to push me to tell them, "Yes, I'll sell my company to you."
>
> Finally, after listening to them talk for long enough, I said, "Stop, just stop a minute. I'm trying to make you understand this. I can't operate like this; I can't give you an answer right now because I'm afraid that if I do, I'll wake up tomorrow morning and say, Oh my God, what have I done?" After you've given it away, you can't get it back. For that reason, I wouldn't even let them tell me how much they were thinking of offering me for my company. I guess I was afraid that if the price was too high, I'd sell out. I can't say exactly what it was, but there was a number I wouldn't have turned down. So that was the end of that, and I still have no desire to sell.

Given Valerie's commitment to Morgan Publications and her desire to remain as president of the company, there were a number of dilemmas she faced.

> I really feel as though we need more professional management here. I need to figure out how to structure our operations so that I can let the department managers just manage. They need to stop guarding their own turf and realize that they are playing on the same team.
>
> Our approach to management has to change. When we passed 20 or 30 people, we hit this huge need for structure. People want to know how their performance is being reviewed, when their salary will be reviewed, and what exactly they are responsible for. These questions didn't come up several years ago. People would just do what needed to be done. When we moved into our new offices, everyone was aghast that I hadn't planned on a coffee machine and a fridge. But, we had been bringing in coffee and lunch for four years.
>
> So, people want much more structure, systems, and order in their lives than they once did. On the other hand, they don't want to feel that their freedom is being taken away.
>
> I think we have to change if we want to grow. We must to decide what formal structures and systems are needed, and then put them in place. We

have had problems in the past, for instance, when we fired people and didn't have any documentation to back it up. We went through a big effort a while back to decide how many vacation days everyone should get. Today, my assistant asked me who checks to see what people are actually taking. I don't know, and I don't really care.

We need to decide what kind of people to bring in, and at what level. Is the organizational structure right? What new people and positions do we need?

I have too much to do, and I'm not doing everything. I am not analytical or detail-oriented. I often ignore the administrative component and just tell someone else to make a decision.

MIDDLE MANAGEMENT'S PERSPECTIVE

The various managers who worked for Valerie shared their perspectives on her and on the firm.

Jane Silbert, Circulation Manager: When I joined the firm, I was the fourth employee. I helped Valerie plan the first conference. Following this, we moved to getting our own computer and bringing the circulation and fulfillment function in-house.

From the start, I had a great deal of independence and autonomy. Valerie would get interested in something, and we would work on it together; but by and large, she stayed out of the day-to-day decision making. She is very involved in the company because she is the type of person that people will naturally stop in to talk with.

We do annual budgeting now and use this process to set other goals for the department. But these are not explicitly tied into performance appraisal or compensation. In fact, the performance appraisal system is not in place at the management level. I do develop an operating—or action—plan that underlies the budget, but Valerie doesn't see or approve this.

All of the managers work closely together. Our actions affect each other a great deal. Occasionally, we do conflict, but we try to work these situations out without going to Valerie.

Margaret Rapp, Production Manager: Just about everything we are involved in comes through here: magazines, directories, conference books, even meal tickets for the conferences.

I was hired two years ago when there was no production department. I was in the editorial area, in charge of coordinating the outside typesetters. Now, we have brought everything in-house.

Valerie gives me a lot of independence. We spent about $1 million in here last year, and there really are no formal cost controls. Valerie knows I'm pretty cheap, and she trusts me to do a good job saving money. We meet our deadlines and the quality looks good, so she is happy to leave us pretty much alone.

If we get caught up in a deadline, and two different people are putting pressure on me that we can't meet, Valerie will give me lots of support and back up whatever decision I make.

We do have a budget, but the accounting system doesn't give me much information that I can really use. The numbers are cut in a way that bears little relationship to the decisions I have to make—they are aggregated at too high a level to allow me to make anyone accountable. I just keep track with a paper and pencil.

At any rate, no one ever really reviews performance against budget anyway.

Frank Kendall, Editor: I started working here when the company was only Valerie, Ken Dryden, Jane Silbert, and one other editor. I was responsible for managing the free-lancers and our vendors—printing, typesetting, and art. We have brought all of these functions, and a lot more writers, in-house.

During our growth, Valerie has trusted me to manage the department. She makes no bones about telling me about problems and issues she sees, but she stays out of the day-to-day decision making. Valerie has always been a leader and a supporter of people, more than an administrator.

Lately, however, I've detected more of an effort to put some formal structures into the organization. I think this is a mistake. We all want to produce excellent products, and to work as professionals. If we make sure that people have the right values, the rest will take care of itself. As long as I can look at someone in a particular situation and say that they did the same thing that I would have done, I am satisfied. What more do you want?

I spend a lot of time supporting people, encouraging them, praising their good work. It's much harder to shape someone's performance with criticism. Often, the first time I read something is when it actually appears in print.

We meet frequently with people in other departments to ensure that we all know what is going on and to hammer out issues that need to be resolved.

David Metcalf, Sales: I joined in 1981 to sell two products—ads in *Computer Training* and exhibit space at our conference. From the start, Valerie gave us lots of autonomy. Still, she is extremely involved in the business because she is sincerely interested in the people who work here.

As the sales department has grown, we have developed our own approaches to setting objectives and monitoring performance. I will go to Valerie when we need more people for the department, but she trusts the day-to-day operating decisions to us.

It's my job to see that people are selling for the maximum amount of time every day and to insulate my people from whatever bureaucratic pressures and burdens may arise.

Lynn Williams, Conferences: I started working here in the summer of 1981. Valerie had just organized the first conference and was gearing up for the second one. I was hired to help out, stuffing envelopes and running around to prepare for the conference.

I really learned a lot from Valerie via that experience. She took me to all the meetings and was extremely involved in every decision. Following that second conference, I was put in charge of that area. Since that time, we have grown dramatically, and she is far less involved in the day-to-day operations.

Still, it is difficult for Valerie to maintain a distance between herself and this operation. She trusts and supports me and knows that she shouldn't be involved, but she *likes* to be involved. And her input is valuable.

The problem comes when she wants to have input but doesn't just make a decision. She will give us her opinion, and we will work on something, and then we get more input. We just keep going back and forth.

We have formalized some of the processes through which we interact. She approves an annual budget, and I monitor my area's performance against this monthly.

Valerie used to pull together the conference program (60 or so speakers) in a pretty informal way. Now, we have a very formal process in which speakers develop proposals, and the editorial and conference departments meet with Valerie to develop a final program.

I feel as though we do need these formal processes in place in order to allow us to focus more clearly, less ambiguously, on specific objectives.

Valerie shared the concerns of her middle management:

I know we need more formal systems, but I don't want to lose the small business feeling. I do not want to implement strict controls at the expense of creativity. This company is a lot of fun, and I enjoy my job very much.

EXHIBIT 1   Chronological Outline of Significant Events

Date	Event
1967	Begins teaching at Ashford High School.
1972	Stops teaching and takes a year off to take interesting courses.
1973	Starts her language company.
1977	Forms a partnership to acquire management training skills; begins teaching foreign cultural aspects.
1979	Forms a partnership and starts her publishing company; first newspaper called *Human Resource News*.
1981	Puts on first Training Conference; launches *Computer Training* newspaper.
1982	Faces near-bankruptcy; puts on first telemarketed conference.
1983	Company has positive net worth for the first time.
1984	Partnership ends; launches glossy magazine called *End-User Computing*.

EXHIBIT 2   Summary Balance Sheets

	12/31/79	12/31/82	12/31/86
Assets			
Current assets:			
Cash	$ 1,283	$ 5,535	$ 346,633
Accounts receivable.............	8,768	55,763	422,717
Inventory	—	10,420	35,312
Prepaid expenses................	639	91,402	101,743
Total current assets..........	$10,690	$163,120	$ 906,405
Property and equipment	$ 2,084	$ 58,977	$ 329,676
Less accumulated depreciation .	86	14,068	96,637
Total PP&E...................	$ 1,998	$ 44,909	$ 426,313
Other assets.....................	150	4,600	20,387
Total assets	$12,838	$212,629	$1,353,105
Liabilities and Stockholders' Equity			
Current liabilities:			
Notes payable—bank	$32,500	$ 20,457	$ 23,667
Notes payable—equipment	456	2,278	10,565
Accounts payable	8,908	128,836	183,033
Deferred conference income.....	—	115,910	53,231
Deferred subscription income...	—	57,547	62,990
Other..........................	228	68,114	8,654
Total current liabilities.......	$42,092	$359,352	$ 342,140
Long-term liabilities			
Notes payable—bank	$ —	$ 42,006	$ 17,778
Notes payable—equipment	229	11,794	106,463
Total long-term liabilities	$ 229	$ 53,800	$ 124,241
Stockholders' equity			
Common stock	20,000	20,000	200
Additional paid-in capital.......	—	—	19,800
Treasury stock	—	—	—
Retained earnings prior.........	—	(95,483)	351,487
Retained earnings current......	(49,483)	(105,030)	515,237
Total stockholders' equity	(29,483)	(200,513)	886,724
Total liabilities and stockholders' equity	$12,838	$212,629	$1,353,105

EXHIBIT 3   Summary Income Statements

	1979	1982	1986
Income			
Ad placement	$ 25,122	$ 182,328	$1,149,919
Subscriptions......................	—	86,441	154,286
Conference registrations	—	121,320	1,674,703
Conference expositions............	—	38,680	439,435
Lists..............................	—	20,366	174,272
Interest...........................	—	—	14,684
Miscellaneous	—	14,534	9,980
Total income	$ 25,122	$ 463,669	$3,617,279
Direct Costs			
Printing..........................	$ 8,841	$ 115,089	$ 557,680
Postage and mailing services	7,734	31,019	95,775
Conference*	—	112,212	1,021,586
Other.............................	—	12,486	65,208
Total direct costs...............	$ 38,907	$ 270,788	$1,740,249
Gross profit	(13,785)	192,881	1,877,030
SG&A			
Salaries	—	$ 227,789	$ 738,864
Other.............................	35,698	70,122	430,929
Total SG&A....................	$ 35,698	$ 297,911	$1,169,793
Net profit (loss) before tax	$(49,483)	$(105,030)	$ 707,237
Tax	—	—	$ 192,000
Profit after tax	$(49,483)	$(105,030)	$ 515,237

*Conference expenses include hotel and meals for conference participants, as well as all other costs associated with conferences.

EXHIBIT 4 Morgan Publications Organization Chart

Valerie Morgan
President

Conferences	Sales	Editorial	Production	Circulation	Marketing	Accounting
Lynn Williams	David Metcalf	Frank Kendall	Margaret Rapp	Jane Silbert	Rod Leneo	Jill White
Operations manager	*End-User Computing*	*End-User Computing* (3)	Typesetters (2)	Data entry (4)		
Program coordinator	*Computer Training*	*Computer Training* (2)	Assistants (2)	Acquisition		
Registrar	*Human Resource News*	*Human Resource News*	Art director	Training		
Exhibits coordinator	Conferences		Graphic artist			
Department secretary	Assistant					
	Department secretary					

EXHIBIT 5   Morgan Publications—Monthly Budget Results for
Publications

	April Results		
Item	*Human Resource News*	*Computer Training*	*End-User Computing*
Graphics.....................	$ 264.00	$ 483.25	—
Writer (freelance)...........	300.00	1,161.17	$ 1,086.33
Paper and printing..........	5,436.67	16,465.56	33,884.55
Printing/other...............	434.00	1,338.54	599.77
Postage.....................	35.52	3,303.76	307.15
Mailing services.............	543.06	491.37	1,588.34
Agency commission	895.50	7,075.06	10,762.51
Lists........................	296.50	4,181.46	720.00
Postage.....................	841.00	4,337.32	10,200.00
Photography/illustration	400.00	975.00	2,991.91
Travel and entertainment...	2,304.87	1,447.27	2,552.00
Consultants	1,800.00	—	1,531.90
Marketing and advertising..	719.11	312.00	2,740.57
Shipping and delivery.......	—	1,729.51	1,002.75
TOTAL DIRECT COSTS	$14,270.23	$43,301.27	$69,967.78
PROFIT	$ (3,677.79)	$17,647.20	$ 4,497.22

EXHIBIT 6   Portion of Circulation Departmental Budget

1986 Budget Planning Sheet

Goal/project (include completion date)

To obtain a net gain of 1,000 paid subscribers for <u>Human Resource News</u>
by 12/31/86

Item/Activity	Amount	Justification	
Direct mail campaign	$12,090	Copywriter	2,500
May		Postage	1,875
(15,000)		Bus. reply	70
		Lists	1,125
		Mail house	520
		Photography	500
		Printing	5,500
Direct mail campaign	$16,690	Postage	3,750
July		Bus. reply	140
(30,000)		Lists	2,250
		Mail house	1,050
		Printing	9,500
Direct mail campaign	$ 9,090	Postage	1,875
Nov.		Bus. reply	70
(15,000)		Lists	1,125
		Mail house	520
		Printing	5,500
Post card decks	$ 5,600		
(3 at 100,000 each)			
Advertising, 2 publications	$ 735		
(3 times each)			

The Johnsonville Sausage Co.

Ralph Stayer hung up the phone and leaned back in his chair, deep in thought. One of Johnsonville Sausage's private label customers— Palmer Sausage—was considering increasing its purchases from Johnsonville by a huge amount. In fact, the company was talking about placing an order that, if accepted, would account for 25 percent of Johnsonville's annual sales volume. Ralph wondered how he should react.

OVERVIEW

The Johnsonville Sausage Co. was purchased in 1945 by Ralph's parents and was located in Johnsonville, Wisconsin, a small town about 60 miles north of Milwaukee. The company was a rural meat market—a family home with a storefront, a sausage kitchen, and a slaughter shed and smokehouse out back.

At the time it was purchased, the business was small—roughly $50,000 per year in sales—but quite profitable: The shortage of meat and consequent rationing had inflated meat prices. Soon after the Stayers purchased the business, however, the U.S. government eliminated the rationing system, and prices and profits began to fall.

In order to survive, the Stayers opened a retail food store in 1946 with a local man who sold groceries. The Stayers supplied all of the meat and managed the meat counter. This business did well, and the

This case was prepared by Michael J. Roberts.

Stayers opened two more retail stores in conjunction with this grocery business in 1948 and 1952.

Thus, for quite a time, the business was a full-line retail butchering business. Mr. Stayer would buy livestock from local suppliers, slaughter the animals, and sell meat in the three retail stores. Mr. Stayer also made fresh sausage, which had acquired an excellent reputation in the area. He managed these stores, and Mrs. Stayer kept the books for the business.

Ralph was interested in running the business with his father and worked with him summers during high school and college. When Ralph graduated from Notre Dame in 1965 with a bachelor's degree in business, he and his father took a hard look at Johnsonville's operations. Essentially, there were two aspects of the business—wholesale and retail. They concluded that it would be difficult to grow the retail meat business without opening grocery stores as well. The Stayers had no interest in getting involved in this aspect of the business, and retail supermarkets had evolved to the point where they typically had their own full-line meat departments.

The wholesale business, however, looked more promising. Ralph had begun selling some sausage products to other stores in the area (but not local establishments competing directly with the Stayers' retail business). The product had been well received, and Ralph was confident that he could increase sales. The Stayers decided to focus their efforts on building this segment of the business.

Ralph built the wholesale business to the point where it accounted for $4 million in sales in 1975, $15 million in 1980, and $50 million in 1985. Between 1980 and 1985, return on equity had climbed relatively steadily from 18 percent to 27 percent. Long-term debt had remained a fairly constant portion of the capital structure, as the debt-to-equity ratio hovered between 55 percent and 65 percent. The company had been transformed from a small family of workers to a business of well over 500 employees. Ralph was officially named president in 1978, but had assumed most of the day-to-day decision-making authority for the wholesale business in the early 1970s.

The remainder of this case describes the business in more detail and the changes that transpired as the company grew.

THE BUSINESS

Products

Johnsonville Sausage's product line consisted of three types of sausage, which in total accounted for approximately 120 SKUs:

Fresh sausage: Made from freshly butchered pork and beef cuts. Popular fresh sausage products included bratwurst, Italian sausage, breakfast links and patties, and kielbasa. Fresh products had a shelf life of approximately three weeks.

Smoked sausage: A sausage made in the same manner as a fresh sausage, but to which nitrates and nitrites were added as a "cure"; this preserved the meat and gave it a characteristic red/brown color. The sausage was then cooked for two to four hours in a hot oven with smoldering wood chips to impart a smoked flavor. Smoked sausage had a shelf life of approximately two months.

Semidry sausage: Semidry or *summer* or *slicing* sausage was made like a smoked sausage, but was cooked for three or four days. This removed most of the moisture and preserved the sausage while giving it a strong flavor. Semidry sausage was typically much larger than an average sausage and could be sliced like a salami. Semidry sausage had a shelf life of at least four months.

Product varieties within each category were created by the use of different spices and by varying the "link length" and the sausage casing.

Production

All sausage began as a combination of beef and pork cuts. Johnsonville slaughtered its own hogs and its own beef up until 1973, when it decided to purchase these cuts from local suppliers. Then, in 1980, the company purchased a slaughtering operation in order to provide its operations with fresh pork. Live hogs were purchased weekly and slaughtered daily at the company's slaughterhouse in Watertown, Wisconsin, 80 miles south of Sheboygan. The butchered pork was shipped daily in 2,000-pound bins to the Johnsonville plants.

The processing plants ran on a two-shift basis, so that the fresh meat could be turned into sausage on a continuous basis. Fresh meat was delivered to the plant by 10 P.M. when the first shift began to turn this meat into sausage filler: Meat was ground, and spices and flavorings added.

At 6 A.M., the second shift would arrive and begin making sausages by stuffing casings with this mixture.

— The sausage meat was emptied into a large hopper and was extruded into the casing.

— For fresh sausage, the links were then placed on styrofoam trays, flash frozen, wrapped in cellophane packages, and packed in boxes to be shipped.

— For smoked or semidry sausage, the links were placed in the smokehouse and cooked/smoked for a time with a seasoned wood.

USDA inspections were also a part of the manufacturing process. Workers had to test samples of each product for fat, protein, and moisture content, and report the results to the USDA. This entire process was carried out in large refrigerated rooms. Sausage production was typically finished by 3 or 4 P.M., a scant 24 hours after the hog had been butchered.

Fresh sausage was stored in large refrigerated rooms. Because of its relatively short shelf life, and Johnsonville's desire to sell a fresh product, inventory was kept at a minimum—two days or so—and all products were made in response to customer orders. During the summer months, fresh sausage was extremely popular, particularly the bratwurst for which the company was famous in Wisconsin. Johnsonville had the ability to produce on a two-shift basis if required during these summer months.

All of the company's production had originally been produced in the plant that was attached to the original Stayer home. The Stayers had moved out while Ralph was a youngster, but he still pointed out his old bedroom, which was now used as the purchasing office.

Johnsonville had built a new plant in 1978, which was now used only for fresh products; the old factory was used strictly for smoked and semidry products.

Sales and Distribution

The company relied on a combination of brokers and its own direct sales force to sell its product. The firm employed 25 salesmen in 1985. Food brokers were used outside of Wisconsin. Part-time "demonstrators" were used by the company to cook and distribute free samples of product in retail stores. The product was initially sold primarily by word of mouth, but the company began print advertising in 1975. Johnsonville also worked with stores to develop promotions, which typically included a discount on the price of certain products as well as co-op advertising.

Fresh bratwurst was the product most responsible for Johnsonville's growth; "brats" were sold at Milwaukee Brewers' Stadium and were extremely popular. In fact, several annual polls of sportswriters and broadcasters revealed that Johnsonville's bratwurst was the favorite "stadium food" available anywhere:

> Bratwurst is one of the passions that consumes, and is consumed by, Bob Costas [NBC sportscaster]. Name a ballpark, and Costas will tell you the best item on the menu. . . . And when it comes to ballpark food, no other stadium occupies a more hallowed spot in Costas's heart, on his palate, or in his stomach, than Milwaukee's County Stadium. "The single best ballpark item anywhere, at any ballpark, hands down, is the bratwurst with the sauerkraut and red sauce, at County Stadium," he said. "It's not even close."[1]

In addition to publicity like this, the firm inaugurated a TV ad campaign in 1981 that focused on the "brat fry" as a social event. The commercials featured uninvited guests overwhelming a man who is cooking Johnsonville brats. The brat fry had become a popular Milwaukee area social event, and local papers described the phenomenon:

> In east central Wisconsin, spring is marked not by returning robins or budding willows, but by frying bratwurst. . . . Brat fries are prevalent in this four-county area year round. . . .[2]

Sausage was distributed by a fleet of company-owned trucks, which left the Johnsonville plant each morning. The trucking operation was separately incorporated and run as a distinct business. In order to permit the carrying of full loads, the company carried nonJohnsonville products to some neighboring states.

Markets

Initially, the company served only the Sheboygan market through its retail outlet there. Several more retail outlets were added in that area in 1948–52, and the firm did not start wholesaling until Ralph began selling to other stores in 1965. Some other jobbers were added between 1968 and 1972. Initially, only Ralph sold the products; he worked first with small retailers and then local chains to convince them to carry the products. Once they had been signed on as an account, jobbers took weekly orders for the products.

By 1975, Johnsonville was serving two of the largest grocery chains in Wisconsin, as well as a host of other, smaller accounts in the greater Milwaukee area. Still, the company operated solely within that state. In order to sell outside of Wisconsin, Johnsonville would have to comply with stricter federal inspection standards, which would

---

[1]The *Milwaukee Journal*, July 21, 1985, p. 6.
[2]*Chicago Tribune*, April 8, 1984.

require the opening of a new plant. In 1978, Johnsonville decided to open a new plant and began serving the state of Indiana; Ralph's sister Launa was the sales rep for that state.

As time went on, the company continued to expand its distribution both within and out of the state. Johnsonville expanded to Iowa, Indiana, Illinois, and Minnesota, and several other neighboring states. Meanwhile, the firm's market position in Wisconsin continued to strengthen. Their share of the bratwurst market in the greater Milwaukee market rose from 7 percent in 1978 to 46 percent in 1985. The company's Italian sausage was number two in this market, and its breakfast sausage ranked number four.

MANAGEMENT

As the company grew, it underwent a series of changes, both in its structure and in its philosophy. Ralph described his early approach to managing the business:

> I ran the business from the sausage stuffer. I made all the decisions about purchasing, production scheduling, pricing, and advertising. I called on our major accounts. We had some office help to handle the payroll and receivables and payables. But I made all the decisions. As the company grew, I did hire a financial person and a sales manager. I still made all the decisions and let them handle the implementation details.

In 1980, however, Ralph began to feel uncomfortable with the business and the manner in which he was managing it:

> I was fed up with the business. The quality of our product was slipping and no one seemed to care. I had always been proud of the fact that people seemed to enjoy their jobs and took pride in their work. But that seemed to change. People were careless—equipment was being poorly cared for and bad product was making its way into the market. We did an attitude survey, and general morale was just even with the national average.
>
> One incident particularly sticks in my mind. I'd hired someone early on, who was very competent. Then one day it struck me that he was just a soldier, carrying out my orders. I tried to get him to take more responsibility, but he couldn't; I'd ruined him. A few years of my style had beaten the independence out of him. I vowed I'd never do that again to a man.

During the time that Ralph was attempting to work through his thoughts and feelings about the business, he happened to hear a lecture by a professor from the University of Wisconsin. Dr. Lee Thayer was addressing the issue of how managers could change their philosophy and style of management. Dr. Thayer taught and did research in the organizational behavior field and had training in the

psychology area as well. Thayer began working with Ralph to change
Johnsonville. He described the process:

> It was a long, slow process. The philosophy that we were trying to
> implement had several dimensions.
>
> — First, performance is key. And in a well-developed system, there is no
>   conflict between what is best for the company and what's best for the
>   individual. If there is, there is a problem with the way things are being
>   defined, or the way the system is set up.
> — The second element is the idea that people do need help to accomplish
>   their objectives, and that *this* is the job of management. The way we
>   can help them is to define very carefully what their job is, define
>   explicitly what the performance standards are, and then give them the
>   resources they need to accomplish their objectives.

Thayer described the change process at Johnsonville:

> The first task was to develop a new model of managerial performance in
> Ralph Stayer's mind. There were several elements to the process. First, he
> participated in several seminars where we reviewed the new philosophy.
> Next, he would call me frequently with questions regarding particular
> decisions that had to be made. We discussed how these issues should be
> handled if we wanted to be true to the philosophy we were trying to
> implement. It was very difficult work. As much as Ralph wanted to
> change, it was still difficult to do.

Ralph described the role that Lee Thayer played in the process:

> Lee Thayer played a vital role in this organizational transition. First, he
> was a touchstone for me personally. We talked at least several times a
> week. He helped me understand my own role as a leader, and the
> importance of that role to the organization. Even more importantly, he
> was a sounding board for working through specific issues and problems.
> He was there at the inception of the program and encouraged the entire
> company and kept the process going. He was an objective voice that could
> help us see when we were making progress, and when we were slipping
> back toward our old ways. We wouldn't be where we are today without him.

Ralph spoke about how he had come to view his job:

> The most important step was developing the understanding that if I was
> dissatisfied with the way people in the company were performing, it was
> my fault, not theirs.
>
>   My first task is as a developer of people, our organization's "members."
> I spend a lot of time with people in the organization just talking things
> through. I don't tell them what to do anymore; I send them out to make
> their own decisions. If two people come to me—say manufacturing and

marketing—to resolve a dispute, I send them back out; I'm not paying them to push tough decisions up to me; I'm paying them to think.

My job is as a coach, a supporter, a resource. I'm here to help them do their jobs better. I've figured out the few key things I need to know and don't bother with the rest. I'm proud of the fact that there are a lot of details about the business that I just don't know—advertising and promotion plans, for example.

We have a motto here that "Your job is to eliminate your job!" By that, we mean that a manager should delegate so much of his responsibility, and develop the capability of his people to work together to such an extent that his existing job virtually disappears—it has been delegated to those who work with him or her. Of course, that person's job continues to evolve as the people they work with delegate new responsibilities to them.

Whenever I see a problem, I look at myself, not "them." First, I assume that if people aren't achieving the performance results we've decided upon, that some of the problem is my fault—I'm not creating the right environment or giving them the kind of support they need. I need to figure out what part of the problem I am, and how I can change to eliminate it.

It's my job to ask questions, to surface and describe issues, and to create an environment where all of the relevant parties can discuss these issues.

THE ORGANIZATION

The Johnsonville Philosophy

Ralph firmly believed that the change in philosophy was the most important thing that was happening at Johnsonville. The root of that philosophy was a deep moral commitment to the individual. Change at Johnsonville was initiated in an effort to make *people* better, not to make the business better. Ralph spoke about this philosophy and the impact it has had on the business:

> We have gone from a company where I made all of the decisions to one in which responsibility for decisions is distributed to the area best suited to make them. Rather than having one entrepreneur on top, we are trying to have an organization where everyone is an entrepreneur. We want each person to see him or herself as the instrument of his or her own destiny.
>
> Instead of looking outward for more and more business, I am looking inward at our organization and the people that comprise it. We are on the leading edge of developing a far better way for our people to live and work together. The beauty of the system is that it builds on itself. As people grow, opportunities for sales and profits grow, which in turn provides more opportunities for people to grow.
>
> The key to this philosophy is that *people see Johnsonville as a means to their ends, not vice versa.* We are not the means to the end of profit. It's the

other way around: profit is the means to our ends. It is not that profit is unimportant. It is the seed corn that makes everything else work. Our increase in profits has allowed us to increase our investments in the business and increase the compensation for our people at the same time. This has all occurred in a mature, consolidating industry where both profit margins and compensation have been declining overall.

The first step in implementing our philosophy, then, is getting together and deciding what our ends are.

We begin at a fairly high level of abstraction: Clearly, what we all want is job security, increasing compensation, and a job that's rewarding. We have attacked each of these objectives and spent a lot of time thinking about each one in more detail, understanding how we can achieve it.

Job security comes from having customers who value the product. We can all work at this by keeping our eye on the customer. It is everyone's responsibility to make a quality product, to innovate, and to think about the future. The key here is performance. We need to be clear about what our performance objectives are and how we are meeting them.

Compensation is the bottom line in this company, not profit. We will work to make this as big as we can. The smarter we work, the better we become at making customers, the bigger the payoff will be. As we each become more skilled, the performance of the whole company improves. Job security and compensation will both increase.

Finally, the job should be rewarding. Work is a very large part of our lives—all of our lives. It provides the things we want for ourselves and our families. But if we cannot make our lives more fulfilling, more challenging, more rewarding—more fun—then we're all losers in the game of life. We've got to put life back into our work. We've got to put meaning and worthwhileness and purpose back into the one thing we do most with our lives—our jobs. We spend more of our waking hours in our jobs than in any other single thing in life. If all we had to show for it was a paycheck, we would be poor indeed.

We believe that the objective is to develop a non-adverserial company—where everyone's best interest is served by the whole. Whenever we encounter a conflict, we analyze it to determine what changes should be made to resolve it.

The beauty of this philosophy and our objectives is that they all fit together—there is no conflict in achieving these goals. Working toward one is working toward them all. That is because they all revolve around performance. With good people, who have the tools and help they need, working toward superior performance improves job security, improves compensation, and most importantly, makes for rewarding work.

Structure

As the organization structure evolved, there was a great deal of emphasis placed on allocating responsibility properly, or, to use Ralph

Stayer's phrase, "deciding who owns the problem." As an example, customer letters of complaints or praise were typically sent to direct line workers. If a letter complained about too much salt or a "flavor pocket" (i.e., all the spices in one bite of sausage), the letter was routed to the employees in the meat-grinding room who added the spices. If the complaint was relative to a tough or split casing, the letter went to the sausage stuffers. They wrote a letter explaining the cause of the problem, the steps that were taken to avoid it, and apologized for the inconvenience. Employees were able to send out coupons for a free product to such customers.

During the early stages of the organization's transition, Ralph attempted to delegate responsibility to the people he had in place below him, but found that some of these individuals were unable to accept the kind of responsibility that Johnsonville's new philosophy required. In response, Ralph brought in new people to the three key positions that reported to him. All of these individuals had a great deal of experience in their respective functions. Moreover, Ralph screened them carefully to be sure that they would enthusiastically embrace the firm's philosophy.

— Bob Salzwedel, director of Information and Financial Services, was brought in to Johnsonville in late 1981. He had been with a CPA firm.

— Russ Wiverstad joined Johnsonville in mid-1982 as its director of Product Acquisition and Manufacturing.

— Mike Roller, director of Sales and Marketing Services, joined Johnsonville in mid-1984.

The following sections describe how each area of the organization evolved.

Manufacturing

In the late 1960s, the manufacturing operation had been carried out by Ralph and three or four workers who performed all operations, from slaughtering to stuffing and smoking the sausage. This operation was entirely contained within the original Stayer home/factory. (See Exhibit 1.)

When Ralph began working at Johnsonville in 1965, his father supervised production. Ralph gradually took on more responsibility and was responsible for most operations by 1973. Ralph took the president's position in 1978. Then there were 70 to 80 individuals working at Johnsonville, organized as shown in Exhibit 1.

When the second plant was opened in late 1978, Jim Gebler was elevated to the position of plant manager for this facility; Jim had begun working at Johnsonville as a truck driver and had worked making sausage with Ralph for 10 years. Ralph continued to manage the old plant. Then, in 1980, Ralph hired Pat Weiss to supervise both plants. He formalized the manufacturing organization, developing supervisor positions that had previously not existed.

In response to Ralph's attempts to delegate more responsibility, and his dissatisfaction with the way in which Weiss was managing the manufacturing organization, Ralph hired Russ Wiverstad in May of 1982. Pat Weiss was let go.

Russ had been with Oscar Mayer for 30 years, rising to a plant manager position where he was responsible for 700 employees. Russ talked about the reasons he had left Oscar Mayer and joined Johnsonville:

> My job at Oscar Mayer was essentially the enforcement of company policy—policy doesn't exist unless it's enforced. They had standards based on time and motion studies, and if a group wasn't up to par, it was my job to yell at the supervisor. I got sick of it.

Russ talked about the changes that had transpired since he joined Johnsonville:

> When I joined the company, Ralph was making all of the day-to-day operating decisions in the manufacturing area: ordering, scheduling, and the like. It took a little while for Ralph to develop trust and confidence in my abilities, but once he did, he delegated a lot of responsibility to me. Over the years, he's become even less involved in the day-to-day operations. Our relationship works on the principle that it's my job to keep him informed, not his job to ask me the right questions to find out what he needs to know. I think one of the factors that allowed our working relationship to evolve so well was that Ralph didn't *have* to delegate. He was doing it out of choice, not necessity. So, it could happen slowly, at a pace he was comfortable with, and that let him develop confidence in me. As Ralph delegated to me, I delegated to my subordinates. Where all the budgeting and planning used to be done by the vice president of manufacturing, those numbers now come from the shop floor.

Originally Russ had been responsible for manufacturing at Plant 1 (old), Plant 2 (new), and the slaughtering operation. Over the years, as new functions in the organization had been articulated, Russ also assumed responsibility for:

— Engineering—developing plans for new plant and equipment;

— Research and Development—including USDA testing, packaging, product and process development;

— Purchasing—buying meat, spices, and packaging; and,

— Personnel Development—education and training.

The supervisor position in the manufacturing area had been eliminated. Each function—grinding, packing, stuffing, and so forth—had a designated "lead person." Within a given function, workers worked as a team—they would alternate specific jobs (i.e., a worker who picked sausages off a conveyor belt and placed them on a styrofoam tray would switch jobs with a person who wrapped the sausage or who packed the wrapped trays in boxes). This was something that the workers themselves had proposed, and that helped eliminate the routine of some of the jobs. This fit with the company's philosophy in a number of ways. If the workers had true responsibility for performance, then it was up to them to organize the line how they saw fit. Doing so increased their own enjoyment of their jobs, and improved performance. By broadening the scope of their knowledge and skills, workers had come up with new ideas for organizing the work and for new equipment that would make them more productive.

The lead person's responsibilities were not to supervise the other workers, but to collect data, help train new workers, and get information to workers.

A group of workers met each morning to taste a sample of the previous day's production and discuss any ideas on how the product could be improved. Recently, the firm had begun an effort to break jobs up even further, and the lead people were disappearing. Their responsibilities were spread over all of the workers.

Manufacturing workers were evaluated in comparison to budget. On an annual basis, beginning each fall, two or three people from each of the main areas within the manufacturing area would become part of a budget team, together with people from sales and accounting. Working with the sales force, the line workers would develop a sales forecast for the coming 12 months, by product line. They would then develop budgets and set goals for certain key measures, including:

— Labor efficiency: pounds of sausage per man-hour;

— Yield: pounds of meat used per pound of sausage produced; and,

— Labor cost: dollars of labor per pound of sausage.

Workers collected the data required to measure their progress toward these goals and analyzed and posted results versus budget on a monthly basis. Daily figures for yield, efficiency, and cost were produced. Again, all of these steps were taken to ensure that workers had all of the information and help that they needed to understand and improve their own performance.

The capital budgeting process was part of this cycle as well. Line workers developed proposals for new capital equipment. They justified qualitatively why the purchase of the equipment is warranted and then performed a more complex financial analysis, estimating return on assets. Income-producing projects were judged against a 25 percent ROA (pretax) hurdle rate, while safety and quality-oriented investments were evaluated in a less quantitative measure.

During this process, the finance area was viewed as a resource to be used; they were not managing the budgeting process, but were providing service as needed to the line workers.

Sales and Marketing

Ralph performed the retail sales function during the first several years of the company's attempts to expand sales in this area. Following success locally, two of the state's largest chains began distributing Johnsonville products.

In 1975, Ralph hired Dick Gustafson from one of Johnsonville's meat suppliers to help build sales to retail accounts. By 1978, Gustafson was managing two other salesmen; the number grew to five in 1980.

As Ralph began to delegate more responsibility, however, Gustafson was unable to grow into the job; Ralph replaced him in 1981 with Paul Brandon, who began to shift the firm away from direct store sales and delivery to a focus on grocery warehouses. The effect of this shift was an immediate volume surge, followed by a reduction in items carried by retailers and a consequent increase in promotion and related marketing expenses. The effect of this policy error was still being felt when Brandon resigned in late 1983.

Ralph hired Mike Roller in mid-1984 to supervise the sales force and to take on the responsibility for marketing, which Ralph himself had been managing. It fell upon Roller to reorganize sales and marketing operations in order to set the stage for further growth and development. During his first year, he concentrated on rebuilding distressed customer relations; building a management team with well-defined responsibilities, adding performance measures and accountability; putting a marketing and administrative structure in place; building internal and external information systems; and initiating an entry-level training program. Roller also developed the product line in response to suggestions from retailers and the sales force, and significantly reduced operating expenses.

Roller's second-year efforts focused on improving the caliber of individuals in the sales organization and expanding marketing operations to new geographic areas and product segments. The company's first formal marketing plan was developed, including volume and expense budgets that had been developed by the line managers. Timely information systems were developed to allow the monitoring of actual results against this plan.

Staff was added to address operating problems and/or pave the way for further expansion:

— Food service director: added in late 1985 to spearhead the company's expansion into food service institutions, a lucrative market.
— Sales coordinator: added in early 1986 to eliminate coordination problems between sales and manufacturing.
— Marketing coordinator: added to coordinate the implementation of the company's promotional activity—couponing, demonstrations, and the like.
— National account manager: added to begin to develop Johnsonville's business with major national accounts.

Roller had divided the sales force into three groups: food service (restaurants and ballparks), retail, and food processors. Each of these three groups reported to him, as did the marketing, sales administration, trucking/distribution, and internal operations staff. Roller also managed the sales coordinator. Each Tuesday the sales force would send in its sales projections for the coming week. The sales coordinator would get inventory data from the manufacturing department. He would also look at the details of promotions and advertising planned for the next 90 days. Based on this data, the sales coordinator would develop:

— A 90-day rolling forecast of sales to give manufacturing and purchasing a "best guess view";
— Production requirements for the following week; and,
— Estimates of production requirements for each day.

This information would then be sent to each of the two plant coordinators who would develop a production schedule for the week, based on the requirements developed above as well as their own knowledge of manufacturing efficiencies. This information was then used by the purchasing area to make arrangements for purchasing the necessary hogs and beef.

Individual salespeople developed their own plans and budgets and received monthly data—broken down by account and expense item (i.e., travel and entertainment, promotions, advertising).

Finance and Administration

Richard Bassuener was hired to work for Mrs. Stayer as a bookkeeper in 1976. The job consisted primarily of general ledger work, as well as payables and receivables. As Ralph began delegating more responsibility, he felt the company needed to develop financial information systems to collect profitability and return-on-asset data by product line. In addition, he wanted to develop more detailed budgets and timely status reports.

Bob Salzwedel was hired in 1981 to manage the finance function. His responsibilities included acquisitions, cost and financial accounting, as well as accounts credit and collections, and data processing. Richard Basseuner remained in charge of the accounting functions.

Bob felt that the job of the finance area was to provide people with the information that they needed to run the operation themselves.

Several of the traditional accounting functions were in the process of being transferred to sales or manufacturing:

— Billing and credit were being placed under the sales function; and,

— Cost accounting was part of manufacturing.

In Ralph Stayer's words, "We do two things here—make sausage and sell it. They are the two line functions, and as close as possible to 100 percent of what we do should fall under one of these two areas. All support functions—including me—are here to serve these two functions. We work for them."

Personnel

The personnel function had undergone a dramatic shift over the years. In 1980, Donna Schwefel, a secretary, had started the personnel department. This department kept salary records and did the hiring for most of the direct labor jobs. The department also administered the performance review that was used as a basis for hourly wage increases and promotions. This department was also responsible for administering the benefit programs and maintaining the other personnel records that were required by law.

As the organization developed, and as Johnsonville placed more emphasis on individual acceptance of responsibility, the nature of the personnel function changed dramatically. Ralph felt that the personnel function was too important to be delegated to a staff area—it was a line function: "The only difference between Johnsonville and its competitors is our people."

First, many of the typical personnel functions left the personnel department and became the responsibility of "the line."

— Lori Lehmann, who was a packer on the bratwurst line, expressed a frustration shared by many of her fellow workers: New workers were typically thrown on to the production line with no training or orientation. Lori suggested developing a training/orientation program for new hires. She was encouraged to do so and developed a training/orientation guide for all the manufacturing workers in the new plant, as well as specific training for the direct positions. Lori presented this program to all new employees.

— Following success with this project, Lori suggested that people on the line have the opportunity to interview prospective hires. This effort was a success and, in early 1986, plans were under way to dismantle the role of personnel in the hiring functions.

The performance review process was also removed from the personnel area. The new process worked as follows:

— Each individual worker was responsible for developing his or her own job description. This listed responsibilities, the performance objectives for each responsibility, and the standard measures along which performance would be judged.

— Individuals were responsible for updating their job descriptions whenever their responsibilities changed.

— Individuals were also responsible for measuring their own performance and analyzing any deficiencies that they found, and for suggesting ways in which they will improve in these areas.

— At least semiannually, individual workers met with their leader and reviewed these results, and agreed on the performance evaluation. This was supplemented with almost daily discussion regarding objectives and performance.

— Based on this semiannual review, workers were assigned points, from 1 to 100, for their performance. The total number of points was then totalled on a companywide basis, and the bonus pool ("company performance share") was allocated in proportion to points earned.

Because Johnsonville's business was seasonal, there were wide swings in employment levels during the course of the year. To deal with this variation, the firm had a large pool of part-time and seasonal employees who were not considered full-time "members" of Johnsonville. When there were openings in the permanent work force, workers would select the best of these part-time employees.

Still, the company did not have an "employment security" policy. Ralph explained:

The best people—people who are really good at what they do—always have job security. To rely on the company to provide this, rather than one's self, is foolish. We provide an opportunity and environment where people can learn and become great; this is what the company can do.

The personnel function had shifted its focus to the human development area. Terri Case, a local high school teacher, had been hired in mid-1985 in response to a Johnsonville ad seeking an individual "committed to life-long learning."

Terri reported to two individuals:

— Bob Salzwedel, finance and administration, for compensation and personnel issues, such as group insurance, benefits, and profit sharing; and,

— Russ Wiverstad, manufacturing, for personnel development.

Ralph Stayer, as part of his emphasis on "people development," wanted Johnsonville to be a vehicle through which individuals could accomplish their own personal goals, whatever they may be. Every individual in the company was given an $80 educational allowance, to be spent in whatever manner they wished. Some took cooking or sewing classes; others signed up for flying lessons. Magazine subscriptions were another popular use for these funds. The company had also arranged for all workers to receive a free economics course, taught on plant premises by a local professor.

The hiring process was also unusual. In addition to the typical questions about prior experience, potential hires were asked:

— Why do you want to work for Johnsonville?
— How do you spend your leisure time?
— What would you like to be doing in five years?
— How do you define cooperation?
— How do your friends describe you?
— What do you have to offer a group?

In Terri's words, "If someone isn't sharp enough to write a well-thought-out paragraph on why they want to work here, they are probably not qualified to handle the kind of responsibility we give people."

Compensation

Prior to the transition, workers had been paid strictly on an hourly basis, which was about equal to the local average. Hourly increases were typically granted once a year. In 1979, a profit-sharing plan was introduced that contributed toward a worker's pension fund. Management viewed it as unsuccessful, because it did not tie compensation to individual performance; it seemed not to affect worker motivation, perhaps because its effect was not immediate.

In 1982, the company instituted a policy of no across-the-board wage increases. Increases would only be given for an increase in responsibilities. This was tracked via the workers' job descriptions, which were formally reviewed twice a year.

In addition to wages, workers received a company performance share, which was a function of both the firm's and the individual's performance. There were three "pools" to which a share of the company's profits was added semiannually:

— Hourly workers.

— Salaried workers.

— The three senior-level managers (did not include Ralph Stayer).

Ralph described the philosophy behind the compensation system:

> Nothing happens without necessity. To get great performance, it is necessary to build a system where only great performers can survive. Our compensation system is a good example. In the executive group, Russ, Bob, and Mike split their bonus completely upon the basis of what they did to build people during the year. This same percentage was used to compute their share of a net worth incentive—they can each get an additional bonus of up to 5 percent of the company's annual increase in net worth.

Everyone's performance was reviewed, based on his or her own job descriptions and performance targets, and that performance was rated on a scale of 0 to 100. Each pool was then assigned a number of points, which equaled the sum of every worker's point rating. Each worker then received a share of the pool that was equal to his or her point rating divided by the total number of points in the pool. Since the plan was introduced, payments to production workers had averaged as follows (this was the average payment; individual payments varied +/– 35 percent, depending on performance:

1982–$200
1983–$700
1984–$350
1985–$800

In 1985, this payment represented 4–5 percent of the average worker's annual wage. Management hoped to increase this percentage to 25 percent over the next several years. Ralph gave his views on the compensation levels at Johnsonville:

Our "average" wage has improved over the last five years, both with respect to our local area and the industry. Because we've grown so quickly, a relatively high proportion of our work force is new, and they haven't had the chance to work their way up through responsibility and pay levels.

But, if you compare someone who has been here for two years with the average local employee, we've moved from about average to the 80th percentile or so. Only workers in heavy industry represented by the big, national unions do much better.

With respect to the industry, we are below the national master union contract that binds Oscar Mayer and Hormel. Still, we've moved from about 50 percent of the national master contract level to 85–90 percent of that level. During a time that competitive pressures have forced them to decrease their wages, we've been able to *increase* ours.

Some workers were very enthusiastic about the company performance share (CPS). Typically, they had increased their responsibilities over the years, and received hourly increases as well, so they viewed the CPS as a true "bonus." Other workers, however, complained that they had not received any wage increase over the past three to four years. They felt that the CPS was a poor substitute for the annual wage increase that they had formerly enjoyed. In addition, workers seemed to think that there was not much variation between the best and worst performers. The compensation system did seem to have broadened individuals' perspective on the company, however. People questioned Ralph Stayer on the impact of acquisitions and capital investments on the company's performance and the CPS.

Research and Development

Prior to the transition, the research and development area was not formally delineated in the organization. Ralph would work on his own ideas. Now R&D was viewed as the responsibility of everyone in the organization. One of the company's recent, and successful, new products, Beer 'n Bratwurst, was developed by a team within the company. The product consisted of a bratwurst that was made with beer, instead of water, to replicate the flavor that many brat fans achieved by soaking the product in beer.

The idea for the product came out of a brain-storming session held during the summer of 1984. Together with individuals from the sales and research area, this team tested and refined the product, which was introduced six months later.

A similar process resulted in the company's ham and cheese sausage, a mild bratwurst containing bits of ham and cheese. Ralph Stayer wasn't even aware that the product was under development until he was presented with samples.

Systems and Controls

There was an emphasis at Johnsonville on "self-control." In Ralph Stayer's words, "The notion of control systems is an illusion; the only real control is when people control themselves." In line with the company's philosophy, individual performance was key to the achievement of both the individual's and the firm's goals. Thus, the system began with a great deal of emphasis on describing responsibilities and performance targets at an individual level:

— Individual salespeople developed the budgets and forecasts to which they were willing to be held accountable.

— Manufacturing employees used these forecasts to develop budgets and production targets to which they agreed to be held accountable.

Out of these individual commitments, firmwide projections and budgets were developed. These budgets were used as a yardstick against actual performance, and as a control on spending. Nonbudgeted items over $500 had to be approved at the vice president level.

Employees wrote their own job descriptions, set their own performance objectives, and described the measures that would be used to evaluate performance against these objectives. It was the subordinate's responsibility to demonstrate his or her own performance to his or her superior, not vice versa. There was a great deal of emphasis on monitoring one's own performance:

— Manufacturing workers collected the data to evaluate their own performance daily.

— Salespeople received weekly and monthly reports on their performance versus budget.

It was viewed as the individual employee's job to analyze these data and understand them. If there was a shortfall compared with expectations, what was the cause? If plans were being exceeded, what could be learned from this?

Through this approach, individuals could improve their own performance and better their own skills and abilities; it was their responsibility to keep their supervisor informed of any problems.

Workers did punch a time clock, but they didn't punch out for lunch, and their hours were no longer tallied by accounting. It was each individual employee's responsibility to total his hours weekly.

Ralph described the issues the firm faced in developing its systems:

Traditional flows of information are totally inappropriate for what we are trying to accomplish. Traditional information systems transfer the problems away from those individuals that are best-suited to deal with them effectively. The key is to develop systems to push problems back to where they belong. We divide information into two types—history and control. Control data are developed to help each person or group control their own operations. They are generated and kept at the operational level. Historical information shows trends and overall performance, and flows to whoever is interested.

One example of the manner in which Johnsonville worked was a specific problem that the firm had with "leakers"—vacuum-packed plastic packages of sausages that leaked air back into the package, thereby shortening shelf life. One worker described how the problem would have been handled in the days prior to the transition:

> Someone from Quality Assurance would have been measuring the total quantity of leakers, and when it reached a certain point, they would yell at the foreman and tell him to reduce the number of leakers, and the guy wouldn't have a clue what to do about it, so he'd just yell at the people who worked for him. That's the whole reason you need a foreman, so you have someone to yell at when there's a problem.

The problem, however, was handled very differently. A "Pride Team" of volunteers was formed around the leaker problem. This team of first-line workers, with the help of a manufacturing specialist, investigated the leakers and discovered four possible sources:

— The die, which punched out the plastic package;

— The plastic film, which was used for the plastic packages;

— The packaging machine, which actually shrink-wraps the sausage; and

— The actual placement of the sausage in the wrapper.

Only this last cause was a "man-made" source of leakers; the rest were machine- or materials-related. The workers developed a set of priorities for attacking these problems, based on their analysis of the frequency with which each of these causes contributed to the leaker problem.

The workers attacked each problem, working with materials suppliers, making adjustments to equipment or the manner in which it was used. Within two months, the machine/materials problems, which accounted for over 80 percent of the leakers, had been completely eliminated.

New practices were developed for line workers, and this solved the "man-made" leaker problems as well. As a final step in the program, some representatives from the Pride Team visited retail outlets to educate them on how to handle and store the product once it had left the plant, in order to decrease problems that were caused at the store level.

During this process, the workers collected, analyzed, and posted the data every day to determine how they were progressing on the leaker problem.

Summary

Although a great deal of responsibility was delegated to the functions, there were naturally still decisions that cut across these specific areas of responsibility. Ralph described how he viewed such decisions:

> When we have an issue that involves several different areas, I try to get together the key functional managers and let them work on it. I'd rather not make a decision, but expose it to them and let them decide and learn from it. I believe I have a certain responsibility to the shareholders— including myself—and if I thought a decision was endangering the economic health of the organization, I would veto it. But—so far at least—that hasn't happened.
>
> Basically, I don't want to rob the organization of the opportunity to learn.
>
> The greatest joy for me has been watching people take the program and run with it. Seeing people's expectations of themselves and of what they might become being lifted to levels hat would not have been possible any other way.

THE PALMER SAUSAGE DECISION

The employees of Palmer Sausage had gone out on strike in mid-1985, and the company had farmed out its production of sausage items to a number of subcontractors. Johnsonville had produced ring bologna and wieners for Palmer, and the products had sold so well that Palmer asked Johnsonville to continue making the product even after the strike was settled. Palmer sold these products outside of the geographic regions in which Johnsonville competed.

In mid-1986, Ralph Stayer received a phone call from Palmer's vicé president of manufacturing, informing him of the fact that Palmer was thinking of closing one of its midwestern plants and would consider giving the lion's share of the business to Johnsonville. As per standard practice in the industry, any contract for private label production would permit cancellation of the business with 30 days' notice.

Ralph described the thoughts that raced through his mind:

> On one hand, we would love to have the business. We make a 25 percent ROA on this private label business—it is profitable for us. But in our last business plan, we decided that we did not want to push private label business over 15 percent; after that point, it would begin to compete for

capital with the rest of our business. This order alone is for a dollar volume that will represent 25 percent of our sales.

We are running at a very high capacity utilization now. In order to process this business, we will have to run two long shifts, six or seven days a week. (Johnsonville could not operate more than 18 hours per day because it was necessary to break down the equipment and clean it on a daily basis.) This will really push us to our limits. It could have a demoralizing impact on our own people and cause the quality of our own products to suffer.

Longer term, it will force us to build another plant much sooner than we had anticipated. Suppose we build for this business, and then they cancel our contract? Our return on that investment will drop dramatically, and we will have to lay off the workers we hired for this business.

Ralph wondered what he should do.

EXHIBIT 1   Johnsonville Organization over Time

Johnsonville Organization in Early 1960s

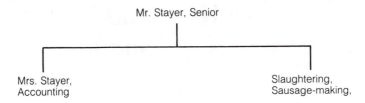

Mr. Stayer, Senior

Mrs. Stayer, Accounting

Slaughtering, Sausage-making,

Johnsonville Organization in 1978

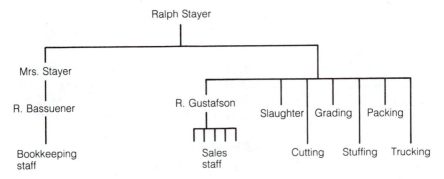

Ralph Stayer

Mrs. Stayer

R. Bassuener

Bookkeeping staff

R. Gustafson

Sales staff

Slaughter | Grading | Packing

Cutting   Stuffing   Trucking

Johnsonville Organization in 1985

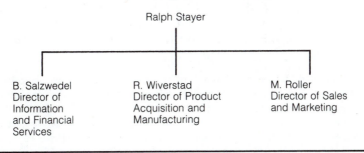

Ralph Stayer

B. Salzwedel
Director of
Information
and Financial
Services

R. Wiverstad
Director of Product
Acquisition and
Manufacturing

M. Roller
Director of Sales
and Marketing

Howard Head and Prince Manufacturing Inc.

"We can own the tennis world," Howard Head told Prince Company president Jack Murray and Jim Baugh, director of marketing. Unfortunately, Mr. Head was not sure that these key people shared his dramatic vision. They were quite satisfied with Prince's recent 100 percent growth rate, and they were not inclined to risk change.

In the spring of 1982, Head had begun to think seriously about the future of Prince. Having already achieved success with his oversized Prince Classic tennis racket, he now envisioned an empire greater than any the industry had ever seen. A small company called Kennex had just approached Mr. Head to ask if Prince would consider promoting their rackets. Although Head found the Kennex racket to be an "excellent and aesthetically beautiful product," he declined their offer. As he put it:

> I was afraid to accept Kennex's offer for fear that word would get out that I was promoting a midsize racket that wasn't mine. Unfortunately, Prince company management didn't want to listen to my ideas for an expanded line of Prince tennis rackets. I had written about 80 pages of company objectives which laid it all out very clearly. However, Prince's director of marketing was afraid that plans for promotion of the 110 would falter unless the company ruled out consideration of any size other than the 110. He felt that a leak concerning the possible consideration of any other size

---

This case was prepared by Susan Harmeling under the direction of Howard H. Stevenson.

would be detrimental to Prince's marketing plans. That was why he thought we should tell Kennex no. I, on the other hand, declined their offer mainly because I had no interest in marketing any racket other than one designed by, built by, and carrying the name of Prince.

Mr. Head's company objectives included plans for aggressive experimentation with a series of 93- and 100-square-inch rackets to go along with the original 110-size Prince. With the standard racket size of 70 square inches on one end and Head's successful 110 square inch Prince on the other, Head felt sure that there was a market for these midsize versions, and he didn't want to miss out on an obvious opportunity. Head's objectives told of his "growing feeling that Prince should expand to a full line of 93s and 100s." He saw the possibility for Prince to "move at once to blanket the entire tennis market, simply taking over and making all other rackets obsolete and unnecessary." This was Head's plan, but he felt that his own company was getting in the way.

Howard Head also felt that Prince's officers were taking an overcautious stance with regard to his plans for expanding the company's telephone-answering force to include computerized information on every dealer. In addition, he envisioned other improvements that involved Prince's public relations and customer service departments. He wanted to fine tune Prince to the very limits, but his own people were stopping him.

Head's now famous oversized racket had taken his young company from $1 million to $35 million sales in just five years, and 1982 projections were for gross sales of close to $60 million. (See Exhibit 1 for Prince Financial Summary). Should he, at the age of 68, set forth to implement these ambitious goals, or should he sell while the value of his business was on the rise? Should he finally "give up the 'thing' world and move into the 'people' world," breaking his addiction to the "powerful drug of creativity"?

Head certainly wasn't thinking of going into business again when the Head Ski Company and its famous name were sold to AMF, Inc. in 1969 for $16 million. On the contrary, he was ready to throw in the towel, for success was sweet, but it was not without its strains. "If a logo had to be designed," Head explained, "I did it. If a selling tour had to be made, I did it. If the factory floor had to be swept, I did it. You can't run a frantically expanding business that way." Maybe not, but the inventor had done something right, for "when AMF took the broom out of Head's hands in 1969, he personally realized more than $4 million in cash."[1] The opening chapter of his amazing story was

---

[1]Walter McQuade, "Prince Triumphant," *Fortune,* February 22, 1982.

complete, and Howard Head's sometimes frustrating experience with his first company was history. Or was it? Actually, this initial business experience with Head Ski Company proved to be a valuable asset as Mr. Head set out a few years later to create yet another superior sporting implement. But did he really want to invest the time and energy in Prince Manufacturing Inc. to take it to the heights he knew were possible?

PRINCE COMPANY HISTORY

Howard Head came to the tennis industry largely by accident. He initially made himself known in recreational circles in the early 50s when he designed the first metal ski. As an aircraft engineer during World War II, he had become an expert on the various uses of aluminum. Using this knowledge, he produced a metal sandwich ski in 1950, which, by the 1960s, had all but crushed its wooden competitors. As Head described it,

> This success had nothing to do with promotion, but stemmed from the fact that the product was almost magically easier to use, making the sport accessible to millions of skiers. Heretofore the extreme difficulty of skiing on the laminated hickory skis of the prior era had limited the sport to the hearty elite. The Head ski was later credited as a key factor in the growth of the sport from perhaps a total of 10,000 U.S. skiers in the 1940s to millions in the 1960s.

Head retired in 1970, a year after selling Head Ski Company to AMF, but his retirement didn't last very long. As he told the story:

> I put in a court and decided to take up tennis, but I found that it wasn't as easy as I thought. Even after I took a lot of lessons, I still had trouble. . . .
>
> My tennis pro must have gotten tired of trying to hit against me, because in the summer of 1971 he suggested that I get a tennis ball machine to practice against. He put me in touch with a little company called Prince up in Princeton, New Jersey. I called them up and told them I wanted to buy one of their machines. They said it would cost $285.00. I said, "All right, you put a machine on the truck today, and I'll put a check in the mail today." That's the way we got started.
>
> They sent a machine down, and I recognized almost immediately that it was a carefully thought-through and well-designed piece of equipment, but about as crude as the first Head ski. Everything went wrong with it: the ball would jam, the ball would glunk, the ball would drop. *Everything* went wrong—I spoke with them over the phone and within two months I

joined the company as chairman of the board and de facto chief engineer. I had gotten into a thing I loved, which was debugging and perfecting a piece of equipment. A year and a half later, Prince had captured half the ball machine business.

One indication of Howard Head's ongoing devotion to innovation and quality was illustrated by this initial contact with the Prince Manufacturing Company. He did them the service of fixing their flawed product before he had invested in the business. In October of 1971, after Head had successfully "debugged" the Prince ball machine, he bought 27 percent of the company for $27,000. (See Exhibit 2 for Chronological Outline and 1971 Balance Sheet.) The company averaged a 15 percent net profit for the first three years from 1972 to 1974. Head explained:

> The reason we were able to do that was because our business was based on the ultrasimple process of someone calling up and saying, "Can I buy a machine?" and we would say, "Sure, put a check in the mail, and when it hits our mailbox we will ship you a machine." We basically had no distributors and no advertising. We just waited for checks and then shipped the machines so we could market the machines at low cost and make a whopping profit.
>
> That ball machine company taught me how to run a profitable business because it was so simple. Furthermore, I was just sitting down in Baltimore smiling and saying, "Well done, fellows; it's great to see this money piling up. . . . "

Mr. Head explained that he had not been particularly anxious to get back into business, and it was clearly not a financial necessity. Rather, it was the result of his own personal struggle with existing sports equipment. This was the crux of Howard Head's whole motivation . . . to fine-tune the existing equipment for each individual user. Head's first invention transformed the ski world, and Prince rackets opened up the same possibilities in the tennis world. As Head put it, "God had smiled on two occasions."

Mal Bash, who came to Prince in 1974 as quality control manager and who was later promoted to chief engineer and chief of manufacturing, had this to say about Howard Head's early role with the company:

> We had this fellow, Howard Head, who came up once in a while and looked around and helped with the company. He offered suggestions on how to improve our product, our ball machine. He came up from Baltimore at least once a month and spent a day or two. I remember we had a lot of discussions about the ball-throwing machine and the ways he thought it could be improved. He was always asking us to try different things. He

would never accept a no. If I said I couldn't do something, he'd ask why? I'd say it wouldn't work, and he'd ask why? again. I found it quite challenging, and it often led to accomplishing things I didn't think could be accomplished.

Mr. Bash went on to tell of Prince's later attempts to develop a more advanced model of the ball machine. It was to be called the Professional and was to have a greater ball capacity. There were problems with the design of this model—the balls constantly jammed as they were feeding into the machine, and as Bash pointed out, it was the "eleventh hour." The company had presold these machines and were now ready to go into production before the jamming problem was fixed. Bash recalled that Howard Head averted the crisis.

> There was a little part of the machine called the spring pin, which kept more than one ball at a time from feeding into the machine. One of Howard's suggestions was to take a couple of spring pins and bolt them into the top of the rotor. He thought it would stir everything up enough to prevent the jamming. I didn't think it would work, but Howard insisted that it would. Sure enough, it solved the problem, and we went into production the next day.

Howard Head's enthusiasm for fixing things, for creating a better product, had started a generation earlier when a different sport caught his fancy. From skis to ball machines to rackets, Head explained that his success was the result of an obsession with performance. He said:

> Sports-minded people will simply gravitate toward a product that works better. Give them a better piece of fly casting equipment, and they will buy that fishing rod. Give them a better ski-down-the-hill design, and they will buy that ski. A better tennis ball hitting implement, and they'll buy that racket when it becomes available. It's performance that counts, and word of mouth that sells the product. No amount of promotion or advertising or other pizzazz will alter this fundamental truth.

TENNIS—THE INDUSTRY

During the late 1960s and the early 1970s, another revolution was taking place in tennis, which had nothing to do with equipment. Gone were the days when the sport was synonymous with country clubs, white garb, strawberries and champagne; tennis was no longer reserved for the elite. Courts were springing up everywhere, and amateur athletes from all walks of life were heading out in droves with rackets in hand. Tennis was starting to sell, and as the sport moved from exclusive circles into the mass market, the possibilities for innovation were endless. As early as the mid-1960s, tennis was clearly "in." Courts were being built in record numbers, especially indoor courts made to accommodate the serious, year-round player. A 1965 *Business Week* article noted the trend:

> Tennis, anyone? This winter, the answer has been a resounding "yes." From its traditional home in grim and drafty armories scarred by National Guard drills, indoor tennis has moved into plush, well-lighted clubs and has attracted thousands of new players. "The demand is so great the new courts aren't even coming close to taking care of all the people who want to play," says an official of the U.S. Lawn Tennis Association. A spokesman for Wilson Sporting Goods estimates that there are some 200 indoor courts in the country, most of them built in the last five years, and about one third of them in the last 12 months.

By 1966, *Newsweek* estimated that there were 8.5 million tennis players in the United States, and among this group, the population of "insiders" was growing rapidly.

This was just the beginning of the craze. The long-standing tradition of "tennis whites" was made obsolete in the late 1960s. "I'm a progressive," claimed Arthur Ashe when he showed up at a January 1968 exhibition match wearing snazzy powder blue shorts and shirt. And though many U.S. clubs were still sticking to the old belief that "whites were right," even some of the most traditional members of the tennis community had decided to jump on the bandwagon, as *Time* reported in February of 1968:

> Said Walter Elcock, president of Brookline's Longwood Cricket Club where players have worn only whites since 1877, "So many changes are being made in tennis, I can't see that a few more will hurt the game. I might even try a colored outfit myself."

The fashion trend from whites to brights signified another trend taking place in the world of tennis, which had deeper implications for the future of the sport. By the early 1970s, things had changed in a sport that had remained the same for a long time. In the summer of 1972, *Life* magazine reported that 100 years earlier, "There was just one tennis court in the United States. It was shaped like an hourglass, as were the ladies playing on it." By the time the article was published, there were an estimated 100,000 U.S. courts in all and 5,000 new ones being added each year.

Whatever the reasons, the trend continued, and by the mid-1970s, it looked as though there was no end in sight. Was it really more than a passing fad? A 1974 *Sports Illustrated* article claimed, "Now Everybody Has the Bug," and warned:

> Once, like gout, it afflicted only the rich, but today tennis fever is epidemic. And it will sneak up on you, too, if you don't watch out.

Twenty-one million Americans, drawn like fruit flies to a vast ripening vine, now play tennis at one level of incompetence or another. This national mania is not without value. Golf courses are no longer as crowded, for one thing, and there aren't as many drunks driving home after a match. Unlike golf, tennis has no par to alert man to his inferiority. He can reach new depths without the need of a 19th-hole elixir to ease the pain. A swig of Gatorade will usually do it.

Of course, all the enthusiasm generated by the sport brought the prospect of endless opportunity for inventors, businessmen, and consumers alike. A 1976 *Time* magazine article called "Those Super Rackets" told of the increasing popularity of rackets "designed to bestow court greatness on weekend hackers."

The names—YFG-50, Boron XT, and the XRC—conjure up visions of supersonic test plans or supersonic racing cars. But the sobriquets belong to tennis rackets, crafted in strange shapes of exotic materials.

In search of a bigger "sweet spot," more power, and control, manufacturers have imbedded boron fibers in an epoxy matrix, reinforced nylon throat pieces with quartz, turned to builders of nuclear reactors for ultrasonic welding techniques, and altered the spacing of strings. The physics laboratories at Princeton where Albert Einstein once worked have been used to experiment with variants of torque and longitudinal flex.

There was a technological revolution occurring in the tennis world during the mid-1970s, reflecting the will of inventors who felt that if colored clothes and neighborhood courts were gaining acceptance, then tennis rackets would have to keep up with the times. Head was one of those inventors. Yet precisely as this period of technological innovation was reaching its peak, the popularity of the sport began to decline sharply. Prince came on the scene in the midst of the turmoil:

The enormous, swelling U.S. tennis boom peaked in the late 1970s; total sales of rackets dropped precipitously from 8.3 million in 1977 to 4.9 million the next year and continued to drift downward to 3.2 million in 1981. (See Exhibit 3.)

The manufacturers are anything but sure why this has happened, but they cite a couple of possibilities. The sport became such a social craze that many would-be players bought rackets before they found it wasn't as easy on the court as it seemed to be on TV. Beyond that, the manufacturers point to the cyclical nature of individual sports in general. Among recent fads, roller skating has hit the skids and racquetball has fizzled (ruining a secondary market for many racket manufacturers). Today, indoor exercise equipment is the rage.

The simultaneous collapse of the market and the fact that the oversize Prince was just beginning its roll, left the giants of the industry searching for defensive strategies. The small, tightly strung world of tennis-racket makers is haunted by a paralyzing question: how to compete with that peculiar, triumphant slammer of the fuzzy yellow ball, the oversized Prince racket. Invented just six years ago by technological iconoclast Howard Head and at first considered nothing more than an amusing novelty, the Prince last year grabbed the commanding share of the high-priced market.

Prince's share of the market for upper-bracket rackets—those selling for $50 and up—exploded from 8.5 percent in 1979 to 30.7 percent in 1981—AMF Head's share meanwhile slipped from 31.6 percent to 26.3 percent while Wilson's fell like a dropshot, from 19.2 percent to 10.7 percent.

This left industry strongmen trying to persuade customers to trade up to more expensive "weapons," as manufacturers call rackets.[2]

Still, not everyone was convinced that Prince was the ultimate weapon. While many players swore by their new rackets, most experts during this peak period of experimentation agreed with Chicago tennis pro Calvin Head (clearly no relation to Howard Head), who claimed that the advantages of the new designs and materials were largely psychological.

"We're all trying to find that little secret, but it's all in the mind," he said. Another pro, disgusted by the stampede to new rackets said, "People will do anything to improve their game except work on their strokes."

Head's oversized racket enjoyed its immediate success even though this professional skepticism had combined with a general decline in the tennis industry. Prince succeeded even though a majority of pros agreed with renowned California teacher Vic Braden who insisted:

I don't care what kind of racket it is. I once saw Bobby Riggs beat a guy with a broom . . . the only difference the Prince rackets make is that now when you serve, you will hit both your legs rather than just one.

DESIGN—PRINCE RACKETS

Head arrived at the ultimate design of his oversized racket after a period of persistent trial and error. This was not, however, his first shot at racket design, as *Fortune* magazine noted:

Head had fooled with tennis rackets before. While still with the Head Company, he had taken to shaving the wooden rims of cheap Korean imports and tacking on aluminum siding in an unsuccessful attempt to strengthen them. By 1974, he was frustrated enough with his own game to give the racket another try. It was either that or take up golf, and Head hated golf.

---

[2] Ibid.

Just as he had looked for a ski that would keep him from tumbling down the mountain, he was searching for a racket that would save him from embarrassment on the court:

> The parallel story in Prince, to compare it with Head, was that I was simply looking for a racket that would be more stable to an off-center hit. I tried to fix it by putting weights on the rim of the frame. It didn't work.
>
> Then, I had a genuine breakthrough. I realized that I shouldn't add any weight, but should spread the weight out. I knew this would increase the inertia and therefore, the stability of the racket. That was my invention.

The only problem was that the result was a funny-looking contraption resembling a snowshoe, not a tennis racket. As one journalist observed:

> He knew it sounded silly (who would play with a paddle the size and shape of a snowshoe?), but he had to give it a try. The result was a racket two inches wider than conventional models, made of aluminum to bear the extra strain of the longer strings. Displeased with the too-round lines of his first designs, Head extended the strung area of the racket into the handle region to soften the curve.[3]

Although Howard Head's Prince racket was later expanded into various materials (his graphite racket was the first of its kind), it was the new shape as well as the dimensions of the racket that were its engineering breakthroughs. By making the racket only two inches wider with a three inch longer hitting surface in the throat, Head had increased the torsional stability of the racket and the size of its "sweet spot" by an extraordinary degree. The earlier 70-square-inch racket had a mean way of twisting in the hand to an off-center hit. As Head described it, "Suddenly, a sport, which had a somewhat limited following because of technical difficulty, became accessible to a much broader range of players. The market expanded, and the sport was just plain more fun. The parallels with the metal ski were obvious." But while the new racket worked very well, its appearance, as one tennis buff wrote, sparked a very important question:

> "Is it legal?"
>
> That's what they asked me when I stepped onto a tennis court brandishing the new Prince racket. It's not a surprising reaction. For the last 75 years or so, tennis players had been used to seeing rackets of roughly the same size and shape. The first really radical change in that geometry is the Prince—an outlandish object resembling a deranged snowshoe. The surface area of the head is a full 50 percent larger than

---

[3]Arthur Fisher, "Super Racket," *Popular Science,* Spring 1977.

that of a conventional design. Reason? To let you hit more balls and hit them better.

Is that legal? Absolutely. The rules of the game specify all sorts of things about the court, the net, and the ball, but state only that the player must strike the ball with an "implement." You are entitled, if the fancy takes you, to whack a tennis ball with a pool cue, butterfly net, or the door off an old pickup.[4]

THE PATENT

It was legal, yes, but the patent office initially said that it wasn't a novel enough idea to merit the issuance of a coveted patent. It did no good simply to assert that this racket was better than the old fashioned kind. The question, "How much better?" had to be answered, and Howard Head was not to be denied. After working with Princeton consulting engineer Ken Wright, Head determined that the racket's "coefficient of restitution" could supply the quantifying data. (The coefficient of restitution at any spot on the racket head is the ratio of the velocity of the incoming ball as compared with the velocity of the ball leaving the strings.)

Using high speed photography, he measured the size of where the coefficients were .3 and .4 and .5 on his new Prince racket as compared with these same zones on ordinary rackets. He found that in every case, these zones on the Prince were three to four times bigger than corresponding zones on conventional 70-square-inch rackets. He even found that there was one zone of .6 on his new racket that didn't exist on an ordinary racket. That was the crucial point. There was now measurable proof that at least by one criterion the Prince racket produced more than three times improved performance with only a 60 percent increase in area. (See Exhibit 4.)

Students of business might have thought it strange that Head seemed to have a great idea which he was taking out and showing to anyone he came in contact with, apparently unconcerned that his invention could be copied. But his experience in development led him to take the necessary precautions of meticulous documentation and also to go through the required legal groundwork. He had actually applied for patents as early as 1974, and the patent was finally issued as Patent No. 3,999,756 in May of 1976. It was good for 17 years, covered a wide range of racket shapes and sizes, and was, according to a 1977 *Popular Science* article, "the broadest tennis racket patent ever granted."

---

[4]Ibid.

Where the Prince was not able to achieve patent protection, for example in Germany and Japan, other companies began to produce rackets of Prince's size and shape. Prince's lawyers were, however, able to secure judgments that prevented those adaptations from being sold in the United States, causing one competitor to muse, "Howard's brilliance really shone at its brightest when he got that patent. It's like getting a patent on a size 9 shoe."[5]

Head explained that this discovery was more "a bit of black magic" than a work of brilliance. He had given the Prince its new shape with the intention of achieving a more aesthetically pleasing design, and it was this alteration that had made the racket's sweet spot 3.78 times bigger than that of a conventional racket. The enlarged sweet spot, combined with the racket's wider head, gave players four times the chance of hearing the clear sound of a center hit shot.

With good feedback from experimental rackets in the field, and with patent in sight, the decision was made to move Prince full speed ahead into the racket business. It was none too soon, as Howard Head explained:

> It was a dramatic moment in this little million-dollar company called Prince Ball Machine Company. We had noticed that our sales of ball machines had remained virtually constant for the last year but that profits had diminished from 15 to 7 percent. Luckily we faced up to the fact that the problem was simply an inherent limit to the size of the ball machine market. There just weren't that many players out there who were interested in that form of practice. The market wasn't there.

Sales of the Prince racket took off just in time, for it had become clear that the ball machine market was saturated. Head had discovered two things simultaneously: that he could not propel the ball machine onto an expanding sales trajectory, and that the potential for racket sales was enormous. The Prince racket had picked up precisely where the ball machine left off, but if Mr. Head was to realize the racket's potential, there were still many obstacles to overcome.

MARKETING

Howard Head consistently emphasized the fact that at no time in his career did he stress a growth imperative:

> I will never try to make my company grow for growth's sake, but I have people who do—marketing people. My compulsion is simply to make the

---

[5]McQuade, "Prince Triumphant."

best sliding-down-the-hill implement for skiers and the best tennis ball-hitting implement for tennis players, and in both sports a different piece of equipment fine tuned to each category of athlete.

At Prince, Head did encounter problems in achieving the latter aim—of providing a racket for players in all segments of the market:

> In 1976, we went into production. In that year, we sold 70,000 rackets, in 1977 we sold 160,000 rackets. I expected to be going up to 250,000 and then 400,000 in the years following, but suddenly there was a leveling off.

Why this slowdown? For one thing, very few young people were buying the new rackets, including the oversized Prince. A Beverly Hills tennis shop salesman reported in November of 1976 that most Prince sales were made to men over 40 "searching for a tennis fountain of youth." A young tournament player summed it up by saying, "When somebody shows up with a fancy stick, some other kid will say, 'Oh you need a bionic racket, huh?' Nobody wants to look like a sissy."

Prince was well aware of this problem:

> Sitting afar I had the perspective and the vision to know that the problem with this racket was that it was being swallowed up by lady club players, elderly men, and beginners, but it was not being accepted by professionals, young college players, or class A players. It finally sank into me, and more quickly than in the case of the Head skis, that these guys had a valid complaint that the rackets were too spongy, strung too softly, and had a frame that was too flexible for the hard hitting young players.

Mal Bash explained further:

> I can remember in early 1976 that we started to get complaints from our customers. They said that the racket didn't play well, that it vibrated badly, and that it made noises when the ball was hit.
>
> Howard and I did some investigation on the problem and came to the conclusion that Prince rackets were not being strung tightly enough. The Prince needed to be strung 15 to 20 pounds tighter than a conventional racket.
>
> So we wrote and rewrote extensive stringing instructions in an attempt to educate the consumer on how the racket should be strung.
>
> Then people started complaining that the racket couldn't be strung on certain machines. Howard said that we had to solve this problem, and I said that I didn't know enough about all of the different kinds of machines. He told me to go out and buy them all, and I did just that. After stringing the rackets on every single machine on the market, we modified our stringing instructions accordingly.

This was not enough, however, to attract the segment of the market that was missing. Mr. Head described the aging group of players who still composed the majority of his most visible customers:

These guys were moderately gentle players anyhow—they were either seniors or getting along. They were not the kind of people who were going to lead the class A players, the younger touring pros, the college players, and the juniors to us. In any case, we increased the string tension, but it still did not attract many of the really good players to our racket. About 1977, I felt this slowdown taking place, and I decided that we must go on a search for a new racket, a stiffer racket with a stiffer frame and a frame that could be strung much tighter. I approached that in two ways. We wanted the tubular aluminum frame racket, which later became the Prince Pro, and we wanted the graphite fiber racket, which later became the Prince Graphite.

Just a couple of years later, Mr. Head's goals for reversing this slowdown in sales had more than been realized, and while he may never have stressed growth per se, he had a strong feeling that even more people should be using his racket. The slowdown was over, and he was now dreaming of even greater market penetration and hoping that every tennis player in the world would soon be using a Prince. The Pro and the Graphite were selling like hotcakes, adding to the Classic's steady share. Further growth seemed inevitable, prompting Head to envision an expanded line of new rackets in an assortment of different sizes, shapes, and colors designed to cater to players in every category. His main obstacle in achieving this goal would come from within his own company:

> In 1979, we were past our leveling-off period, with sales soaring from $9 million to $18 million and with a great increase in profits and margins. It was late in the fall of 1980 that my president, who was a superlative administrator, organizer, leader, and motivator said to me, "Howard you ought to look through the profit plan." I said all right, and I looked at it. I said, "Tell me what it means, give me the gist of it, and what is our sales increase projected for next year?" "Howard, we are projecting a 25 percent sales increase," he said, and I said, "Say that again!" He said, "You know Howard, I am responsible for the company, and I am working for you, and I don't want to overpromise you. I am willing to project a 25 percent sales increase, and I'm sure we may do even better."
>
> I said, "I don't think I'm hearing you right. We grew 100 percent last year, didn't we?" He said, "Yes, but Howard, I don't want to promise you too much." Honest to God, my head started swimming. I told him that we were going to project a continuation of the 100 percent growth and that I would be responsible for it. That's how the thing went. Where would we have gotten the product to sell if I hadn't pressed the issue?

For Mr. Head, the word *marketing* conjured up images of a mindset very different from his own. When asked about the marketing department of his company, he responded:

It is not my favorite area just because of the kind of thinking they do. They are much more timid than I would be if I were in the marketing department. If I felt that we could make a better tennis ball-hitting implement for a wider number of players, I would not be worried about the fact that the image of Prince is a 110-size racket. I would make the better implement first and worry about the marketing effect later. I don't like the word *marketing,* but I do like products.

Mr. Head's ongoing obsession with simplicity and with the efficient delivery of product to consumer was also evident in his attitude toward distributors and sales representatives:

> Past experience led us to conclude that marketing through distributors was an error and that we should standardize on shipment through the home office in Princeton.
> The country was divided quite early into about eight territories with a sales rep from each area in charge. Some of these were from big organizations and some were individual reps, but this is not an area in which I have been strongly interested. It has remained my conviction that the product either sells itself or it doesn't.

MANUFACTURING

It was in the area of manufacturing that Howard Head had learned perhaps the most valuable lesson of his years at the Head Ski Company. The time and energy wasted on problems related to manufacturing was said to be one of the main reasons that Mr. Head, so accustomed to being at the front of the pack, was kept from capitalizing on a major technological breakthrough in ski design. He said:

> If we had not been doing our own manufacturing, we could have ordered this company and that company to do research and switch us over into fiberglass. The fact is that we were unable to do that fast enough. I think I knew that since I had this compulsion to direct everything and do everything myself that I would not succeed in that conversion.

The second time around, he realized the importance of doing what he did best and letting someone else do the rest. He explained:

> At Prince, we do not waste our energies on the frustration of manufacturing. At Head, we ate ourselves up in the manufacturing process I had invented, and we remained total amateurs at it. In the case of Prince, our manufacturing is done exclusively by pros responsible for their own work.

At the beginning, these "pros" were the Maark Corporation, no strangers to Mr. Head. Late in the 1960s, during his final days at the Head Ski Company, Howard Head became interested in tennis and began selling conventional-sized aluminum rackets under the Head label. He had the rackets made to specification by Maark, an aluminum designer and fabricator near Princeton, New Jersey.

In 1974, when Prince manufacturing was ready to begin selling the oversized racket, Head again turned to his friends at Maark to manufacture the first model, known as the Prince Classic.

Head's previous relationship with Maark proved invaluable. As he once said, he would have been too tired to start the project from scratch had he not known someone who could make that first batch of rackets for him. After presenting the idea of the Prince racket to Prince's board of directors in the fall of 1974, the decision was made to get some test rackets produced by Maark the following year. When asked what kind of expenditure that involved, Head explained the nature of this "strategic alliance":

> Maark was smart. They wouldn't charge me a cent for the first experimental racket, nor for the next 6, nor for the final 100 experimental rackets that we needed for confirmation. They were putting me under a moral obligation so that if this racket worked they were going to get the business.
>
> They knew that I was trustworthy, and I think they thought from my history that, goofy as this thing looked, I must have had a good reason for pursuing it. My track record with Head skis was a good one.
>
> Maark's initial pricing policy paid off well. They developed a great relationship with Prince, and they supplied the first production Prince racket, which was known as the Classic. They made it from aluminum extrusion of their own design. It was a good serviceable frame and reached wide acceptance with the beginner and the average player. However, this is the racket that turned out to be too flexible and was unable to be strung tightly enough to make it acceptable to the good player.

In 1978, aware of the flattening in sales and the need for a stiffer racket that would withstand tighter stringing, Mal Bash went to Maark and asked them to make a tubular racket as opposed to their extruded frame. They rejected this design. Bash became indignant at Maark's rejection of his plans for the new racket. As he explained it:

> I walked out of the meeting at that point. I was really feeling like I was going down the wrong track. Here were two guys who had made and designed the first really successful aluminum racket (the Head Pro), and both of these guys had previously come from Alcoa. They had a lot of knowledge about aluminum, but they were just too old and tired to listen.

Head explained the ramifications:

> Maark was getting reasonably fat and they were enjoying our relationship with them. Then we came to them with a change which we knew was the future of the tennis racket world. This is like it was with Head back

in 1965 when I knew in my gut that the wave of the future was going to be the fiberglass ski. But we were unable to make the leap to a totally new technology. This is what was happening with Maark.

The people at Prince knew they needed a tubular aluminum frame. But where would they get it? Mal Bash looked through the *Thomas Registry* and contacted 15 to 20 aluminum fabricators. They all said they were not interested because the new design would be too prone to stress corrosion, a propensity toward internal cracking. Bash then tried Alcoa itself but they wouldn't do it. So he reached out overseas and found the largest tennis racket manufacturer in the world in Taiwan, Kunnan Lo. Kunnan produced beautifully crafted rackets but only in cheap soft alloys. They knew nothing of the high-tempered alloy that Prince would need for its new tubular frame. Head explained how they finally got the product they were looking for:

> Almost at wit's end, Bash thought of an extremely imaginative solution. He decided that what we had to do was to buy high-strength aluminum tubing from Alcoa who would draw it for us, put it in an intermediate temper condition, and ship it over to Taiwan. We would then have Kunnan Lo take over to form the racket for us, put on the handle, anodize it, polish it, put on all the cosmetics, and ship it back to America where we would sell them. The best thing is that we made Kunnan Lo responsible for working its way successfully through the stress corrosion problem so we didn't have to worry about it. We didn't go to Taiwan because we could get rackets cheaper there; we went to Taiwan because the work ethic was so strong. I still remember watching them in that plant—they were dedicated to their work the way earlier American craftsman were. Furthermore, they demonstrated an entrepreneurial capacity to work their way successfully through all problems.

Howard Head and Mal Bash breathed a gigantic sigh of relief when their relationship with Kunnan Lo was firmly established and they could get an unlimited supply of rackets from them. Once established with them, the Maark association continued out of an old loyalty, but it was no longer essential to the survival of Prince. Eventually, the relationship with Maark broke down altogether. This was at least in part due to a strange turn of events. A year after Maark had begun to manufacture the Prince Classic, they were acquired by AMF and so, incestuous though it seemed, Prince and Head rackets were popping out of the shipping door of the same factory.

With the supply problems of the tubular aluminum alloy for the Prince Pro out of the way, Prince turned its attention to the possibility of a graphite racket which, in some respects, would outperform even the Pro in stiffness and resilience. They got the first rackets produced by a large American company. The racket was immediately successful, which led to a small crisis for Prince. The supplier abruptly tried to hold Prince up with an arbitrary 50 percent price increase. Mal Bash solved the problem by withdrawing all the tooling from the company and trucking it down the road to another outfit called Grafalloy who, even though their experience had been solely in graphite golf club shafts, were willing to take on tennis-racket design. The transition was successfully completed.

With the advent of the superior Pro and Graphite models, Howard Head had attracted the kind of young professional and college players for whom he had designed this new product.

Mr. Head's success in achieving this end was perhaps best demonstrated by the success of Pam Shriver who, with Prince Pro in hand, became the youngest player ever to get to the finals of the U.S. Open beating Martina Navratilova along the way. The Prince Graphite was now enjoying a strong position on the market, boosting sales out of the previous slump. Head proudly told the story:

> In 1980, we had profits of $2 million on $18 million in sales. The very next year, with the new rackets, sales doubled again to $34 million with profits of $4.5 million, which is 15 percent after taxes.

FINANCE

In the area of finance, Prince was vastly different from the Head Ski Company. Head Ski was financed initially with $6,000 from Howard Head's personal funds.

During the winter he had moved into a $20-a-month basement apartment, living in his father's old overcoat when his wore out. He borrowed money, and when that ran out, he could no longer pay the airplane mechanics who had been helping him. They worked for over a year without a cent of pay.

But through the next two years, when ski after ski failed, they labored with Head to build the ski he was determined to make. To help make ends meet, Howard Head got a part-time job designing special research equipment for Johns Hopkins University. This paid for the aluminum, glue, plywood, and some special new components and equipment.

After the company got off the ground, things were a little easier for Head and his employees. In 1953, Mr. Head sold 40 percent of the stock in the company for $60,000. This, together with retained earnings and normal bank debt, financed expansion until there was a public offering of common stock and convertible debentures. With the outside financing, Head's stock position was diluted to 18 percent.

Prince was financed very differently—solely out of earnings, even with the stupendous growth. Prince had no outside financing, and there were no outside investors. After Howard Head's initial purchase of stock, no additional capital was raised. Eventually, Howard Head bought out most of the original stockholders who cofounded the company and, at one point, he wound up with about 80 percent. This later diminished to 67 percent, due to stock bonuses that he gave to employees. "I totally owned the company in a sense," he said. "There were no outside stockholders, and no board of directors except in an advisory way."

ORGANIZATION

Whereas Mr. Head's problems with finance and manufacturing had improved dramatically based upon lessons learned at the Head Ski Company, delegation and management continued to be a burden for him. Head believed that any improvement in these areas at Prince was mainly a result of his physical location:

> I recognized shortly after the sale that in the early days of Head I was hurting my own company by glowering over everyone's shoulders.

Head recognized the classic problems of the entrepreneur when he spoke of the Head Ski Company as it was in 1967:

> I think this is typical of the kind of business that is started solely from an entrepreneurial product basis, by someone with no interest or skills in management or business. Such an entrepreneur never stops to plan. The consuming interest is to build something new and to gain acceptance. The entrepreneur has to pick up the rudiments of finance and organizational practices as he goes along. This type of business is fantastically efficient as long as it remains at a certain level. One man can make all of the important decisions.
>
> At Head Ski Company, this approach worked quite successfully until about 1955 when we sold 10,000 pairs of skis and reached the $500,000 sales level. The next five years from 1955 to 1960 saw a number of disorganized attempts to acquire and use a more conventional pyramidal organizational system. To put it succinctly, what was efficient at the $500,000 level was increasingly inefficient as we reached $1 million, then $2 million in sales. One man just couldn't handle it. It was like trying to run an army with only a general and some sergeants. There were just no officers, to say nothing of an orderly chain of command.
>
> With Prince, fates have decreed that I live in Baltimore while the company is up in Princeton. If I lived in Princeton and went into that office every day, no matter what I learned at Head, it would not stop me from impeding the effectiveness of the company by nitpicking and impeding my own effectiveness by wasting all my energy on details that somebody else could handle better.

Looking toward the future, Head had reached the point where he did have to address himself to the difficult task of reviewing the people he had chosen to be his "officers." He often found himself at odds with them, first at Head Ski Company and now at Prince Manufacturing Inc.

He had learned a valuable lesson at Head Ski about the necessity of compatability of objectives among the owner and the top officers within an organization. In January of 1967, Howard Head appointed Hal Seigle to be chief executive officer of Head Ski Company, and though Head himself called Seigle a man with "proven professional management skills," he also felt that Seigle did not place a strong enough emphasis on product. "Under Seigle," Head explained, "I got increasingly frustrated because we were so diametrically different. He was a manager who focused on broad aspects of company organization and expansion by acquisition. From my standpoint he did not pay enough attention to detail and he was not product oriented."

Head had hoped that his problems with the top officer of his first company would not repeat themselves with those at his second, but this was not to be.

Jack Murray became the president of Prince in early 1979, and Howard Head credited him with "shepherding the company through its spectacular growth, partly on his own ability and partly because there is a great marriage between his motivational character and my vision and creativity." Head claimed that Murray's leadership was "absolutely essential" and that the results in the company during his time as president "speak for themselves about how effective he is." Furthermore, Head pointed out one of Murray's strongest assets—and one which Head claimed that he himself would like to possess—Murray "knows the names of everybody in the company."

But it was Murray who was reluctant to project the 100 percent increase in sales, which Mr. Head felt was sure to occur in 1981. Head also disagreed with Murray on the issue of an inflationary price increase of 10 percent. Murray felt that the profit margin at the time was sufficient and that a price increase was unwarranted. Head maintained that the company enjoyed the position of having an exclusive product and that he merely wanted to keep up with inflation.

Jim Baugh was the marketing director under Jack Murray, and as Head claimed, a "strong ally" of Murray's. Head explained:

> He is a very conservative thinker, even more conservative than Jack, in terms of projection. He is very, very afraid that Prince will kill itself by expanding its image to include a midsize racket line. The midsized racket has already hit the market, and for Prince to admit that this racket might have something is frightening to a marketing man.

Mal Bash, who came to play a vital role in the development of Prince, was called by Head the "single most important man at Prince.

He had been hired back in the ball machine days as head of quality control. Within a couple of years, he got the title of factory manager, and then quite soon he became vice president of engineering and manufacturing." Head praised Bash profusely:

> Actually he is less of a manager than a doer. What *vice president* doesn't reflect is the initiative and the drive and the toughness with which he personally went to see Grafalloy and forced them to make a good graphite racket for us. He would take nothing but excellence. He dug them out and grappled with them, and he wouldn't take anything but good results from them. He also went to Taiwan, and instead of doing what a normal Taiwanese customer does, which is to get wined and dined and womened all over the place, he shocked them by insisting that he personally go in and out of the shop day after day. He was watching what these guys were doing and how they bent the aluminum and how they heat-treated it. I give Mal a very high ranking as a major force in the company. . . .

Even after his experience in hiring the various officers within his organization, Head still maintained this idealistic vision:

> I always had the dream that right out there would be a different chief executive officer who would have all my imagination and all my vision and all my critical judgment and all my creativity and all my positives, and who at the same time was a superlative manager, remembered faces, knew all the boys, loved people, people loved him back. . . . It's only as I look back on it in a philosophical way that I see how crazy it is to expect all these qualities in one person. It would be like expecting Leonardo DaVinci to play a great game of soccer. . . .

Head also said that if there was one thing he would emphasize, it would be that his first requirement in hiring someone to be a part of his vision of growth would be

> their attachment to me, either because they were like me or because they respected me or were fascinated by the project. I would avoid people whose views were diametrically different from mine, as in the case of Seigle and some of the earlier marketing people at Prince. . . .

TOWARD THE FUTURE

Mr. Head had done well financially from a personal standpoint. He earned a handsome sum in royalties on top of retained earnings, and as he explained the financial structure of this income:

> The royalties were indeed earnings to me, quite independent of my share in the earnings of the company. There is an interesting point regarding the royalties—they were received by me as capital gains (i.e., 22 percent), but they were expense to the company (50 percent). Originally I assumed

that when the patent was issued I would give ownership of it to Prince. But my patent attorney was adamant that I keep title to the patent in my own name in order to take advantage of the tax law that provides for the above anomaly.

Howard Head didn't like the word *marketing,* he "never had a sales quota," and he believed that "word of mouth was always the primary salesman."

The Prince racket, like the Head ski, was a better product, and Head's only interest was in exclusive products that worked better for the consumer, even if they looked a little funny:

> The skis broke, they were shiny, and the bottom froze, but people found something magic about them. The parallel in Prince is that it looked ludicrous, as evidenced by a big article in the *New York Times* called "Tennis Racket or Barn Door?" which appeared after the company was in production.
>
> I think word of mouth has clearly been the key to boosting sales at Prince, because we've always been faced with a faint snobbism of using that "unfair racket" or that "big racket" or that "oversized racket."

In 1981, Head saw the company through the $35 million mark. He predicted gross sales of $60 million for the following year, and while he was excited about the prospects such enormous growth would bring, he was justifiably concerned about his ability to continue to manage an operation of this size. (See Exhibit 5 for consolidated balance sheets and 1982 business plan.)

The issue wasn't financial. The question was, how much was possible? In his own mind, Head questioned if the company was prepared to grow, or if there were further measures he would have to take in order to reach the next plateau. Did he have the right people working within an effective organizational framework? Was the distribution process running smoothly enough to handle the enormous volume such rapid growth would bring? And perhaps most importantly, what would his own role be if he were to stay on at the helm? How should this role adapt to the inevitable changes soon to occur? Was it within his capacity to broaden the organization or was it time to sell and exit gracefully while luck was with him? It had come time to answer these difficult questions, and he had no one with whom he could share these concerns.

EXHIBIT 1 Prince Financial Summary

Year Ended	Rackets	Gross Sales	Net Earned	Percent
July 1971		$ 32,200	$ 830	2.6%
July 1972		100,000	15,000	15.0
July 1973		580,000	106,000	18.3
July 1974		1,151,000	150,000	13.0
July 1975		1,165,000	74,000	6.4
July 1976	70,000	2,946,000	227,000	7.7
July 1977	160,000	5,051,700	329,000	6.5
July 1978	180,000	7,142,900	200,500	2.8
December 1979	190,000	9,411,800	340,900	3.6
December 1980	300,000	17,785,900	1,668,000	9.4
December 1981	600,000	34,937,800	4,397,600	12.6
(December 1982 projected)	1,000,000	58,675,000	6,560,000	12.2

EXHIBIT 2   Chronology

1969	Howard Head sells Head Ski Company to AMF for $16 million.
1970	Retires. Renovates new home. With new tennis court.
July 1971	Orders Prince ball machine upon advice of tennis pro; began dialog to "debug" machine.
October 1971	Buys 27 percent of Prince for $27,000; becomes chairman of the board and de facto chief engineer.

	Gross Sales	Net Earned	Percent
1972	$ 100,000	$ 15,000	15%
1973	600,000	100,000	17
1974	1,100,000	150,000	14
1975	1,200,000	75,000	6

1974	Begins racket experimentation, first using weights, then conceived spreading weight out (thus increasing area).
1974–75	Controlled testing of experimental model begins.
May 1975	HH decides to go into production: 35,000 rackets necessary minimum order from Maark. (Sold 70,000)
1976	Patent #3,999,756 granted: Import of patent in scope and ownership.

	Rackets	Gross Sales	Net Earned	Percent
1976	70,000	$3,500,000	$250,000	8%
1977	160,000	5,000,000	330,000	7
1978	180,000	7,000,000	200,000	3
1979	190,000	9,500,000	350,000	4

1978	Noted need for Pro and Graphite. Also, exclusive license with Wilson.
1979	Manufacturing problem is solved (Kunnan Lo and Grafalloy).

	Rackets	Gross Sales	Net Earned	Percent
1980	300,000	$18,000,000	$1,700,000	9%
1981	600,000	35,000,000	4,400,000	13
(Projection)				
1982	1,100,000	$58,000,000	$7,000,000	12

EXHIBIT 2 (*concluded*)

Balance Sheet, July 31, 1971
(unaudited)

Assets

Current assets:

Cash	$ 902.95	
Accounts receivable.........................	4,764.74	
Inventory, at cost	7,442.87	
Total current assets......................		$13,110.56

Other Assets:

Patents.....................................	502.56	
Organization expense.......................	132.50	
Security deposits...........................	450.00	
Total other assets........................		1,085.06
		$14,195.62

Liabilities and Stockholders' Equity

Current liabilities:

Accounts payable	$ 5,402.43	
Loans payable—stockholders	10,600.00	
Accrued federal and state income taxes	307.41	
Other accrued liabilities	355.88	
Total current liabilities..................		$12,165.72

Stockholders' equity:

Capital Stock	1,200.00	
Retained earnings—net income for year ...	829.90	
Total stockholders' equity		2,029.90
		$14,195.62

EXHIBIT 3   Industry Overview

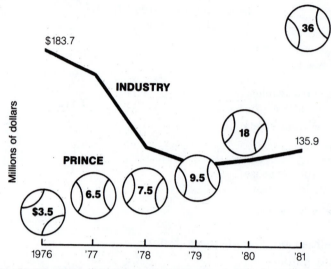

Tennis stumbled in 1977 and racket sales fell severely. But Prince Manufacturing, represented by the bouncing tennis balls, came on like a summer storm, starting behind the mountain in 1976 and drenching the competition. Industry sales are reported at retail. Prince's are its wholesale receipts, the only figures available; a common retail markup is around 40%.

Sources: National Sporting Goods Association, Prince Manufacturing Co.

EXHIBIT 4   Prince vs. Conventional Racket

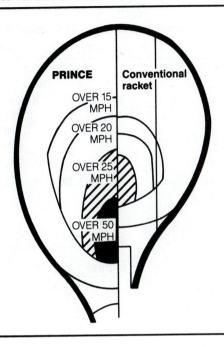

EXHIBIT 5   Financials

Consolidated Balance Sheets as of December 31, 1977–1981

	1981	1980	1979
Assets			
Current assets:			
Cash	$ 924,815	$ 410,212	305,964
Receivables	5,324,384	3,299,985	1,618,597
Inventories..................	4,478,500	2,178,769	858,842
Prepaid expenses	156,163	100,486	57,867
Total current assets........	$10,883,862	$5,989,452	$2,841,270
Plant and equipment, at cost:..	1,181,022	$ 693,779	$ 576,192
Less accumulated depreciation and amortization	287,225	171,104	104,210
Net plant and equipment..	$ 893,797	$ 522,675	$ 471,982
Other assets...................	40,097	80,409	134,334
Total assets...................	$11,817,756	$6,592,536	3,447,586
Liabilities and stockholders' equity			
Current liabilities:			
Notes payable	—	—	$ 450,000
Current installments of long-term debt.............	$ 42,723	$ 42,723	97,208
Accounts payable	1,212,955	813,237	670,548
Accrued expenses	1,268,375	733,998	367,645
Taxes currently payable	1,343,651	1,485,131	266,878
Deferred income taxes	283,499	206,499	87,499
Total current liabilities....	$ 4,151,203	$3,281,588	$1,939,778
Long-term debt, excluding current installments	$ 42,041	84,084	127,607
Deferred income taxes	—	9,000	4,000
Stockholders' equity:			
Common stock without par value.....................	249,643	299,643	75,965
Retained earnings	7,373,869	2,976,221	1,308,236
	$ 7,623,512	3,225,864	$1,384,201
Less cost of shares in treasury	8,000	8,000	8,000
Total stockholders' equity .	$ 7,615,512	3,217,864	1,376,201
Total liabilities and stockholders' equity..........	$11,817,756	$6,592,536	$3,447,586

EXHIBIT 5 (*continued*)

Consolidated Statement of Earnings
and Retained Earnings
1981, 1980, and 1979

	Years Ended December 31,		
	1981	*1980*	*1979*
Net sales	$34,937,800	$17,785,896	$9,411,759
Cost of sales	16,905,951	8,818,221	5,443,393
Gross profit	18,031,849	8,967,675	3,968,366
Selling expenses	5,816,675	3,019,782	1,738,475
Administrative expenses	3,477,287	2,142,262	1,337,883
	9,293,962	5,162,044	3,076,358
Operating profit	8,737,887	3,805,631	892,008
Other income (expenses):			
Royalty income	437,597	253,341	108,252
Royalty expense	(1,119,945)	(574,580)	(274,492)
Interest expense	(22,969)	(71,943)	(76,818)
Miscellaneous	115,078	4,536	1,965
Net other income (expenses)	(590,239)	(388,646)	(241,093)
Earnings before income taxes	8,147,648	3,416,985	650,915
Income taxes:			
Current	3,673,000	1,626,000	249,584
Deferred	77,000	123,000	60,416
	3,750,000	1,749,000	310,000
Net earnings	4,397,648	1,667,985	340,915
Retained earnings beginning of year	2,976,221	1,308,236	967,321
Retained earnings end of year	$ 7,373,869	$ 2,976,221	$1,308,236

EXHIBIT 5   (*concluded*)

1982 Business Plan
Statement of Earnings
Foreign and Domestic

	Total	*Domestic*	*Foreign*
Total			
Racquets	$58,359	$39,601	$18,758
Racquet accessories	2,999	2,549	450
Machines	1,450	1,234	216
Total	$62,808	$43,384	$19,424
Cost of sales	31,540	19,626	11,914
Gross profit	31,268	23,758	7,510
Percent of net sales	50%	55%	39%
Operating expenses			
Sales and marketing	11,220	8,522	2,698
Warehouse and shipping	697	481	216
Administrative and			
general	3,937	2,949	988
Research and engineering	791	546	245
Total	$16,645	$12,498	$ 4,147
Operating profit	14,623	11,260	3,363
Percent of net sales	23%	26%	17%
Royalty and interest			
Royalty income	$ 450	$ 310	$ 140
Royalty expense	1,975	1,412	563
Interest income	200	138	62
Total	$ 1,325	$ 964	$ 361
Income			
Pretax income	$13,298	$10,296	$ 3,002
Percent of net sales	21%	24%	15%

Case Index

Subject Index